Pope Innocent III and his World

Pope Innocent III and his World

Edited by

JOHN C. MOORE

Editorial Committee

Brenda Bolton
John C. Moore
James M. Powell
Constance M. Rousseau

Prepared under the auspices of Hofstra University

Ashgate

Aldershot • Brookfield USA • Singapore • Sydney

Published by
Ashgate Publishing Limited
Gower House
Croft Road
Aldershot
Hants GU11 3HR
England

Ashgate Publishing Company
Old Post Road
Brookfield
Vermont 05036-9704
USA

The authors have asserted their moral right under the Copyright, Designs and Patents Act, 1988, to be identified as the authors of this work.

British Library Cataloguing in Publication Data

Pope Innocent III and his World
    1. Innocent III, Pope—Influence. 2. Popes—Biography.
    3. Popes—Temporal power. 4. Popes—Primacy. 5. Christianity
    and other religions—Islam—History. 6. Europe—Church
    history—600-1500. 7. Europe—History—476-1492.
    I. Moore, John C.
    282'.092

Library of Congress Cataloging-in-Publication Data

Pope Innocent III and his world/edited by John C. Moore: editorial
    committee, Brenda Bolton et al.
        Includes bibliographical references and index.
        ISBN 1-84014-646-X (hardcover)
        1. Innocent III, Pope, 1160 or 61-1216—Congresses. I. Moore,
    John C. (John Clare), 1933-   . II. Bolton, Brenda. III. Title:
    Pope Innocent III and his world.
    BX1236.P57   1999
    282'.092—dc21   99-20427
    [B]   CIP

ISBN 1 84014 646 X

This book is printed on acid free paper

Printed and bound in Great Britain by MPG Books Ltd, Bodmin, Cornwall

Contents

Part Two   Shepherding the Flock

Part Three   Defining and Using Papal Power

Contents

Contributors

FRANCES ANDREWS is a Lecturer in Mediaeval History at St Andrews University, Scotland.

JESSALYN BIRD did her undergraduate work at the University of Pennsylvania and is completing her Oxford University DPhil thesis, 'Crusade and Reform in the Circle of James of Vitry'.

BRENDA BOLTON is Senior Lecturer in History at Queen Mary and Westfield College, University of London.

JOSEPH CANNING is Senior Lecturer in History at University of Wales, Bangor, and Director of the British Centre for Historical Research in Germany at Göttingen.

ROBERT CHAZIN is Scheuer Professor of Hebrew and Judaic Studies at New York University.

GIULIO CIPOLLONE is a Professor at Gregorian University and Urbanian University, Rome.

PETER D. CLARKE is a research associate of the History Faculty and a senior member of Robinson College at Cambridge University.

DEIRDRE COURTNEY-BATSON is an adjunct Assistant Professor of History at Pace University, New York.

CHRISTOPH EGGER is *Universitätsassistent* at the University of Vienna (Department of History) and the Institut für Österreichische Geschichtsforschung.

ANTONIO GARCÍA Y GARCÍA is a Professor of History of Canon Law at the Pontificia Universidad of Salamanca.

MICHAEL GOODICH is a Professor of History at the University of Haifa.

RICHARD KAY is Emeritus Professor of History at the University of Kansas, Lawrence.

CHRISTOPH T. MAIER is a *Wissenschaftlicher Assistent* and *Lehrbeauftragter* in Medieval History at the University of Zurich.

ALBERTO MELLONI teaches the history of Christianity at the University of Rome and is a member of the Istituto per le Scienze Religiose in Bologna.

GILLIAN MURPHY is a doctoral student at University College London and is researching 'Monks and Pastoral Care in the Middle Ages'.

JOSEPH F. O'CALLAGHAN is Professor Emeritus of Medieval History at Fordham University, New York.

BRIAN A. PAVLAC is an Assistant Professor of History at King's College in Wilkes-Barre, Pennsylvania.

EDWARD PETERS is the Henry Charles Lea Professor of History at the University of Pennsylvania, Philadelphia.

JAMES M. POWELL is Emeritus Professor of Medieval History in Syracuse University, Syracuse, New York.

E. C. RONQUIST is an Associate Professor in the Department of English, Concordia University, Montreal.

CONSTANCE M. ROUSSEAU is an Associate Professor of History at Providence College, Providence, Rhode Island.

HANS-JOACHIM SCHMIDT is a Professor of Medieval History at the University of Fribourg, Switzerland.

CLAIRE TAYLOR is doing research towards a PhD at the University of Nottingham, England.

Abbreviations

A thorough explanation of the sources of canon law and the way they are cited can be found in James A. Brundage, *Medieval Canon Law* (London, New York, 1995), 190-202. Suffice it to say here that citations from Gratian's *Decretum* appear in forms like these three examples from Brundage: D. 24 dict. ante c. 5; C. 23 q. 8 d. p. c. 25; D. 2 de cons. c. 82. Five later compilations of decretals (*Quinque compilationes antiquae*) are cited as 1 Comp., 2 Comp., and so forth. The Decretals of Pope Gregory IX (*Liber extra*) are cited as is shown in this example: X 1.18.7.

AASS	*Acta Sanctorum.*
BMCL	*Bulletin of Medieval Canon Law.*
COD	*Conciliorum Oecumenicorum Decreta.* Ed. Joseph Alberigo, et al. Bologna, 1972.
CSEL	*Corpus Scriptorum Ecclesiasticorum Latinorum.*
Gesta	*Gesta Innocentii III.*
Maleczek, *Papst*	Werner Maleczek. *Papst und Kardinalskolleg von 1191 bis 1216. Die Kardinäle unter Coelestin III. und Innocenz III.* Vienna, 1984.
MGH	*Monumenta germaniae historica.*
LL	*Leges.*
SS	*Scriptores.*
Const.	*Constitutiones.*
PL	*Patrologia latina.* Cited by volume and column number.
Pott.	*Regesta Pontificum Romanorum.* Ed. A. Potthast. 2 vols. Berlin, 1874-1875. Usually cited by item number.

Reg.   *Die Register Innocenz'III.*   Ed. Othmar Hageneder et al.
                              Five volumes to date, each numbered according to the
                              register year: 1, 2, 5, 6, 7.   Graz, Rome, Vienna, 1964-
                              1997.   Cited by register year and letter number.   E.g.:
                              6:190 (192) – the number in parentheses being the
                              corresponding number in PL when it is different from the
                              number in Reg.

RHDFE   *Revue historique de droit français et étranger.*

RHGF   *Recueil des Historiens des Gaules et de la France.*

RNI   *Regestum super negotio Romani imperii.*   Ed. F. Kempf.
                              Miscellanea Historiae Pontificiae, 12.   Rome, 1947.

RS   Rolls Series.

Tillmann, *Pope*   Helene Tillmann.   *Pope Innocent III.*   Trans. W. Sax.
                              Amsterdam, 1980.

ZRG   *Zeitschrift der Savigny-Stiftung für Rechtsgeschichte.*
  Germ.   *Germanistiche Abteilung.*
  Kan.   *Kanonistische Abteilung.*
  Rom.   *Romanistische Abteilung.*

Introduction

In May of 1997, a conference entitled 'Pope Innocent III and His World' was held at Hofstra University in anticipation of the eight-hundredth anniversary of Innocent's election as pope in 1198. This volume is the product of that conference.

Lotario dei Conti di Segni was only thirty-seven years old when he was elected pope, but few men or women in the early history of Europe played a larger role in shaping their society. He set in motion two great crusading armies; he sat in judgment of kings and emperors; he struggled mightily to make individuals and society conform to his Christian ideals; he issued a constant stream of legislation that governed the lives of countless Christians for centuries thereafter. But for all that, one can argue that few of his efforts produced the results he hoped for.

If there is any unifying theme that unites all studies of Innocent III, it is that he considered it his right and responsibility to look after all humanity. Christianity was and is a 'universal' religion, claiming to offer salvation to all humankind, and Innocent believed it his duty to nurture the faithful and to defend them from their enemies, within and without. He also looked to the conversion of those enemies, although the danger they presented often seemed to him to call first for forceful restraints. The energetic and resourceful way in which Innocent carried out these responsibilities provoked criticism in his day and has done so ever since.

At the heart of the matter are three questions. The first, perhaps the least difficult, is the factual matter: who the man was – how he was formed, how he actually behaved. Much in this volume addresses this question.

The second question has to do with the proper role of religious authority in the world. The history of religious persecution has convinced most historians that priestly authority should be rigorously excluded from the political arena, that church and state should be sharply separated. But those ideals are not so easily implemented. Do religious leaders – Christian, Jewish, Muslim – forfeit their right to roles of leadership in political, economic and social matters, especially when those matters clearly involve basic human values and moral judgments? Where does legitimate pastoral action end and the illegitimate pursuit of power begin? Where these lines are drawn continues to divide the modern world, so it is not surprising that modern historians cannot agree on whether Innocent went too far or, if so, by how much. This second question is rarely addressed directly in this volume, but it lies behind many of the papers.

The final major question still under debate is the acceptability and the viability of a 'world' government, or more generally the relationship between any 'central' government and regional governments. The medieval Roman emperors could claim authority over the world ruled by their classical and Carolingian predecessors: nearly all of the European peninsula, with adjacent islands, and the entire coast of the Mediterranean. The popes could claim truly universal authority, aspiring to bring all non-Christians into the Christian fold and to subject all Christians to the pastoral authority of the pope. In either case, were these claims the arrogant assertion of authority over peoples who wanted their own independence, or a wholesome effort to create a universal society of peace and harmony, bound together by a single body of law (Roman or canon) and regulated by the benign authority of emperor or pope? Historians, reflecting their nationalist inclinations, long saw both papal and imperial pretensions as mischievous, but having tasted the bitter fruits of nationalism, regionalism and tribalism in the wars of the twentieth century, some may now show a bit more sympathy for efforts to bring warring European princes under a single authority and to create world-wide harmony under international law. Had either the popes or the emperors succeeded in their political ambitions, Europe and perhaps the world might have seen less strife in ensuing centuries. The great world wars of modern times have been basically wars among European powers, transported to other continents. Here too, the papers that follow do not often directly address this question of how the world should be governed, but it provides their context. Innocent III took positions on both of these last two great and controversial questions. He articulated those positions, defended them and vigorously sought to implement them.

The papers in this volume were all presented at the Hofstra conference, but they were not presented in the order nor according to the subject headings found here. The editor hopes that the organization imposed upon them, albeit artificial and somewhat arbitrary, will help readers to form a more coherent picture of 'Pope Innocent III and His World'. The papers do not describe all the events or major issues of his pontificate, but they illuminate his personal formation and his understanding of his world and they show him playing a powerful role in his society.

PART ONE. INNOCENT III AND HIS MILIEU

Edward Peters (who was named for the conference 'Joseph G. Astman Distinguished Conference Scholar') examines the evidence and the scholarship concerning the life of Innocent III before he was elected pope. With rich bibliographic detail, he offers a wide-ranging discussion of the many influences that acted upon the young man so as to produce the pope of history. Some of those influences, especially the schools and the curia, are discussed further in several of the papers that follow.

The theological interests Lotario developed in the schools were not abandoned when he became pope. Christoph Egger argues that although Innocent has been criticized for lacking theological originality, originality is not a proper standard for judging the pope. He offers evidence that as pope Innocent remained an active and perceptive student of theology in the service of his pastoral responsibilities. Similarly, Richard Kay analyzes two works of Innocent to show that Innocent was primarily a theologian. He also concludes, taking a position on a much disputed question, that Innocent seems not to have been a trained canon lawyer. In reaching these conclusions, Kay also illuminates some of the concerns that occupied the pope and his curia.

The inner life of the curia is further revealed by James M. Powell, who addresses two areas of Innocent's pontificate that have remained obscure: the inner workings of Innocent's government and the authorship of the *Gesta Innocentii tertii*, the biography of Innocent written about 1208 by someone within the curia. Building on the work of Werner Maleczek, Powell finds in the career of Petrus Beneventanus some insights into both of these mysteries. He shows that the service of Petrus in the papal government before 1208 makes him a likely candidate for the authorship of the *Gesta*, the contents of which match up with the areas of Petrus's involvement, and he suggests that the growing responsibility of Petrus, with the corresponding demands on his time, accounts for the shift in the content of the *Gesta* from narrative to the bare quotation of documents.

The Fourth Lateran Council (or Lateran IV) was one of the great achievements of Innocent's pontificate, the instrument by which he and like-minded clergy hoped to organize and reform the world according to their own Christian vision. Alberto Melloni looks closely at *Vineam domini*, the encyclical letter announcing the council. He shows that in this area (as in many others), Innocent and his curia followed past traditions of papal government but at the same time went beyond those traditions so as to cast Lateran IV in a slightly different role from the Lateran councils that preceded it.

The papal curia was a place where the problems of the world were discussed and addressed, but it was not only a center of pastoral and political concern. E. C. Ronquist traces the career of a little-known abbot so as to show that the curial milieu fostered cultural and intellectual interests beyond the pragmatic and that it had its own distinctive character, different from those of the schools and of the imperial court in southern Italy.

PART II. SHEPHERDING THE FLOCK

Among the images used to describe papal authority were those of mother and shepherd. Constance Rousseau shows that Innocent, like many other celibate males of his day, appreciated the nurturing, instructing and governing aspects of motherhood, and that he used those qualities to describe and implement his responsibilities as pope. She also points out that despite his distaste for the sexual and reproductive aspects of motherhood, he showed some sympathy for mothers and occasionally tried to lighten their burdens.

Brenda Bolton further stresses the nurturing aspects of Innocent's pontificate. She reviews the many gifts he bestowed on churches and clergy as well as the building programs he undertook for the religious welfare of the faithful. She concludes that these material things, large and small, are in fact evidence of Innocent's serious commitment to pastoral and spiritual values.

Bolton mentions how Innocent stressed centralized organization as the way to preserve the moral quality of monastic houses. The same theme is developed by Gillian Murphy, who traces the fortunes of some Irish monks in Ireland and Germany. She shows that Innocent was aware of these monks, encouraged them and sought to guarantee the quality of their spirituality by pressing upon them the Cistercian type of organization, one that placed all member monasteries under the supervision of a 'general chapter' of abbots.

Michael Goodich also finds Innocent pursuing the spiritual improvement of his flock. He shows that through papal canonization, Innocent hoped to use the examples of saints to inspire believers and non-believers. But because the pope was concerned that the faithful might be misled by heretics, he insisted on the cautious evaluation of evidence of sanctity – visions, miracles and a virtuous life – before canonizing anyone.

It is a commonplace that Innocent's two great concerns were the recovery of the Holy Land and the reform of Christendom. Jessalyn Bird looks at the men who carried those concerns to the general public, the men who preached the crusade and called for reform, and she shows that the two messages could work at cross purposes. In the process, she also shows how the Paris schools, where Innocent and many of the preachers were formed, had not yet found a way to come to terms with the new urban and commercial culture that surrounded them. The distinction between usury and price-gouging on the one hand and legitimate money-lending and fair market practices on the other still lay in the future. The preachers offered crusading and voluntary poverty as the role to salvation, but, ironically, they also opened the perilous road that offered spiritual benefits in return for money.

The heritage of Paris is unfortunate in another regard. Robert Chazan suggests that Innocent absorbed at Paris a more intensive anti-Jewish animus than had moved his predecessors and that this bigotry lay behind the unusual and more vigorous measures he took against Jews. In this case, a form of pastoral zeal, aimed at protecting the Christian faith, was severely detrimental to the Jews of Europe. Innocent's role in the history of anti-Semitism is not a proud one.

Grass-roots religious enthusiasm among European Christians presented a problem that was both religious and political. It could easily wander into heretical opinion, and that, according to the common belief of the day, would jeopardize the salvation both of the heretics and of others whom they might infect. A successful heretical movement would also undermine the entire ecclesiastical structure over which the pope presided.

Innocent's efforts to protect the faith against heretics were both punitive and irenic, and they were always influenced by the interests of local powers. The highly destructive Albigensian Crusade against the heretics of southern France is not discussed directly in these papers, but Claire Taylor's paper shows how that papal campaign fit into the political competition among dynastic leaders, high and low. The well-known opposition between King Philip of France and King John of England had a role in the Albigensian Crusade. King John could not afford to oppose openly a papally sanctioned crusade against heretics, but neither could he allow his enemies to assume power in southern France, where he had his own claims. Hence, he pursued a quiet and unobtrusive policy of supporting the count of Toulouse and opposing the crusading forces – thus giving his enemies the chance to paint him as a supporter of heretics. Taylor concludes, however, that Innocent was able to draw out of all this maneuvering a more secure, peaceful and orthodox regime in southern France.

Although Innocent approved and expanded oppressive and coercive measures (that were further expanded by popes who followed him), he is also given credit for seeing the possibilities of peacefully guiding popular religious enthusiasm into orthodox channels. The best-known example is the Franciscan movement, but there were many others. Frances Andrews takes up this subject in order to point out that the more temperate policy that Innocent showed to a number of popular movements was not entirely his work. In this area, as in all the others, the role of the pope's agents cannot always be clearly distinguished from that of the pope himself, but Andrews shows that the papal agents, as well as other prelates, were unquestionably promoting irenic approaches to new religious groups.

PART THREE. DEFINING AND USING PAPAL POWER
Joseph Canning has been persuaded that Innocent III was not merely a political operator, that he did in fact have a genuine pastoral concern for the people over whom he presided. But he is not willing to concede that 'pastoral' is an adequate word for the pope's understanding of his office or for the way he actually exercised his power. Brian Pavlac goes further. He describes Innocent and the papal curia as pursuing an imperial domination of Christendom and of the world and as doing so at the expense of spiritual reform and peaceful relations with secular princes.

The idea that Innocent sacrificed principle for power receives some support from Peter Clarke, whose paper shows that Innocent was willing to punish the innocent in order to coerce proper behavior from the guilty. Clarke argues that Innocent was not always comfortable with this policy, recognizing that his efforts at coercion could work against his pastoral purposes. Unfortunately, Clarke concludes, Innocent's coercive measures found a place in canon law while his misgivings did not.

The enduring consequences of Innocent's pontificate in canon law are also illustrated in the essay of Deirdre Courtney-Batson. She discusses a single letter of Innocent, one that made its way into the official body of canon law to the considerable perplexity of the canon lawyers who followed after. In *Per venerabilem*, Innocent seemed to be claiming an unlimited power while at the same time acknowledging its limits. Canon lawyers of the thirteenth century tried to explain that subtlety, and in doing so showed that they were serious thinkers, not mere ideologues or lackeys of the curia. Courtney-Batson finds in their ruminations the basis for her own interpretation.

Hans-Joachim Schmidt finds in Innocent's definition of his office a model for his secular counterpart Emperor Frederick II and then for other secular rulers of the West. He shows how the well-known papal phrase *plenitudo potestatis*, the fullness of power, was taken over by the imperial chancery to describe the imperial office. At the same time, he argues, the phrase brought with it its counterpart, *pars sollicitudinis*, a phrase that granted to subordinates a 'share in the solicitude', thereby moderating the power of the monarch.

PART FOUR. ENCOUNTERING THE MUSLIM WORLD

The papers in this volume do not deal directly with the crusades initiated by Innocent III, but several show that Innocent's responses to the Muslim world had far reaching ramifications. Joseph O'Callaghan's paper reminds us that the 'Muslim threat' was not merely a remote, overseas danger. The progress of the Almohad Muslims in Spain made necessary the end of inter-Christian warfare there and an all-out effort from the Christian West. That objective drew Innocent deeply into the internal politics of the Iberian peninsula, where he achieved mixed success. Dealing with the same geographical area, Antonio García y García surveys the extensive range of subjects that led to interaction between Innocent and Spain. The reconquest of Muslim-controlled territory in particular produced complicated questions of political jurisdiction as princes and prelates competed with one another for wealth, power and prestige. These papers can remind us that the role of fifteenth-century popes in mediating between Spanish and Portuguese monarchs in the Oceanic Age had its origins many centuries before in the Iberian peninsula.

Jessalyn Bird's paper indicated that the crusades were for Innocent more than a military response to the presence of Islam. Christoph Maier shows further that the pope tried to integrate the crusading effort into a broad theological framework and to make it an integral part of the spirituality of all Christians. The idea of 'total war', a war-effort that involves the entire population in a common effort has often been associated with the twentieth century, but in Maier's article, we see that, for better or for worse, the crusading movement as led by Innocent anticipated that phenomenon.

Innocent's response to the Muslim world, however, was not uniformly hostile. Giulio Cipollone shows that although Innocent was always committed to recovering from the Muslims lands formerly under Christian dominion, he found it useful at times to seek the cooperation of Muslim rulers and people. His support for the Trinitarians, a religious order founded for the ransoming of prisoners, is a case in point. Perhaps one can find in this flexibility some willingness to find a common humanity between Christians and Muslims, but if so, it did not soften Innocent's determination to end the Muslim occupation of the Holy Land.

How do these papers affect history's final judgment of Innocent? Most of the 'big' questions remain open. Some historians will see unprincipled expediency where others see responsible flexibility. Where some see a man reacting reasonably and energetically to the problems he faced, doing as well as can be expected given the assumptions of his time and place, others will see a man vigorous pursuing the expansion of his own power at the great expense of other governments, groups and individuals. Perhaps most of us will see something in the middle, some human mixture of the egotistic and the altruistic. In any case, these papers show how wide and how deep were his contacts with his world.

* * *

A word of thanks is appropriate here. The conference could not have taken place without the professionalism and thoroughness of the directors and staff of the Hofstra Cultural Center, especially that of Athelene Collins-Prince, who served as Conference Coordinator. Brenda Bolton, James M. Powell and Constance M. Rousseau first suggested the idea of a conference at Hofstra, and they then served on the Planning and Editorial Committees. My Hofstra colleague Linton S. Thorn was, as always, a constant source of advice and support. My heartfelt gratitude goes to all of these people, and to all the others who helped make possible the conference and then this volume.

John C. Moore   Emeritus Professor of History
Bloomington, Indiana   Hofstra University

Part One
Innocent and his Milieu

Lotario dei Conti di Segni becomes Pope Innocent III: The Man and the Pope

Edward Peters

I

How did a medieval *papa electus* become the kind of pope he became? The theological answer – that his electors and he were moved by the Spirit – is unsatisfactory to the historian and was not intended for him or her in any case. Two of the dangers of posing the question at all have been recently signalled by Edward Synan:

> In one direction, the imposing file of eminent popes might seduce us into a prosopography without intelligible pattern; in the opposite direction, the majesty and continuity of the papal office, hypostasized in imagination as 'the papacy', might mask the existential diversity of those who held the office . . . 'the papacy' might seem to be more real than were the flesh-and-blood popes in whom the abstraction was incarnate.[1]

---

[1] Edward A. Synan, 'The Pope's Other Sheep', *The Religious Roles of the Papacy: Ideals and Realities 1150-1300*, ed. Christopher Ryan, *Papers in Mediaeval Studies* 8 (Toronto, 1989), 389-412, at 390-1 (hereafter: Ryan, *Papacy*). Cf. Thomas F. X. Noble, 'Morbidity and Vitality in the History of the Early Medieval Papacy', *Catholic Historical Review* 81 (1995):505-40, an essay of much value for the later history of the papacy as well. The best general studies are I. S. Robinson, *The Papacy 1073-1198: Continuity and Innovation* (Cambridge, 1990) (hereafter: Robinson, *The Papacy*); Werner Malezcek, *Papst und Kardinalskolleg von 1191 bis 1216. Die Kardinäle unter Coelestin III. und Innocenz III.* (Vienna, 1984) and Colin Morris, *The Papal Monarchy: The Western Church from 1050*

One aspect of Synan's second danger is illustrated by the famous observation of Baronius that often seems to inform much of the work of the late Walter Ullmann and others, that there is 'one spirit among all Roman pontiffs'.[2]

But Synan's dilemma does not have only two sides. There is also the theory of papal self-modelling based on earlier popes, an aspect tantalizingly suggested (but far from being as clearly reliable as we might wish) by the choice of papal names after the late tenth century, one most eloquently expressed by another Innocent, the Innocent XII in Book Ten of Robert Browning's *The Ring and the Book* (a poem which commemorates a papal trial in 1698).

> Like to Ahasuerus, that shrewd prince,
> I will begin, – as is these seven years now,
> My daily wont, – and read a History
> (Written by one whose deft right hand was dust
> To the last digit, ages ere my birth)
> Of all my predecessors, Popes of Rome:
> For though mine ancient early dropped the pen,
> Yet others picked it up and wrote it dry,
> Since of the making books there is no end.
> And so I have the papacy complete
> From Peter first to Alexander last;
> Can question each and take instruction so.
> Have I to dare, – I ask how dared this Pope?
> To suffer? Suchanone, how suffered he?
> Being about to judge, as now, I seek
> How judged once, well or ill, some other Pope;
> Study some signal judgement that subsists
> To blaze on, or else blot, the page which seals
> The sum up of what gain or loss to God
> Came of His one more vicar in this world.[3]

---

to 1250 (Oxford, 1989).

I am grateful to the Planning Committee for the invitation to contribute to the Hofstra University conference 'Pope Innocent III and His World', and particularly to James Powell, James Muldoon and Richard Kay for extensive bibliographical assitance and long, informative conversations on the problem of the life of Lotharius, as well as to Joseph Dyer for his very useful study of the Lateran *schola cantorum*. The paper is printed largely as delivered, with a few corrections and changes. The essay is dedicated to Leonard E. Boyle, O. P.

[2]Walter Ullmann, *A Short History of the Papacy in the Middle Ages* (New York, 1972), 1.

[3]Robert Browning, *The Ring and the Book*, ed. Richard D. Altick (Harmondsworth-Baltimore, 1971), Book X, p. 477.

Our earlier Innocent, too, read the *Liber Pontificalis* and evidently considerable other Roman and papal history.[4]

Then there are the particular agendas that each pope planned or encountered, as well as the institutional or other material resources which he had at his disposal, some agendas perennial, others (perhaps most) immediate and particular in time and place. Consider the surprising, dismaying and intractable marital problems of Philip Augustus and Ingeborg of Denmark that Innocent encountered at the beginning of his pontificate (the problem itself had begun several years earlier, in 1193) and worked on intermittently until almost the end, or the surprising reversal of positions in papal favor between Philip Augustus and John between 1199 and the end of the pontificate (or those between Otto IV and Philip of Swabia and later Frederick II), or the consequences and opportunities offered by the equally surprising death of Henry VI on 28 September 1197.[5]

There are still other theories about becoming pope in medieval Europe, few of them satisfactory, partly because we do not have enough biographical data on most medieval popes before their papacies – a lack that has sometimes led to some serious errors on the part of historians and others, most spectacularly, perhaps, in the case of the alleged Pope Joan.[6]

Finally, there is (at least from the mid-eleventh century and in some respects far earlier) the question of personal and professional experience, either outside of Rome (as in the cases of Leo IX or Urban II) or in papal service (as in the case of Hadrian IV), what might be termed the apprenticeship – or managerial – model, and we must remember that Lotharius spent nearly a dozen active years in the curia, probably from the age of twenty-six in 1186 or 1187 until his election as

---

[4]Brenda Bolton, 'Rome as a Setting for God's Grace', in Bolton, *Innocent III: Studies on Papal Authority and Pastoral Care* (Aldershot-Brookfield, 1995), art. I.

[5]On the reversal of positions, see Brenda Bolton, 'Philip Augustus and John: Two Sons in Innocent III's Vineyard?' in Wood, *The Church and Sovereignty*, 113-34, rpt in Bolton, *Innocent III*, art. V. On the death of Henry VI, see Gerhard Baaken, *Ius Imperii ad Regnum. Königreich Sizilien, Imperium Romanum und Römisches Papsttum vom Tode Kaiser Heinrichs VI. bis zu den Verzichterklärungen Rudolfs von Habsburg* (Cologne-Weimar-Vienna 1993), 27-84. The imperial problem was indeed serious; there had been no disputed imperial election since that of Lothar III in 1125. In 1198 both electors and pope faced a very different world. See also Friedrich Kempf, 'Innocenz III. und der deutsche Thronstreit', *Archivum Historiae Pontificiae* 23 (1985):63-91. On Philip Augustus, see John W. Baldwin, *The Government of Philip Augustus: Foundations of French Royal Power in the Middle Ages* (Berkeley-Los Angeles-London, 1986), and *idem*, 'Persona et Gesta: The Image and Deeds of the Thirteenth-Century Capetians, 1. The Case of Philip Augustus', *Viator* 19 (1988):195-207.

[6]Alain Boureau, *La papesse Jeanne* (Paris, 1988). But some myths prove impervious to historical research: see most recently Donna Wolfolk Cross, *Pope Joan* (New York, 1996), an old argument disguised as a novel.

pope on 8 January 1198.[7] His awareness of the papacy dated from the pontificate of Alexander III, and his immediate knowledge of its workings from that of Gregory VIII in 1187. This early experience is important; as Pennington observes, Innocent 'had come to the papal throne with a clear conception of the papal prerogatives he wished to accentuate'.[8] But how and under what circumstances had he formulated it?

The unique surviving letter of Lotharius as a cardinal – written to Henry VI in 1195 or 1196 – unfortunately offers little evidence on this point, except for its iteration of the dangers of heresy and the need for a crusade being the two grounds on which papal and imperial agreement was essential.[9] The letter, evidently a response to a communication from Henry, offers little more. Failing greater evidence from the letter, one must seek the development of Lotharius' ideas on the papacy in other areas.

The question is worth asking, particularly in Innocent's case, because the problem is especially teasing: the pontificate began busy and remained busy – at its very outset it faced one of the most complex sets of diplomatic and administrative problems of any pontificate. The first few pages of Pennington's *Pope and Bishops* sum up the early papal activity dramatically: Innocent immediately begins to expound the theories of papal authority that characterize the papacy after him; he reforms the papal household and the curia, reorganizes the government of the city of Rome, reunites the papal states, restructures the Roman chancery, begins a style of papal rhetoric that influences subsequent canonist rhetoric, creates, in Pennington's felicitous musical metaphor, 'a melodic line to which canonists [later] responded', begins to revise the papal liturgy and adopts – and modifies – the title *vicarius Christi*.[10]

---

[7]On Lotharius as cardinal, see Maleczek, *Papst*, 101-4. The work of Alfons Becker and others has enabled historians recently to recognize the importance of the early career of Odo of Cluny/Ostia in the pontificate of Urban II. See Alfons Becker, *Papst Urban II*, 2 vols (Stuttgart,1964,1988); Ernst Dieter Hehl, 'Was ist eigentlich ein Kreuzzug?', *Historische Zeitschrift* 259 (1994):297-336, and Marcus Bull, 'The Roots of Lay Enthusiasm for the First Crusade', *History* 78 (1993):353-72.

[8]Kenneth Pennington, *Pope and Bishops: The Papal Monarchy in the Twelfth and Thirteenth Centuries* (Philadelphia, 1984), 78. Pennington further argues (89-90) that Innocent did not use earlier decretals or canonistic case law, but rather 'his vision was theological, not legal'.

[9]Werner Maleczek, 'Ein Brief des Kardinals Lothar von SS. Sergius und Bacchus (Innocenz III.) an Kaiser Heinrich VI.', *Deutsches Archiv* 38 (1982):564-76. The letter reflects Lotharius' rhetorical expertise and the common topics of the need for peace between emperor and pope, especially in the matter of the call for a crusade and the prosecution of heretics. Maleczek suggests that Lotharius' letter was in response to a letter sent by Henry VI to individual cardinals.

[10]Pennington, *Pope and Bishops*, 11-16, and for the early date of the political decretals, 48. Pennington describes how his own original plan for the book was changed by the figure of Innocent, p. 11. James Powell has also emphasized Innocent's 'institutional pastoralism': James M. Powell, '*Pastor Bonus*: Some Evidence of Honorius III's Use of the Sermons of Innocent III', *Speculum* 55 (1977):522-37. On Rome and the patrimony, see Daniel Waley, *The Papal State in the Thirteenth*

Innocent was also one of the youngest of all popes. Like John Paul II he left a youthful paper trail. Among the items on that paper trail were surprisingly varied works of theology, homiletics and exegesis. He also left an extensive and interesting anecdotal history, one that invites speculation (if not categorical judgments) about his personality.[11] There are a few interesting physical descriptions and portraits, perhaps two that are likenesses – and Gerhart Ladner has taught us how to read them – but there is no deathmask.[12] His extraordinary political and legal vision invites questions as to its origin, questions not yet finally settled by Pennington, Imkamp or Maleczek.[13] He was, after all, Innocent III, not Innocent IV, and it would be unrealistic to expect his expertise in canon law in 1198 to be that of a professor at Bologna in the late twelfth or early thirteenth century. What seems to be needed is to compare Innocent to other students of theology and canon law of his generation and to consider seriously the extent and character of his participation in the meetings of the consistory both before and after his election.

His astonishing flexibility and devotional artistry in accepting radical religious movements in the face of considerable opposition, as well as his sympathy for Greek devotional practices if not the Greek ecclesiastical hierarchy, asks the same question. The sheer bulk of his official correspondence, his care for its organization and preservation, and especially some of its legal innovations suggest again the career before the papacy, especially if Innocent's own hand can

---

Century (London, 1961), 23-67; Peter Partner, *The Lands of St. Peter: The Papal State in the Middle Ages and the Early Renaissance* (Berkeley-Los Angeles, 1972), 224-43. Michele Maccarrone, 'Papato e regno di Sicilia nel primo anno di pontificato de Innocenzo III', and 'Innocenzo III e gli Avvenimenti di Romagna del 1198', in Maccarrone, *Nuovi Studi su Innocenzo III*, ed. Roberto Lambertini (Rome, 1995), 137-70, 171-207; Brenda Bolton, '"Except the Lord keep the city": Towns in the Papal States at the Turn of the Twelfth Century', in Bolton, *Innocent III*, art. III; Christian Lackner, 'Studien zur verwaltung des Kirchenstaates unter Papst Innocenz III.', *Römische historische Mitteilungen* 29 (1987):127-214; John C. Moore, 'Pope Innocent III, Sardinia, and the Papal State', *Speculum* 62 (1987):81-101. On the liturgy, see S. J. P. Van Dijk and J. Hazelden Walker, *The Origins of the Modern Roman Liturgy* (Westminster-London, 1960), 91-128, and Van Dijk-Walker, *The Ordinal of the Papal Court from Innocent III to Boniface VIII and Related Documents* (Fribourg, 1975), 89-485.

On the title, see Michele Maccarrone, *Vicarius Christi: Storia del Titolo Papale* (Rome, 1952), to which may be added the pre-thirteenth-century inscription cited by Pierre Jounel, *Le culte des saints dans les basiliques du Latran et du Vatican au douzième siècle* (Rome, 1977), 352, n. 15.

[11]The most ambitious attempt has been that of Helene Tillmann, *Pope Innocent III*, trans. Walter Sax (Amsterdam-New York, 1980), 289-315. See also Jane Sayers, *Innocent III: Leader of Europe 1198-1216* (London-New York, 1994), 1-29, and Robert Brentano, *Rome before Avignon: A Social History of Thirteenth-Century Rome* (New York, 1974), 148-55.

[12]Gerhart Ladner, *Die Papstbildnisse des Altertums und des Mittelalters*, Bd. II (Vatican City, 1970), 53-79. Sayers, *Innocent III*, 2.

[13]See below, n. 25.

be detected in some of the key decretals.[14] At the very least, the Registers and the legal collection sent to Bologna indicate Innocent's strong concern for order and record – a concern expressed even in such details as seeing to it that each church in the *patrimonium* possessed a silver chalice, which it was not allowed to pawn. This idea of order in details great and small seems a distinctive characteristic of Innocent, and of Lotharius.[15] And he dreamed – at least three times while pope and with significant results, and presumably before.[16] Innocent also remained sensitive and responsive to the dreams and visions of others throughout the pontificate. Those who dream – or are said to dream – are also interesting.

With good reason, the entire pontificate of Innocent, rather than the youth of Lotharius, has been the focus of most scholarship, particularly since most historians first encounter it in the dramatic contexts of Lateran IV and the early political decretals. But during the past two decades, that pontificate has been extensively rethought, from the work of Pennington, Imkamp, Roscher, and Maleczek to that of Brenda Bolton, Christoph Egger, Jane Sayers, Constance Rousseau and John Moore. In some respects all these changing views of Innocent seem to recapitulate the thought and interests of one great historian, Michele Maccarrone, whose own Innocent has moved from the *Chiesa e stato* of 1940 to the more recent studies of pastoral theology and the Petrine tradition in Rome.[17]

---

[14]On the Register, see Imkamp, *Kirchenbild*, 71-90, with full references. Most scholars agree that Innocent's own words are to be found in many of the official letters, although caution in the attribution of particular words and phrases by the pope must always be used. Innocent's care for the compilation of the registers is equalled by his care for the collecting of his own decretals in the *Compilatio Tertia* by Petrus Beneventanus in 1210-1211 and by his rejection of the *Compilatio Quarta*.

[15]On the Registers and the *Compilatio tertia*, see Imkamp, 32-46.

[16]On the dream of St Francis, see Edward Peters, 'Restoring the Church and Restoring Churches: Event and Image in Franciscan Biography', *Franziskanische Studien* 68 (1986):213-36. On the dream of the hospital, see Brenda Bolton, 'Received in His Name: Rome's Busy Baby Box', *The Church and Childhood*, ed. Diana Wood (= *Studies in Church History* 31)(Cambridge, 1994), 153-67, rpt in Bolton, *Innocent III*, art. XIX (further on children, Constance M. Rousseau, 'Innocent III, Defender of the Innocents and the Law: Children and Papal Policy (1198-1216)', *Archivum Historiae Pontificiae* 32 [1994]:31-42); on Gilbert of Sempringham, see Raymonde Foreville and Gillian Keir, *The Book of St. Gilbert* (Oxford, 1987), 174-77. On the general problem, Robert E. Lerner, 'Himmelsvision oder Sinnendelirium? Franziskaner und Professoren als Traumdeuter im Paris des 13. Jahrhundert', *Historische Zeitschrift* 259 (1994):337-67, with extensive references; Carlo Bertelli, 'Römische Träume', and Julian Gardner, 'Päpstliche Träume und Palastmalereien: Ein Essay über mittelalterliche Traumikonographie', both in Agostino Paravicini-Bagliani and Giorgio Stabile, eds, *Träume im Mittelalter. Ikonologische Studien* (Stuttgart-Zurich, 1989), 91-112, 113-24; Steven F. Kruger, *Dreaming in the Middle Ages* (Cambridge, 1992). Gardner points out (p. 114) that Innocent could also be sceptical about dreams and expressed some scepticism in *De miseria*, I. 24, and he omitted any reference to the dream of Constantine in the Sylvester-sermon, PL 217:481-6.

[17]Thomas F. X. Noble, 'Michele Maccarrone on the Medieval Papacy', *Catholic Historical Review* 80 (1994):518-33, a review-article of Michele Maccarrone, *Romana Ecclesia / Cathedra Petri*. ed. Piero Zerbi, Raffaello Volpini, Alessandro Galuzzi, 2 vols (Rome, 1991). See also Zerbi's survey,

Perhaps the same may be said about the two editions of James Powell's *Innocent III: Vicar of Christ or Lord of the World?* in 1963 and 1994. And the most important key to the revised, rather than the older Innocent, seems to be Lotharius. There was no marked change in the man after the election, although there was continuing intellectual, political and devotional development. The life before the pontificate seems deserving of some new consideration.

II

We have, of course, some assistance in the eulogistic and shrewd biographical narrative, the *Gesta Innocentii Tertii*, written in 1208 by someone fairly close to the pope with full access to the registers, and from it and other sources the biography of Lotharius can be constructed (some of its dating has been revised very recently, by Professors Moore and Bolton, among others, in interesting ways), although it will not tell us everything we wish to know.[18] But it is a substantial work, 'too important to neglect', as Bolton has said, and it was written in a recently developed biographical tradition that includes Boso's *Life of Alexander III*, the *Gesta Friderici* of Otto of Freising, the works of Suger, Guillaume le Breton, and Rigord on Louis VI and Philip Augustus, and the biographies of Bernard and Becket. The life can be easily and quickly summarized.

Lotharius was a son (we do not know the birth-order, although we do know of a brother named Richard and a sister who married into the Annibaldi family) of Trasimondo dei Conti di Segni and Claricia dei Scotti, his father part of a family of landowners in the Anagni region about fifty kilometers southeast of Rome, and his mother a member of the Romani de Scotta family, to which Pope Clement III (1187-1191), was also said to have belonged.[19]

'Michele Macccarone, il cammino di uno storico', 1:xxiii-lix.

[18]Brenda Bolton, 'Too Important to Neglect: The *Gesta Innocentii PP III*', rpt in Bolton, *Innocent III*, art. IV, with full literature. See also Imkamp, *Kirchenbild*, 10-20. John C. Moore, 'Lotario dei Conti di Segni (Pope Innocent III) in the 1180s', *Archivum Historiae Pontificiae* 29 (1991):255-8. On the redating of the Grandmont dispute I have relied on information provided by Brenda Bolton in a personal communication in late 1996. Martinus Polonus designates Innocent as *natione Campanus*, in contrast to Clement III, Celestine III and Honorius III, whom he designates as *natione Romanus*; Louis Duchesne, ed., *Le Liber Pontificalis*, 2 (Paris, 1955):451, 453. The life of Innocent is 451-3. The *Gesta* is printed in PL 214:xvii-ccxxviii. There is a new edition by David Gress-Wright, *The "Gesta Innocentii III": Text, Introduction and Commentary*, PhD Diss., Bryn Mawr University, 1981.

[19]There is a survey of the known relatives and a convenient map and genealogy in Marc Dykmans, 'D'Innocent III à Boniface VIII. Histoire des Conti et des Annibaldi', *Bulletin de l'Institut historique belge de Rome* 45 (1975):19-211 and in Sayers, *Innocent III*, 33-7. Michele Maccarone, 'Innocenzo III prima del Pontificato', *Archivio della R. Deputazione romana di Storia Patria* 66 (IX della Nuova Serie)(1943):59-134, at 67, and 83-4, rejects the relationship. Nothing is known of the age of Clement III. See Volkert Pfaff, 'Papst Clemens III. (1187-91)', ZRG Kan., 97 (1980):261-316. Age and illness had allegedly prevented his election earlier in 1187. There is a possibility that his age might make it

Lotharius himself was born at Gavignano, near Segni and Anagni, in 1160 or 1161. He may have been dedicated to the church early, and he was sent to study at the monastery of Sant' Andrea in Rome under Peter Ishmael, whom Lotharius/Innocent as pope later made bishop of Sutri. Innocent consistently remembered his teachers and fellow-students with appreciation and gratitude. At Sant' Andrea Lotharius would have studied letters and may have come to the attention of his putative relative Cardinal Paul Scolari, who later became Pope Clement III (1187-1191).[20] Lotharius also may have studied liturgy in the Lateran *scola cantorum* and may have become a canon of St Peter's.[21] His life from a very early date was Roman (and Roman largely in the absence of both pope and curia), but not entirely.

Lotharius went to the schools of Paris in the late 1170s or 1180. A few earlier popes had been in contact with the Paris schools, but by the last quarter of the twelfth century these schools had developed considerably and were on the eve of becoming the University of Paris, a move that Innocent later supported.[22] At Paris Lotharius studied under Peter of Corbeil (whom Innocent later made bishop of Cambrai and still later archbishop of Sens) and under Peter the Chanter and Melior of Pisa. Among his fellow students were Stephen Langton, whom Innocent later made archbishop of Canterbury and a cardinal, Robert of Courson, whom Innocent also used as a legate and later made a cardinal, and Eudes de Sully, whom Innocent later used as a *visitator*. All of these were powerful thinkers and forceful personalities.[23] While at Paris, Lotharius also made a pilgrimage to the shrine of Thomas Becket at Canterbury in 1185 or 1186. Thomas had been canonized by Alexander III at Segni in 1173, and it is possible that Lotharius had witnessed the canonization – he would have been twelve or thirteen at the time. Hence his later interest in the saint and the rapidly expanding cult as well as his interests in the cause for which Becket had been martyred. Innocent also certainly knew – and perhaps remembered – something about the

---

unlikely that he was the uncle of Lotharius. Of Richard's three male children, one, Stephen, became a cleric in papal service, and two became secular lords. On the family, see Thumser, cited below, n. 36, and on Stephen, see Maleczek, *Papst*, 195-201.

[20]On the curriculum, see Maccarrone, 'Innocenzo III prima del pontificato', 68-70.

[21]Imkamp, *Kirchenbild*, 20-3, and on the *schola cantorum* below, n. 39.

[22]Peter Classen, 'Rom und Paris: Kurie und Universität im 12. und 13. Jahrhundert', in Classen, *Studium und Gesellschaft im* Mittelalter, ed. Johannes Fried, Schriften der Monumenta Germaniae Historica, Bd. 29 (Stuttgart, 1983), 127-69, esp. 153-4; Imkamp, *Kirchenbild*, 23-32; P. Osmund Lewry, 'Papal Ideals and the University of Paris 1170-1303', in Ryan, *Papacy*, 363-88. Further on Becket, *Gesta*, 131.

[23]John W. Baldwin, *Masters, Princes, and Merchants: The Social Views of Peter the Chanter and His Circle*, 2 vols (Princeton, 1970); *idem*, 'Masters at Paris from 1179 to 1215: A Social Perspective', *Renaissance and Renewal in the Twelfth Century*, ed. Robert L. Benson and Giles Constable, with Carol D. Lanham (Cambridge, MA, 1982), 138-72.

strength of English beer, as he pointedly reminded Robert, the advocate of Mauger bishop of Worcester.[24]

Lotharius returned to Italy in December 1186, as Moore's revised dating has it, and his last act in France was the mission to the papal legates at Grandmont perhaps slightly earlier in 1186. If Lotharius indeed arrived in northern Italy in December 1186, this revised chronology gives him slightly more time to study canon law at Bologna – almost three years – than previous discussions have allowed, although it is too early to be sure, and in any case the argument from chronology is not Pennington's main argument, since Pennington admits that Innocent studied *something* at Bologna. He suggests that it might have been theology or the notarial art, although the former is doubtful, after his five or six years in Paris and the unknown quantity that theology at Bologna was in those years, and the latter improbable). It is worth pointing out in support of Pennington's argument that Innocent later spoke of taking advice as pope from *iuris periti et alium prudentum*.[25] Between 21 October and December 1187, Lotharius was made a sub-deacon by Gregory VIII and he joined the itinerant curia in northern Italy, not Rome, as Moore has pointed out, possibly in recognition of his role in the Grandmont mission, but just as possibly because of his great promise as a scholar-curialist and his status as a member of a prominent Campano-Roman family. The papal curia was itinerant in these years, and Lotharius could have studied at Bologna and joined the curia in northern Italy when needed. Lotharius' association with Gregory VIII also coincided with Gregory's issuing in October 1187 the decretal *Audita tremendi*, the great crusade call in the wake of the

---

[24]Generally, see Christopher R. Cheney, *Pope Innocent III and England*, Päpste und Papsttum, Bd. 9 (Stuttgart, 1976), esp. 26-43, and for France, Raymonde Foreville, *Le pape Innocent III et la France* Päpste und Papsttum, Bd. 26 (Stuttgart, 1992). Of the four saints canonized by Innocent, two – Gilbert of Sempringham and Wulfstan of Worcester – were English, Wulfstan particularly appearing as Innocent's ideal prelate and pastor. See Emma Mason, *St. Wulfstan of Worcester c. 1008-1095* (Oxford-Cambridge, Mass., 1990), 278-81.

[25]Kenneth Pennington, 'The Legal Education of Pope Innocent III', BMCL, n.s. 4 (1974):70-77; *idem*, 'Pope Innocent III's Views on Church and State; A Gloss to *Per Venerabilem*', in *Law, Church, and Society: Essays in Honor of Stephan Kuttner*, ed. Kenneth Pennington and Robert Somerville (Philadelphia, 1977), 49-68; *idem*, review of Werner Maleczek, *Papst und Kardinalskolleg*, in ZRG Kan. 73 (1987):381-4, rpt as 'Further Thoughts on Pope Innocent III's Knowledge of Law', in Kenneth Pennington, *Popes, Canonists and Texts, 1150-1550* (Aldershot-Brookfield, 1993), art. II. The first article is reprinted in the same collection as art. I. See also Imkamp, *Kirchenbild*, 32-46. On Innocent's consulting experts in the law, see Reg. 1:314, cited in James A. Brundage, ZRG Kan. 112 (1995):37, n. 33. Richard Kay's research has suggested that Lotharius may have had more time available for study in Bologna than even Moore's and Bolton's revised dating has allowed, perhaps as much as an additional year.

disaster at Hattin, that launched the Third Crusade and that certainly echoes in Innocent's own later concerns for the Holy Land.[26]

In December 1189 or January 1190 Clement III made Lotharius cardinal-deacon of SS. Sergius and Bacchus. He immediately began rebuilding both the church and the diaconate (*quae nimis erat deformis et ruinosa, ut magis crypta quam basilica videretur*), working on several of his theological writings, not, as far as is known, on canon law, and participating in the work of the curia, even, perhaps, as Moore has argued, producing in the *De miseria* a *speculum curiae*.[27]

At the end of 1197, Roger of Hoveden relates, Celestine III proposed to the cardinals that he would resign the papacy on the condition that the cardinals agreed to elect John of St Paul, cardinal-priest of Sta Prisca, as his successor.[28]

---

[26]On Innocent and *Audita tremendi* see Helmut Roscher, *Papst Innocenz III. und das Kreuzzug* (Göttingen, 1969), 41-4, 270-2, and Penny J. Cole, *The Preaching of the Crusades to the Holy Land, 1095-1270* (Cambridge, Mass., 1991), 62-97; for the papacy and the crusade generally, Robinson, *The Papacy*, 322-49, esp. 348-9. Most recently, see Norman Housley, 'Crusades Against Christians: Their Origins and Early Development, c. 1000-1216', *Crusade and Settlement*, ed. Peter Edbury (Cardiff, 1985), 17-35, esp. 27-31, in which Housley emphasizes Innocent's drawing on eleventh- and twelfth-century crusading ideas, and John Gilchrist, 'The Lord's War as the Proving Ground of Faith: Pope Innocent III and the Propagation of Violence (1198-1216)', *Crusaders and Muslims in Twelfth-Century Syria*, ed. Maya Schatzmiller (Leiden-New York-Cologne, 1993), 65-83, in which Gilchrist, like Pennington, sees Innocent as primarily a theologian. Further, Giulio Cipollone, *Cristianità – Islam: Cattività e Liberazione in Nome di Dio: Il Tempo di Innocenzo III dopo 'il 1187'*, Miscellanea Historiae Pontificiae 60 (Rome, 1992), and *idem*, 'Innocenzo III e i Saraceni: Attegiamenti differenziati (1198-1199)', *Acta Historica et Archaeologica Mediaevalia* 9 (1988):167-88.

Gregory VIII was also the first pope to issue formal decretals of the type later issued by Innocent III. See Robinson, *The Papacy*, 200-1, and for the regular use of Gratian's *Decretum* in the curia (under Clement III), ibid., 483, citing Walther Holtzmann, 'Die Benutzung Gratians in der päpstlichen Kanzlei im 12. Jahrhundert', *Studia Gratiana* 1 (1953):323-49.

[27]John C. Moore, 'Innocent III's *De Miseria Humanae Conditionis*: A *Speculum Curiae*?' *Catholic Historical Review* 67 (1981):553-64. The point is worth making that during Lotharius' time away from pastoral and curial duties he chose to work on his theological projects, the *De miseria*, the *De missarum misteriis*, and the *De quadripartita specie nuptiarum (Dqsn)* and perhaps some of the sermons and the commentary on the seven penitential psalms. Such a concentration of intellectual effort may reflect either a lack of interest in furthering his study of canon law or an alternative to the law he encountered in his curial duties. The description of the fabric of SS. Sergius and Bacchus is in the *Gesta*, IV, PL 214:xviiiB.

[28]The fullest discussions are those of Volkert Pfaff, 'Papst Coelestin III. Eine Studie', ZRG Kan. 78 (1961):108-28, and *idem*, 'Der Vorgänger: Das Wirken Coelestins III. aus der Sicht von Innocenz III', ZRG Kan. 91 (1974):121-67; see also Pennington, *Pope and Bishops*, 11. Whether Hoveden is to be believed in all matters concerning the last days of Celestine III and the election of 1198 is not certain. But the story of the abdication-designation offer is unusual and needs further examination. On the early history of papal abdication, see Pennington, *Pope and Bishops*, 101-10; Peter Herde, 'Election and Abdication of the Pope: Practice and Doctrine in the Thirteenth Century', *Proceedings of the Sixth International Congress of Medieval Canon Law*, ed. Stephan Kuttner and Kenneth Pennington, Monumenta Iuris Canonici, Series C: Subsidia, 7 (Vatican City, 1985), 411-36, at 429-36; Martin Bertram, 'Die Abdankung Papst Cölestins V. und die Kanonisten', ZRG Kan. 56 (1970):1-101;

Roger's version of events in Rome between late 1197 and early 1198 is of great interest, but it is also not universally accepted. If we separate his discussion of Celestine III's alleged offer of resignation from Roger's later account of the conclave that elected Innocent III, it is possible to see in the former episode one of the two great events in the last three months of 1197 – the other being the death of Henry VI – that must have greatly concentrated the curia's attention on the problem of papal succession.

According to Hoveden, the cardinals rejected Celestine's offer, and when the pope died on 8 January 1198, they removed to the fortified Septizonium on the Palatine Hill in order to hold a secure election. Lotharius remained at the Lateran to attend the funeral rather than immediately joining the conclave. None of the leading candidates for the papacy – a group which may have included John of St Paul (the candidate of Celestine III himself), John of St Stephen, Peter of Gallocia (to whom the *De miseria* had been dedicated), Cencius Savelli (later Honorius III, the chancellor of the two preceding popes) and Octavian of Ostia – can have received a significant vote, since Lotharius appears to have received a majority on the first ballot and the necessary two-thirds on the second – hardly a compromise candidate.[29] The author of the *Gesta* (VI) states that immediately after the election three doves flew into the place where the cardinals had voted, the whitest of which settled near Innocent's right side. Might this be a discreet way of indicating that there had been only three candidates, including Lotharius, nominated at the original vote? A holy man was also said to have had a vision in which Lotharius married his mother. The images of *mater ecclesia* and the bishop's marriage to his church are thus the first ecclesiological images associated with the pontificate in the *Gesta*, images always close to Innocent's vision of the church.[30] The *Gesta* author also notes that many other similar revelations were

---

John R. Eastman, *Papal Abdication in Medieval Thought* (Lewiston, 1990). It is worth noting that as Pope Innocent later observed that the marriage of the pope and the Roman Church is so stable and firm that it can be broken only by death (cited from the *Dqsn* by Principe, 'Monastic, Episcopal, and Apologetic Theology', 152-3, n. 135).

On Celestine III and Henry VI, see Gerhard Baaken, 'Die Verhandlungen zwischen Kaiser Heinrich VI. und Papst Cölestin III. in den Jahren 1195-1197', *Deutsches Archiv* 27 (1971):457-513, with a full review of the literature, and Baaken, *Ius Imperii ad Regnum*.

[29] On these men, see Maleczek, *Papst*, 114-17(John of St Paul); 107-9 (John of St Stephen); 95-6 (Peter Gallocia); 111-13 (Cencius Savelli); 80-3 (Octavian of Ostia).

[30] On the image, see Peters, 'Restoring the Church', and Imkamp, *Kirchenbild*, 260-9, 300-23. Robert Benson's discussion of papal marriage-imagery in the context of ecclesiastical office in *The Bishop-Elect: A Study in Medieval Ecclesiastical Office* (Princeton, 1968), 144-7, illustrates an Innocent whose concerns for the authority of the *electus* may well have stemmed from his own experience. Benson cites the *Sermo 3 De diversis*, Innocent's sermon on the first anniversary of his own coronation in 1199, as abounding in marriage-imagery. See also Richard Kay's essay in this volume.

made to pious men, but that these are omitted in the *Gesta* at the wish of the pope, who had evidently read a draft of at least part of it.

Lotharius was elected pope on 8 January. Although there has been some disagreement as to the cardinals' estimation of Innocent and his youth, I suggest that the conclave knew exactly what it was doing; the cardinals may have preferred youthful vigor to age and experience, and they certainly knew Lotharius.[31] He may have been something of an unknown quantity elsewhere in Europe, but the cardinals surely knew him. He chose – or more probably was given (one wishes that we knew about the choice of name more exactly) – the name Innocent.[32] He announced his election when he issued his first papal letter on 9 January. He was ordained priest at the next Ember day, on 21 February, and bishop and pope the following day, the feast of St Peter's Chair.[33]

The Tor' dei Conti was begun shortly afterwards. The family of the (probably not yet Conti di) Segni either then or earlier, settled on the western slope of the Viminal and in the area behind the forum of Nerva, also possessing property and influence in the *rione* Monti.[34] Innocent also began to build his own residence on

---

[31]Maleczek, *Papst*, 101-4.

[32]Maria L. Taylor, 'The Election of Innocent III', *The Church and Sovereignty, ca. 590-1918: Essays in Honour of Michael Wilks*, ed. Diana Wood (= *Studies in Church History, Subsidia* 9)(Cambridge, 1991), 96-112. Taylor argues persuasively that only twenty-one cardinals were present for the election. On the process of election, see Robinson, *The Papacy*, 84-90. The *Ordo Romanus* XII prescribed that the senior cardinal deacon was to name the *papa electus*, and Taylor points out that in 1198 that deacon was Gratian of SS. Cosma e Damiano. Taylor also assumes that the name was given to indicate previous papal models that the new pope should keep in mind. However, it is worth pointing out that three of the last four popes elected at the end of the twelfth century were given (or took) names that had been used earlier in the century by antipopes: Gregory VIII ('Gregory VIII', 1118-1121), Clement III ('Clement III', 1080-1084), and Innocent III ('Innocent III', 1179-1180). On the term, see Michael Stoller, 'The Emergence of the Term *Antipapa* in Medieval Usage', *Archivum Historiae Pontificiae* 23 (1985):43-61. That the memory of antipopes was strong at the end of the twelfth century is indicated by the fact that Gregory VIII expressed great hostility to 'Victor IV' when he exhumed the remains and scattered them (Robinson, *The Papacy*, 506). It is possible that Lotharius was present. It is pointless to speculate about whether 'Victor IV' was still too potent a name and too recent a memory to obliterate by renaming the new pope Victor IV. And there were other antipapal names that had yet to be replaced. 'Innocent III', however, had been quite recent but had only a short and relatively colorless pontificate. It is not at all clear that the choice of papal names invariably intended to echo the pontificates and policies of earlier popes with the same name. Gregory VII, for example, appears to have chosen his papal name from his early patron and predecessor Gregory VI. I share the scepticism of Maccarrone, 'Innocenzo III prima del pontificato', 131-2.

[33]Taylor, 'The Election of Innocent III'. See also Bolton, 'Rome as a Setting for God's Grace', 5, and Agostino Paravicini Bagliani, *La cour des papes au XIIIe siècle* (Paris, 1995), 19-20. Innocent later raised the rank of sub-deacon to that of a major order. On Innocent's consecration of Innocent II's church of Sta Maria in Trastevere, see Taylor, 110-11, Bolton, 'Rome as a Setting', 10-13.

[34]Sayers, *Innocent III*, 33-7; Paravicini Bagliani, *La cour des papes*, 18, suggests an earlier move to Rome on the occasion of the marriage of Lotharius' parents and the mother's Roman connections. See also Richard Krautheimer, *Rome: Profile of a City, 312-1308* (Princeton, 1980), 157.

the Mons Saccorum at the Vatican. His interest in the Vatican began early and continued throughout the pontificate, a reminder of Innocent's Petrine devotion.[35] He was instantly plunged into the problems of the church and the world in the late winter and spring of 1198. And that is the life before the papacy.

III

What can we make of it? For all of the detail about Lotharius it does not tell us, it does allow us access to him through several smaller prosopographies, thus avoiding one of Synan's concerns – the prosopographies of Roman and Campanian families, possibly those of Sant' Andrea and the *scola cantorum*, the schools of Paris, possibly those of Bologna, the curia, and the college of cardinals. In several of these what we do not learn about Lotharius we can learn about the group, even when, as he often does, Lotharius/Innocent seems unrepresentative. Some of these have been well studied: the Roman families by Matthias Thumser and Étienne Hubert, Paris by John Baldwin, Stephen Ferruolo and Walter Principe; Bologna by Stephan Kuttner; the college of cardinals and the curia by Werner Maleczek, the bishops by Pennington.[36]

There are at least echoes of the others: much of the later use of language and rhetoric and the linguistic wit and verbal sarcasm that comes out again and again to the end of the life has the air of the schools and the court about it.[37] There is something of the same quality in the account of Innocent's summer working days and leisure hours at Subiaco in the well-known letter discovered by Karl Hampe

---

[35]Christopher Walter, 'Papal Political Imagery in the Medieval Lateran Palace', *Cahiers archéologiques* 20 (1970):155-76, and 21 (1971):109-36, rpt in Walter, *Prayer and Power in Byzantine and Papal Imagery* (Aldershot-Brookfield, 1993), art. VIIa-b; Gerhart B. Ladner, 'I Mosaici e gli Affreschi ecclesiastico-politici nell'Antico Palazzo Lateranense', rpt in Ladner, *Images and Ideas in the Middle Ages: Selected Studies in History and Art*, 1 (Rome, 1983):347-66; Brenda Bolton, 'Advertise the Message: Images in Rome at the Turn of the Twelfth Century', *The Church and the Arts*, ed. Diana Wood (= *Studies in Church History* 28) (Cambridge, 1992), rpt in Bolton, *Innocent III*, art. XVII, pp. 117-30; Krautheimer, *Rome*, 203-7 and figs 255-8, 260; Bolton, 'Rome as a Setting', 18-19; and Sayers, *Innocent III*, 10-15. On saints, see Pierre Jounel, *Le culte des saints*. On Peter, see Maccarrone, 'La "cathedra sancti Petri" nel Medioevo: da simbolo a reliquia', *Romana Ecclesia / Cathedra Petri*, 2:1249-1374, esp. 1349-55.

[36]Matthias Thumser, *Rom und der römische Adel in der späten Stauferzeit* (Tübingen, 1995), esp. 75-97, 196-7; Étienne Hubert, *Espace urbain et habitat à Rome du Xe siècle à la fin du XIII siècle* (Rome, 1990), 233-64, 281-96; Baldwin, above, n. 15; Stephen Ferruolo, *The Origins of the University; The Schools of Paris and Their Critics, 1100-1215* (Stanford, 1985); Principe, below, nn. 45-6; Stephan Kuttner, *Repertorium der Kanonistik* (Vatican City, 1937); Maleczek and Pennington, above, n. 8, and, for the cardinalate, Robinson, *The Papacy*, 33-120, and Maleczek, *Papst*, 57-204.

[37]Sayers, 2-3, citing Stephan Kuttner, 'Universal Pope or Servant of God's Servants: the Canonists, Papal Titles and Innocent III', *Revue de droit canonique* 32 (1981), rpt in Kuttner, *Studies in the History of Medieval Canon Law* (Hampshire-Brookfield, 1990), art. VIII.

and eloquently cited by Tillmann.[38] Innocent's interest in and skill at liturgy and chant, particularly that of papal Rome – a priest with a voice and a fine ear, *exercitatus in cantilena et psalmodia* as the author of the *Gesta* tells us – probably reflects Lotharius' experience at the *scola cantorum* at the Lateran and its continuing significance to him.[39] There is also substantial evidence of deep personal piety and theological interests reflected in the sermons and theological works – on baptism, marriage and the doctrine of Purgatory, for instance.[40] There is also Innocent's profound concern for the condition of the clergy and the papal household; a remarkable responsiveness to the laity and its own distinctive needs; church reform generally, interestingly conceptualized in Innocent's concern for the rebuilding and refurbishing of both material and figurative churches; the crusade – Innocent was twenty-seven or -eight when Hattin occurred, and he was present at the issuing of *Audita tremendi*. He knew that God tests Christians by demanding penance of them and willingness to lay down their lives for their brothers and that the crusade was impossible without the necessary preliminary penance and reform. Crusade and moral reform are always closely linked in his thought.[41] He possessed an elevated and articulated concept of authority that was expressed very early in the pontificate and must have been developed well before it began, perhaps initially in relation to bishops and to Rome and the patrimony, but quickly extended to other fields as well. The question of legal study at Bologna may also be clarified by considering these smaller prosopographies more closely and in context.

---

[38]Karl Hampe, 'Eine Schilderung der Sommeraufenthaltes der römischen Kurie unter Innocenz III. in Subiaco 1202', *Historische Vierteljahrschrift* 8 (1905):509-35, extensively discussed by Tillmann, *Pope Innocent III*, 288-315.

[39]Imkamp, *Kirchenbild*, 20-3. See also Bernhard Schimmelpfennig, 'Die Bedeutung Roms im päpstlichen Zeremoniell', in *Rom im hohen Mittelalter. Studien zu den Romvorstellungen und zur Rompolitik vom 10. bis zum 12. Jahrhundert*, ed. Bernhard Schimmelpfennig and Ludwig Schmugge (Sigmaringen, 1992), 47-61. The use of the phrase *exercitatus in cantilena et psalmodia* by the author of the *Gesta* is, I suggest, rather strong evidence that Lotharius had spent some time at the Lateran *schola cantorum*, since the phrase was used frequently in precisely this context. See Joseph Dyer, 'The Schola Cantorum in Its Roman Milieu in the Early Middle Ages', *De Musica et Cantu. Studien Zur Geschichte der Kirchenmusik und der Oper Helmut Hucke zum 60. Geburtstag*, ed. Peter Cahn and Ann-Katrin Heimer (Hildesheim-Zurich-New York, 1993), 19-40.

[40]Christoph Egger, 'Papst Innocenz III. als Theologe. Beiträge zur Kenntnis seines Denkens im Rahmen der Frühscholastik', *Archivum Historiae Pontificiae* 30 (1992):55-123, and *idem*, 'Die Taufe bei Papst Innocenz III. Theologische und kanonistische Probleme', paper presented to the X International Congress of Medieval Canon Law, Syracuse, 1996. On Innocent and Purgatory, see Jacques LeGoff, *The Birth of Purgatory*, trans. Arthur Goldhammer (Chicago, 1984), 174-5, and Sayers, 19-20. See also Giles Constable, *Three Studies in Medieval Religious and Social Thought* (Cambridge, 1995), 97-100.

[41]See the discussion in Hehl, 'Was ist eigentlich ein Kreuzzug?', 316, and Christoph Maier's essay in the present volume.

The life also tells us a few other things about Lotharius. His was a life of remarkable travel for a future pope, not, as in the cases of Adrian IV or Alexander III, in papal service or papal or curial exile, but as a student and pilgrim, through northern France, possibly southern Flanders, Normandy, southeastern England and northern Italy. And Lotharius was elected pope while young enough to have these experiences and places fresh in his memory, two generations younger, as Volkert Pfaff has reminded us, than his immediate predecessor, Celestine III, who had been born just after the beginning of the twelfth century. Celestine III had himself thus known the papacy from Calixtus II to Clement III.[42] Innocent also ruled in a world contended for and ruled by other young men – Philip of Swabia and Otto of Brunswick (both around twenty in 1198), Philip Augustus and Henry VI (both b. 1165), four or five years younger than Innocent, John of England (b. 1167), six or seven years younger than Innocent.[43] And some of these young men had grown up very quickly. As a number of scholars have pointed out, Innocent's great pronouncements on papal authority all come from the very early pontificate – they are those of a young pope speaking firmly to young lords as well as to distant rulers. Pennington is surely right: Lotharius had been thinking hard about the papacy long before he became pope. One can only wonder about Lotharius' future role in the curia if he had not been elected pope in 1198. John of Gaeta did not die until 1214. Lotharius would surely have become a bishop – or a monk – perhaps bishop of Ostia, a Hostiensis *avant la lettre*, but a very different Hostiensis!

IV

He did become a bishop, and a bishop of Rome quite unlike any of his predecessors or successors. Here again, the smaller prosopographies may signal some of that distinctiveness, even when the evidence suggests Innocent's differing from the main concerns of the groups identified. Karlfried Froelich has demonstrated convincingly that Innocent's use of exegesis to define papal authority differed from both the exegetical understanding of the schools and from earlier traditions of papal exegesis, which resulted, Froelich argues, in the fact that 'Innocent III fused both lines of papal interpretation, reading the task of "strengthening" specifically as part of the pope's universal teaching ministry', in an 'imaginative fusion of exegesis and papal ideology'.[44] Innocent learned the methods of

---

[42]Celestine III had been made a cardinal in 1144. Pfaff, 'Der Vorgänger', 124; Maleczek, *Papst*, 68-70.

[43]On the ages of these rulers and Innocent's own awareness of his youth, see Bolton, 'Philip Augustus and John', 114-15.

[44]Karlfried Froelich, 'Saint Peter, Papal Primacy, and the Exegetical Tradition, 1150-1300', in Ryan, *Papacy*, 3-44, at 25 and 43.

interpreting the *sacra pagina* at the schools of Paris, but he was not bound to all of their exegetical areas of concentration.

Nor does Innocent seem to have shared the views of the Paris moral theologians concerning the papacy. Walter Principe has considered the school theologians' views of the papacy, particularly their general lack of interest in it.[45] But when Principe treats monastic, episcopal and apologetic theology, we find a very different tradition, one that seems much closer to Innocent and perhaps to Lotharius.[46] Particularly striking appears the influence of Bernard of Clairvaux.[47] Such influences are not surprising. Since the eighth century at least, many of the most important assertions concerning the nature and authority of the papal office were articulated by writers outside of Rome, and even outside of Italy, from Bede and the early Carolingians through the authors of the Pseudo-Isidore collection to Bernard, Gerhoch of Reichersberg, Anselm of Havelberg and Hildegard of Bingen. Principe himself discusses Innocent's theology of the papacy in this latter context, rather than in that of the schools.[48]

Principe's discussions, with the observations of Maccarone, Jacqueline and Froelich, point to an Innocent (and hence to a Lotharius) much influenced by some strands of twelfth-century monastic thought, particularly that of Bernard of Clairvaux, as does the favor he showed toward Cistercians and his replacement of much of the papal household by monks and his reform of papal household

---

[45]Walter H. Principe, 'The School Theologians' Views of the Papacy, 1150-1250', in Ryan, *Papacy*, 45-116.

[46]Walter H. Principe, 'Monastic, Episcopal, and Apologetic Theology of the Papacy, 1150-1250', in Ryan, *Papacy*, 117-70.

[47]*Idem*, 118-29, 149-54; Froelich, 'Saint Peter', 41-2; Michele Maccarone, *Chiesa e Stato nella Dottrina di Papa Innocenzo III* (Rome, 1940), 19-22, 29-31, 35-47, 51; Stanley Chodorow, *Christian Political Theory and Church Politics in the Mid-Twelfth Century: The Ecclesiology of Gratian's Decretum* (Berkeley-Los Angeles-London, 1972); Bernard Jacqueline, *Episcopat et papauté chez saint Bernard de Clairvaux* (Saint-Lo, 1975), esp. 304-5; Walter Ullmann, *The Growth of Papal Government in the Middle Ages*, 3rd edn (London, 1970), 426-37, Annamaria Ambrosioni, 'Bernardo e il papato', *Bernardo Cisterciense: Atti del XXVI Convegno storico internazionale* (Spoleto, 1990), 59-79; *idem*, 'San Bernardo, il papato e l'Italia', *San Bernardo e l'Italia: Atti del Convegno di studi*, ed. Pietro Zerbi (Milan, 1993), 25-50; Sabine Teubner-Schoebel, *Bernhard von Clairvaux als Vermittler an der Kurie: Eine Auswertung seiner Briefsammlung* (Bonn, 1993); Giulio Silano, 'Of Sleep and Sleeplessness: The Papacy and the Law, 1150-1300', in Ryan, *Papacy*, 343-61, esp. 343-9; Jeannine Quillet, 'Saint Bernard et le pouvoir', *Mediaevalia Christiana XIe-XIIIe siècles: Hommage à Raymonde Foreville*, ed. Coloman Étienne Viola (Paris, 1989), 246-59; James A. Brundage, 'St. Bernard and the Jurists', *The Second Crusade and the Cistercians*, ed. Michael Gervers (New York, 1992), 25-33; Jean Leclercq, 'Saint Bernard's Attitude toward War', *Studies in Medieval Cistercian History* II, ed. John R. Sommerfeldt, Cistercian Studies 24 (Kalamazoo, 1976), 20-2.

[48]Principe, 'Monastic, Episcopal, and Apologetic Theology', 149-54. See also Noble, 'Morbidity and Vitality'.

dress to simple white wool clothing.[49] Innocent's first confessor was the Cistercian Rainier of Ponza, his chaplain was the Cistercian Nicholas, and the first cardinal he created was the Cistercian Gerard of Pontigny, Cardinal Deacon of St Nicholas in Carcere Tulliano in 1198 and later Cardinal Priest of S. Marcello in 1199.[50]

The letter from Subiaco discovered by Hampe also underlines Innocent's close association with monasticism generally. The sermon *In resurrectione Domini* delivered at Subiaco and the Subiaco fresco in the *Sacro Speco* are two other pieces of evidence. So is the fourteenth-century gloss of Petrus Bohier to the *vita* of Gregory IV in the *Liber Pontificalis*. Glossing the word *visitator*, Petrus observes that, 'Today, this is not an office of the pope. However, Innocent III personally visited and reformed the monastery at Subiaco'.[51] Innocent's concern with and interest in monasticism was enduring.[52] It is worth emphasizing this aspect of Innocent's personal interests because it reminds us of the place of omens, visions and dreams in the pontificate. The *Gesta* author was permitted by Innocent to describe only one of these concerning the election, and evidence for the others comes from slightly later sources. But they tell us that the author of *Novit, Solitae, Per venerabilem, Vergentis in senium,* and *Venerabilem* was also sensitive to the content of dreams and visions, his own and those of others, again in contrast to the direction of much early thirteenth-century oneirology.[53]

---

[49]In general, see Michele Maccarrone, 'Innocenzo III e la Vita Religiosa', in Maccarrone, *Studi su Innocenzo III* (Padua, 1972), 223-337, and Brenda Bolton, '*Via ascetica*: A Papal Quandry', *Studies in Church History* 22 (1985):161-91 (rpt in Bolton, *Innocent III*, art. VI). On the monastic personal servants and the white wool robes, see *Gesta*, CXLVIII; Bolton, '*Via ascetica*', 168. Most recently, Olivier Guyotjeannin, 'Innocent III', *Dictionnaire historique de la papauté*, ed. Philippe Levillain (Paris, 1994), 877-82. On Innocent and the Cistercian Order, see John C. Moore, 'Peter of Lucedio (Cistercian Patriarch of Antioch) and Pope Innocent III', *Römische historische Mitteilungen* 29 (1987):221-49, at 222, and Brenda Bolton, 'For the see of Simon Peter: The Cistercians at Innocent III's Nearest Frontier', in Bolton, *Innocent III*, art. II; on Rainier of Ponza, pp. 11-19.

[50]Maleczek, *Papst*, 124-5. In the *Gesta* (CXXVI) Innocent restores the monastery of St Martin in Viterbo and affiliates it with Pontigny.

[51]*Liber Pontificalis Glossato*, ed. Ulderico Prerovský, vol. 3, *Glosse, Studia Gratiana* XXIII (1978), p. 401, *glo. ad v. visitator*: 'Hodie non est officium papae. Innocentius tamen tertius per se monasterium Sublacense visitavit et reformavit . . .'. The editor cites Innocent's decretal of 1202 to Subiaco, *Accedentes cause devotionis* (Pott. 1720), which Bohier claimed to have seen. Bohier's own credentials as a reformer perhaps explain his interest in Innocent's monastic reforming activities. On Innocent and Subiaco, see Bolton, 'Via ascetica', 177-9. The reformed monastery was that of Sta Scholastica.

[52]See Maccarrone, 'Primato romano e monasteri dal principio de sec. XII ad Innocenzo III', *Romana Ecclesia / Cathedra Petri*, 2:821-928, esp. 895-928; Brenda Bolton, 'Daughters of Rome: All One in Christ Jesus', in Bolton, *Innocent III*, art. XVI.

[53]See the sources cited above, n. 16, especially Kruger, *Dreaming in the Middle Ages*, 83-123, and the essay by Michael Goodich in the present volume.

His sermon collection, which also both resembles and differs from the homiletic concerns of the Paris schools, was sent to the abbot of Citeaux.[54] It is also striking that the Pauline text cited in terms of religious in the *Sermo in Resurrectione Domini* edited by Moore, based on the text of Phil. 3:20, *Nostra conversatio in celis est*, is cited by Innocent in terms of himself and his clerical – perhaps monastic – audience in *Sermo XIV De tempore*.[55] The papal court described in the Hampe letter and other sources is certainly not a monastic institution – it could not have been – but it surely appears under Innocent to have operated according to that *gravitas* that Bernard of Clairvaux had urged in the *De consideratione*.[56]

The appeal of Citeaux and Bernard should not be surprising. Bernard's ascetic views and allegorical method found a remarkably sympathetic student in Lotharius, and the *De consideratione* was the greatest *speculum papae* of the twelfth century. It would have been unavoidable by anyone in the curia thinking seriously about the papacy, especially during a troubled and increasingly ineffective pontificate like that of Celestine III. Bernard had also urged the pursuit of wisdom in the small leisure afforded by the press of public affairs (I. 12), a description that fits well the *Gesta* portrait of Lotharius working on theological studies in the leisure he could get from the business of the curia.[57]

A second kind of influence, represented (and claimed for himself on Innocent) by Gerald of Wales, focused on sacramental theology and pastoralism, particularly pastoral failures, represented respectively in the first and second distinctions of Gerald's *Gemma Ecclesiastica*, which he presented to Innocent in Rome in 1199.[58] Gerald was nearly a generation older than Innocent, also a product of

---

[54]John C. Moore, 'The Sermons of Pope Innocent III', *Römische historische Mitteilungen* 36 (1994):81-142. On the differences between the sermons of Innocent and those of the school tradition, see Moore, 99, 106, and on the image of the papacy in the sermons, 105-9. See also Synan, 'The Pope's Other Sheep', esp. 391-8.

[55]Moore, 'Sermons', 135-42, at 137. *Sermo XIV* is in PL 217:382B, a sermon resembling the Moore sermon in other respects as well.

[56]Bernard of Clairvaux, *Five Books on Consideration: Advice to a Pope*, trans. John D. Anderson and Elizabeth T. Kennan (Kalamazoo, 1976), IV. 22. On the courtly context of such *gravitas*, see C. Stephen Jaeger, *The Envy of Angels: Cathedral Schools and Social Ideals in Medieval Europe, 950-1200* (Philadelphia, 1994). On citations from the *De consideratione* in the work of Innocent III, p. 187, and above, n. 40. Cf. *Sermo 32 De sanctis*, the sermon for All Saints' Day preached at Subiaco.

[57]Maccarrone, 'Innocenzo III prima del pontificato', 89, 120.

[58]Geraldus Cambrensis, *Gemma Ecclesiastica*, ed. J. S. Brewer, RS 21/1:119. See the translation by John J. Hagen: Gerald of Wales, *The Jewel of the Church: A Translation of "Gemma Ecclesiastica" by Giraldus Cambrensis* (Leiden, 1979), xvi. Gerald characterizes Innocent as 'copiose literatus est et literaturam dilexit'. On Gerald, see Robert Bartlett, *Gerald of Wales, 1146-1223* (Oxford, 1982), and Richard Kay, 'Gerald of Wales and the Fourth Lateran Council', forthcoming in *Viator*.

the Paris schools, but also a man of wide experience as a trained canonist and sharp-eyed observer of the clergy in Wales, England, Ireland and the schools of Paris. The *Gemma*, from which Gerald says Innocent refused to be parted, is a substantial 'mirror for clergy', and its appeal to Innocent seems readily explicable because of these qualities.

V

So far, I have tried to emphasize those aspects of Lotharius' life before the papacy that seem to have been most influential when he became pope. Prominent among these have been the city of Rome and the perspective on the world that it offered, specific courses of study, several of which provided him with an extraordinarily extensive familiarity with Scripture and an exegetical method and vocabulary of metaphors in which he later expressed his ideas about ecclesiology and politics, particular life-experiences both before and after his appointment to the curia, his close curial observations of three pontificates, his devotional sympathies that seem to have lain especially close to monasticism and his own scholarly theological interests. Out of these came his great concerns as pope: the reform of clergy and church, the crusade, the condition of Rome and the patrimony, and the larger diplomatic problems of Sicily, the Empire and other kingdoms and principalities of Europe. Innocent's pontificate was so complex that it usually invites us to look at his interests and activities as at tunnels which do not much connect with one another. But as Egger pointed out in a paper delivered at the tenth International Congress of Medieval Canon Law at Syracuse in August 1996, it is rather our own imperfect ability to connect these aspects of Lotharius' life with Innocent's concerns that leads us to pose such questions as whether he was *either* a theologian *or* a canonist. This is, as Egger said, *eine Frage überhaupt falsch gestellt*. Rather, Egger argues, we should see Innocent as the 'master of a discipline that he had acquired at Paris and Bologna, a single discipline, one that was not yet subjected to the modern organization and classification of sciences'. The fathers of this single discipline were Peter Lombard, Gratian, *and* Bernard of Clairvaux and Gerald of Wales.

The narrative pattern of the *Gesta* introduces these concerns dramatically in a strong and highly focused narrative line. After describing the election, ordination and coronation, it conveys Innocent's immediate commitment to papal business: *statim post electionem . . . sequenti die post consecrationem . . . statim post . . .* Innocent immediately deals with and dismisses the Roman request for a donation and receives the oath of the Prefect of the city (VIII). He then sends out messengers to Markward of Anweiler (IXa) and Conrad of Urslingen in the patrimony (IXb).[59] Innocent himself leaves the city on the feast of the Apostles and moves through the patrimony, dedicating churches, preaching and reconstituting territories long lost to the papacy (X). He does the same in Tuscany (XI), and elsewhere (XII-XVII), then turns his attention further outward, toward Sicily (XVIII-XXI) and to the problem of the imperial election (XXII). This strong narrative line omits most of the other details of the early pontificate, those reflected abundantly in the first few volumes of the Register, but it reveals a decisive, firm pope in action, and it notes that the working of the pontificate began on the day after the election and the day after the consecration. This is not a portrait of a pope pausing to deliberate policy and strategy in consultation with the curia, but of a pope who came to the chair of Peter with a conception of office and an agenda already laid out.[60] Lotharius had already met Bernard's criteria for a curialist, and the *Gesta*-narrative shows him meeting the criteria for a pope as well, at least those required of a pope in the late winter and early spring of 1198.

I will conclude with two citations. Lotharius began work on the *De missarum misteriis* before the pontificate and either completed or revised it later, during the pontificate.[61] Book I, Chapter 8 '*De primatu Romani pontificis*', seems to me to be a later addition, but it contains a view of the papacy that is not inconsistent with Innocent's earlier approach. It is an exegetical explanation of Jesus' establishment of Peter's primacy *ante passionem*, *circa passionem*, and *post passionem*. Because Peter is a *magister*, his faith and that of the Roman Church can never fail – a point that Innocent made several times in other statements.[62] Just as the head has a plenitude of senses and members of the body only part of the fullness of the *sensorium*, so other priests are called *in partem sollicitudinis*, but only the *summus pontifex* to the *plenitudo potestatis*. *Solus Petrus* . . . Peter alone walked to the Lord across the waters; Peter alone, taking up the sword, struck the servant of the high priest; Peter alone threw himself into the water to reach Christ.

The author of the *Gesta* designates Innocent's sermons as works composed after he became pope. In one of these, *Sermo XXII De sanctis*, the second for the feast of Peter and Paul, 29 June, perhaps in 1199 or 1200, Innocent returns to the sea that Peter courageously entered:

---

[59] The PL edition of the *Gesta* has two chapters numbered IX. I here designate them as IXa and IXb.

[60] Maccarrone, 'Innocenzo III prima del pontificato', 130-1.

[61] PL 217:763C-916A; Imkamp, *Kirchenbild*, 46-53; Maccarrone, 'Innocenzo III prima del pontificato', 110-18.

[62] *Mater Ecclesia* and *Magister Petrus* seem to be Innocent's reading of the phrase *Mater et magistra*, coined, apparently, by Gregory VII, Ep. 64 Extra Reg., PL 148:710, cited by Jounel, *Culte des saints*, 351, n.14.

For even as the sea itself is always turbulent and bitter, so the *saeculum* consists always of turbulence and bitterness: never is there peace and security, never tranquility and rest, but everywhere fear and trembling, everywhere hardship and grief . . . In the sea the lesser fish are devoured by the greater, and *in saeculo* lesser men are oppressed by the mighty.[63]

Much of this may seem conventional, coming as it did from the author of the *De miseria*, but the image of the big fish eating the little fish (later made pictorially graphic in the design for an engraving by Pieter Bruegel) was not common. In the seventeenth century such a view might be termed Hobbesian, but Hobbes spoke of the state of savage nature, and Innocent about a world of Christian lords, monarchs and emperors, hardly Leviathans, but able to oppress the weak very effectively. How is this world to be ordered? Innocent is not proposing a papal Leviathan, but, *ratione peccati*, he is getting the attention of worldly rulers so that they will respond to a grander moral vision of their responsibilities than he had seen them demonstrate so far. Innocent spelled out its meaning explicitly in the phrase that followed the image.

The deeps of the sea are Rome, which has been given primacy and principality over the universal *saeculum*, 'lest men, like fishes, should consume one another . . .'.[64] The prince of the church sits in the former seat of Roman princes, holding the keys of the kingdom of Heaven and, by means of these keys, possessing the rule of the circle of the lands, the *orbis terrarum*. The ship is the church, the sea is the world, its depths Rome, that is, if the sermon is rightly understood.

Innocent breaks his chain of metaphors at this point and offers a brief disquisition on the duties of the preacher. The techniques of exposition are the lines and chords that connect the metaphors. The *egregius praedicator* must speak in this instance as if to carnal people, since his audience is not ready for the meat of truth (1 Cor. 3:1-3). The preacher's duty is to recall the luxurious to

---

[63]PL 27:555C-6C.

[64]In his extensive study of the history of the phrase, Wilfrid Parsons did not note Innocent's use of the image and suggested that the image fell out of rhetorical usage among political theorists after the end of the eleventh century: Wilfrid Parsons, '"Lest men, like fishes . . ."', *Traditio* 3 (1945):380-8. Innocent may have taken his usage from Galatians 5:15, or, more likely, from Augustine's commentary on Psalm 64 (*Enn. in Ps. LXIV*, PL 36:780-1). The latest citations that Parsons found were those of the Synod of Trosly in 909 and Atto of Vercelli's comment on Romans 13 (Parsons, 382-3). A speech attributed to Osbert of Milan at the Diet of Roncaglia in 1158 offers another example of 'the logic of the fish' in twelfth-century thought; Philippe Buc, *'Principes gentium dominantur eorum*: Princely Power Between Legitimacy and Illegitimacy in Twelfth-Century Exegesis', *Cultures of Power: Lordship, Status, and Process in Twelfth-Century Europe*, ed. Thomas N. Bisson (Philadelphia, 1995), 310-28, at 315: 'How many kings, nay tyrants . . . favor the fish of the sea, that is to say, smooth rascals, grasping and given over to filthy pleasures . . .'. On other aspects of Innocent's political thought, see the essay by Joseph Canning in the present volume.

continence, the proud to humility and the violent to gentleness, not for mortifica-
tion, but so that they may live, not for killing, but for feeding, not to abandon
them, but to guard and protect them. This is what Peter and Paul did for pagan
Rome. This is what their successor does today. Peter and Paul should be
honored, *quasi primos et praecipuos, quasi patres et patronos.* These two texts,
I suggest, represent the core of the ideas concerning the papacy that Lotario dei
Conti di Segni, Campano-Roman nobleman, Cardinal deacon of SS. Sergius and
Bacchus, and master of a single discipline, brought to the pontificate of Innocent
III.

A Theologian at Work: Some Remarks on Methods and Sources in Innocent III's Writings[1]

Christoph Egger

'Fuerat prefatus Innocentius . . . sapientissimus in trivio et quadrivio, in theologia ceteris prestantior, ingenio velocissimus, eloquentissimus, facundus, lingua expeditissimus . . .' With these words an anonymous writer in Perugia praised the intellectual abilities of Pope Innocent III, who recently had died in the city.[2] Some years earlier the author of the *Gesta Innocentii III* stated that the cardinals had elected Lothar of Segni because of his learning, despite his rather young age. He was a 'vir perspicacis ingenii et tenacis memorie, in divinis et humanis litteris eruditus, sermone tam vulgari quam litterali disertus', whose writings show his outstanding learning in theology and philosophy: 'super coetaneos suos tam in philosophica quam theologica disciplina profecit, sicut eius opuscula manifestant

---

[1]The bibliography has been restricted to the most necessary titles. Innocent's theological writings will be quoted from Migne's *Patrologia Latina* (PL), vol. 217, except for *De miseria humane conditionis*, for which the critical edition of Michele Maccarrone (see below, n. 4) is used. The pope's letters from the registers will be quoted as Reg. with indication of the year of pontificate and the number of the letter: for the first, second, fifth, sixth and seventh year the critical edition prepared under the direction of Othmar Hageneder (Publikationen des Historischen Instituts beim Österreichischen Kulturinstitut in Rom II/1/1, 2, 5-7, Vienna 1964-1997). For the other years, the text of PL, vols. 215-16, will be used.

[2]The text was edited by Massimo Petrocchi, 'L'ultimo destino perugino di Innocenzo III,' *Bollettino della deputazione di storia patria per l'Umbria* 64 (1967):207.

que diversis temporibus edidit et dictavit.'³ In fact, in the middle ages, Innocent was an author of some renown. During his cardinalate, he wrote a treatise about the misery of the human condition, another one about the fourfold meaning of marriage and a commentary on the mass. After his election, his sermons were collected. In the last months of his life, he wrote a commentary on the penitential psalms. Some of these texts were real 'bestsellers' throughout the middle ages. The great number of manuscripts of *De miseria humane conditionis* (approximately seven hundred have survived) and of *De missarum mysteriis* proves their popularity.⁴

Most modern scholars think quite the opposite about the merits of Innocent's writings. Those who have read them criticize the allegorical style and the lack of originality: 'His theological speculations are hardly breathtaking; in fact, if one examines his sources closely, it is difficult to find an idea which is uniquely Innocent's.'⁵ But we should be careful in reproaching Innocent for lack of originality. It might be that our understanding of 'originality' is not appropriate to judge the writings of medieval authors but is rather anachronistic. If we really want to use this notion, we have to ask whether Innocent wanted to be an original writer or whether his intentions were different.

And worse, many scholars have not even read Innocent's theological writings but simply ignore them, as does Gary Macy in his otherwise excellent book about the theologies of the eucharist in the early scholastic period.⁶ Macy, whose primary concern was to find out 'what use or uses the educated Christian

---

³Gesta Innocentii III: *Text, Introduction and Commentary*, chs. 1 and 2, ed. David R. Gress-Wright, PhD Diss. (Bryn Mawr College, 1981), p. 1, ll. 7-9, 17-19 = PL 214:XVIIAB.

⁴Innocent's theological works have been printed by J. P. Migne in his *Patrologia Latina*, vol. 217. *De miseria humane conditionis* was edited by Michele Maccarrone: *Lotharii Cardinalis (Innocentii III) De miseria humane conditionis* (Lucani, 1955), and again by Robert E. Lewis, *Lotario di Segni (Pope Innocent III), De miseria condicionis humane* (Athens [Georgia], 1978), esp. 236-53 (list of manuscripts). For a part of *De missarum mysteriis*, David F. Wright has attempted to establish a critical text: *A Medieval Commentary on the Mass: Particulae 2-3 and 5-6 of the* De missarum mysteriis *(ca. 1195) of Cardinal Lothar of Segni (Pope Innocent III)*, PhD Diss. (Notre Dame [Ind.], 1977). I am preparing a critical edition of Innocent's theological works, especially his *De missarum mysteriis*.

⁵Kenneth Pennington, 'Pope Innocent III's Views on Church and State: A Gloss to *Per Venerabilem*', in *Law, Church, and Society. Essays in Honour of Stephan Kuttner*, ed. Kenneth Pennington, Robert Somerville (Philadephia, 1977), 51-2. It should be stated that Kenneth Pennington's articles about Innocent's legal education have provided the initiative to emphasize the pope's theological learning: Kenneth Pennington, 'The Legal Education of Pope Innocent III', *Bulletin of Medieval Canon Law*, n.s., 4 (1974):70-7; review of Imkamp, *Kirchenbild* (see below, n. 10), ZRG 103, Kan. 72 (1986):417-28; both reprinted in his *Popes, Canonists and Texts, 1150-1550* (Aldershot, 1993).

⁶Gary Macy, *The Theologies of the Eucharist in the Early Scholastic Period. A Study of the Salvific Function of the Sacrament according to the Theologians c. 1080 - c. 1220* (Oxford, 1984).

community in the early scholastic period see in the inherited ceremony of ritual offering and communal eating known as the Eucharist',[7] would have found a rather thorough treatment of his question in the fourth book of the *De missarum mysteriis*.[8]

Only a few historians have really appreciated and dedicated thorough studies to Innocent's theological thoughts, historians like Michele Maccarrone, who wrote about his sacramental theology,[9] or Wilhelm Imkamp, who studied Innocent's ecclesiology[10] (Imkamp's book is a good example of the importance of knowing the intellectual background in order to achieve an adequate understanding of Innocent's personality and his religious and political activities). But Maccarrone and Imkamp are also not free of conceptual prejudices. For them Innocent was an 'antidialectic theologian', fighting against the threats of Aristotelianism, a theologian who is characterized by his 'timidità teologica', his especially cautious dealing with theological problems: 'Melius est tamen deo totum committere, quam aliquid temere diffinire.'[11] In this respect I do not agree with Maccarrone and Imkamp, because their opinion depends on a limited, very schematic and therefore somehow anachronistic understanding of intellectual history of the later twelfth century. I cannot discuss this issue in detail here, but I shall do so elsewhere. I think that the question is put the wrong way: it is more important to know Innocent's intellectual background and his skills in contemporary scholarly methods than to make statements about the quality of his theology or whether he liked or disliked logic and dialectics.

Of course it is not an easy task to give a clear answer to this question. I would just like to point out briefly a few problems connected with it. Firstly, there is the problem of authorship. Actually there is no reason to doubt that Lothar of Segni/Innocent III is really the author of his theological treatises. But it cannot be taken for granted that Innocent is the author of all the letters written in his name. Some of his most interesting theological statements are to be found in letters;[12] so we have to look for criteria – for instance, quotations from the

---

[7]Ibid., 16.

[8]See *De missarum mysteriis* 4.41-4, PL 217:882-6.

[9]Michele Maccarrone, 'Innocenzo III teologo dell'Eucaristia', in *Studi su Innocenzo III.*, Italia sacra 17: (Padova,1972), 339-431.

[10]Wilhelm Imkamp, *Das Kirchenbild Innocenz' III. (1198-1216)*, Päpste und Papsttum 22 (Stuttgart, 1983).

[11]*De missarum mysteriis* 4.30, PL 217:877A. Maccarrone, *Innocenzo teologo* (see above, n. 9), 368-70; Imkamp, *Kirchenbild*, 91.

[12]See for instance the letters *Apostolice servitutis officium* (Reg. 3:216, see below, n. 35), *Cum Marthe circa, Quod pietatem colendo* and *In quadam nostra*: Reg. 5:120 (121), 6:190 (191), 12:8.

theological writings or the use of the first person singular – which might help us to establish the pope's authorship.[13]

There is another problem connected with the question of authorship. Even if Innocent is the author of a certain letter, he could have had essential advice from some specialist. We know very few details about the process of composing letters like the long theological letters in the fifth and sixth volumes of the register,[14] and at present we can only guess who the men behind the pope might have been.

Lastly there is the problem of the literary genre of the letters. Most of them reply to questions asked by ecclesiastical persons and therefore are concerned with very special theological problems. They are not systematic expositions of some dogmatic treatise like those produced in the schools. So what we read is often only scattered remarks from a context which was evident to the contemporary reader but is not to us. Many of these remarks are unique and therefore allow no comparison. So it is extremely difficult sometimes to put them into their context and to interpret them. In any case, we must be aware of the fact that they allow only limited insight into Innocent's intellectual background.

With all that in mind, I shall now give some examples from Innocent's works in order to demonstrate the range of his knowledge of contemporary scholastic methods and discussions. Based on these observations, I shall then propose an interpretative frame for Innocent's theological writings, which I hope will avoid anachronistic assumptions like those described above. Perhaps this frame will seem rather trivial, but sometimes even trivial things have to be said explicitly.

In a long letter written in December 1203, Innocent answered the questions of the retired archbishop of Lyon, Jean de Bellesmains.[15] The part of the letter I shall mention here was also used in a sermon Innocent preached on the feast of Epiphany.[16] Among many other interesting problems the pope is dealing with is the extent to which the ancient philosophers – the 'naturales philosophi' as he calls them – were able to know the Holy Trinity. They knew the Father, whom they called 'togaton' (that is the Greek 'to agathon', the Good) and the Son, whom they called 'noim' (that is 'Nous', reason). They did not know the Holy Spirit – perhaps except for the one who said: 'The first monade generates the second monade, and the first and the second monades are reflecting their ardour

---

[13]See Imkamp, *Kirchenbild* (see above, n. 10), 87-9; Christoph Egger, 'Papst Innocenz III. als Theologe. Beiträge zur Kenntnis seines Denkens im Rahmen der Frühscholastik', *Archivum historiae pontificiae* 30 (1992):113-18.

[14]Reg. 5:120 (121), pp. 234-9; Reg. 6:191(193), pp. 320-7.

[15]Reg. 6:191 (193), pp. 320-7. I have dealt with this letter in some detail in the article mentioned above, n. 13, pp. 100-13.

[16]Reg. 6:191 (193), p. 324, l. 30, p. 325 l. 13; *Sermo VIII de sanctis*, PL 217:483-90, esp. 486, l. 54 and 487, l. 18. About Innocent's sermons, see John C. Moore, 'The Sermons of Pope Innocent III', *Römische Historische Mitteilungen* 36 (1994):81-142.

between each other' – 'Prima monas secundam monadem genuit, prima et secunda suum in se reflectunt ardorem'.[17] The possible source of this sentence is not a standard textbook of the schools around 1200 but the 'theological avant-garde': the *Liber XXIV philosophorum* is a collection of axiomatic sentences put together by an anonymous author at the end of the twelfth or the beginning of the thirteenth century.[18] It is difficult to find out if Innocent made direct use of the *Liber* or if he took the sentence from another text, for instance from the *Regule celestis iuris* of Alanus of Lille.[19] Anyway, that the pope knew sentences like this shows his acquaintance with contemporary theological discussions and is therefore worth noting.

In another part of this letter there is a short quotation from the *Expositio in Apocalypsim* of Joachim of Fiore.[20] But there is another letter which even better testifies to Innocent's aquaintance with this author or at least with his writings. In November 1204, the pope sent to the bishops and the clergy of the crusader army a long and thorough interpretation of what he thought was the meaning of the recent capture of Constantinople.[21] The whole text, being an exposition of the Easter narrative according to the gospel of John (20:1-17), is inspired by Joachim's *Expositio*, two lengthy litteral quotations included.[22] Joachim of Fiore is certainly not what we call a scholastic author but is a rather singular figure because of his exegetical methods, the complexity of his thought and the fortune of his writings. In fact it is difficult to characterize the role he played in the intellectual world around 1200.[23] Therefore the use Innocent made of his texts is a striking example of the pope's range of knowledge.

Another example: in 1208, Innocent inaugurated a stational liturgy in the church of S. Maria in Sassia in order to support his foundation the hospital of S.

---

[17]Reg. 6:191 (193), p. 325, ll. 11-13; *Sermo VIII de sanctis*, PL 217:487B.

[18]*Le livre des XXIV Philosophes*, ed. and trans. Françoise Hudry (Grenoble, 1989), 89. See Mechtild Dreyer, *More mathematicorum. Rezeption und Transformation der antiken Gestalten wissenschaftlichen Wissens im 12. Jahrhundert*, Beiträge zur Geschichte der Philosophie und Theologie des Mittelalters, NF. 47 (Münster, 1996), 147.

[19]Alanus of Lille, *Regulae caelestis iuris*, ed. Nikolaus M. Häring, *Archives d'Histoire doctrinale et littéraire du Moyen-Age* 48 (1981):127, Regula 3.

[20]Reg. 6:191 (193), p. 324, ll. 8-10; Joachim of Fiore, *Expositio in Apocalypsim* (Venice, 1527), fol. 35va. There is a very close parallel to this part of the letter in Innocent's *Sermo IV de sanctis*, PL 217:467BD. See Egger, Innocent III (see above, n. 13), 106-9; Fiona Robb, 'Did Innocent III Personally Condemn Joachim of Fiore?', *Florensia* 7 (1993):77-91.

[21]Reg. 7:154, pp. 264-70.

[22] Reg. 7:154, p. 267 ll. 4-20, p. 268 ll. 8-16; Joachim, *Expositio*, fols 143vb-144ra.

[23] From the extensive bibliography about Joachim, I shall mention only Marjorie Reeves, *The Influence of Prophecy in the Later Middle Ages. A Study in Joachimism* (1969, repr. Notre Dame and London, 1993).

Spirito.[24] On this occasion he preached a sermon about the lesson from the gospel of the day, the wedding of Cana (John 2:1-11).[25] Innocent interpreted the text in the moral sense. Especially interesting is his interpretation of the 'architriclinius', the person who was in charge of the food and drink and tasted the water converted into wine by Jesus. According to Innocent, he signifies the 'synderesis', which forms a part of the human mind, being the conscience that recognizes good or bad, which even in the worst sinner cannot be extinguished.[26] The term *synderesis* originates from a writing error in Jerome's commentary on the book Ezechiel. The word should be read as *syneidesis* and means conscience. The first author known to have used *synderesis* is the theologian Master Udo who wrote around 1160. Then there are Peter of Poitiers, the canonist Simon of Bisignano, Peter Capuanus, Stephen Langton and Innocent. As far as I presently know there is only one other text where Innocent uses *synderesis*: the commentary on the penitential psalms.[27] Apparently the pope is among the first users of this notion, which became very important in thirteenth-century moral theology.

Another example: in the fourth book of *De missarum mysteriis*, Innocent is dealing with the question of the exact moment of the transubstantiation of bread and wine into Christ's flesh and blood.[28] Almost every master of the schools felt obliged to write about this question, and Innocent's way of discussing it is very similar to their texts. After the consecratorial words for the bread, Christ's body is present on the altar, but without blood, because the consecratorial words for the wine have not yet been said. Hence, the wine has not been transubstantiated. Here Innocent makes a short remark concerning a similar problem in the writings of the logicians, who discuss the sentence 'Hoc vivum est mortuum'. In Migne's edition this part of the text is rather enigmatic, because he prints 'vinum' instead of 'vivum'.[29] It is worth noticing that in some contemporary logical treatises,

---

[24]Reg. 10:179, PL 215:1270-1. See Brenda Bolton, 'Hearts not purses: Innocent III's Attitude to Social Welfare', in *Through the Eye of a Needle: Judaeo-Christian Roots of Social Welfare*, ed. Emily Albu Hanawalt and Carter Lindberg (Missouri, 1994), 123-45, repr. in Brenda Bolton, *Innocent III: Studies on Papal Authority and Pastoral Care*, Variorum Collected Studies Series 490 (Aldershot, 1995), article XVIII; Christoph Egger, 'Papst Innocenz III und die Veronica. Geschichte, Theologie, Liturgie und Seelsorge', *The Holy Face and the Paradox of Representation*, ed. Herbert L. Kessler and Gerhard Wolf, Villa Spelman Colloquia 6 (Bologna, forthcoming).

[25]*Sermo VIII de tempore*, PL 217:345-50.

[26]*Sermo VIII de tempore*, PL 217:347AB. See Christoph Egger, 'Dignitas und Miseria. Überlegungen zu Menschenbild und Selbstverständnis Papst Innocenz' III.', *Mitteilungen des Instituts für Österreichische Geschichtsforschung* 105 (1997):340-1.

[27]*Commentarium in septem psalmos poenitentiales*, on Ps. 31.4. PL 217:1012A; Egger, 'Dignitas', p. 341.

[28]*De missarum mysteriis* 4.17, PL 217:868B-869B: 'Quando fiat transsubstantiatio'.

[29]PL 217:868C. I have checked the text in some manuscripts, e.g. Admont, Stiftsbibliothek, MS 341, fol. 47r; Vatican City, Biblioteca Apostolica Vaticana, MS Vat. lat. 4925, fol. 46v and MS Ottob. lat. 4, fol. 41vb.

which their editor Lambert de Rijk called *Tractatus Anagnini* and *Tractatus Monacensis*, the sentence about the 'vivum mortuum' is discussed as an example.[30] Again there is no indication that Innocent made use of these treatises. But as a student of the schools of Paris, he must have had some knowledge of logic and dialectic. This knowledge is part of Innocent's intellectual background even if it is only rarely recognizable.[31]

In chapter nine of the fourth book of *De missarum mysteriis*, Innocent is dealing with the breaking of the eucharistic host. Connected with this question is another one concerning the relationship between the substance of Christ's body and the accidents of the bread. This problem was often put forward in asking what would a mouse be eating if it managed to get hold of a consecrated host, the true body of Christ or just a piece of bread?[32] In discussing this problem, Innocent points out that there is a difference between the meaning of accident 'in physica facultate' and 'in theologica veritate'.[33] Maccarrone interpreted this statement as polemics against the audacious and superfluous questions of the logicians,[34] but I do not think that he was right.

Let us first have a look at a letter from the third volume of Innocent's registers. It is an answer to several theological questions raised by Archbishop Peter of Santiago de Compostella on problems of Christology and of the Trinity.[35] Because of its highly technical language and the subtlety of the problems dealt with, the text is rather difficult to understand and to interpret. With some

---

[30]Lambert M. de Rijk, *Logica Modernorum. A Contribution to the History of Early Terminist Logic*, Wijsgerige Teksten en Studies 6 & 16/1-2 (Assen, 1962-1967), 2/2:263-4 (*Tractatus Anagnini* III, 1), p. 344 (*Tractatus de univocatione Monacensis*).

[31]There are more examples that I shall describe elsewhere. About the place of logic in the curriculum of the twelfth-century schools, see Rolf Köhn, 'Schulbildung und Trivium im lateinischen Hochmittelalter und ihr möglicher praktischer Nutzen', in *Schule und Studium im sozialen Wandel des hohen und späten Mittelalters*, ed. Johannes Fried, Vorträge und Forschungen, 30 (Sigmaringen, 1986):203-84; Klaus Jacobi, 'Logic (II): the Later Twelfth Century', in *A History of Twelfth-Century Western Philosophy*, ed. Peter Dronke (1988, repr. Cambridge, 1992), pp. 227-51.

[32]*De missarum mysteriis* 4.9, PL 217:861D-2C; see 4.11 (ibid. 863BC). This is also a standard question of twelfth-century eucharistic theology; see Artur Michael Landgraf, 'Die in der Frühscholastik klassische Frage Quid sumit mus', in *idem, Dogmengeschichte der Frühscholastik* (Regensburg, 1955), 3/2:207-22; Gary Macy, 'Of Mice and Manna: Quid Mus Sumit as a Pastoral Question', *Recherches de théologie ancienne et médiévale* 58 (1991):157-66.

[33]'Hi facile solvunt quaestionem illam, qua quaeritur quid a mure comeditur, cum sacramentum corroditur: Comeditur secundum illos illa panis substantia, sub qua corpus Christi esse mox desinit. Porro qualem significandi modum habet nomen accidentis in physica facultate, talem existendi modum habet accidens nominis in theologica veritate.' PL 217:862B.

[34]Maccarrone, *Innocenzo III teologo* (see above, n. 9), 367.

[35]The letter was contained in the lost part of the third volume of Innocent's registers (see the Rubricella in Augustinus Theiner, *Vetera Monumenta Slavorum Meridionalium Historiam illustrantia* [1863, repr. Osnabrück, 1968], 1:53, no. 216); the text is known from some decretal collections. I shall quote from the collection of Rainer of Pomposa 1. un., PL 216:1175A-1179B.

probability, we can assume that Innocent himself is the author of the letter, because it is one of the two letters presently known in which the pope makes use of the first person singular: 'Ego vero solebam concedere quando scholasticis studiis incumbebam . . .'[36] The focal question is whether the names of the triune God should be understood as proper names. How could the relationship between such a name and the named person be described? In order to solve this question Innocent first makes a statement about theological language (and in my opinion this statement provides the background for the above-mentioned sentence about the different meanings of the notion 'accidens' to natural philosophers and to theologians): 'Habent enim singulae facultates proprias rationes, nec in eis in uno modo significant nomina semper et verba' – every faculty has its own modes of expression. Therefore the same word could have a different meaning when used in a discussion of natural philosophers or when used in a theological discussion.[37] This principle was first developed by Gilbert of Poitiers in his commentaries on Boethius' theological treatises,[38] and it became common knowledge of academic theology during the second half of the twelfth century.[39] Innocent himself explicitly stated that he is treating the problem 'scholastico more' – like the masters of the schools. At the end of the letter, Innocent gives an example of how to deal with the problem in a different way.

This statement gives us a clue to an interpretative frame for his writings. He says that after having discussed the problem 'more scholastico' he could also handle it 'more apostolico'.[40] In this part the pope emphasizes the impossibility of making affirmative statements about God. All we can say about God with certainty is what he is not: 'Iuxta sapientiam cuiusdam sapientis verior sit de celo negatio quam affirmatio'.[41] The tradition of negative theology as it is expressed here can be traced back to Pseudo-Dionysius Areopagita. His writings were known in the twelfth century through translations, through a commentary written by Johannes Scotus Eriugena and through Hugh of St Victor's commentary on the 'Hierarchia coelestis'. To my knowledge, this explicit statement in favour of negative theology is unique in Innocent's writings.

---

[36]PL 216:1175D. The other letter is Reg. 7:203, p. 355, ll. 11-21, p. 356, ll. 18-24.

[37]PL 216:1175C.

[38]See Nikolaus M. Häring (ed.), *The Commentaries on Boethius by Gilbert of Poitiers*, Studies and Texts 13 (Toronto, 1966), see index s.v. *facultas*.

[39]Bernhard Geyer, 'Facultas theologica. Eine bedeutungsgeschichtliche Untersuchung', *Zeitschrift für Kirchengeschichte* 75 (1964):133-45.

[40]'Haec ergo tibi scholastico more respondemus. Sed si oporteat nos more apostolico [apostolica PL] respondere, simplicius quidem sed cautius respondemus . . .' PL 216:1178B.

[41]PL 216:1179B. See for instance Hugh of St Victor, *Expositio in hierarchiam coelestem*, PL 175:974BC; Alanus of Lille, *Regulae caelestis iuris*, ed. Häring (see above, n. 19), 136, Regula 18.

But what does 'more apostolico' mean? In the part which Innocent described as 'scholastico more', the formal and thematic vicinity to the discussions of the schools is obvious. Speaking 'apostolico more', Innocent says that he will argue 'simplicius quidem sed cautius', in a more simple and cautious manner.[42] In this context, 'apostolico more' cannot be interpreted in the usual meaning of the adjective 'apostolicus' as 'speaking like the successor of saint Peter', 'speaking as pope'.[43] There is no apparent reason why the pope should adopt a more simple manner of speaking when explaining matters of doctrine and faith.   Rather 'apostolicus' might be understood as 'speaking like an apostle', that is like somebody who has to communicate theological doctrines to a wider audience, like somebody who has to preach. In a letter to his legate in Spain Rainer of Ponza, Innocent says that preaching is part of the apostles' office, because Christ himself ordered them to do so.[44] The apostle Paul is an example of an excellent preacher; he is the 'predicator egregius'.[45] Therefore preaching is part of the life of those who are successors to the apostles in the office of pastoral care.[46] As far as we know, Innocent wrote no treatises of scholastic theology in a narrow sense, and I wonder why he should have done so, not being a teacher at Paris or elsewhere, but subdeacon of the Roman church, cardinal deacon of SS. Sergio e Bacco in Rome and finally pope. His writings aim to be understood by many people, not only by the masters of the schools. If we do not read Innocent's texts as scholastic theology, that is, theology of the schools, but – to borrow Father Leonard Boyle's expression – as 'applied theology', we use an interpretative frame the background of which has already been explained: it is Innocent's concern for pastoral practice and care. Therefore, his writings provide us with the unique opportunity to watch a former student of the schools putting into practice what he has learned there. We can watch a theologian at work.

---

[42]PL 216:1178B.

[43]See L.-M. Dewailly, 'Notes sur l'histoire de l'adjectiv apostolique', *Mélanges de science réligieuse* 5 (1948):141-52.

[44]Reg. 2:113 (122), p. 238, ll. 12-15; see Reg. 2:132 (141), p. 272, ll. 16-19; dedicatory letter of the collection of Innocent's sermons, PL 217: 311.

[45]See e.g. Reg. 1:44, p. 68; Reg. 2:60 (63), p. 112, ll. 9-10. Alberto Forni, 'Kerygma e adattamento. Aspetti della predicazione cattolica nei secoli XII-XIV', *Bullettino dell'Istituto storico italiano per il medio evo* 89 (1980-1981):281: 'San Paolo diventa il simbolo del predicatore competente.'

[46]The importance of preaching and pastoral care was emphasized by Peter the Chanter, who was one of Innocent's teachers in Paris. See John W. Baldwin, *Masters, Princes and Merchants. The Social Views of Peter the Chanter and his Circle*, 2 vols (Princeton, 1970), 1:107-16.

Innocent III as Canonist and Theologian: The Case of Spiritual Matrimony

Richard Kay

No one doubts that under Innocent III the papacy brought about many great changes in Latin Christendom, which this conference is celebrating. Our celebrations are haunted, however, by the spectre raised by Kenneth Pennington, who has led us to wonder about the extent of Innocent's knowledge of canon law. Pennington began, in 1974, by pointing out that there is no firm evidence that Innocent studied law under the great canonist Huguccio.[1] His conclusions were challenged in 1983 by Wilhelm Imkamp,[2] and Pennington defended them persuasively in 1986,[3] so today no one can assume that Innocent's debt to Huguccio is a proven fact. But gradually and cautiously Pennington has pursued the implications of his original thesis, probing to see just how extensive Innocent's knowledge of canon law really was. One approach has been to argue that 'it is unlikely that two years would have been an adequate period of study to learn Roman and canon law well enough to have produced some of the superb

---

[1] Kenneth Pennington, 'The Legal Education of Pope Innocent III', BMCL 4 (1974):70-7; reprinted in *idem, Popes, Canonists and Texts, 1150-1550*, Variorum Collected Series 412 (Aldershot, 1993), art. 1. My references are to the reprint.

[2] Wilhelm Imkamp, *Das Kirchenbild Innocenz' III. (1198-1216)*, Päpste und Papsttum 22 (Stuttgart, 1983).

[3] Kenneth Pennington, 'Further Thoughts on Pope Innocent III's Knowledge of Law', in his *Popes, Canonists and Texts*, art. 2; first published as a review of Imkamp's *Kirchenbild* (see above, n. 2), in ZRG Kan. 72 (1986):417-28.

decretal letters which we find in his registers'.[4] Although John Moore has recently shown that Innocent had almost three, rather than two, years during which he might have studied law at Bologna,[5] probably we will never know whether he ever did so, much less for how long. Pennington accordingly pioneered another approach by seeking to determine the extent of Innocent's personal knowledge of canon law. In one instance he was able to show that, at the end of Innocent's first year as pope, his interpretation of one canon was less than professional.[6] Most recently, Pennington has insisted that Innocent's knowledge of law simply remains an open question. 'The point', he concluded, 'is that we should squeeze as much evidence as possible out of Innocent's works.'[7]

When I heard this question being hotly debated in August 1996 at the Syracuse canon law congress, I decided to do some squeezing myself. Much of the evidence for Innocent's personal views has come from the sermon he preached on the first anniversary of his consecration as pope. It occurred to me that this might fruitfully be compared with some of the views he expressed before he became pope, and that is what this paper proposes to do.

Accordingly, the first problem is to find a comparable subject with possible legal, and specifically canonistic, content among the authentic writings of Innocent the theologian. His most popular work, *On the Misery of the Human Condition*, which survives in 672 manuscripts, is purely theological,[8] but offers nothing of ecclesiological, much less legal, interest.[9] Another work, *On the Mysteries of the Mass*, was somewhat less popular, with 194 known manuscripts,

---

[4]Kenneth Pennington, 'Pope Innocent III's Views on Church and State: A Gloss to *Per venerabilem*', in *Law, Church and Society: Essays in Honor of Stephan Kuttner*, ed. Kenneth Pennington and Robert Somerville (Philadelphia, 1977), 51; reprinted in *Popes, Canonists and Texts*, art. 4 (quotation on p. 5). He quotes this passage in ibid., art. 2, pp. 6-7.

[5]John C. Moore, 'Lotario dei Conti di Segni (Pope Innocent III) in the 1180s', *Archivum historiae pontificiae* 29 (1991):255-8.

[6]Pennington, *Popes, Canonists and Texts*, art. 2, pp. 12-14. The canon is D.79 c.3, cited by Innocent in his anniversary sermon (PL 217:663b); see below, at nn. 34 and esp. 54. Pennington has identified two other instances of Innocent's lack of juristic orientation: one in *De missarum misteriis* (ibid., art. 2, p. 14, at n. 42), the other in his translation decretals (X 1.7): ibid., art. 2, pp. 11-12, and *idem, Pope and Bishops: The Papal Monarchy in the Twelfth and Thirteenth Centuries* (Philadelphia, 1984), 85-100.

[7]Pennington, *Popes, Canonists and Texts*, art. 2, p. 14.

[8]Jane Sayers, *Innocent III: Leader of Europe 1198-1216* (London, 1994), 19-20. Latin text most recently ed. and trans. Robert E. Lewis: Lotario dei Segni (Pope Innocent III), *De miseria condicionis humane*, The Chaucer Library (Athens, Ga., 1978); Latin text only ed. Michele Maccarrone: Lotharii cardinalis (Innocentii III), *De miseria humane conditionis* (Lugano, 1955).

[9]Without comment, Imkamp excludes the *De miseria* as a source for Innocent's ecclesiology (*Kirchenbild*, 19, 46-90).

but it relates more to liturgy than to law properly speaking.[10] Instead we must turn to a third work, which is devoted to matrimony, a subject about which both Innocent and the canonists had much to say.

DE QUADRIPARTITA SPECIE NUPTIARUM

This is the treatise *On the Four Species of Nuptials*, which survives in three manuscripts, only one of which is complete (Bologna, Bibl. Univ. 1194). Trombelli's accurate transcript of this manuscript, made in 1755, occupies some 48 columns of Migne's *Patrologia* (217:921-68).[11] The *De quadripartita* was apparently written during Innocent's last years as a cardinal. Certainly it was circulating at the curia in February 1199, when he cited it in *Sermo 3 de diversis*, which celebrated the first anniversary of his consecration;[12] on the other hand, it was written after the *De missarum misteriis*, which it cites,[13] and, according to Maccarrone, that work was written some time between 1195 and 1197.[14] Thus most probably the *De quadripartita* was written during the year or so just before Innocent was elected pope on 8 January 1198.[15]

The *De quadripartita*, at least in the form we know it, appears to be two works loosely combined and given an epistle dedicatory (2 columns, PL 217:921-2). The first part is the core of the work and treats the four species of nuptials, as the title states (26 columns, 923-48); the second part, subtitled 'Epithalamium in laudem sponsi et sponsae', is a commentary on Psalm 44 (20 columns, 949-68) and for the present purpose is irrelevant. Let us therefore concentrate on the first part.

Innocent begins abruptly by announcing that, because nuptials (*nuptiae*) are mentioned in the Bible, there should accordingly be four species of them, since

---

[10]On Innocent's *De missarum misteriis* (PL 217:763c-916a), see Imkamp, *Kirchenbild*, 46-53.

[11]A more recent edition has been done by Connie Munk, 'A Study of Pope Innocent III's Treatise *De quadripartita specie nuptiarum*', 2 vols (PhD diss. in History, University of Kansas, 1975), Xerox University Microfilms, no. 76-16,758. I cite the Migne edition, which is widely available and an accurate transcript of Bologna, Bibl. Univ., MS. 1194, fols 110-43 (see Imkamp, *Kirchenbild*, 54-7). Unaware of Trombelli's source and paleographical expertise, Munk tended to prefer the readings of other manuscripts; when I agree, I will emend the Trombelli-Migne text with [square brackets] and cite the Munk edition.

[12]*De quad.* is quoted at length in *Sermo 3 de diversis* (PL 217:661a-d). The two texts are printed in parallel by Imkamp, *Kirchenbild*, 214-16.

[13]*De quad.* cites *De missarum misteriis*: PL 217:941a.

[14]Although Maccarrone dates the *De missarum misteriis* 1195-1197 (Imkamp, *Kirchenbild*, 57); Sayers opts for 'c. 1195' (*Innocent*, 21). The citation of *De missarum misteriis* in *De quad.* (see above, n. 12) may, however, date from a second redaction; the title of the only complete manuscript of *De quad.* says it is the book 'domini Innocentii papae tertii' (PL 217:921-2).

[15]Imkamp gives 'als Abfassungzeit das Jahr 1197 – Februar 1198' (*Kirchenbild*, 57), evidently calculating from Innocent's consecration (22 February 1198) rather than from his election. But, as his administration began with his election, 8 January 1198 is a more accurate *terminus ad quem*.

biblical texts can be interpreted in four different senses. (1) The basic sense was literal; at this lowest level, of carnal matrimony, a man and his lawful woman are united in one flesh. (2) In the allegorical sense of Scripture marriage is a figure of Christ's union with the Church, so that head and members are joined together in one body, which type Innocent labels 'sacramental marriage'. (3) Read 'tropologically', that is, in a moral sense, marriage typifies the union of the just, or righteous, soul with God, or more often in Innocent's subsequent treatment, with Christ, in what he calls 'spiritual marriage' because the two are one in spirit. (4) The fourth sense is 'anagogical', and in this sense marriage signifies the union of the Word and human nature in Christ's person, and hence it is termed 'personal marriage'.

There is nothing particularly original about all this, as twelfth-century exegetes were forever discerning the four senses of Scripture. Indeed, the idea that Christ's union with the Church is a figure of human marriage goes back to St Paul (Ephesians 5:23).

What is original is Innocent's determined attempt to elaborate the metaphor systematically and at great length. After the introduction (PL 917:923c-4b), he first shows in twenty-two chapters (with a rubric for each) how the matrimonial metaphor applies to the Incarnation (924b-8a), and having thus worked out the fourth sense, he devotes the rest of this part to the second and third senses, which are treated together under fifty-four further topical headings (928a-48d).

These topics seem to have been his unit of composition. Apparently he assembled a list of the various aspects of human marriage, such as the dowry, the witnesses, the best man, and particularly the trappings of the wedding ceremony and the subsequent banquet. To this list of *realia* he added other related but more abstract topics, such as fidelity, fornication, bigamy, separation and consent. Innocent's method was simple: armed with this list of marriage-related topics, he composed a paragraph on each topic, showing, often with great ingenuity, how the topic that he had derived from literal, carnal marriage has its counterpart in a given form of figurative matrimony. For example, the best man (*paranymphus*) in Christ's wedding to the Church was John the Baptist, as he himself had declared (John 3:29); in Christ's wedding to the just soul, the *paranymphus* was fear of the Lord (PL 217:942c-3b), while in his Incarnation it was the archangel Gabriel (926a). The challenge was to justify each identification with one or more proof texts drawn from Holy Scripture.

Since the topical paragraphs are presented as individual units with little or no express principle of order, it would appear that Innocent composed them individually and then arranged each in a convenient, somewhat systematic order, beginning in each series with the consensual contract and ending with the moment when the bride is handed over to the custody of her husband (*traditio*). Within this general plan, however, the two series often treat the same materials in a different order. The second series concludes with the wedding feast (*convivium*), from which Innocent segues into his third part, a commentary on Psalm 44, which he takes to be an epithalamium to be sung, as it were, at the festivities. It is noteworthy that in this chronological arrangement of his material, in both series Innocent omits the last stage of a carnal marriage, namely its sexual consummation. Although some twelfth-century canonists had maintained that coitus as well as consent was necessary to effect a marriage, by 1197 canonists, led by Huguccio, had accepted the doctrine of Peter Lombard and the Paris theologians, who maintained that coitus was not an essential element.[16]

There can be no doubt that the *De quadripartita* is essentially a work of biblical exegesis that displays the skills Innocent had acquired in Paris. In view of the Pennington thesis, however, it is worth inquiring whether there is any trace of canonistic learning in this work, composed just before Innocent became pope. As far as I can ascertain, nothing in the *De quadripartita* indicates that Innocent's training was anything but theological. To be sure, theologians often dealt in their way with the same subjects as canon lawyers, but when Innocent's source can be identified, it invariably turns out to be theological.[17] In fact, as far as I can tell, his only literary source other than the Bible seems to have been the *Sentences* of Peter Lombard, which was the standard theological textbook at Paris. Although many parallel passages could be cited, one will suffice. Innocent's dependence on the *Sentences* is placed beyond doubt by at least one direct quotation of the Lombard's *ipsissima verba*: in *Sent.* 4.26.6, it is Peter and not one of his *auctoritates* who declares that 'inter coniuges coniunctio est secundum consensum animorum et secundum permixtionem corporum'.[18] Innocent echoes this phrase under the rubric *De consensu animorum et commixtione corporum*: 'Caeterum duo sunt in conjugio: consensus animorum, et commistio corporum.'[19]

---

[16]James A. Brundage, *Law, Sex, and Christian Society in Medieval Europe* (Chicago, 1987), 268; Constance M. Rousseau, 'The Spousal Relationship: Marital Society and Sexuality in the Letters of Pope Innocent III', *Mediaeval Studies* 56 (1994):89-109, at 91-2.

[17]An exception might seem to be the *quaestio* Innocent argues, 'Whether Christ is to be called a bigamist (*bigamus*)' because he repudiated *Synagoga* in favor of *Ecclesia* (PL 217:935c-6c). *Bigamus* might seem to be a legal term; certainly Peter Lombard avoids it when discussing the concept, even though he borrows his material from Gratian (*Sent.* 4.33.4.1-2, ed. Brady, 2:461). Nonetheless, the term was in current use by Paris theologians: e.g. Peter Comestor, *Historia scholastica*, Genesis 28: 'Lamech . . . [Genesis 5:28-31] qui primus bigamiam introduxit . . .' (PL 198:1078d).

[18]Peter Lombard, *Sententiae* 4.26.6, ed. Ignatius Brady et al., *Magistri Petri Lombardi Parisiensis episcopi Sententiae in IV libris distinctae*, 3 vols, Spicilegium Bonaventurianum 4-5 (Grottaferrata, 1971-81), 2:420.

[19]*De quad.*, ed. PL 217:930a.

Assured by this clear case of borrowing, many other parallels between the two texts may be safely assumed to have been borrowed as well.[20]

Consequently, our conclusion from this brief analysis of Innocent's *De quadripartita* must be that its literary sources are the Bible and the *Sentences* of Peter Lombard, and its method is that of the Paris school of theology. Hence it would seem that the author, on the eve of his pontificate, was innocent of canonistic proclivities, much less training. It should be noted in passing, however, that the work does afford the social historian an interesting profile of contemporary marriage practices, since Innocent apparently drew on them in selecting his topics. For example, he indicates that for the sake of completeness at her betrothal (*desponsatio*) a sponsa should be given three things: a ring, an embrace and a kiss.[21]

SERMO 3 DE DIVERSIS

Innocent's *De quadripartita* has a pendant, or corollary. To celebrate the first anniversary of his consecration, which fell on 22 February 1199,[22] Innocent extended his matrimonial analogy to cover the mystical marriage of the pope to the Roman Church, and incidentally, of other bishops to their dioceses as well. This consecration sermon presents a curious contrast to the *De quadripartita*, for Innocent now expressly cites canon law, as well as the Bible, to support his arguments. There can be no doubt about this, for in three instances he says that his authority is *in canone* and in a fourth it is *canonica auctoritas*.[23] Moreover, much of the sermon is devoted to questions that are more canonistic than theological. Yet this sermon, like the *De quadripartita*, is not an official

---

[20]E.g. *De quad.*, ed. PL 217:932a, where Innocent lists the three benefits of marriage as faith, offspring and sacrament, to each of which he devotes a separate chapter (932a-3c). The treatment is ultimately derived from Augustine, via Peter Lombard, *Sent.* 4.31.1-3. Gratian, to be sure, quotes another passage from Augustine to the same effect (Munk, ed. cit., 2.36), but very briefly (8 lines = C.27 q.2 c.10, ed. Friedberg, 1:1065); Innocent does not echo the passage.

[21]*De quad.*, ed. PL 217:942a: 'His ergo ornata virtutibus Ecclesia desponsatur, et ad plenitudinem desponsationis omnimodam annulatur, amplexatur, et osculatur . . .'

[22]Innocent explains that the sermon was not delivered on 22 February, however, because that day was the feast of St Peter in Antioch; instead, the anniversary celebration was moved to some less prestigious day (PL 217:663c), perhaps 23 February, as Imkamp assumes (*Kirchenbild*, 57). The printed editions (*princeps* Cologne 1552; reprinted Cologne 1575 and PL 217:659d-66d) indicate that this anniversary was the first: 'Anniversarium ergo diem, quo fuit hoc conjugium spirituale consummatum, hodie mecum primum celebratis . . .' (PL 217:663c); but Munk, who edits the text as an appendix to her study of *De quad.* (see above, n. 19), omits *primum* because it occurs in neither of the extant manuscripts (ed. cit., line 134) though it was undoubtedly in the lost exemplar of the *editio princeps*. The present paper will show that topical allusions link this sermon to events of Innocent's first year (below, nn. 39 and 43).

[23]PL 217:633ab. Munk, wrongly I think, prefers the variant 'cautum tradit auctoritas' to 'canonica tradit auctoritas' (ed. cit., line 127 vs. PL 217:663b). Cf. nn. 32-34, 52, below.

document; Innocent is speaking in his own voice. Indeed, when he collected his early sermons (1202-1204), Innocent described them as 'certain sermons . . . which I have preached and written down',[24] which certainly emphasizes their personal character. Thus there can be no doubt that Innocent in his private capacity could and did display a knowledge of canon law. But it does seem remarkable that his canonistic competence appears so abruptly in this sermon, hardly a year after the composition of the exclusively theological *De quadripartita*. If we can explain the difference, perhaps we can come to a better understanding of Innocent the canonist. Let us begin by analyzing the anniversary sermon in detail.

It is not long – less than five columns in Migne's format. Innocent begins by announcing the text, or pericope, on which the sermon will be based. It is well worth noting, if only as the key to the sermon's structure, for Innocent returns to it four times, in each case in order to view his theme from a different perspective. The pericope is John 3:29a: 'He that hath the *sponsa* is the *sponsus*: but the friend (*amicus*) of the *sponsus*, who standeth and heareth him, rejoiceth with joy because of the voice of the *sponsus*.'[25] Innocent tersely expounds the literal meaning: Christ is the *sponsus*, the Church his *sponsa*, and John the Baptist who said these words is their best man (*paranymphus*), the *amicus sponsi*. Innocent then places this in the context of 'the little book we have published on the four species of nuptials' (PL 217:661a) by repeating its first two introductory chapters *in extenso* and practically verbatim (661a-d), which are the ones in which the four species of matrimony are distinguished and identified. This replaces the conventional preacher's *divisio thematis* and demonstrates that Innocent's text concerns the second species, namely sacramental matrimony between Christ and the Church, which unites two in one body (*in una corpore*).

The pericope is then repeated to signal that Innocent will now begin to elaborate his chosen theme (*dilatio thematis*) by offering two alternative allegorical interpretations of the literal text, in which John was the friend of the bridegroom. In the first allegory, Innocent proposes that as pope he himself is the *amicus sponsi* in Christ's marriage to the Church (PL 217:661d-2c). The pope can be said to rejoice, like the best man in the pericope, because as Peter's successor he has the keys of the kingdom of heaven (Matt. 16:19) and, in the words of Jeremiah 1:10, has been 'set over the nations and kingdoms . . .'. These two proof texts were mainstays of papal ecclesiology, familiar enough to canonists and indeed to all curialists. Matrimony only leads into this first allegory but plays no further part in it.

---

[24]PL 217:311-12: 'quosdam sermones ad clerum et populum, nunc litterali, nunc vulgari lingua proposui et dictavi . . .'. See Imkamp, *Kirchenbild*, 64.
[25]John 3:29a, trans. Douay-Rheims, altered.

For our purpose, the most noteworthy feature of this section is that Innocent begins his exposition by announcing: 'Ego, fratres, sum amicus Sponsi' – 'I, brothers, am the friend of the Bridegroom' (PL 217:661d).[26] Since it is qua pope that he is *amicus Sponsi*, it follows that in this context his brothers are the pope's *fratres*, the cardinals, who are regularly so addressed by the pope.[27] At the end of the sermon, after the last pericope, he will indicate that others, who are addressed as his 'sons', are also in the audience ('Vos autem fratres et filii', 666b). These indications of the intended audience are significant because I would argue that it influenced his choice of *auctoritates*. For it was a principle of medieval preaching, propounded by Gregory the Great, that 'the discourse of teachers ought to be fashioned according to the quality of the hearers'.[28] Consequently the most effective sermon was one addressed to a specific, homogeneous target audience, in this case, a curial one in which the cardinals were the most prominent element. After a year's experience of conferring with them, Innocent surely knew that this was an audience that appreciated canon law, probably more than theology.

He brings the cardinals into the picture with his second allegorical reading of the pericope, which runs almost to the end of the sermon (PL 217:662c-6b). He announces his new thesis abruptly: 'Am I not the *sponsus* and any one of you the *amicus sponsi*?' he asks, and immediately answers his rhetorical question in the affirmative.[29] Just as Christ is married to the universal Church in the literal text, so in the allegory the pope is joined to the Roman Church in a sacramental marriage[30] at which the cardinals function as friends of the bridegroom.

The cardinals' role in the allegory is not elaborated. Instead, Innocent justifies his analogy by raising three objections to it, which he answers with his most overt display of canonistic learning. The first is the rather playful paradox that Innocent can be married even though he has taken a vow of celibacy. This objection is summarily brushed aside by observing that, because spiritual marriage does not involve sexual intercourse, it is compatible with celibacy.

The second objection is wholly based on canon law. 'A carnal marriage, between a man and a woman, is customarily said to be initiated, ratified and consummated. It is initiated in betrothal, confirmed in consent and consummated

---

[26]Munk (ed. cit., line 50) rightly emends the Trombelli-Migne text, which reads 'Ego factus sum amicus Sponsi', (661d) to *fratres*.

[27]Imkamp, *Kirchenbild*, 60.

[28]*Regula pastoralis 3*, proem, ed. PL 77:49: 'Pro qualitate igitur audientium formari debet sermo doctorum . . .'. See Richard Kay, *Dante's Swift and Strong* (Lawrence, 1978), 99 and 348, n. 159.

[29]PL 217:662c: 'An non ego sponsus sum, et quilibet vestrum amicus sponsi? Utique.'

[30]Significantly, perhaps, he here (PL 217:662d) describes the Roman Church by the same set of attributes ('Sara maturior', etc.) that he had ascribed to the Church universal in *De quad.* (PL 217:941a).

in copulation. Likewise a spiritual marriage between a bishop and church is said to be initiated in election, ratified in confirmation and consummated in consecration' (PL 217:663a). In both cases Innocent seems to be reporting a *communis opinio*.[31] Innocent's marriage, however, does not seem to conform to this marital pattern, because it was initiated and confirmed simultaneously, since the pope is confirmed when he is elected and vice versa. For proof of this, Innocent asks his audience, 'Don't you remember what you've read about this in a canon *(in canone)*?' And he summarizes Gratian's D.23 c.1: a pope-elect has the same authority as 'the true pope' (663a).

The third paradox is that in carnal marriage close relatives cannot marry, whereas in spiritual marriage it is the outsiders who are excluded. This is proved by three references to canon law. On the one hand consanguinity is prohibited 'in a prudent canon you have read';[32] on the other, 'canonical authority' permits the clergy of a diocese to oppose the intrusion of an outsider,[33] and accordingly 'it is found in a prudent canon' that the pope himself must be chosen from among the cardinal deacons or priests.[34] Again, the audience is assumed to be familiar with the authorities cited, and the fact that all three are canons is particularly stressed.

Perhaps the most significant feature of these three objections, or paradoxes, is how irrelevant they are to Innocent's argument. In the spirit of a scholastic debate, needless objections are raised only to be answered. Here they serve to demonstrate Innocent's skill as a canonist and nothing more. He is playing to the strength of his audience.

With these objections removed, he picks up his main theme by recalling the occasion for the present celebration (PL 217:663c). Then, at length, he shows that the pope's marriage to the Roman Church possesses the traditional three benefits

---

[31]Who was accustomed to distinguish three stages in carnal marriage? Not Gratian, for although he uses all three terms – *initiatum, ratum, consummatum* – he and the canons he excerpts never link all three together: *Wortkondordanz zum Decretum Gratiani*, ed. Timothy Reuter and Gabriel Silagi, MGH, Hilfsmittel 10 (Munich, 1990), esp. vol. 4, s.v. 'reri'. Cf. Robert L. Benson, *The Bishop-Elect: A Study in Medieval Ecclesiastical Office* (Princeton, 1968), 124, n. 21, and 147-8. However, the three stages of marriage formation that Innocent sketches (though not his terminology) are characteristic of Parisian theologians from Abelard on: Brundage, *Law, Sex, and Christian Society*, 237. Innocent's application of these stages of carnal marriage formation to the spiritual marriage of a bishop to his church was first proposed by Huguccio, and by 1199 this compromise solution was coming to be widely accepted by canonists: Benson, *Bishop-Elect*, 121-36.

[32]PL 217:663b: 'legistis in canone cautum'. Identified by Munk (ed. cit., line 124) as C.35 q.2-3 c.16, ed. Friedberg, 1:1268.

[33]PL 217:663b: 'canonica tradit auctoritas'; identified by Munk (ed. cit., line 127) as D.61 c.13, ed. Friedberg, 1:231; she reads *cautum* for *canonica* (see above, n. 23).

[34]PL 217:663b: 'reperitur cautum in canone'; identified by Munk (ed. cit., line 130) as D.79 c.3, ed. Friedberg, 1:277.

of matrimony – fidelity, progeny and a sacramental bond.[35] The treatment is generally theological, with several noteworthy exceptions.

The most curious benefit is Innocent's spiritualized version of the conjugal debt (*debitum conjugale*), which for canonists always and invariably referred to the claim each partner had on the other for sexual intercourse.[36] According to Innocent, however, the conjugal debt has a non-sexual equivalent in the pope's obligation to provide for his Church (*debitum providentiae*) and in his Church's reciprocal obligation to reverence him (*debitum reverentiae*).[37] Interestingly enough, this interpretation is based on the canon *Per singulas* that states that a bishop should provide for his diocese and receive reverence from it in turn.[38] That canon does not refer to these obligations as *debita*, however, and in fact it is altogether free of marital imagery. Evidently Innocent knew Gratian's *Decretum* well enough to see that this canon could provide a non-sexual analogue to the conjugal debt of carnal marriage. Actually, it is hardly surprising that he knew this canon, for only seven weeks earlier, on 5 January 1199, he and the cardinals had been discussing it in connection with the decretal *Duo simul*.[39] No doubt not a few in the audience caught the allusion, recognized how Innocent had come by it, and perhaps smiled at his desexualized interpretation of the conjugal debt.

In the same section, on marital fidelity, Innocent interacts with his audience more overtly.[40] After asking 'whether one bishop can have two bishoprics', he replies, presumably with a smile, that an example can readily be found in the bishop of Ostia and Velletri, whose two sees had been united in 1150. As the dean of the college of cardinals, the cardinal-bishop of Ostia (Octavian in 1199) would have been the most prominent member of Innocent's audience.[41]

---

[35] Already mentioned in *De quad.* (see above, n. 20).

[36] James A. Brundage (personal communication).

[37] PL 217:663d-4a: '[Ecclesia Romana] recipiens et reddens debitum conjugale, recipiens ab eo [Romano pontifice] debitum providentiae, et reddens debitum reverentiae.'

[38] Gratian, *Decretum* C.9 q.3 c.2, ed. Friedberg, 1:606; identified by Munk, ed. cit., line 155.

[39] X 1.31.9 = Reg. 1:515, pp. 749-50, citing in n. 3 *Decretum Gratiani* C.9 q.3 c.8 *Per singulas*.

[40] At the place (PL 217:664a) where Innocent asks whether his audience has read how Abraham had two wives ('Nonne legistis . . . ?'), Munk points out (ed. cit., line 168) that canonists could have read this in C.32 q.4 c.3 and dict. ante c.1. Although canonists sometimes did cite the Bible indirectly through the canons, still in this case Innocent is clearly referring directly to the Old Testament, which he cites by name in the preceding sentence ('secundum quod legitur in Veteri testamento').

[41] PL 217:664b. Munk, 'Study', 1:187-8; Maleczek, *Papst*, 80-3. Innocent goes on to cite the case of St Augustine, who was made bishop-coadjutor of Hippo while Valerian, his predecessor, was still living. As Munk noted (ed. cit., lines 181-4), the circumstances of Augustine's promotion are recorded in one of Gratian's canons (C.7 q.1 c.12, ed. Friedberg, 1:571); but I note no verbal echoes that would suggest this was Innocent's source.

The section on the three goods of marriage concludes with a pair of canonistic allusions.   Although in Christian carnal marriage a couple 'may never be separated from each other except by death' (PL 217:664d), the spiritual bond between the pope and the Roman Church can in fact be severed in the case of an heretical pope (665a).[42]

Another repetition of the pericope marks the end of the long section on the goods of marriage (PL 217:665a); Innocent continues with his analogies. His bride, the Roman Church, has brought him *plenitudo potestatis* as the vicar of Christ's dowry (665ab) – a claim that only a month earlier Innocent had incorporated in his decretal *Inter corporalia* on the translation of bishops (21 January 1199).[43] Again the audience would understand this to be a topical allusion to Innocent's ambitious program to enhance the conception of papal power.[44] The preacher next reminds the cardinals of his own prodigious activity during the first year of his pontificate: 'The Roman Church brought me an ample dowry', he observes, 'but you have seen whether I have made her a wedding gift in return; I will not boast about it myself.'[45]

The anniversary celebration ends with these words, but the sermon goes on with a coda of sorts devoted to another question suggested by the recent discussion of

---

[42]The best known case was that of Pope Anastasius, whom God struck down for seeking to end the Acacian schism. Innocent could have read the account in D.19 c.9 (ed. Friedberg, 1:64) or, more likely, in Gratian's ultimate source, the *Liber pontificalis*. Many other canons also indicate that a pope can err in matters of faith: e.g. D.21 c.7, D.40 c.6, C.2 q.7 dict. post c.39, C.24 q.1 c.9-18 (ed. Friedberg, 1:71, 146, 495-6, 969-72). In his anniversary sermon, Innocent goes on to observe that 'I would not readily believe, however, that God would permit a Roman pontiff to err against the faith', on which see Brian Tierney, *The Origins of Papal Infallibility, 1150-1350*, 2nd edn (Leiden, 1988), 36, n.1.

[43]X 1.7.2, *Inter corporalia* (21 Jan. 1198), ed. Friedberg, 2:99, and Reg. 1:335, pp. 495-8. See Kay, *Swift and Strong*, 126.

[44]Eventually the concept of the pope's spiritual marriage to the Roman Church, which Innocent first developed in this sermon, was marvellously expressed in the apse mosaic that Innocent commissioned for Old Saint Peter's, as Brenda Bolton explains elsewhere in the present volume (pp. 125-7). See also Gerhart B. Ladner, *Die Papstbildnisse des Altertums und des Mittelalters*, Monumenti di antichità cristiana, 2d ser., no. 4, vol. 2 (Vatican City, 1970):56-68. This figure of *Ecclesia Romana* is beautifully reproduced in color from the 'Album Grimaldi' (Arch. Cap. di S. Pietro, A 64ter, fol. 50) in Michele Maccarrone, *Romana ecclesia, cathedra Petri*, ed. Piero Zerbi et al., 2 vols (Rome, 1991), vol. 1, frontispiece. Note that the dowry Innocent mentions in his sermon is graphically suggested in the mosaic by the papal keys. Peter holds them in heaven, while Innocent holds them on earth; but the pope bears the keys in virtue of his marriage to the Roman Church, to whom they belong, as is evident because she bears them on her banner as a feudal heiress might display the insignia of her hereditary honor or *dignitas*. Note also that Christ himself is present on earth only as the Eucharistic Lamb, i.e. in the sacrament, as the chalice in front of him indicates; in other respects, Christ in heaven is represented on earth by his vicar, the *claviger*.

[45]PL 217:665b: 'Amplam mihi tribuit dotem, sed utrum ego donationem aliquam sibi fecerim propter nuptias, vos videritis. Ego nolo [nolim] asseverare jactanter [iactanciam]' (Munk prefers the variant readings: ed. cit., lines 235-6).

episcopal translation. Innocent proposes a pair of paradoxes: a man can be a bishop before he is the *sponsus* of his church, and contrariwise he can be the *sponsus* before he is bishop. In the first case, Innocent explains, if a man is provided to the bishopric by the pope, the clergy have not elected him and consequently have not given their consent, which is the act that makes the church his *sponsa*. In the other case, the *sponsus* is only the bishop-elect until he has been consecrated and 'will claim neither the name of bishop nor the office' (PL 217:666a).   This was the traditional view currently being challenged by Huguccio's doctrine that the bishop's spiritual marriage was consummated when his election was confirmed by the metropolitan, his ecclesiastical superior.[46] Innocent concludes his sermon by offering the assembled canonists his own solution as to when the bishop's spiritual marriage was consummated.[47]   'In spiritual matters, one can distinguish between a *sponsus* and a husband (*vir*), and between a *sponsa* and a wife (*coniunx*),[48] because a *sponsus* is called *electus* before confirmation, namely before he knows by experience (*cognoscat*),[49] i.e. before he administers; he is called a *vir*, however, after confirmation, and especially after consecration, when at last he administers fully.'[50]   As Robert Benson long ago explained, from this passage 'It is apparent that Innocent felt compelled to transform the Huguccian doctrine by assigning to electoral confirmation the effects which Huguccio has ascribed to "mutual consent": the "spiritual marriage" is contracted after canonical election and confirmation.'[51] Doctrinally speaking, this is the principal novelty in the sermon; evidently, for maximum impact, Innocent had saved his best for last.   The point of this gratuitous digression would seem to be to display Innocent's ability to correct the leading canonist of the day, not with canonistic expertise but with commonsense and with logic.

---

[46]Benson, *Bishop-Elect*, 126-8, 147-9.

[47]PL 217:666a: 'Sed an ita sit, sollicitudo nostra disquirat.' Munk reads instead *uestra exquirat*, with the extant manuscripts (ed. cit., line 254); however, since Innocent does not drop the question but goes on to answer it, these words clearly introduce his solution.

[48]Here Munk rightly improves on the Migne text, which pointlessly distinguishes between *sponsa* and *vir*, and between *sponsus* and *coniunx*. She reads: 'Inter sponsum autem et uirum, et inter sponsam et coniugem distingui potest in spirituali coniugio . . .' (ed. cit., lines 254-6). Cf. PL 217:666a-b: 'Inter sponsam autem et virum, et inter sponsum et conjugem distingui potest in spiritualibus . . .'.

[49]The argument turns on the twofold sense of *cognoso*: 'to investigate judicially' and 'to get to know carnally' (*Oxford Latin Dictionary*).

[50]PL 217:666b: 'Inter spons[u]m autem et virum, et inter spons[a]m et conjugem distingui potest in spiritualibus: quod sponsus appellatur electus ante confirmationem, videlicet antequam cognoscat, id est antequam administret; vir autem appellatur post confirmationem, et maxime post consecrationem, cum jam plenarie administrat' (emended from Munk; see above, n. 47).

[51]Benson, *Bishop-Elect*, 148-9.

A final pericope signals the end of the sermon, which concludes with a now broadened appeal not only to *fratres* but also to *filii*, who now are all described as *amici sponsi*. They all are exhorted to rejoice with Innocent the bridegroom and to pray that he may attain salvation by paying his conjugal debt to the Church (PL 217:666bc).

CONCLUSIONS

What, then, can we conclude from this reading of Innocent's anniversary sermon?

(1) First, and most certain, is the canonistic character of the sermon. It is remarkable for its numerous references and allusions to the canons. What is more, it appears to be exceptional in this regard, for there is little or no canonistic content in Innocent's three other consecration sermons – one apparently preached at his own installation in 1198 and the others at undated consecrations of unnamed bishops.[52] Indeed, an electronic search of the text of all his sermons reveals that this is the only one in which a canon is cited explicitly.[53]

(2) The canonistic character of the anniversary sermon, therefore, is an anomaly that requires an explanation, which is readily supplied by the special circumstances of the occasion. Evidently it was an intimate, in-house celebration by a team that had worked together now for a year. Innocent addressed his remarks primarily to his 'brothers', the cardinals, and only as an afterthought to the other *curiales* present, who were his 'sons'. What they had shared over the past year was an ongoing discussion of points of canon law, and consequently it was entirely appropriate that Innocent stress this common interest.

(3) But what does this sermon tell us about Innocent's knowledge of canon law? First of all, it shows that by February 1199 he could cite canons readily, but because he did so only on this one occasion and not in his many subsequent sermons, it is clear that he could and did know the canons without always flaunting his knowledge. As a preacher, his usual persona was that of the theologian, not the canonist.

(4) Consequently, it is possible that he already knew his canons before he became pope, perhaps by hearing cursory lectures on the *Decretum* at Bologna, perhaps by participating in curial business during his almost eight years as

---

[52]Innocent, *Sermones de diversis 1, 2*, and *4* (PL 217:649-60, 665-72).

[53]I am indebted to Thomas Izbicki (Johns Hopkins) for searching the electronic version of Migne's *Patrologia Latina*, vol. 217. Canons are, however, explicitly mentioned five times in Innocent's *De missarum misteriis*: 2.25 (812d), 3.6 (845a), 4.13 (865c), 4.32 (877c), and 4.42 (883b). The first four are citations by the author; the last occurs in an excerpt from St Augustine: 'cautum est in canone, quod . . .'. Note that Innocent himself employs variations of Augustine's formula (see above, nn. 32-4).

cardinal.[54] But I am inclined to doubt this because in that case there would then have been little point to this display of canonistic learning in his anniversary sermon. Furthermore, if Innocent had been a proficient canonist on the day of his consecration, why did he not display it in his sermon on that occasion (PL 217:653d-60d) in order to establish a bond of sympathy with the canonists at the curia? But he did not.

(5) This argument *ex silentio* can be buttressed by several hints in the anniversary sermon that suggest that Innocent's knowledge of the canons had been acquired quite recently. His use of the obscure canon *Per singulas* is best explained by its use in a decretal dated 5 January 1199. And his unnecessary coda on the spiritual marriage of a bishop (as opposed to the pope) is best understood as his solution to questions raised in connection with the fashioning of the decretal *Inter corporalia* (21 January 1199).

(6) Even more persuasive are the repeated indications that, although Innocent could cite certain canons, still his understanding of them was that of an amateur, not a professional canonist. Thus his spiritual interpretation of the conjugal debt as one of providing for his spouse, rather than attempting to produce progeny with her, was contrary to the canonists' understanding of the *debitum coniugale*. Again, as Pennington established, Innocent showed himself to be an amateur in interpreting the canon *Oportebat* (D.79 c.3) literally, whereas no contemporary canonist was convinced by it that the pope must be selected only from the existing cardinal deacons or priests.[55] Finally, the triumphant distinction between *sponsus* and *vir*, with which he resolved the question raised in his irrelevant coda, brushes aside the legal complexities with the self-assurance of a Parisian logician.

---

[54]Maleczek lists six cases in which Celestine III supposedly appointed Cardinal Lotario as auditor, plus another when he was a subdeacon: *Papst*, 104, nn. 360 and 364; cf. Michel Maccarrone, 'Innocenzo III prima del pontificato', *Archivio dell Società romana di storia patria*, 66, n.s. 9 (1943):59-134, at pp. 89-91. In fact, Lotario was clearly not an auditor in two of these cases: Reg. 1:85 (he professes his past good will for Milan but is not named in the detailed case history recited in Reg. 1:37) and Reg. 1:103 (he helped Magister P. de Castaneto – probably a friend from his Paris days – to secure a benefice at Sens). That leaves five cases in which Lotario was actually named an auditor: Reg. 1:150, 267, 317, 2:30, and 8:86. In the first three, two other auditors were also appointed; in the fourth, only one other (Reg. 2:30); and in the last, Lotario was sole auditor in a local Roman case (8:86). Although Maleczek takes these commissions as certain proof of Innocent's legal training (*Papst*, 104), this is not necessarily so. His knowledge of French may have been useful in the examination of witnesses, which is expressly said to have been done in the case concerning Vézelay that he heard as a subdeacon (Reg. 1:150). Moreover, there were more cases at the curia than there were cardinals in residence: e.g. in March 1192, a third of the cardinals (nine) were absent from the curia (*Papst*, 333). Evidently the resident cardinals would have to share the caseload; a commission provided only the expertise that the case required.

[55]Pennington, *Popes, Canonists and Texts*, art. 2, pp. 12-14.

Innocent emerges from this analysis, then, as a theologian who had spent a year conferring with canonists. He had learned much from them, but his field of professional expertise was nonetheless theology.

Innocent III and Petrus Beneventanus: Reconstructing a Career at the Papal Curia

James M. Powell

The pontificate of Pope Innocent III presents numerous challenges to historians. His great energy, which drew him into virtually all the major issues of his time, has made it difficult to form a coherent picture of his reign, beyond the general recognition of his strong commitment to reform. The result has been a tendency to focus on specific issues, treating his pontificate in a topical manner, with the figure of the pope himself moving dramatically across the stage as the main character, while those associated with him play only minor roles. In recent years, however, this approach has begun to change, due in considerable part to the work of Werner Maleczek.[1] His detailed study of the college of cardinals under

---

[1]Werner Maleczek, *Papst und Kardinalskolleg von 1191 bis 1216: Die Kardinäle unter Coelestin III und Innocenz III* (Vienna, 1984), is exceptional in this regard. The biographers of Innocent III from Friedrich Hurter, *Geschichte Papst Innocenz des Dritten und seiner Zeitgenossen*, 4 vols (Hamburg, 1841-1844) and Achilles Luchaire, *Innocent III*, 6 vols (Paris, 1904-1908) to Helene Tillmann, *Papst Innocenz III.* (Bonn, 1954, English translation, Amsterdam, 1980) and Jane Sayers, *Pope Innocent III: Leader of Europe, 1198-1216* (London, 1994), have taken a topical approach. More specialized works such as Christopher Cheney's *Pope Innocent III and England* (Stuttgart, 1976) and Raymonde Foreville's *Innocent III et la France* (Stuttgart, 1992), do examine changes of policy, but not usually from a curial perspective. Karl Wenck, 'Die römischen Päpste zwischen Alexander III. und Innocenz III, und der Designationsversuch Weihnachten 1197', *Papsttum und Kaisertum* (Munich, 1926), 415-74, advanced a thesis concerning political differences within the college of cardinals in this period, but this view has been criticized and virtually rejected by Tillman (*Pope*, 291-2) and W. Maleczek (*Papst*, 264). Maleczek argues that there is no evidence for an ideological split in the college under

Celestine III and Innocent has revealed a significant change in the role of the cardinals after 1203. Whether this represents a turning point in policy terms is hard to say, since Maleczek finds no evidence for any ideological differences among the cardinals under Innocent.[2] These were chiefly cardinals of Innocent's creation and included such important figures as Hugolino of Ostia, Benedict, cardinal-priest of Santa Susanna and later cardinal-bishop of Porto, Guala Bicchieri and Pelagius of Albano.

The mid-point of Innocent's reign is also marked by a number of events, some of which may indicate that this was a period of difficulty. In the first place, there is the fact that the *Gesta Innocentii III*, a major source for Innocent's pontificate, has long troubled scholars because it ended in 1208.[3] Coincidentally, the *Regesta super negotio Romani Imperii* (RNI) ended in 1209, thus omitting materials relating to the conflict with the Emperor Otto over the Kingdom of Sicily.[4] Innocent III's announcement of the authoritative collection of his decretals for the first twelve years of his pontificate, entrusted to Petrus Beneventanus, also falls

---

Innocent III.

[2]Ibid., 335.

[3]Work on the *Gesta* has been reviewed most recently by Brenda Bolton, 'Too important to Neglect: The Gesta Innocentii PP. III', *Church and Chronicle in the Middle Ages: Essays presented to John Taylor*, ed. G. A. Loud and I. N. Wood (London, 1991), 87-99; reprinted as essay IV in Brenda Bolton, *Innocent III: Studies on Papal Authority and Pastoral Care* (Aldershot, 1995). The literature on the *Gesta* has grown slowly, beginning with Hugo Elkan, *Die Gesta Innocentii III im Verhältnis zu den Regesten desselben Papstes* (Heidelberg, 1876). The work of Elkan was severely criticized for its partisanship by Yves Lefèvre, 'Innocent III et son temps vus de Rome: étude sur la biographie anonyme de ce pape', *Mélanges d'archéologie et d'histoire de l'école française de Rome*, 61 (1949), 242-5, esp. 243. Volkert Pfaff, *Die Gesta Innocenz III und das Testament Heinrichs VI*, ZRG Kan., 50 (1964), 78-126, esp. 84, is much less critical of Elkan. Agostino Paravicini-Bagliani, 'La storiografia del secolo XIII: prospettive di ricerca', *Römische Historische Mitteilungen*, 18 (1976), 45-54, discusses the relationship of thirteenth-century papal biographies to the *Liber Pontificalis*. David R. Gress-Wright completed a doctoral dissertation, 'The "Gesta Innocentii III": Text, Introduction and Commentary', at Bryn Mawr College in 1981. There is also an extended discussion of the *Gesta* in Wilhelm Imkamp, *Das Kirchenbild Innocenz' III. (1198-1216)* (Stuttgart, 1983), 10-20. The introduction to Gress-Wright's thesis is quite helpful. He made extensive use of earlier works, especially that of Elkan, and adds to the suggestions of Lefèvre regarding the structure of the *Gesta*. On the ending of the *Gesta* in 1208/9, see Lefèvre, 'Innocent III', 242, and Bolton, 98-9. Gress-Wright provides a somewhat fuller discussion, 41*-5* and 109*-10*. He has a lengthy discussion of the *Gesta*'s statement that Innocent 'made . . . books of sermons, letters, registers, and decretals', after his accession to the papal throne (*Gesta*, PL 214, Chap. i). He suggests that this reference is an interpolation. He may be right, but it could have been added by the author *c.* 1209. This would account for its presence in Vat. Lat. 12111.

[4]*Regestum Innocentii III super negotio Romani Imperii*, ed. Friedrich Kempf, S.J. (Rome, 1947). The final document, no. 194, is a letter of Innocent III to Otto dated 11 October 1209. This letter clearly leaves things 'in medias res'.

in 1209/10.[5] Moreover, the decretals which have long attracted the interest of those studying relations between church and state were issued prior to 1210.[6] Though the second half of Innocent's pontificate witnessed the climax of the conflict with King John of England over the archbishopric of Canterbury, it did not produce decretals that evoked the same interest either among contemporary canonists or modern researchers.[7] Nor should we forget that 1208 marked the beginning of the Albigensian Crusade, which some have suggested served to trigger a change in the papal approach to heresy.[8] This approach might especially be taken if we consider it in relation to the policies Innocent pursued in the patrimony, culminating in his parliament at Viterbo in 1207.[9] Finally, in a recent article on 'Papal *Adventus* at Rome in the Twelfth Century', Susan Twyman has wondered if Innocent III did not face an internal Roman crisis in 1208 that delayed his return to the city. Monsignor Maccarrone has cited the account in the *Gesta* concerning a serious disturbance in the city precipitated by the actions of the Orsini at precisely this time.[10] But even if we go so far as to label this period as one of unusual significance for Innocent's reign, we must still deal with the question of how to achieve a better understanding of these events.

As I have indicated, Werner Maleczek has pointed the way by his emphasis on Innocent's use of the college of cardinals.[11] Taking his suggestion as a starting point, I believe that it is possible to improve our understanding of Innocent's pontificate if we focus on his use and promotion of personnel. From these choices, we may get further insight into his policies. In the course of this paper, I wish to develop this line by making a case study of one individual who has not received as much attention as others but whose career, as reconstructed here, sheds considerable light, not merely on the process of selection and promotion at the papal court, but also on the way in which policy was shaped and implemented.

---

[5]On the dating of *Compilatio Tertia*, see Stephan Kuttner, 'Johannes Teutonicus, das Vierte Laterankonzil und die Compilatio Quarta', *Miscellanea Giovanni Mercati*, vol. 5, *Studi e Testi*, no. 125 (Vatican City, 1946), 608-34, esp. 621. Maleczek, *Papst*, 172, and no. 361.

[6]Of course, the emphasis on certain decretals reflects the development of historiography. But Innocent's own views are reflected in his letter authenticating *Compilatio Tertia* and his attitude toward later compilations by John of Wales (*Compilatio Secunda*) and Johannes Teutonicus (*Compilatio Quarta*). Sayers, *Innocent III*, 108-9.

[7]Cheney, *Innocent III*, 383, has an interesting comment suggesting that Innocent was willing to rest on his earlier decretals as precedents in this period.

[8]Foreville, *Innocent III*, 249-50.

[9]Gress-Wright, 64*; Sayers, 158; *Gesta*, PL 214:cxxiii; Tillmann, *Pope*, 135.

[10]Susan Twyman, 'Papal *Adventus* at Rome in the Twelfth Century', *Historical Research* 69 (1996), 233-53, esp. 251-2. Michele Maccarrone called attention to the account in the *Gesta*, which says that 'nel 1208 sorsero a Roma gravi torbolenze contro il papa, suscitate dai "filii Ursi"' that is, the Orsini. See his 'Innocenzo III prima del pontificato', *Archivio della società romana di storia patria*, n.s., 9 (1943), 59-134, at 87. *Gesta*, PL 214:clxxxiv.

[11]Maleczek, *Papst*, 315-16, 334-5.

Although he was promoted to the cardinalate and played a critical role in the Albigensian affair in the years leading to the Fourth Lateran Council, Petrus Beneventanus has been chiefly known for his role in the preparation of *Compilatio Tertia* (3 Comp.). In large measure, this has been due to a lack of evidence from the papal registers and other sources that would provide us with the skeleton of a biography for the early years of Innocent's pontificate.[12] Yet I believe it is now possible, with fragments we have and only two additional pieces of possible evidence, based chiefly on an analysis of internal evidence in the *Gesta* and on some inferences, to reconstruct the early career of Petrus as an important background figure in the pontificate of Innocent III, one who first rose to prominence as the author of the *Gesta Innocentii III*, though he may earlier have known the pope in Bologna. The question of his authorship of the *Gesta* is, in my opinion, a key to understanding his role during the latter part of Innocent's reign.

The problem of the authorship of the *Gesta* has tempted a number of conjectures of a general kind, but only David Gress-Wright has been willing to single out a particular individual as the possible author: Octavian, cardinal deacon of SS. Sergius and Bacchus (created a cardinal in 1206), who was related to Innocent and who served as papal chamberlain from June 1200 to April 1204.[13] Octavian apparently began his career in the papal chapel. In 1199, he accompanied Cardinal Jordanus of S. Pudenziana on a journey to collect troops in the March and the Kingdom of Sicily against Markward of Anweiler.[14] These qualifications certainly suggest him as a viable candidate for authorship of the *Gesta*. What follows is not so much a rebuttal of this suggestion as an alternative, one that, in my view, sheds light on the conjunction of policy and personnel during the pontificate of Innocent III.

The case for Petrus Beneventanus is much more complex than that for Octavian but incorporates some similar elements. Most scholars since Hugo Elkan have accepted the view that the author of the *Gesta* was a south Italian or had special knowledge of Southern Italy.[15] Among those meeting this criterion, in addition to Octavian, are such important figures as Cardinal Hugolino of Ostia, the later

---

[12]A. Teetaert, 'Colevacino, Pierre', *Dictionnaire de droit canonique*, 3: 1000-2; Friedrich Heyer established the identity of Petrus Beneventanus with the cardinal deacon of S. Maria in Aquiro and traced his later career. 'Veber Petrus Collivaccinus von Benevent', ZRG Kan. 6 (1916):395-405; Maleczek, *Papst*, 172-4.

[13]Gress-Wright, 112*-14*; Maleczek, *Papst*, 163.

[14]Reg. 1:554 (557), 555 (558), pp. 802-9; *Gesta*, PL 214:XLII, chap. xxiii.

[15]Elkan, *Gesta*, 47-56, has a detailed discussion of Innocent's involvement in the *regno*, which suggests that the author was well informed; see also Gress-Wright, 55*-62*. Lefèvre, 243, however, disagrees with Elkan's view that the *Gesta* was written 'to justify and magnify the policy of the pope in Sicily'. Pfaff, 'Die Gesta', 89, shows that the author was well informed about south Italian affairs.

Pope Gregory IX, as well as other cardinals involved in the affairs of the *Regno*. Of lesser figures, Master Philip, the papal chaplain, spent some time in Southern Italy before and after his return from England.[16] Finally, as his name shows, Petrus Collovicensis came from a prominent Beneventan family with strong ties to the law.[17] Given the traditions of Benevento and Capua as centers of legal studies in the South and the importance of southerners like Cardinal Petrus Capuanus in the early pontificate of Innocent III, we should not be surprised at his presence at the curia. We cannot find evidence to support a connection between Petrus and the Cardinal Priest of St Marcellus but neither can we rule out the possibility.[18] There is also agreement that the author of the *Gesta* was a member of the papal chancery and had access to the papal registers.[19] While such a qualification would not itself eliminate cardinals from consideration, the circumstances of Innocent III's pontificate, in which cardinals played a much less visible role in the chancery, make it less likely that a cardinal could fill this role.[20] Moreover, Master Philip must be eliminated because he spent much of the first two years of Innocent's reign in England. Where was Petrus Beneventanus?

Until now, our first clear mention of Petrus, as Professors Cheney and Maleczek have shown, occurs in the Evesham Chronicle, which reports that in October 1205 Thomas of Marlborough, prior and later abbot of Evesham, briefed several lawyers in the case which he was then pursuing in Rome against Bishop Mauger of Worcester. They included Petrus Beneventanus, chaplain of the lord pope, 'qui primus habebatur in advocatos curiae . . .'. In fact, Thomas's opponent complained to Pope Innocent III that Thomas had made it impossible for him to secure adequate legal representation. The pope laughed and said, 'There has

---

[16]Philip was sent to southern Italy 'so that peace would be reestablished and justice restored', as we learn from Innocent III's letter to Berard, master justiciar of the Terra di Lavoro dated ca. 1-10 November 1199 (Reg. 2:374-5). In 1200, Innocent dispatched him to England to expedite the collection of the clerical fortieth for the crusade (Cheney, *Innocent III*, 41). He returned from England only in 1203, which reduces the likelihood that he was author of the *Gesta* (Cheney, *Innocent III*, 95-6, 243-5). Tillmann (*Pope*, 225, n. 136) discusses the accusations of extortion made against him in England. Cheney has a lengthy treatment (*Innocent III*, pp. 244-5). The *Gesta* (PL 214:lxviii-lxix) notes that the pope sent 'Brother Rainer and Master Philip the notary to the Terra di Lavoro' to absolve Diupold in 1203, after his return from England. The *Gesta* continues: '. . . Soffridus proditorie cepit magistrum Philippum, notarium domini papae, quem ad petitionem ipsius Diupuldi, dominus papa direxerat im Apuliam et Terra Laboris, committens eidem in temporalibus vices suas, ut inter Theutonicos et Latinos pacem et justitam faceret observari; quem dictus Soffridus vix tandem, extorta gravi redemptione, dimisit.'

[17]Maleczek, *Papst*, 172, n. 360. This was apparently a family with strong ties to the law.

[18]Cf. Maleczek, *Papst*, 334.

[19]Lefèvre, 243; Gress-Wright, 112*.

[20]Maleczek, *Papst*, 263-4.

never been a shortage of lawyers in the Roman Curia'.[21] From this episode it seems safe to infer that Petrus Beneventanus was already by late 1205 a well-known and established figure in curial legal circles, one of the most desired lawyers in Rome. One reason for his eminence may well have been the knowledge that he was someone the pope listened to on legal questions. This would explain Thomas's pleasure at his choice as well as his opponent's concern.

There are now two other pieces of possible evidence that may shed light on Petrus Beneventanus in Rome before October 1205. Just a few months earlier, in July 1205, as Raymonde Foreville tells us, Innocent III sent his chaplain, Petrus, to Queen Ingeborg of France, then imprisoned by Philip Augustus in the castle of Étampes, to console that unhappy lady.[22] Both the date and the reference to Petrus as papal chaplain suggest that this is our Petrus. Further, the detailed knowledge and the strength of personal feeling evident in the *Gesta* account of Philip's treatment of Ingeborg make this a valuable witness to Peter's participation in that affair and supports the view of him as author of the *Gesta*. Moreover, in a letter dated 10 January 1203, Innocent appointed Bishop Lanfranc of Chiusi, Oddo the castellan of Radicofani and the papal scriptor, Master P., to absolve Pepo of Campiglia and his brothers from excommunication under certain conditions.[23] I have not been able to find any other evidence of a Magister P. as a papal scriptor in this period. However, the case pursued here continued to develop and was discussed in considerable detail in the *Gesta* as part of the events

---

[21]Cheney has a very full discussion of this case, but does not discuss Petrus's role, with the exception of a single reference: *Innocent III*, 109-11, 117-20, 162, 187-8, 195-9, 226, 230, n. 200, esp. pp. 195-9. He mentions on p. 105 that Petrus Beneventanus was 'briefed'. Maleczek, *Papst*, 259, 172, n. 360. Evesham Chronicle, RS, 29:153. 'Respondit dominus papa subridendo, "Nunquam deficit alicui copia advocatorum in curia romana"'. This case was incorporated into canon law (X 5.33.17; 'Ex ore sedentis'), which is found in 3 Comp. 5.16.7. There is a Magister P. in Innocent III's letter to the archbishop of Cologne of 20 May 1199. He was part of the delegation sent to the pope with letters on the election and coronation of Otto IV. RNI, 27-9, no. 11. Bernard Barbiche, *Les actes pontificaux originaux des archives nationales de Paris*, 2 vols (Città del Vaticano, 1975-8), 1:419-32, does not list any papal *scriptores* for this period that would alter the conclusion reached here.

[22]Foreville, *Innocent III*, 301, calls him Petrus, but PL 215:680 (July 5, 1205) states: 'we have sent you our beloved son, Master P., our chaplain, a man of foresight and loyalty, to bring you the consolation of our visitation.' Peter is normally abbreviated with a 'P.' in the registers; Philip, for example, is usually abbreviated 'Ph.' or 'Phil.'. Cf. the account of this delegation in the *Gesta*, PL 214:cii, which does not, however, identify the pope's representative (Elkan, *Gesta*, 77). We should, however, note two remarks from that section of the *Gesta*, PL 214:cii: 'et licet rex plures et maiores advocatos haberet, non tamen defuit qui, propter Deum, verbum faceret intrepidus pro regina.' And a few lines later, we find: 'ut eam faceret honorariconcolaterias et confortatorias ei literas saepe tranmittens, et per proprios nuntios eam faciens visitari . . .'

[23] Reg. 5:137 (138), pp. 272-4.

leading up to the parliament of Viterbo in 1207.[24] If Master P. was Petrus Beneventanus, his role in this case would have helped to inform his account in the *Gesta*. Also, the fact that Master P. was a papal scriptor in 1203 is not at all inconsistent with the notion that he could have been promoted to the papal chapel by 1204/5. This evidence accords with the fact that it was as papal notary and subdeacon that he was named as the compiler of the decretals of Innocent III in 1209.[25]

If we pursue the chronology of the career of Petrus Beneventanus further, we may note that the period at which the *Gesta Innocentii III* ends and *Compilatio Tertia* begins not only dovetails quite neatly but suggests why Petrus Beneventanus, if he was the author of the *Gesta,* would be pressed to put it aside.[26] Moreover, a number of scholars have also noted that the *Gesta* itself had already undergone an important structural change in 1203.[27] Until that time, it was a narrative composed on lines similar to that of other papal *Gesta* of the twelfth century. After that date, it took on the character of a dossier of letters. David Gress-Wright has suggested that its author may have been forced to this expedient by the press of business. This situation mirrors the career changes we have already suggested for Petrus Beneventanus in this period. If 'Master P., scriptor noster' was the author of the *Gesta* and our Petrus, there is evidence that in 1203 he was beginning to advance in his career. Also, he was becoming involved in the curia.[28] Time constraints may have led him to shift from a narrative organization to an emphasis on collecting materials. When he undertook to edit the decretals, he had to bring the *Gesta* to a conclusion.[29] Thereafter, his career took off when he was raised to Cardinal Deacon of S. Maria in Aquiro in

---

[24]*Gesta*, PL 214:xxvii-xxix, shows how early this interest developed. But there is no mention of heresy at this point in the *Gesta*. *Vergentis*, addressed to clergy and people of Viterbo (1199), was, however, included in 3 Comp. 5.4.1.

[25]Maleczek, *Papst*, 172, 361. Sayers, *Innocent III*, 108, suggests the pope commissioned the collection.

[26]Kuttner, 'Johannes Teutonicus', 621-2. Pott. 4157, 1:358.

[27]Lefèvre, 243-4, advanced this view. He connected it with Innocent's illness and near death in 1203. Cf. Pfaff, 'Die *Gesta*', 79-80. Gress-Wright, 109*-10*. I have recently come to question this position. On the basis of my examination of the correspondence between Innocent and the Emperor Alexius III, as well as that with Calojohn of Bulgaria, another hypothesis has emerged that better fits the view that Petrus was the author of the *Gesta*. I would like to suggest that the extensive use of papal letters seems to occur when Peter was not directly involved and may, indeed, have been occupied elsewhere. Hence, he would have to rely more upon archival materials. This argument cannot be settled here, but I believe it deserves to be noted.

[28]Evesham Chronicle, RS, 29:153.

[29]Cf. Gress-Wright, 109*, suggests the press of business as the reason. The evidence presented here seems to support that view.

1212.[30] Early in 1214, he undertook his important legation in southern France.[31] Here, previous legates had faced difficulties in dealing with the crown, the French bishops and Simon de Montfort.[32] The choice of Petrus Beneventanus seems to have been dictated by the increasing tensions between the papacy and the local bishops and leaders of the Albigensian Crusade. Interestingly, the attitude and positions he took in his relations with the French crown are entirely consistent with the strong line taken by the author of the *Gesta* against Philip Augustus in the matter of his marriage.[33] On Petrus's return from France, he participated in the Fourth Lateran Council, in which the pope clearly attempted to pursue policies similar to those previously advanced by his legate, policies which were opposed by Simon de Montfort and were generally favorable to the interests of the count of Toulouse.[34] That he continued to enjoy the confidence and support of Innocent III is shown by the fact that the pope promoted him to be cardinal priest of S. Lorenzo in Damaso early in 1216.[35]

Kenneth Pennington, in his study of the French recension of *Compilatio Tertia*, has discussed a change in the decretal *Quia diversitatem*, that sheds interesting light on the high regard of the pope for this canonist.[36] As Pennington has shown, this change represented a significant difference in the meaning of the decretal and must, therefore, have had at least the tacit approval of the pope. It is not at all surprising, therefore, that the pope stressed the fact that Petrus's collection enjoyed his full support in *Devotioni vestrae*, which he addressed to the masters and scholars of Bologna and which accompanied the collection.[37] Clearly, Petrus was the pope's man.

Finally, we must ask whether the *Gesta* itself provides any support for our effort. First, there is the matter as to what is treated and what is not. This has been often discussed.[38] One point that deserves some thought concerns the possible relationship between the *Gesta* and the RNI. Although it is evident that the author of the *Gesta* was well informed concerning the business of the empire, he does not utilize the RNI when discussing problems in papal and imperial relations in the *Gesta*. This suggests that he saw the RNI as a work that was

---

[30]Maleczek, *Papst*, 172.

[31]Ibid., 172-4. Foreville, *Innocent III*, 267-9.

[32]Foreville, *Innocent III*, 217-70; see also James M. Powell, *Anatomy of a Crusade* (Philadelphia, 1986), 33-47, which deals with the legation of Robert Courçon.

[33]Gress-Wright, 63*; *Gesta*, PL 214:xci-cviii.

[34]Maleczek, *Papst*, 174. Foreville, *Innocent III*, 269.

[35]Maleczek, *Papst*, 174.

[36] Kenneth Pennington, *Pope and Bishops* (Philadelpia, 1984), 127; see also his 'The French Recension of *Compilatio Tertia*', BMCL 5 (1975):53-71, esp. 60-4.

[37]Emil Friedberg, *Quinque compilationes antiquae* (Leipzig, 1882), 105.

[38]Elkan, *Gesta*, *passim*; Lefèver, 242-5; Gress-Wright, 29*-35*; Bolton, 97.

already treating that matter and he deliberately omitted it from the *Gesta*.[39] Could we even suggest that he may have been one of those involved in the editing of the RNI at some point? If we look at the *Gesta* from this perspective, we may find support in the suggestion made by David Gress-Wright, that it took the RNI as a model in its dossier of materials from the registers. In addition to focusing attention on the important topics that it treats, whether concerning the patrimony, the fourth crusade, the marriage of the French king or others, we should also stress that the *Gesta* functioned primarily as an internal document.[40] Those who have sought in it a propagandistic purpose have tended to overlook this point. As recent scholars have pointed out, the *Gesta* was at times critical of decisions.[41] Only someone in a position to look closely at the decision-making process, perhaps someone not directly involved, could make such observations.

There seems to be a closer relationship between the *Gesta* and *Compilatio Tertia* than has been previously noted. A number of the cases and topics dealt with in the *Gesta* furnished material to *Compilatio Tertia*. Of the cases discussed in the *Gesta*, in chapters XLI-XLV, decretals regarding the conflict over Lambeth between the archbishop of Canterbury and the monks of Christ Church and between the archbishop of Milan and the abbot of Scozula are in *Compilatio Tertia*. The case of the suspension of the patriarch of Antioch over the unauthorized transfer of the bishop of Apamea to the diocese of Tripoli and the dispute among the Iberian bishops are included as well. Finally, the case of Conrad of Hildesheim, who was excommunicated because he tried to move to the diocese of Würzburg, provided the decretal *Illud Dominus*. In the cases discussed in the *Gesta*, the decision whether or not to include them in *Compilatio Tertia* may have been taken on the basis that no better cases occurred in the period from 1203 to 1210. What may carry even more weight than the mere listing of these cases with a brief summary of each is the fact that the decretals selected for *Compilatio Tertia* sometimes deal with rather obscure legal issues not likely to be known to someone who had not had some direct connection with them. An excellent example is the decretal *Cum in partibus*, which deals with the meaning of words and was addressed to the bishop of Coimbra and other Portuguese bishops. The case itself involved a jurisdictional dispute between the archbishops of Braga and Compostella. The selection of this decretal suggests considerable familiarity with the situation. All of the decretals from the first and second years of Innocent's pontificate – the third and fourth years are lost – are found in his register for those

---

[39]Gress-Wright, 33*-4*, 110*. Note especially his comments on the RNI as a model for the dossier of letters in the *Gesta*.

[40]Cf. the summary of its transmission in Bolton, 89 and 97, where she refers to it as an 'official work'.

[41]Lefèvre, 244-5, esp. regarding the crusade. Bolton, 89-90.

years.[42] It may well be that the cases discussed in this section of the *Gesta* represent some of those in which Petrus was personally involved in these years. This point, however, is not susceptible to proof, because a number of these decretals, including *Cum in partibus*, are found in the decretal collection compiled by Bernardus Compostellanus in early 1208, but not accepted by Innocent as authentic.[43] There is no evidence, however, that Petrus Beneventanus drew on this collection, since these letters are found in the register. They might still have been part of a dossier put together by Petrus. It is even possible that Bernardus drew on some such collection made by Petrus himself.

Following this line of thinking, we should note that *Compilatio Tertia* contains a number of decretals from the period following 1203 that refer to the same parties. The compiler seems to have had a continuing interest in the archbishopric of Milan, in Canterbury and in dioceses in the Iberian peninsula.[44] Most of the decretals referring to these dioceses are concentrated in the period before 1203. But the inclusion of so many from the later period appears to be distinctive in *Compilatio Tertia*. Interestingly, the *Compilatio Romana*, does not, for the most part contain these post-1203 decretals relating to these dioceses found in *Compilatio Tertia*.[45] Awareness of the legal significance of decretals by the author of the *Gesta* carries over to his inclusion of other decretals that are well known to scholars. The inclusion of *Novit ille — suscepisset* and *Novit ille qui nichil*, addressed to the king of France in 1200 and *Novit ille — puniemus*, sent to the French hierarchy in 1204, all dealing with the matter of the royal divorce, should not surprise us because of their importance, but also because of the evidence presented here that Petrus had intimate knowledge of the case.[46] The involvement of Petrus Beneventanus with the case of Queen Ingeborg and the extensive account of this matter in the *Gesta*, along with the marked sympathy shown the queen, deserve serious consideration in establishing ties between the *Gesta* and the canonist. We should also note that the decretal *Vergentis*, sent to the clergy and people of Viterbo in 1199 and dealing with the problem of heresy,

---

[42]Reg. 1:50, pp. 77-8; 1:551 (554), pp. 797-8; 2:1, pp. 3-5; 2:37, pp. 60-5; 2:72 (75), pp. 126-34; 2:96 (104), pp. 207-8. See below, note 45 for references to *Compilation Tertia*.

[43]Heinrich Singer, *Die Dekretalensammlung des Bernardus Compostellanus antiquus* (Vienna, Hölder, 1914), Sitzungsberichte der K. Akademie der Wissenschaften in Wien, 171, 2, pp. 64, 96, 102-3, and 113. See note 46 below, 3 Comp. 2.13.2, 5.2.2, 5.12.1, 5.23.1. I would like to thank Kenneth Pennington for the loan of his copy of Singer.

[44]For Milan, cf. 3 Comp. 3.16.2; for Canterbury, 1.18.6; for Spain, 3.31.3 and 3.38.3.

[45]Singer, *Deketalensammlung*, 68.

[46] *Novit ille — suscepisset* and *Novit ille qui nichil* (3 Comp. 1.19.5; 2.19.1) and *Novit ille — puniemus*, sent to the archbishops and bishops of France in 1204 (3 Comp. 2.1.3).

though not mentioned in the *Gesta*, is included in *Compilatio Tertia*.[47] The *Gesta* does, however, deal briefly with the subject of heresy in Viterbo. Also, *Solitae*, addressed to the Emperor of Constantinople is found in *Compilatio Tertia*, and is included in the *Gesta*. Further research along these lines may add to our understanding of possible relationships between these works.

If the picture we have sketched here has any value, it is to fill out further what we know about the way in which Pope Innocent recruited, employed, promoted and rewarded those who worked for him and to demonstrate how, in this instance, as in the case of such legates as Nicholas of Tusculum, Guala Bicchieri or Hugolino, he solved problems by choosing capable agents and working with them. In many instances, they not only carried out papal policy but also, no doubt, influenced its direction. Innocent's judgment is amply justified by the trust these men enjoyed under Honorius III, who, in 1217, promoted Petrus Beneventanus to be cardinal bishop of Sabina.[48]

As a result of this effort, some points emerge more clearly. The career of Petrus Beneventanus suggests a continuity of policy on crucial issues that extends from the very early years of Innocent's pontificate up to Lateran IV. If Petrus was the author of the *Gesta*, we must conclude that he was one of the best-informed figures in the curia. His expertise on French affairs reached back to his mission to Queen Ingeborg and provided the basis for a better understanding of subsequent developments there. If the editor of *Compilatio Tertia* was already such an important figure in the curia, Innocent's confidence in him becomes more understandable. Moreover, his importance suggests that further study of *Compilatio Tertia* as a policy statement is warranted. Pennington's work already indicates that an effort was being made to fine tune some aspects of Innocent's legal decisions, probably with an eye to local courts. But what about the overall content of these decretals? Was this an effort to make the transfer of papal policy to the local level more efficient? Does this purpose perhaps explain why other compilations were rejected? Certainly, Petrus Beneventanus was a papal agent. Was he also an active participant in the making of policy? Clearly, we need to move research on figures like Petrus Beneventanus to a more central position, recognizing their role in shaping, under papal supervision, the road travelled by the papacy under Innocent III. In this particular case, we can only conclude that

---

[47]For the dossier of cases, see *Gesta*, PL 214:lxxx-lxxxix. The cases cited are found in 3 Comp. 5.14.1, 2.13.2, 1.5.1, 5.4.1, 1.21.1, 5.23.1, 4.15.1, 5.12.1. Cf. also, note 21 above for the Evesham case. 3 Comp. 1.7.1 (X 1.8.3) deals with the use of the pallium by the bishop of Troya, also treated in the *Gesta*, and 3 Comp. 1.19.1 (X 1.30.3) deals with his effort to move to Palermo. For the mention of heresy in Viterbo, see *Gesta*, 214:clxi-clxxii.

[48]Tillmann, *Papst Innocenz III*, 3; Sayers, *Innocent III*, 18, and 40; Maleczek, *Papst*, 293-4.

Innocent demonstrated his consistency of purpose by the way he furthered the career of one of his leading experts.

Vineam Domini – 10 April 1213: New Efforts and Traditional *Topoi* – Summoning Lateran IV

Alberto Melloni

When Emperor Alexius Comnenus and the patriarch of Constantinople wrote to the thirty-nine-year-old pope that a council could be fruitful for Christendom, only twenty years had passed since the previous general council of the Latin church.[1] Such a request (1199) was one of the signs that Lateran III[2] had left many tasks undone, especially the crusade to repel the Muslim threat to Constantinople's lands and to recover Jerusalem, lost in 1187.

THE CRUSADE
The crusading impulse was a heritage of the previous century. Innocent III did not renounce this project, and he did not see it as being in conflict with his attempt to promote unity within Christendom.[3] He did, however, align it among his own priorities. So the crusade could be seen as one of the fields in which Innocent III expressed his capacity as *reformer*. The redemption and commutation of the crusader's vow and the collection of money as a way of partial

---

[1]Reg. 2:201.
[2]*Le troisième concile du, Latran (1179)*, ed. J. Longère (Paris, 1982).
[3]On the program of the pope see Helene Tillmann, *Papst Innocenz III.* (Bonn, 1954); M. Maccarrone, *Studi su Innocenzo III* (Padova, 1972); E. Kennan, 'Innocent III and the First Political Crusade', *Traditio* 17 (1981):231-49.

indulgence were some of the places where crusade and reform met.[4] Innocent III knew the lasting value of this effort. He had personal experience of the crusading impulse in Western Christendom. On 5 October 1199, he authorized the crusade in defense of Livonia's church, land and patrimony of Mary.[5] The shocking experience of the Fourth Crusade of 1204 – which was directed at the Holy Land but instead ended bloodily in Constantinople – did not in the short run arouse in Innocent serious mistrust of this 'tool'.[6] It is after this date, however, that we can perceive in the sources a difference (if not a separation) between the crusade as ideology of an operational Christendom and the earlier notion of the crusade as carrier of military effectiveness. Episodes like the Children's Crusade[7] and the Albigensian affair did not shake the pope's confidence; rather they convinced him that a serious effort should be made to centralize the management of the *negotium crucis* as ideological demonstration.[8]

THE COUNCIL

That a council could be useful for such a purpose was obvious enough; but it was not enough to make the gathering more challenging than a twelfth-century general council. Two letters at the end of 1199 give witness that the new pope was thinking about summoning a council 'pro multis necessitatibus ecclesiasticis'.[9] In a letter to the archbishop of Köln three years later,[10] Innocent III said that it had been suggested 'by a number of people' (*a plerisque*) that a general council be summoned to curb the disobedience of the bishops. The pope asked the archbishop to attend personally if such a council was called. As Kempf has stressed, these letters are not irrelevant for the prehistory of Lateran IV.[11] They show that along with the idea of the council as the 'natural' place to solve conflict, there is in Innocent III something innovative: he plans to establish the 'venerable' general council as a new means to improve legislation, discipline and politics. After a century during which Lateran councils always arose from

---

[4] J. A. Brundage, *Canon Law and the Crusader* (Madison, 1969), 69-70, 162-3, 185-6. For the effect, see Ch. Meier, *Preaching the Crusades. Mendicant Friars and the Cross in the Thirteenth Century* (Cambridge, 1994).

[5] W. Urban, *The Baltic Crusade* (Illinois, 1975); E. Christiansen, *The Northern Crusade. The Baltic and the Catholic Frontier 1100-1525* (London-Basingstoke, 1980).

[6] L. and J. Riley-Smith, *The Crusades: Idea and Reality 1095-1274* (London, 1981).

[7] W. Stürner, *Kreuzzugsgelübde und Herrschaftssicherung. Friedrich II. Und das Papsttum im letzten Pontifikatsjahr Innozenz' III.*, in *Papsttum, Kirche und Recht im Mittelalter. Festschrift für Horst Fuhrmann* (Tübingen, 1991), 303-15, esp. 304.

[8] B. Bolton, 'Tradition and Temerity: Papal Attitudes to Deviants, 1159-1216', in *Schism, Heresy and Protest*, ed. D. Baker (Cambridge, 1972), 79-91.

[9] Pott. 862-3 (12-13 Nov. 1199).

[10] Pott. 1767 (20 Nov. 1202).

[11] RNI, no. 80, p. 219 n.

schismatic emergencies, Innocent III is planning a different council, one where the 'reform' refrain is to move in new directions.

No sources give us a single reason for Innocent III's decision to summon a council. It is likely that the military defeats of 1212 in the East (but also the spontaneous movements of the very same year) meant that the Christian faithful were ready to take crusading vows. As Powell wrote, Innocent sought 'the fusion of the ideology of crusade with the movements of lay piety, that had begun by the middle of the twelfth century' and this 'achieved a theology of the crusade'.[12] A link between the reform of the church and the recuperation of Jerusalem made the pope understand in a new framework the pulse of renewal in spiritual life, so frequently manifest in past years.

A link so important requires a big event. What could have been better than a council? The council could not, however, be a Gregorian council, a short, general council proclaiming new laws and launching old appeals. It had to be something new and different, something great and universal in a renewed meaning. Innocent III had already announced that a council could have been a magnificent opportunity to show the 'justice' of the pope.[13] But the problem was not simply to draft a constitution to be read in front of the fathers.

THE LETTER *VINEAM*

The result of Innocent III's research is a sophisticated document, dated 19 April 1213. It is a letter that the papal chancery sent to bishops, abbots, princes and patriarchs. The announcement of the council,[14] at first glance, seems painted with new colors on an old canvas. The assembly, the letter says, will be held in Rome; that is obvious. Crusade and reform (*recuperatio* and *reformatio*) are the two main issues on the agenda. This is not a novelty, but the two items are presented as the outcome of a threefold process: prayer with God, analysis with the cardinals, consultation with prudent men. The purpose of the council is described in a very 'classical' way:[15] the extermination of vices, the renaissance of virtues, faith, peace, freedom, the adhesion of princes to the crusade, the apostolic

---

[12] J. M. Powell, *Anatomy of a Crusade 1213-1221* (Philadelphia, 1986), 16, see also 15-32.

[13] For Burgos, see A. García y García, *Constitutiones concilii quarti Lateranensis una cum Commentariis glossatorum* (Città del Vaticano, 1981), 9. For York, C. R. Cheney and W. H. Semple, *Selected Letters of Pope Innocent III Concerning England* (Edinburgh, 1953), 210 and Cheney and Cheney, 171 and 273.

[14] The letter is in Reg. Vat. 8 fo., 142r, n. 30 (olim 26); notes from Cheney and Semple, *Selected letters,* 144-7.

[15] For the crusade theme as a key to the *Gesta,* see B. Bolton, 'Too Important to Neglect: The *Gesta Innocentii PP III*', in *Church and Chronicle in the Middle Ages*, ed. I. Wood and G. A. Loud (London, 1991), 87-99.

intention to create consent on the *recuperatio* issue.[16] All the bishops are urged to attend; chapters and temporal powers are invited to be represented.

I think we can try to separate and discern within these general messages three different groups of lexical choices, words and expressions (sometimes arguments). Some of them were an expression of a definite tradition, some pointed out a change in direction and some others were quite new.

SOME REPETITION

It is reasonable and proper to start with some characteristics of the text which should prevent us from overestimating *Vineam Domini*. The letter, as was inevitable, was modeled on stereotypes already established, with language and tradition well known to Innocent III's chancery. Of course even repetition, insofar as it is not a general repetition of everything that has been said, represents a little choice that should be duly noted.

First of all the idea of *reform*. After momentous success in Gregorian years, reform did return to conciliar acts in the projects of Alexander III. For his Lateran council, he announced on 21 September 1178 that he was willing to *reformare reformanda.*[17] Innocent III followed this pattern but stressed the pairing of *reformatio* and *recuperatio*.

The second meaningful repetition involves an image rather than an ecclesiastical refrain: the *vineyard*. But what vineyard? It has sometimes been suspected that the vineyard image is something new in this context because it does not fit the twelfth-century pattern. In fact, the biblical image of the vineyard was often used in relation to the necessity of repressing heresy, very often as an application to the church of a verse of the Song of Solomon (2:15): 'Carpite nobis vulpes parvulas quæ demoliuntur vineas, nam vinea nostra floruit'. An example (and possibly a path from the Scripture to the papal chancery) can be found in Gratian, C. 24 q. 1 c. 25). Here the Master quotes a passage from Jerome: 'Christi vineam vulpes exterminant', and it is likely that decretists and commentators are the ones who contributed the image to Innocent's literary capital.[18] Brenda Bolton has suggested on this basis that through the vineyard image one can detect a link between the summoning of Lateran IV and *Vergentis*, the famous decretal on

---

[16]The situation of those who were *captivi* seems a major issue only to G. Cipollone, *Cristianità - Islam. Cattività e liberazione in nome di Dio. Il tempo di Innocenzo III dopo 'il 1187'* (Rome, 1992), 349.

[17]PL 200:1184-5.

[18]See B. M. Bolton, 'Philip Augustus and John: Two Sons in Innocent III's Vineyard?', in *Church and Sovereignty c. 590-1918. Essays in Honour of M. Wilks*, ed. D. Wood (Oxford, 1991), 113-34, especially 113; repr. in B. Bolton, *Innocent III: Studies on Papal Authority and Pastoral Care* (Aldershot, 1995), art. V.

heresy,[19] which quotes the image of vineyard foxes. In fact, vineyards and foxes can be found elsewhere in papal acts. *Die Register Innozenz' III.* contains five quotations from the Song of Solomon 2 in 1198-1199 and seven in 1199-1200.[20] Innocent's *Sermons* also often refer to the vineyard, together with foxes, a typical symbol of the heretic.[21] So is Innocent III leaving the conciliar tradition by treating schism? Is he shifting to a link between council and heresy? The answer is no: the vineyard does represent a repetition, but that of a different source. In *Vineam* there are beasts (instead of foxes), because Innocent III in 1213 does not quote S. of S. 2, but rather Isaiah 5. There the prophet compares Israel to a vineyard which gave bitter grapes *(uva labruscam)* instead of wine; the vineyard deserved devastation and pain. No matter of heresy, indeed; rather, strictly a problem of reform.

The image of the council used by Innocent III is that of an instrument concerning the *status ecclesiæ*; he repeats the idea that the ordinary welfare of the church can be secured through the bishops.[22] The pope does not need their approval and help to draft the decrees (and he will proclaim the conciliar constitutions as 'decreta domini Innocenti etc. in generali concilio Lateranensi edita');[23] but only through their reception can the canons be effective for that *status*. Instead of a council to curb disobedience, as some had suggested, Innocent III follows the conciliar tradition of seeking consent.

The tears of the pope (the last repeated image) are more effective than the usual image of sorrow and desperation; but they are not foreign to papal style. Anthropomorphism of the office and dramatization are tools to improve effectiveness.

POSSIBLE NEW DIRECTIONS
Some aspects of *Vineam*, however, do not simply repeat usual *topoi*. Compared to the twelfth-century documents announcing a general council, *Vineam* presents a different degree of literary accurateness. Innocent III's text has some characteristics which need explanation. *Vineam* is not a prayer to take part in the council; it makes multiple references, sometimes awkward ones.

---

[19]See K. Pennington, *Pope and Bishops. The Papal Monarchy in the XII and XIII Centuries* (Philadelphia, 1984) and more recently *The Prince and the Law 1200-1600. Sovereignty and Rights in Western Legal Tradition* (Berkeley, 1993).

[20]Indexes to Reg., first and second years.

[21]See L. Kolmer, *Ad capiendas vulpes. Die Ketzerbekämpfung in Südfrankreich in der ersten Hälfte des 13. Jahrhunderts und die Ausbildung des Inquisitionverfahrens* (Bonn, 1982).

[22]Y. Congar, 'Status Ecclesiæ', in *Post Scripta, Studia Gratiana*, 15 (1972):3-31, and 'Quod omnes tangit ab omnibus tractari et approbari debet', *RHDFE*, 35 (1958):210-59.

[23]See García y García, *Constitutiones*, 139.

Innocent has clearly decided to summon a council based on the most venerable tradition of the 'big seven' ecumenical councils: the *consuetudo patrum* had never been used in the previous century for a papal (general, but also universal) council.[24] The merging of the council's and the pope's powers had never been thought of as something which required a common definition. Nonetheless, the pope combines the program of an eighth council (a *universale concilum*) with a mention of the Lateran (III) laws on the economic costs of the traveling bishop.

Another indication of the type of council he is considering comes from a literary reference to the council as an 'apostolic file', *apostolica lima,* to correct vices. Innocent III had asked for the use of a *lima* to correct serious abuses long before drafting *Vineam.*[25] After summoning Lateran IV, the pope describes the council's work to Philip of France as a rasp file; to preserve lasting tradition he recommends 'limam omnium generali concilio reservando'.[26] It is a new image, which passed through conciliar history very quickly, but it shows a creative intention for Lateran IV.[27]

Other questions arise from different details. Does the proverb closing the letter mean something about the type of council Innocent III is summoning? Why does the pope use the technical term of *provisio* for the council?[28] Is the *saeculum* in which the pope wants the *recuperatio/reformatio* definitely a life term? Or a chronological indication? Or (better?), an echo of Joachimite speculations on the six centuries (666) of success granted by God to the Muslim but now arriving at its end?

SOME CHANGES

Within a framework of choices and intentions, the curia is inserting real and very important departures from twelfth-century tradition.

A first one pertains to the timing: the council is not summoned for the same year or for 'the next Lent', as was usual, but for 1 November 1215. Two and a half years in advance! Such a long delay is offered in order to ensure a very general participation; the bishops will not be excused. They have the time to arrange their own attendance and to persuade others who are invited.

---

[24] See A. Hauck, 'Die Rezeption und Umbildung der allgemeinen Synode im Mittelalter', in *Historische Vierteljahrschrift,* 10 (1967):468-9; F.-J. Schmale, 'Systematisches zu den Konzilien des Reformpapsttums im 12. Jahrhundert', in *Annuarium Historiae Conciliorum,* 6 (1974):23-7, 36-9; H. J. Sieben, *Die Konzilsidee des lateinischen Mittelalters (847-1378)* (Paderborn, 1984), 5.

[25] For instances in the registers of his letters, see no. 154 from the year 1207 (PL 215:1249), no. 175 from 1210 (PL 216:344), no. 66 from 1213 (PL 216:868).

[26] PL 217:230, no. 190 (14 May 1214).

[27] The only source I can mention is in the prologue of Joannes Michaelensis to the Templars' *Regula* (PL 166:860). In patristic writings, the rasp is an image of personal conversion.

[28] On bishops' rights of provision, see Pennington, *Pope and Bishops,* 120-5.

A change in the announcement implies a change in participation: the letter specifies that each portion of the Christian world must be fully represented. The chapters must send deans and provosts or other delegates and procurators. Representation can express sacramental powers. The juridical correctness that can make a great universal council calls for a plenary audience, no matter how great the cost.

These requirements make irrelevant the placement of the council in the liturgical year. The classic 'Gregorian' summoning was for a Lenten synod. Lateran councils were opened (I) on 19 March 1123, (II) on 3 April 1139, and (III) on 5 March 1179.[29] Of course this practice meant that the participants had to travel across the Alps and/or the Apennines or even to sail during the winter. *Vineam* makes it clear that bishops and procurators are summoned for late fall so as to have the opportunity to reach Rome during the summer.[30]

Vineam offers good arguments for taking part in Lateran IV. The council will be (and to a certain extent is) prepared. Even if the pope and his jurists have a certain numbers of decretals ready to became constitutions and solutions of juridical *cruces*, Innocent stresses that he has received the counseling of his brothers the cardinals. This role of the cardinals in shaping the agenda is important. While masters like Alanus considered the cardinals as an institution that could never prevail over the pope's will, one should remember that they would not have bothered to advance the argument unless cardinals had a real role in papal procedures.[31] *Vineam*'s statement concerning the cardinals' role in the preparation does not imply a strictly 'collegial' procedure; but we should not forget that there was no need to mention and no tradition of mentioning a place for the *consistorium*. This organ, which shortly after will be interpreted as part of the divine parliament, marks a difference between the pope – as summarizing the Roman church – and other bishops.[32]

A 'prepared' council does not mean that Innocent III is not thinking of a 'democratic' council. His idea – it will be clear during the sessions – is to introduce some laws and programs and have them approved by the council in a *liturgical* form. Some expressions of *Vineam* will be quoted in the constitutions.[33] The title of Lateran IV will not change (*PP. sacro approbante concilio*) but the

---

[29] Among the big local councils, the use of the Lenten synod was widespread. Councils at Reims, for example, were held on 19 October 1119 and 21 March 1148.

[30] B. Bolton, 'A Show with a Meaning: Innocent III's Approach to the Fourth Lateran Council, 1215', *Medieval History* 1 (1991):53-67, esp. 55; repr. in Bolton, *Innocent III: Studies*, art. XI.

[31] Pennington, *Pope and Bishops*, 53

[32] Maleczek, *Papst*. As Hostiensis will say the bishop has an *auditorium*, whereas the pope has a *consistorium*, Pennington, *The Prince and the Law*, 51.

[33] I have added some references to COD in the text printed in the appendix to this article.

preparation opens a door to some external inputs.[34] *Vineam Domini* invites all the bishops to attend (only two have to remain in each province) and to take with them to Rome written reports concerning what needed reforming. Unfortunately, nothing of such a consultation has apparently survived, but it confirms the idea of a double role of the assembly (to listen/to speak),[35] a double role which will find room in the actual procedure of the Lateran sessions.

Nothing about heresy is explicitly stated in *Vineam*. As Brenda Bolton has shown, the papal attitude to deviants has changed between 1159 and 1216. Innocent III has equated heresy and treason, but he has also opened a dialogue with Christian 'disobedience' and with groups pursuing the poor and mendicant life.[36] He will not use military language in presenting either crusade or reform.[37]

Another novelty appears concerning the crusader's vow. The recipients of *Vineam* are asked to grant their support to the crusade preacher, but the crusade does not appear as the main issue of the announcement. Details and plans about the crusade will find their place in another encyclical (*Quia major*), which parallels the summoning.[38] By 1 November 1215, the pope has to recover his control over the crusade-movement, and the two years of preparation will be used to organize the different regions sketched by the papal chancery. The list of addresses shows that Rome had divided Europe into large regions for the purpose of promoting order in the crusade's preparation.[39] Crusade is definitely on the papal agenda, but the *double pas* of *Vineam* and *Quia major* indicates that plans for the future are different from the memories of the past.

A final remark can be made concerning a couple of adjectives: Innocent III refers to his 'subditi seculares et regulares'. In this parallelism there is no place

---

[34]M. Maccarrone, 'Il IV concilio Lateranense', *Divinitas* 2 (1961):225-63.

[35]Sieben, *Die Konzilsidee*. For some of the most important points debated at Lateran IV there are only suspicions concerning the impact of preparation. See H. Schrekenberg, *Die christlichen Adversus-Judaeos-Texte (11. Bis 13. Jh). Mit einer Ikonographie des Judenthemas bis zum 4. Laterankonzil* (Frankfurt, 1988); J. Avril, *Quelques aspects de l'institution paroissiale après le IVe concile du Latran*, in *Crises et réforme dans l'église de la réforme grégorienne à la préréforme. Actes du 115e Congrès national des Sociétés Savantes Avignon* (Paris, 1990), 93-106; G. Baaken *Der deutsche Thronstreit auf dem IV. Laterankonzil (1215)*, in *Ex ipsis rerum documentis. Beiträge zur Mediävistik. Festschrift für Harald Zimmermann* (Sigmaringen, 1991), 509-21; R. M. Frahe, 'IV Lateran's Revolution in Criminal Procedure: The Birth of "Inquisitio", the End of Ordeals, and Innocent III's Vision of Ecclesiastical Politics', in *Studia in Honorem Eminentissimi Cardinalis Alphonsi M. Stickler* (Rome, 1992), 97-111.

[36]Bolton, 'Tradition and Temerity', 86.

[37]G. Grado Merlo, 'Militia Christi come impegno antiereticale (1179-1233)', in *'Militia Christi' e Crociata nei secoli XI-XIII* (Milan, 1992), 358-69. J. Bird rightly stressed this point during our symposium.

[38]Riley-Smith, *The Crusades*, 118-24.

[39]On the exclusion of Spain, see Powell, *Anatomy*, 17. On the destiny of the idea, see E. Siberry, *Criticism of Crusading 1095-1274* (Oxford, 1985).

for a subtle way to suggest a theological or canonistic position. One can, however, understand from such a perceptive reference (to an issue which will grow as a crisis factor between friars and secular clergy in the following decades)[40] another symptom of the perceptiveness and the perfectionism of the draftee and the signer.

SOME FINAL REMARKS

Vineam is one of the major texts that was drafted in the curia of Innocent III. It was not to become law or part of the teaching of law, and it is usually dealt with in a few lines in the histories of Lateran IV.[41] Of course this is perfectly legitimate. The great work which has been done on Innocent III allows us today to use it to test some assumptions about his pontificate and its guidelines. It seems to me that in such a perspective, *Vineam* cannot be considered an 'innocent' letter; it is rather a *manifesto*. This 'political' use of the papal summoning is one of the lasting heritages that on 19 April 1213 could not easily be foreseen.[42]

---

[40]On the bishops attempt to regain old prerogatives see Pennington, *Pope and Bishops*, 156-71. *Regulares* appears in the councils' language with Lateran IV; see *Thesaurus Conciliorum Oecumenicorum et Generalium Ecclesiæ Catholicæ*, curante Cetedoc (Louvain-La-Neuve, 1996) s. v.

[41]R. Foreville, *Latran I, II, III, IV* (Paris, 1965).

[42]See G. R. Evans, 'The Attack on the Fourth Lateran Council', *Annuarium Historiae Conciliorum* 21 (1989):241-66.

APPENDIX

Archiebiscopo Episcopis, Abbatibus Prioribus.
per vinnensem provinciam constitutis
Indictio concilii generalis.
(Laterani, XII Kal. Maii.)[43]

Vineam Domini Sabaoth multiformes moliuntur bestie demoliri, quarum incursus adeo invaluit contra ipsam ut ex parte non modica pro vitibus spine succreverint, et, quod gementes referimus, ipse jam vites proferant pro uva *labruscam* [Is. 5:4], infecte multipliciter et corrupte. Illius ergo testimonium invocamus *qui testis est* in celo *fidelis* [Rev. 1:5, Ps. 88:38] quod inter omnia desiderabilia cordis nostri duo in hoc seculo principaliter affectamus, ut ad recuperationem videlicet terre sancte ac reformationem universalis Ecclesie valeamus intendere cum effectu: quorum utrumque tantam requirit provisionis instantiam ut absque gravi et grandi periculo ultra dissimulari nequeat vel differri. Unde supplicationes et lacrimas frequenter effudimus coram Deo [cf. Heb. 5:7], humiliter obsecrantes quatenus super hiis suum nobis beneplacitum revelaret, inspiraret affectum, accenderet desiderium, et propositum confirmaret, facultatem et opportunitatem prestando ad ea salubriter exsequenda. Quapropter habito super hiis cum fratribus nostris et aliis viris prudentibus frequenti ac diligenti tractatu, prout tanti sollicitudo propositi exigebat, hoc tandem ad exequendum predicta de ipsorum consilio providimus faciendum, ut quia hec universorum fidelium communem statum respiciunt, generale concilium juxta priscam sanctorum Patrum consuetudinem convocemus propter lucra solummodo animarum op[p]ortuno tempore celebrandum; in quo ad exstirpanda vitia et plantandas virtutes, corrigendos excessus, et reformandos mores (COD 237:6), eliminandas hereses, et roborandam fidem, sopiendas discordias, et stabiliendam pacem, comprimendas oppressiones, et libertatem fovendam, inducendos principes et populos Christianos ad succursum et subsidium terre sancte (COD 234:14) tam a clericis quam a laicis impendendum, cum ceteris que longum esset per singula numerare, provide statuantur inviolabiliter observanda (COD 256:11) circa prelatos et subditos regulares et seculares (COD 260:32) quecunque de ipsius approbatione concilii visa fuerint expedire *ad laudem et gloriam nominis ejus* [Phil. 2:10], remedium et salutem (COD 245:16) animarum nostrarum, ac profectum et utilitatem populi Christiani.

Quia vero ante biennium universale non posset concilium commode congregari, disposuimus interim per viros prudentes in [*V: et*] singulis provinciis plenius explorare que apostolice provisionis limam exposcunt, et premittere viros idoneos ad terre sancte negotium procurandum, ut si, exigente necessitate sacrum concilium approbaverit, nos personaliter ipsum negotium assumamus efficacius promovendum. Credentes igitur hoc salutare propositum ab illa descendere a quo *est omne datum optimum et omne donum perfectum,* [Iac. 1:17] universitati vestre per apostolica scripta precipiendo mandamus quatenus vos taliter preparetis quod a presenti Dominice Incarnationis millesimo ducentesimo decimo tertio anno usque ad duos annos et dimidium, prefixis vobis pro termino Kalendis Novembris, nostro vos conspectui presentetis cum modestia et cautela, ita quod in vestra provincia unus vel duo de suffraganeis valeant episcopi remanere pro Christianitatis ministeriis exercendis, et tam illi quam alii qui canonica forte prepeditione detenti personaliter venire nequiverint, idoneos pro se dirigant responsales, personarum, et evectionem mediocritate (COD 250:23) servata quam Lateranense concilium definivit, ut nullus omnino plures, quivis autem pauciores secum adducere possit; nec quisquam superfluas faciat et pomposas [*BT*], sed necessarias tantum et moderatas expensas, ostendendo se actu et habitu verum Christi cultorem, cum non secularis applausus, sed spiritualis profectus in hoc sit negotio requirendus. Injungatis autem vos, fratres archiepiscopi et episcopi, ex parte nostra universis Ecclesiarum capitulis, non solum cathedralium, sed etiam aliarum,

---

[43]Cheney and Semple, *Letters*, 144: based on Reg. Vat., fo. 142 r, n. 26 (*olim* 30); Bosquet I.555 (lib IV, reg. XVI, ep. 30) = Migne PL 116:823; Bodleian, Tanner ms 8, fo. 723r.

ut prepositos vel decanos aut alios viros idoneos ad concilium pro se mittant, cum nonnulla sint in ipso tractanda que specialiter ad Ecclesiarum capitula pertinebunt (COD 240-1). Interim vero et per vos ipsos et per alios viros prudentes universa subtiliter inquiratis que correctionis aut reformationis (COD 237:8) studio indigere videntur, et ea fideliter conscribentes, ad sacri concilii perferatis examen, circa subventionem necessariam terre sancte, ubi *Deus rex noster ante secula salutem in medio terre* [Ps. 73:12] dignatus est operari, opem et operam efficaciter impensuri, assistendo fideliter et prudenter iis quos deputaverimus ad hoc negotium specialiter procurandam. Nullus itaque se fallaciter excusando ab esecutione tam sancti operis subtrahat, si canonicam vult vel itinerum impedimenta causetur, que, *Domino faciente signum in bonum* [Ps. 85:17], ex magna jam parte cessare coeperunt. Nam et quanto imminent majora pericula, tanto potiora remedia convenit adhiberi. *Nunquam enim navigavit per equora qui semper exspectat ut mare non concitet ex se fluctus* [cf. Jas. 1:7].

Datum Laterani, XIII Kal.Maii, pontificatus nostri anno decimo sexto.[44]

---

[44]*Im eumdem modum illustri Constantinopolitano Imperatori, usque* ex se fluctus. Cum ergo deceat et expediat ut tua imperialis sublimitas ad synodum tam solemnem nuntios dirigat speciales, serenitatem tuam monemus et exhortamur attentius quatenus prescripto termino, vita comite, viros idoneos dirigere non postponas, per quos tue nobis aperias beneplacitum voluntatis; quia quantum cum honestate poterimus, ad tuum libenter et efficaciter intendemus commodum et honorem.

Vineam Domini Sabaoth, etc., *usque* donum perfectum, universis archiebiscopis et episcopis ac aliis ecclesiarum prelatis per universas fere Christianorum provincias constitutis per apostolica scripta precipiendo mandamus ut se ipsos taliter preparent, etc., *verbis competenter mutatis, usque* requirendus. Injungant etiam archiepiscopi et episcopi ex parte nostra universis Ecclesiarum capitulis, etc., *usque* fluctus. Cum igitur in hoc generali concilio sint multa tractanda que ad statum vestri ordinis pertinebunt, decet et expedit ut ad idem concilium viros idoneos destinetis, qui negotia vestra debeant fideliter procurare.

In eumdem modum capitulo Costantinopolitano usque cum modestia et cautela. Qui vero canonica forte prepeditione detenti personaliter venire nequiverint, idoneos pro se dirigant responsales; nec quisquam superfluas, etc., *usque* requirendus. Ideoque discretioni vestre per apostolica scripta mandamus quatenus ei qui, auctore Deo, constantinopolitane Ecclesie presidebit, ex parte nostra que premissa sunt fideliter nuntietis, ut et juxta priscam formam nostro se conspectui representet; nihilominus de collegio vestro viros idoneos pro vobis ad hoc sacrum concilium transmissuri, cum nonnulla sint in ipso tractanda que specialiter ad Ecclesiarum capitula pertinebunt. Interim vero per vos ipsos et alios viros prudentes, etc., *usque* perferatis examen. Nullus itaque se fallaciter, *usque* ex se fluctus.

Learning and Teaching in the Early Thirteenth-Century Papal Curia

E. C. Ronquist

What in the time of Innocent III would the papal curia – *scriptores*, cardinals, diplomats – or the pontiff himself consider worth knowing? A great deal, it is easy to suppose, about modes of address, tactful adjustments and political government – things that are matters of prudence; about the points of confession and absolution and judgements of canon law – clerical, curial concerns; about liturgy, the sustaining of pious action in sermons and the maintenance of orthodoxy – priestly concerns, as well. Running through these interests is a capacity for rhetoric, for systematization and for theology.[1] Although these are now distinct domains of scholarly enquiry – history, law, theology, literature – I must venture into all of them in an attempt to sketch some features of the intellectual skills and accomplishments of the illustrious clerisy, led by Innocent III in the early thirteenth century, as they studied and held authority well beyond central Italy.

Permit me to use an anchronistic term and call some of these clerics intellectuals (I have seen the term used by Anthony Grafton, discussing the sixteenth-century curia). They show a delight in and devotion to knowledge and the arts that surpassed institutional utility. And in any case practical measures of persuasion, ordination, orientation all required information, doctrines and

---

[1]Thus, the importance of clarity and order in the thought of Innocent III was noted by Robert Brentano, *Rome before Avignon* (New York, 1974), 150.

methods of greater generality, especially if it is universal jurisdiction itself and authority that is being claimed. As a subsidiary contribution to discussions in this volume, the clerical skill and knowledge I should like to investigate will be of the theoretical sort, concerned with nature, biblical interpretation and theology. I will look here at instances of training in broader reaches of eloquence and intellectual confidence that might nevertheless support the practical work of legates and administrators of the thirteenth-century church, particularly given the very special sort of power that reinforced its capacity to persuade and the faith and moral bearings to which it was directed.

These active figures have left evidence of a pleasure in learning that went beyond the needs of practice, while they also engaged in modes of teaching designed for already busy young people. Learning and teaching, enquiry and application, were reciprocal activities. In the theoretical direction, practical arts of nature –medicine, astrology – might be investigated more for their lore than for their effects. Practical rhetoric, a useful clerical skill, might be refined into verse, replacing commanding persuasion with the cultivation of elevated attitudes, while reinforcing certitude with continuing research into evidence and authoritative backing.[2] Yet it was also the case that doctors of what has come to be called 'scientific theology' wrote hymns and preached sermons, practising what Gregorius de Monte Sacro, whom we shall be considering, called 'theologia et theurgia'. And traditional texts were being indexed in order to become reference repertories for practical application.

I will discuss some cultivated personages and their relations, but I will not much deal with Innocent III himself, who was, quite apart from the tests of prudence he faced, a learned and eloquent figure both before and during his papacy.[3] I can also not promise a full catalogue of the many people who were styled 'magister' in the papal court. I will instead recall data about some cardinals, and I will deal particularly with some implications of the encyclopedic poem by Gregorius de Monte Sacro that gives elaborate evidence of a specific

---

[2]It was during the second stage of his education in the liberal arts that the student was introduced into the work of the '*philosophi et poetae*'; Helene Wieruszowski, 'Rhetoric and the Classics in Italian Education of the Thirteenth Century', *Collectanea Stephan Kuttner* 1 = *Studia Gratiana* 11 (1967):171-207 at 184, though she is chiefly discussing secular and legal education. For the relationship of *dictamen*, verse and music, see Hans Martin Schaller, 'Die Kanzlei Kaiser Friedrichs II: Ihr Personel und ihr Sprachstil', 2, *Archiv für Diplomatik* 4 (1958):322-4. Cf. F. X. Seppelt, 'Das "Opus Metricum" des Kardinals Jacopus Stefanescki', *Monumenta Coelestiana – Quellen zur Geschichte des Papstes Coelestin V*, Quellen und Forschungen aus dem Gebiet der Geschichte (Paderborn, 1921) for verse-writing after study in Paris and Bologna.

[3]For the diversified writing of Innocent III at leisure, possibly, and in earnest, see, e.g., John C. Moore, 'Innocent III's *De miseria humanae conditionis*: A *Speculum Curiae*?', *Catholic Historical Review* 67 (1981):553-64, and his 'The Sermons of Pope Innocent III', *Romische historische Mitteilungen* 36 (1994):81-142.

range and style of learning inspired by early intellectual stimulation in Rome. It appears that the papal court had a way of using learning relatively distinct from that of the imperial court and the universities, though techniques were also shared.

In the next section, I will give evidence particularly from Gregorius de Monte Sacro of his education through members of the curia. The final section will attempt some generalizations about the quality of such education, with emphasis on the methods, typically analogical and hierarchical, by which there was a specific form for organized knowledge and reinforcement of practical persuasion. Particularly, we will see use of and collections of the *distinctio*, a device that collected instances of the use of a word in a text (the Bible, but also Gregory the Great's *Moralia on Job*) and then differentiated the meanings into lower and higher senses.

I. INTELLECTUAL CIRCLES IN THE CURIA

My guide to the milieu of learned enquiry in Rome at the end of the twelfth century and through the papacy of Innocent III will not be the findings of the Fourth Lateran Council, but the less official record of his fostering in Rome by a Petrus who took the name Gregorius. Gregorius by 1220 was abbot of the Benedictine monastery of the Holy Trinity on Monte Sacro in Apulia, a monastery directly dependent on the Holy See. He died sometime before 1248. I have for several years been put to school by Gregorius de Monte Sacro's major piece of writing, the encyclopedic *Peri ton anthropon theopoieseos* or in one of the original spellings *Peri ton anthropon theopijsis*, regularly glossed *De hominum deificatione*. As it comes to be published, this encyclopedic text will prove to be a rich account of the range and orientation of learning an Italian cleric of the period found worth recording in some 13,000 Latin hexameter verses set amid short and longer glosses that point back to sources of the information.[4] The

---

[4] See Filippo Tamburini, 'Gregorio, Abate del monastero della SS. Trinità di Monte Sacro sul Gargano († 1250 c.) e la sua opera poetica', *Miscellanea Bibliothecae Apostolicae Vaticanae* 1, Studi e Testi 329 (Città del Vaticano, 1987), 147-95, with all the introductory prose texts; E. C. Ronquist, 'The Early-Thirteenth-Century Monastic Encyclopedia in Verse of Gregorius de Monte Sacro', *Studi medievali* Ser. 3.29 (1988):841-71, with the prose 'Prologus' (proceeding, as here, from 'Gregorius de Monte Sacro, *Peri ton anthropon theopoieseos*: A Study and Partial Edition', dissertation, University of Chicago, 1975); and Hans Martin Schaller, 'Studien zur Briefsammlung des Kard. Thomas von Capua', *Deutsches Archiv für Erforschung des Mittelalters* 21 (1965):393, 499-502, with the letter to Thomas. Udo Kindermann has presented editions of the shorter poems and hymns, 'Das Poema geminum von den Heiligen des Heiligen Berges: Zwei frühe poetische Patrozinien-Reliquienkataloge', in Irene Vaslef and Helmut Muschhausen, eds, *Classica et Mediaevalia: Studies in Honor of Joseph Szövéffy*, Medieval Classics: Texts and Studies 20 (Washington, 1986), 77-90 for two hymns, one of which has the name of Gregorius de Monte Sacro in acrostics, 'Gregors Gebet', in *Festschrift für Paul Klopsch*, Udo Kindermann et al., eds, Göppinger Arbeiten zur Germanistik 492 (Göppingen: Kümmerle, 1988), 175-206, *Der Dichter vom heiligen Berge* (Nürnberg, 1989) and

text was ready to be glossed in the early 1230s. Works of Gregorius (and possibly others) are preserved in two manuscripts from Monte Sacro now in the Biblioteca Apostolica Vaticana, Barb. lat. 2089 (B) and Vat. lat. 5977 (V).[5]

Gregorius de Monte Sacro's account of his development in the prose prefatory material to the long verse treatise affords a picture of learning and teaching in the circle of the cardinalate, which gave his early life a different pattern of experience from that of a monastic school or distant university.[6] The record is mainly given in the dedicatory letter to Thomas of Capua, which has been edited by Hans Martin Schaller. Here Gregorius emphasized the ecclesiastical and theological implications of his experiences in learning. I will use his statements to make a series of sketches. At the end of this section there will be brief discussion of the key term in the title of the verse encyclopedia, *Theopoiesis*, glossed *Deification*, a focus that other medieval encyclopedias might not claim.

Thomas Capuanus, known also as Thomas de Episcopo, was identified by Gregorius de Monte Sacro as cardinal presbyter of Santa Sabina, as he was from 1216 to his death at Anagni in 1239. Gregorius did not mention that Thomas was also archbishop of Naples, papal chancellor and an important figure in negotiations between the papacy and the empire.[7] He was a nephew of Honorius III.[8] He had done practical work as a *notarius*[9] and rose to be an important figure in papal affairs; in 1230, for example, his legation succeeded in reconciling Gregory IX and Frederick II. He was also a man of letters – according to

---

Flores Psalmorum: A Hitherto Unknown Jesu-Psalter (Concord NH, 1990).

[5]Manuscript V, which shares hands with the slightly earlier or imperfect B, was in Monte Sacro in 1366 when it was lent out to a 'palatino comiti' (V 4v) whom Tamburini (153) has identified with Nicolò Orsini, a correspondent of Petrarch's circle, so in all probability both had been prepared and preserved there. V ascribed the collection of shorter hymns headed 'Flores psalmorum' and a 1100 line 'Cur Deus homo' to 'petrus carus Gregorius Abbas Montis Sacri', cancelling the 'petrus carus'. Jane E. Sayers, *Papal Government and England during the Pontificate of Honorius III (1216-1227)* (Cambridge University Press, 1984), 45, 201, noted a papal scribe P. C. active in 1217, and a 'Petrus Greg.' who was delivering mandates in Paris 1222 and 1224 while residing there. In the letter to Thomas of Capua Gregorius de Monte Sacro noted that his original name had been Petrus.

[6]Cf. Brian Stock, *The Implications of Literacy* (Princeton, 1983), 488-9: 'The wandering between two periods of relative stability was also essential . . . In all three stages of the "rites of passage," as instability increased, there arose a corresponding desire to internalize inherited religious values.'

[7]See, e.g., Clemente Schmitt, 'Tomasso di Capua', *Enciclopedia Cattolica* (Vatican, 1954). Thomas was the last chancellor of the curia. Though archbishop of Naples, he preferred to stay in the curia, according to Norbert Kamp, 'Monarchia ed episcopato nel Regno svevo di Sicilia', in Cosimo Damiano Fonseca, et al., eds, *Potere, società e popolo nell'età sveva* (Bari, 1985), 123-49 at 135; similarly Klaus Ganzer, *Die Entwicklung des auswärtigen Kardinalats im hohen Mittelalter: Ein Beitrag zur Geschichte des Kardinalkollegiums vom 11. bis 13. Jahrhundert*, Bibliothek des Deutschen Historischen Instituts in Rom 26 (1963), 202.

[8]Sayers, *Papal Government*, 5.

[9]Reinhard Elze, 'Die päpstliche Kapelle im 12. und 13. Jahrhundert', ZRG, Kan. 36 (1950):145-204 at 176.

Salimbene, the 'melior' and 'pulchrior dictator de curia'.[10] His hymns evidence his mastery of verse, particularly an antiphon, two hymns and a sequence from the Office honouring St Francis of Assisi, composed for Gregory IX in 1228. But Salimbene's term *dictator* should refer above all to Thomas' position in the chancery from Innocent III to Gregory IX, where he remained a friend of his imperial counterpart Petrus de Vinea.[11] He left treatises on the *dictamen*: the *Ars dictandi* has been edited,[12] but not the *Summa dictaminis*, a formulary in ten books with some 625 examples that was compiled 1260-1270 in the curia.[13] His participation in the work of ecclesiastical communication was not merely formal, for he was the author, it is supposed, of a *Summa penitentie* and was major penitenciar under Gregory IX.[14]

Gregorius de Monte Sacro offered his work to Thomas of Capua for correction, with humble apology for its being a 'meagre and poorly documented treatise that claims to be about everything, composed with backward understanding and expressed with inept diction, and fearing the document-scanning eyes and metre-measuring ears of an acute judge'.[15] Despite the humility, the act of dedication to Thomas of Capua shows a sense of a continuity of interests between the verse encyclopedia and the work of the papal chancery. Gregorius took up chancery techniques, turning them to the higher purpose of formal exposition of what he called *Theopoiesis*. He showed skill in the control of prose by the *cursus*, regulating the endings of clauses (where in his prose, like Thomas of Capua, Gregorius de Monte Sacro preferred the *cursus velox*), but tested himself further by the demands of the classical hexameter. As he declared, 'Since, as I worked, anxiety increased that the composition might grow beyond measure, I metrically

---

[10]Salimbene de Adam, *Cronica*, ed. Giuseppe Scalia, Scrittori d'Italia 232/1 (Bari, 1966), an. 1247, p. 265, an. 1250, p. 554.

[11]Hans Martin Schaller, 'Zur Bestehung der sogenannten Briefsammlung des Petrus de Vinea', *Deutsches Archiv für Erforschung des Mittelalters* 12 (1956):114-59 at 146.

[12]Emmy Heller, *Die Ars Dictandi des Thomas von Capua*, Heidelberg, Akademie der Wissenschaften, *Sitzungsberichte, Philos.-hist. Klasse*, 4 (Abhandlung, 1928-1929).

[13]Maleczek, *Papst*, 201-3, Heller, 1, and Schmitt.

[14]To him C. H. Haskins assigned the first formulary of the papal penitentiary, 'The Sources for the History of the Papal Penitentiary', *American Journal of Theology* 9 (1905) 429-32, text ed. H. C. Lea, *A Formulary of the Papal Penitentiary in the Thirteenth Century* (Philadelphia, 1892). Sayers, *Papal Government*, 24-5, has suggested that the position of penitenciar was a 'demoted office' of chancellor.

[15]My English versions here will be interpretations more than strict translations. Gregorius had written: 'Exilem igitur et inconptum quasi de uniuersitate tractatum sensu tardiore compositum, imperitiori sermone prolatum, uestro nomini dedicatum, aures et oculos arguti iudicis formidantem, sensus uester beniuolus pie inspiciat et benigne corrigat, quia uestre correptioni dirigitur et iudicio, non fauori' (V 8r). If I render *inconptum* 'poorly documented', it is remembering that the *computus* was an early form of medieval encyclopedism, one studied particularly by Faith Wallis, e.g. 'Images of Order in the Medieval Computus', in Warren Ginsberg, ed., *Ideas of Order in the Middle Ages*, Acta 15 (Binghamton, 1990), 45-67.

bound it in.'[16] One notes that the text was here called a *dictamen*, though by title it is *poesis*, or more exactly *theopoiesis*. It was thus a mode of rhetorical composition, but competitively sublime and of a higher range than a 'practical' attempt at persuasion. Gregorius de Monte Sacro had emulated Thomas of Capua in the writing of hymns, but the *Peri ton anthropon theopoisesos* is a turn from lyrics of affective devotion to elaborate exposition in sustained verse.

Discussing his education, Gregorius de Monte Sacro declared that:

> I was the vilest of things and of scarcely any weight, when, with the gift beyond the merits of any individual by which He moves and teaches each person science (as the font of the sciences without human schooling in the manner of the love of letters), the unspeakable amplitude of Divine Grace made me learned in understanding through the pages of the Scriptures, and ornamented me at the age of ten with gifts of honour in the ring of sacred exercises, through the once venerable man, Gregorius de Sancto Apostolo, cardinal deacon and legate of the Apostolic See, adopted as a son by him and signed with his name, while up to then I had been called poor Peter.[17]

The formula of adoption used by Gregorius de Monte Sacro suggests that Gregorius de Sancto Apostolo fostered him with particularly personal care. It is likely he had been an oblate, one born in the Apulia to which he later returned, since he described himself as 'ciuis garganicus natione apulus'. A parallel case of a well-educated orphan is Albinus, who was cardinal bishop of Albano from 1182 to 1196.[18]

Gregorius de Sancto Apostolo was cardinal deacon of Santa Maria in Portico 1188-1202.[19] He was a legate to Hungary, Lombardy, the Marches of Ancona and

---

[16]'Et ut maior michi anxietas succresceret cum labore, ne dictamen cresceret in immensum, illud metrice coartaui' (V 7r).

[17]'Ineffabilis diuine gratie amplitudo, . . . me, uilissimum rerum et fere nullius momenti, munere, quo preuenit merita singulorum et docet omnem hominem scientiam utpote fons scientiarum absque humano magisterio post amorem litterarum, sacra pagina intellectualiter erudisset, ac sacri tyrocinij cingulo per olim uenerabilem uirum Gregorium Sanctorum Apostolorum diaconem cardinalem tunc Apostolice Sedis legatum, adoptatum sibi in filium suo nomine insignitum, cum Petrus pauper admodum uocitarer, decennem munificentius decorasset' (V 7r). The passage can be variously punctuated to set the moment at which literacy succeeded naive inspiration, a frequent topos in mystical discourse, as also in the subsequent quotation.

[18]Albinus was a *magister* in Verona and switched to theology; for the young orphan a monastic uncle provided rudiments of instruction and then a relative who became bishop of Orvieto. See Uta-Renate Blumenthal, 'Cardinal Albinus of Albano and the "*Digesta pauperis scolaris Albani*" MS. Ottob. lat. 3057', *Archivium Historiae Pontificiae* 20 (1982):7-49.

[19]Maleczek, *Papst*, 93-4; Helene Tillmann, 'Richerche sull'origine dei membri del collegio cardinalizio nel XII. secolo', *Rivista di Storia della Chiesa in Italia* 29 (1975):383 (the whole study 24 [1970]:441-64, 26 [1972]:313-53, 29 [1975]:363-402).

Rimini, and Cisalpine Gaul, where he had a hand in suppressing heresy. After the death of the Empress Constance, he was given, though only briefly, care of the realm and 'custody' of the young ward of the pope, Frederick II.[20] I do not know of any writing by Gregorius de Sancto Apostolo, but it appears he did foster the learning of the young tiro who took his name while describing his promising gifts as if his capacity for rhetoric were a miracle:

> Without delay beyond my powers I began to express the celestial gift in rude and rustic speech, the rhetorical resources, a docile heart, and matter for discourse divinely given me. For it was not as one schooled in grammar and the other liberal arts that I attempted to write something, but rather by a divine gift and infused instinct.[21]

Viewing this as a miracle suggests he saw his writing as going beyond what arts training would call for, perhaps as it originated in a childlike capacity for faith. Gregorius de Sancto Apostolo must, nevertheless, have provided both instruction in scriptural narrative and the training in full literacy that led to the capacity to attempt formal writing.

It would appear that with grounding in sacred expression Gregorius de Monte Sacro then entered a monastery.[22] Yet he remained ready for further intellectual training from the cardinalate. Thus as Gregorius described it, 'I attended to the words of most illustrious men of blessed memory.'[23]

The first of these two subsequent patrons was 'Roger, who took me into his household from the monastery, discussing the Seven Penitential Psalms with his

---

[20]Epistles of Innocent III at the Lateran, 25 January 1199 and 17 February 1199, announce his mission to Sicily, 'constantiam tue mentis, prudentiam, dispositionem in arduis negotiis Apostolice Sedis experti', committing to him the *tutela* of Frederick and the *dispositio regni*: cited J.-L.-A. Huillard-Breholles, *Historia Diplomatica Friderici Secundi* (Paris, 1852) 1.1, pp. 24, 28-9, who notes from the *Res gestae Innocentii Tertii* that 'Verum quia non bene intendebatur ei a familiaribus regis et praesertim a cancellario qui dedignabatur eum superiorem habere, cum et omnes non regiis, sed propriis utilitatibus insudarent, post non multum temporis ad Sedem Apostolicam est reversus', so that 'Gregorius . . . ineunte mense julio hujus anni Romam regressum comperimus' (p. 29, n. 2).

[21]'Parumper supra uires cepi celeste donum rudi et rustico sermone quasi balbutiens experiri, copia discendi corde docili et materia michi celitus attributa. Non enim gramatice [sic] uel aliarum liberalium artium laribus per humanum magisterium educatus, scribere aliquid attemptaui, set potius divino munere uel instinctu' (V 7r).

[22]Alfredo Petrucci, *Cattedrali di Puglia*, 551, n. 32, recorded his stay at the monastery of Santa Maria de Pulsano.

[23]'Audiui siquidem gloriosissimos uiros sancte recordationis' (V 7r).

familiares.[24] This was Roger, cardinal presbyter of S. Anastasia 1205-1212.[25] A German canonist, he was papal legate in Sicily in 1209 and Apulia in 1210 and also had missions in Denmark, Sweden and Bohemia. Praepositinus – Prévotin of Cremona – cited him for what he regarded as an erroneous position on the Eucharist.[26]

The statement that Roger was in some fashion working on the Seven Penitential Psalms with the people around him – 'disserens suis familiaribus' – is singular evidence of mixed learning and teaching in the late-twelfth-century curia, both for the social organization and for the subject being discussed. In the passage we see Gregorius again taken into a household rather than a school, as it would appear Roger was holding, as it seems, discussion seminars with people associated with him for more practical tasks, his *familiares*.[27] This household had become an independent centre of enquiry, earlier than the evidence we have that by the end of the thirteenth century individual cardinals might have quite extensive libraries, primarily of legal texts.[28] Roger's household was thus functioning like a miniature papal curia, of which we have better evidence of how it functioned as an informal school. Innocent III had some fifty chaplains, and according to Salimbene he reproved them for neglecting reading. Yet according to the Latin poet Heinrich of Würzburg in the time of Urban IV, the *curiales* were all too busy

---

[24]'Magistrum Rogerium, cum me in suum a monasterio assumpisisset, septem penitentiales psalmos Rome suis familiaribus disserentem.'

[25]Maleczek, *Papst*, 150; he subscribed to documents through 30 December 1211. Confusing the notice of Alfonso Chacon (Ciaconius), *Vitae et res gestae Pontificorum Romanorum* (Roma, 1630) 2:642, 656, Louis Moréri, *Le grand dictionnaire historique*, 19th edn (Paris, 1748), ascribed to Roger the works of Gregorius de Monte Sacro.

[26]Georges Lacombe, *La vie et les oeuvres de Prévotin* (Le Saulchoir, 1927), 180-1, with details about Roger – unless this was Roger, titular of S. Eusebio (1178) and archbishop of Benevento (d. 1221), whence Carmelo Ottaviano, 'A proposito di un libro sul Prepositino', *Rivista di filosofia neoscolastica* 20 (1978):366-71 at 370.

[27]For the social structure, see Agostino Paravicini Bagliani, *Cardinali di curia e 'familiae' cardinalizie*, Italia Sacra: Studi e documenti di storia ecclesiastica 18-19 (Padua, 1972); for chaplains with the title 'magister' 2:492-3. Borwin Rusch thought 'simple monks' (like Gregorius) might serve as helpers to cardinal-penitenciars, *Die Behörden und Hofbeamten der päpstlichen Kurie der 13. Jahrhunderts*, Schriften der Albertus-Universität, Geisteswissenschaftliche Reihe 3 (Königsberg, 1936), 39. Evidence for a papal *schola*, c. 700, was cited by D. A. Bullough, *Settimani di Studio del Centro per lo Studio del Alto Medioevo* 19 (Spoleto, 1972):479, n. 49; Innocent IV set up a *Studium Generale* for theology and law in Lyon, 1245 (Rusch, 131).

[28]See Richard Mather, 'The Codicil of Cardinal Comes of Sasate and the Libraries of Thirteenth-Century Cardinals', *Traditio* 20 (1964):319-50, and Agostino Paravicini Bagliani, 'Le biblioteche dei cardinali Pietro Peregrosso († 1295) e Pietro Colonna († 1326)', *Zeitschrift für schweizerische Kirchengeschichte* 64 (1970):104-39.

passing hours reading and speculating about celestial matters.[29] A fourteenth-century collection of *distinctiones* glossed 'curiales' 'curiosi et iocundi'.[30] But for their skills Innocent III and Honorius III increasingly used *familiares* of the curia instead of cardinals for varied missions, and the *curiales* themselves might rise to the rank of cardinal.[31]

As to the material Roger was taking up with his *familiares*, the Psalms were the most elementary texts of literacy and useful for the basic interpretation of the liturgy. The *Commentary on the Psalms* of Cassiodorus had been marked for its stylistic terms and rhetorical analysis, so providing a training instrument for composition.[32] In the description Gregorius de Monte Sacro gives of Roger's teaching, the concentration on the Penitential Psalms suggests possible specific training both in the hearing of confession – the practice given new importance by the Fourth Lateran Council – and in its analysis through penitential manuals and canon law. We meanwhile also have a treatise on the Seven Penitential Psalms by Innocent III himself, with elaborate numerical parallels and *distinctiones* that may have been the sort of analysis Roger of St Anastasia was also working out (Gregorius's glosses do not correspond with those of the Innocentine treatise). A simpler earlier *Expositio in Psalmos penitentiales* by Gilbert de Reggio was attributed to Gregory VII in the *Patrologia Latina*, vol. 79. That by Innocent III was marked by a gesture that makes its construction itself an act of penitence, as it was dated 10 April 1216, Good Friday, as Brenda Bolton has reminded us in another paper in this collection.[33]

The work of Roger has not been traced, but we may recall the efforts of canonists not only in the organization of their own field of study but also in the

---

[29]'A causis si quando patres et litibus aures / Expediunt, studii protinus arma petunt. / Hinc ubi librorum pertransit hora, pererrant / In terra posito pectore claustra poli / Celestes speculantur opes, mundoque labanti / Succurrunt humili sedulitate precum', Heinrich of Würzburg, *Liber de statu Curie Romane*, 645-50, ed. Hermann Grauert, *Magister Heinrich der Poet*, München, Academie, *Sitzungsberichte, Philos.-hist. Klasse* 27/1 (1912):90.

[30]See Jacques Chaurand, 'Latin médiéval et context social: le campagnard et l'homme de cour d'après un receuil de distinctions du XIVᵉ siècle', in *La Lexicographie du latin médiéval et ses rapports avec les recherches actuelles sur la civilisation du Moyen Age*, Colloques Internationaux du CNRS 529 (Paris, 1981), 59-75 at 67.

[31]This information from Elze, 151, 164, 175, 178, and from Norbert Kamp, 'Soziale Herkunft und geistlicher Bildungsweg der unteritalienischen Bischöfe in normannisch-staufischer Zeit', in *Le Istituzioni ecclesiastiche della 'Societas christiana' dei secoli XI-XII: Diocesi, pievi e parrochie*, Pubblicazioni dell' Univ. Cattolica del Sacro Cuore, Miscellanea del Centro di Studi Medioevali 8 (Milano, 1977):89-116 at 111. There were 200 chaplains by the time of Innocent IV (Elze, 188).

[32]Ann W. Astell, 'The Rhetoric and Poetics of *Concessio*: Cassiodorus's *Commentary on the Psalms*', paper in the 11th Biennial Conference, International Society for the History of Rhetoric, Saskatoon, 25 August 1997.

[33]For the date of Innocent's treatise Michele Maccarone, *Studi su Innocenzo III* (Padova, 1972), 342, cites a manuscript note.

transmission of information more generally. Thus Gregorius de Monte Sacro found concepts of twelfth-century cosmologists explained and reduced to verbal information in the *Magnae derivationes* of the canonist Huguccio of Pisa, whose alphabetical dictionary was carried on in the mid-thirteenth-century *Summa* or *Expositiones vocabulorum Biblie* of the Franciscan Guillelmus Brito and in Giovanni Balbi's *Catholicon*, the text Gutenburg printed first after the Bible. Huguccio also wrote on grammar, hagiography and the Creed.[34] The range of his work is exemplary of an intellectual style, such that 'twelfth-century scholarship is characterized by the effort to gather, organize, and harmonize the legacy of the Christian past as it pertained to jurisprudence, theological doctrine and Scripture.'[35]

The second 'gloriossimus vir' with whom Gregorius engaged in higher studies, this time 'scientia divina', was the younger of two cardinals, kinsman both named Petrus Capuanus. Of him Gregorius recalled:

When I paused, returning to him from England, I also attended the lectures of my lord, the master of theology, Petrus, cardinal deacon of San Giorgio in Velabro, who at that time was in Paris holding the clair of the correct faith, teaching theology and *theurgia* to the people.[36]

Gregorius here reveals further experiences, first another turn away from formal schooling, perhaps to accompany a legation in England though we have no record of his name, and then in Paris returning to studies with a person ultimately of the papal curia. The younger Petrus Capuanus, according to Gregorius de Monte Sacro, was both as a theologian and – to interpret his word *theurgia* – a preacher. He taught in Paris, 1200-1218, and was friendly with the theologians Stephen Langton and Robert de Courson, who also became cardinals. As to *theurgia* we

---

[34]The *Magnae derivationes* with some 194 manuscripts has never been edited into print. See G. Cremascoli, 'Uguccione da Pisa: Saggio bibliografico', *Aevum* 42 (1968):123-66. There are excerpts in Claus Riessner, *Die 'Magnae Derivationes' des Uguccione da Pisa und ihre Bedeutung für die romanische Philologie, Temi e testi* 11 (Rome, 1965), and Roswitha Klinck, *Die lateinische Etymologie des Mittelalters* (München, 1970). Some of Huguccio's other texts, *De dubio accentu* et al., were edited by Giuseppe Cremascoli, Biblioteca degli Studi Medievali 10 (Spoleto, 1978). For someone both canonist and 'minor theologian' at Oxford, see R. W. Southern, 'Master Vicarius and the Beginning of an English Academic Tradition', in J. G. Alexander and M. T. Gibson, eds, *Medieval Learning and Literature: Essays Presented to Richard William Hunt* (Oxford, 1976), 257-86.

[35]Mary A. Rouse and Richard H. Rouse, *Authentic Witnesses: Approaches to Medieval Texts and Manuscripts*, Publications in Medieval Studies 17 (Notre Dame, 1991), ch. 6, '*Statim invenire*: Schools, Preachers, and New Attitudes to the Page', 191.

[36][Audiui etiam] scientie diue semel dominum meum magistrum Petrum Sancti Georgij ad Uelum Aureum diaconem Cardinalem apud Parisius regentem cathedram orthodoxe, cum ad eum reuertens ab Anglia diuertissem, theologiam et theurgiam populis edocentem (V 6v).

may note the case of Langton as another 'moral or pastoral, rather than systematic theologian'.[37] Nevertheless, the sermons that survive in a Paris manuscript and the better witnessed *Summa theologie* have generally been ascribed to the elder Capuanus.[38] When this Petrus Capuanus was made cardinal deacon of S. Giorgio in Velabro (1219-1236), Gregorius de Monte Sacro might have followed him back to Rome.[39]

It is useful for this survey of intellectual possibilities to pause for further consideration of the two Petri Capuani, though attribution of their work to one or the other is slightly uncertain. Werner Maleczek has provided a full account of both of them.[40] They were of an Amalfitan patriciate family, traders with Muslims in the tenth century and originally from the Langobard nobility of Capua.[41] The elder Petrus was legate to the kings of both England and France (and many other places). He was cardinal deacon of S. Maria in Via Lata (1193), then cardinal presbyter of S. Marcello (1200) and patriarch of Constantinople (1211); he died in 1214.[42] In 1198, Gregorius de Sancto Apostolo came to his aid

---

[37]F. M. Powicke, *Stephen Langton* (Oxford, 1928), 54. Langton's chapter divisions of the Bible were made standard by distinctio-treatises, Rouse and Rouse, 214.

[38]The sermons are in Paris, Bibliothèque nationale, MS. nouv. acquis. lat. 999. The *Summa theologie* has the incipit 'Vetustissima veterum comeditis [comederitis, Glorieux, *Répertoire*] et novis supervenientibus vetera abicietis [Leviticus 26:10] – Vetustissima veterum sunt tres personae.' See Friedrich Stegmuller, *Repertorium Commentariorum in Sententias Petri Lombardi* (Wurzburg, 1947) 1:321, no. 667, adding several manuscripts to the list in Glorieux, 1:265, no. 108. Lacombe, *Prévotin*, 69, placed Petrus' *Summa* before 1193, as an influence on Praepositinus. For a further text in that circle, see Artur Landgraf, 'Eine neuentdeckte Summa aus der Schule des Praepositinus', *Collectanea Franciscana* 1 (1931):289-318, also noting a later influence on Franciscans.

[39]Gregorius cannot be identified in C. R. Cheney and W. H. Semple, eds, *Selected Letters of Pope Innocent III concerning England (1198-1216)* (London, 1953). At the end of 1198 Petrus Capuanus the Elder was ordered from England to France, Helene Tillmann, *Die papstlichen Legaten im England bis zur Beendigung der Legation Gualas (1218)*, Inaug. Diss., Bonn, 1926, p. 88.

[40]*Petrus Capuanus: Kardinal, Legat am vierten Kreutzzug, Theologe († 1214)*, Publikationen des hist. Instituts beim österreichischen Kulturinstitut in Rom, Abhandlungen 8 (Wien, 1988). Beilege A notes of the younger Petrus Capuanus that while Honorius III named him patriarch of Antioch, he never left Rome, where he functioned as a judge. See also Norbert Kamp, 'Capuano, Pietro', *Dizionario Biografico degli Italiani* 19 (Roma, 1976), the Elder, pp. 258-66, the Younger, pp. 266-8. In 1206 the younger renounced a benefice in favour of a chaplain of Roger of S. Anastasia. Conrad Eubel, *Hierarchia Catholica* (Münster, 1913) 1:4-5, corrected Chacon on Petrus Romanus.

[41]Norbert Kamp, 'Capuano, Giovanni', *Dizionario Biografico degli Italiani* 19 (Roma, 1976):257-8.

[42]Maleczek, *Papst*, 117-24; Kamp, 'Capuano, Pietro', 258-66; cf. Heinrich Zimmermann, *Die päpstliche Legation in der ersten Hälfte des 13. Jahrhunderts von Regierungsantritt Innocenz' III. bis zum Tode Gregors IX. (1198-1241)*, Görres-Gesellschaft, Veröffentlichungen der Sektion für Rechts- und Sozialwissenschaft 17 (1913):47. For his election as patriarch of Constantinople, see also Maria Morselletto, 'Pietro di Capua', *Enciclopedia Cattolica* (Vatican, 1953). He was already active in the crusade that led to the capture of Constantinople (1204); see Tillmann, *Papst*, 227-30. The relationship of the two Capuans was reversed in John W. Baldwin, *Masters, Princes, and Merchants: The Social Views of Peter the Chanter and his Circle* (Princeton, 1970), 1:45.

after he had been robbed in Piacenza.[43] In later life he founded in Amalfi a school of the 'liberal arts' for both laymen and clerics.

The elder Petrus Capuanus was one of those who toward the end of the twelfth century were constructing reference works for the Bible that were vast organized collections of *distinctiones* of biblical terms, though his treatise has also been ascribed to the younger Capuanus. It is an *Ars concionandi* or *Alphabetum in artem sermocinandi*, with words in each letter of the alphabet arranged hierarchically from God down to the abyss – in the first set, *a (alpha)* to *abyssus*.[44] The *Ars concionandi* was completed after becoming a cardinal, by 'Petrus divina permissione sanctae Romanae cardinalis ecclesiae indignus', a man of many cares, its later edition dedicated to a 'clerus romanus'. In the Preface he laments that the cares of practical tasks made it difficult to complete a work begun during his studies.[45]

There has recently been a discovery by Rouse and Rouse of a very early revision (1208-1213?) of the *Ars* by the Waldensian 'heretic' who became a *Humilatus*, Durand of Huesca. It was dedicated to the canonist Bernard of Pavia.[46] One may also mention a collection of *distinctiones*, more random in selection of words and briefer than the *Ars*, but very ingenious in discussion, by a Magister P[etrus], and dedicated *in absentia* to an Archbishop Walter of Palermo, the notable archbishop of that name reigning there 1169-1190 (another, though unconfirmed by the pope, 1200).[47] The incipit of this shorter collection

---

[43]Maleczek, *Papst*, 93, 119.

[44]The title assigned by Glorieux, *Répertoire des maîtres en théologie de Paris au XIIIe siècle*, *Études de philosophie médiévale* 17 (Paris, 1933), 1:265. It is also referred to as *Alphabetum in arte sermocinandi* (perhaps to be preferred) and the *Rosa alphabetica*; incipit 'Dilectis plurimum et diligendis semper.' For additional manuscripts, see E. M. Martini, 'Intorno à Pietro Capuano, cardinale scrittore (sec. XII-XIII)', *Archivio storico della provincia di Salerno* 1 (1921):302-3, giving a full list of variant titles and ascriptions. Excerpts were published by Jean-Baptiste Pitra, *Spicilegium Solesmense* (Graz, 1852-1855), indexed 3:496-8. The Rouses give a succinct account of the text, 211-14.

[45]'Olim in scholasticis studiis incoeptum sed absoluendum inter negotiorum curas', Pitra, *Spicilegium*, 3:498.

[46]Mary A. and Richard H. Rouse, 'The Schools and the Waldensians: a New Work by Durand of Huesca', in *Christendom and Its Discontents: Exclusion, Persecution, and Rebellion, 1000-1500*, ed. Scott L. Waugh and Peter D. Diehl (Cambridge, England, 1996), 86-111.

[47]For Walter of Palermo, see L. J. A. Loewenthal, 'For the Biography of Walter Ophamil, Archbishop of Palermo', *English Historical Review* 87 (1972):75-82, questioning the view he had been sent by Henry II as a tutor to William II. Kamp, 'Capuano, Pietro' the elder, and 'Soziale Herkunft', 106, supposes he was of Sicilian origin and that his encouragement of Capuano shows he also had studied abroad. Joan daughter of Henry II Plantagenet did marry William II of Sicily. She received the Apulian Monte Sant'Angelo as a dowry, Pier Fausto Palumbo, 'Honor Montis Sancti Angeli', *Archivio Storico Pugliese* 6 (1953):304-70.

uses the same figure of Rachel and Leah as the revised preface to the *Ars concionandi*, so it was also the work of a cleric in the active life.

The elder Petrus Capuanus was also likely the author of the *Summa theologie*, sometimes ascribed to his nephew. It showed considerable theological ability, in the expert judgment of Martin Grabmann. It represented a third and consequently a crucial stage in the establishment of commentary on the *Sentences* of Peter Lombard as a standard school method (the elder Petrus Capuanus had been a student of Petrus Pictaviensis, as the Parisian master and chancellor [1169-1190] had been a disciple of the Lombard and others; like Petrus Pictaviensis himself, Petrus Capuanus was not the slavish imitator of his master).[48] An engagement both with discursive theology and the making of distinctions had also been characteristic of Petrus Pictaviensis and Praepositinus.[49]

To add slightly to the list of cardinal-theologians, mention may be made of Laborans, canon in Capua *c.* 1160-1173 and a cardinal 1173-91, with a pithy and rhetorical style; he also reordered Gratian in a *Compilatio decretorum*.[50] The *Ars concionandi* was ascribed by some manuscripts to Petrus de Morra (d. 1206), a canonist also known as Petrus Scolasticus, cardinal deacon of S. Maria degli Angeli 1205-1213.[51] Albinus, cardinal bishop of Albano, was mentioned earlier. The two Capuani were of course by no means the only Italians to be practitioners of the theological style of the universities. Aristocratic families saw fit to give young people destined for the clergy an advanced education of that sort, Lothar of Segni being another such student, without receiving an Arts Licence, but adding, as some did, the study of law in Bologna, where it remains tempting to speculate he might have met with Huguccio.[52] Among Paris-trained theologians,

---

[48]See Martin Grabmann, *Die Geschichte der scholastichen Methode* (Freiburg im Breisgau, 1909), 532-4, and Artur Landgraf, 'A study of the Academic Latitude of Peter of Capua', *New Scholasticism* 14 (1940):57-74, 'Die Quellen der anonymen *Summe* des cod. Vat. lat. 10754', *Mediaeval Studies* 9 (1947):296-300, and the article cited above. The second preface of the *Ars concionandi*, suggesting a reedition after becoming cardinal, is found in a manuscript together with the *distinctiones* of Magister P, Capuanus's *Summa theologie*, the *Summa contra haereticos* by Praepositinus, and the *Distinctiones Psalterii* by Petrus Pictaviensis, Vat. lat. 4304, s. XIII (1/2).

[49]Distinctions were added as glosses to Praepositinus's *Summa contra haereticos* 'Vt producit uentos', MS. Vat. lat 1174 (s. XIII), ff. 9-64. For sermonic presentation of the *Summa super Psalterium* of Praepositinus, see Lacombe, 105-6, 113-22.

[50]*Laborantis Cardinalis Opuscula*, ed. Artur Landgraf, Florilegium Patristicum 32 (Bonn, 1932).

[51]The two Petri Capuani and Petrus de Morra are 'da non confondere', August Pelzer reminded us, s. n. 'Pietro de Capua' (junior), in Angelo Mercati and Augusto Pelzer, eds, *Dizionario ecclesiastico* (Torino, 1948), cf. Martini, 90. The ascription of the *Ars concionandi* to Petrus de Morra in MSS. Chalon-sur-Saone 15 and St Omer 217, cited Martini, 302-3, was accepted by Pitra, *Spicilegium*, 2:xxviii; as was in addition the Summa, 'Vetustissima veterum', by Glorieux, 1:265, no. 108.

[52]See, e.g., Peter Classen, *Studium und Gesellschaft im Mittelalter*, ed. Johannes Fried, Schriften der Monumenta Germaniae Historica 29 (Stuttgart, 1983), esp. ch.3, 'Rom und Paris: Kurie und Universität im 12. und 13. Jahrhundert', 127-69, giving many instances of cardinals being styled

Roland Bandelli had become Alexander III.[53] Arnold of Brescia, a student of Abelard, became a Roman of a different and hostile sort.

Gregorius de Monte Sacro did not himself become a *magister* or cardinal. He instead became abbot of the monastery of the Holy Trinity on Monte Sacro, one of the many in Apulia directly dependent on the Holy See.[54] He is named as abbot in a document of Honorius III, dated 19 May 1220 at Viterbo, entrusting him with the reform of the monastery of Santa Maria of Pulsano.[55] The election must have occurred after August 1218, when the previous abbot of Monte Sacro was still living. Gregorius continued to be mentioned in documents through 30 December 1241. A request in 1249 for a record of 1248 refers to customs *tempore abbatis* so he must by then have been defunct.[56]

It is worth mentioning that the Apulia to which he returned as an experienced adult was being claimed linguistically and religiously as Latin, not Greek. It was also the centerpoint of Frederick II's power.[57] Gregorius de Monte Sacro would be there as a defender of Latinity and of papal interests. Quite as much as the busy diplomat the elder Petrus Capuanus, he complained about practical interruptions to his writing. But though Gregorius served on various investigatory commissions and did some building that may have been a cause of driving the monastery into debt,[58] his main activity would seem to have been the composition of his encyclopedic poem and supervision of its explanatory glosses. The poem was certainly completed by 1236, the death date of the younger Petrus Capuanus and probably that of Bishop Risandus of Molfetta, one of the dedicatees. A gloss to the last book of the poem recorded a flood that had occurred in Rome in 1230, suggesting an even earlier *terminus*.[59]

'magister', and in particular, Michele Maccarone, 'Innocenzo III prima del pontificato', *Archivio della R. Deputazione Romana di Storia Patria* 66 (1943):59-134.

[53]See *Die Sentenzen Rolands nachmals Papstes Alexander III*, ed. Ambrosius M. Gietl (Freiburg im Breisgau, 1891).

[54]Petrucci, *Cattedrali*, 551, n. 32. Cf. Volkert Pfaff, 'Das Verzeichnis der romunmittelbaren Bistümer und Klöster im Zinsbuch der römischen Kirche (LCnr.XIX)', *Vierteljahrschrift für Sozial- und Wirtschaftsgeschichte* 47 (1960):71-80 at 72.

[55]Domenico Vendola, *Documenti Vaticani relativi alla Puglia* 1 (Trani, 1940):106-7, no. 115, cited by Salvatore Prencipe, *L'abbazia benedettina di Monte Sacro nel Gargano* (Santa Maria [Città Vecchia], 1952), 70-1 and 144.

[56]Ibid., 78.

[57]Schaller, 'Die Kanzlei Friedrichs II', 1, *Archiv für Diplomatik* 3 (1957):207-86 at 221-2.

[58]See Maria Stella Calò Mariani, *L'arte del duecento in Puglia*, with photographs by Paolo Monti, Bruno Calò and Giuseppe Gernone (Torino, 1984), 59-61, and F. Fiorentino, 'Una epigrafe mediovale da Monte Sacro [of 1225]', *Archivio Storico Pugliese* 32 (1979):253-7.

[59]'Huius temporibus inundante tybero flumine aqua fere totam urbem usque ad supremos gradus Basilici beati petri occupauit, sicuti quondam tempore Pelagii predecessoris beati primi Gregorii', V 136r in margin. Cf. Ryccardus de S. Germano, *Chronica*, ed. G. H. Pertz, MGH SS 19:358, ad an. 1230: 'Mense Februarii, primo die mensis eiusdem, Rome Tyberis fluvius per alluvionem usque adeo

What did Gregorius de Monte Sacro's distinctive schooling lead to? It appears he had already been thinking of an encyclopedic project when with Gregorius de Sancto Apostolo. It was finally completed, with a feeling of accomplishment that would let him finally rest in a sabbath of contemplation, like the Deification at which the title of the completed work aims. His description suggests the layered complexity of the verse treatise:

> I rested, as if having completed the parallel work of the six days through the six ages of the world, and as, after the six phases of human life have been accomplished and created anew through the six works [of mercy], on the seventh day we may rest in the Lord, our souls on holiday.[60]

Here he explains the scheme of the work which matches the seven days of creation with seven ages of the world. Each book provides both natural lore appropriate to the class of beings for that day of the haexaemeron, and also summaries of the life of Christ and of biblical and finally ecclesiastical history. The treatise thus subordinates its abundant information about created nature to biblical history (and at the end that of the church and the empire), and these to moral and theological doctrine. At any point of information reached, there may be a *distinctio* of the term as it is used in the Bible or is appropriate to the Blessed Virgin.

The arrangement doubles and raises the natural to the spiritual. That begins to explain the title, *Peri ton anthropon theopoieseos*, 'On the Making Divine [or the Divine Poetics] of Mankind'. The text is a large-scale allegorical elaboration and justification of procedures of parallelism of lower to higher classes of knowledge, as nature is redeemed by revelation, and human nature by divine intervention. Analogy (which might elsewhere be dramatic allegory) provides the organization in which any item may be found. As said, the margins of the manuscripts of *Peri ton anthropon theopoieseos* carry further the work of elaboration with

---

inundavit, quod occupavit de domibus Urbis usque ad Sanctum Petrum et usque ad Sanctum Paulum; quod tanti causa timoris Romanis omnibus extitit, ut mox de communi consilio, metu mortis, dominum papam ad urbem de Perusio revocarent.' See further Friedrich Gregorovius, *Rome in the Middle Ages*, Book 9.4.2, trans. A. Hamilton, 2nd edn (London, 1906) 5.1.153-4. A similar detail Gregorius de Monte Sacro did not mention was the visit of Frederick II to Apricana in Gargano, 1232-1233, mentioned in the *Chronica* of Ecelinus and Albericus, *Rerum italicarum scriptores* 8.4, p. 29. Norbert Kamp, *Kirche und Monarchie im staufischen Königreich Sizilien*, Münstersche Mittelalterschriften 10/2 (München, 1975):645-7 has Risandus as bishop October 1222 to 5 August 1271 (!).

[60]'Applicanti igitur animum ad scribendum, materia michi occurrit diuinitus opera sex dierum, ut iam conceperam animo adolescentulus, Domino predocente, de quibus disserens quadriformiter in sex libris, in septimo, facto fine, quieui, ut per sex etates mundi sex dierum operibus iam patrati, sex etatibus hominis iam peractis sex operibus recreati, in septima, feriatis animis, in Domino quiescamus' (V 7r).

distinctiones. Marginal glosses also present quotations that repeat the sources of information used by Gregorius de Monte Sacro, treating them as undifferentiated tradition, since they are rarely ascribed to distinct authors. Old information is ennobled by the new versification, the poetry in turn becoming prayer and admonition of salvation, the remaking of an eternal life.

II. ARTICULATING A COMMON WORLD

Along with the works of the two Petri Capuani and of Innocent III the glossed codices of Gregorius de Monte Sacro are important evidence for the state and method of learning in the curial milieu. As an encyclopedia, the *Peri ton anthropon theopoieseos* displays shared and accumulated information worth knowing through a method that organizes items in a hierarchy. This is a different handling from the scientific theology that was developing in universities and the empirical and physical enquiries of the imperial court. It is also different from the practical ethics of public sermons. It does, nevertheless, resemble the manner of some kinds of monastic writing that were being done in Germanic territories in the twelfth century. And it resembles the style of thinking of treatises and sermons of Innocent III and of the papal scriptorium (the imperial scriptorium too, which had learned techniques from the other).

Remarks here on these matters may serve as a preliminary sketch of a specific shared world of lore and commonplaces and the use of analogies to give them hierarchical rank. A full picture (and edition of Gregorius' work) will make possible a better understanding of the methods by which Latin Christianity imagined the world. I avoid the word ideology, which has often come to suggest a constellation of ruling concepts, platonistic hierocratic Ideas or consolidated Hegelian *Geistesgeschichte*. Methods, instead, provide paths for the discovery and negotiation of information; they are ways of learning and working with teachable doctrines.

The enterprise of encyclopedism has a bias toward the conception of a unified world – the notion that there can be a full and complete array, to various degrees of complexity, of items of nature or of history. The model provided by Gregorius de Monte Sacro suggests Roman encyclopedism was conservative in preferring a collection closed within doctrine. A similar instance was the *De universo* of the Carolingian Hrabanus Maurus, who kept material of Isidore's *Origines* intact but encased it in a second order of allegorical doctrinal applications for items of the natural order. I have elsewhere speculated more generally about two sorts of encyclopedism, one of which treats information as such a treasure to be kept and enclosed, while the other makes it a sort of capital for investment in practical verbal or investigative projects.[61]

A further distinction is between the display of information for purposes of verbal adornment and the practical use of it as a resource for identifying objects and practices in the field. Treatises produced in the imperial court tended to be of the latter practical type. Thus the *Sphere* of John of Sacrobosco gave a way of finding astronomical data, perhaps then to be interpreted in the finding tables of astrology. The imperial treatise on hunting birds, *De arte venandi cum avibus*, presented recognizable sketches of hunting birds and practical details of their habits.[62]

The error of Gregorius de Monte Sacro in neglecting an entry for the item *falco* would not have occurred in a treatise on hunting birds, but it marks for Gregorius a different sort of mistake, namely that his accumulating of vocabulary for the multitude of birds in general was incomplete. Gregorius de Monte Sacro's text was not for practical identification and care, but rather to assemble the raw materials for verbal display, closed and somewhat hemmed in by verse. The verse display was a strenuous model of epideictic rhetoric, persuasive by its impressiveness and richness, like a ceremony. A long unordered list of bare words such as he typically fell into may demonstrate the plenitude of divine power in creating the surprising variety of natural species. Still, Gregorius de Monte Sacro was not unique in giving little horizontal linkage to items of natural history; the series was instead determined vertically, by an ethical or ontological allegory, as when 'lion' is the first of the beasts, or the four rivers of Paradise first among rivers.[63]

---

[61]E. C. Ronquist, 'Patient and Impatient Encyclopedism', in Peter Binkley, ed., *Pre-Modern Encyclopaedic Texts* (Leiden, 1997), 31-45.

[62]The two courts, papal and imperial, and their styles of thought were not in absolute contrast. Michael Scot, who translated Aristotle's *History of Animals* and wrote on astrology, physiognomy and possibly alchemy from around 1198 into the 1220s, also had benefices arranged for himself by Honorius III and Gregory IX. If a fifteenth-century manuscript thought it probable to ascribe miscellaneous natural experiments to Frederick II, another of the fourteenth gave those of a 'chancellor and cardinal'. See Lynn Thorndike, *A History of Magic and Experimental Science during the First Thirteen Centuries of Our Era* (New York, 1923), vol. 2, ch. 51, and p. 803. And compare Charles Homer Haskins on the complex network of secular interests: 'Frederick II and Henry III [of England] have the same Latin *versificator*, Henry of Avranches, who also writes for the Pope and various baronial patrons; while Frederick brings the poets of his *Magna Curia* into contact with the troubadours and Minnesingers of his Transalpine dominions, welcomes Theodore the Philosopher from Antioch and Michael Scot from Spain, and maintains a learned correspondence with the scientists and philosophers of the various Mohammedan sovereigns of North Africa and the East', *The Renaissance of the Twelfth Century* (1927; Cleveland, 1957), 61.

[63]Both the case for the *PTAT*: 'Rex leo perualidos fortissimus exit in armos', though a rooster may terrify him. Albertus Magnus apologized for using the alphabet and so giving no hierarchy to his commentary on *De animalibus*, Rouse and Rouse, *Authentic Witnesses*, 202.

Gregorius de Monte Sacro's kind of encyclopedism was more rhetorical than scientific or 'scholastic'; it remained true to the verbal trivium of the 'liberal arts' that he had first acquired after his initial religious intuition.[64] One instance: there were cardinal physicians in the thirteenth century, so that this practical physical art was known in the papal curia.[65] In contrast, while Gregorius devoted extensive sections of his encyclopedia to medical lore, the lore was a verbal accumulation and implicit demonstration of the 'miseries of the human condition', not for the conservation of health. Lothar of Segni too accumulated natural miseries of the human condition in a rhetorical tour de force, with the cure of the miseries not healing but transcendence.

The differentiation of items and kinds of information into a hierarchy was a widespread intellectual practice. Arrays of differentiated hierarchical terms were used in the construction of *arengae* or persuasive instances in rhetorical discourse. Here there was a Capuan style used both in papal and imperial courts, marked by elaborate periodical sentences, and a 'biblical-liturgical style', with heavy use of the Vulgate, and almost sheerly ornamental citation of multiple parallel instances of natural, historical and biblical lore.[66]

Particularly important was the use of the hierarchical distinction of senses of a biblical word. John C. Moore has shown the procedure to have operated in the construction of the sermons of Innocent III. But Gregorius was conservative in not detaching the words elaborated into *distinctiones* from their context in a hexaemeral sequence. They were not arranged in alphabetical order as they were in the innovative twelfth-century methodology for reference works, nor indexed.[67]

---

[64]Cf. Elze, 198, for examiners who were experienced in the arts rather than in law. Later in the century in imperial circles one might compare Henricus de Isernia, who in Naples around 1258 'had studied neither theology, Medicine, nor law, but only the liberal arts, by which he acquired the title "magister"', translating Karl Hampe, *Beiträge zur Geschichte der letzten Staufer: Ungedruckte Briefe aus der Sammlung des Magisters Heinrich von Isernia* (Leipzig, 1910), 24.

[65]Maleczek, *Papst,* recorded Joannes of St Paul, from the end of the twelfth century, who wrote on medicine. Agostino Paravicini Bagliani, 'Medicina e scienza della natura alle corte di Bonifazio VIII: uomini e libri', in Angiola Maria Romanini, ed., *Roma anno 1300* (Roma, 1983), 773-89, noted that by then practically all cardinals had a *medicus* among their familiares.

[66]Schaller, 'Die Kanzlei', 2, 284-7, for a Capuan style, also 308-10, 324, and for the *distinctio,* 317; see 285-6, 238-9, for a comparison of the court to the orders of angels. The same topics articulated the sacralizing and imperializing of both church and empire (325). See further for the influence of the style of Innocent III, Otto Vehse, 'Die antike Propaganda in der Staatkunst Kaiser Friedrichs II', *Forschungen zur mittelalterlicher und neuerer Geschichte* 1 (München, 1929); for hyperbole and biblical citation, K. Pivec, 'Der Diktator Nicolaus von Rocca: Zur Geschichte der Sprachschule von Capua', *Innsbrucker Beiträge zur Kulturwissenschaft* 1 (1953):135-52.

[67]Cf. Rouse, *Authentic Witnesses,* 204: 'The use of alphabetical order was a tacit recognition of the fact that each user of a work will bring to it his own preconceived rational order, which may differ from those of other users and from that of the writer himself. Applied to distinction collections, this notion meant recognition that while one might teach in the order of the text of the Bible, one did not

Even commentaries on the Psalms, primary texts a cleric might know more or less by heart, did add indices, though that does not seem to have been the case for the treatises by Innocent III, which are thus similarly conservative. In contrast, we have seen that the elder Petrus Capuanus gave evidence of less conservative advanced intellectual enquiry being carried out in Rome, producing a reference work that would not be read sequentially.

For an instance of thinking through a pyramidal array of parallel sets of distinctions, one upon the other, beginning with a division of a verse of the Scriptures (as manuals on sermon construction advocated), it is tempting to cite all of the progressive development of Innocent III on 'The Resurrection of the Lord', working with Mark 16:1, the women who brought spices to anoint Jesus. Consider just one stage of the analogical argument, which had an important practical outcome in the ranking of religious vocations:

These three women signify the three lives: lay, regular, and clerical. The life of laymen is active and secular; the life of religious is contemplative and spiritual; the life of clergymen is rather mixed and shared, partly secular inasmuch as they possess worldly things and partly spiritual inasmuch as they administer divine things.[68]

Using this method of differentiated sequencing Joachim of Fiore could take the same items and put monks, the regular religious, at the culmination of the sequence, while for Innocent they were placed earlier at what he took as a stage of leisure, not yet engaged with religious work in the world.[69]

---

preach thus.'

[68]Innocent III, Sermon 27, 'In Resurrectione Domini', ed. and trans. Moore, 'The Sermons', 135-42 (the punctuation is mine): 'Quoniam que mulieres corporaliter egisse leguntur, nos debemus spiriualiter adimplere, considerandum est nobis que sunt moraliter adimplete iste tres mulieres....Tres iste mulieres designant tres vitas: laicalem regularem et clericalem. Vita laicorum activa est et secularis; vita religiosorum contemplativa et spiritualis; vita clericorum quasi mixta est et communis, que partim est secularis in quantum mundana possident, et partim est spiritualis in quantum divina ministrant. Iste tres vite alibi desinnantur in Evangelio, ubi dicitur, Duo sunt in agro, duo in mola, duo in lecto – unus assumetur et alter relinquetur [Luke 17:34-35]. Mola que iugiter volvitur significat mundum, qui semper mutatur [muttatur *JCM*]. Unus in mola, sunt laici, quo cum multis laboribus et angustiis rebus mundanis utuntur. lectus designat quietem, unde in lecto sunt religiosi, qui occupationibus seculi derelictis in contemplationis otio delectantur. In agro vero sunt clerici qui nunc *in curis secularibus laborant, nunc* in spirituali suavitate quiescunt, tanquam illi, qui in agro cultura nunc segetis fatiscunt, nunc arborum umbra delectantur', with variant 'in seculari anxietate laborant et'.

[69]Thus Joachim of Fiore, *Liber de concordia Noui ac Veteris Testamenti* 3.1.3 (203-12) ed. E. Randolph Daniel, Transactions of the American Philosophical Society 73/8 (1983), 247. See further for divergent interpretation of the pair of Mary and Martha, Fiona Robb, '"Who Hath Chosen the Better Part?" (Luke 10,42): Pope Innocent III and Joachim of Fiore on the Diverse Forms of Religious

For the Benedictine Abbot Gregorius the leisured compilation of an encyclopedia was meant to articulate the principles of hierarchy and transcendence. While
in practice the abbot and bishops would find themselves working together on
commissions of enquiry, in writing a dedicatory letter to his neighbour Bishop
Risandus of Molfetta, in whose diocese Monte Sacro had dependencies but to
whom Gregorius was not subordinate, he began by stating inequality and
subordination to be the chief principle of the created world.[70] The powerful initial
sentence of the letter to Risandus proclaimed in appropriately complex
hypotactical syntax that 'as the Creator of universality, unique Being, did not
uniformly create all out of nothing, neither did he distribute everything equally'.[71]
By using the allegorical procedures by which the 'spiritual sense might be elicited
from the Scriptures' developed by the likes of Gregory the Great and Augustine,
the resulting poem would be one in which 'the things it contains may stimulate
the spirit of a hearer or reader, and beyond the text get the mind's hand to scratch,
that is, to do something well' (Gregorius had just said to Risandus that his text
had the comparative value of a bug in comparison to the wisdom and judgement
of the bishop).[72]

Gregory the Great's enormous allegorical *Moralia in Hiob* was particularly on
the mind of the renamed Gregorius de Monte Sacro. Throughout the codices
there are glosses derived from Garnerus de Sancto Victore's *Gregorianum*, a late-
twelfth-century compilation of encyclopedic classes of *distinctiones* which takes
terms not directly from the Scriptures, but from Gregory the Great's *Moralia in*

Life', *Monastic Studies* 2 (1991):157-70. Much earlier, for Pseudo-Dionysius, monks were the
perfected class of the laity, but lower than clergy, Paul Rorem, *Pseudo-Dionysius: A Commentary on
the Texts and an Introduction to Their Influence* (New York, 1993), 18-24.

[70]For Thomas of Capua, *Ars dictandi*, ed. Heller, 5-6, in salutations the greater name should come
first; for Peter of Blois, bishops are exalted and of the second rank, abbots only in the third. See
further Giles Constable, 'The Structure of Medieval Society According to the *Dictatores* of the
Twelfth Century', in Kenneth Pennington and Robert Somerville, eds, *Law, Church and Society:
Essays in Honor of Stephan Kuttner* (Philadelphia, 1977), 253-67, reprinted in *Religious Life and
Thought* (London, 1979).

[71]'Dum non uniformiter vnus Ens, uniuersitatis Conditor, in quo nullus numerus nulla pluralitas,
cui quidlibet quod est est omne esse quod est, incomprehensibilis inuestigabilis et inmensus, non
accipiens aliquid aliunde set superhabundans in omnibus et nullius egens, bonitate sua sapienter
ordinans uniuersa, ex nichilo simul omnia produxisset, non omnibus eque omnia distribuit, set optimus
Ens prout uoluit cuique decentia contulit uariantibus qualitatibus atque modis, et competenter naturalia
uniuersitati gratifice subdistinxit, omnia disponendo pondere numero et mensura [Wisdom 11:21], ut
quasi dissona qualitatibus iuncturis uero a se inuicem non discrepantibus et se quasi quibusdam
brachiis amplexantibus amicabiliter consona unum alternata pace efficerent armonice membra corpus,
locis et terminis inlocalis et interminabilis distinguens et collocans uniuersa, ad quem quasi ad entem
et causam sui currunt omnia sponte sua' (V 3v).

[72]'Continentur enim in eo que stimulent audientis animum et legentis, et mentis manum suscitent
ad pruritum, ad bene scilicet aliquod operandum, et ex doliis Scripturarum eliciant spiritualem sensum
clausum quo uitiosorum argumenta subtilia elidantur, et hanelent ad eterna gaudia superorum' (V 4r).

Hiob. One may note parenthetically that this treatise thus shows that texts of human authority might be treated with scriptural methodology even before Dante's *Commedia*. Yet it maintains similarities to a collection of biblical *distinctiones* that has been ascribed to a different Garnier de Rochefort.[73] To return to the influence of Gregory the Great, it would seem Gregorius de Monte Sacro was prompted by consciousness of the name he had taken when one of his codices paused at more or less the middle of the poem for an extended prose gloss on 'Job "dolens"' ('dolens' an etymological gloss), which turns out to be a condensation of the *Moralia*, somewhat fuller than a similar effort by Rupert von Deutz.[74]

Connections of Gregorius de Monte Sacro's compilations to Gregory the Great, a text of St Victor in Paris, the alternative Cistercian Garnerius and the work of Rupert von Deutz are all telling, since none of these manifest 'scientific', let alone Aristotelian, theological thinking. Rupert von Deutz in the twelfth century worked out an enormous allegorical historical treatise in the manner of Augustine's *City of God* that would have been supportive of the papacy. Another such papalist in Germanic territories was the encyclopedist Honorius Augustodunensis. Both Rupert and Honorius were used by Arno von Reichersberg (d. 1175), whose *Hexaemeron* was elaborated with a three-fold exposition of Creation, Consummation, Restoration and saw the Creation recapitulated in the Pater Noster.[75] Innocent III also held to the *sacra pagina* and to allegory, instead of dialectic.[76] All these thus share an organizational procedure by ranked analogy, subordinating nature to revelation and divine pre-eminence.

---

[73]I have consulted both the handsome *Gregorianum, hoc est, Allegoricae omnium pene rerum in Biblijs contentarum explanationes, promptae ex uniuersis D. Gregorii Papae scriptis*, Ioannes Picard, ed. (Parisiis: Carolius Seuestre, 1608), and PL 218. This compilation has some strong resemblances to the *Allegoriae in totam sacram Scripturam*, attributed in PL 212 to Hrabanus Maurus, but by Richard and Mary Rouse with much more probability to the Cistercian Garnier de Rochefort; meanwhile, Otfried Lieberknecht in correspondence has suggested to me both that its Prologue is identical with that of the *Gregorianum* and that the whole of it might have been compiled by Adam Scot (d. 1212). M.-D. Chenu objected to a 'scholasticism' of allegory that detached images from historical context, 'La décadence de l'allégorisation: un témoin, Garnier de Rochefort († v. 1200)', in *L'Homme devant Dieu: Mélanges offerts au P. Henri de Lubac* (Paris, 1964), 2:129-35.

[74]Rupertus Tuitiensis, *Super Job commentarius*, PL 168:963 ff.

[75]See Israel Peri, ed., 'Das Hexameron Arnos von Reichersberg: Eine Exegese aus dem 12. Jahrhundert', *Jahrbuch des Stiftes Klosterneuberg*, NS 10 (1976):9-115. A further platonising Hexaemeron of the period influenced by Rupert and Arno and in verse was by Andreas Suresøn, *Andreae Surosis Filii 'Hexameron'*, ed. Stan Ebbesen and L. B. Mortensen, Corpus Philosophorum Danicorum Medii Aevi 11, 2 vols (Copenhagen, 1985-1986); see further Lars Boje Mortensen, 'The Sources of Andrew Suresen's Hexaemeron', *Cahiers de l'Institut du moyen âge grec et latin* 50 (1985), 112-216.

[76]Wilhelm Imkamp, *Das Kirchebild Innocenz' III (1198-1216)*, Päpste und Papsttum 22 (Stuttgart, 1983), 92.

Cistercians bring in another multiple connection. They were favoured by popes of the thirteenth century,[77] and they maintained an interest in Joannes Scotus Eriugena, even if doubts had been declared about his orthodoxy.[78] In the style of Joannes Scotus the title of the *Peri ton anthropon theopoieseos* uses an ingenious Greek formation of 'theo-poetics' both to name the text a 'sacred and didactic poem' and to focus its discourse on the 'making divine of the human person', glossed in Latin as *deificatio*.[79] Texts of Joannes Scotus more regularly use *theosis* for the concept, which risks unorthodox gnosticism but affords a Platonic account of salvation.

The preceding paragraphs have assembled neo-platonists, Augustinian historians and allegorists, all of whom use a method of hierarchical analogy. The observation is not new that the method of hierarchical Platonic analogy was a strong means to imagine and to justify the claim of the papacy to theocratic superiority and for the detachment of the office from its practitioner.[80]   A countering Aristotelianism might later find the theocentric claims of the papacy to political priority over the nations to be 'inorganic', though the platonizing principle Karl Morrison has called Mimesis might still be saved and survive into modern times.[81]   If the elaborate work of Gregorius de Monte Sacro was

---

[77]For affection for Cistercians, Ursmer Berlière, 'Innocent III et la réorganisation des monastères bénédictins', *Revue Bénédictine* 32 (1920):23-42, 145-59; Brenda Bolton, 'For the See of Simon Peter: The Cistercians at Innocent III's Nearest Frontier,' rpt in her *Innocent III: Studies on Papal Authority and Pastoral Care*, Variorum Collected Studies Series CS 490 (Aldershot, 1995), and Robb for Rainier of Ponza and Joachim of Fiore. See C. H. Lawrence, 'Stephen of Lexington and Cistercian University Studies in the Thirteenth Century', *Journal of Ecclesiastical History* 2 (1960):164-78, for intellectuals who joined the Cistercians.

[78]For hesitations about John the Scot, see Paolo Lucentini, *Platonismo medievale: contributi per la storia dell'eriugenismo*, 2nd edn (Firenze, 1980) 14 ff., 37 ff. Honorius Augustodunensis gave his views greater respectability (80). For survival, see also H. F. Dondaine, *Le Corpus dionysien de l'Université de Paris au XIIIe siècle*, Storia e letteratura 44 (Roma, 1953).

[79]Cf. the Eriugenian formula of distinctions made by Honorius Augustodunensis, *Libellus VIII. quaestionum* 2, PL 172:1187-8, 'Christi incarnatio fuit humanae naturae deificatio, eius mors nostrae mortis destructio, eius resurrectio vitae nostrae reparatio', cited Lucentini, *Platonismo*, 67.

[80]Marta Cristiani, *Dall'unanimitas all universitas da Alcuino a Giovanni Eriugena: Lineamenti ideologici e terminologia politica della cultura del secolo IX*, Istituto Storico Italiano per il Medio Evo, Studi Storici, fasc. 100-2 (Roma, 1978), 186, noted how John the Scot's thought could yield either theocracy or Byzantine imperial theology. For a term that leads from Bernard of Clairvaux to Innocent III, see Yves Congar, '*Homo spiritualis*: Usage juridique et politique d'un terme d'anthropologie chrétienne', in *Aus Kirche und Reich: Studien zu Theologie, Politik und Recht im Mittelalter: Festschrift für Friedrich Kampf*, ed. Hubert Mordek (Sigmaringen, 1983), 1-10.

[81]See, e.g. Walter Ullmann, *A Short History of the Papacy in the Middle Ages* (London, 1974), 268-9, for the thesis that 'in the second half of the thirteenth century there also occurred an intellectual revolution which at least indirectly contributed to the growing estrangement of contemporary Europe from the papacy', with such manifestations as 'the conception of man as a product of nature', 'the appearance of the citizen and the State', 'properly understood natural science' and 'the spread of the vernacular and vernacular literature', all of which Gregorius de Monte Sacro was innocent of. See also

symptomatic of the circle of his education and edification, it shows both the strength and the vulnerability of curial intellection: a strength, for instance, in the assertion of theopoiesis, that is, salvation, as the goal of an assemblage of information and teachings, a claim other encyclopedic treatises would not make; a weakness in the slighting of the value and accuracy of single items considered in themselves.[82] Philosophy might never resolve similar quarrels between Idea and specific Substance.

Nevertheless, we should be slow to take any one work as the synthesis of the mentality of a group and historical moment. The allegorical construction of hierarchies, stacking subordinate and overriding concepts, does give evident support to what is theocratic, feudal, aristocratic and paternalistic. Accurate historical observation of specific data, however, may find nuances and compromises in the practice of hierarchy, whether by popes, emperors or the knights of romance.[83] As noted above, a bolder abbot than Gregorius de Monte Sacro in south-eastern Italy was Joachim of Fiore, using analogical constructions of biblical data to argue that the perseverance of the apostolic church was now succeeded by the perfection of monasticism, a claim that would divide the later thirteenth-century papacy between Boniface VIII and the renunciation of Celestine V and be cited by Spiritual Franciscans against the worldly glory of the curia. Earlier, perhaps, there was encyclopedic diversity rather than opposition: Innocent III encouraged Francis of Assisi, and Thomas of Capua celebrated his memory. And the Franciscan Bonaventure worked out Platonic allegories while teaching in scholastic Paris.

From this incomplete survey, one may draw a variety of conclusions. It appears that the material of curial thinking does include speculative hypotheses, as with the continuing citation of the work of Joannes Scotus Eriugena. If we look to the *method* by which data, references and authoritative texts are connected, the circle of common thinking includes both friends and opponents, Innocent and Joachim of Fiore, the papacy and the empire, all habitually working through analogies drawn from the same biblical and natural body of lore, the sun and the moon, Moses and Joshua, Mary and Martha and any other commonly accepted sets that

---

Ullmann on the *Dictates* of Gregory VII: 'In the Roman system it was a strict hierarchical ordering of society which was held to be of divine origin' (153). For the continuing survival of hierarchy through analogy, see Karl F. Morrison, *The Mimetic Tradition of Reform in the West* (Princeton, 1982), e.g. chs. 7 on Thomas Aquinas and 15 on Marx and Newman. Cf. Martin Grabmann, 'I Divieti ecclesiastici di Aristotile sotto Innocenzo III e Gregorio IX', *Miscellanea Historiae Pontificiae* 5 (Roma, 1941).

[82]'Symbolic theology is not argumentative, or conclusive', observed Rorem, 37, in the course of a stimulating survey of the variety of applications of the concept of hierarchy (18-46).

[83]Thus Tillmann, *Pope*, 27, noted that 'Innocent came to see things differently, to recognize the limits of papal power and to respect an autonomous sphere of temporal power.'

might be ranked in a hierarchy.[84] A shared practical resource for argument was thus the *distinctio*, which arrayed a body of differentiated instances tied back to a common term, frequently in a climactic sequence. Underlying the *distinctio* was the common content arranged in encyclopedias of lore, synopses of biblical history, dictionaries, concordances, collections of canons. Practical training would be needed for the discretion needed to make decisions and discourse on the basis of such organized information. In the case particularly of Gregorius de Monte Sacro, I have sketched how in the curia such familiarization with resources for research and training in modes of rhetorical exposition, canon law and theology might take place in 'familial' settings without there being a formal school.

---

[84]So to a question posed by Huguccio whether Christ's body poured forth *phlegma* or water, Innocent resolved it was water (Reg. 12:7, 5 March 1209, PL 216:16-18) using both an Old Testament analogy, as reported by Achille Luchaire, *Innocent III*, 3rd edn, 1 (Paris, 1907):247, and also the physical distinction of *elementum* and *elementatum* developed by the encyclopedist Guillaume de Conches, according to the more thorough analysis by Christoph Egger, 'Papst Innocenz III. als Theologe: Beiträge zur Kenntnis seines Denkens im Rahmen der Frühscholastik', *Archivum Historiae Pontificiae* 30 (1992):84-100. For an often cited politically crucial distinction, see Othmar Hageneder, 'Das Sonne-Mond Gleichnis bei Innocenz III', *Mitteilungen des Instituts für österreichische Geschichtsforschung* 65 (1957):340-68.

Part Two
Shepherding the Flock

Pregnant with Meaning: Pope Innocent III's Construction of Motherhood

Constance M. Rousseau

Towards the end of the first book of his *De miseria humane conditionis* (1195), Lotario dei Conti di Segni, cardinal of SS. Sergius and Bacchus, later to become Innocent III, included an account from Flavius Josephus' history concerning the plight of a mother.[1] According to this historian,[2] during the Roman siege of Jerusalem a certain wealthy noblewoman, driven to madness and desperation by extreme starvation and the loss of all her possessions, slew her nursing infant, roasted and ate half of him. She excused her action as a means of delivering her son from war, famine and the yoke of Roman slavery. When plundering thieves broke into her home, attracted by the smell of roasted flesh, and threatened her on pain of death to surrender the food that she had prepared, the woman offered the remains of the child and the men fled in repulsion and terror.

Perhaps the dire state in which the woman found herself had caused her to consider that death for her child was preferable to a life of misery. In the

---

[1] I would like to thank Brenda Bolton, Norma Kroll, Thomas McGonigle, O.P. and John Carmi Parsons for their helpful suggestions and criticism concerning an earlier version of this paper.

There are three editions of the *De miseria*. I have used Lotario dei Segni (Pope Innocent III), *De miseria conditionis humane*, ed. Robert E. Lewis (Athens, Georgia, 1978). Less recent editions include Lotharii Cardinalis (Innocentii III), *De miseria humane conditionis*, ed. Michele Maccarrone, Thesaurus Mundi Bibliotheca Scriptorum Latinorum Mediae et Recentioris Aetatis (Lucca, 1955) and PL 217:701-46.

[2] Lotario dei Segni, *De miseria*, 1.28, pp. 138-41; Flavius Josephus, *De bello Iudaico*, VI.3.4; ed. G. Dindorfius (Paris, 1865), 2:286-7.

immediately preceding chapter of the *De miseria*, Lothario had discussed earthly punishments and tortures and lamented the fate of miserable mothers who gave birth to unhappy children.[3] Yet, he wished his readers to recognize the immorality of the woman's action during the siege and so referred to it as a 'horrible deed' (*horrible facinus*).[4] We too, like the male robbers who ran away, are filled with horror at the retelling of this story. Lothario described a cruel and monstrous mother whose lack of nurturing overturned all those traditionally associated qualities of motherhood – caring, protection and self-sacrifice.[5]

The maternal activity of nurturing and rearing children appears as the major focus in much of the scholarly literature concerning medieval motherhood.[6] In 1982, Caroline Walker Bynum observed how twelfth-century male Cistercian writers linked pastoral responsibility and authority with maternal care and suggested that they used maternal symbols as a means of humanizing this authority.[7] A more recent collection of essays offers a further explanation for this appropriation of mothering imagery by men: male writers regarded mothering primarily as nurturance rather than sexual and biological reproduction, since men could take over the former female role while the latter two roles were patently impossible.[8] The specific research of Parsons and Hale suggests further that male appropriation of the caring role of mothers and the lack of emphasis on biological motherhood continued well beyond the twelfth century and are discernible in

---

[3]Lotario dei Segni, *De miseria*, 1.27, pp. 136-9.

[4]Ibid., 1.28, p. 139.

[5]We will define motherhood for our purposes here as the state of being a mother – from conception through gestation and pregnancy, to birth and the rearing and nurturing of children.

For a discussion of cruel mothers see Christiane Klapisch-Zuber, 'The "Cruel Mother": Maternity, Widowhood, and Dowry in Florence in the Fourteenth and Fifteenth Centuries', in *Women, Family, and Ritual in Renaissance Italy*, trans. Lydia G. Cochrane (Chicago, 1985), 117-31.

[6]For general background see the excellent survey of motherhood in Clarissa W. Atkinson, *The Oldest Vocation: Christian Motherhood in the Middle Ages* (Ithaca, 1991); a collection of essays on sainthood and maternity, Anneke B. Mulder-Bakker, ed., *Sanctity and Motherhood: Essays on Holy Mothers in the Middle Ages* (New York, 1995); for the theory of motherhood and mothering, see Julia Kristeva, '*Stabat Mater*', in *The Female Body in Western Culture*, ed. Susan Rubin Suleiman (Cambridge, 1986) and Nancy Chodorow, *The Reproduction of Mothering: Psychoanalysis and the Sociology of Gender* (Berkeley, 1978). A recent review article Alice Adams, 'Maternal Bonds: Recent Literature on Mothering', *Signs* (1995), 414-27 is also helpful.

[7]Caroline Walker Bynum, 'Jesus as Mother and Abbot as Mother: Some Themes in Twelfth-century Cistercian Writing', in *Jesus as Mother: Studies in the Spirituality of the High Middle Ages* (Berkeley, 1982), 110-69, esp. 147-60.

[8]John Carmi Parsons and Bonnie Wheeler, eds, *Medieval Mothering*, The New Middle Ages Series 3 (New York, 1996), xi-xii, xv.

sources as diverse as the fourteenth-century literary works regarding pregnant English queens and the fifteenth-century cult of St Joseph.[9]

Nevertheless, unlike some medieval male writers, Innocent III had a much more comprehensive understanding of motherhood than mere care, although nurturing continued to play a significant role in his conception of pastoral responsibility and the exercise of papal power. His letters, sermons, hymns and theological treatises reveal that he discussed motherhood and maternal behavior from three particular perspectives, linking it to authority, generation and nurturance and then placed these within three very different contexts – the metaphorical, the miraculous and the mundane, that is, ordinary maternal experience.

Patristic writers often characterized the church as a fertile mother, whose children were spiritually reborn in the context of baptism.[10] Throughout the corpus of Innocent III's letters we find this representation of metaphorical motherhood implied in the *arengae* formulas, although they also intimate much more – that is, the claim to authority and primacy.

The pope utilized two formulas expressing maternal authority and mothering of Christians as a means of emphasizing the primacy and rank of the Apostolic See as well as its pastoral mission. Often treating the Apostolic See and the Roman Church as one interchangeable entity, the pope saw both as possessing authority as the 'mother and teacher of all churches' *(mater sit Ecclesiarum omnium et magistra)*[11] or the divinely established 'mother and teacher of all the faithful' *(cunctorum fidelium mater est et magistra)*.[12] To a much lesser degree, we find the same feminine images in Innocent's theological treatises and the sermon literature.[13]

Bare phrases which were widely used in such a formulaic way reveal little of why Innocent considered the church or his papal office in such maternal terms.

---

[9]John Carmi Parsons, 'The Pregnant Queen as Counsellor and the Medieval Construction of Motherhood', 39-61, and Rosemary Drage Hale, 'Joseph as Mother: Adaptation and Appropriation in the Construction of Male Virtue', 101-16, both in *Medieval Mothering*.

[10]For valuable background see Wilhelm Imkamp, *Das Kirchenbild Innocenz' III (1198-1216)*, Papste und Papsttum 22 (Stuttgart, 1983), 260-72, esp. 260, 268; See also the older work of K. Delahaye, *Ecclesia mater chez les pères des trois siècles* (Paris, 1964).

[11]Reg. 1:27, pp. 40-1 = PL 214:21 (1198); Reg. 1:349, pp. 520-2 = PL 214:322 (1198); PL 216:605 (1212); Reg. 1:393, pp. 592-3 = PL 214: 372 (1198). This last example uses the words 'ceterarum mater et magistra' rather than 'ecclesiarum omnium' but the meaning is the same.

[12]Reg. 1:15, pp. 25-7 = PL 214:14 (1198); Reg. 1:69, pp. 100-3 = PL 214:59 (1198); Reg. 1:351, pp. 525-8 = PL 214:326 (1198); Reg. 1:375, pp. 568-9 = PL 214:355 (1198); Reg. 1:426, pp. 636-7 = PL 214:400 (1198); Reg. 1:455, pp. 679-80 = PL 214:429 (1198); Reg. 2:43 (45), pp. 82-3 = PL 214:585 (1199); Reg. 2:48 (50) pp. 88-9 = PL 214:588 (1199); Reg. 5:159 (160), pp. 311-14 = PL 214:1177 (1203); PL 215:913 (1206); PL 215:1044 (1206). PL 216:872 (1213) uses 'mater est omnium fidelium' rather than 'cunctorum fidelium' but again the meaning is the same.

[13]PL 217:341, Sermo VII Dominica II In Adventu Domini; PL 217:774, *De sacro altaris mysterio*.

The pope seemed to be applying the teaching role of human mothers to the church. Women such as Dhuoda (9th c.) had long been educators in the family, teaching their children Christian doctrine and moral principles, but that was in the private sphere.[14] Innocent was asserting a teaching authority and primacy of motherhood for the church in the public sphere – a very different matter. He thus appeared to be expanding the notion of maternal authority into the ecclesiastical sphere and for the male apostolic office.

To ascertain Innocent's reasoning behind the usage of these two formulas, we will look at a specific case, the pope's correspondence to the Byzantine emperor and the patriarch of Constantinople concerning the proposed reunion of the Greek and Roman churches. In urging the Emperor Alexius III Comnenus (1195-1203) to end the schism and return to the Roman fold so that the Greeks could give aid to the western crusade in the Holy Land, Innocent referred to the Roman Church as the 'mother and teacher of all the faithful' as established by God.[15] In a similar vein, he exhorted the patriarch of Constantinople George II Xiphilinus (1191-1198) that the daughter the Greek Church should return to her mother, the Roman Church.[16]

The following year, George's successor, John X Camaterus (1198-1206), responded to the pope, desiring an explanation for Innocent's assertion of the authoritative primacy of the Roman Church as *mater et magistra*.[17] John X questioned the papal claim since the church of Jerusalem clearly possessed this title on account of her historical precedence and dignity.[18]

Innocent's answer to the patriarch pointed out that the primacy of the Apostolic See and the church of Rome had been instituted by God, not by man, and was proven by the Petrine Gospel texts and apostolic testimony. He asserted that the Roman Church was called 'mother of all churches' not for reason of time but rather for superior dignity since Peter was considered first among the apostles. Peter was thus given precedence, even though his brother Andrew actually came to the faith before him.[19]

The apse mosaic which Innocent would commission for the basilica of Old St Peter's reconfirmed this special title for the Apostolic See. Below an enthroned

---

[14]Dhuoda, *Handbook for William: A Carolingian Woman's Counsel for Her Son*, trans. Carol Neel, Regents Studies in Medieval Culture (Lincoln and London, 1991); David Herlihy, *Medieval Households* (Cambridge, 1985), 122-4.

[15]Reg. 1:353, p. 527 = PL 214:326 (1198).

[16]Reg. 1:354, pp. 529-30 = PL 214:328-9 (1198).

[17]Reg. 2:199 (208), pp. 379-82 = PL 214:756-8 (1199). For John X Camaterus' career and original Greek correspondence, see A. Papadakis and Alice Mary Talbot, 'John X Camaterus Confronts Innocent III: An Unpublished Correspondence', *Byzantinoslavica* 33 (1972):26-41.

[18]Reg. 2:199 (208), p. 380 = PL 214:757-8.

[19]Reg. 2:200 (209), pp. 382-9, esp. 387-8 = PL 214:758-65 (1199).

Christ and the figures of Sts Paul and Peter, we find a 'Nilotic' landscape where Innocent and the female figure of Ecclesia flanked the Lamb of God standing on a hill. The inscription running below the mosaic emphasized the theme of papal primacy and apostolic succession. It read 'This is the See of St Peter's, this the Temple of the Prince [of the Apostles], the glory and mother of all churches'.[20]

In explaining to the patriarch the second title of the Roman Church as 'the mother of all the faithful', the pope further appropriated for the church the human functions of reproduction and care, including the giving of instruction and food, and associated these with her maternal authority.[21] These human maternal activities possessed allegorical significance for the pope whose understanding of the reproduction of the church was closely related to her spiritual marriage to Christ, the bridegroom, an idea previously developed in his earlier treatise on the four types of marriage written during his cardinalate.[22] Since one of the three Augustinian marital goods was the good of offspring[23] and since marriage was first instituted by God for procreation, the church in uniting with Christ her Spouse, was transformed from sterile to a joyful and fruitful mother.[24] According to the pope's metaphorical exegesis to the patriarch, the church, like a mother, conceived by catechizing, gave birth by baptizing and nourished by offering communion to the faithful.[25] Such ideas echoed those in Innocent's earlier treatise when he had emphasized that the church instructed Christians in the doctrine of salvation and morality; she fed them with the bread of life and gave them saving water to drink.[26] As Wilhelm Imkamp noted, Innocent's maternal imagery embraced the whole of the church's activities in terms of the cure of souls and the administration of the sacraments for salvation.[27] Thus, the church, as a powerful mother, held the source of all life.

The church's unique status also had jurisdictional ramifications which the pope pointed out to the patriarch. Innocent concluded that just as the members of the

---

[20]Richard Krautheimer, *Rome: Profile of a City, 312-1308* (Princeton, 1980), 205-6, and fig. 163 on p. 205. See also S. Sibilla, 'L'iconografia di Innocenzo III', *Bolletino della sezione di Anagni della Società Romana di Storia Patria* 2 (1953):79-82; G. Ladner, 'Innocenz III 1198-1216', *Die Papstbildnisse des Altertums und des Mittelalters* (Vatican City, 1941-84), 56-68, for discussions of this mosaic.

[21]Reg. 2:200 (209), p. 388 = PL 214:764 (1199).

[22]PL 217:931-3, *De quadripartita specie nuptiarum*; Imkamp, *Kirchenbild*, 262-4.

[23]St Augustine, 'The Good of Marriage', in *Treatises on Marriage and Other Subjects*, ed. and trans. R. J. Deferrari, Fathers of the Church Series, 27 (New York, 1955), 13.

[24]PL 217:931-2, *De quadripartita*. 'Et [Jesus] adhaesit uxori suae, id est Ecclesiae se conjunxit . . . Eamdem et sterilem et matrem filiorum [the Psalmist] appellat: sed prius sterilem antequam Christo copulata fuisset; postea vero matrem filiorum laetantem'.

[25]Reg. 2:200 (209), p. 388 = PL 214: 764 (1199); see also PL 217:929, 963, *De quadripartita*.

[26]PL 217:933-4, *De quadripartita*.

[27]Imkamp, *Kirchenbild*, 264.

body were commanded by the head and a daughter should return to her mother, so the Greek Church as a daughter church owed obedience and reverence to her mother, the Roman Church.[28] Thus, the pope claimed not only the authority of the Roman Church over those within her embrace but also supplanted the power and authority of other churches.[29]

The protective care of the church and the Apostolic See over Christians flowed from this maternal authority. The church held the spiritual power to grant apostolic protection to those who sought it. According to Innocent, using another formula, the Roman Church was 'a pious mother' who cherished and fostered the welfare of believers, defending and granting security to them.[30]

In analyzing the pastoral treatment of his flock, the pope discussed maternal and paternal tendencies in his metaphorical personification of the Apostolic See. His juxtaposition of affection as maternal and of correction as paternal seemed to suggest that as a masculinized and therefore powerful mother, the church's affectionate nurturing could turn into subordination and punishment. Using his characteristic word-play, he declared that his papal office had both the softness of the maternal breast (*ubera*) and also the rigorousness of paternal blows (*verbera*).[31] Consequently, the Apostolic See, as a father, would inflict punishment but as a mother could not forget the children of her womb and awaited their return to her maternal bosom when they were disobedient.[32] Certainly, Thomas of Marlborough would echo these words after his return from Rome, where he had appeared during 1204-1206 for his Bendictine monastery of Evesham in its dispute against its bishop over the issue of monastic exemption. Thomas compared the conduct of the papal court of Rome to a solicitous mother who gave consoling embraces to children punished by their father.[33]

Maternal reproductive, nurturing and authoritative qualities also figured significantly in the second context of miraculous motherhood. In this case, only through divine mediation could reproductive motherhood even occur. Sterile women of advanced age, such as Sarah and Elizabeth, became fruitful, bearing sons through God's holy power.[34] Of course, the unique motherhood of the

---

[28]Reg. 2:200 (209), p. 389 = PL 214:764 (1199); Reg. 2:202 (211), pp. 394-7 = PL 214:771 (1199).

[29]After the Fourth Crusade of 1204, Innocent would announce that the Byzantine Church had finally returned to her mother and that Roman primacy was fully restored in the East. See Walter Ullmann, *The Carolingian Renaissance and the Idea of Kingship* (London, 1969), 172.

[30]Reg. 1:426, pp. 636-7 = PL 214:400 (1198); PL 214:858 (1199); PL 215:1115 (1207); PL 215:1517 (1208); PL 215:1555 (1208); PL 216:163 (1209); PL 216:281 (1210); PL 216:293 (1210); PL 216:320 (1210).

[31]PL 214:922 (1200). See a somewhat similar gendered juxtaposition, Reg. 2:55 (57, 58), pp. 102-4 = PL 214:595 (1199).

[32]Ibid., 923 (1200).

[33]W. D. Macray, ed., *Chronicon abbatiae de Evesham, ad annum 1418*, RS 29 (1863):229.

[34]PL 217:541-2, Sermo XIX, In Festo S. Joannis Baptistae.

Virgin Mary which transcended ordinary human generation in every way was the most miraculous of all.[35]

The miraculous motherhood of Mary obliterated the sexual aspect. Emphasis of this point was seen in Innocent's distinction between women who conceived a child internally by sexual intercourse with an external male agent and Mary who conceived Jesus internally through divine intervention and who enclosed (*circumdedit*) the child in her womb.[36] The pope offered a metaphorical image of Mary's singular status as that of an enclosed garden (*hortus conclusus*) since she was a virgin before birth, during birth and after birth.[37] Moreover, the pope pointed out the paradoxes in her motherhood that contributed to its miraculous nature – as a mother, the virgin bore a child, the star produced a sun, a daughter conceived a father, a creature brought forth the Creator. Mary through her motherhood was simultaneously mother, daughter, bearer and handmaid.[38] Not only was this motherhood miraculous because of its exceptional circumstances, but also most importantly, it was miraculous because it provided salvation for all. Just as death entered the world through Eve, mother of the human race, so new life in the person of Christ entered the world through Mary his mother.[39]

Despite this miraculous motherhood which superseded anything an ordinary woman could experience, Mary fulfilled the other maternal nurturing functions. As this hymn attributed to Innocent III attested, she loved and nourished her baby Jesus as would any human mother:

> Per amorem tuae matris,
> Cujus venter te portavit,
> Et te dulci lacte pavit:
> Te per ipsam oro supplex,
> Quia tu es salus duplex,

---

[35]For a complete study of Innocent's mariology in the sermon literature, see Wilhelm Imkamp, "'*Virginitas Quam Ornavit Humilitas*'": Die Verehrung der Gottesmutter in den Sermones Papst Innocenz' III', *Lateranum* 46 (1980):344-78. On the Virgin Mary in general, see Atkinson, 101-43; Marina Warner, *Alone of All her Sex: The Myth and the Cult of the Virgin Mary* (New York, 1983) and the most recent Jaroslav Pelikan, *Mary Through the Centuries* (New Haven, 1996).

[36]PL 217:460, Sermo II, In Nativitate Domini; PL 217:460, Sermo III, In Nativitate Domini; PL 217:577, Sermo XXVII, In Solemnitate Assumptionis Gloriossimae semper Virginis Mariae.

[37]PL 217:583, Sermo XXVIII, In Assumptione B. Mariae.

[38]PL 217:457, Sermo II, In Nativitate Domini; PL 217:522, Sermo XIV, In Solemnitate Annuntiationis Gloriosissimae semper Virginis Mariae; PL 217:506, Sermo XII, In Solemnitate Purificationis Gloriosissimae semper Virginis Mariae.

[39]PL 217:581, Sermo XXVIII, In Assumptione B. Mariae; PL 217:506, Sermo XII, In Solemnitate Purificationis Gloriosissimae semper Virginis Mariae; PL 217:317, Sermo I, Dominica I in Adventu Domini.

Rerum dator mundanarum,
Atque salus animarum.[40]

In his sermons as in the preceding hymn, Innocent stressed an important and far-reaching implication which resulted from Mary's position as Mother of Christ. She possessed an intercessory authority of cosmic magnitude through which she mediated between the fallen mortal and the male divine power, Jesus Christ. Anyone who was besieged by lust or pride, or any other sin, could pray to the chaste and humble Virgin and she would hear his plea and intervene with her Son to send assistance.[41] The pope asked, 'Who has invoked her and has not been heard? She is the mother of beautiful love and holy hope who prays for the wretched, aids the afflicted and intercedes for sinners.'[42]

The Virgin's motherhood went far beyond that of bearing Jesus and extended spiritually to all believers – the lowly, the mighty, even the pope himself. On the day of the pope's death, Lutgard of Aywières, a Cistercian nun, experienced a vision where she saw Innocent tormented in the flames of Purgatory. When the nun asked him why he was punished so, the pope answered that although he deserved eternal fire, through intercession of the Mother of Mercy, he had escaped such a fate.[43] Thus, according to contemporaries of the pope, the intercession of Mary applied to all sinners.

If the motherhood of Mary was desexualized in Catholic doctrine, Innocent did not shrink from pointing out sexual and generative aspects in addition to nurturing behavior in the third context of mundane or ordinary motherhood. Rather than marginalizing reproductive motherhood as Parsons and Wheeler contend was the tendency of many male writers, Innocent, as the cardinal Lothario, focused on the sexual and biological but also simultaneously deprecated these in his first book of his ascetical treatise, *De miseria humane conditionis*. We must beware of the problematic nature of this text in ascertaining Innocent's views of ordinary human motherhood since the first and third books were rooted in the *contemptus mundi*

---

[40]PL 217:919, *Innocentii III Papae Hymnus*. 'Through the love of your [Christ's] mother, whose womb bore you and who trembling, nursed you with sweet milk, I, a supplicant, pray to you through her, since you are the twofold salvation – the giver of things of this world and the deliverer of souls.' This hymn is attributed to Innocent III in Migne, PL.

[41]PL 217:578, Sermo XXVII, In Solemnitate Assumptionis Gloriossimae semper Virginis Mariae; PL 217:584-6, Sermo XXVIII, In Assumptione B. Mariae.

[42]PL 217:578, Sermo XXVII, In Solemnitate Assumptionis Gloriossimae semper Virginis Mariae.

[43]Imkamp, '*Virginitas*', 346 citing AASS, 1701, 16 June, 3:245; Thomas de Cantimpré, *The Life of Lutgard of Aywières*, trans. Margot H. King (Toronto, 1987), 37-8.

tradition stressing the negativity of all human life.[44] With this caveat in mind, the fact that the pope treated the sexual in motherhood at all is still instructive.

In the process of appropriating many human maternal behaviors for the church and Apostolic See and desexualizing procreation in the case of the Virgin, what did the pope leave for ordinary mothers? What remained was the transmission of original sin through reproduction, a notion which was Augustinian in origin and had a long theological tradition.[45] According to Lothario, a mother conceived a child in sin because the very process of procreation involving sexual intercourse was lustful.[46] Such a harsh view was based on the scriptural text from the Psalms: 'For behold I was conceived in iniquities and in sin did my mother conceive me.'[47] The cardinal therefore queried:

> Who does not know that copulation, even conjugal, is never performed entirely without the heat of desire, without the fervor of the flesh, without the stench of lust? Because of this conceived seeds [*semina*] are made filthy, defiled, and spoiled, from which seeds the soul ultimately imparted [*infusa*] contracts the blemish of [original] sin.[48]

In emphasizing this sexual side of reproduction at the time of conception, the text seems to imply from the plural form of 'semina' that both the mother and the father provided the seeds of conception. This suggests that Lothario might have supported the Galenic two seed theory of reproduction.[49] The cardinal also claimed that *both* mother and father (*parentes*) were ultimately responsible for the corruption of the soul of the child as a result of their lustful activities.[50]

Lothario's negative understanding of female aspects of reproduction was also found in his disparaging depiction of fetal gestation where he suggested that a

---

[44]Constance M. Rousseau, 'Gender Difference and Indifference in the Writings of Pope Innocent III', in *Gender and Christian Religion*, ed. Robert Swanson, Studies in Church History 34 (forthcoming 1998); Robert Bultot, 'Mépris du monde, misère et dignité de l'homme dans la pensée d'Innocent III', *Cahiers de civilisation médiévale* 4 (1961):441-56. See also John C. Moore, 'Innocent III's *De miseria humanae conditionis*: A *Speculum curiae*?', *Catholic Historical Review* 67 (1981), 556-7, 563, who has proposed that Book II describes the corruption of the Roman curia seen by Lothario during his career.

[45]Pierre J. Payer, *The Bridling of Desire: Views of Sex in the Later Middle Ages* (Toronto, 1993), 53-9.

[46]Lotario dei Segni, *De miseria*, 1.3, pp. 98-9.

[47]Ps. 50:7.

[48]Lotario dei Segni, *De miseria*, 1.3, pp. 98-9. Translation by Lewis.

[49]Ibid. For a discussion of the various theories of conception see Joan Cadden, *Meanings of Sex Difference in the Middle Ages: Medicine, Science and Culture* (Cambridge, 1993), 11-167 and John W. Baldwin, *The Language of Sex: Five Voices from Northern France around 1200*, The Chicago Series on Sexuality, History and Society (Chicago, 1994), 88-96.

[50]Lotario dei Segni, *De miseria*, 1.3, p. 99.

woman's body was a *locus* not only for sin but also for pollution. Lothario noted that the fetus was fed with menstrual blood in the mother's womb, blood which was detestable and unclean.[51] The negative attitude continued in his recounting of the birth process as very painful, laborious and dangerous, as revealed in the stories of biblical women such as Rachel who had died in childbirth.[52] He concluded his discussion of mundane human motherhood in this text by noting that not just biological processes but also motherly nurturing was fraught with difficulties: '[she] feeds with difficulty and labor, and protects with constancy and fear.'[53]

Perhaps it was this recognition of the burdens of motherhood first articulated in the Flavius Josephus story which caused Innocent as pope to develop pastoral policies which would facilitate, at least to some degree, the broad range of mothering activities of actual women. These pastoral policies must also be considered in the context of power for it was through them that the faithful became aware of the papal presence.

Innocent did not consider the actual birth process as sinful and was sensitive to the mothers' spiritual needs. He revealed this attitude in his response of March 1198 to Thomas archbishop of Armagh who had questioned whether parturient women should be allowed access to the church to give thanks without observing a waiting period as stipulated in the Old Testament.[54] According to Innocent, since the grace of Christ prevailed over the Mosaic law, the archbishop should not prohibit the new mothers' access to the church since otherwise they would seem to be punished for their birth pangs as if for some misdeed.[55] The pope seemed to imply in his decision that, unlike conception which involved sexual pleasure, lust and the transmission of original sin, the birth process was so painful and difficult that women should not suffer further by being denied entrance to the church.

The pope's acknowledgement that the failure to give birth for reasons of sterility could have severe repercussions on the protection of inheritance rights to the patrimony was demonstrated in another case.[56] The apostolic legate to Sicily Cinthius the cardinal priest of St Laurence in Lucina (1191-1217)[57] reported to Innocent that during confession, a certain woman had admitted that she feared that her husband's property would be inherited by others rather than herself and therefore she had obtained an herbal potion from a sorceress which

---

[51]Ibid., 1.4, pp. 100-1.
[52]Ibid., 1.6, pp. 102-5.
[53]Ibid., 1.6, pp. 104-5, translation by Lewis.
[54]Reg. 1:63, pp. 93-4 = PL 214:55 (1198).
[55]Ibid.
[56]PL 215:1570 (1209).
[57]Maleczek, *Papst*, 104-6.

caused her womb to swell and give the appearance of pregnancy. At her appointed delivery time, the woman substituted an unrelated child for her own. The woman now feared to tell her husband since he believed the child was his heir. The pope ruled that, just as penance could not be denied to a woman who bore a child by adultery without her husband's knowledge, so this woman, despite the continuation of the fraud, could not be denied penance, especially if the legate determined from the non-relatives who would have inherited the property that her testimony was indeed the truth.

In this case, the pope appeared to recognize the patrimonial and perhaps even personal concerns of a woman who went to great lengths to simulate motherhood. It is most surprising that he somehow tolerated the woman's unilateral adoption and substitution of an heir by a false pregnancy and did not require her to tell the truth to her husband. Discreet imposition of penance was the only requirement.

A degree of papal sympathy to the burdens of mothers to provide nurturing care to their children was revealed in Innocent's second response to the supplications made in the same year, 1209, from a woman Maria living in northern France.[58] This woman was so poor and sickly that she could no longer fulfill her maternal duties (*maternae sedulitas officium*). Therefore, she had previously requested Innocent to order that her son be placed in a monastery so as to obtain nourishment and support. Since the abbot of St Médard, Soissons, had failed to follow the pope's order, Innocent now reiterated the command, adding that the boy should be received as a monk at fifteen years of age. The pope's stipulations for the monastery's provision of the child indicate what he considered part of a mother's duty in providing for her children. These provisions included not only food and clothing but also instruction.[59] The pope, however, failed to require any financial arrangements to be made so that the poor mother could continue living with her child in the outside world. Perhaps this was because of the mother's specific request for a monastic life for her son, or because Innocent wanted to increase the number of men in religious life, or probably most likely, because the pope himself had been educated in a Benedictine monastery of S. Andrea on the Celian Hill in Rome and thoroughly approved of such an arrangement.[60]

Innocent's other attempts to prevent and rectify maternal neglect and the even more deadly practice of infanticide were found in his policies dealing with the problems of many desperate Roman mothers who abandoned their unwanted children by throwing them into the Tiber River. In an effort to curb this expression of cruel and murderous motherhood, Innocent established the Hospital

---

[58]PL 216:35-6 (1209).
[59]Ibid.
[60]Brenda Bolton, '*Via ascetica*: A Papal Quandary?' in *Innocent III: Studies on Papal Authority and Pastoral Care*, Collected Studies Series (Aldershot, 1995), art. VI, p. 166.

of the Holy Spirit as a refuge for the foundlings who were fished from the waters.[61]

The rule of this foundation, approved by Innocent, went even further in aiding mothers and mothers-to-be. This text stipulated that mothers who might stay at the hospital while on pilgrimage to Rome would receive separate cradles for their infants, a measure to prevent accidental death by overlaying.[62] Impoverished pregnant women were likewise to be given care at the hospital and receive charity such as food and clothing.[63] Conceivably, we can regard Innocent's pastoral care of these mothers as a measure to deter any degree of monstrous motherhood as was first recounted in the story of the Roman siege of Jerusalem. We must also keep in mind that these pastoral policies were useful in making the papal presence an experienced reality for the women. The papal foundation of a hospital for the needy and his approval of its rule was one way of achieving this, his institution of a liturgical station for the celebration of solemn mass there was another.[64]

As our survey of Innocent's works has shown, he viewed motherhood positively as a position of authority only in the metaphorical context of Mother Church and in the miraculous context of Mary as intercessor. Innocent took maternal authority, which in its ordinary human reality was domestic, private, constricted by the boundaries of the family, and articulated its public, far-reaching and, in the singular case of Mary, cosmic dimensions. The pope regarded the reproductive aspect of motherhood favorably only in the metaphorical and miraculous contexts where Mother Church or holy women brought forth children through divine intervention. He had a negative evaluation of sexual and biological aspects of ordinary human motherhood but at least did not ignore or marginalize these as was the tendency of many medieval male writers.

We have seen that the pope explored and stressed the nurturing aspect of motherhood and indeed it seems to be the focus in his own pastoral policies where he tried to encourage maternal behavior to some extent. The pope by trying to 'nurture the nurturers' not only appropriated the nurturing activities of mother-hood in his policies but also attempted to humanize his authority and have it recognized by Christians. This papal care was not only limited to individuals in need. It would extend much more widely to the care of the entire church through Innocent's delegation of Cistercian and Dominican preachers, his recognition of the Franciscan order and the decrees of the Fourth Lateran Council.

---

[61]PL 214:200-3, *Gesta Innocentii PP. III*. On Innocent's founding of this hospital, see Brenda Bolton, 'Received in His name: Rome's Busy Baby Box', in *Innocent III: Studies in Papal Authority*, art. XIX.

[62]PL 217:1148, *Regula Ordinis S. Spiritus de Saxia*.

[63]Ibid., 1145-6.

[64]PL 217:350, Sermo VIII Dominica Prima Post Epiphaniam; PL 214:200-3, *Gesta Innocentii PP. III*.

Qui fidelis est in minimo: The Importance of Innocent III's Gift List

Brenda M. Bolton

In two chapters at the end of the *Gesta Innocentii*, the pope's anonymous biographer records a long and impressive list of offerings given by Innocent III to enhance the worship and decoration of numerous churches, monasteries and institutions in Rome and throughout the Patrimony of St Peter.[1] Not since the Catalogue of Donations of 807,[2] made by Leo III (795-816) to all the ecclesiastical institutions of Rome and to some outside the city walls, had any one pope's donations been compiled in such careful detail. The list followed the fundamental and ancient custom of the *Liber Pontificalis*, by which formulaic entries of papal generosity and benefactions had been recorded from the earliest period. With Innocent's biographer, the practice of listing, with its long and respectable history under popes from the seventh to the ninth centuries, was once again important. Delogu has shown that, for the period 687-868, ample gift lists were used in the *Liber Pontificalis* to give a quantitative evaluation of each pope's achievements in the maintenance and embellishment of the city of Rome.[3] During the Carolin-

---

[1]*Gesta Innocentii PP III*, PL 214:xviii-ccxxviii, esp. chapters CXLV, cols cciii-ccxi and CXLIX, cols ccxxvi-ccxxviii.

[2] L. Duchesne, ed., *Le Liber Pontificalis*, 2 vols (Paris, 1886-92); *The Lives of the Eighth-Century Popes (Liber Pontificalis)*, trans. Raymond Davis (Liverpool, 1992), 175-8, 209-18; Herman Geertman, *More Veterum: il 'Liber Pontificalis' e gli edifici ecclesiastici di Roma nella tarda antichità e nell'alto medioevo* (Groningen, 1975).

[3] Paolo Delogu, 'The Rebirth of Rome in the Eighth and Ninth Centuries', *The Rebirth of Towns in the West AD 700-1050*, Council for British Archaeology Research Report 68 (1988), 32-42.

gian period, the papacy progressively assumed political and judicial authority over Rome and its surrounding region. The works of which the popes were patrons now stressed Rome's ideological position, providing material which could be used for a qualitative evaluation. The Carolingian passion for listing[4] established a precedent which may be used to emphasize the significance of the varied multitude of small gifts made by Innocent III. These spiritually revealing donations often occurred in those little churches which abounded in Rome. Guided by Christ's words that there is value in being faithful in small things (the least),[5] we need to examine the spiritual implications and importance of Innocent's gift list.

Iacobini, in his excellent work, has dealt comprehensively with the architectural importance of Innocent's buildings.[6] In so doing, he joins others in the field of art history in general and of architectural history in particular, in focusing on large-scale works of importance which can be attributed to Innocent's patronage or otherwise dated to within the pontificate.[7] The provenance of several small 'sumptuary' pieces of metal work associated with the pope, either stylistically or by inscription, which has provoked much debate in the past, seems now to have been resolved.[8] The greatest problem, however, arises in any consideration of the

[4] Janet L. Nelson, 'Literacy in Carolingian Government' in Rosamond McKitterick, ed., *The Uses of Literacy in Early Medieval Europe* (Cambridge, 1990), 258-96, esp. 296.

[5] Luke 16:10.

[6] Antonio Iacobini, 'Innocenzo III', in *Enciclopoedia dell'Arte Medioevale*, 7 (Rome, 1996):86-392; *idem*, '"Est haec sacra principis aedes"': La Basilica Vaticana da Innocenzo III a Gregorio IX (1198-1241)', in *L'Architettura della Basilica di San Pietro: Storia e Costruzione.* Atti del Convegno Internazionale di Studi, Roma Castel S. Angelo (7-10 novembre, 1995), *Quaderni dell'Istituto di Storia dell'Architettura*, n.s., 25-30, 1995-97 (Rome, 1997), 91-100.

[7] D. Redig de Campos, 'Les constructions d'Innocent III et de Nicholas III sur la colline vaticane', *Mélanges de l'Ecole française de Rome* 71 (1959):359-76; Maria Bonfioli, 'La diaconia dei SS Sergio e Bacco nel Foro Romano: fonti e problemi', *Rivista di archeologia cristiana* 50 (1974):55-85; C. Rebecchini, 'Il ritrovamento del palazzo d'Innocenzo III in Vaticano', *Monumenti musei e gallerie pontificie* 2 (1981):39-52; H.Geertmann, 'Richerche sopra la prima fase di S. Sisto Vecchio in Roma', *Pontificia Accademia Romana di Archeologia. Rendiconti* 41 (1968-1969), 219-28; Pio Francesco Pistilli, 'L'architettura tra il 1198 e il 1254', in *Roma nel Ducento: L'arte nella città dei papi da Innocenzo III a Innocenzo IV*, ed. Angiola Maria Romanini (Turin, 1991), 1-72, esp. 1-29; Anna Maria Voci, *Nord o Sud? Note per la storia del medioevale* Palatium Apostolicum apud Sanctum Petrum *e delle sue capelle* (Vatican City, 1992), 45-104.

[8] Marie-Madeleine Gautier, 'Observations préliminaires sur les restes d'un revêtement d'émail champlevé fait pour la Confession de Saint Pierre à Rome', *Bulletin de la Société Archéologique et Historique du Limousin* 91 (1964):43-70; *idem*, 'L'art des émaux champlevés en Italie à l'époque primitive du gothique', *Il Gotico a Pistoia nei suoi rapporti con l'arte gotica italiana, Atti del secondo convegno internazionale di studi* (Pistoia, 1966), 271-93; *idem*, 'La clôture émaillée de la Confession de Saint Pierre au Vatican, lors du Concile de Latran IV, 1215', *Bibliothèque des Cahiers Archéologique* II *Synthronon: Art et Archéologie de la fin de l'Antiquité et du Moyen Age* (Paris, 1968), 237-47; F.Vitale, 'Il frontale della confessione Vaticano', *Federico II et l'arte del duecento italiano*, 2 vols (Rome, 1980), 2:159-72; Julian Gardner, 'L'architettura del Sancta Sanctorum', in *Il*

very smallest gifts – the precious jewels, the richly-textured fabrics, the liturgical furnishings, the decorated bindings and ecclesiastical vestments – which have all perished or been replaced over time, leaving nothing to be definitely associated with Innocent. The *Gesta* Gift List provided by his biographer is all that now remains.

This list appears in two separate chapters containing forty-seven entries in the first and forty-eight in the second. The first chapter records several multiple donations and single offerings, ending with a final spectacular gift of chalices to all the churches of Rome which lacked them.[9] The second chapter records the distribution of his own treasure.[10] Both chapters generally deal with benefactions in order of the importance of the recipient or the size of the gift. The five major basilicas, the *Constantiniana* or Lateran, St Peter's, St Paul's outside the Walls, S. Maria Maggiore and S. Lorenzo *fuori le Mura*, head the first list and are followed by the churches of the city and those of the Patrimony. Sums of money mentioned in the list for repairs and, in a few cases, for *ab initio* building projects, although impressive, are far outnumbered by vestments and equipment for the work of the altar.[11] Innocent donated ten *vestes*, altar cloths made of silk or other fine material and woven with gold threads, for hanging on hooks or rods around the altar or in front of the altar, to the major basilicas and other important churches.[12] He presented at least eight 'noble' altar cloths and frontals for the celebration of the Eucharist, executed in the technique known as 'white-work'. 'White' or 'German' work, produced in convents such as Altenberg on the Lahn, was characterized by the great variety and skill in both scale and conception.[13] The resulting designs were uniquely powerful compositions with images woven in white linen stitches on unbleached linen. Other embroideries utilized gold thread, wound around a core of silk for additional flexibility and depth of colour. Innocent gave twenty-three red silk copes, ten other coloured copes, five dalmatics, twenty *palla* or other sorts of altar cloth, four pluviales, four *ampulae*, at least ten other items of liturgical equipment, seven crosses and 140 silver chalices. There were many other smaller and similar items.

Sancta Sanctorum, ed. C. Pietrangeli (Milan, 1995), 19-37, esp. 19-20; Antonio Iacobini, 'Le porte bronzee medievali del Laterano', in *Le Porte di Bronzo dall'Antichità al Secolo XIII*, ed. Salvatorino Salomi, Istituto della Enciclopedia Italiana (Rome, 1990), 71-95; *idem*, 'La Pittura e le Arti Suntuarie: da Innocenzo III a Innocenzo IV (1198-1254)', in *Roma nel Duecento*, 237-319.

[9]*Gesta*, CXLV, cols cciii-ccxi.

[10]Ibid., CXLIX, cols ccxxvi-ccxxviii.

[11]J. Braun, *Der christliche Altar in seiner geschichtlichen Entwicklung*, 2 vols (Munich, 1924); C. E. Pocknee, *Liturgical Vesture: Its Origins and Development* (London, 1960); *idem*, *The Christian Altar in History and Today* (London, 1963).

[12]Compare L. Edward Phillips, 'A Note on the Gifts of Leo III to the Churches of Rome: *Vestes cum storiis*', *Ephemerides Liturgicae* 102 (1988):72-78.

[13]Beryl Dean, *Embroidery in Religion and Ceremonial* (London, 1981), 9-10.

Papal gifts of gold and silver to churches and monasteries are strikingly reminiscent of Carolingian grants and are recorded in Roman pounds (*librae=c.* 0.327 kg) and ounces (*onciae*=1/12 *libra*). Innocent III's considerable money gifts amounted to 253 ounces of gold, 1000 silver marks, 1006 pounds, 2690 pounds in income from lands and rents with 1000 pounds income in gold. Eight named individuals,[14] a number of religious institutions, [15]convents and even a group of hermits[16] were amongst the beneficiaries of this papal generosity.

The anonymous papal biography which contains details of the Gift List was little known in the Middle Ages.[17] The text of the *Gesta* itself is not without hurdles of ambiguity.[18] Only three medieval copies remain and none of these is contemporary with the likely period of its first composition.[19] The original *Gesta* manuscript, completed *c.* 1208 and deposited in the Papal Archives, was, at a later date, severely mutilated either by fire or by some other unspecified accidental disaster.[20] Much of the latter part of the manuscript was lost. Happily, an archival copy had been made in Rome whilst the original was still complete and this was probably copied at least once more.[21] The earliest surviving copy of the *Gesta* included the six final chapters detailing the Gift List and can be quite precisely dated.[22] It is written in two separate late thirteenth-century hands on watermarked paper from the mills at Fabriano in Northern Italy, which were in

---

[14]The patriarch of Bulgaria and the bishop of Trnovo, Guy and William, rector and procurator of S. Spirito, the cardinal bishops of Portus and Ostia, John Colonna, cardinal deacon of SS. Cosmas e Damiano and the archbishop of Ravenna.

[15]The Roman Fraternity, the *hospitales* of the city and that of Rigo Sanguinaria on the Via Cassia.

[16]The hermits of Albano.

[17]K. W. Pennington, *Pope and Bishops: The Papal Monarchy in the Twelfth and Thirteenth Centuries* (Philadelphia, 1984), 54.

[18]Little has been written on this valuable source. The earliest work, now outdated, is the thesis of Hugo Elkan, *Die Gesta Innocentii III im Verhaltnis zu den Regesten dessleben Papstes* (Heidelberg, 1876). More useful are Y. Lefevre, 'Innocent III et son temps vus de Rome: Etude sur la biographie anonyme de ce pape', *Mélanges de l'Ecole française de Rome* 61 (1949):242-5; Volkert Pfaff, 'Die *Gesta Innocenz' III* und das Testament Heinrichs VI', ZRG Kan., 50 (1964):78-126; Wilhelm Imkamp, *Das Kirchenbild Innocenz' III. (1198-1216)*, Papste und Päpsttum 22 (Stuttgart, 1983), 10-20; Brenda Bolton, 'Too Important to Neglect: the *Gesta Innocentii PP III*', in *Church and Chronicle in the Middle Ages: Essays Presented to John Taylor*, eds G. A. Loud and I. N. Wood, (London, 1991), 87-99; David Gress-Wright, *The 'Gesta Innocentii III': Text, Introduction and Commentary* (Ann Arbor, 1994) (PhD thesis, Bryn Mawr College, 1981). For a highly original and persuasive view on authorship see now James M. Powell, 'Innocent III and Petrus Beneventanus: Reconstructing a Career at the Papal Curia', included in this volume.

[19]Vatican City, Biblioteca Apostolica Vaticana, MS Vat. lat. 12111, ff.1-85r; Paris, Bibliothèque Nationale, MS lat. 5150, MS lat. 5151; Gress-Wright, *Gesta*, 115*-26*.

[20]Ibid., 115*.

[21]Ibid., 116*.

[22]Vat. lat. 12111; Gress-Wright, *Gesta*, 119*-22*.

operation from about 1286.[23] By the later thirteenth century, this manuscript had already received some attention, being copied or recopied, possibly during the pontificate of Nicholas IV (1288-1292). Its *terminus ad quem* is probably around 1310 when the papal bureaucracy moved to Avignon.[24]

This full edition of the *Gesta* is the important one. For most of the next seven centuries it lay surprisingly dormant, appearing at irregular intervals. Even more surprisingly, when these spasmodic appearances occurred, the Gift List appears to have been ignored. It was not until the 1970s that Krautheimer[25] and Brentano[26] mentioned it in passing and then without any substantial comment. Even Maccarrone, that maestro of Innocentian studies, failed to delve further.[27] There seems to be no reason for this neglect except a lack of awareness or, perhaps more correctly, interest. With the move towards a greater understanding of Innocent's spiritual approach, there has been a gradual realization of the potential significance of this part of the *Gesta*. A qualitative examination of the list should surely be worth attempting.

As a preliminary, it is interesting to cite those regular but sparse appearances of the full version of the *Gesta*. By 1369, the manuscript had definitely reached Avignon, for it appeared as Number 1473 in the Catalogue of Urban V, described as 'A Book of Pope Innocent III covered with white vellum and written *in papiro*'.[28] In 1411 and 1594, it was still at Avignon in the Papal Library where, in 1603, a copy was made by the Italian Erasto Andreucci.[29] By 1604, the manuscript had arrived back in Rome and was annotated by Giacomo Grimaldi (1568-1623), archivist of St Peter's, for his *Description of the Basilica of Old St Peter's*[30] and by Cardinal Baronius who used it for his *Annales Ecclesiastici*.[31] Several seventeenth-century copies were made from this manuscript before it dropped out of sight, only to be 're-discovered' once more by Cardinal Angelo

---

[23]Ibid, 120*.

[24]Imkamp, *Das Kirchenbild*, 14.

[25]Richard Krautheimer, *Rome, Profile of a City 312-1308* (Princeton, 1980), 203.

[26]Robert Brentano, *Rome before Avignon: a Social History of Thirteenth-Century Rome* (London, 1974), 151.

[27]Michele Maccarrone, *Studi su Innocenzo III*, Italia Sacra 17 (Padua, 1972), 11.

[28]'Libellum Innocencii pape tercii copertum pelle alba scriptum in papiro'. F. Erhle, *Historia bibliothecae romanorum pontificum* (Vatican City, 1980), 395; Imkamp, *Das Kirchenbild*, 14-15; Gress-Wright, *Gesta*, 120*.

[29]G. Mercati, *Note per la storia di alcune biblioteche Romane dei secoli xvi-xix*, Studi e Testi 164 (Vatican City, 1952), 7.

[30]Reto Niggl, *Giacomo Grimaldi (1568-1623): Leben und Werk des römischen Archäologen und Historikers* (Munich, 1971); ibid., *Descrizione della Basilica Vaticana* (Vatican City, 1972).

[31]*Annales Ecclesiastici ab anno MCXCVIII*, eds. C. Baronio, O. Rainaldi, I. Laderchio, 37 vols (Paris, 1864) 1:1-2; Imkamp, *Das Kirchenbild*, 14-15.

Mai who, in 1841, published this *Gesta*[32] in full including the final six chapters. Following Mai, J.-P. Migne also used the full version with the chapters taking up twenty-six columns of text in the *Patrologia Latina* of 1855. Today, the 1369 manuscript is in the Vatican Library, catalogued as Vat. lat. 12111, the high accession number being explained by its relatively recent transfer in 1920 from the Vatican Secret Archives.[33]

The compilation of such a vivid and extensive gift list comes as a surprise since none of Innocent's immediate predecessors had provided any such detailed exemplar. The Gift List in Innocent's *Gesta* is more reminiscent of the lists of Hadrian I (772-95) and Leo III (795-816) than anything composed closer to Innocent's day.[34] There is an explanation for this. Innocent's own interest in the Carolingians and their history is very marked, going far beyond the *translatio imperii* of Christmas Day 800 to the liturgical writings of Amalarius of Metz[35] and Notker the Stammerer of St Gall.[36] Innocent's reformed 'Roman Office' of the papal court, contained nearly thirty feasts with lessons drawn from lives of the popes as set out in the *Liber Pontificalis*.[37] This not only had the beneficial effect of reducing the length of the services – which may have been pleasing to the varicose-liable papal chaplains with him at Segni in 1211 or 1212[38] – but also increased historical knowledge of a former period in which the gift lists of popes were longer and more detailed than anything to be found in the twelfth century. If the *Gesta* was indeed, as is generally believed, composed by someone close to Innocent in the curia, then it is likely that its author would have been highly conversant with the example set by the *Liber Pontificalis*, having heard such frequent extracts from it. Amongst the complex legacies of the Carolingian Renaissance was a heightened awareness, not only of church building and restoration, but also of what the church should mean to the people's faith.[39] Innocent would certainly have subscribed to this view and, indeed, he followed it. Purists might say that the pragmatic Innocent, working as he did in this way,

---

[32]A. Mai, *Spicilegium Romanum* (Rome, 1841), 6:300-12.

[33]Gress-Wright, *Gesta*, 119*.

[34]Compare Phillips, 'A Note on the Gifts of Leo III to the Churches of Rome', 72-8.

[35]Enrico Mazza, 'L'altare nell'Alto Medioevo: l'interpretazione di Amalario di Metz', *Arte Cristiana* 80 (1992):403-10.

[36]For Innocent's interest in Notker, *Vita B. Notkero Balbulo*, AASS, April I, 6 April, pp. 576-604, at 587.

[37]S. J. P. van Dijk and J. Hazelden Walker, *The Origins of the Modern Roman Liturgy* (London, 1958), 95-112.

[38]Van Dijk and Walker, *Roman Liturgy*, 267-9.

[39]Edward Peters, 'Restoring the Church and Restoring Churches: Event and Image in Franciscan Biography', *Franziskanische Studien* 68 (1986):213-36, esp. 222, 228-31.

was not really so spiritually absolute as, for example, Peter Damian[40] and St Bernard.[41] These two were against the identification of material development with true spirituality, St Bernard being extremely severe against 'useless building and such frivolities'.

Edward Peters has dealt with the place of church building and church restoration in papal pastoral thought in the early thirteenth century, which recognized the spiritual significance of the material fabric. As he says, 'So much restoration carried out in Rome, in spite of every difficulty in the City, reflected the new interest in the church edifice more dynamically than anywhere else in Europe'.[42] Since the sack of Rome of 1084 by the Normans, each pope had, in varying degrees, worked to achieve such restoration, given the limitations of their power in the city and of the money available. Innocent was no exception and indeed, his was not the time for great projects. There were two reasons why this was so. First, the earlier restoration had left little of substance for him to do.[43] Secondly, the two main tasks from the beginning of Innocent's pontificate were the control of Rome, including bringing back the Papal States,[44] and the recovery of the Holy Land for Christ.[45] Although there was little time or money for much else, it would be a superficial error to consider the Gift List as a page-filling exercise by the biographer. Such a conclusion would be to misread the character and faith of Innocent III. He himself was indefatigable in all things and so his every effort merited being chronicled by the biographer. Whilst his contribution as restorer, builder and patron is now receiving more attention, an evaluation of the spiritual content of this work still lags some way behind. In fact, it is in his minor building and related projects forming, as they do, such a large part of the Gift List that the depth of Innocent's faith at work – as it were, in spirit and in stone – can be seen. Where there are precious jewels amongst the gifts, he may well have been using the tradition that these jewels represented the Light of God and Christ in the World.[46]

Beyond Innocent's pontificate, evidence from his official biography, entered in the later so-called *Liber Pontificalis* by Martin of Troppau (d. 1279), is

---

[40]PL 144:165; John Van Engen, 'The "Crisis of Cenobitism" Reconsidered: Benedictine Monasticism in the years 1050-1150', *Speculum* 61 (1986):269-304, esp. 286-7.

[41]St Bernard, *Apologia to Abbot William*, trans. Michael Casey, in *Cistercians and Cluniacs*, (Kalamazoo, 1970), 63-6.

[42]Peters, 'Event and Image', 226.

[43]Ernst Kitzinger, 'The Arts as Aspects of a Renaissance: Rome and Italy', in *Renaissance and Renewal in the Twelfth Century*, eds Robert Benson and Giles Constable (Oxford, 1982), 637-70, esp. 638-45; Krautheimer, *Rome*, 203-6.

[44]Maccarrone, *Studi*, 9-22.

[45]J. M. Powell, *Anatomy of a Crusade 1213-1221* (Philadelphia, 1986), 15-32.

[46]Compare *De sacro altaris mysterio*, PL 217:773-916, esp. 783-6.

helpful.[47] It outlines the pope's career to 1216 as it would have been remembered in the third quarter of the thirteenth century. Like the earliest entries in the *Liber Pontificalis* dating from the sixth century, Martin's slight biographical information must have depended on written sources, easily available to the generality of officials in the papal bureaucracy. He uses little of the material provided by Vat. lat. 12111 (the *Gesta*) and concentrates on three major items. He places amongst the pope's many 'glorious works' the building of the Hospital of Santo Spirito and the reconstruction of the church of San Sisto.[48] He does indeed comment that the pope gave one pound of silver to each church in Rome which did not have a chalice, stressing that Innocent hoped that making such a public statement of a papal gift would prevent the chalices from being secretly sold off.[49] This is an interesting contrast with the *Gesta*'s declaration of motivation. Although the papal biographer noted the number of chalices as 133 and their weight as 100 marks of silver, he is perfectly clear that the purpose of the chalices was for the reverence of the sacred mystery of the blood of Jesus Christ.[50] Actually, Innocent's concern combined the two, not only the practical but also the spiritual.

Other sources from within the period of the pontificate can be used to corroborate, correct or amplify the *Gesta*'s evidence. This is especially so for the years 1208 to 1216, for it should not be assumed that Innocent ceased to make gifts in those years which the *Gesta* did not cover. One contemporary, who viewed Innocent from just inside the Regno, is an anonymous Cistercian from the house of S. Maria de Ferraria near Teano, and his evidence enables a comparison to be made with the *Gesta* in two particular cases.[51] This southern monk was clearly well informed about events at the curia and in his *Chronicle* concentrated on certain spiritual activities which may help in any consideration of Innocent's motivation. His *Chronicle* entry for 1207 records two events which clearly gave the monk much satisfaction. In February of that year, Innocent put aside his rich vestments, his scarlets and silks, his gold and silver vessels, all his pontifical paraphernalia and replaced them with religious clothing consisting of white wool and lambskins.[52] The *Gesta* records the reasoning behind Innocent's actions in using wood and glass for his vessels and lambskins instead of ermine and miniver

---

[47]Duchesne, *Liber Pontificalis*, 2:451-4.

[48]Ibid., 2:451-2.

[49]'Tali pacto quod vendere eos non possunt', ibid., 2:452.

[50]'Pro reverentia sancti mysterii corporis et sanguinis Jesu Christi', *Gesta* CXLV, col. cxx.

[51]A. Gaudenzi, ed., *Chronica Romanorum pontificium et Imperatorum ac de rebus in Apulia Gestia (781-1228) auctore ignoto monacho Cisterciensi*, Società Napoletana di Sancta Patria, 1, Cronache (Naples, 1888), 34.

[52]'Innocentius papa III mensa Februarii dimisit et a se repulit indumenta et vestes pretiosas, id est scarlatum, pelles criseas armenicas, parascipdes, sciphos, cratera, frena, et lora aurea et argentea; assumpsit sibi vestes religiosas idest de lana alba et pelles agniculas', *Auctore ignoto monacho*, 34.

as stemming from his wish to correct any superfluity amongst his bishops and reduce them to modesty.[53] To this end, Innocent removed himself from outside lay influence, even being served at table by 'religious, regular and honest people'. Likewise, the anonymous Cistercian monk informs us that, also in 1207, Innocent instituted a convent in which all the nuns of Rome would be able to unite in developing their spiritual life in strict claustration.[54] Here, his information supplements the generous financial arrangements detailed by the *Gesta*.[55] Innocent's significant personal spiritual demonstration of 1207 was thus followed up by a particular physical manifestation – the provision of a new convent – which would be of value to the religious life of others.

The Gift List, then, has three outstanding components. First is what Peters calls 'on the ground ecclesiology', based on worship and dealing with much church restoration and decoration through the forms and traditions of the church.[56] In some ways this is the transforming of an event into an image in which altars and chalices played significant parts. Second, based on compassion, is the charitable component which allows for the healing of the sick and the care of the poor and needy, whilst the third, the faith, is the pastoral component which includes, as far as the Gift List is concerned, the obligation to provide opportunities for the maturing of the faith of those who wish to live the life of the religious.

These components, in turn, were expressed in the various churches of Rome and the Patrimony, where Innocent attended to the needs for holiness in the worship of God, in the Hospital of Santo Spirito, where the healing of the sick took place, and in the convent of San Sisto, where the spiritual needs of the many women in Rome who sought to undertake the full life of a religious could be allowed to flourish.

All the churches of the city were of significance to Innocent as bishop of Rome. The *Gesta* records his frequent acts of munificence, describing him as *studiosus* – well-informed and willing to research – in practices of worship (*cultus*) and in a concern for the decoration or ornamentation of churches.[57] Although there may be some partiality on behalf of the author of the *Gesta*, there is no reason to challenge this view. Evidence can be used from elsewhere to reinforce the fact that Innocent had an interest in altars, church dedications and consecrations which was, after all, part of the necessary 'job description' of any active bishop. For

---

[53]*Gesta*, CXCLVIII, cols ccxxv-ccxxvi.

[54]'Instituit etiam universale cenobium monalium Rome, in quo omnes moniales conveniant, nec eis inde progredi liceat', *Auctore ignoto monacho*, 34; Brenda M. Bolton, 'Daughters of Rome: All One in Christ Jesus', *Studies in Church History* 27 (1990):101-15.

[55]*Gesta*, CXLIX, col. ccxxvii.

[56]Peters, 'Event and Image', 234, n. 8.

[57]*Gesta*, CXLV, col. cciii. 'Quantum vero munificus et studiosus exstiterit circa cultum et ornamentum ecclesiarum, frequentia dona manifestant'.

example, at Pentecost in 1216, an anonymous eyewitness commented on the outstanding devotion with which Innocent had consecrated the altar of S. Erculano in the cathedral of Perugia.[58] Further, knowledge of the procedures for and the performance of the liturgy in the basilicas of Rome formed a substantial element of his duties as cardinal-deacon from *c*. 1190-1198. The liturgical commentary of Amalarius of Metz (d. 850) placed the altar at the centre of the liturgy and Innocent seems to have been much influenced by Amalarius's idea of liturgical drama as a message for the simple faithful.[59]

Tentative themes of significance can be put forward to make some sense of the apparent jumble of gifts to churches. In addition to that decoration of altars with cloths and the consecration of those altars, there was the equipment for the mass, particularly the provision of chalices.[60] The repair and restoration of the fabric of the churches was an ongoing problem. Churches in Rome required much minor restoration to prevent the need for eventual major restoration. The roof of S. Maria Maggiore was repaired for 20 pounds.[61] SS. Apostoli received 30 pounds[62] for an unspecified repair, whilst S. Pudenziana was given the tiny sum of three pounds.[63] A double operation was carried out at the adjacent churches of S. Constanza and Sant'Agnese, which cost 70 pounds.[64] The author of the *Gesta* uses *reparare* and *reficere* rather than *restaurare* or *renovare* to describe the status of these repairs.

However, one particular church was selected for larger scale renewal or reconstruction in accordance with Innocent's personal predilection. His title church, SS. Sergio e Bacco on the Forum, was in such a ruinous condition that more of the crypt beneath was visible than the church above.[65] As Lothario, Innocent had succeeded to this *titulus* in 1189 or 1190 in succession to his *consobrinus* Octavian, who had held it from 1182 to 1189 before his elevation as cardinal bishop of Ostia. Octavian had succeeded Paolo Scholari who had held

---

[58]In particular, Massimo Petrocchi, 'L'ultimo destino perugino di Innocenzo III', *Bolletino della Deputazione di Storia patria per l'Umbria* 64 (1967):201-7, for the pope's consecration of altars in Perugia in September 1198 and 5 June 1216.

[59]Mazza, 'L'altare nell'Alto Medioevo', 403-10. See my forthcoming article, 'Message, Celebration, Offering: the Place of Twelfth- and Early Thirteenth-century Liturgical Drama as "Missionary theatre"', *Studies in Church History* 37 (1998).

[60]*Gesta*, CXLV, col. cciii. Chalices for the Lateran, St Peter's, S. Maria Maggiore, S. Lorenzo *fuori*, SS. Sergio e Bacco, S. Maria in Sassia and 133 chalices to the churches of Rome. 'Numerus autem eorum fuit centum triginta trium, pondus vero centum marcarum argenti'.

[61]*Gesta*, CXLV, col. ccvi.

[62]Ibid., col. ccx.

[63]Ibid., col. ccviii.

[64]Ibid., col. ccvi. 'Pro reparatione basilicae Sanctae Constantiae et porticus ecclesiae Sanctae Agnetis'.

[65]*Gesta*, IV, cols xviii, cxlv, ccvii; Bonfioli, 'La diaconia dei SS. Sergio e Bacco', 55-85.

it from 1179 to 1180 before becoming Clement III.[66] Perhaps the apparent neglect of this tiny church by its two former occupants, compared with the *Gesta's* record of Lothario's essential repairs to roofs and walls, indicates the more caring attitude of the latter. He had a new altar constructed on new steps, making a new *pectoralia* or enclosure for the *schola cantorum* in front of the choir.[67] On becoming pope, he immediately undertook a second building campaign at SS. Sergio e Bacco, ordering a portico with columns to be erected. When questions were raised about the finances, many wondering from whence, in view of his recent elevation, he had been able to find such money, his biographer came to his defence with the explanation that they were paid for 'from goods which God had conferred on him while he was cardinal'.[68] Innocent gave to this church expensive gifts and exquisite small works for use in liturgical ceremonies, in particular, a Limoges-enamel basilica shrine, various small silver receptacles to enhance the altar, a silver-gilt chalice, and he also guaranteed the church a generous income.[69] An inscription over the portico stressed the importance of this two-staged restoration, first during his cardinalate and then during his pontificate.[70]

Innocent III was the first canon of St Peter's to be promoted so far up the hierarchy.[71] As pope, his gifts to the basilica, where he had held a benefice, were to be of special value, both materially and spiritually. He granted to the canons of St Peter's the power of striking *insignia* in lead or tin and retaining any profits ensuing.[72] The *Gesta's* brief entry is spelled out in greater detail by Innocent himself in a letter dated 18 January 1199.[73] This gave the canons the right to produce pilgrim badges to honour the basilica itself and the apostles Peter and Paul, whose images would serve to increase the devotion of those making their *ad limina* pilgrimage to the tomb.

---

[66]Brenda Bolton, 'Rome as a Setting for God's Grace', *Innocent III: Studies on Papal Authority and Pastoral Care*, Variorum Collected Studies Series, CS 490 (Aldershot, 1995), art. I, pp. 1-17, p. 14.

[67]*Gesta*, IV, col. xviii.

[68]Ibid., 'de bonis quae in cardinalatu contulerat sibi Deus. Multis mirantibus unde in novitate sua tantas invenisset expensas'.

[69]Ibid., CXLV, col. ccvii.

[70]Vatican City, Biblioteca Apostolica Vaticana, MS lat. 3938, fol. 284; Bolton, 'Rome as a Setting', 15.

[71]13 March 1198, '... qui olim in ipsa vobiscum pariter canonici beneficium assecuti', Reg. 1:296, p. 418.

[72]*Gesta*, CXLV, cols cciv-ccv, 'quartem partem oblationum de omnibus ministeriis, potestatem insignia plumbea vel stagnea faciendi et proventus eorum'.

[73]18 January 1199, Reg. 1:534 (536), pp. 772-3.

This badge was of great significance. To the pilgrim, it represented a visible proof of a spiritual journey undertaken and successfully completed in Rome.[74] The language of his letter confirms Innocent's desire that the badges produced by the canons of St Peter's should be regarded as superior to all others, and he strictly forbade anyone other than those approved by the canons of St Peter's to make badges, threatening any who so did with excommunication.[75] Rome had not previously had such a pilgrim-badge emblem, and Innocent, in promoting these for the city, was playing his part in advertising the apostles' tomb. He also granted to the canons the authority either to cast the badges themselves or to concede this right to whomsoever they wished – as long as their nominees remained answerable to the canons in all details.[76] This was a valuable gift and the canons undoubtedly benefited from Innocent's creation and protection of the process of badge production.[77]

All these gifts to churches and basilicas, as recorded in the *Gesta*, were meant for the glorification of God – Father, Son and Holy Spirit. And yet, there is one possible exception, which is certainly not minor and which some might consider to raise questions about the self-glorification of Innocent and his position within the church.[78] The *Gesta* mentions Innocent's restoration of the early, perhaps fourth-century, much-decayed apse mosaic in the Constantinian basilica of Old St Peter's.[79] In 1592, Giacomo Grimaldi, the archivist, wishing to record this great church in every detail before its final destruction, made a drawing of Innocent's apse decoration.[80] Its design reveals several contemporary insertions for Innocent took advantage of this opportunity to place in the apse a representation of himself, the pope, to give an indication of the importance of the papal

---

[74]Esther Cohen, '*In haec signa*: The Pilgrim-Badge Trade in Southern France', *Journal of Medieval History* 2 (1976), 193-214; Michael Mitchener, *Medieval Pilgrim and Secular Badges* (London, 1986). See also Debra J. Birch, *Pilgrimage to Rome in the Middle Ages: Continuity and Change* (Woodbridge, 1998), 187-92.

[75]19 June 1207, Pott. 3121.

[76]Reg. 1:534 (536), p. 773.

[77]Compare the privilege of Peter Annibaldi of 12 March 1224, confirming grants made by Innocent, in Franco Bartoloni, ed., *Codice Diplomatico del Senato Romano dal MCXLIV al MCCCXLVII*, Fonti per la Storia d'Italia, 87 (Rome, 1948), 1:111-5.

[78]Gerhart B.Ladner, *Die papstbildnisse des Altertums und des Mittelalters*, 2 vols (Vatican City, 1970), 2:56-68; S. Sibilia, 'L'iconografia di Innocenzo III', *Società Romana di storia patria*, Bolletino della Sezione per il Lazio Meridionale, 2 (Anagni, 1953), 65-100.

[79]*Gesta*, CXLV, col. ccv, 'absidam ejusdem basilicae fecit restaurari mosibus, quod erat ex magna parte consumptum'; José Ruysschaert, 'L'inscription absidale primitive de S.-Pierre. Texte et contextes', *Atti della Pontificia Accademia Romana di Archeologia. Rendiconti*, 40 (1967-1968), 171-90.

[80]Vatican City, Biblioteca Vaticana, Archivio S.Pietro, Album 64, fols 158v-159r; Grimaldi, *Descrizione della Basilica*, 196-7; Krautheimer, *Rome*, 205-6.

office whilst making the overriding statement about the significance of the Christian life and message of salvation.

The apse consists of two levels. In the upper vault, Christ sits on a central throne, his right hand raised in a Greek blessing and holding in his left a closed book. On either side are Peter and Paul, identified by Greek and Latin inscriptions. Two palms and a meadow set in an odd 'Nilotic' landscape denote the scene as Paradise. Two stags drink from the four rivers of life which proceed from the throne. Such a design is reminiscent of early figural mosaics, and these may indeed be the original figures, although somewhat modified by Innocent.[81]

In the lower zone, along the rim of the apse vault runs a frieze of twelve sheep proceeding from Bethlehem and Jerusalem. In the centre, before a throne surmounted by a gemmed cross, stands the Lamb upon a hill and with its blood flowing into a chalice placed before it.[82] On either side of the Lamb are the figures of Innocent III and *Ecclesia Romana*. Innocent, wearing his tiara, extends his arms to the Lamb in an attitude of *proskynesis*, an attitude of supplication and adoration, derived from the offering of gifts as well as from the seeking of help.[83] *Ecclesia Romana* carries a banner on which are depicted the two keys, the papal symbol. At the rim of the apse is an inscription, flanked by two chalices. It reads + THIS IS THE SEE OF PETER, THE DWELLING OF THE PRINCE, THE GLORY AND ORNAMENT AND MOTHER OF ALL CHURCHES. THE DEVOTED BISHOP WHO SERVES IN THIS TEMPLE GATHERS THE FLOWERS OF VIRTUE AND THE FRUITS OF LIFE +[84]

Clearly, the figure of Innocent and *Ecclesia Romana* were not part of the original design.[85] Their appearance and placing in Innocent's composition carry significant implications, although historians have argued long over what those implications are. While Krautheimer believed that, read together with the inscription, his insertions stress the themes of apostolic succession and papal supremacy,[86] they also appear to represent ammunition for the claim of St Peter's to be the cathedral of Rome and mother of all churches, a title hitherto claimed

---

[81]Ruysschaert, 'L'inscription absidale', 182-5.

[82]José Ruysschaert, 'Le tableau Mariotti de la mosaique absidale de l'ancien S.Pierre', *Atti della Pontificia Accademia Romana di Archeologia. Rendiconti*, 40 (1967-1968), 295-317.

[83]Gerhart B. Ladner, 'The Gestures of Prayer in Papal Iconography of the Thirteenth and Early Fourteenth Centuries', *Didascalie. Studies in Honor of Anselm M. Albareda* (New York, 1961), 245-75.

[84]Anita Margiotta, 'L'antica decorazione absidale della Basilica di San Pietro in alcuni frammenti al Museo di Roma', *Bolletino dei Musei Communali di Roma*, NS, 2 (1988):21-33, esp. 22.

[85]Antonio Iacobini, 'Il mosaico absidale di San Pietro in Vaticano', *Fragmenta Picta: Affreschi e mosaici staccati del Medioevo romano* (Rome, 1989), 119-29.

[86]Krautheimer, *Rome*, 206; compare Walter Ullmann, *The Growth of Papal Government in the Middle Ages* (London, 1955), 308-9.

and jealously guarded by the Lateran, the oldest and greatest of all the churches of Rome.[87]

It is possible that the spiritual significance of the apse mosaic and its inscription goes far beyond a single concentration on the theme of apostolic succession. Innocent is no mere modest donor in this apse, meekly kneeling at Christ's feet. Rather, he is most visibly present as pope, standing with *Ecclesia Romana* as the successors to both apostles. But Innocent takes second place to the Roman church. It is Rome, her church and her patron, St Peter, who are important. The Roman setting of his office and his inheritance from St Peter give him power to minister to the Lamb. Boyle has shown how Innocent's ideal of apostolic service made him the astonishing pastoral pope that he was.[88] Above all, Innocent is the pope of the Fourth Lateran Council, a council which transformed the pastoral face of Europe for more than three centuries.[89] Since this apse mosaic, surely refurbished for the council by November 1215, could be said to depict something of Innocent's view of the *vita apostolica*, his understanding of the Bible and his own profound and serious consideration of the Eucharist, it is of a spiritual nature, and Innocent, representing all popes, needed to be there as pope at the time.[90] The central presence of the chalice can be linked with its increasing importance in the liturgical revisions then taking place in the mass. While Innocent did not, as has frequently been supposed, himself define transubstantiation in the creed which he promulgated at the council,[91] he wished to affirm Christ's presence in the sacrament, not least to curtail the spread of Cathar heresy, which had even penetrated into Tuscia Romana, dangerously near to the see of St Peter itself. Here, in mosaic, the most visible and durable medium, in the basilica dedicated to the Prince of the Apostles, he publicly insisted on the central place of Christ, the Lamb, who, by shedding his sacrificial blood, had made himself saviour of all mankind. Christ's body was in the pyx, at the consecration of the host and in the chalice.[92] The depiction of the Lamb with the blood flowing directly into the

---

[87]Michele Maccarrone, 'La "Cathedra Sancti Petri" nel Medio Evo: da simbolo a reliquia', *Rivista di Storia della Chiesa in Italia* 36 (1986):349-447, esp. 429-32.

[88]Leonard E. Boyle, 'Innocent III and Vernacular Versions of Scripture', in Katherine Walsh and Diana Wood, eds, *The Bible in the Medieval World: Essays in Memory of Beryl Smalley*, Studies in Church History, Subsidia 4, 97-107.

[89]Leonard E. Boyle, 'The Fourth Lateran Council and Manuals of Popular Theology', in T. J. Hoffman, ed., *The Popular Literature of Medieval England* (University of Tennessee, 1985), 30-43.

[90]Brenda M. Bolton, 'A Show with a Meaning: Innocent III's Approach to the Fourth Lateran Council, 1215', *Papal Authority*, 53-67.

[91]Gary Macy, *The Theologies of the Eucharist in the Early Scholastic Period* (Oxford, 1984), 140-1.

[92]Brentano, *Rome before Avignon*, 266-7.

chalice is of considerable interest.[93] There seems to be no discoverable Roman precedent for this, at the time, unique depiction.[94]

With the overwhelming proportion of Innocent's gifts being given to the churches and basilicas for the first component of worship, his motivation becomes clear. He would not have forgotten St Paul's advice to the Ephesians which, paraphrased, states that it is Christ himself who holds the building together and turns it into the holy and sacred temple.[95] This is confirmed by Innocent's many references to the temple, not only as a holy place, but as an example of the dedication of those who wished to serve God. In his opening sermon at the Lateran Council, with so many decrees to be promulgated, he dealt with the restoration of Solomon's temple[96] by King Josiah in the eighteenth year of his reign. Innocent asked that this episode should be considered as a parable of the present time, so that, in the eighteenth year of his pontificate, the church might also be restored as the temple had been.[97]

Many historians have put forward the view that all Innocent III's actions were based on the exercise of his power. Kitzinger, for example, in spite of being more sympathetic to the importance of these gifts than most, regarded them as being 'keyed to themes of power and triumph'.[98] This is too stereotyped a view – neglecting not only the gifts but also the various strands of Innocent's whole personality which underlay his motivation, based on his character and beliefs. His spirituality was the most important, not only because it sprang from his faith but also because it placed him firmly in the spiritual ferment of his time as typified by the *vita apostolica*. Unlike many who were content with such 'lofty ideals', he did not forget where, as shepherd of the sheep, his true responsibilities lay, however routine they may appear to have been. His own personal responsibility to SS. Sergio e Bacco, the property assigned to him, exemplifies this. In this area was his personal responsibility to his family in spite of the possible implication of nepotism.[99] His relationship with his brother was specially close and is instanced by his defence of the Tor dei' Conti.[100] His responsibility as pope – the head of Christ's church on earth – has been accepted by most historians as

---

[93]Ruysschaert, 'Le tableau Mariotti', 304.

[94]Compare the Ghent polyptich of *The Mystic Lamb* by Hubert and Jan Van Eyck (dedicated 6 May 1432).

[95]Ephesians 2:20-2. Compare Peters, 'Restoring the Church', 220.

[96]*Sermones de Diversis VI, In Concilio habitus*, PL 217:673-80.

[97]Ibid., col. 675, 'Templum Domini, quod est Ecclesia, restauretur'.

[98]Kitzinger, 'Arts as Aspect of a Renaissance', 649-50; Karl Nöeles, 'Die Künst der Cosmaten und die Idee der *Renovatio Romae*', *Festschrift Werner Hager* (Recklinghausen, 1966), 13-37, 30-1.

[99]For a more critical view see Matthias Thumser, *Rom unde der römische Adel in der späten Stauferzeit* (Tubingen, 1995), 75-97, esp. 76-84.

[100]Bartoloni, *Codice Diplomatico*, 57, pp. 92-4.

effective, but it should not be regarded as the result of any personal aggrandizement or a search for power.[101] Instead, he has all the attributes of the born administrator, who, given responsibility for a function in an organisation, sets out to achieve (or manage) the purpose of that organisation to the optimum. Given Innocent's belief that he was empowered by the Holy Spirit, it is not to be wondered that he was both successful and faithful in those things which were little – the least as well as those that were great.

Although there are many gifts for the charitable duty of caring for the sick and setting up conditions for their healing, the most important single item is the Hospital of Santo Spirito.[102] The very first gift in this part of Innocent's list was for the work of the sick and poor. He bestowed and endowed benefices, possessions, rents, treasure, ornaments, books and privileges which seemed sufficient to him so that the religious atmosphere and necessary hospitality were always abundant. The *Gesta* states that Innocent had the hospital building reconstructed at his own expense for the care of the poor and the infirm, contributing 1000 silver marks.[103] These 1000 silver marks were broken down into vessels worth 600 marks and gold plate worth 400 marks. He gave 200 pounds' income to Brother William, procurator of the hospital[104] and two great German altar cloths to the church of S. Maria in Sassia, associated with the hospital by his bull *Cupientes proplurimis* of 8 December 1201.[105] The hospital was placed under the charge of the Order of Saint-Esprit, the brothers being responsible to the pope alone. However, for all his detailed provisions for the great Roman foundation by the Tiber, even Innocent recognized that his own financial support would not be sufficient to cover the full costs of caring for the sick in the hospital of Santo Spirito. Consequently, he wished to spread almsgiving amongst a much wider circle. This was to be serious almsgiving with a serious purpose.[106] Those Roman brothers of the hospital delegated for the collection of alms were to restrict themselves in their fund-raising, travelling only to Italy, Sicily, England and Hungary. Innocent issued prescriptions about the collection of alms in any city or place where an interdict was imposed and granted an exceptional privilege. In honour of Almighty God, at the coming of the

---

[101]See in general Michele Maccarrone, *Vicarius Christi: Storia del titolo papale*, Lateranum NS 18, 1-4 (Rome, 1952), 109-18.

[102]For a brief account see Brenda M. Bolton, 'Hearts not Purses? Pope Innocent III's Attitude to Social Welfare', in Emily Albu Hanawalt and Carter Lindberg, eds, *Through the Eye of a Needle: Judaeo-Christian Roots of Social Welfare* (Kirksville MO, 1994), 123-45, esp. 136-41.

[103]*Gesta*, CXLIV, cols cc-cciii.

[104]Ibid., CXLIX, col. ccxxvii.

[105]Pietro de Angelis, *L'Ospedale di Santo Spirito in Saxia*, 2 vols. *1. Dalle origini al 1300* (Rome, 1960), 380-1.

[106]*Inter opera pietatis*, 19 June 1204, Reg. 7:95, pp. 151-5.

hospital collectors, interdicts were to be suspended once a year. The bells were to be rung and the churches opened so that words of exhortation about the raising of alms might be put to the people in the church. The collectors were placed under special protection, and privileges were granted to members of the hospital confraternity including tithe exemption.

In 1208, Innocent raised the image of the Hospital of Santo Spirito in Rome by instituting a new and solemn liturgical station on the Sunday after the octave of Epiphany when, with hymns, psalms, torches and tapers, the canons of St Peter's carried processionally the image of the Veronica from their basilica to the church of S. Maria in Sassia and back again.[107] Innocent's sermon for the day, on the theme of the wedding feast at Cana – water into wine – addressed the crowds of Romans and pilgrims with a fund-raising motive which was to have a spectacular charitable outcome.[108] One thousand pilgrims and Roman poor were to be given by the papal almoner three pence each, for bread, meat and wine, every year in perpetuity. The canons who bore the Veronica in this procession were to be given twelve pennies from the oblations made at the *Confessio* or tomb of St Peter, while the acolytes were to have a pound of wax for their lights.[109]

The work of the Hospital of Santo Spirito drew together the threads of Innocent's charitable concerns. In 1208, Guy of Montpellier, who was joint master of Santo Spirito and of a similar hospital in Montpellier, had died, and Innocent himself, contrary to the precepts laid down in *Inter Opera Pietatis* of 1204, named Peter de Graniero, a Roman, as master.[110] On 8 June 1208, the pope declared that Peter, as head of Santo Spirito, was to be the superior general of the order, thereby securing the primacy of the Roman foundation. In so doing, Innocent made the order very much his own. He defined *hospitalitas* as fulfilling the corporeal acts of mercy. Babies were particularly provided for – whether those of pilgrim mothers or the 'lone' parent.[111] Prostitutes also, provided they could remain chaste for Lent and until after Easter, could find brief shelter at the hospital.

Papal generosity to the hospital was quite remarkable. In addition to the 1000 silver marks which was Innocent's contribution from his own resources, Guy as master was to receive 100 pounds and William, the procurator of the hospital, another 200. The *Gesta* Gift List itemizes some of the gifts conferred by the pope on the church of S. Maria in Sassia, dealt with here because S. Maria in Sassia

---

[107]PL 215:1270-1.
[108]PL 217:345-50.
[109]*Gesta*, CXLIV, cols cc-cciii; Brentano, *Rome before Avignon*, 19-21.
[110]Reg. 7:95, pp. 152-3.
[111]Brenda M. Bolton, 'Received in His Name: Rome's Busy Baby Box', *Studies in Church History* 31 (1994):153-67.

was the hospital church and so very important to the patients.[112] These gifts were two altar cloths, richly embroidered in 'German work', a red cope edged in gold, an alb, amice and stole, a chalice of silver gilt, a crystal lavabo, a pair of silver candelabra, two silver patens and a thurible, each worth five marks, and a silver reliquary, decorated with a cross, fashioned from one whole ounce of gold and with the harrowing of hell at its centre, carved in onyx and encrusted with precious jewels. Such magnificence needs to be seen in the context of the comparative frugality imposed by Innocent III on the curia.[113]

Innocent was ever ready to enlist the aid of others in this charitable enterprise. In developing another building for the hospital, the former Saxon School, Innocent was not only utilizing a prime site on the Tiber but he was able diplomatically to use the English connection to obtain money from King John and his successors. At Innocent's invitation, on 25 March 1204, John confirmed the donation of the church of Writtle in Essex as an expectative, promising to pay 100 marks a year from the Exchequer until the church should fall vacant.[114] These payments lapsed during the interdict, but following reconciliation between king and pope, the legate to England, Nicholas de Romanis, secured from John a valuable promise for continued payments.[115] By 25 March 1221, Writtle was in the hands of the hospital, valued at 100 pounds, and John was recorded in the necrology of Santo Spirito.[116]

Although Innocent was generous with his gifts to the hospital, they could never be sufficient. The demand of all hospitals at all times has never been able to be matched by the resources provided. He thus moved towards requesting the provision of alms by others for the healing and care of the sick, poor and needy. In a sermon, composed probably in 1202 or 1203 because of its allusion to a time of famine,[117] he sets out the basis for his views that alms should result from compassion and pity and be given in the name of Jesus. Such alms-giving is righteous in itself. In fact, as Moore indicates, in his sermon on Zachaeus, the publican who gave half his wealth to the poor, Innocent stressed particularly that

---

[112]*Gesta*, CXLV, col. ccix.

[113]*Gesta*, CXLIII, cols cxcvi-cc.

[114]Thomas Duffus Hardy, ed., *Rotuli Chartarum, I (1199-1216)* (London, 1837), 123; C. R. Cheney, *Pope Innocent III and England*, Papst und Päpsttum, 9 (Stuttgart, 1976), 237-8.

[115]A. Mercato, 'La prima relazione del Cardinale Niccolò de Romanis sulla sua legazione in Inghilterra', in *Essays on History presented to R. L. Poole*, ed. H. W. C. Davis (Oxford, 1927), 287-8.

[116]Pott. 5659; P. Egidi, ed., *Liber Annualium di Santo Spirito in Sassia* (Rome, 1908).

[117]Sermo XXIX De tempore, PL 217:441-50, col. 447, 'Omni tempore debemus indigenti subvenire, sed praesertim hoc tempore, in quo Deus sterilitatem et famem induxit'.

so long as the rich had obtained their wealth legally, it was their duty to give alms.[118]

That this approach was maintained by Innocent throughout his pontificate can be seen from his 1216 Commentary on the Penitential Psalms.[119] These psalms he raised from being just a traditional part of the liturgy for Holy Thursday to a matter of crucial importance in the understanding of God's forgiveness. How much notice was taken by others of these comments, both on alms and penitence, is not clear from contemporary sources or from the decrees of the Lateran Council.

In the third group of projects, based upon the component of faith, Innocent felt that he, as the instrument of the Spirit, was carrying out a most important task. The combined enterprises of San Sisto – the restoration of the old church and the building of a new convent in which to house all the nuns of Rome under the same roof – were among Innocent's greatest building projects.[120] He was dedicated to this scheme *ferventissimo animo*, setting aside to pay for it 50 ounces of royal gold and 1100 pounds.[121] This was a huge sum in comparison to his other projects and an amount only to be surpassed in size by his gift to Casamari. He also searched for outside help to assure the continued existence of this new institution for Rome. For example, in 1213, the legate to England, Nicholas de Romanis, sought and obtained from King John the promise of 150 marks each year to be set aside *ad opus monasterii Sancti Sixti*.[122]

Innocent needed to combine both the basilica of San Sisto and the nearby tiny convent of S. Maria *in Tempuli* in order to enable him to realize this great project. The fifth-century basilica, the *titulus Crescentianae*, stood on the Via Appia near the imposing ruins of the Baths of Caracalla and Innocent's monumental project was to reconstruct it completely, not merely to repair or restore it.[123] Excavations have revealed the plan of the ancient basilica. It had three naves without a transept and the central nave was carried by twelve pairs of columns 2.5 metres apart. Innocent's architects reduced the length of this nave by half, suppressed the two outer naves and considerably raised the floor level. They also retained the external north wall of the former basilica as a foundation for one of the sides of

---

[118]John C. Moore, 'The Sermons of Innocent III', *Römische Historische Mitteilungen* 36 (1994):81-142, esp. 96.

[119]PL 217:967-1130.

[120]V. J. Koudelka, 'Le *Monasterium tempuli* et la fondation dominicaine de S. Sisto', *Archivum Fratrum Praedicatorum* 31 (1961):5-81; Brenda M.Bolton, 'Daughters of Rome: All one in Christ Jesus!', *Studies in Church History* 27 (1990):101-15.

[121]*Gesta*, CXLIX, col. ccxxvii; Koudelka, 'Le *Monasterium Tempuli*', 69; Geertman, 'S. Sisto Vecchio', 219-28.

[122]Mercati, 'La prima relazione', 287-8.

[123]Geertman, 'S. Sisto Vecchio', 220-3.

the new cloister. This project was initiated in 1207, according to the monk of Ferraria.[124] The *Gesta* does not mention the building work but only the sum which the pope intended to devote to it in 1207. Yet, Innocent IV in 1244 attributed the building of San Sisto entirely to his predecessor.[125] Certainly, therefore, at Innocent's death in July 1216, the works at San Sisto – both church and monastery – must have been sufficiently far advanced to permit the attribution of the entire work to him. Yet, if the plan for San Sisto was certainly formed by 1207 – and possibly even earlier – why then was it not completed by 1216? The slowness of progress in the building work is surely explained by the size and difficulty of the whole enterprise – the need to fill up the old nave and to raise the ground level to halfway up the columns. [126] The adjoining S. Maria *in Tempuli* was, by the early thirteenth century, in such a bad state of repair that the convent was hardly habitable.

The most interesting aspect of this project of Innocent III was his idea of reuniting and unifying convents and nuns with differing rules and different disciplinary traditions in order to create *a universale cenobium*. Within one single convent, suitable for all the religious women of Rome, the faith of all would grow in maturity.[127] This particular project was not only part of Innocent III's general plan of reform but was also crucial to specific reforms within Rome itself. All the monasteries of Rome, whether for men or for women, came under the immediate jurisdiction of the pope who held power over them in both the spiritual and material fields. Most of these monasteries were Benedictine, and it was their autonomous character which clearly gave Innocent so much cause for concern. He had even felt it necessary to travel outside Rome, to Subiaco in 1202 and to Cassino in 1208, to conduct personal visitations in both these great Benedictine centres and to impose rigorous regulations whenever necessary.[128] In December 1204, Innocent intervened for the first time with regard to the convents of Rome, strictly forbidding abbesses to dispose of their convents' goods and lands.[129] Very little is known about the state of Roman convents at this time but it seems likely that there were not more than eight in all and that they were

---

[124]*Auctore ignoto monacho*, p. 34.

[125]Vatican City, Archivio Vaticano, Reg. Vat. 21, fols 89v- 90v, 'et monasterium Sancti Sixti de Urbe quod, constructum per felicis recordationis Innocentium papam predecessorem nostrum de bonis Ecclesiae Romane'.

[126]Geertman, 'S. Sisto Vecchio', 220.

[127]Maccarrone, 'Il progetto di un *universale cenobium* per le monache di Roma', *Studi*, 272-8.

[128]Brenda M. Bolton, '*Via Ascetica*: A Papal Quandary?', *Studies in Church History* 22 (1985):161-91, esp. 175-81.

[129]Reg. 7:167, pp. 294-5; Cristina Carbonetti Vendittelli, ed., *Le più antiche carte del convento di San Sisto in Roma (905-1300)* (Rome, 1987), 28-104.

tiny with perhaps four to six nuns in each, often not strictly enclosed.[130] Nor were they rich – rather their desire to sell their lands represented their need for money on which to live collectively. Innocent was well aware of the wish for individual but not collective poverty of the monks and nuns of Rome. The *Gesta*, therefore, places them amongst the principal recipients of his gifts.[131] There is also frequent help for other religious men and women who were leading the lives of hermits and recluses.

When Innocent's drastic intervention of 1204 halted all these economic ventures by the convents of Rome, it was a move towards the ultimate objective which he formulated in 1207. His aim then was to unite all the nuns on one site, from which they could develop their religious life under one unified rule.[132] Innocent had already made such a move far from Rome. In 1201, he had encouraged diverse groups of missionaries in Livonia, both monks and canons regular, to unite into one religious community with uniform habits and observance to foster the apostolic ideal.[133] Now, in Rome, amongst women, Innocent wished to impose a stricter observance to adapt them in the most perfect way to their religious life. It seems that Innocent had thought of entrusting the care and supervision of the new convent to the canons of the Order of Sempringham, whose founder, Gilbert, he had canonized in 1202.[134] With its double congregation of nuns and regular canons, this English order must have seemed particularly well adapted to the spiritual guidance of women. Innocent envisaged at San Sisto a house capable of containing at least sixty nuns. How then did he propose to fill this imposing new building? The great new convent on the Via Appia would recruit, at least in part, from amongst the nuns of the older Roman foundations, but their numbers were not great, probably not more than eighty in all seven or eight convents.[135] So the rest would be drawn from those with new vocations – pious women already living in communities without an explicit religious profession and without having embraced a formal rule of life. There were many such women and it was Innocent's desire to find a place for them within the church. It was on behalf of these women that Jacques de Vitry, the well-known preacher, made his hazardous journey from the diocese of Liège to the curia at

---

[130]Koudelka, 'Le *Monasterium Tempuli*', 46-8.

[131]*Gesta*, CXLIII, cols cxcix-cc.

[132]Maccarrone, *Studi*, 272-8; Koudelka, 'Le *Monasterium Tempuli*', 38-46.

[133]M.-H. Vicaire, 'Vie commune et apostolat missionaire: Innocent III et la mission de Livonie', *Mélanges M.-D. Chenu* (Paris, 1967), 451-66; Maccarrone, *Studi*, 262-72 and esp. 334-7.

[134]Raymonde Foreville and Gillian Keir, eds, *The Book of St Gilbert*, Oxford Medieval Texts (Oxford, 1987), 245-53.

[135]Koudelka, 'Le *Monasterium Tempuli*', 46-8. These were S. Andrea in Biberatica, S. Agnese, S. Ciriaco, S. Maria in Campo Marzo, S. Maria *in Tempuli*, S. Bibiana and S. Maria in Maxima.

Perugia to ask Innocent for help and approval.[136] He arrived a day too late. Innocent was dead and San Sisto remained empty.

The building of San Sisto and the programme that this project had symbolized for Innocent was highly relevant to Dominic and to Bishop Fulk of Toulouse.[137] Indeed, Dominic was already founder of a convent for converted women at Prouille and Fulk its benefactor. Innocent himself had taken Prouille into papal protection in 1215 and when Fulk and Dominic were together in Rome in November of that year, it is quite possible that they saw the recently completed great church and the new convent of San Sisto in the process of reconstruction. But it was not until 1217 when Dominic was once again in Rome, and there was still no cloistered community for nuns, that he may have drawn the attention of Innocent's successor, Honorius III, to the desolate condition of the rebuilt church and cloister which were still awaiting the nuns for whom Innocent had planned the building. Action followed.[138] The nuns were finally housed in 1221.

Much of Innocent's expenditure seems to have been on those monasteries in the Patrimony, in particular, the northern Cistercian house of S. Martino *al Cimino* and the great abbeys of Fossanova and Casamari to the south of Rome.[139] In the course of the twelfth century, a close alliance had developed between the papacy and the Cistercian Order. Not only had popes been able to work with these monks to stimulate crusading zeal and to attack heresy but Innocent particularly approved of the Cistercian system of affiliation, mutual visitation and the institution of the Annual General Chapter of all abbots. At the Fourth Lateran Council, he even instituted this chapter for all other Benedictines and Augustinians.[140] Cistercian abbots had served him well on commissions of enquiry and he, in turn, fostered their houses. Most spectacular amongst his acts of generosity to the Cistercians of the Patrimony was that to the abbey of S. Martino *al Cimino*, in the sensitive region close to the heretical city of Viterbo.[141] Whereas the general chapter itself seems to have taken the decision in 1207 or 1208 to abandon this monastery, Innocent, 'wishing rather to encourage the spread of religion than

---

[136]R. B. C. Huygens, *Lettres de Jacques de Vitry (1160/70), évêque de Saint-Jean d'Acre* (Leiden, 1960), 71-8.

[137]Brenda M. Bolton, 'Fulk of Toulouse: the Escape That Failed', *Studies in Church History* 12 (1975):83-93; Patrice Cabau, 'Foulque, marchand et troubadour de Marseille, moine et abbé du Thoronet, évêque de Toulouse (v. 1155/1160 - 25.12.1231)', in *Les cisterciens de Languedoc (xiiie-xive s.)*, Cahiers de Fanjeaux, 21 (Toulouse, 1986), 151-79.

[138]Bolton, 'Daughters of Rome', 113-15.

[139]*I Cisterciensi e il Lazio*, Atti delle giornate di studio dell'Istituto di Storia dell'Arte dell'Università di Roma, 17-21 Maggio 1977 (Rome, 1978).

[140]Norman Tanner, ed., *Decrees of the Ecumenical Councils*, 2 vols (London-Washington, 1990), 1:240-1.

[141]Brenda M. Bolton, 'For the See of Simon Peter: the Cistercians at Innocent III's Nearest Frontier', *Papal Authority*, art. II, pp. 1-20.

to see it removed completely' from such a strategically-placed frontier monastery, stepped in with his offer of the then vast sum of 1000 pounds to redeem its possessions and pay off its debts.[142]

To the south of the Patrimony, where the threat came not from heresy but from the long-lasting German occupation, Innocent was forced to rely mightily on two great Cistercian houses. To Fossanova near Priverno astride the Via Appia, Innocent gave 100 pounds for the completion of its conventual church, begun in 1187, and he was to have the satisfaction of consecrating the high altar there with his own hands on 19 June 1208.[143] To Casamari, near Veroli, along the Via Latina and the Upper Liri Valley, he gave the huge sum of 200 ounces of gold *pro fabrica* to pay for the construction of the new church begun in 1203.[144] The work at Casamari was directed by the monk, William of Milan, and was completed by 1217 when Innocent's successor, Honorius III, consecrated the church.[145] The situation of both these monasteries at the southern limits of papal territory was significant in guarding the approaches to Rome from the Regno. Not for nothing did the papacy regard the Cistercians as the frontier guards of faith, and the monks here served the pope well on sensitive diplomatic missions.

While the Cistercians were the first real monastic order, self-regulating through the statutes of their chapters and with legislation to enforce unanimity, some older Benedictine houses, not being so regulated, posed grave problems. A little detective work may help to make the point. A brief entry in the *Gesta* Gift List for the monastery of Subiaco records a fragmentary offering – 'a chasuble of . . ., a red silk vestment and 30 pounds' income'.[146] Subiaco was (and is) the site of two monasteries, one dedicated to St Benedict and his sister, Scholastica, today known as S. Scholastica, and the other, the Sacro Speco or 'very narrow cave' where Benedict himself had spent three years before moving on to found Monte Cassino. Innocent visited Subiaco, some forty miles from Rome, with his curia from mid-July to mid-September 1202 to avoid the heat of summer.[147] This visit was, however, to play a vital part in the pope's ideas on monastic reform, and its outcome is enshrined in the decretal *Cum ad Monasterium* which was included in Gregory IX's collection.[148]

At S. Scholastica, Innocent was most disturbed by the secular intervention and lax, undisciplined life of the monks.[149] They did not give hospitality as they ought

---

[142]PL 215:1309-12; *Gesta*, CXXVI, cols clxii-clxiv and CXLV, ccviii, ccxxvii.
[143]PL 215:1435-7;*Gesta*, CXLIX, col. ccxxvii.
[144]*Gesta*, CXLV, ccviii.
[145]F. Farina and B. Fornari, *L'architettura cistercense e l'abbazia di Casamari* (Frosinone, 1978).
[146]*Gesta* CXLIV, cols ccix-ccx.
[147]R. Morghen, ed., *Chronicon Sublacense (593-1369)* (Rome, 1991), 213-19.
[148]X 3.35.6 in Emil Friedberg, ed., *Corpus Iuris Canonici*, 2 vols (Leipzig, 1879), 2, cols 599-600.
[149]Reg. 5:80 (81), pp. 156-60.

but he was specially concerned by their possession of private property, legislated against so strictly by St Benedict in Chapter 33 of his Rule.[150] The prohibition against private property was repeated by Innocent in the strongest terms. Any monk caught with personal possessions in his lifetime was to be expelled from the monastery. Worse still, if, after his death, a monk was to have had property or possessions, then Innocent invoked the punishment laid down by Gregory the Great in his *Dialogues*, that the offending monk should be buried in a dung heap outside the monastery.[151]

In *Cum ad Monasterium*, Innocent recognized the important role a monastery should play within a local community. To ensure the provision of hospitality as the Rule required and remedy the deficiencies at Subiaco, Innocent granted as a gift to the monks additional grain from one mill for alms for the poor.[152] Certain churches, assigned as benefices to the local clergy, were to be given back to the monastery and the almoner was instructed to use the income to help the sick. The inherent weakness of the Rule of St Benedict was the autonomy it allowed. This meant that, if the abbot was weak or neglectful, his abbacy could bring disaster. But Innocent was aware that spiritual success also depended upon practical means, in addition to strong leadership. Without making any reference to any particular property and aware of the great patrimony of the abbey, he underlined the need for additional food supplies and the return of benefices in order that the monastery could fulfil its function. The Gift List reveals his concern by giving to S. Scholastica a chasuble and a small income.[153]

The *Chronicon Sublacense* records Innocent's visit and repeats exactly the wording of his letter. However, the chronicler provides additional details – listing the pope's five points of reform: property, silence, the eating of meat, the lack of hospitality and of care for the sick. He then adds that the monks themselves were to have at least two meals a day and that the pope himself had instructed that the income from *Castro Murano* should be set aside for these meals. Should the income be in excess, then it was to be used to provide a third meal. It seems that Innocent had also assigned from other income of the monastery money for clothing so that each brother should receive a cowl, scapula, tunic and cloak, a new cowl every four years and a new cloak every two. Thus, this apparently small gift by the pope appears to have eased the burden of the monks of S. Scholastica, as he must have hoped.[154]

---

[150] J. McCann, ed., *The Rule of St Benedict* (London, 1952), 84-7.
[151] Reg. 5:81, p. 158; *Chronicon Sublacense*, 216.
[152] *Chronicon Sublacense*, 214-15.
[153] *Gesta*, CXLIV, col. ccix, 'Monasterio Sublacensi, unam planetam de . . .'.
[154] *Chronicon Sublacense*, 218.

However, perhaps Innocent's most important gift – tiny but by no means insignificant – is not mentioned in the Gift List but must be reconstructed from a papal letter. On 1 September 1202, while still at Subiaco, Innocent wrote to the prior and brothers of the small community of *Lo Speco*, the upper monastery.[155] In his letter, he reminds them that, having come to the Holy Cave out of devotion, he had found the monks living a holy life there and observing that spiritual discipline enjoined by St Benedict. In addition, he writes of his concern that their spiritual observance should suffer from a lack of temporal support. Hence, he grants them and their successors six pounds annually from the treasury of St Peter's for their sustenance, pointing out that his gift will enable the monks of the Sacro Speco to live independently of the lower monastery of S. Scholastica.

A gift of such importance required clarification, and Innocent reveals in a letter of 24 February 1203, that, following his visit the previous year, Prior John and the brothers of *Lo Speco* had journeyed to Rome to ask the Pope to stipulate the origin of the six pounds they had been promised to ensure their independence from S. Scholastica.[156] Innocent met their request by conceding to them six pounds from the income of *Castro Porziano*. On 3 February 1217, the year after Innocent's death, Honorius III confirmed the donation from *Castro Porziano* to *Lo Speco*[157] and it was reconfirmed in 1227 by Gregory IX.[158] In 1236, Gregory wrote to the bailiffs of Porziano, commanding them to pay the six pounds in money, not in kind, and this injunction was repeated in 1256 by Alexander IV.[159] Subsequent popes had thus ensured the practical needs of the Holy Cave, a small gift first given by Innocent, but one which allowed his spiritual message to continue.

In addition to the gifts on what I have called 'The Gift List', the *Gesta* and other sources contain details of gifts both given and received by the pope. To the individual concerned, the fact that the pope was involved was of particular and special significance, no matter what the status of the participant. These gifts might be part of the diplomatic niceties of the time, features of significant ecclesiastical relationships, special rewards for service carried out or supplications made.

Certain examples are of interest. On 29 May 1198, Innocent wrote to Richard I of England.[160] The pope's letter was accompanied by a gift of four gold rings,

---

[155]Reg. 5:77 (78), pp. 152-3.

[156]Reg. 6:1, pp. 3-4.

[157]V. Federici, 'Dei documenti pubblici e privati dei monasteri Sublacensi', in *I Monasteri di Subiaco*, 2 vols (Rome, 1904) 2, CCLXII.

[158]Ibid., CCLXXVI.

[159]Ibid., CCXXXXII and CCCXXXXVIII.

[160]Reg. 1:206, pp. 295-7; C. R. Cheney and W. H. Semple, eds, *Selected Letters of Pope Innocent III concerning England (1198-1216)* (London, 1953), 1-2.

each one set with different jewels, the significance of which the king was to interpret in a spiritual sense – through shape, number, material and colour. The roundness of the rings was to indicate eternity, the transition from temporal to spiritual things. The number four represented the four main virtues – justice, courage, prudence and temperance. Gold was wisdom, for as gold excels all other metals, so wisdom is superior to all other gifts, as Solomon had shown in requesting it so that he could wisely govern his people. For Innocent, the greenness of an emerald represented faith; the clearness of the sapphire hope; the redness of the garnet charity, and the radiance of the topaz the practice of good works. While Innocent always enjoyed giving advice to kings, this letter to Richard was repeated in identical terms to King John in 1205. It thus may have represented a papal acknowledgement of their joint support for Otto of Bruns-wick.[161] In February 1206, Philip Augustus also received a sapphire as a gift from the pope.[162] The lesson that the French king was supposed to draw from this was that Innocent had hope in him.

In another section of the *Gesta*, one particular gift is detailed as being from Innocent, but not quite so straightforwardly as others on the Gift List.[163] The pope was faced by a moral dilemma. Conrad of Querfurt, formerly bishop of Hilde-sheim, had presumed to translate himself to the see of Wurzburg.[164] Following a four-year battle, by the end of which he had been excommunicated, Conrad was eventually persuaded to come to Rome. Bare-footed and without his pallium, he prostrated himself on the ground to ask and receive forgiveness.[165] On returning to Germany, he sent some very beautiful silver vases to the pope. Innocent was, according to his biographer, briefly taken aback, 'hesitating as to whether he ought to accept the gifts or refuse them'.[166] Eventually Innocent accepted the present but 'lest Conrad should think that he could be corrupted by the giving of a gift, he sent back a precious gold cup, worth more than all the silver ones put together'.

That Conrad's gift was far more generous than most and, therefore, unrepresen-tative of the usual gifts made by bishops can be seen at the other end of the scale in regard to Bishop Wolfger of Passau.[167] It is relevant to gifts at the time of Innocent, since it is dated 1203-1204 and is in the bishop's travelling account

[161]Thomas Rymer, *Foedera, conventiones, litterae . . .*, 10 vols (The Hague, 1739-45), 1:139.

[162]*Les Registres de Philippe Auguste*, John W. Baldwin, Francoise Gaspari, Michel Nortier and Elisabeth Lalou, eds, 1 (Paris, 1992):231. 'Item 27. De papa 1 saphirum'. I am most grateful to Professor Baldwin for bringing this gift to my attention.

[163]*Gesta*, XLIV, cols lxxxvii-lxxxviii.

[164]K. Pennington, *Popes, Canonists and Texts*, art. III, pp. 20-2.

[165]*Gesta*, XLIV, col. lxxxviii, 'prosternens se totum in terram, in modum crucis manus expandit'.

[166]Ibid., 'haesitans utrum deberet illa recipere, an potius refutare'.

[167]Wolfger, bishop of Passau (1191-1204), patriarch of Aquileia (1204-).

with its own little gift list.[168] Wolfger is justly famous for his gift of a fur coat to Walter von der Vogelweide[169] but his other gifts, such as twenty-nine pennies to a bald apostate from Einsdorf and a talent to the *jongleur* Flordamor at Bologna, might just indicate a soft heart. Wolfger became patriarch of Aquileia – not, of course, as a direct result of his gift-giving, although such gifts were undoubtedly exchanged between bishops as a mark of friendship or appreciation as well as to indicate spiritual meanings.

The *Gesta* makes reference to an episode of gift-giving which surrounded the submission to Innocent of Kalojan, king of Bulgaria, in November 1204 and his acceptance of Catholic Christianity.[170] Innocent sent to Basil, archbishop of Trnovo and primate of the Bulgarians, a chasuble, dalmatic and white silk tunic, a great ring with five topazes (indicating the practice of good works), a mitre, camice, amice, stole, girdle, stockings, sandals, gloves and other ornaments which patriarchs ought to have.[171] In return, Kalojan sent Innocent two silk vestments,[172] one red and one white and a *camelus*[173] which may have been another vestment or even a goblet. Whatever it was, it came accompanied by two children, boys called Basil and Bethlehem, entrusted by Kalojan to Innocent so that they could be taught Latin. More conventionally, Peter king of Aragon was likewise fitted out with the regalia and symbols of his office when he came to Rome in November 1205.[174] Although these were the formal gifts of diplomacy, each one had a deeper spiritual meaning which the pope, as usual, was not slow to point out.

At the time of the deposition in the papal archives of the full *Gesta* collection in Vat. lat. 12111, Innocent's *Commentary on the Seven Penitential Psalms* appeared.[175] This *Commentary* occurs in some eight manuscripts, from one of which it is clear that although it was Innocent's last work, he must have been working on it for some time before its completion on Holy Saturday, 9 April 1216.[176] The question arises as to whether Innocent might have regarded it as a consequential complement to his Gift List. The *Commentary* links together the motives for gifts and alms whereas repentance requires confession and penance

---

[168]Helen Waddell, *The Wandering Scholars* (London, 1927), 236-8.

[169]Ibid., 237, 'xiij den. Waltero de Vogelweide pro pellico v. sol. longos'.

[170]*Gesta*, LXV-LXXXII, cols cxxv-cxxxi.

[171]*Gesta*, CXLIV, col. ccix.

[172]August Theiner, ed., *Vetera Monumenta Slavorum Meridionalium Historiam Illustrantia. I, 1198-1549* (Rome, 1863), XL, p. 39.

[173]E. Piltz, *Kamelaukion et Mitra: insignes byzantins imperiaux et ecclesiastiques* (Stockholm, 1977), 19-21, which makes clear that *camelaucus* is a vestment.

[174]*Gesta*, CXX, cols clix-clxi.

[175]PL 217:967-1130.

[176]Vatican City, Vat. lat. 699, f. 86; Maccarrone, *Studi*, 123-6.

with true forgiveness coming only from God, and, therefore, the most important thing was to be right with God. In return for the giving of gifts, no reward should be expected or sought. His view on the place of penance, related indulgences and God's forgiveness seems to have been somewhat at variance with or even omitted from Canon 62 of the Fourth Lateran Council.[177] This must have concerned him considerably and the *Commentary on the Seven Penitential Psalms* may have been the result.

In this context, Innocent, realizing how his motives for giving the gifts on his Gift List might be misunderstood, used the Penitential Psalms to show that forgiveness would come from God and not as a reward for any gift-giving. The reason for the giving of gifts was different.

In conclusion, this portrayal of Innocent's spiritual motivation is atypical amongst historians. Since the subtitles of many books on Innocent III consistently follow the more traditional views, they perhaps emphasize too much that he was all-powerful or at least that he sought to be so. From the nineteenth century to the present day, sub-titles have followed the line from 'Lord of the World'[178] to 'Leader of Europe'.[179] In both these and other works this concentration on his eminence disguises the man of faith and spirituality which indeed Innocent was. To be entirely concerned with his powerful status, with here and there a concession to other facets of his activities, leaves out an important part of his pontificate. The proper understanding of Innocent has suffered thereby. Many of those who have written about him have been attracted by his status, his power and his law-making, in the context of the events of the time as they saw them. This excludes the prospect of a really balanced assessment of the true Innocent. It is to be regretted that Innocent's real intentions have been so neglected. This examination, using the Gift List as a tool, attempts to give a different view of the pontificate. It may be useful as a contribution to a qualitative historical analysis, but, more importantly, it may reveal how Rome and the Romans at the beginning of the thirteenth century benefited from a pope who was trying to make the gospel work in the world of the time.

---

[177] Tanner, *Decrees*, 1:263-4.

[178] James M. Powell, ed., *Innocent III: Vicar of Christ or Lord of the World?*, 1st edn (Boston, 1963) and 2nd expanded edn (Washington DC, 1994).

[179] Jane Sayers, *Innocent III: Leader of Europe 1198-1216* (London, 1994).

The *Coarb* of Peter: Innocent III and Irish Monasticism

Gillian Murphy

The *Annals of Inisfallen* for 1202 report that 'the cardinal of the *coarb* of Peter came this year to reform the men of Ireland'.[1] The cardinal was John of Salerno, cardinal-priest of St Stephen on the Celian Hill, and the *coarb* of Peter was Innocent III. A *coarb* is an heir or successor and is a title used to refer to Irish abbots who were themselves often the heirs of the founding saints of their monasteries. The purpose of this paper is to conduct an investigation into the connection between Innocent III and Irish monasticism.

Even as a youth, Innocent may have been aware that a small community of Irish monks was living in Rome. Directly opposite the monastery of S. Andrea on the Celian Hill, where Innocent may well have been educated, was SS. Trinitatis *Scottorum*.[2] Listed by both John the Deacon and Peter Mallius as amongst one of the most important monastic institutions of Rome in the mid-twelfth century,[3] this house for the *Scotti*, as the Irish abroad were known, was located on the south-east corner of the Palatine Hill. The discovery of this Irish community was made by Dom Wilmart when he examined a Vatican codex (Lat. 378) which had

---

[1]Seán MacAirt, ed., *Annals of Inisfallen* (Dublin, 1951), 331. I would like to thank Brenda Bolton for her encouragement and all her helpful suggestions.
[2]G. Ferrari, *Early Roman Monasteries: Notes for the History of the Monasteries and Convents at Rome from V through the X Century* (Rome, 1957), 333-5.
[3]John the Deacon, *Descriptio Lateranensis Ecclesiae*, and Peter Mallius, *Descripto Basilicae Vaticanae*, in *Codice Topografico della Città di Roma*, R. Valentini and G. Zucchetti, eds, 3 (Rome, 1946):362, 439.

formerly belonged to the monastery of S. Maria in Pallara.[4] This manuscript listed the brethren of a small community – SS. Trinitatis – at the end of the eleventh century, inhabited then by Columbanus, Mauricius, Felix, Donatus and Malchus, names which are common in Irish ecclesiastical history.[5] His possible early contacts with the *Scotti* must, however, have made an enduring impression since he was to show special favour to their communities in Bavaria, Franconia and Austria by granting the privileged and independent status of a *Schottenkongregation*.[6]

Innocent's knowledge of Irish monasticism and how Ireland was incorporated into his aims to reform the church and its exempt monasteries are relatively untouched areas. Scholars such as Gwynn, Watt and Ó Fiaich have contributed greatly to our knowledge of Irish ecclesiastical history but they do not deal with the pontificate of Innocent and Ireland in any depth.[7] P. J. Dunning has concentrated on Innocent's political correspondence and letters on juridical and administrative matters concerning Ireland.[8] Helpful though his work is, a different approach will be adopted here by concentrating specifically on Irish monasticism. Much detective work has had to be undertaken since, of the seventy or so letters addressed to Ireland by Innocent, only twelve are to monasteries, and these are primarily concerned with routine matters of protection and confirmation of privileges.[9]

So what of Innocent, the island of Ireland and of monastic life there? The pope's knowledge of Ireland may have been coloured by his conversations with the brilliant, witty and sarcastic failed bishop, Gerald of Wales (1146-1223). Gerald visited Ireland twice, in 1183 and 1185, and recounted his experiences in lurid detail. From his *Topographia Hibernica* (1188)[10] and *Expugnatio Hibernica*

---

[4]A. Wilmart, 'La Trinité des Scots à Rome et les notes du Vat. Lat. 378', *Revue Bénédictine* 41 (1929):218-30.

[5]Ibid., 229-30.

[6]G. Renz, 'Beiträge zur Geschicht der Schottenabtei St Jakob und des Priorats Weih Sankt Peter in Regensburg', *Studien und Mitteilungen aus dem Benediktiner und Cistercienser Orden* 16 (1895): 258; J. P. Fuhrmann, *Irish Medieval Monasteries on the Continent* (Washington DC, 1927), 102.

[7]A. Gwynn, *The Irish Church in the Eleventh and Twelfth Centuries* (Dublin, 1992); J. A. Watt, *The Church and the Two Nations in Medieval Ireland* (Cambridge, 1970); T. Ó Fiaich, 'Irish Monks in Germany in the Late Middle Ages', *The Church, Ireland and the Irish, Studies in Church History* 25 (1989):89-104.

[8]*The Pontificate of Innocent III and Ireland*, unpublished PhD thesis, University of Dublin, 1960; 'Pope Innocent III and the Ross Election Controversy', *Irish Theological Quarterly* 26 (1956):346-59; 'Pope Innocent III and the Waterford-Lismore Controversy', *Irish Theological Quarterly* 28 (1961):215-32; 'Irish Representatives and Irish Ecclesiastical Affairs at the Fourth Lateran Council', in *Medieval Studies presented to A. Gwynn*, J. A. Watt, J. B. Morrall and F. X. Martin, eds (Dublin, 1961), 90-113.

[9]P. J. Dunning, 'The Letters of Innocent III to Ireland', *Traditio* 17 (1962):229-53 at 251-3.

[10]R. Bartlett, *Gerald of Wales 1146-1223* (Oxford, 1982), 213.

(1189),[11] it is clear that Gerald regarded the Irish as 'a wild and inhospitable people',[12] and at their worst 'filthy and wallowing in vice'.[13] Gerald could have relayed these feelings to Innocent on one of his three journeys to Rome between 1199 and 1203 when he claims to have often had occasion to talk with the pope. Innocent could have been left in no doubt where Gerald's preference lay. Indeed, on his visit to the curia in 1199, Gerald even boasted that he had presented his own books as gifts whilst others had brought only money.[14] The Welshman proudly stated that Innocent kept his books by the papal bedside and did not want to part with them.[15] Surely Innocent's knowledge of Ireland must have been enhanced by such lively bedtime reading!

More up-to-date and certainly less biased information would have reached Innocent through the vegetarian and 'tee-totaller' Cardinal John of Salerno,[16] legate to Ireland between 1202 to 1203.[17] It is significant that Innocent dispatched his legate at the beginning of his pontificate, perhaps to get a more balanced view than he had received from Gerald of Wales.

Innocent was well aware of problems in the Irish church. His letters to Ireland provide ample evidence that prelates were too involved in temporal matters and that hereditary succession to ecclesiastical office was still prevalent.[18] He wished to eradicate both these vices from the Irish church and John of Salerno briefed him on these issues. Various Irish annals record that this cardinal held two synods in 1202, one in Dublin for foreign and Gaelic clerics and another, held at Athlone a fortnight later, for the laity and clergy of Connacht.[19] Innocent wrote to John of Salerno on 20 February 1203 and denounced the *enormitates* in the Irish church, which 'enormities' his legate had found especially in Tuam and other parts of the country.[20]

---

[11]Ibid., 215.

[12]Gerald of Wales, *The History and Topography of Ireland*, trans. J. O'Meara (London, 1982), 101.

[13]Ibid., 106.

[14]'Praesentant vobis alii libras sed nos libros', J. Brewer, ed., *Giraldus Cambrensis Opera*, 8 vols, RS 21/1 (1861):119; Michael Richter, *Giraldus Cambrensis: the Growth of the Welsh Nation* (Aberystwyth, 1972), 122.

[15]H. Tillmann, *Innocent III* (Bonn, 1954), 293. *Giraldus Cambrensis Opera*, 1:119.

[16]'Praedictus vero Johannes non manducavit carnem; vinum et siceram non bibit.' W. Stubbs, ed., *The Chronicle of Roger of Howden*, 4 vols, RS, 51/4 (1871):175.

[17]Maleczek, *Papst*, 107-9.

[18]Reg. 1:364, pp. 548-551; PL 214:342, dated 17 September 1198; M. P. Sheehy, ed., *Pontificia Hibernica: Medieval Papal Chancery Documents Concerning Ireland*, 2 vols (Dublin, 1962-5), 1:93.

[19]W. Hennessy, ed., *Annals of Loch Cé*, 2 vols (Dublin, 1871), 1:223; B. MacCarthy, ed., *Annals of Ulster*, 4 vols (Dublin, 1893), 2:239.

[20]'Litterarum perlecto tenore quas ad nostram destinasti presentiam intelleximus evidenter quod inter alias enormitates quas in ecclesiis Yberniensibus invenisti hanc detestabilem abusionem presertim in ecclesia Tuamensi et in partibus aliis cognovisti vigere quod non solum in minoribus prelaturis verum etiam in archiepiscopatibus et episcopatibus inmediate filii patribus succedebant', PL 214:1172;

How then was Innocent to deal with these problems? It was to the Cistercians that he now turned. He held them in enormous respect, referring to them as 'the best of monks'.[21] Their originality lay in their unique constitution which influenced all subsequent orders.[22] The Cistercians claimed to follow literally the Rule of St Benedict and in order to counter the autonomy allowed by this Rule, they created a strong federal framework which ensured uniform observance throughout all their houses. This uniformity depended upon a two-fold supervision. They held an annual General Chapter at Cîteaux on the Feast of the Exaltation of the Holy Cross (14 September), which all abbots were obliged to attend, whilst a highly regulated system of filiation existed between mother and daughter houses ensuring visitation and oversight.[23]

Mellifont, situated near Dublin, was a daughter-house of Cîteaux. It was the first Cistercian monastery in Ireland, founded in 1142 by St Malachy, friend of St Bernard.[24] Within six years of this foundation, five further daughter-houses were established.[25] By the end of the century this number had increased to thirty-seven, but four of these were to fail by 1228.[26]

Ireland presented particular problems which were to cause many difficulties for the Cistercians. Indeed, the Statutes of the General Chapter at Cîteaux provide examples of this. For instance, they record the frequency of Irish abbots defaulting from their duty to attend the General Chapter.[27] In 1190, it was decreed that Irish abbots should come only once every four years but this was to be in rotation to ensure that Ireland was represented each year.[28] In 1195, Irish abbots were obtaining privileges and yet were failing to come to the General Chapter to seek its approval.[29] The Chapter of 1196 punished the unnamed offenders by excluding them from the abbatial stall for forty days.[30] They were also to perform

---

Sheehy, *Pontificia Hibernica*, 1:121.

[21]'Cum inter omnes religiosos nostri temporis viros Cisterciensis et Carthusiensis ordinum fratres magna per Dei gratiam polleant honestate . . .', PL 216:469, letter of 11 October 1212.

[22]C. H. Lawrence, *Medieval Monasticism* (London, 1989), 176.

[23]Ibid., 187-8.

[24]A. Gwynn and R. N. Hadcock, *Medieval Religious Houses: Ireland* (London, 1970), 115.

[25]Bective (1147), Inislounaght (1148), Baltinglass (1148), Monasteranenagh (1148) and Grellachdinach (1148), ibid., 123-43.

[26]Ibid., 117, 121-3.

[27]J. M. Canivez, ed., *Statuta Capitulorum Generalium Ordinis Cisterciensis*, 1 (Louvain, 1933):351 (1208), 400 (1212), 437 (1215), 449 (1216), 457 (1216), 488 (1218); C. Colmcille, *The Story of Mellifont* (Dublin, 1958), 43-7.

[28]'Abbates de Hibernia tribus annis remaneant et quarto anno veniant, et ita ordinet abbas Mellifontis ut aliqui eorum veniant singulis annis ad Capitulum.' Canivez, *Statuta Capitulorum*, 122. This was modified in 1195; see 196.

[29]Canivez, *Statuta Capitulorum*, 196.

[30]Ibid., 204.

six days in *levi culpa* or light punishment, one day of which was to be on bread and water.

From the beginning of his pontificate, Innocent had held the Cistercian Order in high regard and acknowledged the power and potential of Cistercian organization, which could benefit Benedictines and Augustinians alike.[31] Major disciplinary problems concerning the Irish Cistercians occurred mainly after Innocent's pontificate. He did not write to any Cistercian house in Ireland and so must have been confident that this Order could regulate itself with its system of General Chapters, diffinitors and visitation between mother- and daughter-houses. There was, therefore, no need to interfere with their methods of imposing uniformity in Ireland.

Ireland was also home to the Arrouaisian canons of the Augustinian Order, brought there by St Malachy in the 1140s.[32] Gerald of Wales had comments to make about this order, especially in Armagh. In his *Speculum Ecclesiae*,[33] a work envisaged in 1191 but not finished until 1220,[34] Gerald showed his disgust that no wall separated the double communities of monks and nuns but only branches and blackthorn bushes, and so liaison between the two sections was easy. Gerald looked to the Gilbertines as a model of reform because, as he claimed, this order had achieved almost complete separation between monks and nuns within their double houses.[35] On 9 December 1200, Innocent sent directions to the archbishops of Armagh and Tuam and abbots, priors and canons of the Arrouaisian Order in Ireland stressing that representatives should be sent to the annual General Chapter at Arrouaise in France.[36] This must have been a precursor for Innocent's intentions for the regular clergy in general. Moreover, Innocent must have been assured that Ireland was in good hands under the Arrouaisian canons, who, like the Cistercians, could adequately deal with problems of discipline through their General Chapters.

Innocent's graver problems stemmed from the exempt and autonomous houses of the Old Benedictines. In the summer of 1202, he stayed at Subiaco near Rome and visited the two monasteries there. He had much praise for the upper monastery of Sacro Speco but witnessed grave abuses at the sister monastery of

---

[31]PL 214:334; Canivez, *Statuta Capitulorum*, 221-4.

[32]Gwynn and Hadcock, *Religious Medieval Houses*, 149.

[33]*Giraldus Cambrensis Opera*, 4:183.

[34]Bartlett, *Gerald of Wales*, 220.

[35]*Giraldus Cambrensis Opera*, 4:184.

[36]PL 217:67; Pott. 1189; Sheehy, *Pontificia Hibernica*, 1:112. See also P. Dunning, 'The Arrouaisian Order in Medieval Ireland', *Irish Historical Studies* 4 (1945):297-315.

Santa Scholastica.[37] Innocent believed that the root of the Benedictine problem was possession of personal property. The decretal *Cum ad monasterium* of 24 February 1203 was issued to reform this monastery and became part of his programme of reform for monasticism as a whole.[38] Already on 15 February 1203, Innocent had seized the initiative and ordered the heads of monastic houses to gather together in six provincial chapters in order to improve the discipline in those monasteries which were immediately subject to the Holy See.[39] These houses were exempt from episcopal control and were in a bad state both spiritually and temporally.[40] The only chapter of the six for which a record has survived was that held at Perugia.[41] The plan of 1203 did not materialize into a permanent institution, but Innocent still did not abandon his aim. In November 1208, another limited apostolic visitation was organized throughout Tuscany and even extended to Viterbo and Rieti.[42]

Up to this point, Innocent had omitted the German Benedictines from his plans for monastic reform. However, from studying the collection of documents by Renz, it is apparent that the Irish Benedictine monasteries founded from St James of Regensburg recognized the potential of the General Chapter and this is why they called a meeting of all their abbots at Regensburg in 1211.[43]

Links between Ireland and Regensburg went back to 1067, when St Marianus set out on pilgrimage from Ireland to Rome with two companions.[44] Reaching Germany, the three stayed at Bamberg and then moved to Regensburg. In 1076, the Benedictine abbess of Obermünster gave them the priory of Weih-Sankt-Peter outside the city walls, and by the end of the century the community had grown

---

[37]Pott. 1734; B. Bolton, 'Via Ascetica: A Papal Quandary', in *Monks, Hermits and Ascetic Tradition, Studies in Church History* 22 (1985):161-91 at 178; U. Berlière, 'Innocent III et la réorganisation des monastères Bénédictins', *Revue Bénédictine* 32 (1920):22-42 at 40.

[38]PL 214:1064-6; Pott. 1734.

[39]'. . . monasteria per Tusciam, Marchiam et ducatum Spoletanum constituta, *nullo medio* ad Romanum Ecclesiam pertinentia', G. B. Mittarelli and G. D. Costadoni, eds, *Annalium Camaldulensium* (Venice, 1759), 254-5; PL 214:1173-4; Pott. 1843; M. Maccarrone, *Studi su Innocenzo III*, Italia Sacra 17 (Padova, 1972):328-9; U. Berlière, 'Innocent III et la réorganisation des monastères bénédictins', *Revue Bénédictine* 32 (1920):145-59 at 156-9, and 'Les Chapitres Généraux de l'ordre de S. Benoît avant le IV Concile de Latran (1215)', *Revue Bénédictine* 8 (1891):255-64 at 262-4; C.R. Cheney, *Pope Innocent III and England* (Stuttgart, 1976), 231-6.

[40]Bolton, 'Via Ascetica', 181. Provincial chapters were to be held at Perugia and Piacenza for north and central Italy, at Paris, Limoges and Cluny for France and in London for all English monasteries. Ireland was omitted, amongst others.

[41]Maccarrone, *Studi*, 330-4.

[42]PL 215:1490; Pott. 3539; Maccarrone, *Studi*, 242.

[43]Renz, 'Beiträge zur Geschicht', 255.

[44]A. Gwynn, 'The Continuity of the Irish Tradition at Würzburg', *Herbipolis Jubilans* (Würzburg, 1952), 57-81 at 61; Helmut Flachenecker, *Schottenklöster: Irische Benediktinerkonvente im hochmittelalterlichen Deutschland* (Munich, 1995).

considerably with the influx of monks from Ireland.[45] In February 1089, Emperor Henry IV (1084-1106) granted them a charter of protection which encouraged them to construct a larger monastery. This became known as St James at Regensburg and was consecrated in 1111.[46] It continued to expand during the twelfth and thirteenth centuries and established the following abbeys: St James in Würzburg (1134), St James in Erfurt (*c.* 1140), St Giles in Nuremburg (*c.* 1140), St James in Constance (1142), St Mary in Vienna (1156), Kiev (end of twelfth century),[47] Kelheim (1231) and two priories in Germany, Memmingen (1187) and Eichstätt (1194).[48] Würzburg founded two small priories in Ireland, one at Ross Carbery (*c.* 1134)[49] and the other at the Rock of Cashel (*c.* 1148),[50] as recruitment centres for Irish communities on the continent.

The papacy acknowledged the importance of the congregation of St James and issued bulls of protection. The bull of Lucius III, *Religiosam vitam eligentibus*, dated 10 April 1185,[51] confirmed grants made by Eugenius III (1145-53), Adrian IV (1154-1159) and Alexander III (1159-81). Celestine III (1191-1198) and Innocent followed this tradition.[52] The bull of Lucius had first defined the relationship of St James at Regensburg to its filiations. It further decreed that the abbots of all the Irish monasteries in Germany and Austria were to visit St James once a year for mutual counsel and receive advice on any irregularities they had incurred.[53] There is no evidence that these meetings took place until 1211.

Innocent III clarified the independence of the Irish *Schottenklöster* and placed the organization of all these monasteries on a firmer basis. Canon 12 of the Fourth Lateran Council, *In Singulis Regnis*, recognized the Cistercian General Chapter as an approved model and commended it to all monasteries lacking a similar organization of their own.[54] Abbots and priors of Benedictine and Augustinian houses of each province or kingdom were ordered to hold meetings

---

[45]D. A. Binchy, 'The Irish Benedictine Congregation in Medieval Germany', *Studies* 69 (1929):194-210 at 197.

[46]Ibid., 199.

[47]Kiev was abandoned in 1241. See Ó Fiaich, 'Irish Monks in Germany', 96.

[48]Renz, 'Beiträge zur Geschicht', 64-9. Other foundation dates are given by Gwynn in 'Some notes on the History of the Irish and Scottish Benedictine Monasteries in Germany', *Innes Review* 5 (1954):5-15 at 10, and by Ó Fiaich, 'Irish Monks in Germany', 94-5.

[49]Gwynn and Hadcock, *Religious Houses: Ireland*, 107.

[50]Ibid., 104.

[51]PL 201:1349; Renz, 'Beiträge zur Geschicht', 255.

[52]PL 206:1059 for the bull of Celestine III (1194); Renz, 'Beiträge zur Geschicht', 259 for Innocent's bull of protection.

[53]'. . . ubi et correctiones excessuum et instituta ordinis a vobis suscipiant humiliter et observent . . .', PL 201:1349.

[54]COD, 240-1; Maccarrone, *Studi*, 246-62; Bolton, 'Via Ascetica', 182.

every three years.[55]   Canon 12 ensured that the congregation of Benedictine monasteries was established on a national and territorial basis, but this posed a problem for the Irish Benedictines in Germany.[56] Innocent held these Irish monks in special favour and, at the Fourth Lateran Council, granted another and special bull which gave them independent status from the Benedictines. All monasteries founded from or dependent on St James at Regensburg, now or in the future, were incorporated into the *Schottenkongregation*.[57] The importance of Innocent's bull was to accommodate the unique fraternal relationship of the Irish *Schottenklöster* into his scheme for the Benedictines as a whole. The first General Chapter following Innocent's special bull was held on 28 July 1216, and nine abbots of the *Schottenkongregation* are recorded as attending.[58]

It has taken much routine detective work to show that Ireland, on the fringes of Christendom, was not neglected by the *coarb* of Peter. Innocent's knowledge of Irish ecclesiastical matters was formulated through conversations with Gerald of Wales and John of Salerno. One of Innocent's aims as pope was to reform the church,[59] and he believed this could be best accomplished by breaking down the autonomy of the old Benedictine and Augustinian houses.[60] Ireland and its monks, both at home and abroad, were to be incorporated into this scheme.

From the twelve letters of protection to Irish monastic houses, it would seem that Innocent was not much concerned with the condition of monasticism there. However, one of these letters was significant in that it was to the Arrouaisian canons in Ireland enjoining them to attend their General Chapter at Arrouaise. Innocent must have been confident that the Cistercians and Arrouaisians, with their unique system of General Chapters, were quite competent to regulate monastic discipline in Ireland. The implementation of the General Chapter was the crux of Innocent's policy for monastic life and the *Scotti* or Irish Benedictines in Germany were crucial to this scheme. The establishment of the *Schotten-kongregation* ensured that these monasteries had the means to correct disorders found therein. Moreover, this demonstrated Innocent's concern not to destroy the special fraternal bonds between these Irish houses. He well understood the uniqueness of their position so far from their mother-land. Indeed, the existence in Rome of the Irish community of SS. Trinitatis *Scottorum* must have been an almost daily reminder to him as he passed by the Palatine Hill. To deny

---

[55]Lawrence, *Medieval Monasticism*, 192.

[56]Fuhrmann, *Irish Medieval Monasteries*, 104.

[57]Renz, 'Beiträge zur Geschicht', 258.

[58]Ibid., 259.

[59]B. M. Bolton, 'Too Important to Neglect: *Gesta Innocentii III PP*', *Churches and Chronicle in Middle Ages: Essays Presented to John Taylor*, G. A. Loud and I. N. Wood, eds, (London, 1991), 87-99 at 93-4.

[60]PL 214:334; Canivez, *Statuta Capitulorum*, 221-4.

Innocent's interest, therefore, in Irish monasticism is greatly to undervalue the contribution made by this *coarb* of Peter.

Vision, Dream and Canonization Policy under Pope Innocent III

Michael Goodich

In the view of contemporaries Innocent III had been no stranger to the supernatural. The *Gesta Innocentii Tertii* reported that at the time of his elevation three
doves had appeared at the site where the cardinals were meeting. After he was
named, a white one flew above his head and sat down on his right, a sure sign of
divine election.[1] At the same time, someone reportedly had a vision that Innocent
had married his mother, namely mother church, while there were other revelations
that the newly elected pope did not want bandied about.[2] When during a drought
Innocent was dedicating the cathedral church at Spoleto in late August 1198, the
local citizens had searched about for a spot to dig where they could find water.
They suddenly saw water issuing forth from beneath a pit which had been covered
by a stone and were able to provide for their thirsty horses. In honor of the pope's
visit this was called the *Fons papalis*.[3]

In an apocryphal story found in Salimbene's *Cronica*, but without contemporary confirmation, the pope had reportedly been mocked during a sermon by a

---

[1]PL 214:xx (6). See Brenda M. Bolton, 'Too Important to Neglect: The Gesta Innocentii PP. III',
in *Church and Chronicle in the Middle Ages*, ed. G. A. Loud and I. N. Wood (London, 1991), 87-99,
on the value of this source. She argues that the work is based on papal registers, suggests close
personal contact with the pope and argues that it is therefore a major source for Innocent's reign. For
a recent edition, see David R. Gress-Wright, *The 'Gesta Innocentii III': Text, Introduction and
Commentary* (Bryn Mawr dissertation, 1981).

[2]Ibid.

[3]PL 214:xxvi (9). A letter of 21 August 1198 to the bishop of Bamberg places Innocent at Spoleto
(PL 214:306, no. 135; Pott. 352; Reg. 1:335, p. 495).

necromancer who had learned his art in Toledo.[4] The man boasted that he could
bring the dead back to life and command demons. Innocent secretly met at Rome
with the magician, who proceeded to bring the archbishop of Pietra Bismantova
back to life; the dead man was accompanied by small children, donkeys covered
with treasure, servants, knights and a multitude of chaplains. After the archbishop
reported that he had been damned because of his pride and vainglory, the vision
disappeared. Lutgard of Aywières told her biographer Thomas of Catimpré that
she had seen Innocent himself suffering the flames of purgatory shortly after his
death because of three ill-fated deeds.[5] But he was saved from the greater torture
of Hell through the Virgin's intercession due to his having built a monastery,
presumably Cistercian.

Innocent's most widely known alleged vision or dream occurred before his first
meeting with Francis of Assisi in the spring of 1209. Thomas of Celano's *Vita
secunda,* the *Legenda trium sociorum* and Bonaventure's *Legenda maior* report
that he envisioned a humble and mean-looking man propping up the crumbling
basilica of the Lateran.[6] At first he was unclear about its meaning. But after
meeting St Francis shortly thereafter, he said, 'Truly this is the man who will
sustain the church through the deeds and teaching of Christ', thus giving the papal
blessing to the new order. In Bonaventure's version, this was preceded by an
earlier vision in which the pope saw at his feet a palm tree sprouting, which grew
into a great tree; he understood this to represent Francis and gave approval to the
order, until the second dream led to the order's final confirmation. All of these
accounts were written after 1246, and the story does not appear in Thomas of
Celano's *Vita prima,* written shortly after Francis' death. A similar report appears
regarding St Dominic in Constantine of Orvieto's life, written in the winter of
1246/7 and likewise does not appear in Jordan of Saxony's earlier life.[7]
Tillmann's judgement, shared by Manselli, seems apt that such a 'legend, if not

---

[4]Salimbene de Adam, *Cronica,* ed. O. Holder-Egger, MGH, SS, 32 (Hannover, 1913):32. The editor
notes that the present name of this place is Pietra Bismantova situated near Castelnovo ne' Monti,
about 22 km southwest of Reggio Emilia. I have found no evidence that this had been the site of an
archbishopric.

[5]Thomas of Cantimpré, *Vita Lutgardis,* ii.7, in AASS, 16 June IV, 197; for translation see Margot
H. King, trans., *The Life of Lutgard of Aywières* (Toronto, 1991), 50-5. Innocent died on 16 July 1216.
Thomas reports that Lutgard had told him what grave deeds had led Innocent to purgatory, but he
would not reveal them 'out of reverence for the dead pope'.

[6]Thomas of Celano, *Vita secundi S. Francisci,* 2:17, in *S. Francisci Assisiensi vita et miracula,* ed.
Edouard Alencon (Rome, 1906), 183. This is the earliest version and was written between 11 August
1246 and 13 July 1247; see also Bonaventura, *Legenda maior,* I.3.9, III.10; *Legenda trium sociorum,*
XII.51. For English translations see Marion G. Habig, ed., *St. Francis of Assisi. Writings and Early
Biographies. English Omnibus of the Sources for the Life of St. Francis* (Chicago, 1973). I wish to
thank Sean Kinsella for assistance on this.

[7]Pierre Mandonnet, *Saint Dominique. L'idée, l'homme et l'oeuvre,* 2 vols (Paris, 1937), 1:159.

in the literal, yet still in a deeper spiritual sense, rings true'.[8] In short, this was the kind of 'pious fraud' so common in medieval hagiography.

All of these reports portray Innocent as readily susceptible to vision and the supernatural. Nevertheless, the authenticity of these accounts may be doubted on the grounds of: (1) the traditions of hagiographical stereotype; (2) an absence of secondary confirmatory evidence; (3) the known prejudices and programs of their authors; and (4) the relatively late date of their publication. If we examine the more likely cases of Innocent's brush with the supernatural, a more textured portrait emerges, which places Innocent's experience firmly within the context of the practical issues of papal canonization, which had concerned Innocent even before his elevation to the papal throne. Sometime in the 1180s, the future pope made a visit to Canterbury, where he may have witnessed some of the miraculous events which often occurred at Thomas Becket's tomb; in 1186 or 1187 he was at Grandmont in the Limousin, at the hermitage of Stephen of Grandmont, canonized in 1189.[9] While serving as cardinal-priest of SS. Sergius and Bacchus in 1193, he had been present at the canonization of John Gualberti and had presumably become acquainted with the miracles contained in that saint's canonization record;[10] and his authorship of a collect in honor of Bernard of Clairvaux would also suggest familiarity with Bernard's dossier.[11]

Nevertheless, one of Innocent's earliest papal letters, which has been unduly neglected, may well be regarded as the *locus classicus* of his attitude toward sainthood, heresy, vision and the supernatural. While at Rieti, shortly after 19 July 1198, Innocent addressed a letter to his *consobrinus* and vicar cardinal-bishop Octavian of Ostia, whose involvement in several canonizations would have made him eminently qualified to recognize the miraculous. The trusted Octavian had himself served as papal legate in Germany in the matter of Bernward of Hildesheim; and Celestine III had indicated that he was among those who had recommended the canonization of the Cistercian Stephen of Grandmont.[12]

---

[8]Tillmann, *Pope*, 278; see also Raoul Manselli, *San Francesco di Assisi*, 3rd edn (Rome, 1983), 115-16; *idem*, 'Il sogno come premonizione, consiglio e predizione nella tradizione medioevale', in *I sogni nel medioevo*, ed. Tullio Gregory (Rome, 1985), 224-5. See also Peter Dinzelbacher, *Vision und Visionsliteratur im Mittelalter* (Stuttgart, 1981), 59.

[9]Tillmann, *Pope*, 13-14 and accompanying notes on pilgrimage and his relationship to Octavian.

[10]AASS, 12 July III, 321-2.

[11]PL 185:625; 214:1032, no. 62; Reg. 5:60, p. 116; Pott. 1699 for letter to Archbishop John of Lyons. The collect was written at the request of Ranier of Ponza in 1202.

[12]*Historia canonizationis et translationis S. Bernwardi episcopi*, in AASS, 26 October IX, 1024-34; Eric Waldram Kemp, *Canonisation and Authority in the Western Church* (Oxford, 1948), 96-8; PL 204:1427, no. 113. Jean Becquet, *Scriptores ordinis Grandimontensis*, in *Corpus cristianorum. Continuatio mediaevalis*, 7 (Turnhout, 1968), *De revelatione beati Stephani*, 282-3.

Innocent's letter reads as follows:[13]

A few days before we left the city [of Rome] an aged and frightened priest – so it would appear – visited us and secretly reported that the blessed apostle Peter had appeared to him in a nocturnal vision while asleep saying: 'Go to Pope Innocent and tell him that I have said that I have loved him as a son since his birth and have promoted him through various ranks up to my own see. For this reason he ought to zealously and vigilantly take care to act in order to beautify and honor my home [i.e. St Peter's in Rome]. He should therefore know that in my church very few altars have been consecrated. As a result it happens that the divine mysteries are celebrated on altars that have fallen into decay. He should therefore at least act to have them consecrated with due reverence, and he should be sure that divine office is celebrated on them very often.' In fact that vision appeared to him a second time; but since he did not do as he had been ordered to do, the third time the apostle had taken offense and said, 'Because you have failed to obey my order, I will take away your hearing.'

As a result he became deaf so he could not hear at all. Sighing and crying out, he went to confession vowing to the blessed Peter, requesting tearfully and pitifully that his hearing (should) be restored to him, because he would fulfill what had been ordered of him immediately. Since by the mercy of God this was granted to him he told us in detail what had happened to him.

---

[13]Reg. 1:359, pp. 540-1; PL 214:336, no. 359; Pott. 405. The text reads as follows: '*Oct(aviano), Hostiensi episcopi, vicario nostro.* Paucis diebus ante nostrum ab Urbe recessum sacerdos quidam etate longevus timoratus–ut creditur–ad presentiam nostram accessit, secreto proponens, quod in visione nocturna per somnium ei apparuit beatus Petrus apostolus dicens: 'Accede ad pontificem Inno(centium) et ex mea sibi parte significa, quod a nativitate sua quasi filium illum dilexi et per diversos gradus promotum in mea tandem sede constitui. Quapropter et ipse decorem et honorem domus mee debet diligere studioque vigili promovere. Sciat ergo, quod in ecclesia mea pauca sunt altaria consecrata. Unde contingit, quod in altaribus dissecratis divina misteria celebrantur. Faciat igitur ea saltem cum debita reverentia consecrari, super que novit frequentius officium celebrari divinum." Verum, cum semel et iterum eadem sibi fuisset visio revelata nec ipse, quod mandabatur, impleret, tercio tandem idem apostolus velud offensus intulit dicens: "Quia meum obaudisti mandatum, ego tuum tibi tollam auditum." Extunc ita surdus effectus est, ut penitus non audiret. Gemens ergo vehementer et mplorans ad confessionem beati Petri devotus accessit, cum lacrimis postulans, ut misertus sibi restitueret auditum, quia mandatum ipsius illico adimpleret. Quo per Dei misericordiam exaudito, quod acciderat ei, nobis per ordinem indicat. Licet autem secundum apostolum non sit credendum omni spiritui, quia tamen in tali negocio angelus Sathane non transfiguraret se in angelum lucis et melius est pie credere quam temere dubitare, cum honestum sit quod proponitur faciendum, etsi verum non esset, quod asseritur revelatum, fraternitate tue, de qua plenam fiduciam obtinemus, per apostolica scripta mandamus, quatinus altaria Philippi et Jacobi, Simonis et Jude, beati Gregorii et sancti Andree, que dissecrata dicuntur, tu ipse consecres vel per alios auctoritate nostra facias consecrari. Credimus enim, quod ex hoc nobis fructus eterne reributionis accrescet.'

It is right according to the Apostle that *one should not believe every spirit* [1 John 4:1], because in such matters *the angel of Satan himself may transform himself into an angel of light* [2 Cor. 10:14]; and it is better to piously believe than to fearfully doubt, since it may be honorable to do what has been suggested, even if it may not be true. Oh fraternity, we have therefore obtained enough money concerning what is claimed to have been revealed [and] we have ordered by means of an apostolic letter that you should consecrate the altars of Philip and James, Simon and Jude, the blessed Gregory and the blessed Andrew, which are said to have fallen into decay; or by our authority you should have them consecrated by others.

We believe that from this the fruit of eternal reward will increase.

Innocent thus summarizes the contents of a rather standard miracle of revenge, in which the victim is punished for failing to heed the saint, despite having been warned three times. The credibility of the old man's vision is confirmed by the injury he had suffered due to his failure to act on the saint's request. Such miracles are a common hagiographical *topos* in many miracle collections, and it was, in fact, Innocent who was the first to include those wavering Christians whose faith had grown cold – along with the pagans, Jews and heretics – among those who would benefit from canonization. The convincing fear with which the old man was thus gripped was clearly infectious, and, as a devotee of St Peter, the pope saw where his responsibility lay. He therefore deputed Octavian to repair the altars.

A similar miracle of revenge was to appear in the documents relating to the case of Wulfstan of Worcester, canonized by Innocent on 14 May 1203.[14] It was reported that on the evening of 6 September 1198, that is, shortly after Innocent's letter to Octavian, Bishop John of Worcester and the monks had secretly opened up Wulfstan's tomb without papal permission. They had then deposited his vestments in one reliquary and his bones in another. At the time, a curious cleric had been surreptitiously admitted by the guardians to witness at a distance what was going on. The next night he had a vision of Wulfstan's predecessor Oswald (bishop of Worcester 961-992, archbishop of Canterbury 971-992), saying in a scolding voice, 'What have you done? You have taken my lord out at night? If you had translated him during the day and in public view, you would have found

---

[14]Reginald Darlington, ed., *The Vita Wulfstani of William of Malmesbury* (London, 1928), 183. This is contained in the later collection of miracles prepared in connection with the canonization. See Emma Mason, *St. Wulfstan of Worcester c. 1008-1095* (Oxford, 1990), 278. For the canonization bull, *Cum secundum evangelicam veritatem*, see J. Fontanini, *Codex constitutionum quas Summi Pontifices ediderunt in canonizatione Sanctorum ab anno 993 ad annum 1729* (Rome, 1729), nos. 30, 40 ff.; Reg. 6:63 (62), pp. 87-9; Darlington, 148-50; Pott. 1900; PL 215:59-61, no. 62.

water and oil.' The author notes that to those possessing the grace of understanding, the water signifies the operation of the Holy Spirit, and the oil the cure of the sick. Bishop John died shortly thereafter on 28 September 1198, and his death was regarded as fitting revenge for his presumptuous, secretive fiddling with the tomb at night, rather than in the light of day.

In addition to the warning to skeptics inherent in both the old man's deafness and the bishop's death, the letter to Octavian further reveals Innocent's cautious attitude toward dreams and visions and his fear that Satan may employ his wiles to befuddle believers.[15] This letter to Cardinal Octavian also represents Innocent's first citation of 2 Corinthians 10:14, originally directed against false prophets and agents of Satan. It was to be repeated in all four of his extant bulls of canonization, dedicated to Homobonus of Cremona, Wulfstan of Worcester, Gilbert of Sempringham and Empress Cunegunda, and it was then used by subsequent popes. These verses laid the scriptural groundwork for an important innovation in papal policy. No prior canonization bull, going back to the first bull issued in 993 by John XV in the case of Ulrich of Augsburg (the first extant papal bull), contains these passages which refer to the possibility of devilish mischief, thus requiring the testimony of reliable witnesses. As Kuttner and others have pointed out, it was Innocent who introduced into the canonization process this stress on the interdependence of the virtuous life and posthumous miracles of the saint as a means of validating each other. It was during his pontificate that Alexander III's bull *Audivimus* granting the papacy exclusive rights over canonization was introduced into canon law collections, beginning in about 1206; this canon was incorporated into the canons of the Fourth Lateran Council, later to be inserted into the *Decretales Gregorii Noni*.[16]

---

[15] The citation of 1 John 4:1 concerning the unreliability of every spirit was shortly thereafter employed in a letter to Richard the Lionhearted sometime between 15 August and 15 September 1198, warning against detractors and spreaders of lies (Reg. 1:357, pp. 535-8; Pott. 380; PL 214:332, no. 357). Similar phrases appear in a letter to the archbishops of Bulgaria on 27 November 1202 in Reg. 5:115, p. 227; PL 214:1113, no. 116; Pott. 1775.

[16] Stephan Kuttner, 'La réserve papale du droit de canonisation', *Revue historique de droit français et étranger*, N.S., 17 (1938):206-12 ff.; see also his comments in 'Retractatio VI' in *The History of Ideas and Doctrines of Canon Law in the Middle Ages* (London, 1980); R. Klauser, 'Zur Entwicklung des Heiligsprechungverfahrens bis zum 13. Jahrhundert', ZRG Kan., 40 (1954):101; Wilhelm Imkamp, *Das Kirchenbild Innocenz' III. (1198-1216)* (Stuttgart, 1983), 273-89; André Vauchez, *La sainteté en occident aux derniers siècles du moyen âge d'après les procès de canonisation et les documents hagiographiques* (Rome, 1981), 42-7. Roberto Paciocco, *'Sublimia negotia'. Le canonizzazione dei santi nella curia papale e il ordine dei frati minori* (Padua, 1996), 17-39. See also R. Paciocco, 'Miracolo e santità canonizzata nella "Vita prima sancti Francisci"', *Collectanea franciscana*, 54 (1984):261-9. A good account of one case is Jürgen Petersohn, 'Die Litterae Papst Innocenz' III. zur Heiligsprechung der Kaiserin Kunigunde (1200)', *Jahrbuch für Landesforschung* 37 (1977):1-25. For text of *Audivimus*, see E. Friedberg, ed., *Corpus iuris canonici*, 2 vols (Leipzig, 1879), X 3.42.2 (vol. 2, p. 650).

In Innocent's first bull of canonization, devoted to Homobonus of Cremona (d. 13 November 1198), issued on 12 January 1199 at Rome, he argued that the signs and miracles performed by the true saints would especially confound the heretics when they witness the prodigies which abound at the tombs of Catholics.[17] Both good deeds performed in the saint's lifetime and miracles after death are necessary for canonization since, '. . . *the angel of Satan may often transform himself into an angel of light* [2 Cor. 10:14], and some may *carry out good deeds to be seen by men* [Matt. 23:5], and some may even perform miracles, although they may be *men of corrupt lives,* [and] *reprobate* [2 Tim. 3:8], just as is read concerning Pharaoh's magicians [Exod. 7:11, 7:22] and even about the Antichrist, who, *if it were possible, [would] seduce the very elect* [Matt. 24:24; Mark 13:22] into error with their miracles. Therefore neither deeds nor miracles are enough . . .'

This fear that Satan may act through such false prophets to perform miracles became the scriptural justification for the inquiry into the saint's virtues and miracles, which preceded papal canonization. Among Satan's wiles are those visions and delusions with which many of the saints do battle, and which become the source of the evil deeds performed by heretics and other enemies of the faith. Innocent's attitude toward vision was probably informed by Augustine's citation of 2 Corinthians 10:14 in his *De Genesi ad litteram*.[18] Here, the snares of Satan appearing as a good angel are noted, who may even gain the victim's 'confidence in matters that are manifestly good, [and] he may then lure his victim into his snares.' The biblical examples cited by Augustine refer to Moses and the magicians of pharaoh (Exodus 7:8-13), the temptation of Eve and the ass speaking to Balaam (Numbers 22:28).

The desire to distinguish true from false prophets, as Innocent himself admits in his canonization bulls, was a result of his concern with the problem of the heretics in France and Italy, who are likened in his earliest letters to pharaoh's magicians.[19] In 1198, he had appointed Gregory cardinal deacon of S. Maria in Portico, along with the Lombard bishops, to draft a statute which would forbid

---

[17]Reg. 1:528 (530), pp. 761-764 for bull, for citation 762; PL 214:483, no. 530; Pott. 573. Roberto Paciocco, '"Virtus morum" e "virtus signorum". La teoria della santità nelle lettere di canonizzazione di Innocenzio III', *Nuova rivista storica* 70 (1986):597-610.

[18]Augustine, *De Genesi ad litteram duodecim*, ed. Josephus Zycha, CSEL, 28, sect. 3, pt. 1 (Prague, 1894), xxii.13.28 (p. 398), xi.29.37 (p. 161). For translation see Augustine, *The Literal Meaning of Genesis*, trans. John Hammond Taylor, 2 vols (New York, 1982). For Augustine's and Gregory the Great's views of dream and vision, see Steven Kruger, *Dreaming in the Middle Ages* (Cambridge, 1992), 34-56. In Innocent's All Saint's Day sermon no. 31 (PL 217:592-3), the pope deals with various genres of vision, the 'corporeal, enigmatic and comprehensible'.

[19]Reg. 1:94, pp. 135-8 (PL 214:82, no. 94) citing Exodus 7:13-18; cf. PL 214:538-9, no. 1; Reg. 2:1, pp. 3-5 (*Vergentis in senium*).

their occupying public office.[20] On 25 March 1199, he addressed a letter to the clergy and people of Viterbo on this theme of the sly wiles of the heretics who act 'under the guise of piety'.[21] On 12 July 1199, in a letter to the archbishop of Metz, the pope addressed the proliferation of vernacular translations of scripture and of unauthorized preaching, which took place in secret. He asked the archbishop to investigate the orthodoxy of such persons and deputed three Cistercian abbots to deal with the matter. Innocent's letter makes a clear connection between the wiles of both heretics and the Devil, saying 'out of an obligation to both the wise and the foolish according to the apostle, we ought to care about the salvation of all, so that we should remove evil persons from the villages and nourish good persons in their virtues. This work demands great discretion, since bitter vetch secretly subverts with the appearance of virtue, and *the angel of Satan* fraudulently *may transform himself into an angel of light* [2 Cor. 10:14]'.[22] Further warning against the treacherous wiles of the Waldensians, he argued that since one's inner aims are hidden from sight, it is not enough to claim that one is sent by God, but this claim must be confirmed through the operation of miracles, as in the case of Moses, who had turned his staff into a serpent and back again.

This linkage between heresy, the wiles of Satan and the need for miracles to confirm the true aims of the apostle appears in the life of the rector Pietro Parenzo. Innocent had appointed Parenzo to cleanse Orvieto, which city was dominated by Cathars and involved in a dispute with the pope over the jurisdiction in Aquapendente. Pietro's life by Canon John of Orvieto, probably written in 1200, shortly after the rector's assassination by the Cathars, speaks of the deceitfulness of a certain Cathar of Florence named Diotosalvo who 'like Satan has transformed himself into an angel of light' and has propagated his views in the city.[23] While spending Easter with his family at Rome, Peter had allegedly taken the opportunity to speak with the pope on Monday, 19 April 1199, on his way from St Peter's to the Lateran, near the basilica of San Daniele de Forma. According to an ancient Roman custom, in the course of this liturgical procession

---

[20]Reg. 1:298, p. 421; PL 214:256, no. 298; Pott. 286 for letter of 25 June 1198 to archdeacon James of Milan to encourage the Lombards to prohibit heretics from holding public office.

[21]Reg. 2:1, pp. 3-5 (25 March 1199); PL 214:537, no. 1; Pott. 643, *Vergentis in senium*, to the people of Viterbo on the deceptive wiles of the heretics.

[22]Reg. 2:132, p. 273; PL 214:695, no. 141; Pott. 780; Kurt Victor Selge, *Die erste Waldenser*, 2 vols (Berlin, 1962), 1:299; Malcolm Lambert, *Medieval Heresy. Popular Movements from the Gregorian Reform to the Reformation* (Oxford, 1992), 73.

[23]Vincenzo Natalini, ed., S. *Pietro Parenzo. La leggenda scritta dal Maestro Giovanni canonico di Orvieto*, in *Lateranum*, N.S., 6 (Rome, 1936):157.

one may speak with the pope as he passes by.[24] Innocent urged him to continue his pursuit of heretics even though his life had been threatened and prophetically said, 'My son, by the authority of the apostles St Peter and St Paul, I absolve you of all your sins if you die at the hands of the heretics.' Although commissioners visited Peter's tomb and a 'life and miracles' was prepared according to canonical rules accompanied by a public clamor and reports in the pope's presence around 1 May 1216,[25] there is no evidence that Innocent took action to bring about Peter's canonization, despite his murder at the hands of heretics.[26] Orvieto had been under interdict, and the pope died in 1216 while on route to Perugia.

Innocent's next encounter with supernatural vision is found in the dossier of Gilbert of Sempringham (*c.* 1083-1189).[27] Briefly, Innocent's vivid and detailed dream on the eve of Gilbert's canonization describes how, between 2 January and 12 January 1202, during the time when Gilbert's case was being considered, Innocent saw a high tower while asleep. Upon entering, he found a beautiful bed surrounded by a silken canopy covering decorated with images of the saints, on which he attempted to stitch. He began to think about Gilbert's case and heard a voice saying, 'The Archangel Michael will be your helper in this matter'. Because of his uncertainty about the revelation, he turned for counsel to the Cistercian Ranier of Ponza (d. 1207/9), who interpreted the symbols which had appeared, confirming the divine will to have Gilbert canonized.[28] Ranier had served as the pope's legate in missions against the heretics, as papal confessor, and probably as a member of the commission investigating the Humiliati. On another occasion, Ralph of Coggeshall reports that Ranier had been informed of a vision of the Virgin which had appeared to another monk, warning the pope of

---

[24]Michele Maccarrone, 'Orvieto e la predicazione della crociata', in *Studi su Innocenzo III*, in *Italia sacra. Studi e documenti di storia ecclesiastica*, 17 (Padua, 1972):41; PL 214:529.

[25]*Vita* of Pietro in Natalini, op. cit., 200, reports that when the pope visited Orvieto in 1216, a certain physician named Albertinus reported directly to the pope about the cure of a child's fracture which had occurred in 1213: 'Paratus autem erat dictus Albertinus de sua sanitate coram Pontifice fidem facere iuramento; de sanitate pueri cum nobili eius matre se idem facere asserabat.' The author of the latter part of Parenzo's life and miracles is referred to as 'R'.

[26]The last miracle occurred in early May 1216.

[27]Raymonde Foreville and Gillian Keir, eds, *The Book of St Gilbert* (Oxford, 1987), 173-7. For the bull see C. R. and M. G. Cheney, eds, *The Letters of Pope Innocent III (1198-1215) Concerning England and Wales* (Oxford, 1967), no. 574.

[28]Herbert Grundmann, 'Zur Biographie Joachims von Fiore und Rainers von Ponza', *Neues Archiv* 16 (1960):237-546, provides considerable material on Ranier's career. For a letter of Hugolino of Ostia, the future Gregory IX, addressed to the abbots of Fossanova, Casamari and Salem describing Ranier's reputation as a miracle-worker, pious hermit and possessor of spiritual intelligence, edited by E. Winkelmann, see *Analecta Heidelbergensia, Varietà, Archivio della Società romana di storia patria*, 2 (Rome, 1879):363-7. I wish to thank Brenda Bolton for assistance in dealing with the shadowy Ranier of Ponza.

her indignation about certain financial exactions from the Cistercian order.[29] On the way to the curia to deal with this issue, Ranier had himself received a revelation in his sleep that three abbots were on their way to Rome to deal with the matter. He told the pope of these two revelations, and the issue was dealt with satisfactorily. Ranier had thus served as the pope's confidant on several occasions in which dreams were reported and interpreted, when Innocent preferred to seek an expert's advice rather than rely on his own judgement.

The life of Procopius (c. 975-1053), composed about 1240, likewise reports a vision experienced by Innocent.[30] After miracles had occurred at the saint's tomb at the church of John the Baptist in Prague, demands had arisen for his canonization. On the Sunday of the Incarnation, 1203, the saint appeared to Abbot Blasius, provisor and rector of the monastery of Sázava, urging him to go to the Roman curia in order to present written evidence of Procopius' miracles. The vision appeared three times and promised to provide assistance in this mission. Blasius undertook the journey and approached the pope with two companions. Innocent, however, disregarded both the written and oral testimony presented to him.[31] Although the abbot stayed a year and made many attempts, his funds eventually ran out and he decided to abandon his commission. When he was already outside the city walls, the saint, carrying a pastoral staff, allegedly appeared to Innocent while he was in conclave and said: 'Why have you hesitated, why have you delayed, how long have you allowed my body to remain buried in this way, why have you allowed my chaplain to go away empty-handed in this way? Unless you immediately order him to return from the road to the church of S. Lorenzo fuori il Muri and look favorably on the testimony of my body and grant me due honor, I will cut you down in this way.' Procopius raised up his pastoral staff, as if to strike the pope. Innocent, awakening, asked the saint to identify himself, which he did and then disappeared. This staff seems to have acquired some reputation, since immediately after the account of Procopius' canonization, it is reported that on 14 June (the feast of the Nativity of John the Baptist), in an unstated year, an unidentified abbot appeared carrying a staff, whose touch cured the sick, and then disappeared.[32] In the presence of thirteen cardinals, Innocent allegedly then ordered Blasius to return, took note of the testimony of Procopius' sanctity, celebrated a mass and canonized him. He then

---

[29]Ralph of Coggeshall, *Chronicon Anglicanum*, in RS, 66, ed. J. Stephenson (London, 1975):131-2; cf. also Caesarius of Heisterbach, *Dialogus miraculorum*, ed. J. Strange, 2 vols (Cologne, 1890), vii.6, in vol. 2, pp. 7-8.

[30]*De apericione canonizationis S. Procopii*, in František Krásl, ed., *Sv. Prokop. Jeho Klášter a Památka u Lidu* (Prague, 1895), 499-500; see also Václav Chaloupecký and Bohumil Ryba, *Středověké Legendy Prokopské* (Prague, 1953), 158-9.

[31]Ibid., 499: 'papa nihil ducens dicta et scripta, parvipendit tanti viri sanctitatem.'

[32]*Vita*, 501.

sent Guido di Preneste, cardinal priest of Santa Maria in Trastevere as legate to Bohemia in order to handle the canonization. This allegedly occurred on 4 July 1204, although we do not have the bull of canonization, and the life in which it is found was written about 1240.

The late date of this report might raise doubts about its reliability. But there is some evidence taken from the dossier of the next saint canonized by Rome which may lend credence to Innocent's vision. Innocent himself issued no canonizations after 1204. The next papal canonization was therefore that of Archbishop William of Bourges (d. 1209) by Honorius III in 1218.[33] William's case includes a story which bears a striking resemblance to the report of both Innocent's vision of Procopius and the old cleric's encounter with St Peter, and which might confirm the veracity of the Procopius account. It is reported that during the period when Honorius was weighing the results of the inquiry into William's life and miracles, a dean and archdeacon of Prague had come to Rome as messengers of archbishop Andreas of Prague in order to gain assistance against secular encroachments. They had experienced a long delay in the treatment of their case, and the dean tearfully prayed one evening at the church of St Peter's for divine assistance to expedite their business. He then returned to his hospice and, after falling asleep, dreamt that he was visited by a man dressed in white who had spoken to him by name, saying, 'Dean, why are you disturbed about your business? Heed my advice, and it will be expedited shortly.' The specter instructed him to: (1) frequently recite and always bear in mind the entire Psalm 35, which begins, 'Plead my cause, O Lord, with those that strive against me ...', and (2) recite an invocation to William. The dean replied, 'I don't know who this Saint William about whom you speak is, nor am I acquainted with the name of the city.' The vision recurred and he was also told that this saint would be canonized within three days. He was warned that unless he did as he was told, he would return to his homeland without having carried out his mission.

The dean then aroused the archdeacon of Prague, saying they should wake up to say matins. The archdeacon complained of the early hour, and refused to get up. The dean then said, 'While I was resting in my bed a man dressed in white appeared and spoke to me. But I fear that I have been deluded by the deceitful wiles of the enemy: I know that I am not worthy of such an honor, that God and our Redeemer, to whom every heart is open and every will speaks, should deign

---

[33]There are several versions of this story. The fullest is found in 'Sancti Gulielmi archiepiscopi Biturciensis Vita, miracula post mortem et canonizatio', *Analecta Bollandiana* 3 (1884):350-6. See also Anon. monk of Chaalis, *Vita S. Gullelmi*, in AASS, 10 January I, 638-9; Philippe Labbé, *Novae bibliothecae manuscriptorum librorum collectio*, 2 vols (Paris, 1657), 2:379-86. See R. Aubert, 'Guillaume de Bourges', *Dictionnaire d'histoire et de géographie écclésiastiques*, 22:862-3. For bull of canonization see Pietro Pressuti, ed., *Regesta Honorii papae III*, 2 vols (Rome, 1888-95), 1:223, nos. 1343-45; Fontanini, no. 49 ('*Etsi electi*'); Pott. 5803-5.

to reveal such heavenly secrets to me his unworthy servant.' The archdeacon said, 'Go back to sleep . . . since this is surely not a vision (*visio*) but a delusion (*delusio*).' He went back to sleep, and the vision reappeared in the same precise way, warning him that if he did not do as he was told, evil would befall him. Therefore, at dawn, when matins was being sung, he rushed to the bishop of Prague and told him what had happened, asking that because of the secrecy of the confession, he should reveal to no one what had transpired. The bishop nevertheless reported the vision to the pope and the assembled ecclesiastics who were then considering William's case, vouching for the dean's honesty and piety. William was canonized on 17 May 1218. The dean's performance seems to have paid off, since on 13 July 1218 Honorius asked King Ottakar of Bohemia to protect the clergy against noble depredations.[34] The fact that this vision is found in the account of the saint canonized immediately after Procopius, following a fourteen-year hiatus in canonizations, suggests that the story of Innocent's Procopius vision may perhaps have some historical foundation and had been publicized, and it seemed that a further vision would hasten William's canonization.

The dean's admitted fear that Satan was deluding the archdeacon echoes the same attitude of pious caution toward the supernatural which Innocent himself had expressed in his letter to Octavian and in his subsequent canonization bulls. This policy identified the heretics with Satan masquerading as an angel of light, who could be combated through the miracles of the saints. Revelations of both heresy and sainthood demanded similar kinds of cautious inquiry. Among those files which were probably dealt with by Innocent are the cases of Caradoc, William of Malavalle, Peter of Trevi, Peter Parenzo, William of Bourges, Lawrence of Dublin, Virgil of Salzburg, Homobonus, Cunegunda, Gilbert, Wulfstan and Procopius;[35] Peter of Castelnau was not canonized, but was recognized by Innocent III as a martyr after his assassination in 1208,[36] while the cults of Sts Peter and Paul were actively encouraged by the pope.[37] Nevertheless, only four or five cases (if the view here suggested regarding Procopius is

---

[34]Presssuti, op. cit., 1:219, no. 1324.

[35]Theobald, *Vita Guillelmi* in AASS, 10 February II, 450-72 and comments in Kaspar Elm, *Beiträge zur Geschichte des Wilhelmitenordens*, in *Münstersche Forschungen* 14 (Cologne, 1962); Fontanini, 644, no. 30; *Vita* of Peter of Trevi in AASS, August VI, 545 contends that the case was dealt with at the Fourth Lateran Council. 'Vie et miracles de S. Laurent archevêque de Dublin', *Analecta Bollandiana* 33 (1914):157, contends that both Celestine III and Innocent III were petitioned in this case; on Caradoc, AASS, 13 April II, 150-2 and Pott. 1047, for letter of 8 May 1200 asking for investigation; Kemp, op. cit., passim.

[36]PL 215:1355C-56A for bull in which Peter is likened to the first martyr St Stephen.

[37]PL 214:39 no. 44; Reg., 1:44, p. 67; Pott. 44, to bishop Lupold of Worms ordering the celebration of feast of the conversion of Paul in all of his diocese.

accepted) led to a successful conclusion under his pontificate, while much procedural innovation was introduced in order to guarantee that no false prophets, like the heretics, would be identified as saints. In all of these, with the exception of Cunegunda, canonized on 3 April 1200, a vision played a decisive role. Cunegunda, who was regarded as a model of marital chastity, had become the object of a cult in the mid-twelfth century, centered at Bamberg; under Celestine III in 1189 miracles had appeared, and an inquiry was undertaken.[38] Here, Innocent merely concluded a case which had been under consideration for some time.

The visions here discussed were all premonitory and explicit, generally lacking the cryptic symbolism so often found in medieval dream and vision, except for the vision concerning Gilbert (and even this case is rather transparent), although on occasion Innocent did display a penchant for symbolism, as in his detailed description of the hidden meaning of the features of four bejewelled gold rings given as a gift to King Richard of England on 29 May 1198.[39] Nevertheless, Innocent was not the kind of melancholic cleric so often regarded as the recipient of vision and required confirmatory evidence of its truth.[40] He would be willing to act on supernatural sightings, including his own, provided they were examined by an expert such as Ranier of Ponza or had been confirmed by multiple appearances and even by signs of revenge exacted by an offended saint.

---

[38]Petersohn, op. cit., for bull; Fontanini, 37-40 no. 29; PL 210:222; Pott. 1000. For life, based partly on the miracle inquiry, see AASS, 3 March I, 272-9. Innocent also wrote a collect in Cunegunda's honor found in the canonization bull. The revived interest in Cunegunda's cult may have been related to the 1189 canonization of Bishop Otto of Bamberg by Clement III. Her life goes into unusual detail concerning her benefactions to the diocese of Bamberg.

[39]Reg. 1:206, pp. 205-7; Pott. 225; PL 214:179 no. 206: 'in quibus te volumus spiritualiter intelligere formam et numerum, materiam et colorem, ut misterium potius quam donum attendas'. This is referred to in Brenda Bolton, '*Qui fidelis in minimo*: The Importance of Innocent III's Gift List', a lecture published in this volume.

[40]Dinzelbacher, op.cit., passim for a survey. A contemporary dream interpretation manual from about 1165, written at Constantinople, is Simon Collin-Rosset, ed., 'Le *Liber Thesauri occulti* de Paschalis Romanus (Un traité d'interprétation des songes du XIIe siècle)', *Archives d'histoire doctrinale et littéraire du moyen âge* 30 (1963):111-98. This is the kind of manual, because of its provenance, which might have been employed by Ranier of Ponza. A later such text from about 1335, which includes scholastic views is R. A. Pack, ed., 'De prognosticatione sompniorum Libellus Guillelmo de Aragonia adscriptus', *Archives d'histoire doctrinale et littéraire du moyen âge* 33 (1966):237-93.

Reform or Crusade? Anti-Usury and Crusade Preaching during the Pontificate of Innocent III

Jessalynn Bird

Innocent III launched no less than three major crusades before his premature death in 1216, instituting a systematized approach to recruitment and funding. In fact, much of the research on Innocent emphasizes his high estimate of papal power and the resulting steps he took to endow the papacy with real administrative and legal clout, working from the top downwards. Yet his papacy was also permeated with calls for reform from below. One such reform party was the Peter the Chanter's school. Although John Baldwin has placed Innocent among the Chanter's disciples, the demands placed upon him as head of the church could sometimes conflict with his own reforming ideals, and with the more untempered idealism of the men he chose to implement his vision.[1] This paper will pose several questions. Was Innocent primarily a reformer or a pragmatist in the matter of the crusades? Were Innocent's agents simply part of the papal apparatus, or were their missions sometimes contradictory to papal policy? How much freedom was Innocent allowing his appointees leading up to the Fourth Lateran Council (1215), and how did he react when his legates' and preachers' plans were challenged?

I would suggest that Innocent, through the realization that the moral reform of the West was necessary for the success of the crusades in the East, transformed

---

[1] For a historiographical survey, see James M. Powell, ed., *Innocent III: Vicar of Christ or Lord of the World*, 2nd edn (Washington, DC, 1994). For Baldwin, see n. 3 below.

the very concept of the crusade.[2] Although this association had been made in the past, Innocent III, with his penchant for institutionalization and his links with the moral theology school of Peter the Chanter, was able to achieve what Urban II and Gregory VIII could not. By commissioning 'Paris' men such as James of Vitry, Robert of Courson, Stephen Langton, Fulk of Neuilly, and Eustace of Flay to preach the crusade and, in Robert and Stephen's case, to hold regional councils preparatory to the Fourth Lateran itself, he invested them with the authority to combine the crusade with an insistence upon a reformed church and a pastorally guided laity.

For both Innocent and the Paris preachers, usury became one of the prime concerns associated with crusade preaching and the new extension of the vow to non-military classes, including the merchant class.[3] Just as internecine violence had been identified as the prevailing social evil in Urban II's time and calls for peace joined those for the first crusade at Clermont, so Peter the Chanter's circle depicted usury and avarice as undermining the social fabric.[4] Usury could be

---

[2]See Innocent's opening sermon at Fourth Lateran in Stephan Kuttner and Antonio García Y García, 'A New Eyewitness Account of the Fourth Lateran Council', *Traditio* 20 (1964):124, 132; Raymonde Foreville, *Latran I, II, III et Latran IV*, Histoire des conciles oecuméniques 6 (Paris, 1965):261-3; PL 216:823-5; PL 217:678; James of Vitry, *Historia Occidentalis*, ed. J. F. Hinnebusch, Spicilegium Friburgense 17 (Fribourg, 1972), 73-88 (hereafter cited as H.Occ.).

[3]For the vow, see Michel Villey, *La Croisade: Essai sur la formation d'un théorie juridique* (Paris, 1942), 132, 137, 146, and James A. Brundage, *Canon Law and the Crusader* (Madison, 1969), 69-70, 75-8, etc. Usury was defined by theologians as loaning out money or goods in the expectation of receiving anything back over the principal. It could be hidden in various contracts and thus was linked closely to the concept of *turpe lucrum*, or 'shameful gain' in business. The best treatment of Peter the Chanter's circle and its fight against usury remains the magisterial work by John W. Baldwin, *Masters, Princes, and Merchants: The Social Views of Peter the Chanter and His Circle*, 2 vols (Princeton, NJ, 1970), 1:261-343 (hereafter cited as MPM). See also T. P. MacLaughlin, 'The Teaching of the Canonists on Usury (XII, XIII and XIV Centuries)', *Mediaeval Studies* 1 (1939):81-147; 2 (1940):1-22; Lester K. Little, 'Pride Goes Before Avarice: Social Change and the Vices in Latin Christendom', *American Historical Review* 76 (1971):16-49; John W. Baldwin, *The Medieval Theories of Just Price: Romanists, Canonists and Theologians in the Twelfth and Thirteenth Centuries*, Transactions of the American Philosophical Society, n.s. 19.4 (Philadelphia, 1959); Odd Langholm, *Economics in the Medieval Schools: Wealth, Exchange, Value, Money and Usury according to the Paris Theological Tradition 1200-1350*, Studien und Texte zur Geistesgeschichte des Mittelalters 29 (Leiden, 1992), esp. 17-61. To my chagrin, Jacques Le Goff's poetic *Your Money or Your Life: Economy and Religion in the Middle Ages*, trans. Patricia Ranum (New York, 1988), came to hand only after this paper was completed. Although the works cited above emphasize that the questions asked by the Chanter's school led to the gradual justification of the merchant's profession, we must remember that their theories were still heavily tinged with anti-merchant sentiment, particularly on the subject of usury, which did not find an 'official' justification until the late thirteenth century.

[4]Third Lateran Council (1179) c.25, in COD, 223; *Utinam Dominus* (1208), PL 215:1502-3; *Quia Maior* (1213), PL 216:818-19; *Ad Liberandum* in COD, 267-71; H.Occ., 78-9; James of Vitry, sermons to merchants in Douai, Bibliothèque Municipale, Ms. 503, sermon 56, fol. 389v, sermon 58, fols 394v-5v, sermon 59, fol. 397v; Peter the Chanter, *Verbum Abbreviatum*, ch. 50, PL 205:157

practiced by Jews or Christians. And while jurisdiction of the former was the carefully guarded preserve of secular powers, the latter could fall under either secular or episcopal courts. Although Innocent and the Paris circle at times called upon the prince to rein in both types of usurers,[5] they concentrated on exhorting bishops and religious houses to enforce existing laws against Christian usurers,[6] and on promulgating new anti-usury legislation in the diocesan synods and provincial councils both before and after Fourth Lateran. They also joined anti-usury preaching to crusade recruitment.

While these elements were stressed from the beginning of Innocent's pontificate,[7] they converged with particular force in the legation of Robert of Courson. In 1213, Innocent gave Robert a dual commission to hold councils in preparation for the Fourth Lateran and to coordinate crusade recruiting in France. Robert had extensive experience in crusade and reform matters both as a theology master in Paris and as judge delegate for protecting crusaders' rights since 1208.[8] One of these rights, published in crusading bulls from 1145 onwards, was the cancellation of interest on usurious loans, which could keep the crusader from departing. In *Ad liberandum*, published shortly after the Fourth Lateran council, this right was confirmed and specified. Prelates were to enforce it against

---

(hereafter VA).

[5]James of Vitry rebukes secular leaders for shielding Jews and usurers in order to tax them, rather than defending the poor of Christ (a category which included ecclesiastics) (Douai 503, *sermo ad potentes et milites* 51, fols 374v-5r). See also Robert of Courson, *De Usura*, ed. G. Lefèvre, Travaux et mémoires de l'Université de Lille 10 (30) (Lille, 1902), 9, 53, 63, 65, 73 (hereafter *De Usura*); works cited in n. 3 above. I will only occasionally refer to Jewish usurers, although often repression of both groups was linked. See William Chester Jordan, *The French Monarchy and the Jews: From Philip Augustus to the Last Capetians* (Philadelphia, 1989); *idem*, *Louis IX and the Challenge of the Crusade* (Princeton, NJ, 1979); John W. Baldwin, *The Government of Philip Augustus: Foundations of French Royal Power in the Middle Ages* (Berkeley, 1986).

[6]VA, ch. 50, PL 205:158-9; *De Usura*, 18, 35-7, 63, 65; sermon to merchants 58, Douai 503, fol. 395r; H.Occ., 73-81, 83.

[7]For efforts to repress usury before Fourth Lateran (1215), see n. 3 above, VA ch. 50, PL 205:158; McLaughlin, 'Canonists,' 2-4, 13-15; John T. Noonan, Jr, *The Scholastic Analysis of Usury* (Cambridge, Mass., 1957), 13-19; Foreville, *Latran*, 153; John Hine Mundy, *Liberty and Political Power in Toulouse, 1050-1230* (New York, 1954), n. 40, p. 295; *Decretals of Gregory IX*, V.xix.1-19, in Emil Friedberg, ed., *Corpus Iuris Canonici*, 2 (Leipzig, 1881):811-16; Council of Avignon (1209), I.i-iv in Giovanni D. Mansi, ed., *Sacrorum conciliorum nova et amplissima collectio*, 31 vols (Florence and Venice, 1759-1798), 22:785-6 (hereafter Mansi).

[8]Marcel and Christiane Dickson, 'Le Cardinal Robert de Courson: Sa vie', *Archives d'histoire doctrinale et litteraire du moyen age* 9 (1934):61, 68, 78, 83-8, and his legation, 88-116 (hereafter cited as Dicksons).

Christian usurers, while princes were urged to provide a suitable deferral for those crusaders who could not pay their debts to Jews.[9]

In addition to this specific jurisdiction, Robert used his legatine authority to convene provincial councils, combining anti-usury legislation with crusade recruiting, perhaps beginning among fellow reformers in Paris (1213). The decrees of this council were reiterated nearly verbatim at Rouen in 1214, which Robert convoked after preaching the crusade to a combined audience of clergy and laity with great effect. Both councils provide useful insight into how he planned to combat usury through canon law.[10] Part of Robert's success in promulgating such unusually severe anti-usury measures lay in the archbishop of Rouen's active support, which one can infer from the archbishop's wrangling with Philip Augustus over usurers and their wills and possessions, a struggle directly reflected in the council's decrees.[11]

First and foremost, Robert worked to sever the usurer's ties with local churchmen and the nobility. Their relatives were banned from holding church office, and clerks were not to work for usurers by drawing up contracts or by defending them in court.[12] Once he had fixed draconian penalties for prelates who shielded usurers, he called upon bishops to hold inquisitions to ferret them out. If the usurer refused to clear himself in the episcopal court or repent after three publications of his name, he was to be publicly excommunicated, severed from all social contact with fellow Christians and all sacraments of the church, including Christian burial.[13] He was further stigmatized by legal association with Jews and heretics.[14]

---

[9]COD, 267-71; Brundage, *Canon Law*, 82-3, 180-3. On *Ad Liberandum*'s relationship to the rest of the council canons, see Kuttner and García y García, 'Eyewitness Account', 128, 133-4, 156-8.

[10]MPM 1:311; Dicksons, 89-91, 96-8; Council of Paris (1213) in Mansi, 22:889-924; Council of Rouen (1214) in Mansi, 22:889-924. I will cite the Paris canons. Robert may have held a similar council at Reims (1213), as well as councils at Clermont, Limoges, Bordeaux and Montpellier, although one in Bourges (1215) was boycotted (Dicksons, 95, 103, 112-13, 125).

[11]Innocent III supported the archbishop against Philip. See McLaughlin, 'Canonists', 6-7; Baldwin, 'Philip Augustus and the Norman Church', *French Historical Studies* 6 (1969):1-30, esp. 10-15; PL 216:487-8; *Recueil des actes de Philippe Auguste*, ed. H. F. Delaborde, et al., 5 vols (Paris, 1916-1979), 3:#1360 (should be dated 1214), 4:#1510 (1218) (hereafter *Actes*).

[12]Paris Add. V.iii. and 'De Usuris' I.i, I.v., in Mansi, 22:850; c.16, Fourth Lateran (1215), in COD, 243; *De Usura*, 18, 37-9, 67-71, 79. This restriction flowed from the idea that clerks should not be involved in *negotium* at all. On the other hand, monasteries and cathedral chapters were often burdened by interest-bearing debt (Paris I.vii, in Mansi, 22:821; c.59, Fourth Lateran, in COD, 262; n. 74 below).

[13]Paris Add. V.v. in Mansi, 22:850-1 (cf. Third Lateran [1179], c.25, in COD, 223).

[14]More imprecise but no less powerful ideological connections were forged between Jews, usurers, prostitutes and heretics in the harm they caused the members of Christ. For legal sanctions, see Odette Pontal, *Les statuts de Paris et le synodal de l'ouest (XIIIᵉ siècle)*, Les statuts synodaux Français du XIIIᵉ siècle 1 (Paris, 1971):52-92 (hereafter Pontal); Avignon (1209) I.iii, in Mansi, 22:786; Paris Add.

The usurer's family and servants suffered with him. Christians who served a Jew or usurer were excommunicated.[15] Similarly his wife was faced with a quandary. She could live frugally from her husband's usurious possessions only if she were persuading him to make restitution. If he were unrepentant, she could separate from him and live on what she managed to beg from family and friends, or in the last resort, seek bare necessities from her husband if she intended to make restitution.[16]

In order to prevent the circumvention of episcopal justice by the usurer, Robert forbade his parish priest and monasteries to take his alms or provide any sacrament, including Christian burial.[17] In addition, his will was null and void if he died unrepentant, and Robert calls upon the local lord to confiscate dead usurers' ill-acquired possessions at the behest of the church.[18] These measures were intended to force the usurer to make restitution to his victims, as all other channels of spiritual expiation were closed to him until he did so.[19] If *exempla*

V.ii., iv-vi in Mansi, 22:850-1. For ideological connections, *De Usura*, 63, 53, 81; James of Vitry, *Sermones ad mercatores et campsores* 58, Douai 503, fols 394v-5r, and 59, fols 396r-v; Thomas F. Crane, *The Exempla or Illustrative Stories from the Sermones vulgares of Jacques de Vitry*, Publications of the Folk-lore Society 26 (London, 1890), no. 172 (hereafter Crane); VA, ch. 21, PL 205:76, ch. 50, PL 205:150; Peter of Vaux-de-Cernay, *Historia Albigensis*, ed. Pascal Guebin et Ernest Lyon, 3 vols. (Paris, 1926) 1:§13, p. 15.

[15] Paris Add. V.i. in Mansi, 22:851; *De Usura*, 39; V. L. Kennedy, 'Robert of Courson on Penance', *Mediaeval Studies* 7 (1945):309-12, 315, hereafter 'Kennedy'; Jean Longère, 'Deux sermons de Jacques de Vitry (d.1240) "ad servos et ancillas"', in *La femme au moyen âge*, ed. Michel Rouche and Jean Heuclin (Mauberge, 1990) §5, p. 274.

[16] Paris Add. V.x. in Mansi, 22:851; *De Usura*, 41, 43; Kennedy, 320; cf. Thomas of Chobham, *Summa Confessorum*, ed. Rev. F. Broomfield, Analecta Mediaevalia Namurcensia 25 (Paris, 1968):510, and James of Vitry, *Sermo ad mercatos et campsores* 58, Douai 503, fol. 395v, who lamblasts women whose expensive tastes pauperize their husbands, forcing them to become usurers. See also Caesarius of Heisterbach, *Dialogus Miraculorum*, ed. J. Strange, 2 vols (Cologne, 1851) II.vii (1:70-2), XII.xxiv (2:335-6) (hereafter DM).

[17] Paris II.vii and Add.V.i, v, vii in Mansi, 22:827, 850-1; Avignon (1209) I.iii, II.xvii in Mansi, 22:786, 826; Montpellier (1215) I.xxx. in Mansi, 22:946; Third Lateran (1179), c. 25, in COD, 223; VA, PL 205:76; *De usura*, 21, 23-39, 41, 45, drawing partly from VA, ch. 50, PL 205:159; Kennedy, 302, 318-19, 323. Prohibitions against taking usurious alms are ubiquitous in James' sermons to religious orders. He attacks black monks and the military orders for abusing their papal privileges by providing the sacraments to usurers and other excommunicates in exchange for their dirty money (Douai 503, fols 301r-v, 304r-v; H.Occ., 83, 129; *Analecta novissima spicilegii Solesmensis: Altera continuatio*, ed. Cardinal J. -B. Pitra, 2 [Paris, 1888]:409, hereafter 'Pitra'; Crane, no. 176-8). Canons 57-8 and 60 of Fourth Lateran shut down many of the usurers' loopholes. For a monk's view of the problem, see DM, II.vii-viii, II.xxvi, II.xxxi-ii, XI.xli, XI.xlii (ed. Strange, 1:70-3, 98-9, 103-6, 2:300-2).

[18] Paris. Add. V.i, V.v. in Mansi, 22:849-51; *De Usura*, 21, 23; Kennedy, 315; n. 11 above.

[19] Restitution was considered to be the primary component of the usurer's satisfaction. Without it, his sins could be confessed, but not absolved (Kennedy, 307, 309; MPM 1:304-5; Mary Mansfield, *The Humiliation of Sinners: Public Penance in Thirteenth Century France* (Ithaca, 1995), 56-9, 85 (hereafter Mansfield); Paris (*c.*1200), c.34 and Synodal of the West, c.107 in Pontal 1:64, 212. On

are any indicator of popular absorption, the burial and no-alms clauses could be particularly effective. One nugatory warning stars Robert, who while touring the countryside as legate ordered a usurer recently interred in a Christian cemetery to be exhumed and buried in unhallowed ground.[20]

The depth of Courson's anti-usury zeal may be estimated from the local clergy's adverse reaction to his statutes. The Paris circle's rather wide definition of usury was hard on churches and monasteries in urban areas, who were dependant upon the patronage of the merchant class.[21] While Robert easily promulgated his statutes in the north, where he had links with powerful bishops amenable to the Paris reform program, he met with stiff resistance from some local prelates and communes in the Midi.[22] The city of Cahors (infamous for its usurers), forewarned by a circular in which Philip Augustus cautioned them about men who would try to encroach upon their civil liberties under the guise of the crusade, slammed its gates in Robert's face. He promptly burned them in revenge.[23] Robert of Auxerre reported that after Courson had preached the crusade for two years throughout France, his relationship with the local prelates had so deteriorated that they boycotted his council at Bourges and appealed to Rome, asking the pope to relax his legate's excessive decisions.[24]

---

restitution before alms, see DM, II.xxxii-iii, ed. Strange, 1:106-8; VA, PL 205:76,159; James of Vitry, *Sermones ad mercatores et campsores* 57, Douai 503, fols 392v-3r; and 59, fols 396v-7v; *De Usura*, 23, 35, 45-9; Kennedy, 326-7, 331-5.

[20]British Museum, Ms. Royal 7.D.I., fols 129r-v and 130r-v (the first edited in Dicksons, n. 1, p. 99). James contrasts the deceptiveness of monks who promise salvation and burial for alms with the proper reaction of a parish priest who refused to bury an unrepentant usurer despite his relatives' imprecations (*Sermo ad mercatores et campsores* 59, Douai 503, fol. 398r and Crane, no. 176-7).

[21]Note 3 above; Paris II.xxv. in Mansi, 22:832; VA, ch. 50, PL 205:157-8; *sermo ad mercatores and campsores* 58, Douai 503, fols 393v-4v; *De Usura*, 3, 9-20, 53-73, 79. The Chanter's circle assumed that usury was an urban phenomenon. It was not only a sin of merchants, but specifically of burghers and the hated communes, who managed to circumvent episcopal justice by writing their own laws on usury (James of Vitry, sermon 58, Douai 503, fols 394r-v, 395v-6r; sermon 52 to burghers, fols 386v-8r; Crane, no. 244; VA, ch. 50, 205:157, *De usura*, 63-5; DM, V.ix, ed. Strange, 1:289-90; and the anti-communal strictures of Paris Add. V.iii. and 'De usurariis' I.i. in Mansi, 22:851-2; X.V.xix.5 (1207).

[22]*Chronicle of Laon* (1214), MGH SS 26:78-9; Potthast 4922.

[23]The orthodox Cahorsins lent vast sums to Simon de Montfort. Philip Augustus' circular is contemporary with his petition against Robert's anti-usury efforts. In his reply to the latter, Innocent asked him to rescind the circular. See PL 217:229-30 (May, 1214); *Actes* 3:#1332 (perhaps misdated 1-18 August, 1214/1215); Y. Renouard, 'Les Cahorsins, Hommes d'affaires française du XIIIᵉ siècle', *Transactions of the Royal Historical Society* 11 (1961):43-67; Yves Dossat, Simon de Montfort', in *Paix de Dieu et guerre sainte en Languedoc au XIIIe siècle*, Cahiers de Fanjeaux 4 (Fanjeaux, 1969):281-302, esp. 289-90; Dicksons, 100; Potthast 5125; Peter of Vaux-de-Cernay, 2:146, 208, n. 2.

[24]Robert of Auxerre, *Chronicon* (1215), MGH SS 26:280.

In addition to warning his cities, Philip Augustus complained to Innocent about Courson's anti-usury decrees, trying to separate out his campaign against usury from his dual commission to hold local reform councils and preach the crusade. However, Innocent defended his legate. Although Courson had not received a special mandate, he did not need one. Usury was consuming the possessions of both the church and *milites*, and the rulings of the provincial councils gave Courson the authority he needed. While Innocent counselled Robert to moderation, urging him to respect honest custom and reserve important changes for the coming general council, he did not cancel his legation, and even arranged a composition between him and the irate French prelates.[25]

Although that composition is lost, another from 1214 sheds light on the protest from all quarters.[26] With Bouvines looming over the horizon, Philip Augustus was skittish about any erosion of his rights to levy military duties, taxes and tailles. The general package of crusaders' rights threatened his ability to marshall the economic and military resources of his kingdom. Legal and economic jurisdiction over crusaders was central to the provisions of this composition, which followed an inquest made by the bishops of Senlis and Paris and was approved by Robert as a temporary working measure until Fourth Lateran should meet.[27] Yet another reason why Philip Augustus and some barons and prelates opposed Robert's work probably lay in the delicate interlacing of legal jurisdiction over Christian usurers, a Gordian knot which Robert attempted to sever by urging bishops to work on an inquisitional rather than accusatorial basis, while calling princes and communes to defer to them in this matter. Some reform-minded bishops such as the archbishop of Rouen and Fulk of Toulouse welcomed their new powers. However, other secular princes, bishops, and monasteries were irked by an outsider's interference in an area as crucial as their legal jurisdiction over laymen. Undoubtedly some ecclesiastics were tied to the merchant community through blood relations or derived vital income through taxes or donations from such communities.[28]

---

[25]MPM 1:20-3; *Quia Maior*, PL 216:821-2; PL 217:229-30; Pott. 4922; preambles to Paris (1213) and Rouen (1214) in Mansi, 22:817, 899-900.

[26]Only cursory notices survive (Pott. 5161). For the composition of 1214, see PL 217:239-40 (March 1214), also *Actes* 3:#1360 (misdated 1215).

[27]See James M. Powell's outstanding *Anatomy of a Crusade, 1213-1221* (Philadelphia, 1986), 33-50, which informs my discussion below; see also Mundy, *Liberty*, 302, n. 65.

[28]MPM 1:302; *De Usura*, 18; notes 11 and 13 above. For earlier attempts to use episcopal inquisition against usurers, see McLaughlin, 'Canonists', 2, 13-5; X.V.19.c.12,15; Mundy, *Liberty*, n. 41, p. 295. Robert also attacked Jewish usurers, a lucrative source of taxes for Philip Augustus and other prelates and lay lords. For prelates' illicit links to the merchant community, see James of Vitry, *Sermo ad mercatores et campsores* 58, Douai 503, fol. 395v, VA, ch. 50, PL 205:158, and n. 12 above.

Although Robert of Auxerre and other chroniclers crow at the putative humiliation of Courson at Fourth Lateran, the only evidence for this is that no new extensive usury legislation was promulgated there, as had been hoped for by the Chanter's circle, who saw the general council's combination of papal power and secular presence as the only way to extirpate usury.[29] However, the fight against Christian usury predated Fourth Lateran and was not dependent upon new decrees. The existing decrees of Third Lateran (1179) and Fourth Lateran's mandate to hold diocesan synods and provincial councils opened the back door to Paris reformers, as Odo of Sully's synodal statutes and Robert of Courson's provincial councils became templates for the new diocesan and provincial application of the Fourth Lateran's reforms.[30] Bishops associated with the Paris circle, such as the archbishop of Rouen and Fulk of Toulouse, were a crucial part of the solution, as they promulgated new statutes, enforced old ones and arraigned usurers before their episcopal courts, forcing them or their heirs to make restitution.[31]

The Paris circle's fight against usury did not consist merely of legal coercion. Rather, the unedited sermons of James of Vitry to merchants and crusaders illustrate how the Paris circle's assault upon usury coincided temporally and thematically with their crusade preaching and how they sought to communicate their ideals to a lay audience. James of Vitry preached the Albigensian and Fifth Crusades in association with Robert of Courson, and both were heavily influenced by Peter the Chanter's writings on usury.[32] *Quia Maior* and other bulls directed

---

[29]See n. 44 below. For the Fourth Lateran as a partial triumph for the Paris reformers, see MPM 1:315-43; Dicksons, 116, 124-9; Powell, *Anatomy*, 41, n. 35, pp. 49-50; Foreville, *Latran*, 243-4, 290, 294, 296. Contrast with Penny J. Cole, *The Preaching of the Crusades to the Holy Land, 1095-1270* (Cambridge, Mass., 1991), 127-9 (hereafter Cole), and Achille Luchaire, *Le Concile de Latran et la Réforme de l'Église* (Paris, 1908), 45 and 52; *idem, Innocent III. La Question d'Orient* (Paris, 1907), 282-98, who follow Robert of Auxerre.

[30]Third Lateran Council (1179), c. 25, in COD, 223; Fourth Lateran Council (1215), c. 6, 7, 67 in COD, 236, 265-6. See Pontal, esp. lix, lx-lxi, lxxvii, 68-9, 105-7, 136; Mansfield, 63-74; C.R. Cheney, 'Statute-Making in the English Church in the Thirteenth Century', in *Medieval Texts and Studies* (Oxford, 1973), 138-57, esp. 144-7. For textual problems linked to diocesan and synodal legislation, see ibid., 111-37, 148-57, 185-202. Aspects of Robert's anti-usury legislation were promulgated at Montpellier and perhaps at Clermont, Bordeaux, Limoges and Reims (Dicksons, 100, 102-3, 109-10, 125-7; Montpellier (1215), I.v, I.xiv, I.xxx, in Mansi, 22:941, 943, 946; contrast Cole, 127-9).

[31]This may have led to something of a craze for testimentary restitution. James of Vitry calls for personal restitution during one's lifetime, if only for the reason that often the heirs did not follow through (sermon 59, Douai 503, fols 397v-8r). For the archbishop of Rouen, see n. 11 above. For Fulk of Toulouse's anti-usury campaign, see Mundy, *Liberty*, 61-3, 77-85, 88, 165, 290-1, 294-7; *idem*, 'Un usurier malheureux', *Annales du Midi* 68 (1956):217-25; Mireille Castaing-Sicard, *Les contrats dans le très ancien droit Toulousain, Xe-XIIIe siècles* (Toulouse, 1959), 256-60; n. 38 below.

[32]James' *Sermones ad mercatores et campsores* (58 and 59, Douai 503, fols 393v-8v) borrow heavily from the Chanter's *Verbum Abbreviatum*.

crusade preachers to target urban centers, and to stress in their preaching that those who gave money, useful advice or aid were to share in the crusade indulgence according to the quantity of their aid and the degree of their devotion. This included those who built ships or donated them to the crusade, and we know that James of Vitry specifically pursued the Genoese, whom he noted were seasoned sailors and sea merchants and thus extremely useful to the crusade cause. Their devout and wealthy wives were prime sources for vow commutations and donations. Other crusade preachers such as Oliver of Paderborn, Robert of Courson and Cardinal Hugolino of Ostia recruited in urban centers in Flanders, the Île-de-France and Northern Italy. Their success is indicated by Gervase of Prémontré's plaint that there was no one to commute the vows of the militarily unfit or protect burghers and rustics from the abuse of their crusading privileges after Robert's legation ceased in 1215.[33]

The anti-usury stance of the Paris circle was the logical outcome of their insistence upon the *vita apostolica* and voluntary poverty as the sign and expression of spiritual conversion, of their attempt to impose previously monastic values upon the world at large. They fused reform of the West with the promulgation of the crusade vow as one of the new quasi-monastic options offered to spiritual layfolk, a fusion with important consequences. The 'crusade idea' became further abstracted from the physical goal of liberating the holy land, and taking the crusade vow soon became to the Paris reformers preaching the crusade a marker of spiritual renewal or conversion. The specific targeting of non-military classes for crusade recruiting, particularly merchants, meant that anti-usury preaching in one sense logically accompanied the new extension of the vow to those who gave money.

The teaching of Peter the Chanter's circle, as disseminated in James of Vitry's sermons to merchants, stressed that the anxieties and sin associated even with licit business strangle spiritual things.[34] Papal bulls and the crusade sermons of James of Vitry presented voluntary poverty and almsgiving as the cure for usury.[35] They criticized the wealthy for luxuriating in their riches while the cross, the instrument

---

[33]*Quia Maior* (1213), PL 216:818-19; *Pium et Sanctum* (1213), PL 216:822; *Ad Liberandum* (1215) in COD, 267-71; James of Vitry, *Lettres*, ed. R. B. C. Huygens (Leiden, 1960), Ep. 1, pp. 76-8 (hereafter Huygens); Gervase of Prémontré in Karl L. Hugo, *Sacrae Antiquitatis Monumenta Historica, Dogmatica, Diplomatica*, vol. 1 (Stivagii, 1775), Ep. 2, pp. 3-5, Ep. 4, pp. 6-8 (hereafter Hugo); Guido Levi, *Registri dei Cardinali Ugolino d'Ostia e Ottaviano degli Ubaldini*, Istituto storico italiano, Fonti per la storia d'Italia (Rome, 1890), Eps. 8, 11, 17-8, 77, etc.

[34]VA, ch. 19-20, PL 205:72; James of Vitry, sermons to burghers and merchants in Douai 503, no. 52, fols 382r-5r; no. 53, fols 386r, 387v-8r; no. 56, fols 388r, 390v, Pitra, 433-4; no. 57, fols 391r-v; no. 58, fol. 393v; *exempla* from the same in Crane, nos. 157, 159-66.

[35]*Sermo ad cives et burgos* 53, Douai 503, fols 383r-v, 385r; *sermo ad mercatores et campsores* 58, fol. 393v, fols 394v-5r; n. 19 above.

of voluntary poverty that Christ had assumed for their salvation, was in the hands of the Gentiles. The faithful ought to take up the cross in *imitatio Christi* even unto death.[36] This crusading call to voluntary poverty is virtually identical to that in sermons addressed to merchants.[37] In fact, the link between crusade and anti-usury preaching came in that both called for conversion, expressed in the renunciation of riches by adopting voluntary poverty and a quasi-regular existence.

What the ideal response of the merchant was to be is illustrated in the *Vita* of Mary of Oignies. In his preamble, James says that the exiled Bishop Fulk of Toulouse, drawn by crusaders' reports of the beguines in the diocese of Liège, came to Oignies and persuaded James to write Mary's *Vita* as preaching material for the Albigensian crusade.[38] It may have been intended for anti-usury preaching in Toulouse as well, for in describing the religious women of the Liège area, what James stresses most is their hatred of their relations' riches. Mary of Oignies first persuaded her husband to give all their possessions to the poor. Abandoning her family and the world, she embraced a life of manual labor and service.[39] As a quasi-regular she took elaborate measures to avoid usurious alms given to the leper hospital where she worked, to the point of eating wild herbs. She had clearly absorbed the Paris teaching on restitution of usury, as she had visions of two superficially pious widows of usurers who did not make proper restitution to their husband's victims and so burned in hell or purgatory, themes one could

---

[36]Unpublished protheme, *sermo ad crucesignatos vel crucesignandos*, Douai 503, fols 364r-6r; partial edition of the same in Pitra, 2:425-7 and n. 35 above. James uses *religio* to describe both crusaders and religious orders (*Historia Hierosolymitana*, in *Gesta Dei per Francos*, ed. Jacques Bongars, 2 vols [Douce, 1611], 1:1048).

[37]*Quia maior*, PL 216:817; *Post Miserabile*, Reg. 1:336, pp. 499-505; *Utinam Dominus*, PL 215:1501; *sermo ad crucesignatos*, Pitra, 2:425, 427-8; *sermo ad cives et burgenses* 52, Douai 503, fols 382v-4r; *sermo ad mercatores et campsores* 56, ibid., fols 388r-9r, 390v.

[38]*Vita Marie Oigniacensis*, ed. Daniel Paperbroeck, in AASS, June 5 (Paris 1707), 636B-E, 637C-D (hereafter VMO). Nicolette Schulman, currently writing a PhD thesis on Fulk of Toulouse at the University of Toronto, thinks that Fulk may have heard of the *mulieres sanctae* from James as early as the summer of 1210 in Paris or the winter of 1211/1212 in the Liège area. The former date may indicate that Fulk instituted an episcopal anti-usury tribunal at the instigation of the Paris circle (from 1211 onwards, see n. 31 above).

[39]VMO 636E-637A, 639A-D. Matthew 16:24, a favored authority for self-abnegation by means of the monastic life or the crusade vow, is used to describe Mary's renunciation (VMO 640E-F, 645C-E, 647E-48B). She had been denied itinerant mendicancy and the crusade vow (VMO, 648F-49A, 658CD). For contemporary attitudes toward 'pauperes', see Jean Batany, 'Les Pauvres et la Pauvreté dans les Revues des "Estats du Mond",' in *Développement du paupèrisme et organisation de l'assistance*, ed. Michel Mollat, Études sur l'Histoire de la Pauvreté, vol. 1, part 2 (Paris, 1974), 469-86; Jean Longère, 'Pauvreté et Richesse chez quelques predicateurs durant la seconde moitie du XII° siècle', in ibid., 255-73.

easily imagine Fulk of Toulouse preaching with alacrity to the burghers of Toulouse.[40]

We know that usury thrived in urban areas, as did confraternity-like communities such as the Humiliati, whose literacy and emphasis upon poverty suggest that many were from the merchant class, as were many of the lay religious around Oignies, including one merchant who went on the Albigensian crusade and Mary herself.[41] Just as these communities emphasized the need to live from manual labor, so the Paris circle hailed it as the prime component of the *vita apostolica* and the opposite of the usurer's accumulation of interest through inactivity. In a sermon to manual laborers, James says that the *respublica* would not be able to stand firm without manual labor, while usury destroys society. The farmer often works harder than the monks in the cloister, and if he toils with penitential intent, he is promised eternal life.[42] The hardships of lay life, if undertaken with the same spirit as one who enters the monastery to earn penance by prayer and self-imposed hardships, also earn one penance. The same was true of the difficulties endured on crusade, and in at least one *exemplum*, monastic life and the crusade are assigned as equivalent penitential labor.[43]

The Paris reformers wanted to extend this quasi-regular ideal to all layfolk. James warns merchants that they are safer as farmers or artisans, while Robert of Courson suggested that the only way to extirpate usury were if a general council were called where church and secular authorities could force everyone to live

---

[40]VMO 647E-648B, 650EF, 670AB. On inherited usurious money's damning effect, see *sermo ad mercatores et campsores* 59, Douai 503, fols 397r-v; *De usura*, 83; VA, ch. 50, PL 205:159.

[41]Huygens, Ep. 1, pp. 72-3, 74-6; Suppl. to VMO, 667B-E; VMO 639EF, 670AB. See Lester K. Little, *Religious Poverty and the Profit Economy in Medieval Europe* (London, 1978), 188-90, 254-5; Herbert Grundmann, *Religious Movements in the Middle Ages*, trans. Steven Rowan (Notre Dame, 1995), 25, 28, 35, 69-74, 82-8; Brenda Bolton, '*Paupertas Christi*: Old Wealth and New Poverty in the Twelfth Century', in *Renaissance and Renewal in Christian History*, ed. Derek Baker, Studies in Church History 14 (Oxford, 1977):95-103, but see n. 2 above. For the Paris circle's emphasis upon labor as one of the criterion for a legitimate profession and as a penitential process in itself, see the discussion below and Jacques Le Goff, 'Trades and Professions as Represented in Medieval Confessor's Manuals', in *Time, Work and Culture*, trans. Arthur Goldhammer (Chicago, 1980), 107-12; *idem*, 'Merchant's Time and Church's Time in the Middle Ages', in ibid., 29-42 (although I disagree with some of his conclusions); MPM 1:271.

[42]VA, ch. 50, PL 205:157-9; *De usura*, 37; *Sermo ad agricolas et vinitores et alios operarios*, partially edited in Pitra, 2:435-6; *sermo ad mercatores et campsores* 58, Douai 503, fols 394v-5v, 397v. James stresses manual labor and voluntary poverty in sermons to religious and layfolk as an individual and societal panacea.

[43]DM, I.xvi, ed. Strange, 1:23; Kennedy, 307. Penitents were bound by many of the same restrictions as monks (Mansfield, 180-1), some of which crusade preachers sought to impose upon their recruits on campaign.

from manual or spiritual labor. Rid of usury and rapine, the world would return to its pristine state.[44]

These ideals had been applied by members of the Chanter's circle who preached the Fourth Crusade, including Fulk of Neuilly and Eustace of Flay. From 1195 onwards, Fulk campaigned against usury and prostitution with a conversion drive which caused many to take the cross or contribute alms for Jerusalem. He would dun usurers publicly until they confessed, then tell them to make restitution or give their usurious money to the poor.[45] Eustace of Flay's preaching tour in England combined crusade recruiting with a fierce opposition to usury and to trading on Sundays and feastdays.[46] Matthew Paris notes that he made magnates, prelates and wealthy citizens, particularly merchants, the focus of alms-giving campaigns. He had alms trunks put in every church for people to donate for charitable purposes a percentage of money earned from food sold on Sundays, and he stressed social responsibility for the poor, which he may have joined with responsibility for Christian brothers in the East. In fact, Matthew claims that Eustace converted usurers and warned them to take up the Lord's cross.[47]

Innocent not only supported Fulk's reform and crusade preaching, but welded it to a wider anti-usury campaign.[48] He also strove to link the crusade with familiar devotional practices such as alms trunks, processions, and prayers, targeting the class which had the most alms to give – merchants.[49] This is illustrated by the striking similarity of Eustace's letter from heaven to a bull of Innocent III addressed to the archbishop of Canterbury and the English prelates

---

[44]*Sermo ad mercatores et campsores* 57, Douai 503, fol. 393r; *De Usura*, 37.

[45]H. Occ., 89-101, and the sources cited in Milton R. Gutsch, 'A Twelfth Century Preacher – Fulk of Neuilly', in *The Crusades and Other Historical Essays presented to Dana C. Munro*, ed. L. J. Paetow (New York, 1928), 183-206, particularly Roger of Howdon, *Chronica*, ed. William Stubbs, 4 vols, RS 51 (London, 1868-71), 4:76. Robert of Auxerre linked repression of Jewish usury to Fulk's anti-usury and crusade preaching (MGH 26:258, see William Chester Jordan, *Jews and the French Monarchy*, 40-45).

[46]Some have considered his preaching activity to be purely reform-oriented. See Cole, 88; C. R. Cheney, *Pope Innocent III and England* (Stuttgart, 1976), 241 and n. 12. At least two English chroniclers link Eustace to Fulk (Roger of Howdon, 4:123; Ralph of Coggeshall, *Chronicon Anglicanum*, ed. Joseph Stevenson, RS 66 [London, 1875]:133), and Howdon specifically states that 'Ipse etiam praedicatione sua corda multorum convertit ad usurarum relazationem, et ad crucem Jerosolimitanae profectionis capiendam' (4:124), as does Roger of Wendover (Matthew Paris, *Chronica Majora*, ed. H. R. Luard, RS 57 [London, 1872-1882], 2:465). For Eustace's campaign against Sunday and feastday trading (shared by Peter the Chanter's circle), see J. L. Cate, 'The English Mission of Eustace of Flay (1200-1202)', in *Etudes d'histoire dediées à la mémoire d'Henri Pirenne*, ed F. L. Ganshof, E. Sabbe, and F. Vercauteren (Brussels, 1937), 67-89; MPM 1:266.

[47]Roger of Howdon, 4:124, 169; Matthew Paris, *Chronica Majora*, 2:465.

[48]PL 214:375-6.

[49]*Utinam Dominus*, PL 217:1502; *Quia Maior*, PL 216:821-2; *Ad Liberandum* in COD, 270-1.

in 1201, the year of Eustace's reform tour. Eustace's celestial epistle linked the sins of the West to the loss of the East, as did papal bulls. In Eustace's case, improved care of the poor and the ending of Sunday markets were seen as prerequisite to regaining God's favor in the Holy Land,[50] and both Eustace and Innocent call for the conversion of the wealthy to voluntary poverty through assuming the cross. Innocent had commanded this message to be preached throughout England, so that people would take the cross and aid the Holy Land with their possessions.[51]

Eustace and Fulk's emphasis upon the necessity for giving alms in restitution for usury must have resonated with crusade bulls, which stress almsgiving for their new non-military audience. Just as Peter the Chanter asserted that the avaricious incur God's wrath because they refuse to give alms to the poor here on earth, who represent Christ, so *Utinam Dominus* told preachers to assure the city populace of Italy that even a small gift could bring spiritual benefit. The famous mitigation of the crusade vow, where Innocent allowed those who contributed to the Holy Land to share in the remission of sins according to the quantity of aid and the quality of devotion, is justified as the familiar practice of commuting the work of penance into the work of giving alms.[52] If the division posited by Jean-Marc Bienvenu ever existed, where the bourgeoisie channelled their devotion into giving alms to the new urban poor while the nobility met their spiritual needs through the crusades, it disintegrated as the 'crusade idea' evolved and merchants could now participate in the crusade both by going in person and by their favored charitable activity.[53]

However, the usurer was placed in a special situation. He was often wealthy and thus a prime target for crusade recruitment, yet according to the Paris reform circle, his alms were worthless until he had made complete restitution. Preachers stressed this particular point through *exempla* which portrayed the usurer who repented, only to nearly despair when he found that his accustomed route of penance was worthless. Once the severity of his situation hit home, he was willing to do anything to attain salvation and surrendered himself to the discretion of his confessor. These *exempla* were meant to counter the real situation, as James confesses just how hard a nut the usurer was to crack. Concern to maintain their lifestyle and avoid impoverishing their families made them much more willing to give alms which earned them public praise, than to make humiliating

---

[50]Ralph of Coggeshall, 168-9; Matthew Paris, *Chronica Majora*, 4:462-6.

[51]Roger of Howdon, 4:165-7; C. R. Cheney and M. G. Cheney, eds, *The Letters of Innocent III (1198-1216) concerning England and Wales* (Oxford, 1967), no. 318.

[52]*Quia Maior*, PL 216:818; *Utinam Dominus*, PL 215:1502-3.

[53]Jean-Marc Bienvenu, 'Fondations Charitables Laiques au XII⁰ siècle: L'exemple de l'Anjou', in Mollat, *Développement du paupérisme*, 563-9.

restitution to people they had victimized. The ideal pattern was that of Theobald the Rich, infamous usurer of Paris, who repented and went to Maurice de Sully, bishop of Paris, who suggested that he give alms to the bishop's pet project, the construction of Notre Dame. However, Theobald instead chose the counsel of Peter the Chanter, who advised him to have a crier broadcast his willingness to make restitution. After he had repaid all claimants, he could give alms from any remaining money.[54]

Certainly there was confusion on the ground level as to what exactly a penitent usurer ought to do. If he heard a crusade sermon, he would be given three options – going in person, sending a substitute or contributing money.[55] In fact, James of Vitry, in order to reach the commercial mentality of his audience, had presented the crusade indulgence as a spiritual bargain, a golden opportunity to avoid all penance in this world and purgatory in the next, as did *Quia Maior*.[56] James emphasizes how the cross is much more efficacious than any other penitential option, including almsgiving for the dead, fasting and wearing hair shirts, thus situating it in the penitential spectrum familiar to burghers, which ranged from penalties imposed in the relative privacy of the confessional to shaming penitential acts assigned by episcopal courts to humiliate manifest usurers.[57] In some cases, the latter could be commuted into less humiliating almsgiving. However, this avenue was not always open to the usurer, who had sinned by his money, and was bound to make restitution as the first and primary component of his penance. In fact, Robert of Courson suggested the opposite to the above process – if the usurer lacked the funds to make monetary restitution, the impecunious *fenerator* should make what restitution he could, beg his victims' forgiveness, then go on crusade.[58]

---

[54] James of Vitry, sermons 58-9, Douai 503, fols 393v-6r, 396r-8v; DM, II.xxxiii (Theobald) and II.xxxi-ii (Strange, 1:103-8); Otto of Sanblaise on Fulk of Neuilly, MGH SS 20:330; see also *De Usura*, 83.

[55] James changes the official offer of a partial indulgence graded according to quantity contributed and quality of devotion and simply says that those who give money to crusaders receive the indulgence as do *crucesignati* who leave legacies in their wills (Pitra, 2:426-9 and n. 33 above).

[56] *Quia Maior*, PL 216:818; James of Vitry, *sermo ad crucesignatos vel crucesignandos*, partly edited in Pitra, 2:428-30; Bernard of Clairvaux, Ep. 363, PL 182:567. James' sermons to pilgrims, which clearly doubled as crusading sermons, are also crammed with mercantile images (nos. 49-50, Douai 503, fols 368v-74r).

[57] Mansfield, 115-23. The proper audience response is indicated by an *exemplum* in which a man literally jumps at the offer – out the window to avoid his obstructionist wife (Pitra, 2:428-9).

[58] Mansfield, 85-6 and notes 93-4; n. 19 above; Kennedy, 334-5. Robert offers this option in the face of various objections which argue that the usurer or robber ought not to be allowed to commute the penance of restitution 'vel in penam peregrinationis vel in aliam . . . ergo non debet alicui pro restitutione facienda iter peregrinationis Iherosolimitane iniungere' (ibid., 334).

Crusade and reform preaching were intended to effect a conversion, followed by confession and assigned penance, which in the case of someone taking the cross, was 'commuted' into the penance earned by taking the cross as a form of penitential pilgrimage.[59] The privilege to absolve excommunicates, traditionally reserved to the bishop, was granted to crusade preachers, who thus utilized both the private penance of the contrite sinner in the confessional and that penance which had become public by virtue of the penitent's excommunicate state or manifest sin. The public aspect of taking the cross was exploited by crusader preachers, who presented it as an honorable alternative to the shame inherent in the usurer's execrable profession.[60] In a sermon to *crucesignati,* in an argument which must have appealed to usurers, James says that he who corrupted many by his bad example can now make restitution to God by building up many. Why would one be ashamed to take the cross publicly, when one used to sin publicly? The usurer could thus move from a shunned status similar to that of a Jew or heretic to the ideal Christian by becoming a *crucesignatus.* Caesarius of Heisterbach relates how during the preaching campaigns of Oliver of Paderborn and John of Xanten (both acquaintances of James of Vitry), a rustic usurer named Gottschalk took the cross not from devotion, but from the social pressure exerted by those around him.[61]

So if the usurer escaped censure in the legal forum, he could be got at through public opinion and the confessional forum.[62] However, there were problems with

---

[59]Mansfield, 125, 128, 279-81, 284-7; Villey, 145-6. For contemporary cases of the crusade as penitential pilgrimage in Frisia, see DM, VII.iii, XII.xxiv, ed. Strange, 2:3-5, 332-5, and the case of Raymond VI of Toulouse (Mansi, 22:815, 816D). In such instances, proper devotion was in question. James depicts the hordes of criminals who had paid to have their sentences commuted to an exile in the Holy Land as a force detrimental to the crusading cause (*Historia Orientalis,* ch. 83, in *Libri duo quorum prior Orientalis sive Hierosolymitanae alter Occidentalis historiae nomine inscribitur,* ed. F. Moschus, [Douai, 1597; repr. Farnborough, 1971], 162-3).

[60]Usury fell midway between public and private penance due to its practitioners' notoriety (Mansfield, 85, 113-4, 117-23). Public penance suited anti-usury preachers perfectly, who despite the new technology of negotiated penance in the confessional, longed for the usurer's humiliation. Peter the Chanter allowed priests preaching against usury to denounce manifest usurers by name and, as the final touch to Theobald the Rich's penance, enjoined him to process through Paris clad only in a loincloth, while his servant beat him with a rod and proclaimed, 'Behold, this is the man whom the state honored for his wealth, who held nobles' sons hostage' (DM, II.xxxii, ed. Strange, 1:106; Mansfield, 21, 49, 115, 265). In his sermons to merchants, James combines *exempla* illustrating the social opprobrium usurers faced with protestations that paradoxically, some usurers were honored for their riches and sheltered in the courts of prelates and princes. As a result, those who feared the contempt of a world which despises 'pauperes' took up usury (Crane, no. 179, and sermon 58, fol. 395v, which copies VA, ch. 50, PL 205:158).

[61]*Ad crucesignatos vel crucesignandos,* in Pitra, 2:428-9; DM, II.viii, ed. Strange,1:70.

[62]*Sermo ad crucesignatis et crucesignandis,* Pitra, 2:428-9; *De Usura,* 35, 41. The Paris circle's effort to make confession central was one of the leading factors for the adoption of 'Omnius utriusque' at Fourth Lateran. They wrote the earliest manuals for confessors, urging the confessor to question

signing usurers. Would the goal of crusade preaching be humiliation through penitential acts or the funding of the crusade through vow commutations? The deliberate recruitment of the militarily unfit and the resulting widespread commutation of vows threatened to place the merit and emphasis upon the very money with which the vow was redeemed, as in Gottchalk's case. When the papal dispensators were collecting the redemption money from the old, poor and infirm, Gottschalk passed himself off as a pauper and commuted his vow for five talents, because the dispensator had not checked with the parish priest. He then went to the local tavern and jeered at the pilgrims about to depart. 'You stupidly cross the sea, expending your possessions and endangering your lives. I however, will stay at home with my wife and my money, and for the five marks with which I redeemed my cross, will have a similar reward to you'.[63] He had obviously heard and absorbed sermons where the crusade indulgence was presented as a bargain which could be bought by alms, but had missed the crucial insistence upon contrition!

There were other problems as well. Which should come first, restitution to victims or fulfillment of the usurer's crusade vow? In the council of Paris (1213), Courson decreed that by special papal dispensation for converted usurers, the repentant *dives* could hand over the money acquired by usury to a prelate, legate or other intermediary, who should then consider if the converted usurer has many children, is poor or has just taken the cross. In such cases, the intermediary could reserve money for the usurer to live from, then use the remainder to make restitution, a mitigation of Courson's theoretical approach, which demanded that the usurer and his family beg in the streets before they lived from unjustly acquired money.[64] Obviously Robert had moderated his original opinion, due partly to the opposition of prelates responsible for enforcing the legislation, partly to the realization that if usurers were to be converted at all, severity had to be balanced with mercy.[65]

One can imagine how easily the fine distinction could be lost of giving alms through an intermediary and only after restitution, particularly as the roving

---

each profession on the sins to which they were most prone (in the case of merchants, usury and fraud) (Mansfield, 6, 18-53, 62-74, 288-9; Alexander Murray, 'Confession before 1215', *Transactions of the Royal Historical Society*, 6th series, 3 [1993]:51-81).

[63] A neighbor swore that he could have paid 40 marks (DM, II.vii, ed. Strange,1:71).

[64] Paris. Add. V.iv, in Mansi, 22:850; Kennedy, 334; Mansfield, 55-9, 85-91. His *De Usura* offers painfully detailed instructions on restitution (47-9). Other council canons suggest that the indigent usurer ask for his victims' forgiveness from monetary restitution and make satisfaction through non-monetary means such as prayers or fasts for the victims' souls, just as Robert suggested that with his victims' permission he substitute the pilgrimage for any remaining restitution (Mansfield, 86 and n. 89).

[65] See DM, III.lii, ed. Strange,1:169; Kennedy, 326.

preachers commissioned to recruit men and alms for the crusade must have appeared very similar to the very pseudo-preachers they denounced – wandering preachers who offered indulgences in return for donations for building churches. James and Robert of Courson took pains to separate their own activities from those of such men, and worried that the *quaestuarii* provided the usurer with an opportunity to circumvent making restitution, as did religious houses which accepted their alms and provided them with burial.[66]

In order to segregate themselves from the pseudo-preachers, the Paris circle insisted that the reform preacher live a scrupulously upright life. Similarly, in *Pium et Sanctum*, Innocent admonished crusade preachers to limit their entourages and procurations.[67] This was even more crucial when the crusade preacher was collecting money, for as the case of Fulk of Neuilly illustrates, the preacher's credibility could plunge even as the alms he collected amassed.[68] That people did respond to the call to give alms and that Innocent's instructions for placing alms-chests in churches were followed is indicated by chronicle evidence.[69] However, commutation of the vows of burghers and other non-military people proved to be an invitation for alarms about abuses, and some of the French clergy were not enthusiastic about the combination of indiscriminate signing and reform. One chronicler claimed that Courson and others of the Paris circle used to preach throughout the kingdom of France, signing children, old people, women, the lame, blind, deaf, even lepers. As a result, many rich men shunned taking the cross.[70]

In addition, it would seem that the audience could be all too aware of the irony of reform preachers decrying usury while collecting vast sums of money for the crusade effort. The cognitive dissonance which arose from preachers condemning usurious and fraudulent practices while speaking of the crusade in mercantilistic

---

[66]On *questuarii*, see H.Occ., 103-6; Kennedy, 326-7, 330-1, 333. Prohibitions against wandering preachers abound in councils (e.g. Council of Paris [1213] I.vii-ix, in Mansi, 22:820-1). In one sermon to merchants, James stresses that doctors study hard in Paris to seek the sinners' souls, not their possessions (no. 57, Douai 503, fol. 390v). For the circle's detestation of religious houses built from usurious alms, see *De usura*, 35-7; Frederick M. Powicke, *Stephen Langton* (London, 1965), pp.16, 88; DM, VIII.xlvi, ed. Strange, 2:118; Douai 503, sermon 59, fol. 396v; notes 17 and 19 above.

[67]*Pium et Sanctum* (1213), PL 216:822-3; H.Occ., 89-90, 94-101; Walter L. Wakefield, *Heresy, Crusade and Inquisition in Southern France* (London, 1974), 89-90.

[68]H.Occ., 100-1; however, cf. Otto of Sanblaise, MGH SS 20:331, *Chronicle of St. Denis*, RHGF 17:384DE, Eudes Rigord in RHGF 17:48. Many chroniclers concocted elaborate explanations of just where the alms gathered by Fulk of Neuilly and others went (see Gutsch, cited n. 45 above).

[69]For England, see the *Annals of Dunstaple*, in *Annales Monastici*, ed. H. R. Luard, 4 vols, RS 36 (London, 1857-69) 3:40 (1212); *Annals of Waverly*, ibid., 2:281, 289; Ralph of Coggeshall, *Chronicon Anglicanum*, p.168 (1214); for Oliver of Paderborn's preaching campaign, see Emo, *Chronicon*, MGH SS 23:473; *Chronicle of the Kingdom of Cologne, first continuation*, MGH SS 24:18.

[70]William the Breton, RHGF 17:108; cf. Robert on commutation of penance (Kennedy, 326-7, 331-5).

terms and accepting money from merchants for vow commutations and crusade donations (no matter how strictly controlled) would later lead Matthew Paris and other chroniclers to denounce the friars for selling crusade indulgences like Cistercians sold sheep at woolmarkets. However, it would seem that the novelty of the vow commutation and mercantile recruitment saved the Paris preachers from the accusations of mercenary banality which would soon swathe the friars, although the murmurings of Robert of Auxerre and the chronicler of Laon would soon crescendo into the shrill criticisms of Matthew Paris and many others during the pontificate of Innocent IV.[71]

From the strictly practical angle, some of Courson's efforts may perhaps have hindered the crusade. His insistence that crusaders should rather, naked, follow the naked Christ than accept loans from Jews or usurers restricted an accessible source of funding.[72] And, as James Brundage has noted, Innocent's decrees that crusaders could be absolved from interest on their loans while on crusade effectively ruined their credit rating.[73] However, despite Robert of Auxerre's protest above, it would seem that widescale recruiting and the contemporaneous fight against usury did not necessarily alienate rich men and *milites*. Robert of Courson recruited a powerful contingent of nobles from France, and the sermons and recruiting activities of other crusade preachers such as James of Vitry show that noblemen were as susceptible to the new mercantile rhetoric of voluntary poverty as they were to the older themes of loyalty, service and revenge.[74] But perhaps the practical impediments brought about by the anti-usury campaign will help us to reconsider the portrayal of Innocent as above all a goal-oriented organizer of the crusades. For on the subject of usury, his appointment of Paris reformers to preach the crusade and his stipulations against usurious contracts actually helped to alienate some powerful prelates and secular rulers such as Philip Augustus and kept some crusaders from finding the necessary funding to go on crusade. In this respect, reform may have triumphed over crusade in the Innocentian plan before the Fourth Lateran Council.

---

[71] See Barbara H. Rosenwein and Lester K. Little, 'Social Meaning in the Monastic and Mendicant Spiritualities', *Past and Present* 63 (1974):4-32. Matthew Paris contrasts the Paris circle to the friars, particularly on the subjects of usury and crusade preaching (*Chronica Majora*, 5:404-7). I am writing an article on this topic.

[72] *De usura*, 19-20, 39-41, 43, 55, 79; Chobham, 510. However, Robert admitted that if the crusader could find no other source of money to fulfill his vow, he could borrow from a usurer, after first asking him to lend without interest.

[73] *De usura*, 41-3; Brundage, *Canon Law*, 180-3; Noonan, *Scholastic Analysis*, 13-14, 17-18. Crusade and reform also clashed on practical grounds under Eugenius III, who was the first to specify crusaders' freedom from usury on loans and who attacked monasteries' and cathedral chapters' use of the usurious mortgage (the primary source of funding for landed crusaders).

[74] See Powell, *Anatomy*, 34-5, 38-9; Dicksons, 75-6, 106-7, 130-1; RHGF 19:610, 615, 629-30, 661, 663; n. 41 above on the social composition of the Humiliati, etc.

However, at Fourth Lateran itself, it would seem that a composition which Innocent brokered between Robert, some French prelates and Philip Augustus probably involved a stipulation which defanged the reforming and jurisdictional powers of legates for the crusades in France. There would be no more legates with sweeping control over crusaders to interfere in episcopal, royal and communal jurisdiction. Instead, *crucesignati* would be at the mercy of the local episcopal court to protect their rights. Part of the Paris circle's attraction as preachers had been their ability to take the power to protect crusaders' rights and use this to lobby against usury, an activity which won them partisanship from both nobles and bourgeoisie. In the end, it would seem that it was Robert's extensive and willing use of legatine powers, combined with his reform program, which caused the real protest.[75]

Perhaps, stymied by episcopal and secular opposition at Fourth Lateran, Innocent planned to circumvent it by a post-council appointment. Certainly both Gervase of Prémontré and James of Vitry insisted that a new legate was needed to protect the less powerful crusaders, whose legal and financial rights were being abused by the very secular and religious magnates who had promised them money, counsel and leadership when they took the cross. James foresaw that his inability to enforce the spectacular legal and spiritual privileges he preached would undermine his recruiting efforts. However, any hope that James, now bishop-elect of Acre, might succeed Courson as legate was dashed with Innocent's premature demise. Despite a congenial reception, Honorius III claimed that he could not give James special powers in this matter, pointing to the Fourth Lateran pact which entrusted the defense of the crusaders to the prelates of France. James' ties to Courson may have prevented his appointment, for he was shipped out to Acre to prepare for the crusading army's arrival, and by 5 December 1216, Honorius had chosen an outsider as papal nuncio and protector for crusaders in the kingdom of France, Archbishop Simon of Tyre. Gervase of Prémontré portrays the unfortunate Simon as a vacillating interloper bereft of a European support base, dubious about the extent of his own power, completely dependent upon the pope and the by then clearly inadequate provisions of *Ad Liberandam*, too dithering to protect crusaders against exploitation by local secular and ecclesiastical lords.[76]

---

[75]Sources cited in n. 76 below. Robert of Auxerre and other chroniclers who criticized Robert were willing to embrace as reformers theologians such as Peter the Chanter and charismatic preachers such as Fulk of Neuilly, because neither attempted to impose permanent laws. They seem to have resented Robert's willing use of legatine powers more than his actual reforms.

[76]Gervase of Prémontré, Eps. 2 (February 1217) and 4 (July-August 1216) in Hugo 1:2-5, 6-8; Huygens, Ep. 1, p. 74 (October 1216); RHGF 19:615-6; 629-30, 661, 663; *Ad Liberandam*, COD, 269; Joseph Greven, 'Frankreich und der fünfte Kreuzzug', *Historisches Jahrbuch* 43 (1923):15-52, esp. 34-40, 52; Powell, *Anatomy*, 119. Protectors were appointed for specific areas in Germany, e.g.

The progress or collapse of the crusade and reform synthesis depended upon a host of factors: varying success rates for the publication of Fourth Lateran's statutes, prelates' inclination or disinclination to enforce them or extend them by their own statutes, the individual fates of various reformers and the ambivalent relationship of papal and local authority. The cooperation of the archbishop of Rouen and the bishops of Paris and Toulouse and the provisions of Fourth Lateran for provincial councils and diocesan synods illustrate that the implementation of both reform and crusade ultimately devolved upon bishops and their diocesan clergy.[77] Despite the increasing spiritual and legal influence of the papal curia in western Europe, even papal legates and judges delegate depended upon local authorities. For this very reason, judges delegate for the protection of crusaders' rights, of preachers and of tax collectors for the crusade were often chosen from local diocesan office-holders or monastic houses.[78] In the absence of a legate, the checks-and-balances system of diocesan clergy, papally appointed local clergy and papal legate became unbalanced, with the result that the center of gravity swung towards local interest and responsibility. In the case of the kingdom of France, this meant that bishops' involvement in the crusade so absorbed their energies that even the most zealous were too busy to make or enforce reforming statutes.[79] However, in the Languedoc, the continued delegation of strong papal legates who worked in tandem with local prelates united reform and crusade both before and after Fourth Lateran, ensuring continued anti-usury legislation. In contrast, the widespread imposition of anti-usury laws in the kingdom of France would have to wait for the advent of Louis IX, who looked upon the reform of France and the repression of usury as integral to his crusading preparations. While Philip Augustus resented the intrusion of reformers into 'secular' affairs (taxation, jurisdiction over crusaders and usurers), Louis IX simply augmented his kingly jurisdiction and moral authority by adopting the reformers' agenda. Once usury became a royal concern, he could issue anti-usury laws for the entire kingdom of France and could coerce as well as cajole local authorities into compliance by utilizing secular officials and the friars as his publicists and

---

Conrad of Marburg and John of Zanten for the archdiocese of Bremen in January, 1216 (PL 217:255-8).

[77] Eps. 2, 4, 33-5 in Hugo 1:2-5, 6-8, 34-6; Huygens, Ep. 1, p. 74.

[78] J. E. Sayers, *Papal Judges Delegate in the Province of Canterbury 1198-1254* (Oxford, 1971), esp. 100-62; Powell, *Anatomy*, 22-7; see Gervase's suggestions for appointees, n. 2 above.

[79] Gervase and James blame the disorder in funding and departure arrangements on the lack of clear central planning and papal control through either papal letters or an effective legate. See n. 2 above, Powell, *Anatomy*, 91-103. For England and Germany, see C. R. Cheney, *Pope Innocent III and England*, Päpst und Papsttum 9 (Stuttgart, 1976):239-70; M. Gibbs and J. Lang, *Bishops and Reform, 1215-1272* (Oxford, 1934); P. B. Pixton, *The German Episcopacy and the Implementation of the Decrees of the Fourth Lateran Council, 1216-1245: Watchmen on the Tower* (Leiden/New York/Cologne, 1995).

enforcers, thus providing the centralized spiritual and secular authority needed to pursue offenders.[80]

[80]For Louis VIII's involvement in the Peace of Paris (1229) and conciliar work in the Midi, see *L'Église et le droit dans le Midi (XIIIe-XIVe s.)*, Cahiers de Fanjeaux 29 (Fanjeaux, 1994):147-213; William Chester Jordan, *Louis IX and the Challenge of the Crusade* (Princeton, NJ, 1979), esp. 86, 101, 154-5, 176-8, 184-8, 190, 232-5; Mansfield, 55, 277; n. 5 above. I would like to thank Carolyn Muessig and Jean Longère for guiding me through the multifarious manuscripts of James of Vitry, and Michelle Lucey, Alexander Murray, Edward Peters, Norman Tanner, Jean Dunbabin and Christopher Tyerman for generously reading and criticizing various stages of this paper, which would never have been written without the financial munificence of the Fulbright Association and the Thouron family. Dr Jonathan Phillips and the Seminar on the Study of the Crusades and the Latin East were a forgiving first audience. All errors remain my own.

Pope Innocent III and the Jews

Robert Chazan

Pope Innocent III has been regularly recognized by historians of medieval Christendom and the medieval church as a pivotal figure. In Colin Morris's recent volume on the western church from 1050 to 1250 in the *Oxford History of the Christian Church*, only one chapter is devoted to a single pontiff, not surprisingly Innocent III. Yet more striking is Morris's decision to introduce the entire volume with a citation from Pope Innocent III: 'Christ left to Peter not only the whole church, but the whole world to govern.' For Morris, Innocent III provides the leitmotif for an important phase of ecclesiastical and indeed western history.[1] A similar sense of the significance of Innocent III can be found in other recent overviews of the medieval papacy, the medieval church and medieval society and forms the basis, in large measure, of the present conference.

In parallel fashion Pope Innocent III's papacy has been identified by historians of medieval Jewish life as pivotal. With respect to the papacy and medieval Jewry, we possess only one effort at a chronological survey, the brief but valuable study of Edward A. Synan, *The Popes and the Jews in the Middles Ages*. Like Morris, Synan too devotes only one chapter to a single pontificate, once more the pontificate of Innocent III. Synan further echoes the sense of Morris and others as to the importance of that pontificate with the following overall observation: 'Despite the most profound dissent as to the value of his reign for the world or for the church, few would dispute the estimate that makes Innocent III the incarnation

---

[1]Colin Morris, *The Papal Monarchy: The Western Church from 1050 to 1250* (Oxford, 1989), The Oxford History of the Christian Church, vol. 7. Chap. 17 is devoted entirely to the pontificate of Innocent III.

of medieval papacy at its zenith.'[2]   With respect to medieval Jewry, Synan's 'dissent as to the value of his [Innocent's] reign' has been non-existent. There has been, from the days of Heinrich Graetz onward, a sure sense of the pontificate of Innocent III as a turning point, a juncture at which medieval European Jewry began a steady decline from which it never really recovered. For historians of medieval Jewry, the pontificate of Innocent III was much more than simply the locus of decline – it was one of the major causative factors in that unremitting process.[3]

For the purposes of this paper, I would like to examine the thesis that postulates the reign of Innocent III as a crucial turning point in medieval Jewish history by posing a series of questions. First, to what extent and in what ways do the sources on Innocent himself suggest a decidedly anti-Jewish turn in policy and thinking? Second, if such a shift can be documented, how is it to be explained? Finally, what place did the new anti-Jewish turn in ecclesiastical policy and thinking play in the complex process of deterioration of Jewish circumstances in medieval western Christendom? I should indicate at the outset that my analysis of these issues flows from a much broader book-length study of declining Jewish circumstances in medieval northern Europe. In that study I treat Innocent III in passing; here I shall focus upon him and his reign.[4]

* * *

Is it in fact the case that the pontificate of Innocent III represents a hardening of both church policies with respect to the Jews and a sharpening of church anti-Jewish rhetoric? There can be, I believe, little doubt on this score. Let us begin with ecclesiastical policy. The church had long before the reign of Innocent III adumbrated broad policy lines for Jewish circumstances within Christendom. To paraphrase the classic formulation of the *Constitutio pro Judeis*, recurrently conferred upon the Jews by many medieval popes, including Innocent III, Jews were in effect to be protected from untoward infringements on their fundamental rights to physical security and to observance of their religious tradition, while they were at the same time to be prohibited from presuming to behave in a manner

---

[2]Edward A. Synan, *The Popes and the Jews in the Middle Ages* (New York, 1965), 83. Chap. 6 is devoted entirely to the pontificate of Innocent III.

[3]This sense was pioneered by the great pathbreaker in modern reconstruction of the Jewish past, Heinrich Graetz. Graetz treats the pontificate of Innocent III at considerable length in the first chapter of the seventh volume of his classic eleven-volume *Geschichte der Juden*, portraying this powerful pope as the archvillain of medieval Jewish history, indeed the architect of the ills of the medieval western world.

[4]Robert Chazan, *Medieval Stereotypes and Modern Antisemitism* (Berkeley, 1997).

that exceeded their fundamental rights to peaceful existence.[5] The thrust of the specific stipulations of the *Constitutio pro Judeis* was protective, spelling out a series of anti-Jewish behaviors which the church found unacceptable. The countervailing notion of Jews exceeding the limits of their basic rights remained in this particular document purposely nebulous, for it was the protections and not the limitations that were the focus of the *Constitutio*. Within the broad complex of ecclesiastical policy vis-à-vis the Jews, the limitations on Jewish behavior were widely discussed and readily understood to mean those Jewish actions that might in any way threaten the Christian majority that had elected to host the Jewish minority. The vagueness of the concept of harmful Jewish behavior and the balance of protection versus limitation assured for medieval ecclesiastical policy a basic fluidity and flexibility.

Given this fundamental and fluid framework of protection-*cum*-limitation, what do we discern in the policy pronouncements of Pope Innocent III? The first point worth noting is the relative absence of protective exhortations in the correspondence of Innocent III. Out of the twenty-nine letters relating to the Jews from his pontificate, only his version of the *Constitutio pro Judeis* (to be analyzed at some length shortly) and an undated rubric of a letter that enjoined Christians, especially crusaders, from harming Jews have survived.[6] A number of Innocent's predecessors and successors saw fit to offer Jews significant protection in the face of a variety of dangers. We have no evidence of Innocent doing so.

Proceeding from protection to limitation, we encounter considerable emphasis in Innocent's correspondence on limitations both traditional and innovative. Innocent was more than simply sensitive to traditional church teaching. Even in areas of well-established ecclesiastical limitation of Jewish behaviors, Innocent regularly took these timeworn concerns in new directions or addressed them with innovative remedies. Moreover, his papacy added to ecclesiastical policy at least one major new domain of limitation. It can hardly be argued that Innocent was simply an energetic proponent of traditional church doctrine. He was clearly concerned with the Jews and their behaviors and was determined to enforce prior

---

[5] The classic study of the *Constitutio pro Judeis* is that of Solomon Grayzel, 'The Papal Bull *Sicut Judeis*', in *Studies and Essays in Honor of Abraham A. Neuman*, ed. Meir Ben-Horin et al. (Leiden, 1962), 243-80.

[6] All citations of papal documents will come from Solomon Grayzel (ed. and trans.), *The Church and the Jews in the XIIIth Century*, 2 vols (Philadelphia and New York, 1933-89), and Shlomo Simonsohn, ed., *The Apostolic See and the Jews*, 6 vols (Toronto, 1988-90). Translations will be based on Grayzel, with requisite alterations. Grayzel has thirty-two documents, as opposed to Simonsohn's twenty-nine. However, Grayzel's nos. 7 and 16 mention Jews only tangentially, while Grayzel's no. 30 concerns usurers with no sense that Jews are involved. The *Constitutio pro Judeis* can be found in Grayzel, 1:92-4, no. 5, Simonsohn, 1:74-5, no. 71 and in Reg. 2:276 (302); the undated rubric can be found in Grayzel, 1:142, no. 32, and Simonsohn, 1:100, no. 95.

limitations, to stretch them to fuller effectiveness, and – where necessary – to enlarge the range of limitation of Jewish behaviors that could be defined as inappropriate.

Let us commence with traditional ecclesiastical concerns over the Jews and their behaviors. The oldest and most well-established church concern involved possible Jewish subversion of Christian belief, especially through relationships in which Jews exercised power. The classic relationships of power outlawed by the church – Jews as owners of Christian slaves, Jews as spouses of Christians, Jews exercising political authority over Christians – hardly constituted a major problem in medieval western Christendom during the late twelfth and early thirteenth century. Rather, the church at this juncture became anxious over relationships that generated what it viewed as excessive contact between Jews and Christians, with the potential for luring these Christians out of their ancestral faith. The Third Lateran Council of 1179 had prohibited employment of Christians in Jewish homes.[7] Pope Innocent III reiterated this prohibition in a letter of 1205, addressed to the king of France:

> It was decreed in the Lateran Council [the Third Lateran Council of 1179] that Jews are not permitted to have Christian servants in their homes, either under pretext of nursing their children or for domestic service or for any other reason whatsoever, but that those who presume to live with them shall be excommunicated. However, they [the Jews] do not hesitate to have Christian servants and nurses, with whom they at times work such abominations as are more fitting that you should punish than that we should specify.[8]

The principle of obviating potentially problematic Christian-Jewish relations was well grounded in the earliest church legislation with regard to Jews, stemming from the very beginning of Christianity's power in the Roman Empire. Pope Innocent III was very much committed to the enforcement of this traditional limitation on Jewish contact with Christians, in its enhanced Third Lateran formulation.

Like so much church legislation, this principle was amenable to a variety of interpretations and to considerable extension. The Third Lateran Council had extended the early ecclesiastical concern with Christian-Jewish contact in relations where the Jew might exercise power to relations that were simply too regular and intimate. A yet more striking extension was decreed by the Fourth Lateran Council, called and led by Pope Innocent III.

---

[7] Grayzel, 1:296, no. I. The Grayzel collection includes both papal letters (organized in Arabic numerals) and conciliar documents (organized in Roman numerals).

[8] Grayzel, 1:106, no. 14; Simonsohn, 1:82, no. 79.

In certain provinces of the church, divergence in clothing distinguishes Jews from Christians and Saracens from Christians; however, in certain [provinces], there has arisen such confusion that no differences are discernible. Thus, it sometimes happens that by mistake Christians mingle with Jewish or Saracen women, and Jews or Saracens with Christian women. Therefore, lest they, under the cover of error, find an excuse for the grave sin of such mingling, we decree that these people [Jews and Saracens] of either sex and in all Christian lands and at all times be readily distinguishable from others by the quality of their clothing. Indeed, this very legislation is decreed for them [the Jews] also by Moses.[9]

This is a telling development and illustrates strikingly the way in which a traditional policy – obviation of undue Jewish influence through social contact – could be markedly intensified through the utilization of new, more effective, and more extreme techniques for achieving older purposes. Imposition of distinguishing Jewish garb flowed almost naturally from heightened ecclesiastical concern with contact between Jews and Christians. If contact with Jews should be limited, then why not limit it in the most effective possible manner? While there was nothing new in principle about the requirement of distinguishing Jewish garb, the end result was certainly altered circumstances for the Jews of western Christendom.

There was a second kind of harm that the church traditionally feared from the Jews, and that was denigration of Christianity. Jews were utterly forbidden to engage in criticism of the ruling Christian faith. In prior centuries, this concern took the form of limiting Jewish behaviors that could be construed as openly or even obliquely derogatory to Christianity. Once again, we find in the pronouncements of Innocent III the combination of reiteration of traditional prohibitions and institution of wide-ranging new limitations.

As an instance of reiteration of prior regulations, let us again cite the valuable papal letter of 1205, addressed to King Philip Augustus.

Indeed, blaspheming against the name of God, they publicly insult Christians, [saying] that they [the Christians] believe in a peasant hung by the Jewish people. To be sure, we do not doubt that he was hung for us, since he carried our sins in his body on the cross. However, we do not acknowledge that he was a peasant, either by manners or by birth. Surely, they themselves cannot deny that physically he was descended from priestly and royal stock and that his manners were distinguished and proper. Furthermore, on [Good] Friday

---

[9]Grayzel, 1:308, no. X.

the Jews, contrary to former practice, publicly run about through streets and squares and everywhere assemble, as is their custom, and deride Christians because they adore the crucified one on the cross and, through their improprieties, attempt to disturb them from their worship.[10]

It should of course come as no shock that medieval Jews in fact rejected the faith of the Christian majority and expressed their animus in terms as vigorous as those used by Christians in denouncing Judaism. The rules of Jewish circumstances, however, made overt expression of this hostility intolerable.

The Fourth Lateran Council addressed itself broadly to reiteration of this prior general principle and, once more, added new techniques for addressing an old fear. The relation of this Fourth Lateran edict to Pope Innocent III's letter of 1205 is patent.

Moreover, they [the Jews] shall go out in public as little as possible on the days of lamentation [preceding Easter] or the Sunday of Easter. For, as we have heard, certain of them do not blush to proceed on such days heavily ornamented and do not fear poking fun at Christians who display signs of grief at the memory of the most holy Passion. We most strictly forbid that they dare to break forth into insults against the Creator and Redeemer. Since we must not shut our eyes to insults heaped upon him who washed away our sins, we order that such presumptuous persons shall be duly curbed by fitting punishment meted out by the secular rulers, so that they dare not blaspheme against him who was crucified for our sake.[11]

We note here two intensifications of the traditional anxiety. Concern with possible Jewish blasphemy led to limitation on Jewish public appearance during Holy Week, and the secular authorities were enlisted in the effort to minimize the danger of Jewish blasphemy. Once more, the anxieties are old, while the methods of addressing the dangers are innovative.

Let us now turn our attention to an area of unprecedented ecclesiastical disquiet over relatively new Jewish behaviors, namely Jewish moneylending. During the middle decades of the twelfth century, the Jewish immigrants in northern Europe who had been attracted as traders into the burgeoning economy of the north began to gravitate toward moneylending. This shift was supported by many of the temporal authorities of northern Europe, interested in both stimulation of the

---

[10]Grayzel, 1:106-8, no. 14; Simonsohn, 1:83, no. 79.

[11]Grayzel, 1:109, no. X. The reference to heavy ornamentation by Jews may reflect the reality of recurrent calendar overlap between the Jewish celebrations of both Purim and Passover and Christian celebration of Holy Week.

economy of their domains and personal profit.   It was facilitiated by the traditional church prohibition of the giving or taking of usury, operative upon Christians but inoperative upon the Jews.[12] The movement of Jews into finance aroused ecclesiastical concern, partially because it was church policy with regard to Christian moneylending that contributed to opening this opportunity for the Jews, partly because church policy with respect to moneylending in general had ramifications for Jewish usury, and partly because moneylending is in a broad way a problematic and emotion-laden economic activity. Already in the latter decades of the twelfth century, we encounter misgivings voiced with respect to Jewish moneylending activity.   During the pontificate of Innocent III, these anxieties increased markedly, with profound implications for the Jews.

Let us look closely at the innovative legislation adopted by the Fourth Lateran Council.

> The more the Christian religion refrains from the exaction of usury, the more does the Jewish perfidy grow insolent with regard to these matters, so that in a short time they [the Jews] exhaust the financial strength of Christians. Therefore, desiring to protect Christians in this matter, that they should not be excessively oppressed by the Jews, we order by a decree of this synod that henceforth, if Jews under any pretext extort heavy and immoderate usury from Christians, all relationship with Christians shall be denied them, until they properly make amends for this exorbitant exaction. Christians, if need be, shall be compelled by ecclesiastical punishment without appeal to abstain from relations with them [the said Jews]. We also impose upon the princes that they not be aroused against the Christians because of this, but rather they should restrain the Jews from such exaction.[13]

In this edict, we find a clearcut statement of the traditional doctrine of church responsibility to preclude Jews from bringing harm on Christian society. Immoderate Jewish usury constitutes a burden on the Christian populace. Thus, the church is doubly obliged to demand limitation of Jewish usury – in part out of its role as protector of the Christian populace and in part out of its broad responsibility to define Jewish status in Christendom.

While the limitation on rate of interest is the most widely known of Innocent's initiatives with respect to Jewish moneylending, there were others as well.   The papal letter of 1205, addressed to the king of France, offers interesting specifics of Innocent III's further concerns with Jewish usury. Included in this papal letter

---

[12]Chap. 2 of my *Medieval Stereotypes and Modern Antisemitism* contains an extensive description of the Jewish move into usury across northern Europe.

[13]Grayzel, 1:307, no. IX.

are three complaints: compounding of interest by Jewish lenders; appropriation of ecclesiastical goods by Jewish lenders: and distraint on Christian property.[14] Every one of these papal complaints, along with the demand for limitation of Jewish interest rates, eventuated in enactment of legislative safeguards by the Capetian kings of France, loyal supporters of the papacy and ecclesiastical legislation.[15] Innovative church policies were hardly acted upon overnight. The demand for usury limitation by the Fourth Lateran Council acknowledges overtly that the secular authorities under whose jurisdiction Jews lived might be loathe to support the new ecclesiastical thrust. Church leadership, however, was accustomed to the long view, to policies that might initially be resisted and only slowly accepted. The commitment of church leadership to such long-term policies was real, and its success rate impressive. Ecclesiastical concern with Jewish usury augured badly for Jewish business activity, particularly in northern Europe, where moneylending had become so central to the Jewish economy.

Thus the correspondence of Innocent III reveals a considerable imbalance in the fluid relationship between protection and limitation, with little sign of the former and abundant evidence of the latter. In the limitations on Jewish behavior for which he pressed, Pope Innocent III included a series of Jewish actions that had traditionally been of concern to the church, extended these concerns in further directions, and advanced new techniques for combating old ills. Most strikingly, Innocent III opened up Jewish economic activity as a new arena for ecclesiastical regulation, beginning a lengthy process of demanding secular limitation on the purportedly harmful Jewish economic activities attendant upon the move into moneylending.

Assessing the level of Innocent's rhetoric with respect to the Jews is considerably more difficult. In a general way, rhetorical flourishes hardly lend themselves to precise evaluation. Nonetheless, it does seem that he was particularly abusive in his depiction of Jews and Judaism, highlighting the great gulf that separated Christianity from Judaism and Christians from Jews and emphasizing the deficiencies of both the Jewish people and their religious faith.

Perhaps the best place to begin is with Innocent's formulation of the *Constitutio pro Judeis*. As already noted, this was, by Innocent's time, already something of a tradition, rooted perhaps back in the eleventh century.[16] Five twelfth-century popes conferred such a document upon the Jews: Calixtus II, Eugenius III, Alexander III, Clement III, and Celestine III. The documents of the first two and

---

[14]Grayzel, 1:106, no. 14, and Simonsohn, 1:82, no. 79.

[15]For full discussion of the Capetian anti-usury campaign, see Robert Chazan, *Medieval Jewry in Northern France* (Baltimore, 1973), 104-24, and William Chester Jordan, *The French Monarchy and the Jews: From Philip Augustus to the Last Capetians* (Philadelphia, 1989), chaps 6, 8, and 9.

[16]Recall the Grayzel essay cited above, n. 5.

the last have been lost; the documents of Alexander III and Clement III are available to us.[17] They show a stereotyped formula that – as already noted – was intended largely as a statement of protection. Just as in the area of policy, so too in the rhetorical trappings of his *Constitutio pro Judeis*, Innocent II reveals himself as a restless innovator. Once again the force of the innovation, in this instance rhetorical, shows concern with and negativity toward the Jews.

The stereotyped *Constitutiones* enacted by Alexander III and Clement III center on a series of prohibitions of anti-Jewish actions. There is only the briefest introduction to and justification for these pro-Jewish measures. The grounding of these measures lies in a reasonable balance: 'Just as the Jews ought not be allowed to do in their synagogues more than permitted them by law, so too in those privileges granted them they ought suffer no infringement'. The grounding for this set of protections thus lies in considerations of reason, the acknowledged traditional balance between limitation and protection, to use our earlier terminology. This is followed by a brief theological 'to be sure'. To be sure, the Jews 'prefer to remain in their obstinacy rather than to acknowledge the words of the prophets and the secrets of their scriptures and to achieve understanding of the Christian faith and salvation'. Nonetheless, despite this cognitive and spiritual failure on the part of the Jews, the combination of Jewish supplication and Christian charity is portrayed as leading to the enactment of the requested legislation, grounded in considerations of fairness and equity.

Pope Innocent III absorbed the whole of the earlier *Constitutiones*, both the preamble indicating the grounds for the enactment and the specific prohibitions, into his own version. He was, however, not at all satisfied with the prior underpinnings of the *Constitutio*, with the notion of maintenance of a reasonable balance between limitation and protection. For Innocent, there was a profounder theological base for the *Constitutio*.

> The perfidy of the Jews ought in many ways be condemned. Nonetheless, they are not to be severely oppressed by the faithful, because through them our faith is validated. As the prophet said: 'Do not kill them, lest my people forget' [Ps. 59:12]. To put it more clearly, you must not destroy the Jews utterly, lest Christians come to forget your law, which they [the Jews] do not understand but display in their scriptures for those who do understand.[18]

Innocent's innovative preamble to his *Constitutio* grounds the enactment in much more than simple considerations of equity; it grounds the enactment in a serious

---

[17]Simonsohn, 1:44, no. 44 (Calixtus II – lost); 1:47, no. 46 (Eugenius II – lost); 1:51, no. 49 (Alexander III); 1:66, no. 63 (Clement III); 1:68, no. 64 (Celestine III – lost).

[18]Grayzel, 1:92, no. 5, and Simonsohn, 1:74, no. 71.

theological consideration. God himself in fact dictated the requirement that Jews be afforded requisite protection, as a means of advancing the cause of divine truth.

Now, the argument that Jews must be maintained because of the divine command embedded in Psalm 59:12 in order to buttress Christian truth was certainly not introduced by Pope Innocent III. This argument formed the opening ploy in the important argument made by Bernard of Clairvaux in his famed crusade epistle and has even earlier roots.[19] To be sure, Bernard's case for maintaining Jewish safety was somewhat more extended and complex than Innocent's; nonetheless, the argument from Psalm 59:12 was the cornerstone there as well. What has not been sufficiently noted is the drastically negative portrait of the Jews that emerges from this argument, as made by both Bernard and Innocent III. In order to appreciate fully the force of this citation from the Psalms we must attend to its context, as many attentive medieval Christians would have done. Psalm 59 depicts its protagonist as surrounded by enemies, but secure in God's protection. The tone of the psalm is set in its opening verses:

> Save me from my enemies, O my God;
>   secure me against my assailants.
> Save me from evildoers;
>   deliver me from murderers.
> For see, they lie in wait for me;
>   fierce men plot against me
>   for no offense of mine,
>   for no transgression, O Lord;
>   for no guilt of mine
>   do they rush to array themselves against me.

Thus, by making Psalm 59 the basis for his prohibition of anti-Jewish violence, Innocent, like Bernard before him, painted a damning portrait of the Jews. The Jews were a heinous enemy, a foe that had murdered, plotting groundlessly against a guiltless figure. Normally, such an enemy would deserve the worst possible fate. God had ordained otherwise, however, for purposes of strengthening Christianity. Innocent III's new preamble to the *Constitutio* provided a

---

[19]For analysis of Bernard of Clairvaux's complex argument against anti-Jewish violence, see Chazan, *Medieval Stereotypes and Modern Antisemitism*, 42-6.

solider, more theological base for the pro-Jewish enactment, in the process portraying the Jews to be protected in highly negative terms.[20]

In addition to his theologically grounded and damning preamble, Innocent also appended to his *Constitutio* a demeaning conclusion. After detailing the protections to which Jews are rightfully entitled, he concludes: 'We wish to place under the protection of this decree only those who have not presumed to plot against the Christian faith'. While this is a perfectly reasonable condition, one that accords with traditional ecclesiastical policy as we have seen it, it is nonetheless striking that Pope Innocent III found it necessary to add this observation. His sense of the Jews as potentially harmful is obvious from the outset of his papal reign.

Flamboyant expressions of concern with Jewish malevolence dot the letters of Innocent III, of which I shall cite only two. Let us note first the opening of a papal letter of 1205, addressed to the archbishop of Sens and the bishop of Paris:

> Christian piety accepts the Jews who, as a result of their own guilt, are consigned to perpetual servitude because they crucified the Lord, although their own prophets had predicted that he would come in the flesh to redeem Israel. Christian piety permits them to dwell in the Christian midst. Because of their perfidy, even the Saracens who persecute the Catholic faith and do not believe in the Christ whom the Jews crucified cannot tolerate the Jews and have even expelled them from their territory, vehemently rebuking us for tolerating those by whom, as we openly acknowledge, our redeemer was condemned to the suffering of the cross. Thus, the Jews ought not be ungrateful to us and ought not requite Christian favor with contumely and intimacy with contempt. Yet, while they are mercifully admitted into our intimacy, they threaten us with that retribution which they are accustomed to accord to their hosts, in accordance with the common proverb: 'Like a mouse in a pocket, like the snake around one's loins, like a fire in one's bosom'.[21]

The imagery of this passage is relatively simple, drawing on traditional portrayal of the Jewish role in the crucifixion. To this Innocent III adds his strong sense of

---

[20]When I delivered my paper at the conference, John Baldwin privately suggested his reservations as to my argument for the resonances of Psalm 59. I have rethought the matter considerably and have decided to leave my formulation as delivered. I do wish, however, to note the reservations of such a distinguished medievalist.

[21]Grayzel, 1:114, no. 18, and Simonsohn, 1:86-7, no. 82.

the Jews of his own day as steeped in animosity toward the Christendom that has – perhaps mistakenly? – offered its hospitality.[22]

A slightly later letter, written in 1208 to the count of Nevers, holder, protector and partner of a significant number of northern-French Jews, offers us more complex imagery and richer insight into Innocent's negative perceptions of Jews.

> The Lord made Cain a wanderer and a fugitive over the earth, but set a mark upon him, making his head shake, lest any finding him should slay him. Likewise with the Jews, against whom the blood of Jesus Christ calls out. Although they ought not be killed, lest the Christian people forget the divine law, yet as wanderers ought they remain upon the earth, until their countenance be filled with shame and they seek the name of Jesus Christ, the Lord. That is why blasphemers of the Christian name ought not be aided by Christian princes to oppress the servants of the Lord, but ought rather be forced into the servitude of which they made themselves deserving when they raised sacrilegious hands against him who had come to confer true liberty upon them, thus calling down his blood upon them and upon their children.[23]

The central traditional element in this diatribe is again Jewish guilt for the crucifixion and the punishment that act drew in its wake. To this traditionally negative image, Innocent III appends a second, that of the murderer Cain, an image of which we shall speak further shortly. Finally, Pope Innocent III sees the Jews of his day and age as contemporary enemies of Christianity, reflected in their ongoing blasphemy, and as contemporary enemies of Christians, reflected in their oppression of 'the servants of the Lord'.

In both policy and rhetoric, it does seem fair to depict Pope Innocent III as deeply concerned with the Jews, as anxious over their historic and contemporary enmity, as determined to invoke and extend the necessary limtations on Jewish behavior, and as moved to language that was highly negative and inflammatory. Is it then possible to identify those factors that led this powerful and innovative pontiff to these concerns and actions?

* * *

---

[22] In chaps 3 and 4 of *Medieval Stereotypes and Modern Antisemitism*, I argue that transformation of the traditional Christian sense of historic Jewish enmity into a perception of contemporary Jewish hatred and its attendant dangers is at the core of the deteriorating imagery of the Jews during the middle decades of the twelfth century.

[23] Grayzel, 1:126, no. 24, and Simonsohn, 1:92-3, no. 88.

In attempting to identify those factors that influenced Pope Innocent III to his greater concern with and negativity toward the Jews, I believe that we must begin by eschewing oversimplication and by renouncing any possibility of relating these tendencies to personal proclivities. We simply do not know enough about the personal predispositions of this pope to essay any explanations rooted in his psychological makeup. The best that we might hope for is explanation that takes full account of the central thrusts of his papacy and the broad social and cultural context in which his life was embedded. In so doing, we must be alert to the multiplicity of developments of the vibrant decades that closed the twelfth and opened the thirteenth centuries. No simple explanation for Innocent's concerns will do.

The citation used by Colin Morris as an opening to his study of *The Papal Monarchy* offers us a convenient starting point: 'Christ left to Peter not only the whole church, but also the whole world to govern'.[24] Developments in the church and the papacy had conspired, prior to the pontificate of Innocent III, to produce an enlarged vision of the power of the papal office within a more puissant church. While earlier centuries had often found a fairly weak church less than fully concerned with secondary issues like the Jews, the more powerful church of the late twelfth century and the early thirteenth was determined to let no issue, primary or secondary, escape its fullest attention. Thus, the Jews – hardly an overwhelming priority in earlier centuries – came onto the papal agenda, along with a host of other heretofore neglected concerns. From another perspective, multiple facets of societal life were held up to closer scrutiny in this period of enhanced church organization and power. A closer look at the intimate workings of Christian society meant inevitably concern with the impact of the Jewish minority within that society. Thus, both in and of themselves and as a factor on the larger societal scene, Jews had to come to the attention of a more powerful and more militant church and papacy.

To be sure, the scrutiny to which both Jews and society at large were subjected helps explain the papal concern with the Jews, but not necessarily its distinctly negative orientation. For this I would urge recourse to my own analysis of the deteriorating image of European – particularly northern-European – Jewry during the middle and closing decades of the twelfth century.[25] Let me make my broad argument as succinctly as possible. Northern-European Jewry was, it is often forgotten, an immigrant Jewry. From the outset, it was drawn northward by the remarkable efflorescence of northern Europe from the late tenth century onward and was in fact encouraged by many of the most progressive barons of the north. From the outset, this young Jewry encountered considerable resistance, rooted in

---

[24]See above, n. 1.
[25]Chazan, *Medieval Stereotypes and Modern Antisemitism*.

part in the realities of its circumstances and in part in the Christian legacy of anti-Jewish imagery. The reality-grounded bases for anti-Jewish feelings included: the immigrant status of the Jews, their obvious religious dissidence in an otherwise homogeneous society, their business orientation and their close alliance with the ruling class. These real foundations for animosity were exacerbated by the highly charged Christian imagery that portrayed the Jews as the worst of enemies of both God and Christianity. While ecclesiastical policy affirmed regularly the prohibition of anti-Jewish violence, as we have seen, the imagery that it regularly promulgated simultaneously fanned anti-Jewish passions. Thus, from early on the Jewish newcomers in northern Europe encountered pervasive hostility.

A number of important developments during the middle decades of the twelfth century conspired to heighten the animosity felt toward the Jews of northern Europe. Surely the most important of these developments involved the rapid economic growth of these decades and the resultant attraction of northern-European Jews into the money trade. Sanctioned by the church and strongly encouraged by the secular authorities, the Jewish move toward moneylending sharpened the hostility borne by many non-Jews toward their Jewish neighbors.[26] As we have already seen in the pronouncements of Pope Innocent III, many Christians of this period saw Jewish moneylending as damaging to the interests of Christian society. While the impact of Jewish lending was obviously far more complex, with important benefits for northern-European economic and political maturation, the perception of harmfulness is not difficult to comprehend. Overextended debtors were in fact often crushed by their obligations, traditional ecclesiastical revenues were lost, fears of a rapidly changing economic and social order were profound. Given the long Christian tradition that emphasized the malevolence and harmfulness of Jews, simplistic perceptions of damaging Jewish economic activity were readily absorbed by a discomfited Christian majority.

The potent combination of realities, especially the Jewish move into the money trade, and the traditional Christian legacy served to heighten Christian fears of Jews and to produce a set of increasingly negative stereotypes. Most striking of all was the notion that Jews regularly murdered Christian neighbors out of their profound hatred of Christ, the Christian faith and Christians. Although overshadowed by the more imaginative embellishments that involved ritualized murder by crucifixion and – somewhat later – ritualistic utilization of Christian blood, in fact the most widespread and damaging twelfth-century stereotype portrayed Jews as murderers bent on inflicting physical harm on their Christian contemporaries.[27]

---

[26]Again, I treated these developments in ibid., chap. 2.
[27]Ibid., chaps 3 and 4.

It is striking indeed to see the most powerful of medieval popes lending the weight of papal authority to this dangerous new stereotype. In the 1205 letter to King Philip Augustus of France, Innocent III, as part of his litany of Jewish crimes, says the following: 'Settled among Christians, they repay their hosts badly. When the opportunity presents itself, they surreptitiously kill Christians. It was recently said to have happened that a certain poor student was found dead in their latrine'.[28] About three decades earlier, the Jews of northern France – badly shaken by an allegation of murder in the town of Blois, by strange judicial proceedings that proclaimed the Jews of Blois collectively guilty of the murder, and by the execution of more than thirty of these Jews – turned in their distress to major secular and ecclesiastical leaders for protection. Both the king of France, Philip Augustus's father, and the count of Champagne reassured their Jews that they would not accept in their courts the accusation of malicious Jewish murder. A major intermediary in this effort was the archbishop of Sens.[29] Now, some three decades later, the head of the Roman Catholic Church dignified this same accusation by lending it the prestige of his high office.

In this connection, let us look back once more on some of the inflammatory rhetoric that we have already noted. Given this new sense of the Jews as physically dangerous, the proverb quoted by Innocent III in his 1205 letter to the archbishop of Sens and the bishop of Paris takes on added weight: the Jews are 'like a mouse in a pocket, like the snake around one's loins, like a fire in one's bosom', poised to inflict harm on their Christian hosts. Yet more striking is the Cain imagery in the 1208 letter to the count of Nevers. Again, the comparison of the Jews to the first murderer, Cain, was by no means innovated by Pope Innocent III. However, given the spread of the malicious murder allegation during the closing decades of the twelfth century, papal projection of the Jews as suffering the punishment of Cain for the crime of Cain represented significant reinforcement for the damaging new stereotype.

I am thus arguing that what moved Pope Innocent III to his negative stance with respect to the Jews was his acceptance of the augmented twelfth-century sense of Jewish malevolence and harmfulness. I am not suggesting that Innocent was in any way the initiator of these perceptions. They had been widespread from the middle decades of the twelfth century onward. While by no means an innovator, he did play a role in the diffusion of these stereotypes, both through his policies and his rhetoric.

---

[28]Grayzel, 1:108, no. 14, and Simonsohn, 1:83, no. 79.
[29]For a detailed analysis of this incident, see Robert Chazan, 'The Blois Incident of 1171: A Study in Jewish Intercommunal Organization', *Proceedings of the American Academy for Jewish Research* 36 (1968):13-31.

As we have noted, the central thrust of Innocent's policies vis-à-vis the Jews was to identify more boldly avenues of Jewish harmfulness and to legislate limitations that would diminish this purported Jewish harmfulness, whether it took the form of undue contact with Christian neighbors, of blaspheming Christian *sancta*, or of oppressing Christians through the machinations of the moneylending business. The result of all these moves was surely to heighten the sense of potential danger flowing from the Jews. In a vicious cycle, the enhanced perception of Jewish harmfulness was absorbed by this powerful pontiff, served as the motivation for new restrictive legislation and was thus more widely purveyed to the masses of western Christendom.

The rhetorical excesses that we have noted flowed from much the same source and had much the same results. The new preamble to the *Consitutio pro Judeis* highlighted the biblical imagery of murderers plotting against a blameless figure, traditionally understood to be Jesus but now extended by the new stereotype into a fear for the life of every Christian. The concluding addition to Innocent's *Constitutio* indicated that it applied only to those Jews 'who have not presumed to plot against the Christian faith', raising of course the specter of a considerable number of Jews who did regularly plot against the Christian faith. Once more Innocent III absorbed the fears of his environment and gave them further currency through the prestige of his great office.

* * *

Some brief closing observations on the role of the church in the decline of medieval Jewry in western Christendom. For Heinrich Graetz, the first great modern historian of the Jewish people, Pope Innocent III was the arch-enemy, the key figure who set most of the negative developments in the history of medieval western Jewry in motion.[30] Graetz's sense of Innocent's negativity vis-à-vis the Jews was surely not misplaced, as I hope we have seen. What I would challenge, however, is Graetz's sense of the genesis of this negativity and his claims as to its impact. There were, to be sure, good reasons for Graetz's telling the tale as he did. To fasten heavy responsibility for medieval Jewish ills on the church made the Jews fellow-sufferers with those figures in Christian society who were regularly seen as the precursors of the Reformation and who were after all major hero figures in the German society of which Graetz was a part. Moreover, making the medieval church the key to comprehending declining Jewish fortunes ultimately proclaimed a relatively positive message for Graetz's own age and ambience: the declining fortunes of the nineteenth-century church could only

---

[30]See above, n. 3.

mean removal of the major historic anti-Jewish force on the western scene, with the likelihood that its demise would be accompanied by considerable improvement in modern Jewish fortunes.

The portrait that I have offered is hardly so encouraging. I have argued that the deteriorating fortunes of medieval Jewry were rooted in broad societal malaise, the kind of malaise that could and does afflict any society and could and does claim any human group as its victims. The causative factors in this decline are neither personal nor simple. No appeal to a specific human figure, as powerful as he might be, will suffice to explain the deterioration of Jewish circumstances. No appeal to a given sector of society or institution, as powerful as it might be, will explain the shift in circumstances that ultimately destroyed a growing and thriving set of Jewish settlements, pushing their descendants from the burgeoning centers of medieval western Christendom out to its peripheries.

What role or roles did the church and its papal leadership play in this deterioration? The answer is again far from simple. The church and its leadership first of all contributed to the early resistance to Jewish immigration into northern Europe by maintaining and promulgating its doctrine of underlying Jewish enmity and harmfulness. To be sure, the church insisted that this underlying enmity was not to serve as the basis for ill-treatment, that Jewish rights to physical safety and religious expression were to be rigorously safeguarded. This combination of anti-Jewish preaching and practical protection was, however, ultimately unstable. Well-educated clergy might understand the divine mandate for the combination, but popular thinking was not always able to follow such convoluted thinking. Periodically, popular movements such as crusading effaced the sophistication of the combination and elicited a more simplistic emphasis on Jewish crimes and the legitimacy of human retribution.[31] More broadly, the stereotype of historic Jewish malevolence allowed for the possibility of seeing contemporary Jews in similar light, for perceiving Jewish neighbors as harboring the same kind of hatred imputed to the Jews of Jerusalem in the gospels. In considerable measure, the fastening of Christian fears on the Jewish minority of twelfth-century northern Europe – while clearly a popular reaction to the dislocations of the period – owed much of its force to the traditional Christian teachings that predated the Jewish arrival in the area.

Once the new concern with Jewish harmfulness had emerged, the church absorbed it and purveyed it in both its policies and its rhetoric. Pope Innocent III, a student for six years in Paris, learned much from his sojourn in the great intellectual and spiritual center of northern Europe, including some of its broadly

---

[31] See my analysis of the breakdown of the complex church position in certain popular crusading bands during the spring months of 1096: *European Jewry and the First Crusade* (Berkeley, 1987), 65-72.

shared popular doctrine with respect to the Jews. He attempted to combat what was widely perceived as the Jewish danger in his policies and reinforced this sense of Jewish danger in his inflammatory rhetoric. In this sense, his impact and that of the church might well be described as secondary, building on views articulated broadly throughout Christian society. The reinforcement of these views achieved through papal policy and rhetoric was, however, considerable.

Pope Innocent III was hardly the archvillain of medieval Jewish history. He was, in one sense, simply a man of his times, sharing perceptions and fears widely spread throughout his milieu. The power of his office and personality, however, gave potent expression to these views and assured them extended impact on the Jews of his own day and of posterity.

Pope Innocent III, John of England and the Albigensian Crusade (1209-1216)

Claire Taylor

On 14 January 1208 Pierre de Castelnau, the papal legate to the French Midi charged with investigating the Cathar heresy, was murdered by, it was commonly believed, agents of count Raymond VI of Toulouse. In the eyes of Pope Innocent III not only was the Languedoc a haven for the enemies of the church, but their protectors flouted papal authority and murdered the servants of Christ's vicar. The pope had already made many attempts to persuade a royal figure to involve himself in a crusade against the heretics and their supporters, and he had consistently called for a truce between Kings Philip II of France and John of England so that their efforts could be put into such a venture.[1] His attempts were in vain, John's priority being the recovery of territory in northern France which he had lost to Philip, and Philip's being the conquest of more of Aquitaine. Thus, the Albigensian Crusade was apparently devoid of royal intervention during this pontificate. However, there is evidence suggesting very strongly that John was actually involved in trying to undermine the crusade, activity which makes sense when viewed in the context of the defence of his own extensive political interest in the Languedoc and of his war with Philip, and which was also shaped by his relationship with the pope in the period 1205-1215. John's unwillingness to draw papal attention to his anti-crusade activity meant that most of his involvement was

---

[1]See especially PL 215:355-7, 501-3, 1360 and 1545. See also C.R. Cheney, *Pope Innocent III and England* (Stuttgart, 1979), 293, and B. M. Bolton, 'Philip Augustus and John: Two Sons in Innocent III's Vineyard?', *Studies in Church History* 9, ed. D. Wood (Oxford, 1991), 113-34, esp. 113-26.

semi-covert, and its objective thus not immediately clear. This paper attempts to expose and examine the evidence for John's involvement in the warfare in the Languedoc and to explain it in the above contexts. Finally, it will look at John's role in the Fourth Lateran Council of 1215 and the pope's response to his attempted intervention in favour of the family of Count Raymond of Toulouse. First of all, John's connection with the house of Toulouse should be explained.

THE DUKES OF AQUITAINE AND THE COUNTS OF TOULOUSE
Since the late eleventh century the dukes of Aquitaine had asserted a claim to the comital seat of Toulouse, occupied by the house of Saint-Gilles. The basis for the inheritance claim, as understood by the Aquitanian party, was that Philippa of Toulouse, daughter of Count William IV of Toulouse, had been heiress to the county and that it was thus inheritable by the dukes of Aquitaine because of her marriage to Duke William IX in 1094.[2] The counts of Toulouse, however, claimed that their ancestor Raymond of Saint-Gilles, brother of William IV, had bought the county from his brother when the latter set out on the First Crusade. Although the county of Toulouse and the comital seat continued to descend in the line of Saint-Gilles, Philippa and her descendants felt disinherited. Thus in 1141 Louis VII of France supported the right of his wife, Eleanor of Aquitaine, to Toulouse.[3] The claim was then pursued by force by Eleanor's second husband, the Angevin Henry II of England, as duke of Aquitaine, in 1159 and 1167.[4] Pressure in 1172 and 1173 finally forced Count Raymond V to do homage for the county to the Angevins at Limoges.[5] In 1188 their son Richard, as duke of Aquitaine, also went to war against the county and occupied much of Quercy, which had been held by the house of Saint-Gilles,[6] to which occupation Count Raymond retaliated in 1192.[7] By 1196 Count Raymond V was dead and Richard initiated a peace with his heir Raymond VI. He gave his sister Jeanne in marriage

---

[2] The Aquitainian claim is set out in Robert of Torigny, *The History of England*, in R. Howlett, ed., *Chronicles of the Reigns of Stephen, Henry II and Richard I*, 4 vols, RS (1884-1889), 4:201-2.

[3] J. H. Mundy, *Liberty and Political Power in Toulouse 1050-1250* (New York, 1954), 47 and J. H. Ramsey, *The Angevin Empire* (London, 1903), 19.

[4] Robert of Torigny, *History*, 201-3; Roger of Wendover, *Flores Historiarum*, ed. H. R. Luard, 3 vols, RS (1890), 2:75; Gervaise of Canterbury, *The Chronicles of the Reigns of Stephen, Henry II and Richard I*, W. ed. Stubbs, 2 vols, RS (1879), 1:167. See also C. de Vic, and J. Vaissète, eds, and A. Molinier (modern edn), *Histoire Générale du Languedoc* (henceforth cited as HGL), 16 vols (Toulouse: 1872-1915), 5:29-30, 33, 50 and 6:24-5, 34-5, 41; P. Wolff, *Histoire de Toulouse* (Toulouse, 1958), 77-80, 122.

[5] Robert of Torigny, *Histoire*, 225. See also HGL 6:51-5.

[6] Richard justified his attack with the claim that Raymond had been responsible for the mistreatment of pilgrims travelling to Santiago de Compostella. Gervaise of Canterbury, *Chronicles*, 432; Roger of Hoveden, *Chronica*, ed. W. Stubbs, 2 vols, RS (1868-1871), 2:339-40. See also HGL 7:22-4.

[7] HGL 6:144-5.

to the new count and she took with her as her dowry the Agenais, a stretch of the Garonne valley in the marches between Gascony and the Toulousain, which was long disputed between the two families.[8] It was to be held by Raymond VI, and by his heirs after his death, of the kings of England as dukes of Aquitaine in return for service by the count and five hundred of his men for a month per year. In addition, Richard renounced his family's claim to Toulouse and also returned, without vassalic obligation, the parts of Quercy which he had occupied in 1188. Jeanne died in 1199, but the homage was performed again in 1200 by Raymond to John, king of England, as duke of Aquitaine.[9] Thus ended the intermittent wars between the dukes of Aquitaine and the house of Saint-Gilles, now their in-laws and vassals for the Agenais.

Philip of France certainly saw that there was a dangerous connection between the two houses. Capetian influence in the Languedoc had been limited since the 1160s, when Raymond V repudiated his wife Constance, sister of Louis VII of France.[10] In 1207/8 Philip apparently told the pope that he was more than happy for a crusade to enter the heretical Toulousain, for the house of Saint-Giles had greatly offended him.[11] Philip and his father, Louis VII, had given Raymond's family aid against Henry and Richard in the wars before 1196, but in spite of this Raymond VI had taken the part of his brothers-in-law against France: in 1198, when he had entered into a league of nobles supporting Richard, although it is not clear if he actually campaigned;[12] and in 1204, when he had sent troops to help John at the siege of Falaise in Normandy.[13] What must certainly have been clear to Philip, however, was the threat posed by John's status as liege lord of Raymond, for it was liege homage which had been performed in 1173 'au préjudice des droits de la couronne de France'[14] and presumably performed likewise in 1200. By the start of the crusade in 1209, therefore, all parties could have anticipated that antipathy between John and Philip and their wars in the north-west of France might have repercussions in the South. Indeed, only in May

---

[8]No copy of the marriage contract survives, but see William of Puylaurens, *Chronique*, ed. J. Duvernoy, 2nd edn (Paris, 1976), 39-41; Pierre des Vaux-de-Cernay, *Histoire Albigeoise*, eds P. Guébin, and H. Maisonneuve (Paris, 1951), 17-18, 126. The anonymous second author of *La Chanson de la Croisade Albigeoise* also refers to it in his account of the Fourth Lateran Council of 1215, where he states that the agreement was in fact approved by Rome (see below). See also HGL 6:173-5.

[9]HGL 6:189, 190-1.

[10]William of Puylaurens, *Chronique*, 38-9, 58-9 and n. 2.

[11]An unreferenced letter is quoted in A. Luchaire, *Innocent III*, 6 vols in 3 (Paris, 1905-1908), 2:125 and cited likewise without reference in M. Roquebert, *L'Epopée Cathare*, 4 vols (Toulouse, 1970-1989), 1:224.

[12]HGL 6:185-6.

[13]In May 1204 John lost Falaise and consequently the rest of Normandy.

[14]HGL 6:54.

the previous year the French king had quarrelled with Raymond again because of a visit made by the latter to Otto of Brunswick, enemy of Philip and ally of John.[15]

JOHN'S INVOLVEMENT IN THE CRUSADE

We can see this Anglo-Toulousain alliance being realized in the affairs of the Languedoc from 1209-1214, especially from 1213. In the spring of 1209 Archbishop Guillaume II of Bordeaux organized a crusade into the Agenais.[16] Perhaps surprisingly, for John was its overlord as duke of Aquitaine, there is no evidence of a reaction on his part. After that time the crusade continued to threaten John's rights in the Gascon marches, and in 1211 there is circumstantial evidence for his involvement. Two of John's Aquitainian officials were engaged in anti-crusade activities. One was Savary de Mauléon, seneschal for John at Poitiers, whom Raymond had specifically summoned for a substantial reward. It is possible that he aided Toulouse during its brief siege in June,[17] and during the southerner's siege of Castelnaudary he arrived from Bergerac with an army of reinforcements.[18] During the subsequent battle at Castelnaudary the *routier* Martin Algaï, John's seneschal for Gascony and Périgord, defected from the ranks of the crusade.[19] As a result in the following year the crusade pursued him to his castle at Biron, in Périgord, and executed him.[20] John's hand can perhaps be sensed again in the Languedoc in early May 1213. At this point the crusaders were attempting to secure their position at Muret, on the edges of the Gascon Pyrenees, and by this year many Gascon nobles had performed homage to Amaury de Montfort, Count Simon's son.[21] They were faced with the untimely defection of a significant contingent led by the Walloon Alard II de Strépy.[22] De Strépy was a vassal of John[23] and had apparently received a message from his lord

---

[15]HGL 6:271.

[16]William of Tudela et al., *La Chanson de la Croisade Albigeoise*, ed. E. Martin-Chabot, 3 vols (Paris, 1960-1972), 1:38-45. This crusade into lands held by Raymond VI was called off when he took the cross himself in June 1209.

[17]Suggested in Roquebert, *L'Épopée*, 2:150. Kate Norgate states that it was because both John and Otto of Brunswick kept the city of Toulouse so well supplied that the crusaders had to raise the seige (K. Norgate, *John Lackland* [London, 1902], 166). However neither historian cites his or her sources and I am doubtful that John was so committed at this stage.

[18]For the siege see Pierre des Vaux-de-Cernay, *Histoire*, 104-13; William of Tudela, *La Chanson*, 1:214-33. See also HGL 6:368-70; J. Sumption, *The Albigensian Crusade*, (London, 1978), 137-41; Roquebert, *L'Épopée*, 1:436 and 2:122.

[19]William of Tudela, *La Chanson*, 1:226-9. See also HGL 6:371-4.

[20]William of Tudela, *La Chanson*, 1:257-63; Pierre des Vaux-de-Cernay, *Histoire*, 132-4.

[21]HGL 6:419.

[22]Pierre des Vaux-de-Cernay, *Histoire*, 164.

[23]See the earlier Latin edition, with extensive footnotes, of Pierre des Vaux-de-Cernay, *Hystoria Albigensis*, ed. P. Guebin and E. Lyon, 3 vols (Paris, 1926-39), 2:113 and n. 1. De Strépy, lord of a minor seigneury in Hainault, became John's vassal on 6 August 1202 for a rent of twenty-five livres.

in late April, leading to modern speculation that this was the cause of his departure.[24] Contemporaries blamed his defection for the inability of the crusade to undertake a siege of Toulouse in early May.[25]

There is also administrative evidence from the crusade and the English court that John was at least considering involvement from 1212 until the battle of Muret in September 1213. It was certainly thought by the crusaders that this was the case, for the January 1213 council of Lavaur denounced Raymond for having put his faith in John, also making reference to the involvement of Savary de Mauléon at Castelnaudary.[26] It is true that the same council also accused the count of an alliance with al-Nathir, defeated at Las Navas de Tolosa the previous year, a charge which is certainly untrue. However, there is other evidence that John was exchanging embassies with the southerners. Count Raymond had a Provençal official, Vital, at John's court from late 1212 to at least 7 April 1213, when he was making preparations to return home.[27] Vital had replaced another ambassador, Robin, and was himself replaced by envoys from Raymond and also from King Peter II of Aragon whose expenses John paid from 14 to 20 April.[28] These envoys were surely sent in an attempt to involve John in the emerging Aragonese/Toulousain alliance against the crusade. John himself had an ambassador, a Cistercian monk, at the Aragonese court between 14 April and 8 May.[29] On 8 July he again sent embassies, this time travelling in an armed ship,[30] to both King Peter and Count Raymond and on 17 August sent, with letters of accreditation, two more envoys to the southerners.[31] One of them was Geoffrey de Neville,[32] John's chamberlain since 1207, who was to continue to play an important role in the affairs of the Languedoc.

T. D. Hardy, ed., *Rotuli Litterarum Patentium*, 1 (London, 1835):16. His daughter married Philip of Hainault, a cousin of Emperor Baldwin of Constantinople and also Philip II of France. In the dispute over the 'Pseudo Baldwin', de Strépy took the part of the countess Jeanne against the rest of Hainault's nobility. J. Monoyer, *Essais d'Histoire et d'Archéologie, II: Les Villages de Houdeng, Goenies, Strépy*, 2nd edn (Mons, 1875), 120-1 and n. 2.

[24]Roquebert, *L'Épopée*, 2:149.

[25]Pierre des Vaux-de-Cernay, *Histoire Albigeoise*, 164.

[26]PL 213:836-8.

[27]T. D. Hardy, ed., *Rotuli Litterarium Clausarum*, 2 vols (London, 1833-44), 1:126; H. Cole, ed., *Documents Illustrative of English History of the Thirteenth and Fourteenth Centuries* (London, 1844), 258. See also Pierre des Vaux de Cernay, *Hystoria Albigensis*, 2:113-14, n. 5.

[28]Cole, *Documents*, 259. See also Peter des Vaux de Cernay, *Hystoria Albigensis*, 2:113-14, n. 5.

[29]Cole, *Documents*, 262. See also Peter des Vaux de Cernay, *Hystoria Albigensis*, 2:113-14, n. 5.

[30] Rot. Lit. Claus., 1:164. See also Peter des Vaux de Cernay, *Hystoria Albigensis*, 2:134, n. 2.

[31]*Rymer's Foedera*, 20 vols (London, 1704-35), 1:175. See also Peter des Vaux de Cernay, *Hystoria Albigensis*, 2:134, n. 2.

[32]See *Dictionary of National Biography; From the Earliest Days to 1900* (hereafter DNB), 22 vols (London, 1921-1922 reprint), 14:251-2. See also J. C. Holt, *Magna Carta*, 2nd edn (Cambridge, 1992), 131 and appendices 6, pp. 448-9, and 10, p. 485.

After the defeat of the southern alliance at Muret, the Toulousain and the Agenais were overrun by the crusade along with many other lands pertaining to Saint-Gilles. Count Raymond was thus denied the revenues and resources required for a counter-offensive. Several sources tell us that he and his son, also Raymond, fled to England where they sought refuge and aid from John.[33] We are told that Raymond VI now did homage to his brother-in-law for the county of Toulouse, in spite of Richard having renounced the family claim in 1196, and that he received 10,000 marks from John.[34] According to Ralph of Coggeshall, this money was raised as part of a levy of 22,000 *livres* on the Cistercian order imposed because of their support for the crusade.[35] The money was granted on 15 December 1213 at Reading and 16 January 1214 at Winchester.[36] The second grant was arranged by Geoffrey de Neville. We are told by the Waverley chronicler that the two Raymonds were then expelled from England by the papal legate, Bishop Nicholas of Tusculum.[37]

In 1214 John involved himself directly against the crusade, asserting his threatened rights first in the Agenais and then in Périgord. Since February of that year, whilst preparing to engage the French in Poitou, John had been based at La Rochelle.[38] From there he took his army via Saint-Emilion to the borders of the Agenais, arriving at the ducal castle at La Réole on 13 April where he remained until the 16th, receiving the homage of forty-three townspeople on the 13th and 15th.[39] Marmande, the next major town upriver, a bastide founded by Duke Richard, lay within the Agenais and was at this time held by the crusade. John's proximity caused its garrison to surrender, and on 15 April he sent down river a force under Geoffrey de Neville, his new seneschal for Gascony, possibly also accompanied by the seneschal for Poitou, Savary de Mauléon.[40] The occupation

---

[33] William of Tudela et al., *La Chanson*, 2:40-1; *Annales Prioratus de Dunstaplia* in *Annales Monastici*, 2 edn H. R. Luard, RS (1865), 39; *Annales Monasterii de Waverleia*, in ibid., 3:280.

[34] Ralph of Coggeshall, *Chronicon Anglicanum*, J. Stephenson, RS (1875), 164 and 168.

[35] Ralph of Coggeshall, *Chronicon*, 164.

[36] *Rot. Lit. Pat.*, 1:106 and 108. John's itinerary gives us the location of the court and is published unpaginated in T. D. Hardy, *A Description of the Patent Rolls* (London, 1835). The second grant was made specifically for the purposes of the voyage home (Ralph of Coggeshall, *Chronicon*, 168).

[37] *Annales Monasterii de Waverleia*, 280.

[38] See John's itinerary in Hardy, *Patent Rolls*.

[39] See John's itinerary and HGL 6:446.

[40] John's activities on the borders of the Agenais, and of his army at Marmande and the reaction of the crusaders, are described by Pierre des Vaux-de-Cernay, *Histoire Albigeoise*, 198-202. See also HGL 6:446. John only actually entered the Agenais on one earlier occassion. In 1200 after the treaty of Le Goulet, he spent the summer touring his French lands. He travelled into Gascony as far south as St. Sever and was at Agen itself on 11 and 12 August (John's itinerary), perhaps to receive the homage performed to him for the Agenais that year (see above). John also visited La Réole, on 15-16 August 1200 (John's itinerary). Modern sources usually refer to Geoffrey de Neville as the royal chamberlain at this time, but he is given the title also of seneschal for Gascony during much of the

began a wave of defections by towns in the Agenais, including at Mas d'Agenais, which Simon de Montfort, the commander of the crusade, attempted to win back. With great difficulty he crossed the Garonne, hampered not only by the flow but by an armed flotilla of barges from La Réole. He then besieged the town unsuccessfully for three days, but without artillery, which he had been unable to transport.

The siege of Mas d'Agenais was rendered unnecessary, however, for John soon had to take his army north to play its part in Poitou in his alliance with Otto of Brunswick and was unable to give the support which he had promised to Geoffrey de Neville at Marmande. In June, therefore, the crusade was able to begin to reoccupy the Agenais. The townspeople of Marmande fled up river to La Réole and the seneschal was forced to surrender the town. His garrison was granted safe conduct and de Montfort placed his own men in the *donjon* and set about dismantling the abandoned town's fortifications. The crusaders also believed John to have promised support for the town of Casseneuil, the new focus of resistance in the Agenais after the fall of Marmande,[41] which was besieged from 28 June, but help did not arrive.

John's continued neglect of the Agenais from June into July was prompted by several factors. Most obviously, on 2 July John's army was routed by the French royal army in Poitou and he fled back to La Rochelle to recover his nerve. In addition, his activity with regard to the crusade had been noticed by the papal legate to the French kingdom, Robert de Courçon,[42] who had moved into position to thwart him. The legate had joined the crusade in April but left its ranks to preside over the council of Bordeaux of 25 June.[43] To this council he had

---

period of John's 1214 activity in western France, mid-April to late August (*Rot. Lit. Pat.*, 1:120-1; *Rot. Lit. Claus.*, 1:170). Savary de Mauléon is mentioned at Marmande in H. J. Chaytor, *Savaric de Mauleon: Baron of Troubadours* (Cambridge, 1939), 27. De Mauléon later defected from John's side in the war with the Capetians and in 1226 fought as part of Louis VIII's crusade in the Languedoc. J. Sumption, *The Albigensian Crusade* (London, 1975), 216.

[41]Pierre des Vaux-de-Cernay, *Histoire*, 198-202.

[42]Robert de Courçon, an Englishman, was one of the major intellectuals of the period. He had studied at Paris under Peter the Chantor in the 1190s, possibly at the same time as Lotario Segni, the future Pope Innocent III. An experienced and able papal judge-delegate, he had been made a cardinal in 1212, and in 1213 he was charged with preparations for the Fourth Lateran Council throughout France. See J. M. Powell, *Anatomy of a Crusade: 1213-1221* (Philadelphia, 1986), 33-50. See also M. and C. Dickson, 'Le cardinal Robert de Courson: sa vie', *Archives d'Histoire Doctrinale et Litteraire du Moyen Âge* 9 (1934):53-142, esp. 85-116; J. Baldwin, *Masters, Princes and Merchants: The Social Views of Peter the Chantor and his Circle*, 2 vols (Princetown, NJ, 1970), 1:19-25 and 2:7-15.

[43]Mansi, *Concilia*, 22:931-4; *Rymer's Foedera*, 1:186-7. See also Peter des Vaux-de-Cernay, *Hystoria Albigensis*, 2:216-17, n. 1; Baldwin, *Masters*, 1:20; Dickson and Dickson, 'Le Cardinal', 100 and 141.

summoned John,[44] who failed to appear.[45] John was forced to submit nonetheless and in a letter of 6 July to the legate, in the presence of Geoffrey de Neville and the bishop of Périgord, he promised neutrality with relation to the dioceses of Agen and Cahors.[46] In addition the legate sent twenty thousand *sous* to de Montfort for the war effort in John's name, although the money did not come from John's own coffers.[47] At some point later in July, the legate travelled a short distance from the siege at Casseneuil to Saint-Livrade, where he issued a charter granting to de Montfort rights to the conquered lands of the Agenais, Quercy, Albigeoise and the county of Rodez.[48] Indeed, by late August the nobility of the Agenais had done homage for their castles to the crusade's commander.[49]

This legatine activity was apparently undertaken without reference to Rome, or to Peter of Benevento, the official papal legate to the Languedoc, who was at this time absent in Spain. Pope Innocent had made it clear that no decisions regarding possession of lands in the Languedoc would be taken until the Fourth Lateran Council, scheduled for the following year. Indeed, anticipating pre-emptory action by de Montfort if not the legate, a letter sent from the papal curia on 18 January 1213 to the churchmen in the Languedoc pointed out that whoever held Jeanne's dowry lands owed homage to John as Duke Richard's successor.[50] John's letter of 6 July 1214 in no way concedes that anyone but Raymond should hold these lands. In the light of this de Courçon's activity requires explanation. It is likely that he perceived that John's actions, by strengthening the southern hand and thus perpetuating the war, touched upon the success of the planned crusade to the Holy Land for, like the pope, he saw conflict in Europe as a major obstacle to its success.[51] Thus it was that between September 1213 and 1215 he

---

[44]*Rymer's Foedera*, 1:186. See also Dickson and Dickson, 'Le Cardinal', 101. The Dicksons do not make a connection between the legate's activity in relation to John and the politics of the crusade; they see his negotiations with John only in the context of the attempt to make peace with Philip Augustus, even though the king's rights to crusader-held lands was at stake. I do not think that the sources imply this.

[45]John was at La Roche-aux-Moines (see John's itinerary).

[46]*Rymer's Foedera*, 1:188.

[47]In August John ordered that the money paid to de Montfort be recouped from the townspeople of La Réole and paid back to the archbishop of Bordeaux who, by implication, had supplied it (*Rot. Lit. Claus.*, 2:171). See also Pierre des Vaux-de-Cernay, *Hystoria Albigensis*, 2:216-17, n. 1.

[48]A. Molinier, ed., *Catalogue des Actes de Simon et Amaury de Montfort* (Paris, 1873), no. 85, p. 79.; HGL 6:451 and 8:653-5.

[49]HGL 6:448.

[50]PL 216:739. See also Roquebert, *L'Épopée*, 2:64; Sumption, *Albigensian*, 177. James Powell suggests that de Courçon shared Pope Innocent's desire to leave the lands pertaining to the county of Toulouse in the hands of the family of Saint-Gilles, and that this explains why the legate was not popular with the French bishops at the council at Bourges in May 1215 (Powell, *Anatomy*, 44 and 46-7). The contents of the Saint-Livrade charter would seem to dispute this.

[51]See Powell, *Anatomy*, 33-6.

attempted to arbitrate between John and Philip Augustus,[52] and that in the summer of 1214 he was to involve himself in the Agenais. It is certain that he played a constructive and diplomatic role in securing the peace between the kings of France and England in the period immediately after Bouvines,[53] but he was able to achieve this by first weakening John's hand in the Languedoc. However, whilst de Courçon undoubtedly felt duty bound to continue the anti-heretical work of his absent colleague Peter of Benevento, he had neither his tact nor his knowledge of the situation.[54] Having neutralized John with regard to the Agenais and Quercy, he initiated a crusade into other lands pertaining to the duchy of Aquitaine. In this way he almost managed to provoke another military response by John, during the seige of Casseneuil. Perhaps between 20 and 25 July, John was reported to be at Périgueux, there accepting into his court refugee soldiers who had fled the re-conquered Agenais – an action we are told made him the object of scandal and compromised his reputation.[55] Pierre des Vaux-de-Cernay is clear that John's actions were prompted by a desire to relieve the Agenais and thereby avenge his nephew, dispossessed of his mother's dowry.[56]

This was not John's plan, however. His presence in Périgueux was merely a threat, for he must have anticipated that de Montfort needed to control Périgord's southern castles if he was to cut off the Languedoc from Aquitainian aid. Encouraged by the legate, as soon as Casseneuil fell and after John had left Périgord, the crusade indeed moved to attack Périgord, crossing the Dordogne as it did so.[57] The attack was ostensibly justified on the basis of information that several strategically placed castles in the region were harbouring enemies of the

---

[52]On 9 September 1213 John had written to the legate that he had received his envoys, who had been charged with enthusing the king about making peace with France and planning a Franco-English expedition to the Holy Land (*Rot. Lit. Claus.*, 1:165). John took little action on the matter, although the legate's attempts persisted. See also Dickson and Dickson, 'Le cardinal', 92-3; Powell, *Anatomy*, 37-8 and 40; Baldwin, *Masters*, 1:21-2; Bolton, 'Philip Augustus and John', 130.

[53]Baldwin, *Masters*, 1:21-2. In response to this, short of other options after Bouvines, John was to send him an envoy from Périgord on around 22 August, Geoffrey de Neville (*Rot. Lit. Pat.*, 1:114; see also Pierre des Vaux-de-Cernay, *Hystoria Albigensis*, 2:215-16, n. 4; Dickson, 'Le cardinal', 105-8).

[54]The legate was noted for lack of diplomacy in many other situations. See sources for the legate above and H. Mayer, *The Crusades*, trans. J. Gillingham (Oxford, 1972), 206.

[55]Pierre des Vaux-de-Cernay, *Histoire*, 199-200. John's presence at Périgueux is not attested by charters and does not appear in his itinerary. The itinerary does not give a location for John between these two dates, however, on the first of which he was at Saint-Maixent in Poitou and on the second he was at Saint-Jean-d'Angely in Saintonge. This makes it quite feasible that the intervening time could have been spent in Périgord. From Pierre des Vaux-de-Cernay's chronology it is clear only that John was at Périgueux before mid-August, when the siege of Casseneuil ended. See also *Hystoria Albigensis*, 215-16, n. 4; HGL 6:446-8.

[56]Pierre des Vaux-de-Cernay, *Histoire*, 199-200.

[57]Pierre des Vaux-de-Cernay, *Histoire*, 202-5; HGL 6:448-51.

peace and of the faith, that is to say, *routiers* and heretics.[58] There is, however, no longer any credible evidence of Cathars in Périgord in either the twelfth or thirteenth centuries,[59] although some of its local nobility and their men, most notably those of Bernard de Cazenac, lord of Domme, Montfort and Beynac, had become notorious for merciless raids on the surrounding countryside.[60] Certainly the crusade had some authority to bring under control *routier* activity in the lands of its targets, but Périgord was traditionally a *sénéchausée* of Aquitaine. Even though John does not appear to have received homage for its lands, nor to have replaced his dead seneschal Martin Algäi, neither did its land-holders perform homage to Toulouse or to the other enemies of the church in the Languedoc. John was wiser than to actually engage the army of God directly, however, and by this point had retreated back further into Aquitaine to nurse the many wounds his ambition had sustained that summer.

JOHN AND PHILIP OF FRANCE

If John wished to intervene in the Languedoc in his own interests and in those of his vassals and relatives of the house of Saint-Gilles, his activity in this context must be understood in relation also to his major concern in these years, his war against the king of France. At times, for example in the early stages of the crusade, it would have suited John well if Philip Augustus had indeed joined its ranks; to have Philip fighting on two fronts could only increase John's chances of success in Normandy and Anjou. But John, in a sense, was also fighting on two fronts, strategically improbable as this seems to modern historians. His visit to La Réole and the capture of Marmande by his army has caused the most confusion.

Michel Roquebert asks 'allait-il s'engager dans l'affaire albigeoise?'[61] and is inclined to answer negatively, pointing to the difficulty of choosing conflict on both the Gascon and Poitevin borders. It was suggested by Kate Norgate that John's manoeuvres from La Rochelle in April 1214 were in fact part of the wars in the north of France, that they were 'to baffle Philip and to ascertain the extent of his own resources in the south',[62] and other historians have followed her in

---

[58]Pierre des Vaux-de-Cernay, *Histoire*, 202.

[59]See G. Lobrichon, 'The Chiaroscuro of Heresy: Early Eleventh-century Aquitaine as Seen from Auxerre', in T. Landes and R. Head, eds, *The Peace of God: Social Violence and Religious Response in France around the Year 1000* (Ithaca and London, 1992), 80-103.

[60]Pierre des Vaux-de-Cernay, *Histoire*, 203, 215. See also Roquebert, *L'Épopée*, 2:287-8.

[61]Roquebert, *L'Épopée*, 2:257-8.

[62]Norgate, *John Lackland*, 198.

this.[63] In the regions of the Angoumois, Limousin and Poitou his manoeuvres did help him to assert his authority.[64] However, the securing of homages at La Réole makes little sense in this context, for it was many miles from the French royal army and instead on the borders of crusader-held lands. It is surely the case, as Michel Roquebert suggests, that John was considering something of a show-down with the crusaders, perhaps even at the request of his brother-in-law,[65] and Johnathan Sumption follows him in this,[66] but neither sees any deliberate strategy in this, only vain posturing. However, from an Agenais perspective, John's intervention appears rather differently than it does to those writing within either an Angevin-Capetian, i.e. northern French, or purely Occitan context. It appears quite simply that 'Jean-sans-Terre s'était rendu en vain en 1214 dans l'Agenais pour le secourir'.[67]

W. L. Warren has said that 'the chroniclers are not at all clear about John's operations from La Rochelle'.[68] Whilst this may be true for the Anglo-Normans, it is not so for the chroniclers of the Albigensian Crusade, who are far from ambiguous about which side John's army was on. The crusade's apologist Pierre des Vaux-de-Cernay states clearly that John's activity was in opposition to the crusade[69] and in defence of his family interests in the Agenais,[70] and that his seneschal Geoffrey de Neville raised his banner at Marmande in clear defiance of the crusaders.[71] Neither is it true for the French chroniclers. William the Breton makes a direct connection between the wars of John and Philip and the power struggle in the Languedoc, saying that Bouvines was fought against the allies and defenders of the Albigensian heretics.[72]

Thus John was active on two fronts, in two wars as part of the same strategy. Having lost the northern territories of the Angevin Empire since 1204 he was now hedging his bets. He was in danger of losing Poitou but by early 1214 had secured

---

[63]Most notably W. L. Warren who does not discuss John's intervention at Marmande at all and states only that 'he marched into Gascony as far south as La Réole to assure himself of the position there' (Warren, *King John*, [2nd edn, London, 1978], 219). J. Gillingham points out John's claim to the Agenais, but does not see his intervention there as at all significant (*The Angevin Empire* [London, 1984], 78).

[64]Turner, *King John*, 131-2.

[65]Suggested in Roquebert, *L'Épopée*, 2:258.

[66]Sumption, *Albigensian*, 176.

[67]A. Cassany-Mazet, *Annales de Villeneuve-sur-Lot et de son Arrondissement* (Agen, 1846), 54.

[68]Warren, *King John*, 1st edn, 218.

[69]Pierre des Vaux-de-Cernay, *Histoire*, 194.

[70]Ibid., 199.

[71]Ibid., 198.

[72]William the Breton, *Philippide* in *Oevres de Rigord et de Guillaume le Breton*, ed. H. F. Delaborde, 2 vols (Paris, 1882-1885), 2:229, lines 496-9. See also G. Duby, *The Legend of Bouvines*, trans. C. Tihanyi (Cambridge, 1990), 130-1 and 151.

the homage of the counts of Toulouse for their county and for the Agenais. If they succeeded in their own battle against the northern French he would have access to an Occitan empire comprising Gascony, the Agenais and the Toulousain. This access could occur whether or not he managed to secure Poitou and recover Normandy, even though these were his most immediate concerns to which he devoted most of his resources. In garrisoning Marmande John was an overlord acting in defence of his vassal Raymond VI, and yet he was never actually seeking a confrontation with the crusaders. As a strategic first priority this would have proved foolish, weakening him both militarily, before marching his army to Poitou, and politically, in terms of his relationship with Rome,[73] and it is important to note that it was Geoffrey de Neville's standard, not that of John, which appeared on the tower at Marmande.

Therefore he did not linger on the borders of the Agenais, let alone enter it in person, but took his army north into Poitou after making his presence known and causing the defection of the towns in the Agenais. John was reminding the French both in the north and in the Languedoc of his claims in the south, which were long-standing in his family and were renewed as a result of the homages received from Count Raymond and his son. Indeed, 'Geoffrey de Neuville . . . avait ostensiblement arboré sa bannière au sommet du donjon, comme pour rappeler aux Croisés que la bastide que Richard Coeur-de-Lion avait fondée trente ans plus tôt, était toujours de mouvance anglaise'.[74] But it is surely the case that, had he and his allies had success against the French king, he would have attempted to consolidate control of the Agenais for the Anglo-Toulousain party. There can be no other explanation for the stationing of a garrison at Marmande under one of his most important officials than that he intended to hold it for himself or his in-laws, nor for his promise to aid Casseneuil except that it was the next most strategically important town in the Agenais.

JOHN'S ENEMIES TAKE THE CROSS

It should also be noted that John had many personal enemies who took part in the Albigensian Crusade, disinclining him further towards it. The most significant amongst these was the de Montfort faction. The crusade's commander, Simon lord of Montfort-l'Amaury in the Isle de France, had been heir also to the earldom of Leicester, but in the early years of the century John had dispossessed English nobles who also held lands in France. De Montfort still used his Leicester title until at least 1217,[75] the year before his death, but from around 1204, in which

---

[73]See below.

[74]Roquebert, L'Épopée, 2:277.

[75]Paris, Bibliothèque Nationale MS Doat 125, fols 110r-12v. The title was employed by his son and heir Amaury de Montfort from 1220 (ibid., fols 139r-40r).

year he set out on the Fourth Crusade, he and his family had moved very firmly into the French sphere. From 1209 their fortunes were intertwined with that of the Albigensian Crusade. In March 1210 de Montfort's countess, Alice de Montmorency, joined the crusade with a new contingent. Her cousin Bouchard de Marly had been with the crusade from 1209 and received Saissac in Carcassès from de Montfort. Alice's brother, Matthew de Montmorency, was to be summoned to the aid of the crusade during the great siege of Toulouse of 1217-1218, at which time he was constable of France. De Montfort's sons and brother Guy also played extensive and important parts in the crusade, and after summer 1213 especially, their control of the borders between the Toulousain and Gascony looked unshakeable.[76]

Another of John's domestic enemies had also taken the cross. Hugh de Lacy, co-lord of Meath with his brother Walter, had been aided in his ambition in Ireland by John and given the newly created earldom of Ulster in 1204,[77] but the family had since seriously fallen from royal favour. Meath was confiscated from Hugh for taking the part of the rebel William de Braose, and he fled Ireland at the approach of John's army.[78] He was presumably heading for the Languedoc, but there is a problem with the dating of the evidence here. William of Tudela places Hugh with the crusaders at Carcassonne in 1209 and states explicitly that he stayed with the crusade when other nobles returned to the north,[79] but sources for the British Isles are quite clear that the de Lacy revolt and Hugh's flight were both in 1210.[80] What is certain is that de Lacy remained close to de Montfort

---

[76]For the involvement of the de Montfort family see numerous references in Roquebert, *L'Épopée Cathare*, 1: 9, 17, 20-4, 146, 171, 272, 279-89, 296, 301, 345, 375, 442-3, 456, 460-4, 447, 471-4, 481, 488; ibid. 2:39, 93, 117, 152-5, 160, 163, 174, 178, 186, 244, 248, 261, 269, 274-5, 279, 290-3, 328-30, 337-8, 342, 349, 357, 389; ibid. 3:14, 20, 29, 31, 37, 40-3, 70, 75, 81, 91-7, 100, 108, 118, 135, 140-1, 150-1, 155, 178, 283-4, 303, 349, 367, 418-23.

[77]At the expense of the disfavoured John de Courcy, lord of Ulster. For the history of the de Lacy family in Ireland in the first decade of the thirteenth century, see J. Otway-Ruthven, *A History of Medieval Ireland*, 2nd edn (London, 1980), 52-78, 80-6. See also S. Painter, *Reign of King John*, (Baltimore, 1949), 46-7; Holt, *Magna Carta*, 108.

[78]William de Braose was the father-in-law of Walter de Lacy, and John deprived Walter of his lands including the lordship of Ludlow. Walter was restored to his English possessions in July 1213 except for Ludlow, whose town he recaptured in October 1213 and castle in April 1215 (*Rot. Lit. Claus.*, 1:147, 173 and 175; *Rot. Lit. Pat.*, 1:132; see also Holt, *Magna Carta*, 203-4). Hugh was evidently not included in this settlement.

[79]William of Tudela, *La Chanson*, 1:92-3 and n. 4.

[80]*Annales Cambriae*, ed. J. Williams, RS (1860), 66-7; *Annales de Margam* in *Annales Monastici*, ed. H. Richards-Luard, 5 vols, RS (1864-9), 1:30; *Annales Dunstaplia*, in ibid., 3:32; Matthew Paris, *Chronica Majora*, 7 vols, ed. H. R. Luard, RS (1872-83), 2:530.

throughout the remainder of the crusade, was often in counsel and in action with him and was rewarded with the fiefs of Castelnaudary and Prouille.[81]

We find yet another established enemy of John's amongst the crusaders from 1209 into its later stages. William des Roches[82] had supported John's nephew Arthur in the Breton succession dispute of 1199. When Philip Augustus recognized John in Anjou at the Treaty of Le Goulet in January 1200, des Roches changed sides and became John's seneschal for Anjou. He then rebelled against John in 1202 and became one of the most important allies of the French king in his conquest of Poitou, and in 1204 he became seneschal of Anjou again, but this time for France.[83]

In 1211 the crusaders had had another significant addition to their numbers. Walter Langton, brother of Stephen Langton whose appointment as archbishop of Canterbury had caused the quarrel between John and the pope, was captured with another crusader as they menaced the borderlands of Foix.[84] The count of Foix wanted ransom for him, but de Montfort captured several southerners near Pamiers and offered them as an exchange. Thus John's political enemies were conquering and gaining lands even on the Gascon border and, in the case of de Montfort in the Agenais, were usurping his authority where he was the acknowledged suzerain (rights which his ecclesiastical enemies such as the Langtons perhaps felt to be void in view of his hostility towards clerical liberties).

JOHN AND POPE INNOCENT

The arbiter of these affairs was ultimately to be Pope Innocent. The circumstances of the troubled relationship between John and the papacy during the years 1205-1213 cannot be rehearsed here in any detail,[85] but they throw a good deal of

---

[81]For references to Hugh de Lacy see Roquebert, *L'Épopée*, 1:289, 294, 306, 438-9; 2:152, 175, 275, 357; 3:21, 31, 75, 93, 110. Hugh only returned to England in 1222 (*Rot. Lit. Pat.*, 1:134 and 150; *Rot. Lit. Claus*, 1:501 and 527; *Annales Dunstaplia*, 75). In 1223-1224 he invaded royal lands in Ireland and was eventually restored to Ulster in 1227 (Otway-Ruthven, *Ireland*, 92).

[82]G. Dubois, 'Recherches sur la Vie de Guillaume des Roches, Seneschal d'Anjou, du Maine et du Touraine', *École de la Bibliothèque des Chartes*, 30 (1869), 32 (1871) and 34 (1873). See also Gillingham, *Angevin Empire*, 55, 66-7, 69 and 73. For his crusade involvement see numerous references in the sources, esp. Pierre des Vaux-de-Cernay, *Histoire*, 39; William of Tudela et al., *La Chanson*, 3:282-4, n. 4.

[83]When Prince Louis of France beseiged Marmande in 1218-1219 he was again in the ranks of the crusade (William of Tudela et al., *La Chanson*, 3:282-3).

[84]Pierre des Vaux-de-Cernay, 102-3. In 1218 Walter Langton was to serve in a crusader army mustered by Alice de Montfort (Sumption, *Albigensian*, 196).

[85]For accounts and analysis of John's relationship with the pope, which was relatively good in the years 1199-1204, and of the dispute over episcopal elections from 1205 to 1213, see Warren, *King John*, 154-73, 206-17; Cheney, *Innocent III and England*, 147-54 and 298-325; Turner, *King John*, 147, 154-66; Painter, *The Reign*, 151-203. Summaries of relevant letters from the pope to John are to be found in Cheney and C. R. and M. G. Cheney, eds, *Letters of Pope Innocent III (1198-1216)*

light on John's activity with regard to the Languedoc. The dispute over John's refusal to accept Stephen Langton as archbishop of Canterbury stood in the way of his co-operation in the crusade from the very start. When the crusade began in 1209, England had been under an interdict for almost a year and John was resisting attempts to reconcile him with either Rome or Philip of France. On 8 November 1209 he was excommunicated, six months after the archbishop of Bordeaux had led his crusade into the Agenais. John could perhaps have saved himself by involvement on the side of God, but this would not have been straight forward in practice. The lands of Raymond VI were protected by the church from attack from June 1209, when he took the cross, to 1211. John's only other option would have been to send troops along the route taken by the main crusader army, along the Rhône valley to attack the lands of the Trencavel viscounts of Béziers, but this would have subjected his army to the authority of the French crusaders, specifically those who were enemies of John in their own right. In any case, in reality John was less than distraught about the prospect and actuality of excommunication. When he did begin to consider involvement in the Languedoc it was from political not religious motives.

From the summer of 1212 John's position was very difficult. He faced a baronial conspiracy in England, and the Dunstable annalist indicates that the rebels wanted to put Simon de Montfort himself on the throne.[86] Rumours were also circulating that the pope was about to release vassals of the king from their fealty, and at the same time in Europe, a papal, Capetian and Hohenstaufen alliance was emerging.[87] John had no choice but to make his peace with the pope and on 15 May 1213 surrendered to him the realms of England and Ireland, receiving them back as fiefs and promising to take part in the proposed Fifth Crusade.[88] Suddenly his relationship with Rome changed. Pope Innocent appears to have treated him as though he believed the change of heart to be entirely

---

Concerning England and Wales (Oxford, 1967), 37-156 and 272-3. See also translations of important letters in C. R. Cheney and W. H. Semple, eds and trans., *Selected Letters of Pope Innocent III Concerning England, 1198-1216* (London, 1953).

[86]*Annales Dunstaplia*, 33. This source dates the rebellion to 1210, however. See also Holt, *Magna Carta*, 226.

[87]See Turner, *King John*, 166-7.

[88]T. D. Hardy ed., *Rotuli Chartarum*, 1:1, (London, 1831), p. 195; Pott. 4776, 1:416; Roger of Wendover, *Flores Historiarum*, 145; Cheney and Semple, *Select Letters*, no. 53, p.149 and no. 67, pp. 177-83; Cheney, *Letters*, nos. 917-18, p. 152. In April 1214, when John was moving to attack the French army in Poitou, the pope was still pleading with John to make his peace with Philip because of the harm the war did to the planning of the crusade (Cheney, *Letters*, no. 963, p. 160; Pott. 4914, 1:429). When a truce was made after John's defeat at Bouvines, the pope again begged him to set out for the Holy Land, to little avail (Cheney, *Letters*, no. 982, p. 162, no. 1005, pp. 167-8 and nos. 1009-10, p. 168). See also Turner, *King John*, 167-74; Cheney, *Innocent III and England*, 326-57; Bolton, 'Philip Augustus and John', 125.

genuine. He warned the barons and the clergy of England against any actions which would undermine John and withdrew his support for the planned Capetian invasion of England.[89] However, before and after John's submission, even during the days in which it took place, there is evidence that the king was at least considering intervention in the Albigensian Crusade. He was exchanging ambassadors with Raymond of Toulouse and King Peter of Aragon in the same period as negotiating his own surrender to Rome with the papal *nuncio* Pandulf, on 13-15 May. These embassies were surely anticipating the inevitable confrontation which was to come that summer at Muret and seeking John's co-operation. John had great financial problems in 1213 which limited but did not rule out aid, for he gave readily enough later that winter,[90] but he could not afford to be be seen helping Count Raymond in the spring. His own embassy to the southerners in August surely confirmed that, as a new vassal of Rome, he could not give them the support he would undoubtedly have liked to give.

By the winter of 1213/14 John did feel able to act, if covertly. The financial help he gave at this time to his Toulousain kin was relatively discreet and not so obviously war-aid as to alarm Rome. Indeed, it was the legate Nicholas of Tusculum, who had executed John's reconciliation with the pope and with Stephen Langton in the same year and who had received John's homage on behalf of Rome, who diplomatically suggested, apparently without censure, that an extended stay by the Toulousains would not be wise.[91] It appears that he felt that their presence and John's financial aid might be misinterpreted, and was certainly judging the 'reformed' John over-generously.

Likewise, John's motive in intervening in the Agenais in the spring was also concealed from many by his larger war against Philip. But Robert de Courçon saw what was happening. The legate has been called 'le docile instrument des ambitions de Montfort',[92] a charge which, like the complaints of contemporary chroniclers at his interference in French ecclesiastical affairs,[93] has a 'myopic

---

[89]Pott. 4774-5 and 4777, 1:416.

[90]In this same winter John was attempting to raise money for his planned attack on France, an expensive undertaking. In addition, detailed in the documents relating to his submission (see above) he had promised to give the pope 10,000 marks towards the Fifth Crusade, money towards papal building projects and also his annual tribute. Not least, he had to make reparations to the English church, the payment of which was a nessessary prerequisite for the lifting of the interdict on his lands, which was still in place despite his homage to the pope. Indeed, he had promised that 15,000 marks would be paid by Christmas 1213, and the balance by Easter 1214. However, no money was paid to the church until October 1214, as a result of which the pope lifted the interdict, and then only a 6,000 mark instalment on the expected 40,000 (Turner, *King John*, 171-2). This makes the 10,000 mark grant to the two Raymonds appear all the more expensive and thus significant to John.

[91]*Annales Waverleia*, 275-7.

[92]Roquebert, *L'Épopée*, 2:296.

[93]Cited and discussed in Powell, *Anatomy*, 35-6.

quality'[94] when his actions are contextualized by his concern for reform and orthodoxy. Indeed, weakness of character was not behind his encouragement of the attack by the crusade on Périgord in 1214, during the peace under which the Languedoc had been placed.[95] Far from it, for, like the pope, de Courçon was a believer in the war that could impose peace and papal authority. However, unlike the pope, he wished this war to continue over the summer of 1214 in order to put de Montfort in as strong a position as possible, whereas John and the other concerned southern parties were forced to wait until the autumn of 1215 for the fate of the Agenais and the Toulousain to be decided. In the meantime, John had to maintain his good relationship with the pope if his own opinion on the matter was to be taken into consideration.

It has to be said that the rebellion of the English barons in 1215[96] could only help John in this matter. In March and April the pope had written to them stating that they must show loyalty to the king, not least because by then John had finally taken the cross.[97] The pope also wrote to various English churchmen expressing his surprise that so few of them were aiding the king against the barons.[98] On 24 August, he denounced and annulled Magna Carta and ordered the barons to withdraw it.[99] By the time of the Fourth Lateran Council John's secular enemies had been excommunicated[100] and Stephen Langton had been suspended as archbishop of Canterbury.[101] Pope Innocent's vassal John was very much in favour at Rome.

---

[94]Ibid., 36.

[95]See Sumption, *Albigensian*, 172-8; Roquebert, *L'Epopée*, 2:256-9 and 285-9.

[96]For the barons' rebellion leading to Magna Carta see Warren, *King John*, 224-45; Painter, *The Reign*, 17-56 and 203-348. John was still supported at this time by Geoffrey de Neville, by then also seneschal for Poitou. Neville was involved in defending Lincoln, Scarborough and York castles for the king and continued to be a royalist under Henry III as sherriff of Yorkshire during the minority, and he was chancellor and seneschal of Poitou and Gascony until 1219 and then again from c. 1222 (*Rot. Lit. Pat.*, 1:379-83; see also DNB, 252). He was amongst the signatories to Magna Carta in 1215 and witnessed its re-issue in 1217 and 1225 (ibid. and see Holt, *Magna Carta*, 131 and 390 and appendices 6, pp. 448-9, 10, p. 485 and 12, p. 511). He was also in the army of the Fifth Crusade (R. Röhricht, *Studien zur Geschichte des Fünften Kreuzzuges*, 2 vols [Berlin, 1874-78], 1:30, no. 24; Powell, *Anatomy*, 223). He died in 1225 in Gascony.

[97]Cheney, *Letters*, nos. 1001-5, pp. 167-8 and no. 1013, p. 169 (Latin text in full pp. 272-3). John took the cross on 4 March 1215 (Holt, *Magna Carta*, 196). This vow was of course never fulfilled and its 'inheritance' arguably provides a context for the crusader vows of his son Henry III (S. Lloyd,"'Political crusades" in England, c.1215-17 and c.1263-5', in P. W. Edbury ed., *Crusade and Settlement*, [Cardiff, 1985], 113-4 and n. 5).

[98]Cheney, *Letters*, no. 1016, pp. 169-70; Pott. 4990, 1:435.

[99]Cheney, *Letters*, no. 1019, p. 170; Pott. 4991, 1:435.

[100]Mansi, *Concilia*, 22:1076.

[101]Mansi, *Concilia*, 22:1070; Matthew Paris, *Chronica Majora*, 2:633-4; Cheney, *Letters*, no.1026.

THE FOURTH LATERAN COUNCIL[102]

Crusader sources tell us that before the council Count Raymond had sent his son to England again to take advice from his uncle John.[103] John was apparently furious at the threat to the family lands and paid for the young Raymond's transport and furnished him with letters of recommendation for himself and his father to be delivered to the pope.[104] It is clear that further strategies were worked out for the council in order to give the son, if not his father, a chance of asserting his rights to Toulouse and also to the Agenais. We are told that the young Raymond, with his illustrious lineage, made a favourable impression on the pope

---

[102]For the canons of the Fourth Lateran Council in general see *Decrees of the Ecumenical Councils*, 2 vols, ed. Norman P. Tanner (London-Washington, 1990) 1:227-71; Mansi, *Concilia*, 22:953-1086. For the business regarding Toulouse and the Agenais specifically, see ibid., cols 1069-70; C. J. Hefèle, *Histoires des Conciles*, trans. H. Leclercq, 22 parts in 11 vols (Paris, 1907-73), 5:2.1316-98 and 1722-33; *La Chanson*, 2:40-89; Pierre des Vaux-de-Cernay, *Histoire*, 215-17; William of Puylaurens, *Chronique*, 92-3; *Anon.*, *Histoire de la Guerre des Albigeoise*, in RHGF, 19:114-92, 31:160-3. The latter is a later thirteenth-century prose chronicle which follows the better informed Pierre des Vaux-de-Cernay in many details, although it is more critical of the crusade and also gives us far more information about the Fourth Lateran Council, information gathered from a variety of sources. See also the account in the Giessen codex published in S. Kuttner, and A. García y García, 'A New Eyewitness Account of the Fourth Lateran Council', *Traditio*, 20 (1964):124-5, lines 44-59 and commentary pp.138-43. The relative merits of the various accounts are discussed in ibid., 138. The latter account is regarded by Kuttner and García y García as a reliable source for the sentence passed; although it lacks the background knowledge of the anonymous *Chanson* author or of Pierre des Vaux-de-Cernay, both of whom were also present, it is comparatively less partisan in tone. Nonetheless they regard *La Chanson* as authoritative in its descriptions of the tortuous process by which the pope reached his decision. Another account is to be found in William the Breton, *Chronique*, in Delaborde, ed., *Oeuvres*, 1.216, p. 306, although William is deemed to be less reliable, believing that Count Raymond and his son had been condemned as heretics before the council (see Kuttner and García y García, 'Eyewitness account', 138). See also HGL 6:469-75, esp. 473-5. For the role of the English representatives see Roquebert, *L'Épopée*, 2:373-5, and Cheney, *Innocent III and England*, 395-6. The papal judgement on the matter was also published in a bull of 14 December 1215 (Pott. 5009, 1:439).

[103]*La Chanson*, 2:40-1 and footnote 3; William of Puylaurens, *Chronique*, 92-3; *anon.*, *Histoire*, 156. See also HGL 6:458.

[104]*Anon.*, *Histoire*, 156. This is the only source to give us detailed information about John's response to his nephew's visit in 1215. The reference in the anonymous *Histoire* to the letter sent with the young Raymond is perhaps derived from the *Chanson* author's claim that the English churchmen carried a letter from John (see below). According to the anonymous prose chronicler the young Raymond then went to meet his father in Rome. The anonymous *Chanson* author and William of Puylaurens tell us that before travelling to Rome the young Raymond travelled from England to rejoin his father in Provence, having crossed the Languedoc with great difficulty and in secret, in the company of Arnaud Topina, probably a prominent citizen of Agen. The young Raymond, William of Puylaurens tells us, was disguised as Arnaud Topina's servant (William of Puylaurens, *Chronique*, 93). See also Roquebert, *L'Épopée*, 2:362. The reference in the anonymous *Histoire* to the letter sent with the young Raymond is perhaps derived from the *Chanson* author's claim that the English churchmen carried a letter from John (see below).

at the council.[105] To help the family's case John sent two trusted advocates. They were the Cistercian Hugh, abbot of Beaulieu in Hampshire, and Walter Gray, bishop of Worcester.

Hugh of Beaulieu was well known to the pope as John's advocate, having interceded with him on several occasions on John's behalf, not without success. In 1204 John had moved and improved Hugh's abbey at Faringdon, founded in 1203, to Beaulieu in Hampshire as compensation for the king's quarrel with the English Cistercians in 1200.[106] Thus Hugh was the beneficiary of John's only monastic foundation. From 1206 Hugh sided with John against Stephen Langton and travelled to Rome in 1207 and 1208 to put the case before the curia.[107] Hugh was amongst several English Cistercians to ignore the interdict,[108] but this did not entirely weaken his credibility at Rome, for in 1208 he persuaded the pope to issue a privilege which stated that he would not seek to impose his episcopal nominees on John, in return for the king's acceptance of Stephen Langton.[109] In the period 1212-1213, during the negotiations through which John made his peace with Rome, Hugh travelled again to the curia on his behalf[110] and was still co-operating with the king over the matter in January 1214.[111] Hugh had also been proposed as bishop to the see of Coventry and Lichfield in 1213-1214 by the canons of Lichfield, possibly at John's instigation.[112] The journey to the Lateran Council was not in fact Hugh's first visit to Rome of 1215, for in the early part of the year he had again been amongst John's envoys in the matter of the charter for free elections and was the king's ally against the barons, and therefore the pope's.[113]

Walter Gray, also one of John's favourites, had formerly been chancellor, a position which he bought for 5000 marks after the death of the former chancellor, his uncle, in 1205.[114] Walter too supported John loyally through the interdict and excommunication. In 1209 his own election to the see of Coventry and Lichfield

---

[105]*La Chanson*, 2:42-3. The young Raymond was descended from the Capetian line through his grandmother Constance, sister of Louis VII, from the Plantagenet kings of England through his mother and from the crusading house of Saint-Gilles.

[106]D. Knowles, et al., *The Heads of Religious Houses, England and Wales* (Cambridge, 1972), 112 and 115; Turner, *King John*, 148; Cheney, *Innocent III*, 35.

[107]Cheney, *Letters*, no. 725, p. 120, no. 800, p. 132 and no. 823, p. 136; Cheney and Semple, *Select Letters*, no. 36, pp.107-9, no. 37, pp. 110-14 and p. 112, n. 3. See also Cheney, *Innocent III*, 151.

[108]Cheney, *Innocent III*, 306 and n. 12.

[109]Cheney, *Innocent III*, 318, n. 73; Knowles, *Heads of Religious House*, 126.

[110]Cheney and Semple, *Select Letters*, no. 45, pp. 130-1 and no. 63, p. 169; Cheney, *Letters*, no. 940, p. 155. See also Cheney, *Innocent III*, 161 and 329-31.

[111]*Rot. Lit. Pat.*,1:109.

[112]*Annales Dunstaplia*, 38. See also Cheney, *Innocent III*, 131 and n. 38.

[113]Cheney, *Innocent III*, 365, n. 45 and p. 367.

[114]Cheney, *Innocent III*, 130-1 and n. 37.

had been one of those regarding which Stephen Langton, the archbishop of Canterbury, complained to the pope of unfair royal influence. Apparently one of John's knights had locked the chapter in a room declaring 'by God's tongue, you shall not leave until you have made a bishop as the king wants; so go and act quickly'.[115] This coerced election was quashed by the archbishop, as was Walter's second election to the same see in 1213.[116] In 1213-1214, however, he secured the election to the see of Worcester. At the Fourth Lateran the matter of the vacant archiepiscopal see of York was raised.[117] The pope had already rejected the election of Simon Langton, another brother of Stephen, for the practical reason that he would be unlikely to work harmoniously with the king, and had required sufficient of the chapter of York to attend the council with a view to another election. The attendees of the chapter had letters of credence from John and elected Walter Gray, the king's favoured candidate.[118] The difference in the approach of the pope to the king, now his vassal, ten years after he had refused to accept John's nominee, John Gray, for Canterbury and had imposed Stephen Langton, is remarkable. Indeed, pope and king were acting together for political reasons to undermine the perfectly legal election of Simon Langton by the chapter.[119]

The *Chanson* author tells us that on 14 November Walter Gray presented the case for Saint-Gilles in legal terms. The Agenais was the dowry of the young Raymond's dead mother Jeanne and therefore his to inherit, even if the pope judged that the lands of his father were indeed to be forfeit. This was because in 1196 the marriage contract had apparently stipulated that if Jeanne died and in the case of the 'mort civile' of Raymond, which would be the case if the council condemned him, her entire dowry, including the Agenais, would pass to her heir, the young Raymond.[120] The bishop argued that this agreement had been confirmed by Rome. Therefore, even if the supreme pontiff adjudged the lands

---

[115]Quoted in *idem*.

[116]Cheney, *Innocent III*, 131.

[117]Turner, *King John*, 41-2. The former archbishop had been Geoffrey Plantagenet, John's illegitimate half-brother.

[118]Mansi, *Concilia*, 22:1071. See also Turner, *King John*, 57, 78, 162-3, 173, n. 48. Walter Gray spent £10,000 whilst at the curia (Matthew Paris, *Chronica Majora*, 2, p. 635), which has been connected to papal approval for his candidature (H. G. Ramm, 'The Tombs of Archbishop Walter de Gray (1216-55) and Geoffrey de Ludham (1258-65) in York Minster, and Their Contents', *Archaeologia* 103 [1971]:101-47, esp. 105). He acted 'passably well' in his new position for thirty-nine years (Cheney, *Innocent III and England*, 394). Simon Langton consequently defected to the Capetian camp, was at one point excommunicated and was appointed archdeacon of Canterbury by his brother in 1227 (Cheney, *Innocent III and England*, 394 and n. 30; Powicke, *Stephen Langton* [Oxford, 1928], 135-8).

[119]Cheney, *Innocent III and England*, 394.

[120]See above for sources outlining the contents of the marriage treaty, esp. *La Chanson*, 2:73-7.

of Raymond VI to be forfeit, and therefore not inheritable by the young Raymond, there was no basis for the confiscation of Jeanne's dowry or for preventing her son from taking possession of it. The pope made it known to John's representative that he agreed and that his case on behalf of the young Raymond was entirely valid. Hugh of Beaulieu now presented the pope with letters from John, a vassal who loved his lord 'with an ever constant heart',[121] pleading clemency on behalf of his nephew with regard also to the lands of Toulouse. The pope also agreed that it would be unjust to deny the young Raymond his Toulousain inheritance, even if it were to be taken from his father.

During the Albigensian Crusade Pope Innocent had installed several new bishops in the Languedoc. These men had already unofficially elected Simon de Montfort as count of Toulouse[122] and voiced their outrage at the prospect of the pope reinstating Raymond VI. Indeed, the *Chanson* author tells us that they followed the harassed pope into the Lateran gardens where he had retired to think the matter over, and that they threatened rebellion.[123] The pope then returned to the council and announced his decision: that all the conquered territories, not least the Toulousain and the Agenais, were to go to de Montfort. Indeed, he included also the unconquered towns of Toulouse and Montauban, essential for control of the Toulousain and the Agenais respectively. In compensation, he declared that the lands were not necessarily permanently lost to the young Raymond. The anonymous author of the *Chanson* tells us that the pope made it clear that de Montfort should guard his undeserved land well: 'let him keep it if he can, for if any of it is taken from him I will not help him to get it back'.[124] Thus the county of Toulouse and the Agenais were granted to de Montfort as a fief of the French king.[125]

Accounts excuse this apparent miscarriage of justice by emphasizing that the pope was unable to carry the council with him, so strong was the feeling against the house of Saint-Gilles and for de Montfort, amongst the French bishops especially.[126] We are told that the pontiff was forced to act very much against his

---

[121]Ibid., 76-7.

[122]The council of Montpellier, convened by Robert de Courçon in December 1212, made this recommendation to the pope (Mansi, *Concilia*, 22:936-7; see also Dickson and Dickson, 'Le Cardinal', 101).

[123]*La Chanson*, 2:58-61.

[124]*La Chanson*, 2:78-9. Only the traditional family lands of St Gilles of which the crusaders were not actually in possession were given to the young Raymond, most importantly the marquisate of Provence.

[125]Not as a fief of Rome as de Montfort had wished (S. Kuttner and A. García y García, 'Eyewitness account', lines 54-5 and commentary, pp. 142-3).

[126]It has been said that the pope 'could not control the self-interest of those who had already made the south of France a battle-ground' (Cheney, *Innocent III and England*, 396). Other accounts concentrate on the papal recognition of the justice of the claim of the young Raymond.

will. The scene in which the miserable pope, attempting to find in the garden peace in which to wrestle with the legality and morality of the case, is pursued and harangued by the southern French bishops is indeed full of pathos; the pope, with all the wisdom of Solomon, is unable to overcome the need to have the support of those below him, and thus makes an unjust decision.

But Innocent III was a great pragmatist; a ruler as well as a judge; a politician as well as a priest. What he wanted for the Languedoc was stable orthodox rule. He also wanted the kings of France and England to go on crusade to the Holy Land. These things were only possible with the Languedoc, France and England at peace. In recognizing the justice of the young Raymond's claim, he understood what lay behind the support from England. The house of Saint-Gilles was firmly in John's pocket. John, having lost his lands in northern and central France, had his eyes on an Occitan Empire, with the allod of Gascony as its cornerstone. Since 1213 he had been binding Raymond VI and especially the young Raymond ever more closely to him. The pair had become dependent on him financially, had already done him homage for the county of Toulouse and the Agenais and would hold them of the dukes of Aquitaine if they could recover them. The papal decision in 1213 to suspend lordship of the conquered lands and allocate them anew, perhaps to the house of Saint-Gilles, meant that John might indeed have succeeded in gaining actual suzerainty after the titular homage of the count of Saint-Gilles. Nor would John need to be ruthless in this matter, as he was otherwise capable of being, but only clever, in favour at Rome, and indispensable to his Occitan neighbours, fellow enemies of France. Thus the pope had to consider that if he were to hand the Toulousain back to those whom he probably considered its rightful heirs, they would be likely to renew and strengthen further their ties to John, perhaps enabling him eventually to renew his war against Philip II.

John has been portrayed as one of the 'vultures' represented at the Fourth Lateran, picking over the bones of the forfeited lands of the Languedoc, his ambassadors sent there to press for his personal claim to the Agenais.[127] This is not in fact the strategy which appears to have been pursued at Rome, neither is there any real indication that the pope thought John to be self-serving in the matter. However to view the pope as entirely regretful about ignoring John's wishes for his kinsmen also rather assumes that he truly believed that the king had been transformed by his act of homage. It would seem that however obedient John was now being, his position as vassal in no sense inclined the pope towards hearing his pleas more favourably than those of the other interested parties in the dispute. To understand the pope's position with regard to John we must

---

[127]Sumption, *Albigensian*, 179.

understand that he had succumbed to papal authority pragmatically from a position of weakness. It was not the case that since John's submission in 1213 the pope 'regarded his new vassal with the same unrealistic indulgence that he had shown before the Canterbury crisis'.[128] Pope Innocent understood John's motives only too well, for in late 1213, after John's homage, he had warned and threatened him against any further disobedience and persecution of the church.[129] His ambition meant perpetual war in France, and the pope would not allow his vassal to go down that road.

Thus we should not see the pope as having been forced into granting the lands in the Languedoc to de Montfort against his will. Of course it was expedient for him to make expressions of regret, but he had his mind set on higher goals, on peace in Europe and a successful crusade to the East. If he had seen dispossessing the young Raymond as morally wrong, would he have done it? We saw in the case of the election of Walter Gray that justice could be overturned if it would lead to political discord, which the election of Simon Langton certainly would have done. This was a lesson that the pope had learned in dealing with John, for the king was as stubborn about defending and extending his own interests as the pope was about matters of principle. What was ultimately wrong, in the pope's eyes, was the perpetuation of war and heresy, to which, at the time, de Montfort looked most likely to put an end. Indeed, in 1213 the pope had told Christians that the Fourth Lateran Council was to be called, amongst other reasons, 'to eliminate heresies and strengthen the faith, to allay differences and establish peace'.[130] The reinstatement of the house of Saint-Gilles in the Languedoc would not further this aim as readily as would the possession of Toulouse and the Agenais by de Montfort.

Thus it was that the pope, having denied John's wishes for southern France, continued to support his vassal in England against the barons[131] and Capetian

---

[128]Turner, *King John*, 170.

[129]Cheney and Semple, *Select Letters*, no. 63, pp. 169-70.

[130]Cheney and Semple, *Select Letters*, no. 51, p. 145.

[131]In December 1216 the pope excommunicated the rebellious barons (Cheney, *Letters*, no.1029, p. 172). For the civil war see Painter, *Reign*, 349-77.

invasion,[132] until his death on 21 May the following year.[133] This was not because he believed that John was now a worthy ruler in all respects. He supported him now, just as he had failed to support him in the affairs of the Languedoc, in the cause of that great theme of this pontificate: secure and peaceful secular rulership whose first loyalty was to Rome.

---

[132]The barons invited Prince Louis of France to invade England and take its crown (Matthew Paris, *Chronica Majora*, 2:654). The pope forbade either the clergy or the French king and his son from military intervention in support of the barons (Cheney, *Letters*, nos. 1032-6, p. 173, no. 1040, p. 173, no. 1044, p. 173, and nos. 1065-6, pp. 176-7). See also Warren, *King John*, 249-56. This was to follow up plans made late in the council, on 30 November, for peace between the kings of England and France, discussed as a prerequisite to the planning of the Fifth Crusade. John, in his many letters sent to the pope before the council, had explained that enemies at home and abroad made it impossible for him to crusade. Prince Louis was indeed to invade England later in the winter, a matter on which the pope would take further action on John's behalf in December and onwards (Matthew Paris, *Chronica Majora*, 2:656-7; see also Cheney, *Innocent III and England*, 391-2).

[133]Not many weeks after he would have heard that he had failed to prevent Louis from landing in England. John's death on 19 October 1216 changed matters for the Capetians and the English rebels. They could not disinherit the child Henry, not least because of the presence of the legate Guala who ensured that his interests were guaranteed by the pope. Thus Prince Louis was forced to abandon England (Matthew Paris, *Chronica Majora*, 3:2-6).

Innocent III and Evangelical Enthusiasts: The Route to Approval

Frances Andrews

During the pontificate of Innocent III, several new religious groups acquired some form of approval for their way of life. This extended from the oral acceptance of a proposal to the formal recognition of a new order. Those approved in turn ranged from the strictly enclosed monks of the community at Val des Choux in the diocese of Langres to the more outward-looking followers of John of Matha or Francis of Assisi. They also, famously, included groups which had previously been condemned as heretics, notably the *Humiliati* and the followers of Durandus of Huesca and Bernard Prim, but also Bosnian 'Christians' who had mistakenly been called Patarines. There are substantial differences between these groups and some are better known than others, either because of the extent of contemporary documentation or, more often, because the scale of the organization which developed after approval generated great interest in their origins. Yet they are worth considering as a group because, at the time of their first encounters with Innocent III's curia, they were all in the same predicament: people experimenting with new forms of religious life who sought ecclesiastical confirmation of the legitimacy of their actions.

This paper will use the contemporary documentation to re-examine the question of how these groups came to enjoy the ecclesiastical approval which had in some cases previously been denied to them. In the past, consideration of the experience of these movements and their acceptance into the hierarchy has focused on the role of the young and energetic pope, Innocent III. Herbert Grundmann set out

229

to establish 'what decisions brought these religious movements under the rules and forms of life of the medieval Church'. He saw Innocent's pontificate as a break with the past: the new pope frequently reversed the policies of his predecessors, hoping to deal with heresy by 'an intelligent, energetic distinction between heresy and a religious movement true to the Church'. He understood that the 'religiöse Bewegungen' were not to be defeated by condemnation and recognized how to bond them with the hierarchical church, through his 'cleverness and ability, foresight and energy'. Although Grundmann argued that Innocent never adopted a comprehensive policy, at the same time he described him as 'consistent', developing 'a policy which can be followed through the years . . . from the negotiations with the *Humiliati*, through the reconciliation of some Waldensian groups, to the rise of the mendicant orders'.[1] Michele Maccarrone later followed the same line, arguing that the approval of new orders such as the *Humiliati* was the direct responsibility of Innocent III, 'fruit of his careful examination and correction', and that his actions implicitly affirmed 'that canonical legislation on religious was the responsibility of the apostolic see', no longer simply to be left to the bishops. In his view, under Innocent the curia passed from according simple protection to religious houses, to 'direct intervention and elaboration of the ordering and discipline' of their lives.[2]

This understandable emphasis on the role of the pope is also found in the work of Brenda Bolton, who discussed his policy in a series of articles. Like Grundmann and Maccarrone she sees Innocent as seeking to 'bridge the gap between the [protest] groups and the hierarchical church' and as adopting a sensitive approach, showing that he was 'prepared to encounter these protest groups as no other pope had done'.[3] In the case of the *Humiliati* however, she concludes that Innocent 'sowed the seeds of their destruction as a primitive evangelical movement', forcing them into a 'diocesan structure which led to the ultimate vitiation of their early form'.[4] This focus on Innocent's role in such 'spiritual' affairs has also partly been prompted by a desire to redress the balance

---

[1]Herbert Grundmann, *Religiöse Bewegungen im Mittelalter* (Berlin, 1935). English translation of second, revised edition (Darmstadt 1961), *Religious Movements in the Middle Ages*, trans Steven Rowan (Notre Dame-London,1995), Introduction and chapter 2.

[2]Michele Maccarrone, *Studi su Innocenzo III*, *Italia Sacra* 17 (Padua, 1972):290.

[3]Brenda Bolton, 'Poverty as Protest: Some Inspirational Groups at the Turn of the Twelfth Century', *The Church in a Changing Society. Conflict-Reconciliation or Adjustment? Papers Presented at the CIHEC Conference*, Uppsala August 1977 (Uppsala, 1978), reprinted in *eadem*, *Innocent III: Studies on Papal Authority and Pastoral Care* (Aldershot, 1995), XIII/7. See also chapters XII, XIV and XV in the same volume.

[4]Brenda Bolton, 'Innocent III's Treatment of the Humiliati', *Popular Belief and Practice*, ed. G. J. Cuming and Derek Baker, *Studies in Church History* 8 (Cambridge, 1972, repr. 1984):73-82. Reprinted, without notes, in *Innocent III. Vicar of Christ or Lord of the World?*, ed. James M. Powell (2nd edn,Washington, 1994), 114-20.

of this pope's 'political' reputation, which has long been the subject of debate.[5] In what follows, however, I wish to side-step the broader question of the 'spiritual' nature of the pontificate to focus on a smaller and more practical one. Here Innocent's role will be taken for granted: the pope provided the leadership, often set the ball rolling and had the foresight to distinguish between those who were dangerous heretics and some groups with potential as members of the ecclesiastical fold. But beyond Innocent himself, who were the people involved in the approval of these groups, and what contribution did they make to the outcome? Such considerations will I hope enable us to clarify the role of the pope himself by giving a human context to his actions and to the making of policy.

The sources for this undertaking present several difficulties, not the least being their incomplete nature. What survives is almost exclusively material emanating from the papal registers. These were certainly intended to be accurate but form an incomplete series, and the texts themselves often reveal the uncertainty of the information available to the curia, reflected in repeated use of the sub-clause 'if this is the case' (*si est ita*). Only indirectly do the letters give any sense of both sides of an encounter between Innocent and these new religious groups. It is therefore easy to concentrate on Innocent and the curia's own presentation of events in the letters. Yet occasional glimpses in other sources, while not impugning the accuracy of the papal record, often add to the picture, and suggest that others may have played a more central role than is at first apparent.

In one rare case a source gives greater detail about the beginnings of the process of approval: Thomas of Celano's *First Life of St Francis* records the holy man's first encounter with the curia. This gives Cardinal John of San Paolo a crucial role in listening to Francis and then assisting him in gaining access to the pope. Celano is not unproblematic as a source. He was writing nearly twenty years after the event and after the death and canonization of Francis changed the value of the events described. But he certainly reflects later understanding of the process involved and since, as we shall see, this description matches the model for treatment of some other contemporary groups, it seems unnecessary to argue that this part of his account is essentially inaccurate. Francis, who had already drawn up a 'form of life and rule', was offered 'advice and assistance' by his bishop once the latter had overcome the shock of finding this local religious in Rome. He then approached John of San Paolo, a cardinal with a reputation for holiness, who received him 'kindly and charitably and praised highly his will and purpose', but proposed that he adopt the life of a monk or hermit. 'Fearing that he might decline from so great a purpose, he showed him ways that would be

---

[5]For an essential introduction to the arguments, see *Innocent III. Vicar of Christ or Lord of the World?*, ed. Powell, passim.

easier to follow.' Only when Francis had convinced him by his constancy, did the
cardinal 'strive to further his [Francis'] aims before the lord pope'.[6]

Celano's account of Francis' approach is rare as a non-curial source (though
papally commissioned and approved) giving details of the first encounter with the
curia. It praises Innocent as 'a famous man, greatly learned, renowned in
discourse, burning with zeal for justice . . .' but suggests that Innocent became
involved at a second stage, and that much of the initial vetting and negotiation
was undertaken by one of those around him, rather than by the pope himself. In
view of the workload of the average medieval pope and of Innocent III in
particular, this is hardly surprising, and much work has been done on the
increased use of papal judges delegate and *visitatores* in this period.[7] These
works are, however, broadly concerned with formal structures and approach the
question from the point of view of papal policy and the development and
effectiveness of the structures of government in the church. They are rarely
concerned with the individuals involved or the contribution these may have made
to the outcome in the sort of cases under consideration here. In spite of such
studies, the emphasis of most modern historical writing mirrors the emphasis of
the surviving sources on the role of Innocent. Yet closer examination of papal
and non-papal sources reveals that much more can be said about the other people
involved. Some of the groups were well-established before approaching the curia,
and the men whom they initially approached or who were delegated by Innocent
to consider their cases had long experience and understanding of the issues
involved. In some instances these were local men, like Bishop Guy of Assisi,
who had substantial knowledge of the local circumstances involved in Francis'
early career, of which neither John of San Paolo nor Innocent can have been
aware. The contribution of such prelates as the first port of call was thus crucial

---

[6]Thomas of Celano, *Vita prima sancti Francisci*, ed. Quaracchi Fathers, *Legendae sancti Francisci
Assisiensis saeculis XIII et XIV conscriptae, Analecta Franciscana* 10 (1926-41), 1, pp. 1-126, 26. The
role of John of San Paolo is also in Julian of Speyer's *Legenda S. Francisci*, written c.1232-5, but
closely dependent on Celano (*Analecta Franciscana*, 10/4, p. 344); although modified it is still in
Bonaventure's *Legenda maior* (*Analecta Franciscana* 10/5, p. 570) and indeed is enlarged in the
Legenda trium sociorum (AASS October II [1866], cap. 12:47-8). English translations of Celano,
Bonaventure and the Three Companions are in *St Francis of Assisi, Writings and Early Biographies.
English Omnibus of the Sources for the Life of St Francis*, ed. Marion A. Habig (Chicago, 1973),
254-6, 651-2, 934-7. On John of San Paolo, see Maleczek, *Papst*, 114-17. See now also M. Robson,
St Francis of Assisi: the Legend and the Life (London, 1997).

[7]See for example, Jane E. Sayers, *Papal Judges Delegate in the Province of Canterbury, 1198-1254*
(Oxford, 1971); John C. Moore, 'Papal Justice in France around the Time of Pope Innocent III',
Church History, 41 (1972):295-306; James Ross Sweeney, 'Innocent III, Canon Law, and Papal
Judges Delegate in Hungary', *Popes, Teachers and Canon Law in the Middle Ages*, ed. James Ross
Sweeney and Stanley Chodorow (Ithaca-London, 1989), 26-52; Maria Pia Alberzoni, 'Innocenzo III
e la riforma della Chiesa in "Lombardia". Prime indagini sui visitatores et provisores', *Quellen und
Forschungen aus italienischen Archiven und Bibliotheken* 73 (1993):122-78.

in determining the nature of the new entities created. (Had Francis been rejected by Guy, as Valdez was rejected by the bishops of the Languedoc, would his route to approval have been so smooth?)

As the result of recent research in the archives, one of the best documented of these cases is now the experience of the early *Humiliati*, the movement listed amongst the heretics condemned by Lucius III and Frederick Barbarossa at Verona in the autumn of 1184 and brought back into ecclesiastical union in June 1201.[8] The most informative early account of the *Humiliati* still remains an entry under the year 1178,[9] in the anonymous (but probably Premonstratensian) *Universal Chronicle of Laon*:

> At that time there were certain inhabitants (*cives*) of Lombard towns who lived at home with their families, chose a distinctive form of religious life, refrained from lies, oaths and law suits, were satisfied with plain clothing and argued for the catholic faith (*pro fide catholica se opponentes*). They approached the pope and besought him to confirm their way of life (*propositum*). This the pope granted them, provided they did all things humbly and decently, but he expressly forbade them to hold secret meetings (*conventicula*) or to presume to preach in public. But spurning the apostolic command, they became disobedient, for which they suffered excommunication. They called themselves *Humiliati* because they did not use coloured cloth for clothing, but restricted themselves to plain dress.[10]

This account, probably written sometime between 1184 and the return of the *Humiliati* to the church in 1201, concentrates on activities of the lay element in the movement and their preaching. It is an understandable focus since it was the most novel and therefore most newsworthy aspect and perhaps most likely to concern the Premonstratensian author of the text, as it had the pope. Yet Innocent's letters of 1201 show that the *Humiliati* had a strong clerical element, and notarial records imply that this had been the case from the very beginning. Already in 1176 their community at Viboldone near Milan was building a church dedicated to St Peter and agreed to pay the provost of the *pieve* a fixed sum in

---

[8]For an introduction to the Humiliati see Luigi Zanoni, *Gli umiliati nei loro rapporti con l'eresia, l'industria della lana ed i communi nei secoli xii e xiii sulla scorta di documenti inediti* (Milan, 1911, repr. 1971).

[9]Or 1179. The correct date depends on whether we maintain that the *Humiliati* approached Alexander at the Lateran Council which opened on 5 March 1179 in the modern calendar, 1178 in the Easter calendar in use in Laon in this period.

[10]'Chronicon universale anonymi Laudunensis', ed. G. Waitz, MGH SS 26:442-57, 449-50. The translation is adapted from *Heresies of the High Middle Ages*, ed. Walter L. Wakefield and Austin P. Evans (New York, 1969), 158-9.

compensation for the expected loss of first fruits and oblations.[11] In 1189 a house at Rondineto in Como was given responsibility for an already established church, and in 1198 San Cristoforo in Lodi was described as a *canonica* in the will of a local benefactor.[12]

Such evidence suggests that the *Humiliati* were integrated into the local ecclesiastical community, and the list can easily be extended to show that they enjoyed cordial relations with northern prelates. These included the bishops of Piacenza, Pavia and Tortona, who gave them or allowed them to administer properties including hospitals and churches in their dioceses, and the archbishop of Milan, who allowed one of their houses in the city to purchase tithes in 1178.[13] In 1186 the pope himself, Urban III, took their community at Viboldone into papal protection, just two years after the condemnation by his predecessor.[14]

Not all of the early records for the movement of the *Humiliati* are equally solid; some stem from much later copies or concern communities which are otherwise undocumented or only later definitively identifiable as *Humiliati*. Nonetheless, the cumulative impression is that the *Humiliati* had maintained 'normal' relations with several churchmen in the north, included clerics amongst their members and, in one case at least, enjoyed a reputation as worthy recipients of legacies. The representatives they sent to petition the curia, Lanfranc of Lodi and James of Rondineto were the superiors of well-established communities and almost certainly clerics. Their journey followed an earlier submission made to Adelard, cardinal-bishop of Verona.[15] Innocent certainly took a personal interest in the case. His letter establishing a distinction between dangerous heretics and groups which could be retrieved had been prompted by the treatment of the *Humiliati* in the diocese of Verona and was addressed to Adelard.[16] Later, when the *Humiliati* representatives had approached the curia, he requested that they also send the leader of their lay contingent and asked to meet other 'suitable and discrete men,

---

[11] Girolamo Tiraboschi, *Vetera Humiliatorum Monumenta annotationibus, ac dissertationibus prodromis illustrata*, 3 vols (Milan, 1766-68), 2:117-19.

[12] For Rondineto, see Tiraboschi, *Vetera*, 3:303-5. For San Cristoforo see Archivio di Stato, Milan, fondo pergamene, cartella 182, busta 100, Sta Chiara Nuova, 10 December 1198. The will of Albert Niger left half his tithes from Fançago to the *canonica* of San Cristoforo and the poor of the hospital of S. Biagio, the other half to the cathedral works.

[13] On Piacenza see for example, G. Storti, *Arena Po. Lineamenti di storia medievale* (Pavia, 1972), 43-52, 120-1. On Pavia see Zanoni, *Gli umiliati*, 8, n. 3; for Tortona see *Corpus Iuris Canonici*, ed. A. Friedberg, 2 vols (Leipzig, 1881), 2:285-6; and for Milan in 1178 see Tiraboschi, *Vetera*, 2:119-22.

[14] Tiraboschi, *Vetera*, 2:123-5.

[15] Referred to by Innocent: 'qui etiam in manibus tuis [Adelard] stare mandatis ecclesie iuraverunt.' *Licet in agro*, 6 December 1199, *Reg.* 2:219, pp. 424-5 = PL 214:788-9.

[16] Ibid.

cultivators of religion and truth and lovers of justice'.[17] As with contemporary judicial cases, he entrusted the detailed investigation to delegates, in this case two groups of men, first local prelates in the north, then members of the curia. The local men were Albert bishop of Vercelli and Peter Cistercian abbot of Lucedio, one of the major Cistercian foundations of northern Italy (a third man, the Cistercian abbot of Cerreto in the diocese of Lodi, had died before the case was heard). When chosen for this task these two men already had substantial careers behind them. Albert had begun his career as a canon of Mortara in the Lomellina and had been a bishop since 1184 (elected first to Bobbio, in 1185 before consecration, he was transferred to Vercelli). He was an efficient prelate, obtaining privileges from Urban III to protect episcopal property and rights and exercising both the administrative and spiritual duties of a diocesan, settling disputes, holding annual synods, appointing a theologian to teach in his cathedral chapter.[18] Perhaps remarkably for a man later favoured by Innocent, in the late 1180s and 1190s, he seems to have identified with the imperial party, frequenting Henry VI's entourage, travelling extensively with him, witnessing imperial diplomas on over thirty occasions and obtaining privileges. He even planned to go on an imperial embassy to pope Celestine III together with Innocent's later *bête noire*, Markward of Anweiler, though this never took place, since it was pre-empted by the deaths of both emperor and pope.

Peter of Lucedio was also an experienced prelate.[19] He had been abbot of Lucedio in Albert's diocese of Vercelli since 1184, and he had acted as a papal agent at least since 1196 when Celestine III commissioned him to assist Albert of Vercelli in resolving a dispute between the canons of Oulx and the monks of San Giusto in Susa.[20] This may have been the first time that the two men had worked together, but over the next few years they seem to have become accustomed to working jointly, being entrusted in 1199 with untangling the century-long dispute between the monks and canons of Sant'Ambrogio in Milan, which the archbishop had singularly failed to resolve and which had exploded into a riot in the basilica itself in December 1198.[21] The choice of these men to consider the *Humiliati*

---

[17]' . . .viros idoneos et discretos, cultores religionis et veritatis ac iustitie amatores. . .', *Licet multitudini credentium*, December 1200, PL 214:921-2.

[18]See L. Minghetti, 'L'Episcopato vercellese di Alberto durante i primi anni del xiii secolo', *Vercelli nel secolo xiii*, ed. R. Ordano et al. (Vercelli, 1984), 99-112.

[19]See John C. Moore, 'Peter of Lucedio (Cistercian Patriarch of Antioch) and Pope Innocent III', *Römische Historische Mitteilungen* 29 (1987):221-49.

[20]*Le carte della prevostura d'Oulx raccolte e riordinate cronologicamente fino al 1300*, ed. G. Collino, *Biblioteca della società storica Subalpina* 45 (Pinerolo, 1908), no. 207, pp. 215-17.

[21]Annamaria Ambrosioni, 'Controversie tra il monastero e la canonica di S. Ambrogio alla fine del secolo xii', *Rendiconti. Classe di lettere e scienze morali e storiche del Istituto lombardo di scienze e lettere* 105 (1971):643-80, 675.

reflects not a new policy but the continuation of an established one, in both practice and personnel. Innocent may have known them personally: by December 1200 he certainly knew Peter, since in that month he wrote that the abbot had attended the curia to explain *viva voce* some of the legal details of a dispute between the Templars of *Lombardia* and the bishop of Tortona, who had handed a Templar house to the *Humiliati* sometime between 1183 and 1193.[22] Whether he knew Albert at this stage is undocumented. What mattered, however, was that these men were *in situ* and had the pertinent local experience. They were also accustomed to working together and were probably friends. Years later, when Albert had become patriarch of Jerusalem, Peter was appointed to Antioch. Innocent had instructed Albert to ensure that a suitable man was chosen, if necessary from overseas,[23] and his letter informing Albert of the election noted that it had indeed been achieved with his intervention, *tuo studio mediante*, and expressed the hope that they would provide each other with mutual solace.[24]

The rule that these men discussed with the *Humiliati* and which was sent to Rome for approval by the second curially-based delegates was partly new and partly constructed by taking elements from a variety of different texts and regulations, including the rule of St Benedict. It includes elements which suggest that Albert and perhaps Peter played an active part in the construction of the new regime. Members of the first 'canonical' order were to adopt the customs of Mortara, Albert's original community, and the administrative structure of the whole group was to mimic that of Cistercian visitation.[25] The Cistercian element may have been introduced by one of the men delegated to the case at the curia, who included Rainier of Ponza, a Cistercian by training and now the pope's confessor; however the customs of Mortara can only have come from Albert. Although the sources give no further clues, such direct borrowing hints at much more guidance from these two northern prelates. The final text was further examined in the curia by Rainier and two cardinals, Gratian, cardinal-deacon of SS. Cosma e Damiano and Peter Capuanus, cardinal-priest of San Marcello (appointed to this title in December 1200, so the second stage in discussion of the *Humiliati* cannot have taken place before this date). Innocent requested that members of the order should come to the curia both to explain the details of their

---

[22] 'salva ei quaestione proprietatis, de qua in hoc iudicio nihil est actum, sicut praedictus abbas de Locedio nobis exposuit viva voce . . .' The letter was included in *Compilatio tertia* and in the Decretals of Gregory IX. *Olim Causam*, X.2.13.12; CIC 2:285-6.

[23] 'personam idoneam de provincia ipsa vel alia citra mare vel ultra', *Quasi non suffecissent*, 12 July 1208; PL 215:1428-9.

[24] *Gratum gerimus*, 5 March 1209; PL 216:18-19.

[25] 'secundum consuetudinem Mortariensis ecclesie'; 'sicut in Cistertiensi ordine patres abbates in minoribus consueverunt abbatibus obtinere', *Non omni spiritui*, 16 June 1201, ed. Tiraboschi, *Vetera*, 2:139-48.

propositum as drawn up by the first delegation in consultation with the *Humiliati*, and to hear any corrections which might be made so that these could be explained to the other members of the new order back at home. The resulting approval bears the mark of Innocent's own hand in the final stages, though the context of his contribution is unclear. According to the text of one of the three letters sent confirming the new order, the examination of the revised *proposita* took place in the presence of Innocent and the cardinals together,[26] while in another, the two examinations were apparently separate.[27] This letter also states that Innocent had made certain corrections for which he was at pains to win their approval. The basic structure, however, remained the product of the *Humiliati* themselves and the two northern prelates, who were well able to initiate actions and take decisions; that is after all why Innocent had chosen them.

Investigation of the other new groups approved during Innocent's pontificate again implies that the pope was happy to leave the detail to others so that they, as much as he, must be acknowledged as responsible for the character of the outcome. His letter to the prior and brothers of the Val des Choux in the diocese of Langres, approving their way of life and amounting to the foundation of the Valiscaulian order, is simply based on the account of Guy de Paray, a Cistercian whom he had appointed cardinal-bishop of Preneste (1200-1221) and who was archbishop-elect of Reims (1204-1206).[28] Guy had come across the house while travelling through the diocese, had diligently enquired into their merits and, finding nothing untoward (*nil in eo nisi religiosum comperit et honestum*) had written to Innocent who now approved their way of life, including as confirmation an outline of their regulations in his letter.[29] Once again the details seem to have been left to the responsibility of the religious themselves and the prelate on the spot; in this case Innocent does not even appear to have added any personal contribution.

Other cases once more suggest that Innocent took a less prominent role, sometimes for obvious practical reasons. John of Casamari, a papal chaplain, was sent to deal with the case of schismatic Bosnian monks who had been calling themselves Christians and had been subject to suspicions of heresy.[30] They made their oath of obedience to the Roman Church before John and Ban Kulin, the lord

---

[26]*Incumbit nobis*, 7 June 1201, ed. Tiraboschi, *Vetera*, 2:128-34.

[27]*Diligentiam pii patris*, 12 June 1201, ed. Tiraboschi, *Vetera*, 2:135-8.

[28]*Licet nec reprehensibile*, 6 July 1204; PL 215:398-402. On Guy, see Maleczek, *Papst*, 133-5.

[29]*Solet annuere*, 10 Feb 1204; PL 215:531-2; See also *Gallia Christiana*, 4:742-5.

[30]On the context of this legation, see James Ross Sweeney, 'Innocent III, Hungary and the Bulgarian Coronation: A Study in Medieval Papal Diplomacy', *Church History* 42 (1973):320-34, 321.

of Bosnia (c.1180-1204),[31] and then two of their company, Lubin and Brageta, accompanied John and Ban Kulin to the king of Hungary and again swore to observe their new statutes, in the presence of the king and of the Hungarian prelates, the archbishop of Kalocsa-Bacs and the bishop of Pécs. A signed copy of their oath and statutes was then sent to Rome.

The remoteness in political terms of the Bosnian case provides an explanation for Innocent's dependence on the judgement of his chaplain, but in others closer to home, it is again clear that other men made some of the crucial decisions. When John of Matha presented his *propositum* for a new order to ransom Christians captured by the infidel, Innocent referred the question to Absalom, abbot of the Augustinian house of Saint Victor (1198-1203) and Odo of Sully, archbishop of Paris (c.1195-1208). Odo, as Tillmann notes, was a possible fellow student with Innocent during his student days in Paris and became 'one of his men of trust in the French episcopate'.[32] These men examined John's intentions and the *institutio ordinis et vivendi modo* and wrote to Innocent, sending him a copy of the new rule. Before approving it in December 1198, Innocent made some additions of his own and allowed John himself to do so. Like the letters for the *Humiliati*, this rule shows explicit borrowing from rules observed by one of the two local prelates. The Trinitarians were to adopt the customs of Saint-Victor regarding the canonical hours and shaving, details which hint at greater influence from Abbot Absalom.[33]

Another instance once more reveals that while Innocent set out the initial policy establishing a distinction between 'poisonous heretics' and those teetering on the boundaries of heresy, other men were responsible for the practical outcome of this decision. As is well known, Durandus of Huesca approached the curia after a debate with Bishop Diego of Osma in Pamiers in the autumn of 1207.[34] Diego, who had not long since returned from the curia himself, had convinced Durandus both that he needed to be reconciled to the church and that the pope would listen. The role of a prelate 'on the spot' is once more crucial. Recent work also provides clues as to who may have assisted Durandus in the curia itself (in other words, who played the role of John of San Paolo this time). Christine Thouzellier

[31] See N. Malcolm, *Bosnia: a Short History* (London, 1994), 13; John V. A. Fine, *The Early Medieval Balkans* (Ann Arbor, 1983), 247.

[32] Tillmann, *Pope*, 3; on Odo and Absalom, see *Gallia Christiana*, 7:78-86, 672-3.

[33] 'In regularibus horis morem beati Victoris observent . . .'; 'In rasura similiter ordinem sancti Victoris sequantur clerici.'; *Operante divine dispositionis*, 17 December 1198, Reg. 1:481, pp. 707-8 = PL 214:443-9.

[34] See M.-H. Vicaire, *Saint Dominic and His Times*, trans. Kathleen Pond (London, 1964), 133-4.

argued that it may have been Leo Brancaleone.[35] Durandus' prologue to the *Contra Manicheos* thanks several cardinals: Pelagius, Nicholas of Clermont, Stephen of Fossanova, Guala Bicchieri and John of Colonna, but it is indeed dedicated to Leo Brancaleone, who was certainly present at the curia during the period when Durandus came to seek approval.[36] Richard and Mary Rouse have, however, recently found new evidence to add to the range of prelates with whom he may have had contact. Durandus produced a revised version of Peter Capuanus' *Alphabetum* and dedicated it to the canonist Bernard Bishop of Pavia whom he met.[37] In the course of the text he also praised Capuanus, perhaps because he had been the author of the original work, a collection of texts designed to assist in the preparation of sermons. Or was it because Capuanus, famous to historians as the man who provoked Innocent's rage over the Fourth Crusade, was also known to contemporaries as a sponsor of new religious movements? He had after all been involved in the approval of the *Humiliati* and had written a sermon against heresy which was a theme close to Durandus' heart.[38] After his disgrace in Innocent's eyes he concentrated his energies on the foundation of a monastery which later passed to the Cistercians and a *schola liberalium artium* in his home town of Amalfi.[39] After his acceptance of Durandus and the Catholic Poor, receiving their oath in person, Innocent did indeed nurture the new group, writing to bishops and others to remind them of their orthodoxy and defending them against the complaints of prelates such as Berengar of Narbonne.[40] It had, however, been other men who had first brought them to his presence.

---

[35]Christine Thouzellier, *Catharisme et valdéisme en Languedoc à la fin du XIIe et au début du XIIIe siècle*, 2nd edn (Louvain, 1982), 298. See also Kurt-Victor Selge, *Die Ersten Waldenser mit Edition des Liber antiheresis des Durandus von Osca*, 2 vols (Berlin 1967).

[36]Durandus of Huesca, *Liber contra Manicheos*, ed. Christine Thouzellier, *Une Somme anti-Cathare: le 'Liber Contra Manicheos' de Durand de Huesca, Spicilegium sacrum Lovaniense, études et documents* 32 (Louvain, 1964):84; discussed by Richard and Mary Rouse, 'The Schools and the Waldensians: a New Work by Durand of Huesca', *Christendom and its Discontents. Exclusion, Persecution, and Rebellion, 1000-1500*, ed. Scott L. Waugh and Peter D. Diehl (Cambridge, 1996), 86-111, 93-4 and notes.

[37]Yale, MS. Marston 266; Richard and Mary Rouse, 'The Schools and the Waldensians', 87, 95, 109.

[38]Paris, Bibliothèque Nationale, MS Lat. Nouvelles acquisitions 991. Identified by Dr Nicole Bériou of the Sorbonne, to whom I am grateful for this reference. The manuscript is almost entirely illegible.

[39]On Capuanus' career, see Werner Maleczek, *Petrus Capuanus, Kardinal, Legat am Vierten Kreuzzug, Theologe (†1214)* (Rome-Vienna, 1988) and *idem, Papst*, 117-24.

[40]The series of letters concerning Durandus is extensive: PL 215:1510-13, 1514; PL 216:29-30, 73-4, 75-7, 256, 274, 601, 607, 608, 609.

Several other cases would be worth exploring here[41] but one final group will suffice: the Waldensians who returned to the church in 1210, led by Bernard Prim and William Arnald. Once more it is clear that Innocent took a personal interest. Following the example of Durandus, the group swore an oath before Innocent himself, and, like the Catholic Poor, they enjoyed support later on, when Innocent sent them a copy of his letter and their oath as proof that they had been examined and approved by him.[42] Here we have no sources other than the papal letters to guide us, but Thouzellier has suggested that what prompted Bernard and his companions to approach the curia was an encounter with Durandus.[43] Certainly by 1210 Innocent's curia may well have had a reputation for constructive responses to the approaches of such religious, so that other prelates need not be involved.

The cases dealt with here are not the standard dispute-settlements with which so much of the business of judges delegate was concerned. They are not directly concerned with property and the administration of rights. They lie much closer to the spiritual and religious life of the church. Yet here as in the innumerable judicial cases, Innocent is revealed as an effective delegator prepared or perhaps resigned to taking a back-seat role, even in cases involving the problem of heresy. These might lead to more detailed investigation (the appointment of two separate levels of enquiry for the *Humiliati*) or require particular oaths to be sworn (as in the case of Durandus or the Bosnian Christians), but as with the Trinitarians or the community of Val des Choux, most of the vetting was undertaken by others. Sometimes he chose men who were old friends or colleagues, but in other cases those making the decisions were 'self-selected', either because of their experience of office before his pontificate (Albert of Vercelli, Peter of Lucedio, John of San Paolo) or because a religious group lay within their jurisdiction (Adelard of Verona, Guy de Paray, Guy of Assisi) or elected to approach them (John of San Paolo). The precise distribution of responsibility for the outcome between the different elements involved – the religious groups, the local prelates, members of the curia and Innocent himself – can no longer be ascertained. It is often simpler to name Innocent as the man responsible as a sort of shorthand for the whole bureaucracy of his pontificate. But that is no reason to ignore the contribution of the other players, men like Albert of Vercelli, who after all went on to become

---

[41] For example, the Bible readers of Metz. See Leonard E. Boyle, 'Innocent III and Vernacular Versions of Scripture', *The Bible in the Medieval World, Essays in Memory of Beryl Smalley*, ed. Katherine Walsh and Diana Wood, *Studies in Church History, Subsidia* 4 (Oxford, 1985):97-107.

[42] *Cum inaestimabile*, 14 June 1210, PL 216:289-93; *Ne quis de* 23 July 1212, ibid. 648-50. 'Ne quis de caetero vestrum valeat calumniari propositum, sicut olim diligenter examinavimus fidem vestram, ita nunc conversationem vestram prudenter investigare curavimus, et utramque litteris apostolicis fecimus comprehendi, ut illa in testimonium habeatis.'

[43] Thouzellier, *Catharisme et valdéisme*, 232.

patriarch of Jerusalem and to help devise and approve the new rule for a highly successful order, the Carmelites, amongst whom he was later venerated as a *beatus*.[44] Nor should we underestimate the contribution of the religious themselves. The new evidence for the *Humiliati* shows that they had strong links with local prelates before Innocent's pontificate. A recent re-examination of the letters Innocent sent to them has revealed that the structure of three distinct groups existed before the intervention of the curia and must therefore be the work of the *Humiliati* either alone or in discussion with Peter and Albert in the north.[45] Innocent was an energetic pope, but neither omniscient nor omnipresent; he was well aware that he could not deal with every issue himself. Early in his pontificate he wrote to the bishop of Périgueux, stating that as he could not be everywhere in person, he wished the bishops to deal with problems on his behalf. He was surely also aware that advice was important in government: as Bernard of Clairvaux wrote to Eugenius III, 'Do all things with counsel, afterwards you won't be sorry'.[46] The advice he received came not just from his brother cardinals, but from prelates out in the provinces who were as responsible as Innocent III himself for the new approach of the hierarchy towards novel religious movements.

---

[44]'Vita S. Alberti', ed. D. Papenbroek, AASS, April I (Antwerp, 1675), 769-99. See also Andrew Jotischky, *The Perfection of Solitude: Hermits and Monks in the Crusader States* (University Park PA, 1995).

[45]Maria Pia Alberzoni, 'Gli inizi degli umiliati: una riconsiderazione', *La conversione alla povertà nell'Italia dei secoli xii-xv*, Convegni del Centro di studi sulla spiritualità medioevale 27 (Todi, 1991):187-237, 201.

[46]Saint Bernard, *De consideratione*, 4.4.11, ed. J. Leclercq and H. Rochais, *Sancti Bernardi Opera*, 3, *Tractatus et opuscula* (Rome, 1967), 457. Cited by Norman Zacour, 'The Cardinals' View of the Papacy, 1150-1300', *The Religious Roles of the Papacy: Ideals and Realities 1150-1300*, ed. C. Ryan (Toronto, 1989), 413-38, 420-1.

Part Three
Defining and Using Papal Power

Power and the Pastor:
A Reassessment of Innocent III's
Contribution to Political Ideas

Joseph Canning

One of the most important trends in Innocent III scholarship over the last couple of decades has clearly been the treatment of him as a pastoral pope. This orientation has provided a useful addition to the well-worked seam of his involvement in political and governmental matters, and in particular to the mass of scholarship devoted to Innocent's ideas of the relationship between temporal and spiritual power. Brenda Bolton herself through her many articles is pre-eminent among scholars who have convinced us that Innocent accorded a prime position to his own pastoral role. She finally convinced me to look more closely at the pastoral aspect of Innocent III through her moving paper on his initiatives to save abandoned babies in Rome. For me, her paper 'Received in His Name: Rome's Busy Baby Box', delivered at the summer 1993 conference at Oxford of the Ecclesiastical History Society and subsequently published in *Studies in Church History*, was a turning-point.[1]

In that paper Brenda Bolton said of Innocent III, 'he was above all a pastoral pope'.[2] Describing Innocent as a pastoral pope certainly makes him sound more attractive and accessible to modern eyes than does emphasis on his vicariate of Christ and his jurisdictional role within canon law. The question, however, is this: how far can the pastoral interpretation be taken as characterizing Innocent's

---

[1] *Studies in Church History*, 31 (1994):153-67.
[2] Ibid., p. 165.

conception of his role as pope? The problem of course relates to Innocent's understanding of the relationship between the two fundamental roles combined in the papal office: the exercise of the power of the keys and Christ's injunction, 'Feed my lambs, feed my sheep'.

My contention in this paper will be that, for Innocent III, power was the core of the pope's function, that this power, which was jurisdictional in nature, operated through a continuum ranging from its pastoral end to that of coercion. In this paper I can only look at part of the problem and will concentrate on the overtly pastoral end of the continuum in which the pastoral and jurisdictional functions of Innocent were bound together. My focus will be on two groups of texts which were programmatic for his conception of the pope's role. I shall look at certain of his sermons – as James Powell said in his article on Innocent's sermon on Good Shepherd Sunday, sermons are a more secure source of the personal thought of a pope than public correspondence.[3] I shall also investigate two major decretals showing the interaction between the political and pastoral aspects of the papal office: *Solitae* (X.1.33.6) and *Novit* (X.2.1.13), together with *In Genesi* (RNI, 18). John C. Moore in a recent study has maintained that it is likely, but not certain, that Innocent III's collection of sermons dates from the years 1201-1205 (except for that delivered at the Fourth Lateran Council);[4] the other sources I have used were definitely produced in the period, 1199/1200-1204. Innocent's views of the pope's role, as considered here, certainly in part derived from the early years of his pontificate – it may well be that they did so in their entirety. It is possible in this paper only to open up the problem of whether Innocent's conception of the whole range of the pope's function can in any meaningful sense be described as pastoral in some extended way. Certainly, like any medieval pope he saw his role as one of humble service and ministry to lead his flock to salvation: as he said, he was 'the servant set over the household' (*Sermo* 2, *De diversis*).[5]

In his sermons, Innocent treated the concession of the keys as the primary grant made by Christ to St Peter in response to the latter's declaration of faith (Matt. 16:19), whereas the commission of the sheep was secondary, in response to Peter's charity made clear in his avowal of love for Christ (John 21:15-17). For as Innocent said in *Sermo* 2, *De diversis*, it was the pope's faith which was the bedrock and which sustained the church:

---

[3]James M. Powell, '*Pastor bonus*: some evidence of Honorius III's use of the Sermons of Innocent III', *Speculum* 52 (1977):522-37.

[4]See John C. Moore, 'The Sermons of Pope Innocent III', *Römische Historische Mitteilungen*, Österreichische Akademie der Wissenschaften, ed. Otto Kresten and Adam Wandruska, 36 (1994):81-142, at 85-87.

[5]'Servus qui super familiam constituitur' (PL 217:658) – see Matt. 24:45.

For unless I were solid in my faith, how could I confirm others in their faith? This is recognised to belong specifically to my office, as the Lord said, 'I have prayed for you, Peter, so that your faith may not fail, and when you have turned again, strengthen your brothers' (Luke 22:32) . . . And so the faith of the apostolic see has never failed in any time of confusion but has always endured whole and unimpaired, so that Peter's privilege might remain undisturbed. Faith is so necessary to me for the following reason: whereas I have God alone as my judge for other sins, for that sin alone which is committed against faith I could be judged by the church. For he who does not believe has already been judged (John 3:18).[6]

The concession of the keys was fundamental because it was the reward for Peter's recognition of Christ's divinity, the *sine qua non* of the foundation of the church. In *Sermo* 21, *De sanctis* Innocent divided the keys, conventionally, into that of knowledge (*scientia*) and that of power (*potentia*). To Peter alone were these two keys given, but in such a way that the key of knowledge was necessarily combined with that of power:

And indeed the first key is understood to be the knowledge to discern and judge; the second key is understood to be the power to bind and loose . . . But the knowledge to discern is not always a key, because even if some people know how to discern, they may nonetheless not be able to discern, because they do not possess the key of power without which knowledge is not a key. The pastor of the church should therefore look out that he does not receive the key of power without the key of knowledge . . . The key of knowledge was therefore necessary for Peter together with the key of power.[7]

In this sermon Innocent distinguished between the power of binding and loosing conceded to Peter and that to remit sins given to all the apostles (John 20:23), as

---

[6]'Nisi enim ego solidatus essem in fide, quomodo possem alios in fide firmare? Quod ad officium meum noscitur specialiter pertinere, Domino protestante: "Ego, inquit, pro te rogavi, Petre, ut non deficiat fides tua, et tu aliquando conversus confirma fratres tuos (Luc. xxii)" . . . Et ideo fides apostolicae sedis in nulla nunquam turbatione defecit, sed integra semper et illibata permansit: ut Petri privilegium persisteret inconcussum. In tantum enim fides mihi necessaria est, ut cum de caeteris peccatis solum Deum iudicem habeam, propter solum peccatum quod in fide committitur possem ab Ecclesia iudicari. Nam qui non credit, iam iudicatus est (Joan. iii)' (PL 217:656).
[7]'Et quidem prima clavis intelligitur scientia discernendi et diiudicandi, secunda clavis intelligitur potentia ligandi et absolvendi . . . Verum scientia discernendi non semper est clavis; quoniam etsi quidam discernere sciant, discernere tamen non possunt: quia non habent clavem potentiae, sine qua scientia non est clavis. Provideat ergo sibi pastor Ecclesiae, ut clavem potentiae sine clave scientiae non recipiat . . . Clavis ergo scientiae necessaria fuit Petro cum clave potentiae' (PL 217:554).

he did also in *Sermo* 2, *De diversis*.[8] These were examples of the tendency of the papacy to interpret Matt. 16:19 as applying to Peter alone. Yet in his sermons, Innocent was not entirely consistent in doing this: in *Sermo* 13, *De sanctis* he admitted an aspect of the alternative interpretation, that the granting of the power to bind and loose in the Matthean passage was to some extent given to all the apostles, but he also made the proviso that 'Blessed Peter principally received the keys of the kingdom of heaven (and thereby his successor did as well), so that he could bind others, but could not be bound by others'.[9]

Sermo 21, *De sanctis* also gave extensive treatment to the commission of the sheep to Peter, defining the overtly pastoral role of the pope with two slightly different formulae: according to the first, Peter should feed his flock by the word of preaching, by the example of his own turning to God in his own life and by defending his sheep,[10] according to the second, by word, example and the sacrament of the eucharist.[11] The commission of the sheep (like the general granting of the power of remitting sins to all the apostles), having occurred after the resurrection of Christ, was of course second in time to the concession of the keys. Innocent also made it clear that the pastoral commission was secondary to the fundamental concession of the power of the keys, as he said in *Sermo* 7, *De sanctis*,

> But it was said to Peter by the Lord, and in Peter to the successors of Peter: 'I shall give to you the keys of the kingdom of heaven, and whatever you bind upon earth will be bound also in heaven, and whatever you loose upon earth will be loosed also in heaven' (Matt. 16:19). He excepted nothing when he said, 'Whatever'. *On account of this* he said elsewhere, 'Feed my sheep' (John 21:17), not distinguishing between these sheep and those, in order that he might show that those who refuse to have Peter for a pastor do not belong to his sheep.[12]

The pastoral commission was given *because* Peter already possessed the keys. The trend of Innocent's thought was to consider the keys, the response to Peter's

---

[8] PL 217:657-58.

[9] 'Principaliter tamen B. Petrus claves regni caelorum accepit, ac per hoc successor eius, ut ipse possit ligare caeteros, sed ligari non possit a caeteris' (PL 217:517).

[10] PL 217:550.

[11] PL 217:555.

[12] 'Petro vero fuit dictum a Domino, et in Petro successoribus Petri: "Tibi dabo claves regni caelorum: et quodcunque ligaveris super terram, erit ligatum et in caelis: et quodcunque solveris super terram, erit solutum et in caelis (Matt. xvi)". Nihil excepit, qui dixit, "Quodcunque". *Propter quod* alibi dixit: "Pasce oves meas (Joan. xxi)", non distinguens inter has oves et illas: ut ostenderet ad oves suas minime pertinere, qui Petrum recusat habere pastorem' (PL 217:482).

faith, as the fundamental core to which the pastoral commission, the response to his charity, was added later to complete the papal office by entrusting the kingdom of God, in the sense of the universal church, to Peter (*Sermo* 20, *De tempori*).[13]

What is emerging from these texts is that Innocent considered power, as contained in the keys, to be basic to the papal role and that the pastoral function was combined with this. This interpretation is supported by the way in which he used what may be called his signature text – Jer. 1:10: 'I have set thee over nations and over kingdoms, to root up and to pull down, and to waste and to destroy, and to build and to plant'.[14] Innocent was notable for his use of Old Testament texts to elaborate his conception of the role of the pope. Jer. 1:10 had been used by previous popes in the eleventh and twelfth centuries, but in a pastoral sense – indeed, in the context of agricultural or gardening imagery, of weeding out vice and planting virtue. Gregory VII's usages of the text in this way spring immediately to mind.[15] Clearly, the language of Jer. 1.10 also made it peculiarly apt for expressing papal claims to power over secular rulers, and it was Innocent's application of the text in this sense that has attracted most attention from modern scholars. Yet the deep meaning of Innocent's employment of the passage is that he saw it as prefiguring the combination of the power and pastoral aspects of the papal office.[16] This was particularly clear in his response *In Genesi* (RNI 18), given in consistory to Philip of Swabia's ambassadors at the turn of 1199/1200. He set forth a phrase-by-phrase concordance between Jer. 1:10 and Matt. 16:18-19 to demonstrate the superiority of papal power over that of secular rulers in both temporal and spiritual matters. Yet he also referred to Jer. 1:10 in its strictly pastoral sense:

And it was said to him [Peter], 'Kill and eat!' [Acts 10:13]. Kill vice and eat virtue; kill error and eat faith, just as you may root up and pull down, build and plant.[17]

For Innocent, power was always present in the papal role, even if at the overtly pastoral end of the spectrum of the pope's function it could best be described as

---

[13]Cols 405-6.

[14]'Constitui te super gentes et regna, ut evellas et destruas, et disperdas, et dissipes, et edifices et plantes'.

[15]*Registrum* 2:68 (p. 226) , 5:2 (p. 350), 6:12 (p. 415): ed. E. Caspar, MGH, Epp., 2nd edn (Berlin, 1955).

[16]See J. A. Watt, *The Theory of Papal Monarchy in the Thirteenth Century. The Contribution of the Canonists* (London, 1965), 40-1.

[17]'Et dictum est ei: "Macta et manduca". Macta vitia et manduca virtutes: macta herrorem et manduca fidem: quasi evellas et destruas, edifices et plantes' (RNI, p. 48).

being held in reserve. There was a clear progression in Innocent's treatment of sin, especially the public sins of secular rulers. This progression was from pastoral admonition to jurisdictional coercion: from the kid glove to putting the ecclesiastical boot in. The first stage would be a relatively gentle one in all humility as the servant of the servants of God and would involve pastoral rebuke: nagging in short. If this failed, the second stage along the continuum would be more assertive pastoral action. As he said in *Sermo* 21, *De tempore* (on Good Shepherd Sunday, and commenting on John 10:11), the pope as pastor has a crook 'which is sharp at the end', wherewith 'to prod sheep which are slow and fat'.[18] This stage marked the beginning of coercion and the link between the overtly pastoral element and papal power, as was indeed implicit in the pastoral function of defence of the flock, already mentioned in *Sermo* 21, *De sanctis*.[19] The third and final stage, when all else had failed, was the full-blown application of the power of the keys through coercive ecclesiastical sanctions.

The claim to humility, pastoral rebuke of secular rulers and the power of the keys were all present in the decretal *Solitae*, which Innocent addressed to the emperor Alexius of Constantinople in 1201. All three texts (Jer. 1:10; Matt. 16:19; and John 21:17) were used in this decretal which was designed overall to remind the emperor of the superiority of spiritual over all temporal power. Perhaps as a *douceur* to make his words more persuasive to Alexius, at the end of the decretal Innocent stressed the humility of the pope's role:

> We hold our exaltation in humility, and consider our humility our greatest exaltation. Wherefore we also write and avow that we are the servants not only of God, but also of the servants of God.[20]

Yet shortly before this passage, the pope, referring to 2 Timothy 4:2, had also expatiated on his pastoral duty to upbraid kings and emperors:

> We follow out the demands of our pastoral office, when we beg, argue and rebuke; and we seek, whether it is convenient to them or not, to lead not only others, but emperors and kings to those things which please the divine will. The sheep of Christ were committed to us in Blessed Peter, when the Lord said, 'Feed my sheep', not distinguishing between these sheep and others, so

---

[18] 'Acutus, ut pungat oves lentas et pingues' (PL 217:410).

[19] See above, n.10.

[20] 'Propter quod exaltationem nostram in humilitate ponimus, et humilitatem nostram exaltationem maximam reputamus. Vnde etiam servos non solum Dei, sed etiam servorum Dei nos esse scribimus et fatemur' (X 1.33.6, ed. A. Friedberg, col. 198).

that he might show that someone was not a member of his flock, if that person did not recognise Peter and his successors as teachers and pastors.[21]

These words were rapidly followed by a reference to the power of the keys with specific quotation of Matt. 16:19.

It was, however, in the decretal *Novit*, addressed to the prelates of France in 1204 in the context of the dispute between King John of England and Philip Augustus, that Innocent expressed most clearly the progression from pastoral rebuke to jurisdictional coercion, in the process of expanding on his claim, as pope, to be able to intervene in disputes *ratione peccati* ('by reason of sin'). Referring again to 2 Timothy 4:2, he said,

> There is no one of sound mind who does not know that it is part of our office to rebuke any Christian for any mortal sin, and, if he rejects our correction, to coerce him with ecclesiastical penalties. It is clear from the pages of the Old and the New Testament that we should and can rebuke him . . . The Apostle also admonishes us to rebuke the unruly, and says the same elsewhere, 'Argue, beg, rebuke in all patience and desire to teach '.[22]

He then went on to justify the power to coerce by reference to Jer 1:10 and Matt. 16:19. However, the overall purpose of such coercion remained pastoral:

> To recall the sinner from vice to virtue, from error to truth, especially when the sin is against peace, which is the bond of love.[23]

No one, kings included, was to be exempted from this exercise of power by the pope.

Novit's pastoral use of coercion brings us back to a question raised at the beginning of this paper. Can the whole spectrum of the papal role be usefully described as being pastoral in purpose? Should 'pastor' be the first term that

---

[21]'Debitum igitur pastoralis officii exsequimur, quum obsecramus, arguimus, increpamus, et non solum alios, sed imperatores et reges opportune et importune ad ea studemus inducere, quae divinae sunt placita voluntati. Nobis autem in B. Petro sunt oves Christi commissae; dicente Domino: "Pasce oves meas", non distinguens inter has oves et alias, ut alienum a suo demonstraret ovili, qui Petrum et successores ipsius magistros non recognosceret et pastores' (ibid., col. 198).

[22]'Nullus, qui sit sanae mentis, ignorat, quin ad officium nostrum spectet de quocunque mortali peccato corripere quemlibet Christianum, et, si correctionem contempserit, ipsum per districtionem ecclesiasticam coercere. Quod enim debeamus corripere ac possimus, ex utraque patet pagina testamenti . . . Apostolus quoque nos monet corripere inquietos, et alibi dicit idem: "Argue, obsecra, increpa in omni patientia et doctrina"' (X.2.1.13, ed. A. Friedberg, col. 243).

[23]'Vt peccatorem revocemus a vitio ad virtutem, ab errore ad veritatem, praecipue tamen quum contra pacem peccatur, quae est vinculum caritatis' (ibid., col. 244).

comes to mind in characterizing Innocent III? It is certainly true that the pastoral element was strongly present in his conception of the papal office, notably in dealing with sin and in defending the church against heresy. Yet Innocent, as pope, was never simply a pastor. This paper has sought to show that power was at the core of Innocent's understanding of the papal office and that the pastoral aspect was combined with that of power, when he was acting as pope. Is 'pastoral' an adequate word to describe his role as vicar of Christ and his claim to possess plenitude of power? In order to encompass the whole range of the papal office, one is on much firmer ground pursuing the idea of the pope's role as servant and minister, as becomes clear, if one looks again at *Sermo* 2, *De diversis*:

> Now you will see who is this servant set over the household, namely the vicar of Jesus Christ, the successor of Peter, the anointed of the lord, the God of pharoah, set in the middle between God and man, below God but above man, less than God but greater than man; who judges all things, but is judged by no one.[24]

Although part of the function of service was pastoral, it would seem to stretch language too far to equate the two. For one thing, Innocent's own definitions of his pastoral role were quite restrictive, in terms of preaching the word of God, giving good example, consecrating the eucharist and defending his flock. Yet problems remain, as always with Innocent. As we have seen, in *Sermo* 21, *De sanctis*, he referred to the pope as *pastor ecclesiae* when receiving the key of power.[25] Furthermore, the plenitude of power itself had by implication a pastoral aspect, because, as he repeatedly said, other bishops were called only to part of the care.

Despite such ambiguities, it was power which was inherent throughout the whole spectrum of the papal role and provided the dynamic of the pope's function. Power in short was the key to Innocent III's notion of why there was a pope and what he existed for. Papal power existed for a purpose, in part overtly pastoral, but effected through jurisdiction, in order to lead his flock to salvation at Christ's command. Even when Innocent III was performing a pastoral role as pope, he was by definition a wielder of power placed between heaven and earth. But in saying this, I am haunted by those babies he saved. Was he acting then as

---

[24]'Iam ergo videtis quis iste servus, qui super familiam constituitur, profecto vicarius Iesu Christi, successor Petri, Christus Domini, Deus Pharaonis: inter Deum et hominem medius constitutus, citra Deum, sed ultra hominem: minor Deo, sed maior homine: qui de omnibus iudicat, et a nemine iudicatur' (PL 217:658).

[25]See above, n. 7.

pope, as bishop of Rome, or as Lothar of Segni? Perhaps the problem involved in unravelling the pastoral and power aspects of Innocent's view of his office only reflects the ambiguities of the role of any priest and certainly of any bishop: even if his jurisdiction is restricted to the sacrament of penance, the pastor is always a man of power.

Emperor Henry VI (1191-1197) and the Papacy: Similarities with Innocent III's Temporal Policies

Brian A. Pavlac

Between 1191 and 1197 Henry VI of the Staufen dynasty reigned over central Europe and sought to control its destiny as king over Germany, emperor of the Romans and, finally, as king of Sicily. Henry VI has been overshadowed historically by both his father, Frederick Barbarossa, and his son, Frederick II. Nevertheless his brief reign was consequential and decisive. He strengthened his dominion in Germany and northern Italy, conquered southern Italy and Sicily, received tribute from north Africa, sent a crusading army to Syria and made his influence felt in Constantinople. But historians have often been critical of all these efforts, especially since Henry's main contribution to history, allegedly, was to worsen relations between *regnum* and *sacerdotium*, the empire and the church. The leaders of these two institutions at the time increasingly held very different views on political affairs. There were three main areas of disagreement: who was in charge of the German bishops, who was in charge of Italy and who was the leader of Christendom. As Henry VI quarrelled and negotiated with Pope Celestine III, he affected at least one important member of the curia, Lothar of Segni, who would later become Pope Innocent III. This survey of Henry VI's reign and conflicts with the papacy reveals that Innocent's policies and practices were strikingly similar to the emperor's career and goals. While Innocent condemned Henry's expansionism, the pontiff did much the same thing. This brief comparison also illustrates why the conflict between kings and popes proved intractable for so long.

Not that Innocent or Henry began these difficulties, which dated back at least to the so-called Investiture Contest, a hundred years earlier. Henry grew up amidst conflicts between church and empire. He was born in 1165, just a few years after Lothar of Segni. In a carefully planned election, Henry was elevated at the age of four to king, co-ruler and eventual successor to his father.[1] He began formally witnessing documents after 1173 and was present at such key events of Barbarossa's reign as the military defeat by the Lombard League at Legnano and the Treaty of Venice with Pope Alexander III. When he reached adulthood, his father, in an unprecedented step, tried to make him co-emperor. But the papacy, which alone performed the imperial coronation, refused to go along. And indeed, relations between pope and emperor worsened after the election of Pope Urban III in 1185, becoming so bad that open warfare broke out. Henry himself went into battle in papal territories, culminating in a successful two-week siege of Orvieto. Shortly afterwards, however, the succession of a new pope and the impetus to begin the Third Crusade led to better relations. Once more, negotiations for Henry's elevation to co-emperor began.

Three deaths in the few years after 1190 then radically altered Henry's destiny, providing the opportunity to expand his power beyond any previous expectation. First, the death of his father, the great Frederick Barbarossa, left Henry sole claimant to the imperial position. Second, the death of King William II of Sicily, leaving Henry's wife Constance as legitimate heiress to that kingdom, enticed Henry to conquer that realm.[2] Third, the death of Pope Clement III brought into power the aged Pope Celestine III, who would face Henry for the rest of his reign.[3]

The imperial conflict with the papacy overshadowed Henry's whole reign, if not the whole of medieval German history. As stated above, the three main issues of disagreement were the role of bishops, the position of Italy, and the political hierarchy of western European princes. As for bishops, the kings wanted loyal allies in these positions, while the popes wanted suitable colleagues. The Investiture Contest had not really settled who had ultimate power over choosing

---

[1] A good recent biography of Henry VI is Peter Csendes, *Heinrich VI.*, Gestalten des Mittelalters und der Renaissance (Darmstadt, 1993); the classic work is Theodor Toeche, *Heinrich VI.*, Jahrbücher der deutschen Geschichte 18 (1867, repr. Darmstadt, 1965).

[2] Donald Matthew, *The Norman Kingdom of Sicily*, Cambridge Medieval Textbooks (Cambridge, Eng., 1992), 274-5, 286, shows that Constance's claims to inherit Sicily were not clearly defined and could only be decided by force; see also Theo Kölzer, 'Sizilien und das Reich im ausgehenden 12. Jahrhundert', *Historisches Jahrbuch* 110 (1990):3-22.

[3] On Celestine and the curia see Maleczek, *Papst*; Piero Zerbi, *Papato, Imperio e 'Respublica Christiana' dal 1187 al 1198*, Pubblicazioni dell'Università Cattolica del S. Cuore, n. s. 55 (Milan, 1980); Volkert Pfaff, 'Der Vorgänger: das Wirken Coelestins III. aus der Sicht von Innozenz III.,' ZRG, Kan. 41 (1955):121-67.

bishops, especially since German bishops were also secular princes, governors of territories and temporalities as well as pastors in the church. The pope claimed to supervise them by right of his primacy in the church; the emperor claimed to command them as feudal suzerain. While this issue would complicate political and spiritual policies for centuries, in Henry's period it was a comparatively minor nuisance.

Far more important to the papal-imperial conflict of this period was the dispute over Italy. Since the Early Middle Ages, the popes claimed and often exercised real political dominion over the city of Rome and the lands around it.[4] They also asserted rights to numerous possessions in northern Italy, particularly the Mathildine lands in Tuscany after 1102. And after the Norman conquest of southern Italy and Sicily in the eleventh century, they assumed suzerainty and special privileges in that kingdom as well. The growing corpus of canon law nourished this developing papal monarchy. But at the same time the newly recovered Roman law nurtured the evolving German monarchy. German kings, technically called kings of the Romans, disputed papal claims, citing their own imperial legal traditions.[5] Especially after the elevation from king of the Romans to emperor of the Romans by the pope in Rome, German rulers regularly sought to assert their sovereignty over the Italian peninsula. Since the emperors were also kings of Italy they claimed it all, from the north all the way through Rome and on to the south including the island of Sicily.[6]

The comparison of Italy and Sicily to the treasure of the Nibelungs – luring the German kings to their destruction – is somewhat dated.[7] Indeed the Germans only naturally sought to dominate Italy, since someone had to do it. That might seem harsh, but most political states which can exercise dominance will try to do so over areas of perceived political weakness, especially where sovereignty is not sharply defined. Who that someone was for medieval Italy – the German kings, the popes or the Italians themselves (usually as city-states) – was the most serious disagreement. Otto of Brunswick's subsequent Italian policies against Innocent substantiate the natural inclination of imperial power to lay claim to rights in Italy. By the end of the Middle Ages no one had succeeded sufficiently, which

---

[4] See Thomas F. X. Noble, *The Republic of St. Peter: The Birth of the Papal State: 680-825* (Philadelphia, 1984).

[5] Gerhard Baaken, 'Recht und Macht in der Politik der Staufer', in Karl-Augustin Frech and Ulrich Schmidt, eds, *Imperium und Papsttum: Zur Geschichte des 12. und 13. Jahrhunderts* (Cologne, 1997), 157.

[6] Willy Cohn, *Das Zeitalter der Hohenstaufen in Sizilien: Ein Beitrag zur Entstehung des modernen Beamtenstaates* (Breslau, 1925), 6.

[7] Karl Hampe, *Germany under the Salian and Hohenstaufen Emperors*, trans. Ralph Bennet (Totowa, NJ, 1973), 220.

failure meant another series of foreign invasions after 1494. A power vacuum was too irresistible to ignore in those wealthy, sunny lands.

Moreover, Italy and Sicily lured the papacy into a dangerous game with the German kings. Many pontiffs also thought they needed a political territorial base to preserve their independence of action. The popes had especially used the Norman kingdom of southern Italy and Sicily as a check on German domination since the eleventh century. They could draw on vassals and mercenaries from the south to help resist attempts by German rulers to control Rome. But in doing so, the popes were fatefully drawn into the feudal and political affairs of Italy and the empire. As popes haggled over control of the imperial crown and struggled to prevent the unification of the Sicilian kingdom with the empire, the *unio regni ad imperium*, political and military disputes with the Germans were inevitable.

An example of diplomatic manuevering and brute force greeted Henry's first step as successor to his father in getting himself crowned Roman emperor. Before that could be arranged, a distasteful matter had to be settled with the new pope, who was himself delaying his own consecration to put pressure on the king.[8] The Roman citizens were pressuring the Roman curia to get rid of the rival city of Tusculum, which was protected by imperial garrisons. Pope Celestine insisted that Henry turn over Tusculum in order to win his coronation. Henry did so, and the Romans destroyed the city stone by stone, down to its foundations. Historians have described Henry's surrender as an action without honor, done in 'cold political calculation', 'allowing sentiment no influence if it conflicted with reason of state'.[9] Henry is not solely to blame, however, since the papacy mediated and also benefited from this callous deed.[10] Was this betrayal, by which the papacy politically profited, an important lesson for cardinal Lothar?[11]

After his successful imperial coronation, which Lothar witnessed with displeasure, Henry's next efforts were not crowned with success.[12] His subsequent attempt to conquer southern Italy and Sicily failed miserably. Soon the pope's recognition of, from Henry's point of view, the usurper Tancred of Lecce as king of Sicily, along with other incidents, increased tensions between the Roman curia

---

[8]Katrin Baaken, 'Zu Wahl, Weihe und Krönung Papst Cölestins III.', *Deutsches Archiv* 41 (1985):211.

[9]Csendes, *Heinrich*, 99. Hampe, *Germany under the Emperors*, 221-2.

[10]If, according to Daniel Waley, *The Papal State in the Thirteenth Century* (London, 1961), 25-6, the government of the city of Rome mostly benefited from this and other restitutions, the papacy likewise immediately profited from the improved relations with the city leaders.

[11]Peter Partner, *The Lands of St Peter: The Papal State in the Middle Ages and the Early Renaissance* (Berkeley, 1972), 223, describes the transaction 'as one of betrayal and murder'.

[12]Tillmann, *Pope*, 6; *Regesta imperii, IV/3: Die Regesten des Kaiserreiches unter Heinrich VI. 1165-(1190)-1197*, ed. J. F. Böhmer and G. Baaken (Cologne, 1972), no. 145a (hereafter cited as Reg. Imp.).

and the German court.[13] Then Henry's problems in Germany multiplied. First the Welfs/Guelphs provoked rebellion, as Henry the Lion illegally returned from exile and reclaimed his old power in the north. Even wider opposition to Henry's rule broke out after the emperor was implicated in the murder of Bishop Albert of Liége.[14] If Henry had died at this point, his reign would be considered by all to have been a miserable failure.

Henry's place in history was saved by the capture of Richard the Lionhearted, just before Christmas 1192. Henry's brilliant exploitation, or extortion, of this opportunity gained him both a supply of cash and confusion in England and France. Upon the fortuitously-timed death of his rival Tancred in late 1194, Henry swept down on southern Italy like the 'rage of the Northwind' as Innocent III described it later.[15] Opposition collapsed, and he celebrated his kingship in Palermo on Christmas Day 1194. Henry had at last achieved the *unio regni ad imperium*. With Henry's success in Germany and Italy, princely opposition faded away, and foreign princes paid tribute to or petitioned to be crowned kings by the ever-blessed emperor.

But the pope remained concerned about ecclesiastical rights and obligations, and so tensions between the church and the empire worsened once more. Pope Celestine unsuccessfully tried to interfere in the Sicilian kingdom in what he saw as rights granted by Tancred.[16] In return Henry put some military pressure on the pope. He devastated the Campagna in 1194, while his brother, Philip of Swabia, ravaged north of Rome, occupying towns claimed by the papacy.[17]

Flush with success, Henry expanded his vision, proclaiming in early 1195 his intent to lead a crusade to liberate the Holy Land.[18] Historians have suggested various motives for Henry's announcement of this crusade. To some, Henry intended to use the crusade to pressure the Roman curia into negotiating with him.[19] Others suggest that the crusade was aimed against the Byzantine Empire

---

[13]Reg. Imp., no. 206; MGH Const. 1, no. 343, where Henry protests that the abbey of Monte Cassino came under his jurisdiction, while he intended to have peace and concord with the pope.

[14]Raymond H. Schmandt, 'The Election and Assassination of Albert of Louvain, Bishop of Liége', *Speculum* 42 (1967):639-60.

[15]Csendes, *Heinrich*, 190.

[16]Maleczek, *Papst*, 119, and the letter from the regent Empress Constance from 1195, in Josef Deér, ed., *Das Papsttum und die Süditalienischen Normannenstaaten, 1053-1212* (Göttingen, 1969), 100-1; Matthew, *Norman Kingdom*, 292; Gerhard Baaken, 'Das sizilische Königtum Kaiser Heinrichs VI.', in *Imperium und Papsttum* (see above, n. 5), 338-9.

[17]Partner, *Lands of St Peter*, 226.

[18]Claudia Naumann, *Der Kreuzzug Kaiser Heinrichs VI.* (Frankfurt am Main, 1994).

[19]Wilhelm Leonhardt, *Der Kreuzzugsplan Kaiser Heinrichs VI.* (Borna-Leipzig, 1913), 83; Johannes Haller, 'Heinrich VI und die Römische Kirche', *Mitteilungen des Instituts für österreichische Geschichte* 35 (1914):588, 562; Helmut Roscher, *Papst Innocenz III. und die Kreuzzüge* (Göttingen, 1969), 48. Cf. Ernst Perels, *Der Erbreichsplan Heinrichs VI.* (Berlin, 1927), 102; cf. Cohn, *Zeitalter*

or personal conquest of the Levant.[20] A third possibility, usually not considered by papal historians, was that Henry had a sincere desire to fulfill the ideal of the crusading knight, as exemplified by his father.[21]

In any case, before he could venture off on a crusade, Henry needed to guarantee order in both *regnum et imperium*, in particular by getting his infant son recognized as German king. Additionally, he tried to make the empire hereditary in his family, under the so-called *Erbreichsplan*. He got some few promises from the German princes to acquiesce, by granting them inheritance in female lines of their fiefs, but the papacy once more frustrated his plans. Reportedly, the papacy feared that the inheritance plan would reduce the imperial coronation into a mere ceremony and thereby would take away much of its influence.[22] Of course, from the Staufen point of view the papacy should not have any influence: the duly chosen king, by God's grace, should be crowned emperor. Did any dynasty want the papacy to hinder the succession of its family members? Despite this setback, Henry intensively pursued better relations with the papacy, especially from 1195 to 1197.[23]

In contrast to his ruthless reputation, Henry's repeated efforts to work towards peace need to be emphasized. It is impossible to determine Henry's motivation behind these efforts, whether Machiavellian or pure. Compared to Innocent III, we lack a wealth of sources about Henry's lines of reasoning.[24] There were no personal letters, no adequate lives or annals, no sermons to dissect for psychological clues. And little is known about the explicit details of many of his offers. Yet it is obvious that Henry did regularly try to appease church officials, seeking

---

der Hohenstaufen, 7, 11, 24-9, who emphasizes that Henry was using diplomatic means to end the conflict with Rome. Gerhard Baaken, 'Die Verhandlungen zwischen Kaiser Heinrich VI. und Papst Coelestin III. in den Jahren 1195-1197', in *Imperium und Papsttum* (see above, n. 5), 51, sees them as part of negotiations worked out with the pope in advance.

[20]Toeche, *Heinrich*, 380; Walter Kienast, *Deutschland und Frankreich in der Kaiserzeit (900-1270)* (Stuttgart, 1974), 3:674; Edouard Jordan, *L'Allemange au Moyen Age D'Henri L'Oiseleur a la mort D'Henri VI (919-1197)* (Paris, 1936), 161; Ekkehard Eickhoff, 'Die Bedeutung der Kreuzzüge für den deutschen Raum', in *Die Zeit der Staufer* (Stuttgart, 1977), 3:240.

[21]Jonathan Riley-Smith, *The Crusades: A Short History* (New Haven, 1987), 118; Matthew, *Norman Kingdom*, 291. Edgar N. Johnson, 'The Crusades of Frederick Barbarossa and Henry VI', in Kenneth M. Setton, ed., *A History of the Crusades*, 2 (Madison, WI, 1969):116-17, combines this motive with a resentment against Byzantium. Cf. Naumann, 123.

[22]Friedrich Kempf, *Papsttum und Kaisertum bei Innozenz III: die geistigen und rechtlichen Grundlagen seiner Thronstreitpolitik*, Miscellanea historiae pontificae, 19 (Rome, 1954), 8-9.

[23]Cohn, *Zeitalter der Hohenstaufen*, 16; for a detailed study of the negotiations see Baaken, 'Verhandlungen', esp. 48-80.

[24]Jane E. Sayers, *Innocent III: Leader of Europe, 1198-1216*, (London and New York, 1994), 87, notes the effective propaganda machine that Innocent made out of his chancery.

peace, friendship and concord in his official documents.[25]   Ever since Pope
Gregory VIII, Henry had offered respectful loyalty to the Roman Church.[26]   He
returned ecclesiastical possessions to Pope Clement.[27]   He never claimed the papal
patrimony, which would have destroyed the material basis for papal incomes.[28]
He acknowledged an inclination toward the fatherly care of the pope and wanted
to settle all differences as a loving son.[29]   For Henry's own part, he claimed to
offer peace and prosperity, adding that he and his father, Frederick I, were not to
blame for the past differences between church and state.   He denied responsibility
for the attacks by his brother, Philip of Swabia, or by other officers, and he
declared his intention to correct their injustices.[30]   Moreover, he kept coming back
with new offers of his own, seeking to negotiate with various prelates and
cardinals.[31]   He would nonetheless not give in to the extremist papal position.   His
duty was to uphold his own honor and that of the empire and the kingdom of
Sicily.[32]

Given the nature and paucity of sources relating to these issues, we cannot
determine whose terms were more reasonable.   Instead, interpretations have
tended to rely on whether one agreed with papal authority or imperial power.
Each side had plausible legal claims backed by general policies.   Each leader
surely thought he was being reasonable and sincere, and that the other was being
unfair and obstreperous.   Given the rapid papal expansion under Innocent later,
it is unlikely that the church leaders were any more moderate than imperial ones.
Henry presumably saw himself as dedicated and thought that his invasions were
both right and necessary.   Many churchmen saw him as a tyrant or oppressor of
the church in Italy, especially given that ultimate tool of politics, warfare, which
Henry periodically used.   The papacy certainly wanted at least the accustomed
feudal oaths for Sicily.[33]   But Henry was unwilling to insult his imperial dignity

---

[25]For example, MGH Const. 1, no. 371: 'inter ecclesiam Romanum et imperium firmus deinceps
pacis et concordie stabiliretur processus', and 'quod hic indubitanter inter vos et nos ecclesiamque
Romanam et imperium unionis et amicitie nexus firmetur'; no. 375: 'Super reformandam concordiam
ac pacem firmandam inter regnum et sacerdotum personamque vestram et nostram sincerum habentes
animum'; no. 376: 'Cum in tractatu pacis, qui huc usque inter vos et nos habitus est'; no. 377: 'de
stabilitate pacis et concordie inter nos et vos geruntur'.

[26]Reg. Imp., no. 63; MGH Const. 1, no. 411.

[27]Reg. Imp., nos. 83, 84; MGH Const. 1, nos. 322, 324.

[28]Waley, *Papal State*, 23, 25.

[29]Reg. Imp., no. 580; MGH Const. 1., no. 364. He refers to himself as a loving son in, e.g., Reg.
Imp. nos. 505, 520, 534, 569, 572; MGH Const. 1 nos. 370-1, 375-7.

[30]Reg. Imp., no. 534; MGH Const. 1, no. 375; Csendes, *Heinrich*, 183; Baaken, 'Verhandlungen',
68.

[31]Reg. Imp., nos. 212, 520, 560, 572; MGH Const. 1, nos. 344, 371, 376, 377. Maleczek, *Papst*,
86.

[32]Baaken, 'Verhandlungen', 76; MGH Const. 1, no. 377.

[33]Cohn, *Zeitalter der Hohenstaufen*, 17.

with such an oath (just as John of England would refuse Philip II of France). The curia often responded to Henry's attempted offers with recriminations about attacks upon the church and about the many oppressions by Henry's officials.[34] War was, however, the necessary component of rule in the Middle Ages, when so many lords ignored the law or appealed to contradictory or higher laws. And Pope Celestine was at least tacitly supportive of a murder plot against Henry, hardly a morally upright political policy.[35] The history of papal-imperial relations shows that each side wanted as much as it thought fair; and each side, with rare exceptions, either settled for or seized what it thought it could get away with, given the circumstances. Most importantly, Henry recurrently sought negotiation, and not just violent confrontation, even when he had a decisive military advantage. He never officially called for the complete capitulation of the papacy; he did not want to drive the pope from Rome or elect an anti-pope, which predecessors had done. Henry's public proclamations of a desire for peace and negotiation show that at the least he recognized there were points which could be legitimately discussed.

These negotiations culminated in what Henry called 'the highest offer' that an emperor had ever made to a pope.[36] While again the lack of sources prevents historians from knowing for sure what this offer entailed, some of their speculations have ranged from a moderate financial settlement putting canonries and prebends at the disposal of the papacy, to an extreme surrender of the empire as a papal fief.[37] Whatever the offer, Henry insisted he was trying to build peace out of love for God, for the salvation of his soul, and with veneration for the pope and the Roman Church.[38] What Henry held to be the highest price an emperor had ever offered, however, was not enough for the curia. So in the end, Henry got his son elected king the old-fashioned way, with no recognition of a right of inheritance. If Henry had succeeded with the *Erbreichsplan*, some historians fear he might have created a destructive hegemony in Europe.[39] Regardless, Henry

---

[34] Csendes, *Heinrich*, 166.

[35] Baaken, 'Verhandlungen', 74; see also Bernhard Schimmelpfennig, *Könige und Fürsten, Kaiser und Papst nach dem Wormser Kondordat*, Enzyklopädie Deutscher Geschichte 37 (Munich, 1996), 57.

[36] Csendes, *Heinrich*, 184-6.

[37] Concerning the various interpretations about this 'höchste Angebot' see: Hampe, *Germany under the Emperors*, 227; Haller, 'Heinrich und die Römische Kurie', 652; Edouard Jordan, 'Henri VI a-t-il offert a Célestin III de lui faire Hommage pour L'Empire?' in *Mélanges D'Histoire du Moyen Age offerts a M. Ferdinand Lot* (Paris, 1925), 295-301. Baaken, 'Verhandlungen', 79-80, argues against all interpretations, and declares the problem of the nature of the offer insoluble.

[38] Reg. Imp., no. 572; MGH Const. 1, no. 376.

[39] Heinrich Mitteis, *Der Staat des hohen Mittelalters* (Cologne, 1980), 266; Colin Morris, *Papal Monarchy: the Western Church from 1050 to 1250*, Oxford History of the Christian Church (Oxford, 1991), 198.

reached the apogee of his power as he successfully sent off the first crusaders. He even crushed a conspiracy to assassinate him. Indeed, 'all people around him, even across the sea, feared his severity and shook in terror before him'.[40]

Then, at the age of only thirty-two, on 28 September 1197, Emperor Henry VI died. The chronicler Otto of St Blaise said his death 'should be mourned by the Germans and all the peoples of Germania for all time'.[41] His accomplishments crumbled. There began a serious crisis for the German monarchy as warfare between the Staufen and Welf/Guelph dynasties tore central Europe apart. Henry's death marks, for some German historians, the end of the High Middle Ages. Even more, it may have been the 'greatest catastrophe in the history of the German Middle Ages'.[42] Europe was changing, taking a different direction.[43]

One of the most important changes was that, a few months after the emperor's death, Innocent III entered the stage of history. Previously, as a cardinal of SS. Sergius and Bacchus, Lothar of Segni took part in the evolving curial policy toward Henry VI. From his writings we know a little of what cardinal Lothar thought of Henry's actions. At least from the curial point of view, the reign of Henry VI was judged to have oppressed the papacy.[44]

It is certainly interesting that the future Pope Innocent once took up his pen to address the emperor personally.[45] After Henry proclaimed his crusade in April 1195, he had sent offers to the curia to build better relations, urging obedience to the pope and peace for the betterment of Christendom.[46] One response survives; it is from Cardinal Lothar. In a letter cleverly tying together many biblical quotations and allusions, Lothar encourages Henry to continue the crusade (something he was already doing) and also exhorts Henry to persecute heretics. As pope, Innocent certainly devoted much energy to both the crusading movement and the repression of heresies. At this juncture in the imperial-papal

---

[40]Toeche, *Heinrich*, 467. Critics commonly cite Henry's harshness in punishing the rebels. It was a brutal age, however, known for the cruelty of even Richard the Lionhearted at Acre and Chalus. For descriptions of the violence of the age, see Charles Edward Smith, *Innocent III, Church Defender* (Westport, CT, 1971), 1-38.

[41]Cited by Horst Fuhrmann, *Germany in the High Middle Ages, c. 1050-1200*, trans. Timothy Reuter, Cambridge Medieval Textbooks (Cambridge, 1986), 186.

[42]Karl Jordan, 'Investiturstreit und frühe Stauferzeit', in *Gebhardt Handbuch der deutschen Geschichte*, 9th edn (Stuttgart, 1981), 1:422; Hampe, *Germany under the Emperors*, 230; Fuhrmann, *Germany*, 186. Historians who dislike Henry see his death as a 'deliverance for Europe', fearing he could be as powerful as another Napoleon; C. W. Previté-Orton, *Outlines of Medieval History* (Cambridge, England, 1929), 257; E. Jordan, *Histoire du Moyen Age*, 150. See also Arno Borst, 'Die Staufer in der Geschichtschreibung', in *Die Zeit der Staufer* (Stuttgart, 1977), 3:274.

[43]Mitteis, *Staat des hohen Mittelalters*, 268.

[44]Johannes Haller, 'Kaiser Heinrich VI.', *Historische Zeitschrift* 113 (1914):477.

[45]Maleczek, *Papst*, 104; Werner Maleczek, 'Ein Brief Kardinals Lothar von SS. Sergius und Bacchus (Innocenz III.) an Kaiser Heinrich VI.', *Deutsches Archiv* 38 (1982):564-76.

[46]Reg. Imp., no. 410; MGH SS 17:524.

negotiations, however, the cardinal avoids the most important issues at hand: division of authority in Italy and the status of Sicily. And while he somewhat energizes the previous lukewarm papal enthusiasm for the crusade, his introduction of the heresy issue waters down that support. Since heresy was not high on the imperial agenda at that time, it could only serve as a distraction.[47] So the cardinal seemed to be stalling, postponing a true reconciliation between pope and emperor.[48] Eager for any response, nonetheless, Henry replied to Lothar in a letter, picking up themes of crusade and heretics.[49] He intended to take up and wield the sword of Peter, the temporal sword, as was appropriate to his office. But little improvement in relations seems to have resulted.

Lothar's opinions, formed as cardinal, found development in Innocent's papal letters dealing with Henry's successors – his brother, Philip of Swabia, Otto of Brunswick from the Welf dynasty and, of course, his son, Frederick II – who in many ways were continuing Henry's policies. These documents reveal more of what Innocent thought of the emperor, his family and his policies. In the *Deliberatio super facto imperii de tribus electus,* Innocent mentions again the danger of the unification of Sicily and the empire, 'which would shake the church'.[50] Further, he partially discredits Frederick, supposing that because of his imperial dignity, he would not swear fealty and homage to the pope, just as his father, Henry, had not. The papal claims to the overlordship of Sicily clearly figured large in Innocent's concerns. When talking about Philip of Swabia, Innocent relates how 'Henry and Frederick Barbarossa persecuted the church, indeed the whole family were persecutors'. He has one last telling incident about Henry: he had violently invaded the Patrimony of St Peter, many times devastated it and to the injury of the church 'mutilated certain servants of our brothers by having their noses cut off'.[51] Unfortunately we do not know more about whether or why these poor servants lost their noses. Still Innocent distinguishes them from clerics, an attack on whom would have brought immediate excommunication.[52] In any case, Cardinal Lothar had not appreciated Henry's, or his family's, exercise of power in Sicily or Italy.

---

[47]Richard Kieckhefer, *Repression of Heresy in Medieval Germany*, (Philadelphia, 1979), 17.

[48]Waley, *Papal State*, 16, points out how the pope's policy of suspending action aided their success when circumstances changed. Matthew, *Norman Kingdom*, 293, notes the papal interest in protracted negotiations.

[49]Reg. Imp., no. 505; MGH Const. 1, no. 370.

[50]RNI no. 29.

[51]Morris, *Papal Monarchy*, 199.

[52]Smith, *Innocent III, Church Defender*, 2-10, reviews some of Innocent's practices against those who attacked clergy. On the problems of violence against clergy and clerical property caused by the confusion of legal rights, as well as on the church's attempt to punish those guilty of attacks, see Volkert Pfaff, 'Pro posse nostro, Die Ausübung der Kirchengewalt durch Papst Coelestin III.', ZRG Kan. 43 (1957):89-131.

After his elevation from cardinal to pope, Innocent seized the moment to reverse the scenario that Henry had begun.[53] Henry's death created a unique opportunity for the papacy.[54] With Germany caught up in civil war, no one could interfere with papal temporal policies. Instead of seeking cooperation with the empire, the curia advanced an expansionist papal program against the imperial position. First, Innocent interfered in German politics as never before, making the warfare worse in the process, according to Walther von der Vogelweide.[55] Significantly, Innocent asserted papal authority over German bishops, coercing them to his side.[56] Second, papal dominion in Italy had its greatest chance to develop. More than any previous pope, Innocent lorded over southern Italy as regent in the Kingdom of Sicily.[57] And in central Italy he virtually founded the Papal States by securing long-held claims.[58] He expanded power aggressively, capitalizing on resentment against the Germans to bolster weak claims, especially using nepotism on a scale larger than ever.[59] Innocent's nepotism, in fact, led directly to the murder of Philip of Swabia.[60] Third, without the balancing competition of the universal emperor, the papacy spread out and asserted itself all over Europe.

In this last matter, the leadership of Christendom, Innocent would act almost exactly as Henry had. Concerning the emperor, historians have often criticized him for his alleged 'thirst for world dominion', as he erected a *Weltherrschaft* or *dominium mundi* over western Europe and the Mediterranean.[61] Historians have suggested grand aims for Henry VI. First he cowed the princes in Germany. In

---

[53]He also revised numerous policies of his predecessor; see Volkert Pfaff, 'Der Vorgänger: Das Wirken Coelestins III. aus der Sicht von Innozenz III.', ZRG Kan. 41 (1955):156.

[54]Walter Kienast, 'Die Anfänge des Europäischen Staatensystems im späteren Mittelalter', *Historische Zeitschrift* 153 (1936):222; Haller, 'Kaiser Heinrich VI.', 471; Morris, *Papal Monarchy*, 202; E. Jordan, *Histoire du Moyen Age*, 150.

[55]See for example Walther von der Vogelweide, *Die Lieder*, ed. Friedrich Maurer, Uni-Taschenbücher, no. 167 (Munich, 1972), no. 73, p. 222.

[56]Sayers, *Innocent*, 61, 79.

[57]Matthew, *Norman Kingdom*, 298-306, also points out his weaknesses as a politician.

[58]Partner, *Lands of St Peter*, 229; Waley, *Papal State*, 67.

[59]Partner, *Lands of St Peter*, 229-34; Morris, *Papal Monarchy*, 198, 420. On the use of weak claims, especially imperial privileges, see Manfred Laufs, *Politik und Recht bei Innozenz III.: Kaiserprivilegien, Thronstreitregister und Egerer Goldbulle in der Reichs- und Rekuperationspolitik Papst Innozenz' III.* (Cologne, 1980).

[60]Herbert Grundmann, 'Wahlkönigtum, Territorialpolitik und Ostbewegung im 13. und 14. Jahrhundert', in *Gebhardt Handbuch der deutschen Geschichte*, 9th edn (Stuttgart, 1981), 1:434: namely the reputed motive of the murderer, Otto von Wittelsbach, was his anger about his broken engagement with one of Philip's daughters whom the king then intended for one of Innocent's nephews.

[61]Previté-Orton, *Outlines*, 256. Sayers, *Innocent*, 49, (with approval of the concern) cites an 'Imperial Chronicler' as a contemporary source. Others like Cohn, *Zeitalter der Hohenstaufen*, 10, 29, maintain that Henry merely wanted to play power politics and not really gain dominion.

the south he established authority over Sicily and central Italy. In the north, he made England an imperial fief as a result of Richard's capture. In the west, he built new ties with the kingdom of Aragon. And in the east, he organized a crusade to the Holy Land and perhaps intended to use it against Byzantium. Also in the east, he accepted the feudal overlordship of Armenia and Cyprus.[62] For imperial claims, this was nothing new: Frederick Barbarossa had already spoken in this vein, claiming to outrank all other rulers, the 'little kings'.[63] Overall Henry had certainly gone far in continuing or reviving a respect for imperial lordship.[64]

Arguably, Innocent also sought to dominate the world, as he promoted papal power far beyond the claims of most of his predecessors. The recent collection *Vicar of Christ vs. Lord of the World* reviews the disagreements among historians about how much of Innocent's motivations were religious and how much were political.[65] Regardless of the weight given to his political motives, most agree that his decisions altered the foundations of Christendom. According to Innocent, the pope was the '*caput et fundamentum christianitatis*', the enthroned leader above kings and emperors of Christendom.[66] Indeed, papal jurisdiction encompassed the whole globe, while an emperor's was much more limited.[67] And does not Innocent's phrase 'higher than man, but lower than God' indicate a claim for universal authority?[68]

'The heir to Henry VI was Innocent III', said Ranke.[69] When it came to the location of political authority within the feudal hierarchy of Europe, or even the impossible ideal of the lord of the world, Henry paved the way for Innocent III.

---

[62]Peter Halfter, 'Die Staufer und Armenien', in *Von Schwaben bis Jerusalem: Facetten staufischer Geschichte*, ed. Sönke Lorenz und Ulrich Schmidt, Veröffentlichungen des Alemannischen Instituts, 61 (Sigmaringen, 1995):197-200; Elizabeth Chapin Furber, 'The Kindom of Cyprus, 1191-1291', in Setton, ed., *A History of the Crusades*, 2:604; Naumann, 39-46.

[63]Csendes, *Heinrich*, 223; Benjamin Arnold, *Medieval Germany, 500-1300: A Political Interpretation* (Toronto, 1997), 103-7.

[64]Toeche, *Heinrich*, 358; Sayers, *Innocent*, 49.

[65]James M. Powell, 'Introduction', in *Innocent III*, ed. Powell, 1-2. See also Theodor Mayer, 'Papsttum und Kaisertum im Hohen Mittelalter: Werden, Wesen und Auflösung einer Weltordnung, ein kritischer Überblick', *Historische Zeitschrift* 187 (1959):36-7.

[66]Kempf, *Papsttum und Kaisertum*, 309-15.

[67]Kempf, *Papsttum und Kaisertum*, 317, citing RNI, no. 18.

[68]PL 217:657-8.

[69]Leopold von Ranke, *Weltgeschichte*, 4th edn (Leipzig, 1921), 7:162, puts the inheritance in the context of Henry's (Teutonic) plans to dominate the West: 'Dieser Kaiser repräsentierte noch einmal die deutsche Weltherrschaft, mit der es nun für immer vorbei war. Sein eigentlicher Nachfolger war Lothar Conti, der Papst Innocenz III., 1198-1216.' Ranke, 163-5, goes on to claim that Innocent successfully replaced Henry's imperial domination of Italy with a papal one free of German influence, and from there sought to determine the political destiny of Europe. The condensed version of Ranke's assessment is quoted or alluded to, e.g. by Waley, *Papal State*, 30; Morris, *Papal Monarchy*, 420, 438; and Sayers, *Innocent*, 50.

Innocent repeated what Henry did, and his longer reign allowed him to attain more than the emperor. To compare: in Germany he became the arbiter of the kingship, while in the south he regained feudal lordship over Sicily and asserted control in central Italy. Additionally, in the north, he turned England into a fief as a result of King John's incompetence. In the west, he brought the kingdom of Aragon into his orbit.[70] In the east, he successfully promoted crusades, one of which conquered Constantinople, subjecting Byzantium to Innocent's authority.[71] He even brought distant Armenia into further contact with the West. Incidentally, some historians consider Innocent, like Henry, ruthless in enforcing his own conception of church-state relations.[72] The pontiff was not afraid of shedding blood and encouraging warfare for his version of truth and justice.[73] While Innocent might have vigorously denied modelling his ascendancy on the Staufen emperor, the similarities are remarkable.

In transforming Henry's legacy to serve the papacy, Innocent succumbed to the seduction of trying to impose his ideological structure upon the medieval world. The striking similarity in the efforts of these two rulers reflects desires infecting most of the powerful, from which Innocent appears to be no less immune than Henry. Of course, this emphasis on anti-imperial and political exertions ignores Innocent's many worthy accomplishments in church administration, canon law, theology, patronage, charity, pastoral care etc. His political labors, however, are central to his historical reputation, as when Helene Tillmann explains 'History's' denial to Innocent III of the title 'the Great'.[74]

These parallels in papal and imperial goals also guaranteed that the quarrel between church and empire would intensify. There were no easy distinctions between 'religious' and 'secular' for either the papalists or the imperialists. Political practices about bishops and Italy derived from perceptions about justice in this world and about the chances for getting into heaven in the next. Each side thought it was doing what was 'right' and that the other side was 'wrong' about their actions within the divinely ordered system. The emperor had his place; the pope had his.[75] The differences were not in the general ideologies or specific

---

[70] Sayers, *Innocent*, 49, 72, 83.

[71] On Innocent's strengths and weaknesses as a promoter of crusades, see Riley-Smith, *Crusades*, 120. See also Friedrich Hurter, 'Innocent III: Victim of Partisan Historians', in *Innocent III*, ed. Powell, 13.

[72] Geoffrey Barraclough, *The Origins of Modern Germany* (New York, 1963), 207.

[73] Johannes Haller, 'Lord of the World', in *Innocent III*, ed. Powell, 85.

[74] Helene Tillmann, 'The Man', in *Innocent III*, ed. Powell, 183-4.

[75] For a good review of different positions on the nature of the imperial coronation and office, see Ulrich Schmidt, 'A quo ergo habet, si a domno papa non habet imperium? Zu den Anfängen der "staufichen Kaiserwahlen"', in *Von Schwaben bis Jerusalem: Facetten staufischer Geschichte*, ed. Sönke Lorenz und Ulrich Schmidt, Veröffentlichungen des Alemannischen Instituts, 61 (Sigmaringen, 1995), 62-88.

legal precedents and rights, as much as in the details about who could exert direct authority in particular instances. The papacy's increasing policy was to weaken imperial influence in Italy to its own perceived advantage. The empire meanwhile sought to increase its influence in Italy, generally to the papacy's perceived disadvantage. First Henry had been successful, then Innocent.

And while both Innocent and Henry briefly triumphed, both ultimately failed in key ways. These rulers tried to accomplish too much. Emperor Henry's overambitious goals and achievements overawed and worried both his contemporaries and modern historians.[76] His determined imperial policies helped to frighten the curia into a paranoid destruction of the German monarchy. The civil war in Germany after Henry's death, which permanently weakened the crown's prerogatives, arose partly in reaction to Henry's success. In Italy, the imperial system of rule collapsed quickly, as Italians revolted against German law and taxation. Thus (after the brief attempted revival of imperial authority under Henry VI's son, Frederick II) both Germany and Italy seemed irrevocably doomed to disunity until the nineteenth century.

Innocent, similarly, overreached himself. Within the church, Innocent weakened the moral authority of the papacy by his interference in secular politics.[77] As Brian Tierney has written, the papacy created a 'destructive tension in medieval Catholicism' as it sought temporal power.[78] Regarding Germany, the papacy weakened its kingship and government so much that it is not hard to see why German historians blame Innocent for the problems of the thirteenth century.[79] Moreover, a weak Germany was a papal pyrrhic victory, since a powerless king did not make the Germans more religious.[80] A recent study has shown that Innocent's crowning achievement, the Fourth Lateran Council, had very little impact on the German bishoprics, largely because of continuing political unrest.[81] Meanwhile in Italy, Innocent may have founded the Papal States, but they were of little advantage to the spiritual mission of the papacy.[82] Innocent undid much of what Henry had accomplished; in turn, Henry's son, Frederick II, undid much of what Innocent had accomplished, at least in Germany and Italy. And within a century, the papacy's obsession with the Staufens and

---

[76]Barraclough, *Origins of Germany*, 200, 204.

[77]Sayers, *Innocent*, 189.

[78]Brian Tierney, 'Innocent III as Judge', in *Innocent III*, ed. Powell, 100-1, noting that even if Innocent himself had the best of intentions, his decretals significantly supported the developing negative papal tendencies.

[79]Kempf, *Papsttum und Kaisertum*, 324.

[80]Kempf, *Papsttum und Kaisertum*, 325.

[81]Paul B. Pixton, *The German Episcopacy and the Implementation of the Decrees of the Fourth Lateran Council, 1216-1245: Watchmen on the Tower* (Leiden, 1995).

[82]Morris, *Papal Monarchy*, 422, 426.

with Germany allowed France and England to build strong secular monarchies, which would successfully overpower the popes.

Perhaps we cannot fault the thirteenth-century clerics for not knowing that the papacy would never 'hold its own against a major secular power'.[83] Nevertheless the popes had already had many decades of experience with quarrels and warfare with the German kings over land and rights in Italy. Papal princes had only held their own against German encroachment when allied with another powerful government, such as Norman Sicily or France. And in the long run, we do know papal temporal power did fail miserably in creating a more vigorous church. The fear of medieval churchmen, that the restriction of the papacy to a small non-temporal position would dissolve its authority, is belied by modern history. The politically powerless pope in the twentieth century is far more influential than the secularized papal princes of the Middle Ages and Renaissance.

In the end we come back to the insoluble dilemma of church and state: how do Christians divide up authority in this world? Medieval history created this confusing dualism of who was in charge: kings or popes? Both powers shared political and spiritual interests as each defended its own perceived rights.[84] At one extreme was an imperial answer: most power to the state, which is the ultimate temporal authority, while clerics should be confined to religious matters. At the other extreme was a papal answer, which mirrored the imperial: the supreme jurisdiction was a prerogative of the popes, while emperors should serve the will of the church. Neither extreme succeeded, nor probably could succeed, in creating a stable, virtuous commonwealth. Henry VI and Innocent III each tried to become lord of the world, a goal history has proven to be too much for mere mortals, even those who are 'higher than men'.

---

[83] John C. Moore, 'Sardinia and the Papal State', in *Innocent III*, ed. Powell, 172.

[84] For a description of these extremes see Walter Ullmann, *A History of Political Thought in the Middle Ages*, Pelican History of Political Theory (Harmondsworth, England, 1970), 100-15, 130-6.

Innocent III, Canon Law and the Punishment of the Guiltless

Peter D. Clarke

INTRODUCTION

The decretals of Innocent III were of major significance for the development of canon law. This was recognized by contemporary canonists, who compiled collections of them and wrote glosses to them.[1] Indeed, Innocent's decretals formulated new legal doctrines and procedures on a wide variety of issues. One of these was the question of punishing the innocent for others' sins.[2] A decretal of Innocent III's predecessor, Celestine III, had noted the Roman law maxim that 'peccata suos auctores tenere debeant', that is to say, the consequences of a wrongdoing ought not to affect innocent third parties directly.[3] A number of Innocent's own decretals are peppered with similar statements of principle from Roman law, such as 'no one ought to be deprived of their right without guilt', or 'a church ought not to suffer loss as a consequence of one person's wrong'.[4]

---

[1]The collections referred to below are *Compilatio Tertia* (= 3 Comp.), *Compilatio Quarta* (= 4 Comp.) and the constitutions of the Fourth Lateran Council. These and the glosses to them are described in S. Kuttner, *Repertorium der Kanonistik (1140-1234)* (Vatican City, 1937), 355-81.

I am grateful to the Leverhulme Trust for financing the research on which this paper is based and my attendance at this conference.

[2]On the canonistic treatment of this general question, see V. Piergiovanni, *La punibilità degli innocenti nel diritto canonico dell'età classica*, 2 vols, Collana degli Annali della Facoltà di Giurisprudenza dell' Università di Genova, 29 and 38 (Milan, 1971-4).

[3]2 Comp. 3.9.2 (= X 3.11.2). The maxim is cited from Cod. 9.47.22.

[4]The principle that '(iure suo) non debeat sine culpa sua privari' is cited in 3 Comp. 4.9.1, 4.10.3, and 4.14.1, and 'delictum persone non redundat in dampnum ecclesie' in 3 Comp. 1.24.1 and 2.2.5. Another maxim in this vein, 'res inter alios acta non aliis preiudicet', occurs in 3 Comp. 2.12.11 and 3.18.5 and 4 Comp. 1.12.1, 2.5.un, and 3.2.1.

Nevertheless, in contemporary canonistic theory and practice there were a few exceptions to this principle of limiting punishment to the guilty. The most obvious was the general interdict, a sanction which deprived a whole community of religious rites because its leaders were seriously opposing ecclesiastical authority. Innocent III was to develop upon and add to these exceptions so much that he revolutionized the church's policy on punishing the guiltless. He used the general interdict to an extent perhaps unparalleled by any of his predecessors and laid down some of the first legal provisions regarding it.[5] He also brought many other penalties affecting the guiltless into regular ecclesiastical usage, such as disinheritance. Most of these he adopted in response to what he saw as the two big dangers facing the church of his day, namely the growth of popular heresy and secular infringements of ecclesiastical liberty. Such penalties were weapons of self-defence but of a very aggressive kind. The aim of the present paper is to survey this new armoury which Innocent developed to combat heresy and violations of ecclesiastical liberty, to study how contemporary canonists reacted to it, and to consider how they and the pope dealt with the moral and practical problems which it raised.

HERESY

Innocent's major contribution to legislation against heresy was the decretal 'Vergentis' (1199), whose significance has been debated just as much by recent historians as it was by thirteenth-century jurists.[6] It was included in the official collection of decretals from the first twelve years of his pontificate, the *Compilatio Tertia*, was later absorbed into Pope Gregory IX's great law code of 1234, the *Liber Extra*, and remained in force until the inquisition fell into decline during the eighteenth century. 'Vergentis' provided harsh measures against those associated with heretics. Firstly, their defenders, harbourers, supporters and adherents incurred infamy if they disregarded warnings to obey the ecclesiastical authorities, and thus were barred from holding public offices, electing others to the same, testifying in court, making or inheriting from a will. Neither could they practice as judges, notaries or advocates, and they were to be stripped of any

---

[5]On Innocent's use of interdicts, see E. B. Krehbiel, *The Interdict: Its History and Operation with Especial Attention to the Time of Innocent III* (Washington, 1909).

[6]For recent historical debate on 'Vergentis': H. Maisonneuve, *Études sur les origines de l'inquisition*, 2nd edn (Paris, 1960), 157, 279-84; W. Ullmann, 'The Significance of Innocent III's Decretal Vergentis', *Études d'histoire du droit dediées à Gabriel Le Bras* (Paris, 1965), 2:729-41; O. Hageneder, 'Studien zur Dekretale "Vergentis" (X V.7.10). Ein Beitrag zur Häretikergesetzgebung Innocenz III', ZRG Kan. 49 (1963):138-73; K. Pennington, 'Pro Peccatis Patrum Puniri: A Moral and Legal Problem of the Inquisition', *Church History* 47(1978), reprinted in his *Popes, Canonists and Texts 1150-1550* (Variorum, 1993), art. XI, 1-21.

ecclesiastical office or benefice which they held. Anyone associating with them was instantly anathematized. One of the first commentators on 'Vergentis', Vincentius Hispanus (*c*. 1210-1215), justified the pope's imposition of infamy in regard to secular affairs by reason of sin and observed that it was lawful for one person to be punished for another.[7] Joannes Teutonicus (*c*. 1217) and Tancred (*c*. 1220) both followed this line and stated that the pope could intervene in secular jurisdiction on account of other crimes.[8] Given that Lucius III had threatened supporters of heresy with infamy as early as 1184, it is not surprising that canonists found this provision so unremarkable.[9] Indeed, commenting on 'Vergentis', Laurentius Hispanus (*c*. 1210) observed that protectors of heretics were thus deservedly punished since heretics could not survive long without their help. Though he did speculate whether those who sheltered heretics because of some blood or marital relationship might be less harshly punished,[10] Laurentius concluded that such a distinction, based on Roman Law, did not apply in this instance, and so heretics and their harbourers were to suffer the same penalty regardless.

'Vergentis' did contain a further provision which was remarkably novel, the confiscation of property and the consequent disinheritance of sons, even orthodox ones. The original wording of the decretal implied that this penalty extended beyond heretics to their sympathizers. In 1215, the Fourth Lateran Council issued a canon, 'Excommunicamus', which qualified the terms of 'Vergentis': those friendly to heretics were excommunicate and after a year of continued disobedi-

---

[7]Vincentius Hispanus on 3 Comp. 5.4.1, v. *confundantur*: 'nota quod sepe punitur unus in altero, ut ii. q. vii. Qualis, Sententia (C.2 q.7 c.9 and c.12)' (Vatican, Biblioteca Apostolica, Vat. lat. 1378, f. 95ra). *Idem*, v. *precepimus*: 'quod facere potest propter obtentum peccati, supra de iud. novit (3 Comp. 2.1.3)' (same manuscript, f.95va). Johannes Galensis (*c*. 1210) wrote identical glosses on this part of 'Vergentis' (see München, Bayerische Staatsbibliothek, Clm 3979, f. 250va).

[8]Johannes Teutonicus on 3 Comp. 5.4.1, v. *precepimus*: 'quod facere . . . et ita potest papa seculares iudices privare dignitatibus suis non tantum propter heresim sed etiam propter alias iniquitates, ut xv. q. vi. Alius (C.15 q.6 c.3), nam et transfert dignitatem imperii de loco ad locum, supra de electione. venerabilem (3 Comp. 1.6.19).' (Vatican, Biblioteca Apostolica, Chigi E.VII.207, f. 240va.) Tancred on 3 Comp. 5.4.1, v. *precepimus* (Vatican, Biblioteca Apostolica,Vat. lat. 1377, f. 264vb) simply reproduces the glosses of Vincentius and Joannes on v. *precepimus*.

[9]His decretal 'Ad abolendam' (1 Comp. 5.6.11): 'Omnes etiam fautores hereticorum tanquam perpetua infamia condemnatos, ab advocatione et testimonio et aliis publicis officiis decernimus repellendos.'

[10]As reproduced by Tancred on 3 Comp. 5.4.1, v. *receptatoribus:* 'Sine quibus heretici diu manere non possunt et ideo merito puniuntur, ar. ff. de officio presi. congruit (Dig. 1.18.3) et ff. de receptatoribus l.i (Dig. 4.8.1), nisi proximos recipiant, puta agnatos, quia tunc non ita graviter puniuntur, ar. ff. de receptatoribus l. ult (Dig. 4.8.52). Quod in hoc casu non concedo, ar. xxvii q. c. De Filia (C.27 q.1 c.26). Puniuntur enim eadem pena receptatores et heretici, ar. C. de his qui latrones occultant. l. i (Cod. 9.39.1). lau.' (Vat. lat. 1377, f. 264vb.)

ence incurred infamy with all the consequences described in 'Vergentis'; but confiscation of property was not mentioned. Nearly twenty years later, the editor of the *Liber Extra*, Raymond de Peñafort, slightly reworded the confiscation provision in 'Vergentis' to restrict its effect to heretics alone and thus reflect Innocent's tacit change of the law.[11] Hageneder argues that this change was occasioned by the reluctance of the King of France to execute this confiscation provision against his vassal, Count Raymond of Toulouse, as a harbourer of heresy, unless Raymond was convicted of heresy itself. By 1214, Innocent came round to this view, and only after Raymond was convicted by the Fourth Lateran Council did he authorize the leaders of the Albigensian crusade, instead of the king, to conquer Raymond's county.[12] Innocent could be flexible and pragmatic in his means even if he was firm about his aims, and this we will observe in other aspects of his penal law touching the innocent, most notably the interdict.

Nevertheless, even according to the revised text of 'Vergentis', the innocent sons of convicted heretics could still be disinherited. And Innocent had justified this such that 'in many instances even according to divine judgement sons may suffer a temporal punishment because of their fathers, and according to canonical sanctions retribution may be inflicted not only on the authors of crimes but also on the offspring of the condemned.' Ullmann speculated that the divine judgement and canonical sanctions which Innocent adduced in his support were certain passages from Gratian's *Decretum*.[13] One of these (d.p. C. 1 q.4 c.11) cited biblical examples of divine punishments falling upon the persons and property of whole communities, but Gratian did not thereby conclude that sons may be responsible for their father's sins: 'by these examples none are proven to be bound by the sin of others except for the imitators of their wickedness.' Orthodox sons were clearly no imitators of their father's heresy, and Innocent did not even concede their possible ignorance of paternal sin, which many *Decretum* texts had recognized as another reason to excuse sons from its consequences.[14] Nonetheless, it had become a commonplace distinction among late twelfth century canonists that while a 'pena eterna', like excommunication, should not be laid on one person for another's sin, a 'pena temporalis' might be.[15] Even if it is doubted

---

[11]Conc. Later. IV c.3 or 4 Comp. 5.5.2 (= X 5.7.13) §5; 'Vergentis' was included in the *Liber Extra* as X 5.7.10.

[12]Hageneder, 'Studien', 149 ff., esp. 157-60.

[13]Ullmann, 'Significance', 740, n. 43.

[14]See Piergiovanni, *La punibilità*, 1:48-56, 185 ff.

[15]Piergiovanni, *La punibilità*, 1:117-52. Anonymous gloss (*c.* 1185-7) on C. 24 d.a.q.3, v. *Quod autem*, added to Huguccio's *Summa* (c.1188): 'Pena duplex est, eterna et temporalis. Ad eternam non imputatur alicuius peccatum alii. Ad temporalem id imputatur . . .' (Vatican, Biblioteca Apostolica, Vat. lat. 2280, f.253rb). This distinction had probably originated with Stephen of Tournai, who wrote c.1160 on C. 1 q.4 c.1, v. *Nullius crimen*: 'Paternum crimen non imputatur filio ad penam eternam,

that Innocent was well versed in jurisprudence, he had many curial advisors who were and could supply such juristic arguments which he thus adapted to his own needs and purposes.[16]

Certainly, on purely canonistic grounds, most contemporary canonists made no objectection to the disinheritance penalty. Vincentius Hispanus passively accepted it without comment. Johannes Galensis (*c.* 1210) seems to have been alone in observing that it contradicted a canon of the Fourth Council of Toledo (633), which had ruled that the sons of lapsed Jewish converts to Christianity ought not to be deprived of their inheritance, since scripture taught that 'filius non portabit iniquitatem patris' (Ezechiel 18:20). However, he was the first of several canonists who remarked that the disinheritance penalty of 'Vergentis' went far beyond the provisions of the Roman Law on heresy. In 'Vergentis', Innocent argued that the same penalties which Roman law had applied to traitors should be extended to heretics for it was surely worse to betray Christ than some temporal authority. Roman law indeed required that the assets of traitors be confiscated and their sons lose every right of succession, but it did not categorize heresy with treason and even permitted orthodox heirs to succeed to the estate of a heretic, excluding only claimants who imitated his crime. Roman law on apostasy, as Johannes Galensis noted, similarly forbade apostates to make a will but permitted their estate to devolve to their nearest Christian heirs.[17] Innocent had made expedient, selective, even unsound use of jurisprudence, but canonists could not directly contradict papal authority and had to find a way around his legal inconsistency. Johannes Galensis found parallels to the severity of 'Vergentis' in a ruling of Pope Alexander III (1159-1181) on heresy and an ancient imperial decree on apostasy, both of which ordered seizure of offenders' property. Laurentius (*c.* 1210) tentatively observed that Roman laws regarding the property of heretics *seemed* to have been corrected by 'Vergentis', whereas, Johannes Teutonicus firmly stated in a gloss that Innocent had corrected the Roman law on heresy, but did not question his right to do so. Glossing 'Vergentis' itself *c.* 1217, he added to this observation that disinheritance of heirs also applied to other

---

imputatur tamen quoad temporalem.' *Die Summa des Stephanus Tornacensis über das Decretum Gratiani*, ed. J. Schulte (Giessen, 1891), 149.

[16]See K. Pennington, 'The legal education of Pope Innocent III', BMCL 4 (1974):70-7. Indeed, it is generally difficult to know when Innocent's letters speak with his own voice or those of his curial officials, but it will be assumed for the purposes of this paper that Innocent must have approved the sentiments of letters issued in his name.

[17]Cod. 1.5.4 and 19. Ullmann ('Significance', 740) said that Innocent's model was the stringent decree 'Quiquis' (Cod. 9.8.5), which ordered complete confiscation against those who betrayed the emperor. Johannes Galensis on 3 Comp. 5.4.1 v. *statuimus*: 'Hinc videtur statuere contra conci. Tol. i.q. iiii. Iudei (C.1 q.4 c.7), [et] contra legem C. de aposta. Apostatorum (Cod. 1.7.4). Sed ista est cum filiis, cum parentes non habent. Similiter alexand' supra e.t. De Brabanzonibus l.i et C. de apost. l.i (1 Comp. 5.6.7; Cod. 1.7.1).' München, Bayerische Staatsbibliothek, Clm 3879, f. 250va.

crimes, like simony and, according to a canon which Innocent decreed at the Fourth Lateran Council, the murder of clerks.[18] Writing after 1220, Tancred admitted that new law could supersede old but was concerned by the severity of the disinheritance provision. Tancred's theoretical solution was that it should only apply in the lands where the pope exercised temporal jurisdiction but in other lands the Roman laws on heresy ought to prevail since they expressed greater equity, and this was to be preferred to the strict letter of the law. He concluded with the Roman law maxim such that a penalty was to be moderated rather than aggravated.[19] Tancred's solution was presumably based on the fact that 'Vergentis' had originally been addressed to the people of Viterbo, a city in the papal patrimony. Even though it had since been sent to the south of France and circulated widely in *Compilatio Tertia*, given the reluctance of at least one secular ruler Philip of France to comply with its terms, Tancred was perhaps not defying reality in arguing for their limitation. Indeed, with regard to Tancred's solution, Pennington has observed that a canonist's interpretation of a papal law could sometimes influence the manner of its application. But, as Pennington demonstrated, Tancred's lead was not followed by subsequent canonists who argued for the strict enforcement of 'Vergentis'.[20] Nonetheless, Joannes Teutonicus (*c.*

---

[18]Laurentius Hispanus on 3 Comp. 5.4.1 v. *severitatis censuram orthodoxorum*: 'Videntur ergo ex hoc recipere correctionem iura illa que dicunt bona hereticorum devolvenda ad filios fideles, ut C. eodem titulo Manicheos (Cod. 1.5.4), vel si non habent filios fideles ad cognatos vel agnatos fideles, ut C. eodem titulo Cognivimus (Cod. 1.5.19), autem ibi posito quod incipit Idem de Nestorianis (Nov. 115.3.14).' *Apparatus Glossarum Laurentii Hispani in Compilationem Tertiam*, ed. B. J. McManus (unpublished PhD dissertation, Syracuse University, 1991), 579. Johannes Teutonicus on C.23 q.7 d.a.c.1: 'Si ergo condemnatus est laicus de heresi, confiscantur bona eius, ut extra de here. c. Vergentis . . . etiamsi aliquis hereticus habet filios vel agnatos . . . et sic corrigitur lex que dicit bona hereticorum ad filios vel agnatos devolvi, ut C. de here. Auth. de Nestorianis (Nov. 115.3.14) . . .' (from Maisonneuve, *Études*, 280, n. 188). Joannes on 3 Comp. 5.4.1, v. filiorum: '. . . et nota quod in tribus criminibus filii excluduntur, scilicet in crimine heresis et symonie, ut hic et vi. q.i §Verum (C.6 q.1 d.p.c.11), et interfectore clerici, ut const. innoc. In quibusdam (4 Comp. 5.13.2).' (Chigi E.VII.207, f. 240va).

[19]Tancred on 3 Comp. 5.4.1, v. *filiorum*: 'Expresse dicitur hic quod bona hereticorum confiscantur sive filios habeant sive non, nec catholicis filiis hereticorum est aliquid relinquendum. Sed contra dicunt leges C. de hereticis. Manicheos et l. Cognovimus (Cod. 1.5.4 and 19) et aut. Idem est de Nestorianis (Nov. 115.3.14), ubi dicitur quod bona hereticorum devolvuntur ad filios orthodoxos; si <non> habent, devolvuntur ad cognatos vel agnatos catholicos. Ad hoc dixerunt la[urentius] et jo[annes] quod hec decretalis corrigit leges illas, et ius illud antiquum tra<h>itur ad istud novum, ar. ff. de legibus et const. Non est novum (Dig. 1.3.26) et supra. de cognatione spirituali c.i lib. i (1 Comp. 4.11.1). Ego dico hanc decretalem prevalere legibus supradictis in terris illis dumtaxat que subsunt temporali iurisdictioni domini pape, sicut ex littera precedenti probatur. In aliis autem terris prevalent leges predicte que maiori equitate nituntur, et hec decretalis de severitate loquitur ut ex littera patet. Equitas enim iuri stricto preferenda est, ut C. de iudiciis. placuit (Cod. 3.1.8), nam cum hec sit pena, molienda est et non exasperanda, ut supra de pen. di. i §Pene (De pen. D. 1 c.18)' (Vat. lat. 1377, f. 264vb).

[20]Pennington, 'Pro Peccatis', 7 (on Tancred's solution) and 8 ff. (on subsequent interpretation).

1217) had noted a mitigation in the decretal text itself, such that heretics could receive back their confiscated goods *ex indulgentia* if they returned to the faith.[21] Even when Raymond of Toulouse was convicted of heresy, Innocent did not apply 'Vergentis' to the letter, for it appears he did not disinherit Raymond's innocent son completely.[22]

This *indulgentia* perhaps suggests that Innocent's intention was not wholly vindictive but was to coerce heretics back into the church by threatening their sons where threats to themselves and other means of persuasion had failed. He was determined to unite all believers into one church under papal direction, and on other occasions he adopted more moderate means to attain this end. Innocent's attempts to accommodate religious groups with slightly unorthodox views, notably the Humiliati, are well known. In 1199, the very year in which 'Vergentis' was issued, Innocent was advising the bishop of Verona to proceed cautiously against such groups suspected of heresy, since, so he said, 'it is not our intention to condemn the innocent along with the guilty'.[23] How can one explain the striking inconsistency between this statement and the provisions of 'Vergentis'? The latter might be seen as extraordinary measures necessitated by extreme circumstances. For example, when Innocent warned those investigating a group in Metz to beware gathering the tares before the harvest and thereby also pulling out the wheat, that is, not to proceed so hastily that the innocent suffer along with the guilty, he still authorized punishment of the group in the event of its persistent disobedience.[24] A stiff sanction was thus justified as a last resort.

Moreover, 'Vergentis' specifically expressed the pope's alarm at the growth of heresy in his own temporal domain with the apparent connivance of local secular authorities. Indeed, it was aimed more directly at such patrons of heresy than at heretics themselves and even exhorted secular rulers outside the Papal State to aid the church by executing the confiscation order in their lands. Hence, it reflected a desire to secure political as well as pastoral obedience, and its unusually harsh provisions perhaps belie what Tillmann saw as a fundamental tension between Innocent's pastoral aims and his political aspirations.[25] This tension is even more evident in Innocent's usage of penalties touching the innocent in defence of ecclesiastical liberty. Indeed, it is one of several features common to his policy

---

[21]Johannes Teutonicus on 3 Comp. 5.4.1, v. filiorum: 'Sic patet quod secundum canones bona hereticorum sive habeant filios sive non . . . Si tamen reversi fuerint ad fidem ex indulgentia possint ei restitui bona, ut hic dicit et xxiii q.iiii Ipsa (C.23 q.4 c.24) . . .' (Chigi E.VII.207, f.240va). Joannes had made the same point two years earlier in his gloss on C.23 q.7 d.p.c.1 (see n. 18 for reference) and would repeat it on 4 Comp. 5.5.2, v. *confiscentur* (Vat. lat. 1377, f. 310 va).

[22]See H. Tillmann, *Pope Innocent III*, trans. W. Sax (North-Holland, 1980), 238-40.

[23]PL 214:788-9: 'Quia vero non est nostre intentionis innoxios cum nocentibus condemnare . . .'

[24]PL 214:793-5.

[25]Tillmann, *Innocent*, 248.

on punishing the innocent both in this cause and in the fight against heresy, as we shall see below.

THE DEFENCE OF ECCLESIASTICAL LIBERTY

In his many conflicts with the Lombard cities, Innocent applied a whole range of measures affecting the guiltless.[26] Their usage by the papacy was not unprecedented but the frequency with which Innocent used them was,[27] and his example in applying such collective sanctions was much followed by his successors. He mostly resorted to them in defence of clerical immunity from lay taxation, allowing them to be lifted once the offending commune agreed to restore what it had wrongly exacted and to respect clerical immunity in the future. Like the confiscation penalty of 'Vergentis', their aim was coercive rather than vindictive. They were threatened usually where excommunication had failed to move the leaders of the commune, and were designed to turn the aggrieved innocent against them. The interdict is an obvious example.[28] If the leaders persisted in their disobedience, the suffering of the innocent could be aggravated by declaration of a trade ban or the exposure of their goods and persons to seizure by secular rulers, thereby increasing the pressure to submit.[29] As Innocent threatened to these communes, he would proceed against them 'spiritualiter et temporaliter'. Often, the final resort was to threaten the loss of a city's see; Piacenza had defied Innocent for three years over the taxation issue when he made this ultimatum in 1208.[30] In the case of Piacenza, it was very effective since its diocese also constituted a temporal county, and the city capitulated immediately rather than suffer the division of its temporal jurisdiction and its economically vital territory between neighbouring rival communes.

---

[26]See Tillmann, *Innocent*, 95 ff.

[27]Lucius III's 1184 decretal 'Ad abolendam' (1 Comp. 5.6.11) threatened against any city sheltering heretics a trade ban and the loss of its episcopal see, sanctions often threatened by Innocent III. On subsequent papal use of such sanctions, see my unpublished PhD dissertation, 'The Theory and Practice of the Ecclesiastical Interdict in the Age of the Decretalists' (University of Manchester, 1995), 193-200, esp. 193 regarding the trade embargo declared by Pope Martin IV against Sicily in 1283 (see *Les Registres de Martin IV*, eds F. Olivier-Martin et al. [École Français de Rome, 1903-35], nos. 276, 460 and 483.)

[28]Innocent threatened interdicts on Treviso (PL 214:555-8), Bergamo (PL 215:201-4) and Modena (PL 215:323-5).

[29]Threatened by Innocent against Treviso (see n. 28), all Lombard communes (PL 215:47-8), Piacenza (PL 215:487-8) and Milan along with Alessandria (PL 216:710-15). Only the letter to Treviso specifies a trade ban along with the seizure of citizens and their goods. Sentences were threatened on Alessandria and Milan not just for violating ecclesiastical immunity but also for protecting heretics and truce-breaking.

[30]PL 215:995-1001. Also threatened by Innocent against Milan along with Alessandria (see n. 29), and Treviso, Bergamo and Modena (see n. 28)

However, when Innocent came to publish a canon at the Fourth Lateran Council forbidding governors of cities from taxing the clergy without papal permission, he attached none of the collective penalties that he had employed in his struggle with the Lombard communes over this issue. Violators of the canon incurred excommunication but the only measure laid down affecting third parties was the extension of this penalty to those who consented to the violation.[31] Early in his pontificate, Innocent had similarly ruled that the automatic excommunication of those who physically maltreated clerks extended to others who consented to this wrongdoing, even if only tacitly in that they stood by and failed to prevent it.[32] Likewise, the Lateran canon also required excommunication of those who had succeeded its violators and had failed to pay back the illicit taxes within a month of assuming office, since, as Joannes Teutonicus observed on this provision, this neglect signified consent to the violation, or as the wording of the canon punningly explained: 'succedat in onere qui substituitur in honore.'[33]

Why Innocent did not add further penalties falling on those other than the actual wrongdoers is not certain. Perhaps, as Tillmann suggested, he did not wish to regularize usage of the extraordinary measures adopted against the Lombard communes, since he or the council found them too problematic in moral and legal terms.[34] Certainly, one penalty threatened against Bergamo in 1203 and Modena a year later, that the heirs of their offending rulers were to be excluded from the clerical life down to the third and fourth generations, raised an issue much debated by the canonists since Gratian's day, namely whether sons could be held responsible for sins of their fathers.[35] In the decretal 'Innotuit nobis' (1200), Innocent had summarized the main line of this debate in response to the particular question of excluding the illegitimate from clerical office. In the manner of Gratian, he noted the conflict among the authorities on this issue; some canons favoured exclusion of the illegitimate while others did not because 'the fault of the parents is not to be imputed to the sons', a teaching of St Augustine included

---

[31]4 Comp. 3.18.3 (Conc. Later. IV, c.46).

[32]4 Comp. 5.15.3.

[33]Joannes Teutonicus on 4 Comp. 3.18.3 v. *mensem*: '. . . quare statim honus illud non pervenit ad succesorem, ar. extra.i. de officio del. Quoniam (1 Comp. 1.21.19)? Resp. quia illud honus provenit ex delicto unde non descendit ad alios, ut xxiiii q.iii. Si habes (C.24 q.3 c.1). Ideo autem prefigitur mensis quia usque ad illud tempus presumitur consensisse, ut i.q.i. Constat (C.1 q.1 c.111) . . .' (Vat. lat. 1377, f.305ra). I discussed this issue of punishing those who consent to the wrongdoing of others in a paper given at the Ecclesiastical History Society Summer Conference, St Andrews, 16-19 July 1997. I have since developed this paper into a long article which will appear in the 1999 volume of the *Zeitschrift der Savigny-Stiftung für Rechtsgeschichte, Kanonistitische Abteilung*. See also Piergiovanni, *La punibilità*, 1:45-8, 159-62.

[34]Tillmann, *Innocent*, 96.

[35]On the Bergamo and Modena cases, see n. 28, and on this general issue, Piergiovanni, *La punibilità*, 1:29-33; 83-7; 98-103; 161 et passim.

in the *Decretum*.[36] In support of this view, Innocent cited theological rather than canonistic authorities; he noted that Christ was descended from illegitimate forebears and quoted scripture, such as Ezekiel 18:20, which said that a son shall not bear the consequences of his father's wickedness. But he observed that some (*quidam*) had qualified Augustine's teaching, arguing that the illegitimate could be excluded from clerical office if they imitated their fathers' incontinence. And he added that, when, in Exodus 20:5, God spoke of visiting the sins of the fathers on their sons down to the third and fourth generations, this referred to those imitating their fathers' sins.[37] This interpretation was in fact traditional canonistic doctrine.[38] In 1206, Innocent was to cite this same reading of Exodus 20:5 in another decretal in order to justify the dispensation of those illegitimate sons in holy orders 'qui paterna vitia non sequuntur'.[39]

Nevertheless, a canon of the Fourth Lateran Council, aimed at patrons who maltreated clerks of churches under their supposed protection, imposed a ban from admission to the clergy on their heirs down to the third and fourth generation, a sentence which, in common with those threatened against the rulers of Modena and Bergamo, consciously recalled the language of Exodus 20:5. Though the council had not regularized this sanction in regard to taxing the clergy, it obviously considered brutalizing the clergy a far more serious violation of their liberties and therefore more deserving of such a statutory penalty, as the text of the canon reasoned: 'lest the punishment be remembered less than the crime.'[40] Nonetheless, the canon permitted dispensation from this punishment, and Joannes Teutonicus observed that this dispensation could even be granted by bishops since the pope had not expressly reserved it to himself.[41] By seeking such dispensation, the heirs in effect repudiated their forebears' wrongdoing. If the canon's aim was to turn sons away from the sinful behaviour of their fathers, it

---

[36]C.1 q.4 c.10: 'Non imputantur filiis peccata parentum, que post eorum nativitatem a parentibus committuntur; nec pro peccatis parentum spirituali pena filii sunt plectendi'.

[37]3 Comp. 1.6.5 (= X 1.6.20): '... culpa parentum non est filiis imputanda ... Hi etiam scripture divine videntur inniti, qua dicitur: "Filius non portabit iniquitatem patris, et pater non portabit iniquitatem filii" (Ezekiel 18:20), per quam antiquum videtur proverbium removeri, quod inter filios Israel dici solebat: "Patres comederunt uvam acerbam, et dentes filiorum obstupescunt." ... inter illegitime genitos quidam asserunt eos solos a sacris officiis prohibendos, qui paternam incontinentiam imitantur. Et hi quoque videntur auctoritate divine legis inniti, qua dicitur: "Ego sum Deus zelotes visitans peccata patrum in filios usque in tertiam et quartam progeniem in iis, qui oderunt me" (Exodus 20:5), quasi dicat, in his, qui circa me paternum odium imitantur'.

[38]See p. 272 above on C.1 q.4 d.p.c. 11, and Piergiovanni, *La punibilità*, 1:37; 45-8.

[39]3 Comp. 1.8.4 (= X 1.9.10) §6.

[40]4 Comp. 5.13.2 (Conc. Later. IV c.45): '... ne minus vindicte quam excessus memoria prerogetur.'

[41]Joannes on 4 Comp. 5.13.2, v.*dispensatum*: 'cum non determinetur a quo possit dispensari, dico quod ab episcopo potest ex quo papa sibi non reservat ...' (Vat. lat. 1377, f. 315ra).

would accord with St Augustine's gloss on Exodus 20:5, made famous by its inclusion in the *Decretum*. It had claimed that God visiting the sins of fathers on their descendants was a sign of divine mercy not severity, for it meant that God postponed punishment in hope of repentance until the sin of the first generation was repeated in the third and fourth.[42] Furthermore, dispensation made the penalty less controversial since the earliest commentators on the canon did not object to it. However, they all agreed that it should be restricted to those heirs in the direct line of descent, and Joannes Teutonicus (*c.* 1217) further qualified that it only applied to those born after their parents' wrongdoing and not before. As Damasus (*c.* 1220) concluded: 'by means of interpretation penalties are to be mitigated rather than extended.'[43]

By contrast, the rigours of the interdict for the guiltless were mitigated under Innocent III less by canonistic interpretation than by his own rulings.[44] As with his tacit modification of the disinheritance provision in 'Vergentis', these legal innovations were occasioned by practical difficulties encountered in applying the penalty. An illustrative case is the interdict which Innocent pronounced on the kingdom of Lèon in 1198. It was brought about by the refusal of the king of Lèon to break off his betrothal to the king of Castile's daughter, his own niece. Such marriage alliances were common in the late twelfth-century Spains,[45] but, on this occasion, Innocent was determined to enforce the canon law forbidding matrimony between such close relatives. A delegation of Spanish prelates came to the curia to beg a dispensation for the marriage and when the pope refused, they sought instead the lifting of the interdict which they said posed a threefold danger to the kingdom, as the decretal which Innocent subsequently addressed to

---

[42]C. 1 q.4 d.p.c.9: 'In tertia et quarta generatione peccata patrum se Dominus comminatur in lege filiis redditurum, non inequalitate iudicii, ut alii peccent et alii puniantur, sed magnitudine clementie dum semper expectat penitentiam et quod in prima generatione delinquitur non prius corripit et emendat, nisi tertia et quarta generatione evenerit.'

[43]Vincentius Hispanus (*c.* 1217) on Conc. Later. IV c.45, v. *usque ad quartam generationem*: 'Sed non potest intelligi de latere, sed de linea descendenti . . .' (*Constitutiones Concilii quarti Lateranensis una cum Commentariis glossatorum*, ed. A. García y García (Vatican City, 1981), 351). To which point Damasus adds on this canon, v. posteritas talium: 'quia pene per interpretation emoliende sunt, non extendende, ut de pen. di. i §Pene (de pen. D.1 c.18). Item non est hec constitutio extendenda ad alias personas quam exprimat . . .' (*Constitutiones*, ed. García y García, 443). This way of thinking naturally also underlay Tancred's gloss that tried to restrict the penalty clause of 'Vergentis'. Johannes Teutonicus on 4 Comp. 5.13.2 (= Conc. Later. IV c.45), v. *posteritas*: 'per hoc patet quod tantum de descendentibus loquitur, non de collateralibus, et etiam de illis qui postea nascuntur, non de iam natis' (Vat. lat. 1377, f. 315ra). This view accords with St Augustine's teaching that sons are not to suffer for the sins that their parents committed 'post eorum nativitatem' (C.1 q.4 c.10; see p. 277 above and n. 34). It also corresponds with the idea of original sin transmitted by Adam to his descendants.

[44]On interdicts in general in the thirteenth century, see my dissertation, cited above, n. 27.

[45]P. Linehan, *The Spanish Church and the Papacy in the Thirteenth Century* (Cambridge, 1971), 13.

them recounts.[46] Firstly, they claimed that heresy was thriving there because the interdict deprived the faithful of pastoral guidance and made the king disinclined to persecute heretics. Secondly, when the church of Lèon no longer preached holy war and granted remission of sins to its participants, the populace was discouraged from fighting the Moors since they feared falling further into sin than they were already, under the interdict. This was perhaps a sign that the populace felt partly to blame for the penalty perhaps since they supported the king in his marriage. Finally, because the clergy observed the ban on church services and withdrew spiritual things, the laity were witholding temporal things from clergy, namely tithes, first fruits and offerings, and so the destitute clergy allegedly had to beg and do labour services for the Jews presumably in return for loans. The pope responded not by lifting the interdict but with a threefold justification of its continued observance, claiming that it had been well-intentioned, imposed according to due canonical process and modelled on human and divine example. His predecessor had laid an earlier interdict on Lèon which was lifted only after the king had complied with papal orders, and it would set a dangerous precedent if he were to drop this requirement in the present case. Also, he noted that when King David sinned in the counting of the people of Israel, God's anger fell on the people, whereupon David confessed his sin saying: 'It is I who have sinned; the wrong is mine. Those sheep, what have they done? O Lord, let not your wrath fall on your people, I beg' (2 Samuel 24:17, 1 Chronicles 21:17). The interdict was thus intended to compel the king of Lèon to repent likewise, his conscience pricked by the suffering of his innocent subjects. However, the claims that it was having unintended effects on popular devotion and even rendering a Christian kingdom vulnerable to infidel attack prompted Innocent to mitigate its severity for the innocent. He permitted resumption of divine offices and burial of clergy without solemnity. At the same time, he intensified the punishment of the guilty, declaring that the king, his intended and their supporters were excommunicate and that divine offices were to cease at any town where they arrived. Innocent was not thereby conceding that it was wrong to punish the innocent, but by reducing their suffering he was seeking to minimize the negative effects of the interdict. This was a reform designed to make it a more effective means of coercion.

The author of the *Gesta Innocencii III* thought this account of sufficient historical importance to copy it into his chronicle of Innocent's achievements, and he added that the king of Lèon eventually came to terms;[47] but whether the king did so because the interdict had been mitigated is open to question. On the other hand, the editor of *Compilatio Tertia* considered the account juridically irrelevant and the reform of the interdict peculiar to the Lèon case, excluding them from his

---

[46]For a modern critical edition of the full text see Reg. 2:72.
[47]Vat. lat. 12111, f.16r (see also edition in PL 214:cv-cvi).

version of the decretal, hence they were not made known to nor glossed by subsequent jurists.[48] Nevertheless, Innocent III mitigated the interdict in other decretals and Lateran canons which did enter the body of canon law. For example, a decretal of 1209 permitted, at the request of its bishop, confirmation and preaching during an interdict on Ferrara. This ruling was subsequently included in *Compilatio Tertia* and the *Liber Extra* and hence could be extended to similar cases. It expressly encouraged preaching so as to induce those who occasioned the interdict to repent.[49] There is also evidence that preaching was allowed for propaganda purposes during the papal interdict on England (1208-1214): to persuade the populace to take the church's side against King John.[50] In addition, the church valued preaching as a means to maintain pastoral contact with the faithful and guide them away from heresy. In 1210, Innocent had been so concerned that the withdrawal of religious ministrations in Bergamo was promoting the growth of heresy there that he lifted the interdict on the city without requiring the legal precondition of full compliance with papal mandates.[51] He was clearly determined to retain interdicts as expedient means of intervening in secular affairs, but he was also sufficiently pragmatic to reform or even revoke them when they conflicted with his pastoral aims.

---

[48]3 Comp. 4.15.1 (= X 4.20.5). Peter of Benevento, editor of *Compilatio Tertia*, only retained the last part of the decretal, which required the restitution of dowries on the dissolution of illicit marriages. By contrast, this part was quickly passed over in the *Gesta*, a fact which may cast doubt on Professor J. M. Powell's recent identification of Peter as the author of the *Gesta*. On the other hand, it may simply indicate that Peter treated the same text in one way as a jurist and in another as a historian.

[49]3 Comp. 5.21.16 (= X 5.39.43): ' . . . cum Ferrarienses cives excommunicationis et interdicti sententiis sint ligati, liceat tibi [bishop] viros et mulieres semel in hebdomada vel in mense apud aliquam ecclesiam convocare, quibus predices verbum Dei, et eosdem ad correctionem inducas'.

[50]*Thesaurus novus anecdotorum*, eds E. Martène and U. Durand, 5 vols (Paris, 1717), 1:812-13: 'Item convocent capellani parrochianos suos singulis diebus Dominicis et precipuis festivitatibus ad crucem aliquam in villa, vel in cimiterio, et predicent eis cum omni dilgentia patientiam et obedientiam, quia Christus factus est obediens Patri &c. Et doceant plus esse obediendum Deo, quam homini. Nolite timere eos qui potestatem occidendi corpus &c. Facta autem predicatione, dicant sacerdotes preces devotissime pro pace Ecclesie, & pro domino rege, et Dominus Jesus Christus dirigat pedes eius in viam salutis, et det ei spiritum consilii ut que agenda sunt secundum Deum videat et ad implenda que viderit convalescat.' These words come from a document, the *Forma interdicti*, discovered by its editors in a Mont St Michel manuscript and which Cheney convincingly suggests 'may have emanated from one or all of the bishop-executors [of this interdict]' ('King John and the Papal Interdict', *Bulletin of the John Rylands Library* 31 [1948], 298). It expresses the fear of these English prelates that the king's power of physical coercion (*occidendi corpus*) would sway his subjects more than the church's spiritual coercion, i.e. the interdict.

[51]PL 216:230.

CONCLUSION

This tension between politics and pastoral care characterized Innocent's whole policy on the question of punishing the guiltless. Where political difficulties in France were frustrating the pastoral aim of 'Vergentis', which was to drive heretics back into unity with the church, Innocent tacitly altered its disinheritance provision. He moderated the interdict where its use as a political weapon created pastoral problems as we have just seen. In Innocent's view, such extreme measures were excused by extreme necessity. The Fourth Lateran Council was to rule that spiritual sanctions should only be imposed after prior warning had failed to move the guilty and when justified by a manifest and reasonable cause. Tillmann is even of the opinion that Innocent was limiting his own use of interdicts in the later years of his pontificate.[52] Nevertheless, Innocent's adoption of a number of penalties falling on the innocent had set a precedent for the subsequent development of canonical penal law, and his own attempts and those of canonists to limit and moderate their application were not wholly successful. Five years after the Lateran ruling on spiritual sanctions, Honorius III had to warn the German episcopacy not to place lands of Frederick II under interdict 'pro levi causa', and in 1237 Gregory IX advised similar caution to French prelates, for Louis IX had complained that some of them were resorting to interdicts on his lands prematurely.[53] The interdict, which the Fourth Lateran Council had hesitated to make a penalty for unauthorized taxation of clergy, was controversially made so by Boniface VIII in his bull 'Clericis Laicos'. In Boniface's *Liber Sextus*, he decreed that anyone who maltreated a cardinal thereby brought disinheritance and exclusion from ecclesiastical and secular office on his heirs, for 'they may be damned in whatever way along with him'.[54] Such language and the measures which it defended arguably came into regular papal usage under Innocent III. In developing them, he sometimes went against traditional legal doctrine, as canonists of his day observed, notably Tancred, and he even contradicted himself on occasion, as with his inconsistent approach to punishing the innocent in the context of heresy. Nevertheless, his innovation responded to the growing challenges facing the church from the emerging secular polities and from heresy, and as resistance deepened to the hierocratic and interventionist claims of the papacy during the thirteenth century, popes resorted to these harsh sanctions touching the innocent ever more frequently. It might be argued that their use aggravated rather than eased the papacy's increasingly embattled situation. Nonetheless, they helped reinforce the view of Christian society as one

---

[52]Conc. Later. IV c.47 (4 Comp. 5.15.5 [= X.5.39.48]); Tillmann, *Innocent*, p. 248.

[53]*Regesta Honorii III*, ed. P. Pressuti (Rome, 1888-91), no. 2637; *Les Registres de Grégoire IX*, eds. L. Auvray et al. (École Française de Rome, 1890-1955), no. 390.

[54]VI 3.23.3 ('Clericis laicos');VI 5.9.5.

corporate unity, expressed by Innocent III himself in his 1198 decretal 'Cum omnes', one unity in which children might be held accountable for the sins of their parents and subjects bear some degree of responsibility for the faults of their rulers.[55]

---

[55] 3 Comp. 1.1.1: 'Cum omnes unum corpus simus in Christo . . . qui in una ecclesia uni Domino famulantur.'

Per venerabilem: From Practical Necessity to Judicial Supremacy

Deirdre Courtney-Batson

In 1202, Count William of Montpellier presented Innocent III with an unusual though not unprecedented request. He asked the pope to dispense his illegitimate children, not so that they could enter orders, but so that they could inherit his property. Innocent had previously granted a similar request from the king of France Philip Augustus. In William's case, however, he refused to act. The decretal in which he set out the reasons for this refusal, *Per venerabilem*, has been a source of controversy ever since.[1]

The situation which initiated centuries of debate was prosaic enough. William of Montpellier, dissatisfied with his wife Eudoxa, had taken a mistress, a normal occurrence in this period. In a reaction only slightly less common, the good count

---

[1] The bull was a complex and probably deliberately ambiguous piece of work, and historians have long been fascinated by it. Some have focused on the bull's importance for the developing law concerning legitimization. R. Genestal, *Histoire de la legitimation des enfants naturels en droit canonique* (Paris, 1905), 181-227; M. Boulet-Sautel, 'Encore la Bulle *Per Venerabilem*', *Studia Gratiana* 13 (1967):371-82. The broader political implications of Innocent's claim to a role in secular legitimation formed the basis for yet another important historical debate. Walter Ullmann, *Medieval Papalism* (London, 1949), 105-6; Sergio Mochi Onory, *Fonti canonistiche dell idea moderna dello stato* (Milan, 1951), 209-14; James Watt, *The Theory of Papal Monarchy in the Thirteenth Century* (New York, 1965), 37-9, 61-2, 110-17; Kenneth Pennington, 'Pope Innocent III's Views on Church and State: A Gloss to *Per venerabilem*' in *Law, Church and Society*, eds Kenneth Pennington, Robert Somerville (Philadelphia, 1977), 49-67. Finally, Innocent's dramatic but ambiguous claim to supreme appellate jurisdiction, made in the last part of the decretal, has found itself open to a number of different interpretations. For a full discussion of this argument see Brian Tierney, '"Tria Quippe distinguit iudicia . . . " A Note on Innocent III's Decretal *Per Venerabilem*', *Speculum* 37 (1962): 48-59.

found later that he far preferred the eight offspring of this illicit union to the singular fruit of his legitimate marriage. Only at this point did William depart from the accepted norm.[2] For rather than petitioning his secular superior for the legitimization of his later children, as was customary, he asked the bishop of Arles to present his case to the papal curia, citing as precedent Innocent's earlier action in the similar case of Philip Augustus. Though Innocent normally welcomed such voluntary appeals on the part of secular rulers, one suspects that the arrival of this particular petition caused little joy at the curia. With the Albigensian heresy on the rise in southern France, Innocent had reason to cultivate orthodox, though sinful, rulers like William.[3] Nevertheless a number of political considerations would seem to have made the denial of William's request a practical necessity.

One of these considerations involved Marie, William's daughter by Eudoxa and his only legitimate child. The logical heiress to Montpellier, she would lose her claim immediately upon the legitimization of six younger half-brothers.[4] That Marie, through her wronged mother, was a cousin of the current Byzantine emperor, Alexius III, may well have given Innocent reason to pause before effectively disinheriting her.

William's ambiguous feudal status added to the complications. In theory, Montpellier fell under the suzerainty of the French king, a relationship dating back to the Carolingians. But social and cultural factors, together with the weakness of the French monarchy, had long encouraged the counts of Montpellier to link their political interests to those of the Spanish kingdoms to the south.[5] By the twelfth century Montpellier, like a number of her neighbors, had attained a *de facto* if not *de jure* independence from the French crown.[6] During the twelfth century the French kings do not seem to have attempted to interfere in the affairs of Montpellier, nor did the counts ever invite such interference. At the same time, the ties between Southern France and the Spanish kingdoms, ties of blood, loyalty and commerce, had continued to grow in strength and complexity. In the case of

---

[2]Jean Baumel, *Histoire d'une Seigneurie du Midi de la France*, 1 (Montpellier, 1969):189-90.

[3]Baumel, 1:193-4.

[4]Marie had at one point renounced her rights to Montpellier, but, as events were to prove, this was of little importance in the absence of another legitimate heir. On her renunciation, see Baumel, 1:190.

[5]For example, William VII of Montpellier is found among the vassals of Alfonso VII of Castile in the mid-twelfth century; similarly, Alfonso II of Aragon maintained close relations with Montpellier. See Joseph F. O'Callaghan, *A History of Medieval Spain* (Ithaca, 1975), 223, 231, 236, 241.

[6]For a discussion of early developments in Southern France, see Archibald Lewis, *The Development of Southern French and Catalan Society, 718-1050* (Austin, 1965). A briefer discussion can be found in René Nelli, *Histoire du Languedoc* (Paris, 1974), 41-6.

Montpellier, pre-eminently a commercial city, these ties were of particular importance.[7]

It is within this political context that we must view both William's unusual request and Innocent's cautious approach to the feudal issue raised in *Per venerabilem.* William's options were severely limited. To declare his own children legitimate was at best a dubious proceeding, at worst a useless one.[8] On the other hand, it is difficult to see how William could have appealed to any other secular authority. In particular, an appeal to the king of France might revive a moribund but still potentially dangerous relationship and invite future French interference in Montpellier's affairs. Moreover, an admission of vassalage to the crown of France would have considerably hampered William's diplomatic relations with Aragon. The appeal to Innocent was thus by far William's most attractive alternative.

William apparently empowered the archbishop of Arles to offer Innocent a tempting incentive. In *Per venerabilem,* Innocent mentions the archbishop's claim that the count, unlike Philip of France, was subject to the pope in both spiritual and temporal matters, because of William's feudal relationship with the bishop of Maguelone.[9] While under other circumstances, this line of reasoning may well have appealed to Innocent, the pope apparently realized that this case offered the advantages to William and the disadvantages to the papacy. By strengthening William's claim to independence from other secular lords, Innocent would have risked unnecessarily offending Philip. He therefore made note of William's assertion but declined to comment on it, a course in which he was followed by the canonists. At the same time, Innocent deftly avoided taking a stand on the issue of William's feudal relationship with other secular rulers. He did not, as has often been asserted, declare that William was subject to the French king. Rather, he merely stated that William was subject to others. Innocent's use of the vague and

---

[7]In the early thirteenth century, the merchants of Montpellier were as aware of the importance of these ties as the count himself was. After William's death, the commune encouraged and arranged Marie's marriage to Pedro II of Aragon in 1204, apparently feeling that such a match would offer the city increased commercial opportunities. See Baumel, 1:233; H. J. Chaytor, *A History of Aragon and Catalonia* (1933; repr. New York, 1978), 68-9.

[8]This was not, however, as absurd as it sounds. In effect, this is precisely what William did after his petition to Innocent failed. In his will (1202), he declared that his eldest son should succeed him as Count William IX (interestingly enough, he placed his son under the care of God, the Holy See, the king of Aragon and the count of Toulouse). The young count's rule was brief. In 1204, he and his unpopular mother were driven from the city, and Marie and her new husband were installed as the new rulers of Montpellier. Had Agnes been better liked, her son's reputed illegitimacy might not have posed an insurmountable problem. As matters stood, however, the circumstances of his birth gave the Montpellierans the excuse they needed to free themselves from her influence. See Baumel, 1: 228-36.

[9]For a discussion of this feudal relationship, see Baumel, 1:80-1; C. DeVic and J. Vaissette, *Histoire Générale de Languedoc*, ed. Privat, 3 (Toulouse, 1872):457-9.

anonymous plural allowed him to make his legal point while maintaining his neutrality in a potentially explosive situation.

Political considerations, then, provide some explanation for the complexities of *Per venerabilem*. Its ambiguity was necessitated in part by Innocent's desire to produce a bull which could be accepted in all of the various courts touched by William's petition. Yet although the political background gives us a clue as to why *Per venerabilem* is so complex, in the end it tells us neither exactly what powers Innocent did claim for himself in the decretal, nor how revolutionary his claims were. The answer to these questions can best be found in a study of the decretal itself and of its earliest commentaries.

Although any number of subdivisions are possible, *Per venerabilem* can most easily be divided into two distinct sections. The first covers the issue immediately raised by William's petition, the question of the pope's proper role in the secular aspects of legitimization. Can the pope ever legitimize in the temporal sphere? If so, has he the power to grant William's petition? Is William even worthy of such a favor? The second section, on the other hand, is far broader in its scope and in its implications. It is here that Innocent makes his famous claim that the pope, as 'vicar of Him who is a priest forever after the order of Melchisedech', exercises a special judicial role in the temporal as well as in the spiritual sphere. The relationship between the two sections is not immediately obvious. Yet it is within the context of the discussion of papal legitimization that Innocent made his later broad and sweeping claims and it is with this context in mind that the canonists commented upon them. So we turn first to the practical problem of legitimization.

Using language almost identical to that found in his earlier decretal legitimizing the children of Philip Augustus, Innocent began *Per venerabilem* with a defense of the general principle that the pope could, in fact, legitimize in the temporal sphere, pointing out that popes in the past had legitimized even natural sons born of adultery so that they could become bishops, and then going on to say:[10]

> From this it is believed to be more true and reputed to be more probable that the Apostolic See is able to legitimize them for secular acts, especially if they do not acknowledge among men another superior who has the power of legitimizing, except the Roman Pontiffs; because, since greater prudence,

---

[10] X 4.17.13: 'Quod autem super hoc apostolica sedes plenam habeat potestatem, ex illo videtur, quod diversis causis inspectis, cum quibusdam minus legitime genitis, non naturalibus tantum, sed adulterinis etiam dispensavit sic ad actus spirituales illos legitimans ut possint in episcopos promoveri. Ex quo verisimilius creditur et probabilius reputatur, ut eos ad actus legitimare valeat saeculares, praesertim si praeter Romanos Pontifices inter homines superiorem alium non cognoscant, qui legitimandi habeat potestatem; quia, quum maior in spiritualibus tam providentia quam auctoritas et idoneitas requiratur, quod in maiori conceditur licitum esse videtur et in minori'.

authority and suitability are required in spiritual matters, that which is allowed in greater matters would seem to be permitted in lesser ones.

Innocent then added two illustrative analogies which served to illustrate the point that a change in status in the spiritual sphere could, in certain instances, have an effect on one's status in the secular sphere: a man elevated to a bishopric would as a result be exempted from his father's power; likewise a serf ordained to the priesthood would be given his freedom. His choice of examples may have been legally flawed, as Dr Pennington has suggested, but his point was reasonably clear.[11] Innocent then went on to emphasize his point that a man who was worthy of ecclesiastical office should also be worthy of lesser secular honors. 'It would seem monstrous', said Innocent, 'that someone who was made legitimate for spiritual functions should remain illegitimate in respect to secular functions. Whence when someone is dispensed in spiritual matters, he is as a consequence understood to be dispensed in temporal matters'.[12]

Innocent's claim was based on the effects of legitimization, rather than on the nature and dignity of the pontifical office and as such was rather narrow in scope. Nevertheless, it was still fundamentally new and marked a significant incursion into an area previously reserved to the secular power. Both canonists and civilians had long agreed that legitimization for temporal affairs fell within the sphere of the secular authority. Thus, the early decretalists viewed Innocent's innovation with almost universal suspicion. Some rejected it outright. Abbas Antiquus simply declared that, 'the pope does not legitimize in temporals those who are subject to another's jurisdiction'.[13] William Naso agreed, contending that the pope was only free to legitimize within his own jurisdiction.[14] Few, if any, of the other thirteenth-century canonists were willing to say with Alanus that, 'the

---

[11]Pennington, 'Pope Innocent III's Views', 54-5.

[12]X 4.17.13: 'Per simili quoque id videtur posse probari, quum eo ipso, quod aliquis ad apicem episcopalis dignitatis attollitur, eximitur a patriae potestate. Praeterea etiamsi simplex episcopus scienter servum alterius in presbyterum ordinaret, licet ordinator satisfacere domino iuxta formam canonicam teneretur, ordinatus tamen iugum evaderet servitutis. Videretur siquidem monstruosum, ut, qui legitimus ad spirituales fieret actiones, circa saeculares actus illegitimus, remaneret. Unde, quum in spiritualibus dispensetur, consequenter intelligitur in temporalibus dispensatum'.

[13]Abbas Antiquus, *Lectura* (Strasburg, 1511), fol. 193r, X 4.17.13. 'Casus. Papa non legitimat in temporalibus aliene iurisdictioni subiectos'.

[14]X 4.17.13, Oxford, Bodl. MS. lat. th. 6.4 fol. 164v. 'sed certe Jo[annes] non sic dixit indistincte prout hic eum dicunt dixesse, et de hec bene notatur per ipsum x di. Quam idem [D.10 c.8]. Nam dixit quod istud quod hic dicitur factum fuit ad petitionem regis. Sed magister B[ertrandus] stat huic littere dicens quod ex quo legittimus est in spiritualibus et in temporalibus et hoc ex littera ubi dicit monstrum uideretur et magister R[aymundus] idem in summa narrat. Magister G[uillemus] Nas[cus] dicit contrarium quia quamquam animas saluare possimus etc. ii. q. vii. hinc autem [C.2 q.7] Nisi sit de sua iurisdictione supra de re. iudi. Cum te a bartholomaeo [X 2.27.23].'

pope has the power to legitimize in respect to secular acts because he is above the prince'.[15] For the most part, the canonists who wrote between Alanus and Hostiensis took a middle road, seeking to explain this new papal prerogative in ways which, unlike Alanus' theory, would preserve both the theoretical and actual independence of the secular authority. The majority sought to severely limit the practical application of papal legitimization in the temporal sphere.

Three major themes can be discerned in the decretalist discussions of papal legitimization in the secular sphere. The first, and broadest, concentrated on Innocent's notion of the consequential nature of papal secular legitimization. Another, based on Innocent's statement about the greater worthiness required by the priesthood, made a distinction between rights of inheritance and other secular honors. Finally, some canonists felt that such papal legitimization could only take place at the behest of the prince.

Johannes Teutonicus is the canonist most closely associated with the idea that the pope's right to legitimize in the temporal sphere was a mere consequence of his right to legitimize in the spiritual sphere, although Laurentius had earlier produced a version of the basic idea, explaining the pope's consequential jurisdiction by noting that, 'At times jurisdiction may be broadened by the nature of the action being considered'.[16] He clarified this somewhat vague statement by citing a Roman law which dealt with judges whose jurisdiction only extended to claims involving limited amounts of money: when someone brought several claims at once, the total amount of which exceeded these limits, the judge could still hear the case, if each claim taken individually would have fallen within his jurisdiction. The application of this rule to Innocent's theory of consequential jurisdiction was faulty at best. The legitimization issue involved two different types of jurisdiction, temporal and spiritual; only one type of jurisdiction was envisioned in the law cited. Vincentius thought it necessary to point out and condemn explicitly the possible implications of Laurentius' loosely focused argument. 'The pope himself', he wrote, 'acknowledges that this (jurisdiction)

---

[15] 3 Comp. 4.12.2 (X 4.17.13) s.v. *saeculares*. 'Hoc ad litteram concedo, quod qui legitimatus est ad omnes sacros ordines recipiendum eo ipso quo ad actus saeculares legitimatus intelligitur, quia secundum nos Papa super principem est etiam in temporalibus et ideo habet potestatem legitimandi quoad actus saeculares', in Alfonso M. Stickler, 'Sacerdozio e Regno nelle nuove recherche attorno ai secolo XII e XIII nei decretisti e decretalisti', *Miscellanea Historiae Pontificiae* 18 (1954):23.

[16] 3 Comp. 4.12.2 (X 4.17.13) s.v. *non noceret* Paris BN lat. 15398 fol. 182v. 'Quandoque enim ex natura accionis ampliatur iurisdictio cognoscentis ff. de iur. o. Si idem [Dig. 2.1.11]'.

is another's'.[17] It was thus left to Johannes to develop a coherent, and therefore limited, defense of consequential jurisdiction.

Johannes admitted that the pope did not, as part of his office, have the power to legitimize in temporals directly. Nevertheless, he argued that Innocent could legitimize in temporals 'through a certain consequence, but not directly'. Johannes pointed out that, in law, often what is not permitted in and of itself, is permitted as a consequence of other circumstances.[18] Two legal citations served to illustrate his point; both involved cases in which a person, because of a unique set of circumstances, was allowed to do something normally forbidden to him. One, from the canon law, noted that the testimony of a slave should be believed when no other way of discovering the truth was available, even though the slave's dependent position would normally bar him from testifying.[19] A text from the civil law described a similar situation. Normally, a legal guardian could not take any action on behalf of his ward, which, in fact, affected the guardian's own affairs. Nevertheless, he could encourage his ward to accept an estate over which he held a lien. Such an action would indeed affect the guardian's affairs, since his ward would then become his debtor. This, however, was permitted because it was merely a consequential effect of the guardian's normal duties.[20]

In both cases, the effect of the special circumstances described was limited to the situations in which those effects occurred and it seems likely that Johannes felt that the pope's power to legitimize in the temporal sphere was similarly limited in its implications. Johannes allowed this one papal incursion into the secular sphere because he felt, with Innocent, that the circumstances, i.e. the need to preserve the dignity of the priesthood, demanded it. Nevertheless, his citations make it clear that he did not intend this opinion to serve as a precedent for more extensive papal involvement in secular matters.[21]

---

[17]3 Comp. 4.12.2 (X 4.17.13) sv. *archiepiscopum* Paris BN lat. 14611 fol. 122 r. 'Quandoque enim sit aliquo mediante quod aliter non fieret et natura accionis ampliat iurisditionem eius qui habet cognoscere de certa summa tamen ar. ff. de iurisditione o. iu. Si idem [Dig. 2.1.11]. Immo et ipse papa fatetur alienam esse supra de iud. Nouit 1. eodem [3 Comp. 2.1.3; X 2.1.13]. Vincentius'.

[18]Johannes Teutonicus, *Apparatus ad Compilatio Tertio*, ed. Kenneth Pennington, Diss. Cornell 1972, 2:628-629, 3 Comp. 4.12.2 (X 4.17.13) s.v. *potestatem*. 'Ad hoc dic quod papa non habet potestatem legitimandi in temporalibus, set tamen eo ipso quod quis est legitimatus in spiritualibus, intelligitur legitimatus in temporalibus, unde per quandam consequentiam legitimat set non directe. Sepe enim permittitur per consequentiam quod per se non permittitur, ut iiii q. iii Serui (C.4 q.3 c.3) ff. de auctor. tut.1.i (Dig. 26.8.1). jo.'

[19]C.4 q.3 c.3.

[20]Dig. 26.8.1.

[21]For a different interpretation of Johannes' gloss, see Kenneth Pennington, 'A Study of Johannes Teutonicus' Theories of Church Government and of the Relationship between Church and State', Diss. Cornell University 1972, 1:266-71.

Johannes' gloss was widely quoted, although among the canonists who wrote before Hostiensis, only Goffredus Tranensis and Raymond of Pennafort fully accepted Johannes' view without further reservation. Other canonists made use of Johannes' work, but only as a first step on the way to a more narrowly defined understanding of papal legitimization. For the most part, they did not see Johannes' idea as being incompatible with their own; rather they simply did not feel that it went far enough in limiting papal power.

The second, and perhaps the most intriguing, interpretation of Innocent III's stand on secular legitimization seems to have originated with Vincentius Hispanus. Vincentius accepted Innocent's arguments about the superior dignity required by the priesthood, but remained dubious about the immediate implications of Innocent's fundamentally new claim. His solution to the dilemma was ingenious, though unsupported by Innocent's text. Vincentius simply denied that *Per venerabilem* applied to the most important aspect of secular legitimization. Vincentius held that the effects of papal legitimization in the temporal sphere extended only to certain secular acts or *honores,* but not to the inheritance of parental goods and estates.[22] Thus, the pope might effect change in the temporal sphere by legitimizing someone so that he could serve as a judge or as a witness, secular activities from which both the canon and civil law banned the illegitimate. A papal dispensation would not, however, give an illegitimate child the right to succeed to his parent's inheritance.

By stressing the functional aspect of papal legitimization in the temporal sphere, Vincentius managed to preserve the notion that greater worthiness was required for priestly offices than for secular ones. At the same time, he treated the subject of inheritance as a purely material matter having nothing to do with a person's relative worthiness. Thus, the question of suitability and the consequent comparison to the priesthood could be seen as irrelevant to a discussion of parental inheritance. This was indeed an ideal solution for those who, while impressed by Innocent's contentions about the superior dignity of the priesthood, still objected to the creation of additional complications in that most explosive of secular concerns, the question of inheritance.

Vincentius' opinion was, of course, at variance with the original text of *Per venerabilem.* In the opening words of the decretal Innocent referred to William's desire to have his children legitimized so that they would be able to succeed him

---

[22]3 Comp. 4.12.2. (X 4.17.13) s.v. *in patrimonio*, Paris BN lat. 14611 fol. 122v. 'Maxime, ut infra eodem capitulo proximo. Immo contra quia non potest legitimare aliquem quo ad forum seculare ubi iurisditionem non habet temporalem, nisi princeps hoc ei comiserit vt infra eodem titulo uel nisi mediate ut in seruo ordinato. Vel melius erit legitimus quo ad actus seculares ut possit esse iudex testis et huius. Sed quod habeat hereditatem paternam non credo. Vincentius.' Vincentius also included this gloss in his later commentary on the Gregorian decretals, X 4.17.13 s.v. *in patrimonio*, Paris BN lat. 3967 fol. 169r.

and later acknowledged William's contention that his need was greater than the French king's since unlike Philip, William had no legitimate male heir to succeed him. Temporal succession, indeed, was the only specific aspect of secular legitimization mentioned by Innocent and there is nothing in the decretal to indicate that he wished to exclude such succession from the claims he made. Nevertheless, for a number of canonists political reality apparently seemed more important than adherence to the text. This interpretation therefore gained considerable support among the early decretalists.

Unlike Vincentius, Laurentius, in his gloss on the word *dispensatur*, explicitly acknowledged the fact that Innocent claimed the right to legitimize in regard to temporal succession.[23] He did, however, sympathize with the spirit of Vincentius' gloss. Laurentius was remarkably unimpressed with the idea that the ability to inherit worldly possessions could have anything to do with the dignity required by the priesthood. In glossing Innocent's statement that it would be monstrous for a man to be legitimate in regard to spiritual functions, but illegitimate in regard to secular ones, Laurentius commented wryly, 'But what kind of monstrosity it would be if one could be a priest and not have his parents' goods, I do not understand'.[24]

Tancred, so often described as a confirmed hierocrat, was perhaps the most surprising of Vincentius' allies in this matter. Believing that Laurentius and Vincentius had proposed different opinions on the question of succession, he juxtaposed their statements in one gloss and then stated unequivocally that, 'I prefer that which was said by Vincentius'.[25]

Vincentius' formulation merited mention, though not always agreement, in most subsequent commentaries on *Per venerabilem*. Johannes Teutonicus repeated verbatim Vincentius' entire gloss on the word *patrimonio*, as well as Laurentius' apparently contradictory gloss on *dispensatum*. He made no attempt to comment on or compare these two, and he clearly preferred his own idea that the pope could legitimate *per consequens* in the temporal sphere. Nevertheless, his uncritical presentation of Vincentius' idea increased its circulation. Likewise, Raymond of Pennafort, while adhering to Johannes' position, pointed out that, 'nearly all the doctors say that he [someone legitimized by the pope] will not be

---

[23] 3 Comp. 4.12.2 (X 4.17.13) s.v. *dispensatur*, Paris BN lat.15398 fol. 182v. 'Eadem ratione si dispensatur in benefitio et in successione.'

[24] 3 Comp. 4.12.2 (X 4.17.13) s.v. *montruosum*, Paris BN lat. 15398 fol.182v. 'Sed cuiusmodi monstrum esset si posset esse presbyter et non haberet bona parentis non uideo'.

[25] 3 Comp. 4.12.2 (X 4.17.13) s.v. *in temporalibus dispensatum*, Cambridge, Gonville and Caius College MS 28/17 p. 291. 'Eadem ratione cum quo dispensatur in beneficio in succescione intelligatur dispensatum. Laurentius. Vel melius erit legitimus quo ad actus seculares, ut possit esse iudex et testis et huius. Sed quod habeat paternam hereditatem non credo. Vincentius. Ego prefero dictum uincencii'.

legitimate in regard to succession, although he will be legitimate in regard to other legitimate acts'.[26]   Goffredus Tranensis, who also preferred Johannes Teutonicus' solution, discussed, but rejected, Vincentius' idea:[27]

> The decretal says . . . that one legitimized by the pope seems to be legiti-
> mized for all secular matters. Nevertheless, Tancred and Vincentius have
> said that he is legitimized so that he can give testimony; likewise so that he
> can be a judge and for similar matters; not, however, for succession. But
> why in those things and not in this I can find no reason.

In the *Glossa ordinaria* Bernardus Parmensis also cited Vincentius' idea in a critique of Johannes Teutonicus theory of consequential jurisdiction. Bernardus, assuming that Johannes had simply reaffirmed Innocent's own claims, had no apparent misgivings about openly contradicting either pope or fellow canonist in this matter:[28]

> Johannes adheres to the allegation which the lord pope puts forward here,
> but I believe the contrary, namely that the lord pope cannot legitimize
> someone who is not within his temporal jurisdiction so that he will succeed
> to an inheritance as a legitimate heir. Such would be to put a scythe in
> another's harvest and to usurp another's jurisdiction . . . and to deprive
> another of the right of succeeding; whence I believe that he [the pope] cannot
> legitimize except with respect to spiritual acts. Nevertheless, some would
> extend papal legitimization to secular offices, so that through it one would
> be understood to be legitimate so that he could be a judge and have whatever

---

[26]Raymundus de Pennafort, *Summa iuris*, ed. Jose Ruis Serra (Barcelona, 1945), part 2, tit. 22, p. 96. 'Dicunt tamen Laurentius, Vincentius et fere omnes doctores quod non erit legitimatus quoad successionem licet quod actus legitimos alios sit legitimus'.

[27]X 4.17.13 s.v. *dispensatum*, Vienna Cod. 2197 fol. 123 v. 'Satis liberaliter loquitur hec decretalis ut legitimatus a papa uideatur legitimatus ad omnia secularia. Tancredus tamen et vincentius dixerunt legitimatum fore quo ad testimonium ferendum. Item ut possit esse iudex et in similibus non tamen quo ad successionem. Set quare in illis et non in isto non inuenio rationem. Goffredus'.

[28]Bernardus Parmensis, *Glossa ordinaria* (Lyon, 1517), fol. 331v, X 4.17.13 s.v. *habeat potestatem*. 'Joannes adhesit allegationi quam ponit hic dominus papa, sed contrarium credo, scilicet quod dominus papa non possit legitimare aliquem quantum ad hoc vt succedat in hereditate tenquam legitimus heres qui non sit dico de sua iurisditione temporali. Sic enim esset mittere falcem in messem alienam et vsurpare alienam iurisditionem quod esse non debet, supra de iudi. Nouit [X 2.1.13] et vi. q.iii Scriptum est [C.6 q.13 c.1] et priuare aliquem iure succedendi. Vnde credo quod non possit legitimare nisi quo ad actus spirituales. Tamen quidem legitimationem extendunt ad honores seculares, vt per hoc intelligatur esse legitimatus vt possit esse iudex et habere huiusmodi honores temporales quos alias habere non posset. Et in hac sententia fuerunt. Laurentius, Vincentius et Tancredus'.

temporal offices he could not otherwise have. Laurentius, Vincentius and Tancred were of this opinion.

Bernardus here added a new element to the idea that the pope should not act *in preiudicium alterius* in cases of legitimization. While earlier canonists mentioned that papal legitimization in temporals might prejudice the rights of a secular ruler, they had failed to point out that where succession was concerned other rights were at stake as well. For, in creating a new legitimate heir the pope might as Bernardus said, 'deprive another of the right of succession'. Indeed, this is precisely what would have occurred in the case of Count William's daughter Marie.

This idea was, in fact, central to Bernardus' objection to papal legitimization in the temporal sphere, as later canonists realized. For example, Monaldus (who in the long run seems to have preferred Johannes' position) presented Bernardus' warning as the one possible reason for excluding the pope from legitimization for purposes of temporal succession.[29] The notion was particularly important as a recognition of the fact that theoretical discussions of the relationship between the spiritual and secular authorities could have a very real impact on ordinary men's lives.

Unlike Bernardus, Innocent IV seems to have accepted Vincentius' point of view, although he provided a more detailed justification for it. He first used it in discussing one obvious flaw in Johannes' idea of consequential jurisdiction. The pope was not the only person capable of legitimizing in spirituals; bishops could also legitimize, at least in most cases. Johannes simply denied that a simple bishop could legitimize in the temporal sphere, but he did not produce a logical distinction between the pope's power and a bishop's in this regard.[30] Innocent IV attempted to offer a logical solution, one which depended on a more limited vision of papal legitimization. In assessing the problem of whether Innocent III's reasoning would give mere bishops the power to legitimize in the temporal sphere, he concluded, more logically than Johannes Teutonicus, that it did, but

---

[29]Monaldus, *Summa*, tit. Qui filii sunt legittimi, London, Lambeth Palace MS 39 fol.111r. 'Item filii quos legittimat papa in spiritualibus per consequens uidetur quibusdam eo ipso in temporalibus legittimati que sunt spiritualibus minus digna. Nam qui potest quod maius est potest et quod minus. Aliis tamen uidetur quod quamuis papa legittimando quosdam in spiritualibus uideatur etiam in temporalibus logittimas se quo ad quedam puta ut possit esse iudex et alios similes habere corporales honores quos autem habere non posset. Non tamen secundum eos potest papa legitimare ut succedat in hereditate patris, quia hic esset priuare filium legittimum successione sua. Potest tamen hoc facere totum papa in terris sue iurisdictionis subiectis. De hiis habes extra, qui fi. sunt le. Per uenerabilem, ubi de hoc in glossa Bernardi, eo enim quod.'

[30]Johannes, *Apparatus*, 2, 629, 3 Comp.4.12.2 (X 4.17.13) s.v. *dispensatum*. 'Hoc intelligas in dispensatione pape. Set si episcopus dispensauit cum aliquo in spiritualibus, non tamen intelligitur dispensatum in successione. jo.'

argued, with Vincentius, that this legitimization only extended to certain secular offices, not to inheritance, 'because one cannot dispense in cases in which one cannot judge'.[31]

Innocent then developed this idea in a more general and detailed exposition of the effects of legitimization. He argued that the validity of any legitimization, whether ecclesiastical or civil, for a particular purpose, depended on its meeting at least one of two criteria: the purpose in question had to be one which did not prejudice the rights of another, and that purpose had to fall within the jurisdiction of the person granting the legitimization. Thus, either a bishop or a prince could legitimize someone so that he could testify or hold certain civil honors, because these purposes met the first criterion – they did not endanger another's rights. Neither a prince nor a bishop, however, could legitimize someone so that he could inherit intestate property in lands not temporally subject to the prince or bishop in question, since here, as Bernardus had pointed out, a legitimate heir's rights might be harmed. On the other hand, a bishop could legitimize someone so that he could be promoted to priestly orders even outside his own diocese, because such promotion would injure no one else's rights. Despite its non-prejudicial nature, however, such a dispensation could not be granted by a lay prince, since this was specifically excluded from his jurisdiction.[32]

Innocent IV, then, like Vincentius, Bernardus and Tancred, believed that the papacy should not, and could not, interfere in the aspects of legitimization related to the inheritance of property. As he had already said at the beginning of his commentary on *Per venerabilem*, 'temporals and spirituals are different and have different judges, nor can one judge involve himself in things which pertain to another'.[33]

---

[31]Innocent IV, *Commentaria* (Lyon, 1525) fol. 183v, X 4.17.13 s.v. *euaderet.* 'Sic et legitimatus per episcopum effugere debet obiectionem illegitime natiuitatis quo ad actus legitimos scilicet quod possit esse iudex et testis. In paterna autem hereditate vel aliis non intelligitur dispensatum, quia non potest dispensare sicut nec iudicare supra eodem. Lator [X 4.17.5] et c. Causam [X 4.17.7]'.

[32]Innocent IV, *Commentaria*, fol. 183v, X4.17.13 s.v. *euaderet.* 'Et nota quod legitimatus restitutus fame etc. cum quo dispensatum est in quocunque foro siue ecclesiastico siue civili et omnia ea facere poterit super quibus habuit potestatem qui legitimauit vel fame restituit vel dispensauit. Poterit enim in omni iudicio testimonium reddere, et ad ciuiles honores vocari nisi sint talia que sint in alterius preiudicium verbigratia. Nam legitimatus ab vno principe vel ciuitate vel primate non obtinebit ab intestato bona hereditaria in terra que non sit subdita legitimanti, quia sic auferuntur bona consanguineis defuncti vel fisco qui debet succedere ab intestate. Item legitimatus a iudice seculari non intelligitur ad ordines legitimatus quia promoueri ad ordines non est de iurisditione laici iudicis. Sed si unus episcopus legitimet aliquem etiam in alia diocesi poterit promoueri, quia dispensare in ordinibus cum illegitimo de iurisditione est cuiusque episcopi et quod illegitimus promoueatur in nullius preiudicium est.'

[33]Innocent IV, *Commentaria*, fol. 183v, X 4.17.13 s.v. *verisimilius.* 'Non tamen verum est nam temporalia et spiritualia diuersa sunt et diuersos iudices habent nec vnus iudex habet se intromittere de pertinentibus ad alium, licet se adinvicem inuare debeant xcvi distin. Cum ad (D.96 c.6) supra

For a few canonists, even the limitation on papal legitimization suggested by Vincentius was not sufficient. A third point of view was expressed by Laurentius Hispanus. Laurentius held that the pope could legitimize in the temporal sphere only when the ruling prince permitted him to.[34] Thus, Innocent was justified in acting in Philip's case, since Philip, as a prince with no temporal superior, had requested him to do so. The pope was not, however, free to grant William's request because William's secular superior (whoever that might be) had not given Innocent permission to legitimize the count's children.

This interpretation of *Per venerabilem* effectively nullified the implications of Innocent's new claim. It did not, however, gain wide acceptance among the canonists, most of whom seemed to favor one or both of the opinions already discussed. Johannes, Tancred and Vincentius each mention Laurentius' gloss on the subject; nevertheless, they clearly prefer their own interpretations. Still, Laurentius' suggestion did gain one important follower, Bernardus Parmensis. Glossing Innocent's early remark that he had the power to legitimize in temporals, particularly in cases in which he received a request from a prince who recognized no other worldly superior, Bernardus held that the pope could legitimize in temporals only under such circumstances.[35] Likewise, when faced with Johannes Galensis' comment that the pope could legitimize in temporals *maxime* (that is, to the greatest extent, but not exclusively) in the papal states, Bernardus replied, 'But you say "only" as I said above, because [the pope] cannot legitimize in the secular forum unless the prince permits him'.[36]

Unlike Vincentius' gloss, this last opinion was not without support from the decretal itself. Innocent indicated not once, but twice, in the decretal that Philip's temporal independence was a significant factor in his decision to grant the French king's petition. More importantly, he cited William's inferior political position as a major stumbling block to papal interference in favor of the count's children. Laurentius and Bernardus did not have to go far beyond *Per venerabilem* itself to find a justification for their limitation on the papal power of legitimization in the temporal sphere.

---

eodem Lator [X 4.17.5] supra de iudi. Nouit [X 2.1.13]'.

[34]3 Comp. 4.12.2 (X 4.17.13) s.v. *exequitur*, Paris BN lat. 15398 fol. 182v. 'Maxime dixit ioannes. Sed laurentius contra, quia eo teste non potest legitimate aliquem quo ad forum seculare vbi non habet temporalem iurisdictionem nisi princeps hoc ei commiserit, vt infra eodem capitulo, vel nisi ordine mediate, ut supra notatur in seruo ordinato.'

[35]Bernardus, *Glossa Ord.*, fol. 331v, X 4.17.13 s.v. *presertim*. 'Id est maxime secundum Ioannes. Secundum alios presertim, id est tantum.'

[36]Bernardus, *Glossa Ord.*, fol. 331v, X 4.17.13 s.v. *beati petri*. 'Dicebat Ioannes maxime. Sed tu dic tantum vt dixi supra, quia quo ad forum seculare non potest legitimare nisi princeps ei permitteret, in seruo scienter ordinatio secus est, sed ipse tenetur domino satisfacere, vt hic dicitur. Bernardus'.

It is also interesting to note in this regard that Laurentius' and Bernardus' descriptions of this papal prerogative reflect the way in which it was used by subsequent pontiffs. Honorius III, Innocent IV and Boniface VIII each exercised the power, but only, with minor exceptions, in cases in which the person involved recognized no other temporal superiors. The exceptions proverbially proved the rule. Innocent IV did legitimize Italian subjects of the emperor on several occasions. To do so, however, he did not rely on a general papal right to legitimize in the temporal sphere. Instead, Innocent argued that he could legitmize in these instances because, at the time, the empire was vacant.[37] *Per venerabilem* did not, it seems, set a precedent for any but a very limited papal involvement in legitimization, along the lines described by Laurentius and Bernardus.

As this summary of the canonical commentaries on *Per venerabilem* indicates, the decretalists took a cautious and moderate approach to the notion of papal legitimization in the secular sphere. They did not discuss the theoretical origins of worldly power, an issue over which they profoundly disagreed amongst themselves. It was the practical problem of preserving both justice and right order in the real world which concerned them. Distinctions between hierocrat and dualist are irrelevant here. Johannes, the moderate dualist, was joined in his opinion by Raymond, a noted hierocrat. Tancred, insulted by Vincentius for his hierocratic gloss on the two-swords theory, fully accepted Vincentius' dualistically distorted interpretation of *Per venerabilem*. Bernardus, who adopted Tancred's two-swords gloss, supported Laurentius' narrow restrictions on the pope's right to legitimize in regard to temporals. It would seem that the hierocrat-dualist dichotomy is of limited utility in understanding the decretalists' reactions to fundamental and practical judicial questions.

There was, however, a second part to *Per venerabilem*, in which Innocent made general claims to a far more extensive role in temporal affairs. The pope, he asserted, 'having examined certain cases may exercise temporal jurisdiction *casualiter*'. His argument centered around a section of Deuteronomy which described three types of cases and held that whenever anything difficult and ambiguous arose in such cases the matter was to be referred to the church. Innocent interpreted this section as describing all types of cases, both secular and ecclesiastical, and asserted that all doubtful matters were to be referred to the Apostolic See. He pointed out that he was the successor of Peter, who had been given the power of binding and loosing, in heaven and on earth. Indeed, he was the, 'vicar of Him who was a priest forever, after the order of Melchisedech,

---

[37]Genestal, 205-9.

appointed by God, judge of the living and of the dead'.[38] Finally, Innocent referred to the words of Paul, 'do you not know that you shall judge angels? How much more worldly matters?'[39]

Although some historians have tried to interpret this part of *Per venerabilem* in a dualistic sense, specifically by asserting that Innocent intended the words of Deuteronomy to apply only to mixed cases, Professor Tierney has shown conclusively that this was not the case.[40] Innocent clearly claimed some sort of universal appellate jurisdiction over both spiritual and temporal matters here. It remains to be seen whether the exercise of this jurisdiction was purely discretionary. Did the secular power remain independent only as long as the pope felt it expedient to allow it to?

The effect of Innocent's claims in the second part of the decretal is jarring; it is difficult to correlate such apparently hierocratic language with the relatively moderate tone of the discussion of legitimization. It is even more difficult to understand the decretalists' reaction, or rather lack of reaction, to this second section. The same canonists who were so careful to defend the independence of the temporal power when they glossed the first part of *Per venerabilem* found nothing to disturb them in Innocent's claim to universal appellate jurisdiction in both temporal and spiritual matters. A few canonists, apparently following Laurentius, hastened to point out that in these matters the pope's jurisdiction was appellate rather than ordinary.[41] This, however, would seem to be a fair interpretation of Innocent's own meaning. It is far more significant that in glossing Innocent's assertion that, 'having examined certain cases, we may exercise temporal jurisdiction casually', the early decretalists found no cause for complaint or concern. Laurentius, Vincentius, Tancred and Bernardus each agreed explicitly that the pope could exercise such jurisdiction in secular affairs whenever there was a disagreement among the judges involved, as they felt the

---

[38]X 4.17.13: 'Is vero super eos sacerdos sive iudex exsistit, cui Dominus inquit in Petro, 'Quodcumque ligaveris super terram, erit ligatum et in coelis, et quodcumque solveris super terram erit solutum et in coelis', eius vicarius, qui est sacerdos in aeternum secundum ordinem Melchisedech, constitutus a Deo iudex vivorum et mortuorum'.

[39]X 4.17.13: 'Paulus etiam, ut plenitudinem potestatis exponeret, ad Corinthios scribens ait: Nescitis, quoniam angelos iudicabitis, quanto magis saecularia?'

[40]See Tierney, 'Tria quippe.'

[41]3 Comp. 4.12.2 (X 4.17.13) s.v. *usurpare*, Gonville and Caius MS 28/17 p. 292. 'Immo licet ex certis causis, non ideo ordinarius est quo ad temporalia, ar, supra de of. iudi. ord. pasto. ex parte [X 1.31.11]. Laurentius.' See also Vincentius, 3 Comp. 4.12.2 (X 4.17.13) s.v. *vsurpare*, Paris BN lat. 14611 fol. 123r; Bernardus, *Glossa ord.*, fol. 331v, X 4.17.13. s.v. *certis causis*.

words of Deuteronomy proved.[42] What connection did the canonists, and indeed, Innocent himself, see between the first and second parts of the decretal?

Since Innocent claimed that all difficult and ambiguous matters should be referred to the Apostolic See, it would seem worthwhile to ask what was difficult and ambiguous in *Per venerabilem*. Both William's and Philip's cases seem fairly straightforward; the complications which adhered to it were political, not legal. Were we to assume as Genestal suggests, that the real issue in Philip's case was whether his children were actually legitimate because a putative marriage had existed between Philip and Agnes of Meran at the time of their birth, then we would have a case which was both difficult and ambiguous.[43] This question, however, would have been a primarily ecclesiastical one, requiring no special papal prerogatives. Moreover, although the possibility of putative marriage may have affected Innocent's decision in Philip's case, this was not the major issue involved in *Per venerabiliem*.

Where then did the difficulty and ambiguity enter in? The answer is, in fact, easy to overlook. The difficult question tackled by Innocent, and by the canonists who followed him, involved the circumstances under which the pope could legitimize someone for purposes of succession. This was an issue, Innocent felt, which could only be resolved by the Holy See. There was no doubt in Innocent's mind that he and he alone should decide whether the pope could grant William's request.

Nevertheless, it is important to remember that Innocent turned down William's request and in doing so relied heavily on the fact that, unlike Philip, William had temporal superiors capable of considering his petition. It seems, then, that although Innocent believed that the papacy did indeed have the power to legitimize in the secular sphere, he still felt that he was only free to use that power when no appropriate secular authority existed. The notion that a given act could be valid, but not licit, was, after all, not unknown to the canonists. The ability to perform an act did not necessarily justify the performance of that act in every circumstance. In effect, the judicial decision which Innocent reached on this truly difficult and ambiguous issue was that it would be improper for the papacy to assert jurisdiction over cases such as William's.

Per venerabilem provides one last piece of evidence to support this explanation of Innocent's intentions. Innocent ends the decretal by telling William that he

---

[42]Laurentius, 3 Comp. 4.12.2 (X 4.17.13) s.v. *temporalem iurisdictionem casualiter*, Paris BN lat. 15398 fol. 183r. 'Et cum requirimur, si est inter iudices uariatum quod probat auctoritate deuteronomii.' See also the following almost identical glosses: Vincentius, 3 Comp. 4.12.2 (X 4.17.13) s.v. *inspectis*, Paris BN lat. 14611 fol. 123r; Tancred, 3 Comp. 4.12.2 (X 4.17.13) s.v. *certis causis*, Gonville and Caius College MS 28/17 p. 292; Bernardus, *Glossa Ord.*, fol. 331v, X 4.17.13 s.v. *certis causis*.

[43]Genestal, 175-204.

could not come to a decision concerning his request unless it could be shown that the count's guilt was lighter and that Innocent himself could judge more freely.[44] This would be a peculiar statement coming from one who had just declared that he had an unlimited freedom to judge in both temporal and spiritual affairs. The canonists who glossed the word *liberior* clearly believed that Innocent meant to say that he did not have jurisdiction in William's case. Johannes Teutonicus interpreted the phrase to mean, 'until it is known whether such jurisdiction belongs to him'.[45] Laurentius was more specific, in keeping with his interpretation of *Per venerabilem*. He asserted that Innocent wished to be shown, 'that you may be subjected to us by the authority of those to whom you are subject'.[46] In a similar vein, Vincentius held that the pope would be able to judge the case *liberior*, 'when [William's] immediate lord has given his assent'.[47]

Innocent did feel, as Professor Tierney has suggested, that the papacy was the supreme court of Christendom. He did not, however, argue that his power was purely discretionary. There would be times, as in *Per venerabilem*, when he would decide that he had no right to accept jurisdiction over a case, though no other earthly power could decide this for him. The image of a supreme court with limited jurisdiction is not as paradoxical as it may seem. The real supremacy of a 'supreme' court lies in its ability to define the limits of its own jurisdiction, rather than in the complete absence of such limits. The implications of this in terms of Innocent's claim to universal appellate jurisdiction are subtle, but important. Innocent did claim temporal judicial power of considerable magnitude in the second part of *Per venerabilem*, but it was not an unlimited power. Moreover, the canonists did not object to Innocent's claims to universal appellate jurisdiction because they found them to be both moderate and rational. Innocent was no dualist; neither was he a hierocrat in the classical sense. He recognized and respected the normal independence of the secular authority, though he did not consider it his equal. The limits on his authority in the secular sphere might exist only in the unwritten constitution of Christendom, the law of God, but they were very real, nonetheless. Innocent's decision in William's case, with its implied adherence to those limits, was his declaration that he intended to remain within the boundaries of his office, even though only he could define those boundaries.

---

[44]X 4.17.13. '. . . petitioni tuae non duximus annuendum, donec, si fieri poterit, et culpa levior et iurisdictio liberior ostendatur.'

[45]Johannes, *Apparatus*, 2, 631, 3 Comp. 4.12.2 (X 4.17.13) s.v. *liberior*. 'Scilicet donec sciatur an talis iurisdictio ad ipsum spectet'.

[46]3 Comp. 4.12.2 (X 4.1713) s.v. *liberior*, Gonville and Caius College MS 28/17 p. 292. 'Vt scilicet auctoritate eorum quibus subest, et nobis subicias. Laurentius'.

[47]3 Comp. 4.12.2 (X 4.17.13) s.v. *liberior*, Paris BN lat. 14611 fol. 123v. 'Accedente assensu domini immediate'.

The Papal and Imperial Concept of *plenitudo potestatis*: The Influence of Pope Innocent III on Emperor Frederick II

Hans-Joachim Schmidt

It is well known that there are strong interrelations between the ecclesiastical and the temporal powers. Cooperation and rivalry are the main characteristics of this relationship. Church and state depended on concepts of political theories which are applicable to both systems. The hierarchical system established by the church was until the high middle ages far more sophisticated than that of any temporal rule. A strong hierarchy of offices and competencies, with their corresponding territorial framework, had been established. The system was directed by its head, endowed with the highest degree of authority and power. The relations between ecclesiastical persons and institutions were ruled by the norms of canon law. To be sure, very often this ideal was not attained, but the exercise of administration, jurisdiction and power was nevertheless bound by legal norms and legitimated by religious prestige.[1]

The medieval church inherited the administrative structure of the Roman Empire of late antiquity. More perfectly than any temporal state, the church, dominated by the pope, succeeded in establishing a far-reaching rule, in imposing on a large number of institutions bureaucratic procedures of administration, of

---

[1] Alois Dempf, *Sacrum Imperium. Geschichts- und Staatsphilosophie des Mittelalters und der politischen Renaissance* (Munich, Berlin, 1975-1976).

collecting taxes, of assembling information, of sending out legates, of stabilizing a hierarchical system of jurisdictional instances and of subjecting people to orders issued by the papal court, the *curia ecclesiae Romanae*. For occidental Christianity, that is for the totality of the western world of that period, a common law was established, the *ius canonicus*. From the end of the twelfth century on, the *ecclesia* was described as and called a *res publica*. The church was treated as a state in the theories of thirteenth-century thinkers and in the practice of papal administrators.[2]

Could the church be an example for the concept and the practice of temporal rule? The question was put by Jacques Verger.[3] He proposed more detailed inquiries on this matter. He said that the formation of the state during the late middle ages was a process that could not be understood without taking into consideration the impact of the contemporary ecclesiastical model. The transfer of know-how and of political concepts from church to state was very important. This transfer was put into effect by the great number of ecclesiastical persons and institutions integrated into the personal staff of imperial, royal and princely courts. Experienced people, experts in law and administration, were needed for creating and stabilizing temporal rule, and they were very often recruited from the clergy.[4]

Until now, this theme has been applied to a few specific ecclesiastical institutions. But we need more information about the larger question: in what way did the church as the assembly of many institutions, as the totality of all western Christians – conceived as a *corpus*, as a *res publica* and as a hierarchy of

---

[2] Johann Baptist Sägmüller, 'Die Idee von der Kirche als Imperium Romanum im kanonischen Recht', *Theologische Quartalschrift* 80 (1898):50-60; Sergio Mochi Onory, *Fonti canonstiche dell'idea moderna dello Stato* (Milan, 1951); Elisabeth Herrmann, *Ecclesia in re publica. Die Entwicklung der Kirche von pseudostaatlicher zu staatlich inkorporierter Existenz*, Europäisches Forum 2 (Frankfurt M., 1980); Cesare Alzati, 'Metropoli e sedi episcopali fra tarda antichità e alto medio evo', in *Chiesa e societa. Appunti per una storia delle diocesi lombarde*, ed. Adrianus Caprioli et al. (Brescia, 1986), 47-77; Jürgen Miethke, 'Der Weltanspruch des Papstes im späteren Mittelalter. Die politische Theorie der Traktate De postestate papae', in *Pipers Handbuch der politischen Ideen*, vol. 2, ed. Iring Fetscher, Herfried Münkler (Munich, Zurich, 1993), 351-446.

[3] Jean Gaudemet, 'La contribution des romanistes et des canonistes médiévaux à la théorie moderne de l'Etat', in *Diritto e potere nella storia Europea, Bd. 1. Atti in onore di Bruno Paradisi, quattro congresso intern. della società Italiana di storia del diritto* (Florence 1982), 1-36; Jacques Verger, 'Le transfert de modèles d'organisation de l'Eglise à l'Etat à la fin du Moyen Age', in *Etat et Eglise dans la genèse de l'Etat moderne. Actes du colloque organisé par le C.N.R.S. et la casa de Velázquez Madrid 30 nov.-1 dec.1984*, ed. Jean-Philippe Genet/Bernard Vincent, Bibliothèque de la Casa de Velázquez 1 (Madrid, 1986):31-9.

[4] Peter Moraw, Helène Millet, 'Les clers dans l'Etat', in *Les élites du pouvoir et la construction de l'Etat en Europe*, ed. Wolfgang Reinhard (Paris, 1997), 237-57; *I canonici al servizio dello stato in Europa, secoli XIII-XVI. Les chanoines au service de l'Etat en Europa du 13e au 16e siècle*, ed. Helène Millet (Modena, 1992).

offices – have some impact on the state-building process? The church under papal rule could be an ideal model for any monarchical power. Political concepts might be transferred from one to another sphere.

In order to test this hypothesis on a limited scale, I will present some reflections on the political ideas conceived by Emperor Frederick II, who was also king of Sicily and who was, in the first half of the thirteenth century until his death in 1250, one of the dominant figures on the European scene. His need for ideological arguments for his kingship was obvious because his legitimacy was always threatened, first by the rivals of the Guelf dynasty, second by the opposition of the high nobility in Germany and in south Italy and last by the papacy. No king or emperor before him had made such an effort to provide a theoretical foundation for his rule. In circular letters, which were veritable propaganda texts, and also in many of his mandatory letters, the foundations of his temporal rule were explained.[5] Some years ago, Hans-Martin Schaller proposed the hypothesis that the texts, documents and circular letters issued by the chancellery of Frederick II were largely influenced by the arguments put forward by Pope Innocent III to define papal supremacy. The pope's theories also shaped the ecclesiastical and political *raisonnement* after his death in 1216. Schaller has analyzed the career of some of the collaborators of Frederick II who, before entering in the service of the emperor, worked at the papal court. But the hypothesis of an exchange of arguments and topics has not yet been examined.[6]

In this paper, I cannot present an exhaustive analysis of the whole range of the transfer between papal and imperial ideology. I will only insist on one aspect, on the concept of *plenitudo potestatis*. Beginning with the pontificate of Pope Innocent III, the term described the high-level power of the Roman pontiff, a power which did not accept any limitation and which was placed in connection with and contrast to the *pars sollicitudinis*, the authority assigned to all other

---

[5]Ernst Kantorowicz, *Kaiser Friedrich II.* (Berlin 1927); Otto Vehse, *Amtliche Propaganda in der Staatskunst Kaiser Friedrichs II.* (Munich, 1929); Helene Wieruszowski, *Vom Imperium zum nationalen Königtum. Vergleichende Studien über die publizistischen Kämpfe Kaiser Friedrichs II. und König Philipps des Schönen in der Kurie* (Munich, 1933); Otto Heinrich Becker, *Kaisertum, deutsche Königswahl und Legitimitätsprinzip in der Auffassung der späteren Staufer und ihres Umfeldes (Mit einem Exkurs über das Weiterwirken der Arengentradition Friedrichs II. und seiner Nachkommen und der Angiovinen)*, Europäische Hochschulschriften III, 51 (Frankfurt M., 1975); Wolfgang Stürner, *Potestas und Peccatum. Der Sündenfall und die Entstehung der herrscherlichen Gewalt im mittelalterlichen Denken*, Beiträge zur Geschichte und Quellenkunde des Mittelalters 11 (Sigmaringen, 1987); *idem, Friedrich II.* (Darmstadt, 1992), 198-204, 231-5, 246-54; *idem,* 'Kaiser Friedrich II. und seine Herrschaftsvorstellungen und politischen Ziele' in *Das Staunen der Welt. Kaiser Friedrich II. von Hohenstaufen, 1194-1250* (Göppingen, 1996), 10-39.

[6]Hans-Martin Schaller, 'Die Kaiseridee Friedrichs II.', in *Probleme um Friedrich II*, ed. Josef Fleckenstein, Vorträge und Forschungen 16 (Sigmaringen, 1974):135-66; *idem,* 'Kanzlei und Hofkapelle Friedrichs II.', *Archiv für Diplomatik* 3 (1957):207-86; 4 (1958):264-327.

bishops, whose competence was restricted to the area of their dioceses and to their office. But before the pontificate of Innocent III, *plenitudo potestatis* had a different meaning. It designated the power of a papal legate empowered by the pope to execute a task in some area assigned to him, to carry out reform or to exercise jurisdiction. Vested with the *plenitudo potestatis*, a papal legate was placed above the local clergy. *Plenitudo potestatis* was a term not claimed by the popes themselves but conferred on persons bound in obedience to papal orders and, at the same time, authorized to give instructions to everyone put under their competence as defined by the pope.[7] The juridical construction of this relation was based on the Roman civil law, on the *Corpus iuris civilis*. The definition of the competencies of the *procuratores* invested by the emperor supposed that they were vested with *plenitudo potestatis*.

The concept was transformed by Innocent III. Now the pope himself claimed the *plenitudo potestatis*. The change was due to an enlarged conception of papal monarchy. Its relation to the local bishops and local churches was cast in juridical and theological terms which supposed a stricter control of and a closer connection to the papal court, a bureaucratic handling of all matters everywhere in Christianity. In making such a claim, the pope did not wish to transform his rule into a temporal one. He claimed to possess supreme temporal authority, but without the intention of himself exercising temporal power, which would be delegated to emperors, kings, princes and communities. Because God had ordained that any temporal power was inferior and subject to the spiritual, the pope intervened in temporal matters only by directing the princes in the use of their power, in order to guarantee that the use of power was exercised in a manner beneficial to the spiritual welfare of Christendom. Nevertheless, because papal prerogatives also claimed temporal matters, these prerogatives would always be a risk for the rule of every prince. The pope must be obeyed more than any temporal ruler. If both gave conflicting orders, even if the issue at stake was purely temporal in nature, the pope's authority took precedence. In the *arenga* of many letters, Innocent III described the Roman pontiff as placed above all *proceres singularum provinciarum*. Only the Roman Church could claim the title and the function of the head of the universal church. The difference between the unlimited power and the particular competencies was seen in the terms *plenitudo potestatis* and *pars sollicitudinis*. The bishops were considered to have only a part of the rule of the universal community; they were subject to the *caput*, the pope. The whole world was assigned only to him. The *distributio dignitatum* was

---

[7]Robert L. Benson, '*Plenitudo potestatis*: Evolution of a Formula', *Studia Gratiana* 14 (1967):193-217; William D. McCready, 'Papal *Plenitudo Potestatis* and the Source of Temporal Authority in Later Medieval Papal Hierocratic Theory', *Speculum* 48 (1973):654-74.

administered by the pope, wrote Innocent III.[8] Also Peter had given the apostles distinctive areas of mission. The *distributio apostolorum*, directed by Peter, was in that regard a prefiguring of the papal distribution of offices. The bishops, as the successors of the apostles, were installed in particular provinces and nations; the pope, as the successor of Peter, was responsible for the whole of Christianity.[9]

Plenitudo potestatis supposed a systematic coordination of offices. The aim was to conform the church to a state, the Roman Empire of antiquity. But added to the purely temporal juridical conception, it included also a theological concept. *Plenitudo potestatis* enclosed the whole range of human activities, including matters of faith. The *plenitudo potestatis* was reserved to the pope; no one else had the right to set up a claim to it – not any other bishop, not any prince, king or emperor. The bishop of Rome, the only universal bishop, who claimed to be the *vicarius Christi*, was set in a position of full power. Temporal and ecclesiastical concepts were combined to define a supremacy that could not be surmounted.

Despite the presumption of exclusivity, the concept of *plenitudo potestatis* could not be restricted to the sphere of papal prerogatives. It was too useful to any kind of rulership. And in the hands of the temporal rulers, it could even be transformed into an ideological weapon to resist the papal claim to supreme authority in temporal matters. Transferred to the temporal rule, the concept of *plenitudo potestatis* could also be used to describe the monarchical position of kings or emperors. The awareness of the usefulness of the concept was undoubtedly reinforced by the renaissance of Roman law, which led to a doctrine of public law and public authority, but the secular application of the term in the middle ages was not directly borrowed from Roman law or from the administrative practice of the late antique Roman Empire. The term entered into the sphere of temporal rule in the middle ages through the mediation of the papal church, especially of Innocent III. Emperor Frederick II was the first who used the theory of *plenitudo potestatis* in order to describe his own position in temporal matters and to resist the papal prerogative. Rivalry with the popes as well as imitation of

---

[8]Reg. 1:320, p. 465; Jean Rivière, '*In partem sollicitudinis*. Evolution d'une formule pontificale', *Revue des sciences réligieuses* 5 (1925): 210-31; Alfred Hof, '*Plenitudo potestatis* und *imitatio imperii* zur Zeit Innozenz' III.', *Zeitschrift für Kirchengeschichte* 66 (1954-55):39-71; Benson, 'Plenitudo potestatis' (see above n. 7); Friedrich Kempf, 'Die Eingliederung der überdiözesanen Hierarchie in das Papalsystem des kanonischen Rechts von der gregorianischen Reform bis zu Innozenz III.', *Archivum Historiae Pontificiae* 18 (1980):57-96; *idem, Papsttum und Kaisertum bei Innozenz III. Die geistigen und rechtlichen Grundlagen seiner Thronstreitpolitik*, Miscellanea Historiae Pontificiae 19/58 (Rome, 1954); Michele Maccarone, *Chiesa e Stato nella dottrina di papa Innocenzo III*, Lateranum NS 6/3-4 (Rome, 1940), 4-7, 25; Wilhelm Imkamp, *Das Kirchenbild Innocenz' III.*, Päpste und Papsttum 22 (Stuttgart, 1983).

[9]Willibrord Hug, 'Geschichte des Festes Divisio apostolorum', *Theologische Quartalschrift* 113 (1932):53-72; Adolf Katzenellenbogen, 'The Separation of the Apostles', *Gazette des Beaux Arts* 35 (1949):81-98.

papal concepts were the basis of the new imperial claim. The transfer was obviously managed by some staff members of the royal Sicilian chancellery who had served before in the papal court. The knowledge papal curialists had acquired was handed over to Frederick II and his circle. Some other elements of the terminology used by the papal court were also transferred to the vocabulary of the court of Frederick II.[10]

Some formulas in royal and imperial documents paved the way for the use of the term *plenitudo potestatis*. In a privilege to the cathedral church of Palermo, issued in 1210, *favoris plenitudo* was promised. The constitutions of Melfi, promulgated in 1231, explained the idea involved in the concept of *plenitudo potestatis* in a way that did not conceal the borrowing from papal formulas. Frederick, as king of Sicily, distinguished between the *sollicitudo*, which described the position of any king and consequently his own rank as the monarch of the Sicilian realm, from the *generalis cura*, reserved to him as emperor, the legitimate monarch of the Roman Empire, the only universal monarchy installed above all kingdoms and peoples. The *plenitudo potestatis* was reserved to the emperor, the *sollicitudo* was assigned to other rulers, considered as locally restricted administrators of territories. In the *arenga* of many imperial documents, their duty was defined as subordinate to the imperial one.[11]

But the two terms – *plenitudo potestatis* and *pars sollicitudinis* – were useful not only in defining the relationship between the emperor and other kings in occidental Europe. It was far more suitable for the definition of all kinds of imperial delegates directly invested by Frederick II. The *capitani generales*, installed for special regions of nothern Italy, were endowed with a share of the imperial authority. Their position was described as assuming *partem sollicitudinis*, while the emperor possessed the *plenitudinem potestatis*. He gave the *merum imperium* to his subordinate legates. They received a delegated and subordinate authority under the control of the emperor.[12]

The difference from the classical terminology of Roman Law is quite clear. The holder of the title of *plenitudo potestatis* was not some plenipotentiary agent with delegated power, as in ancient law, but rather the summit of authority. The concept entered the documents of the imperial chancellery of Frederick II not directly from the *Corpus iuris civilis*, but indirectly from the usage introduced in ecclesiastical law. It was not an imitation of Roman civil law, but an adoption of the papal concept.

---

[10]Schaller, *Kanzlei* (see above n. 6).

[11]J. L. A. Huillard-Bréholles, ed., *Historia diplomatica Friderici secundi*, 6 vols (Paris 1852-61), 2:180; Hermann Conrad et al., eds, *Die Konstitutionen Friedrichs II. von Hohenstaufen für sein Königreich Sizilien* (Köln, Wien 1973), 350.

[12]MGH LL Const. 2, no. 343, pp. 450-1.

This terminology was very suitable for describing the relationship of the medieval Roman emperor or king to the princes of the Holy Roman Empire, especially to those in Germany. When Frederick II promised to raise the duke of Austria to the rank of a king, but a king still under the suzerainty of the *imperator romanus,* he insisted that *plenitudo potestatis* was reserved to himself, while the rulers of the projected Austrian kingdom would exercise the *partem sollicitudinis.* The hierarchical difference would thus be maintained. The honour of the Roman emperor enabled him to integrate royal rule, placed in a subordinate position within the institutional framework of the empire and under the control of the emperor.[13]

The relationship between emperor and princes was described most clearly in the *arenga* of the document which, issued at the diet of Ravenna in April 1232, prohibited the creation of urban communities. The *arenga* claimed the imperial fullness of power. The formula is even a word-for-word imitation of papal statements. The emperor was positioned *super gentes et regna* – a citation of the Old Testament, one that appears in many documents issued by Innocent III. Also the juxtaposition of the *plenitudo potestatis* of the emperor and the *pars sollicitudinis* of the princes of the empire strictly followed the papal formula. Frederick integrated the position of the princes into a hierarchical order which supposed a legal system of formalized relations.[14] The princes were subordinated to the emperor not by personal loyalty, but by a system of different levels of rank and authority. The empire was not formed by feudal bounds, but by a hierarchy of offices. The state-building process, pushed forward by Frederick II, claimed a stricter definition of all kinds of competencies, which were considered to be derived from the imperial authority alone. At the same time, the formula contained an offer of cooperation to the princes, who were invited to take part in the rule of the empire, to assume their part of responsibility. At the diet of Mayence in 1235, Frederick raised Otto of Brunswick to the rank of an imperial prince, inviting him to take part in the *sollicitudo* of the realm.[15]

The claim of Emperor Frederick to rule *super gentes et regna* did not imply any real claim to direct rule over other kingdoms outside the triad of German, Italian and Burgundian kingdoms. For that reason, the formula of *plenitudo potestatis* is used only in documents addressed to imperial princes, not to other kings, not, for example, to those of France, Castile or England. *Plenitudo* did not mean a

---

[13]MGH LL Const. 2, no. 223, 261, pp. 306-8, 358-60; Friedrich Haussmann, 'Kaiser Friedrich II. und Österreich' in *Probleme* (see above n. 6), 225-308.

[14]MGH LL Const. 2, no. 197, 229, pp. 263, 413-14.

[15]MGH LL Const. 2, no. 197, pp. 263-6; Egon Boshof, 'Die Entstehung des Herzogtums Braunschweig-Lüneburg' in: *Heinrich der Löwe,* ed. Wolf-Dieter Mohrmann, Veröffentlichungen der Niedersächsischen Archivverwaltung 39 (Göttingen, 1980), 249-74.

universal world-wide power, but a set of competencies ordered hierarchically under the highest authority within one state, the state which Frederick was trying to build. The concept was integrated into a state-building process, not into a merely illusionary attempt to achieve universal rulership. To be sure, the presumption of *plenitudo potestatis* distinguished the emperor from other kings, but not in such a way that they were subordinated to him. The higher rank of honor must be distinguished from an effective exercise of competencies or power.[16] The *plenitudo potestatis* reserved to the emperor had a more limited aim, namely to strengthen his position within the heterogeneous ensemble of the empire, comprised of Germany, Italy and Burgundy, which was threatened by the power of many temporal and ecclesiastical princes. The feudal ties between king and princes did not suffice to establish a rule which could combine power with administration. The feudal subordination was still important, but it needed a more hierarchical system of several levels of political competence, each under the control of the supreme authority vested with the fullness of power. But the cooperation of princes in managing the affairs of jurisdiction, administration, tax-collection, punishment of enemies and so on was needed. Their authority was not only granted by the emperor but was also based on original rights reserving them a share in the rule of the state. This concept supplied the princely powers with genuine legimitacy. It gave them a solid position in a state without degrading the princes to subordinate functionaries. They kept their independent political position of co-rulers, but at the same time they received the subordinate position of collaborators with the emperor. In both aspects, the system was now defined in terms of an administrative procedure of rule.[17]

This definition of the relationship between emperor-king and the princes was probably pure theory, but it nevertheless provided a strong argument in establishing state-modelled power. It would not be based on an absolutist political theory. The combination of *plenitudo potestatis* and *pars sollicitudinis* suggested the existence of intermediary powers which could not be reduced to mere subordinate subjects but were rather placed in the position of partners in the exercise of state-power. The emperor, asserting the highest rank in a hierarchical system of competencies, had the duty and the right to coordinate the work of his collaborators the princes in the framework of an institutional, iurisdictional and

[16]Othmar Hageneder, 'Weltherrschaft im Mittelalter', *Mitteilungen des österreichischen Instituts für Geschichtsforschung* 93 (1985):257-78; Helmut G. Walther, *Imperiales Königtum, Konziliarismus und Volkssouveränität* (Munich, 1976), 35-9; Dieter Berg, *Deutschland und seine Nachbarn 1200-1500*, Enzyklopädie deutscher Geschichte 40 (Munich 1997):5-15.

[17]Karl-Friedrich Krieger, *Die Lehnshoheit der deutschen Könige im Spätmittelalter (ca. 1200-1437)* (Aalen 1979); Heinrich Angermeier, 'König und Staat im deutschen Mittelalter', *Blätter für deutsche Landesgeschichte* 117 (1981):167-82; Egon Boshof, 'Reichsfürstenstand und Reichsreform in der Politik Friedrichs II.', in *Blätter für deutsche Landesgeschichte* 122 (1986):41-66.

administrative form of rulership. The emperor played an essential role in the process whereby leadership in a 'state' was acquired and brought under the control of the highest authority. In comparision to the other rulers within the empire, the emperor acted as the source of legitimacy, but he also claimed the right to act immediately in every affair he wished to reserve to his domain. The emperor did not receive his power from the Great Electors; on the contrary, they received theirs from him.

The *plenitudo potestatis* was manifested especially in the competence of promulgating law. Legislation as a monarchical right was assumed; the emperor was not merely an executor of pre-existing law. Here too, the parallel between papal and imperial practice is obvious. Almost at the same time, the *Liber Extra* was promulgated by Pope Gregory IX in 1234 and the *Constitutiones* of Melfi in 1231 by Frederick II. Both are legislative texts issued from the fullness of power; both sustained this claim; both tried to revitalize the former legislative competence of the emperors of the ancient Roman Empire; both were the effect of legislative competence.[18]

The result, however, was disappointing for establishing a new base for imperial power in the late middle ages. Although the princes were in reality quite independent, the real rulers of their territories, Frederick had to continue to insist on the integration of these princes into a theoretically full-powered authority if he did not want to renounce his authority. *Plenitudo potestatis* became not in reality the basis of a powerful policy, but a compensation for the loss of power. The claim was ambitious, but in fact it could not stop historical evolution. Finally, the death of Frederick II in 1250 and the end of the Staufen dynasty cut off any chance of a kingship strong enough to master centrifugal tendencies in the Holy Roman Empire.[19]

Nevertheless, the concept of *plenitudo potestatis*, imitating the papal model introduced by Innocent III, continued to influence the ideology of royal and imperial power in Europe. The concept was useful for defining the legitimacy of any medieval monarchy which did not accept a higher authority. The concept was

---

[18]Conrad, *Konstitutionen* (see above n. 11); Georges LeBras, Henri Levebre, Jacqueline Rambaud, *L'Age classique 11490-1378. Sources et théorie du droit*, Histoire du droit et des institutions de l'Eglise en Occident 13 (Paris, 1971); Kurt Wolfgang Nörr, 'Päpstliche Dekretalen und römisch-kanonischer Zivilprozeß', in *Studien zur europäischen Rechtsgeschichte* (Frankfurt M., 1972), 53-65; John Anthony Watt, *The Theory of Papal Monarchy in the Thirteenth Century. The Contribution of the Canonists* (New York, 1966); Kenneth Pennington, 'Gregory IX, Emperor Frederick II and the Constitution of Melfi', in *Popes, Teachers and Canon Law in the Middle Ages. Festschrift for Brian Tierney*, ed. Stanley Chodorow, James Ross Sweeney (Ithaca, NY, 1989), 53-61.

[19]Dieter Willoweit, *Rechtsgrundlagen der Territorialgewalt. Landesobrigkeit, Herrschaftsrechte und Territorium in der Rechtswissenschaft der Neuzeit* (Köln/Wien, 1975); Benjamin Arnold, *Princes and Territories in Medieval Germany* (Cambridge, Engl., 1991); Ernst Schubert, *Fürstliche Herrschaft und Territorium im späten Mittelalter*, Enzyklopädie deutscher Geschichte 35 (Munich, 1996).

a key-term, introduced in documents issued by many royal chancelleries and used by political thinkers in order to give a juridical and theoretical foundation for the state which was emerging from the thirteenth century on. The concept prepared for the development of princely and royal sovereignty. Even in the sixteenth century, the French monarchist theorist Jean Boudin put the term at the center of his reflections.[20]

What Pope Innocent III had introduced thus became an ideological instrument in the hands of political thinkers and practitioners who tried to define political competence and to support state power. Originally a term of Roman law, then used by the papal court, *plenitudo potestatis* was now at the disposal of temporal rulers. It was not possible to reserve the claim to the popes because the concept was too well suited to describing the highest authority in the state. This contribution of ecclesiastical theory to secular political theory was a fundamental step in establishing the 'modern state'.[21]

---

[20]Jean Bodin, *Les six livres de la République* (Paris, 1986), 1:179-228, 295-341; H. Quaritsch, *Staat und Souveränität*, vol. 1: *Die Grundlagen* (Frankfurt, 1970), 41-9.

[21]*L'Etat moderne: Le droit, l'espace et les formes de l'Etat. Actes du colloque Baume Les Aix, 11-12 oct. 1984*, ed. Nicolas Coulet, Jean-Pierre Genet (Paris, 1990).

Part Four
Encountering the Muslim World

Innocent III and the Kingdoms of Castile and Leon

Joseph F. O'Callaghan

The relationship of Pope Innocent III with the Spanish kingdoms has not drawn much attention, even though he had to deal with several complex issues.[1] Among them was the troublesome connection between the Spanish realms of Castile and León. United since the middle of the eleventh century, the two monarchies had been divided in 1157 and in the ensuing fifty years an intense rivalry had developed between them. Animosity between the kings of Castile and León reached a peak in the years just preceding Innocent's accession to power. It was a most inopportune time for quarreling because the Almohads, a Muslim sect that dominated Morocco, invaded the Iberian peninsula and set about re-establishing unity among the fractured states of al-Andalus. The Christians found themselves on the defensive, and the controversy between the kings of Castile and León placed the whole of Christian Spain at grave risk of assault and possible conquest by the Almohads. That was the situation when Innocent III ascended the papal throne in 1198. His task was threefold: to dissolve the Leonese marriage, to pacify Christian Spain, and to encourage the prosecution of the war against the

---

[1]Abbreviations:

BRAH – Boletín de la Real Academia de la Historia.

ES – España Sagrada, ed. Enrique Flórez et al., 51 vols (Madrid: A. Sancha, 1754-1759).

Spanish affairs receive only cursory mention in the following books dedicated to Innocent III: Leonard Elliott Binns, *Innocent III* (London, 1931); Joseph Clayton, *Pope Innocent III and his Times* (Milwaukee, 1941); Sidney Packard, *Europe and the Church under Innocent III*, rev. edn (New York, 1968); Brenda Bolton, *Innocent III: Studies on Papal Authority and Pastoral Care* (Aldershot, 1995); Jane Sayers, *Innocent III* (New York, 1994). Other studies having direct relevance to the Spanish situation will be cited below.

KINGS OF NAVARRE, LEON, CASTILE AND PORTUGAL
IN THE ELEVENTH, TWELFTH AND THIRTEENTH CENTURIES

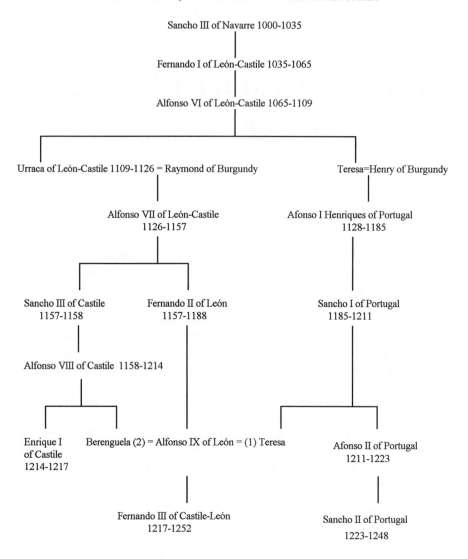

Sancho III of Navarre 1000-1035

Fernando I of León-Castile 1035-1065

Alfonso VI of León-Castile 1065-1109

Urraca of León-Castile 1109-1126 = Raymond of Burgundy

Teresa=Henry of Burgundy

Alfonso VII of León-Castile
1126-1157

Afonso I Henriques of Portugal
1128-1185

Sancho III of Castile
1157-1158

Fernando II of León
1157-1188

Sancho I of Portugal
1185-1211

Alfonso VIII of Castile 1158-1214

Enrique I
of Castile
1214-1217

Berenguela (2) = Alfonso IX of León = (1) Teresa

Afonso II of Portugal
1211-1223

Fernando III of Castile-León
1217-1252

Sancho II of Portugal
1223-1248

Almohads. The achievement of the first two goals, without which the third was impossible, occupied more than half of his reign.

THE LEONESE MARRIAGE

Let us begin with the marriage question. As was so often the case with medieval marriages, this one was arranged with the hope of bringing about peace between the kings of Castile and León. For many years Alfonso VIII had enjoyed an ascendancy among the Christian states of Spain, so much so that when his first cousin Alfonso IX succeeded to the Leonese throne in 1188 he felt compelled to become a vassal of the king of Castile, kissing his hand as he did so. Ever after, he regarded that as a terrible humiliation and tried to thwart Alfonso VIII in every way possible.[2] Such an opportunity arose when the Almohads invaded Castilian territory in 1195. While they inflicted a major defeat on Alfonso VIII and ravaged the Tagus valley, Alfonso IX took advantage of the discomfiture of his Christian neighbor to enter an alliance with the Almohads. That prompted Pope Celestine III (1191-1198), Innocent's immediate predecessor, to excommunicate the king of León, to release his subjects from their oath of allegiance and to proclaim a crusade against him (31 October 1196).[3] The papal legate, Cardinal

---

[2] Alfonso IX, who was seventeen at his accession, feared that Alfonso VIII might attempt to dispossess him and so reunite the inheritance of Alfonso VII. The two kings agreed to some sort of peace at Soto Hermoso in May 1188. Then in June Alfonso IX pledged homage and fealty to Alfonso VIII at Carrión but bitterly regretted it and thereafter became one of the principal enemies of the Castilian ruler. *Chronique latine des rois de Castille jusqu'en 1236*, ed. Georges Cirot (Bordeaux, 1913), ch. 11, pp. 38-40; Rodrigo Jiménez de Rada, *Historia de rebus Hispaniae sive Historia Gothica*, 7.24, ed. Juan Fernández Valverde, Corpus Christianorum, Continuatio Mediaevalis 72 (Turnholt, 1987), 166-7; Lucas of Tuy, *Chronicon Mundi*, in Andreas Schott, *Hispaniae Illustratae*, 4 vols (Frankfort, 1603-8), 4:110; *Chrónicon de Cardeña, ES* 23:379; Julio González, *Alfonso IX*, 2 vols (Madrid, 1944), 1:52-8.

[3] The bull was addressed to Archbishop Martín of Toledo and his suffragans. A similar bull probably was sent to the archbishop of Compostela. The excommunication was to be announced on Sundays and holy days throughout all the dioceses. In response to the request of King Sancho I of Portugal, Celestine III, on 10 April 1197, conceded to those who attacked the king of León the same remission of sins given to oriental crusaders. Whatever lands were conquered from him while he persisted in his obstinate behavior would never be restored to him. Francisco Martinez Marina, *Teoria de las Cortes, Biblioteca de Autores Españoles*, 223 vols thus far (Madrid 1846 ff.), 220:85, no. 3; Ramon Riu, 'Dos bulas inéditas de Celestino III', *BRAH* 11 (1887):457-8; Fidel Fita, 'Bulas históricas del reino de Navarra en los postreros anos del siglo XII', *BRAH* 26 (1895):423-4; Carl Erdmann, *Papsturkunden in Portugal,* Abhandlungen der Gesellschaft der Wissenschaften zu Göttingen, Philologisch-Historische Klasse, Neue Folge, Band XX, 3 (Berlin, 1927):376, no. 154. A month later, the pope informed the archbishops of Bordeaux and Auch and the people of those provinces that they might fulfill the crusading vow by going to Spain rather than to the Holy Land; Paolo Zerbi, *Papato, Impero e 'Respublica christiana' dal 1187 al 1198* (Milan, 1955), 156-8; Juan Francisco Rivera Recio, *La Iglesia de Toledo en el siglo XII* (1086-1208), 2 vols (Rome, 1966), 1:233-5; José Goñi Gaztambide, *Historia de la bula de la Cruzada en España* (Vitoria, 1958), 101; González, *Alfonso IX*, 1:83-5; Jonathan Riley-Smith, *The Crusades. A Short History* (New Haven, 1987), 139-40.

Gregory of S. Angelo, placed the kingdom of León under interdict.[4]   These threats, coupled with the refusal of the Almohads to assist him, persuaded Alfonso IX to make peace with Castile.[5] The keystone of their pact was the consanguineous marriage of Alfonso IX and Berenguela, celebrated at Valladolid in October 1197. While politically expedient, the marriage flouted the canons, as Berenguela was a first cousin once removed of her husband. Celestine III died before taking any action against it,[6] but Innocent III was not likely to ignore it. Alberic of Trois Fontaines' statement that Innocent III initially accepted the marriage out of necessity but condemned it only after children were born is clearly in error.[7]

Soon after his election, the new pope, determined to 'reform peace and to dissolve alliances of iniquity among the princes' of Spain, dispatched his legate, the Cistercian Rainier, with orders to bring about the separation of Alfonso IX and Berenguela and to end their 'turpid contract, abominable in the sight of God and detestable in the judgment of the faithful'. Should the kings of León and Castile persist in upholding the marriage, the legate was instructed to excommunicate them and to impose an interdict on both their kingdoms. Inasmuch as Celestine III's legate, Cardinal Gregory of S. Angelo had already excommunicated and interdicted Alfonso IX and the Leonese bishops Lope of Astorga, Vidal of Salamanca, Mauricio of León and Martín of Zamora, not because of the marriage, but because the king had joined the Almohads in attacking Alfonso VIII of Castile, Rainier was authorized to lift those sentences if they indicated their willingness to obey the papal mandate concerning the marriage.[8] The bishops mentioned evidently had ignored Celestine III's condemnation of their king, but

---

[4]Innocent III made that point on 16 April 1198; Demetrio Mansilla, *La documentación pontificia hasta Inocencio III (965-1216)* (Rome, 1955), 170, no. 138 = PL 214:79. Bishop Martín of Zamora went to Rome to be absolved. Bishop Juan of Oviedo refused to abide by the interdict and was forced into exile by the king.

[5]Rodrigo Jiménez de Rada, *De rebus Hispaniae*, 7.30, pp. 252-3; *Chronique latine*, 15, pp. 49-50.

[6]Rodrigo Jiménez de Rada, *De rebus Hispaniae*, 7.31, p. 253; *Chronique latine*, 15, p. 50; Lucas of Túy, *Chronicon Mundi*, 4:110; Julio González, *El reino de Castilla en la época de Alfonso VIII*, 3 vols (Madrid, 1960), 1:197-9, 722-5, and *Alfonso IX*, 1:91-100; O'Callaghan, *Medieval Spain*, 242-3.

[7]Alberic of Trois Fontaines, *Chronica*, MGH SS, 23:895: 'Et sciendum est quod dicta Berengaria et maritus eius rex Legionensis Alfonsus in secundo et tertio gradu fuerunt. Quod matrimonium licet papa Innocentius III de necessitate primo concesserit, tamen postquam liberos fecerant, illud prohibuit, et ipsius regine incontinentia de qua multa dicebantur, potuit esse in causa. Que tamen a viro suo dimissa fecit abbatiam monialium Cisterciensis ordinis in civitate Burgensi.' Berenguela's first child, Leonor, was likely born in the second half of 1198. The monastery of Las Huelgas de Burgos had been founded by her parents, Alfonso VIII and Leonor.

[8]Innocent III was elected on 8 January 1198. See his letter *Auctor novi* to Rainier in Mansilla, *Documentación pontificia*, 168-70, no. 138 (16 April) = PL 214:79; González, *Alfonso VIII*, 1:384-5, 726. The pope informed Archbishop Martín of Toledo and his suffragans of the legate's mission on 15 April; Archivo de la Catedral de Toledo A.6.G.1.8; Rivera Recío, *Iglesia de Toledo*, 236.

Bishop Martín of Zamora came to Rome to plead his case and was absolved by Pope Innocent.[9] A week later Innocent III left it to the legate's discretion to determine whether Alfonso IX gave a sufficient guarantee of obedience.[10] As a condition of absolution, Alfonso IX had to allow Bishop Juan of Oviedo, who had been driven into exile for his insistence on observing the interdict, to return home.[11] The English chronicler Roger de Hoveden alleged that Alfonso IX offered 20,000 silver marks to the pope and promised to maintain at his cost for more than a year two hundred knights for the defense of Christendom, provided that the pope allow the royal couple to live together until a child was born or at least for three years, but Innocent refused. The accuracy of that report is difficult to assess, but Linehan thinks that Hoveden 'may have been right', because in May 1199 Innocent praised his legate Rainier 'for having spurned all gifts that he was proffered'.[12]

In spite of Innocent III's evident expectation that the Christian kings would promptly submit to him, they did not. Speaking of the persecution by the pagans as a scandal afflicting the Christian people in both East and West, the pope lamented that the situation was worsened by the incestuous marriages of Alfonso IX and Berenguela and of Queen Isabelle of Jerusalem, first with Conrad of Montserrat and then, after his assassination, with Count Henry of Champagne.[13] The pope noted that Rainier time and again tried to persuade Alfonso IX to give up 'that detestable and wicked union'. When the king failed to appear at the time and place fixed by the legate, Rainier promulgated the sentence of excommunication against Alfonso IX and placed an interdict on the kingdom of León. Rainier did not take similar action against Alfonso VIII of Castile because that king intimated that he was prepared to accept his daughter's return to the kingdom of her birth. In the meantime, Archbishop Martín of Toledo and Bishop Enrique of

---

[9]Mansilla, *Documentación pontificia*, 162, no. 131 (26 March 1198) = PL 214:51. Bishop Martín had journeyed to Rome to appeal to Celestine III. The bishop had celebrated after Cardinal Gregory of S. Angelo, Celestine III's legate, imposed sentences of interdict and excommunication on him: 'ex eo quod celebraveras post interdicti et excommunicationis sententias quas in te post appellationem interpositam eundem cardinalem tulisse decebas'.

[10]Mansilla, *Documentación pontificia*, 171-2, no. 140 (21 April 1198) = PL 214:81.

[11]Mansilla, *Documentación pontificia*, 175-6, no. 144 (2 May 1198) = PL 214:115. See also the papal letter of 28 May 1198, ibid., 181-2, no. 152 .

[12]Roger de Hoveden, *Chronica*, 4 vols, RS, 51/4 (London, 1868):78-9; Peter Linehan, *History and the Historians of Medieval Spain* (Oxford, 1993), 258; González, *Alfonso IX*, 1:101, accepts the report without comment.

[13]Queen Isabelle, the sister of Baldwin IV (1174-1185), was married four times. Her first marriage to Humphrey of Toron was dissolved in November 1190 on the grounds of lack of consent due to her tender age; she was next married to Conrad of Montferrat, and on his assassination in April 1192, to Henry of Champagne. When Henry died in September 1197 she was married to Amaury II, king of Cyprus. See Steven Runciman, *A History of the Crusades*, 3 vols (Cambridge, 1952), especially vol. 3.

Palencia, representing the king of Castile, and Bishop Martín of Zamora, a canonist acting on behalf of Alfonso IX,[14] had come to Rome to request a papal dispensation for the marriage, even though Celestine III had refused to give it. The prelates also asked the pope to lift the interdict on León because of a threefold threat from heretics, Saracens and Christians. The bishops argued that the interdict prohibited them from preaching against heresy and from exhorting the people to take up arms against the Muslims or to offer remission of sins to those who did so. Inasmuch as the clergy could not minister to the laity, Christians withdrew their offerings, first fruits, tithes and other temporal support from the clergy, who in consequence were forced to beg and to forage and to serve the Jews, to the opprobrium of the church and of all Christendom.[15]

Innocent III indicated that it was difficult to consent to this petition because he did not wish to give the appearance of failing to proceed in accordance with justice and honesty, especially as Rainier, after legitimate warnings and delays, had imposed ecclesiastical penalties as he had been instructed to do. The pope cited the divine punishment of King David for his adultery with Bathsheba (2 Samuel 24:17) and Celestine III's imposition of similar censures on the kings of Portugal and León because Alfonso IX had first been married in 1190 to his second cousin Teresa of Portugal.[16] Rather than be accused of showing favor to certain persons and not to others, the pope denied the petition except in part. In order to determine whether the parties were prompted by God, as the bishops told him, Innocent agreed to relax the interdict temporarily by permitting the celebration of divine services. Nevertheless, burial in consecrated ground was denied to the laity but not to the clergy, who could be buried there but without the usual solemnities.[17] As the sentence of excommunication against Alfonso IX, Berenguela, their counsellors and supporters would remain in effect whenever they came to a city, town or village, no one was allowed to celebrate in their

---

[14]Linehan, *History*, 257, noted that the bishop of Zamora was the canonist Martín Arias.

[15]Mansilla, *Documentación pontificia*, 209-12, no. 196 (*Etsi necesse*, 25 May 1199) = PL 214:610. Linehan, *History*, 255-6, pointed out that in one of his sermons Santo Martino of León (Sermo X, 'De diversis,' PL 219:134) made much the same argument as the Spanish prelates.

[16]Teresa (the daughter of Sancho I of Portugal) and Alfonso IX were married at Guimaraes on 15 February 1190. Rodrigo Jiménez de Rada, *De rebus Hispaniae*, 7.24, pp. 246-7, declared that 'in odium regis Castellae fuit hoc contubernium procuratum'. Bishop Juan of Oviedo opposed the marriage and was forced into exile. Celestine III excommunicated the kings of León and Portugal and placed an interdict on both kingdoms so long as the marriage remained in effect. Alfonso IX separated from Teresa in 1194, after three children were born, Sancha, Fernando and Dulce. González, *Alfonso IX*, 1: 61-7. Roger de Hoveden, *Chronica*, 3:90 stated that Celestine III placed an interdict on the kingdom of León because of this marriage and that Alfonso VIII forced Alfonso IX to abandon Teresa and to marry Berenguela, 'permissione domini papae Coelestini pro bono pacis'. I doubt that Celestine III gave his permission for the marriage.

[17]In support of his decision he cited the II Lateran Council, canon 20, which prohibited Christian burial of those killed in tournaments.

presence. If Alfonso VIII and Queen Leonor reneged on their promise to obey the pope, he pledged to order their excommunication and the imposition of the interdict on Castile. The castles given to Berenguela as her dowry should be restored to Alfonso IX, but any children born to the couple would be considered illegitimate. Pope Innocent revealed that he was prepared to take further action if they refused to submit, but he chose not to discuss the possibilities at this time. In his letter of 25 May 1199 summarizing the situation he admonished Archbishop Pedro of Compostela and the other bishops in the kingdom of León to punish any cleric who violated the interdict, but he reserved the punishment of Bishop Gonzalo of Salamanca to himself.[18]

The pope's threats failed to achieve the effect he hoped as neither Alfonso VIII nor Alfonso IX acquiesced in his demands. Rather than disrupt the fragile harmony between the two kingdoms, Alfonso IX and Berenguela remained together. In the latter half of 1198 Berenguela had given birth to her first child, Leonor.[19] The two kings met at Palencia on 8 December 1199 to confirm the marriage contract and the dowry granted to Berenguela, without making the slightest reference to papal objections to the match.[20] The marriage probably was discussed when the two kings met again at Medina del Campo in January 1201 and during the Council of Salamanca held in June-July.[21] In August of that same year Berenguela gave birth to the future Fernando III (1217-1252), who would reunite the kingdoms of Castile and León in 1230.[22]

After so many years passed without acceptance of his demands, Pope Innocent III addressed a bitter complaint on 5 June 1203 to Alfonso VIII of Castile whom he saw as the principal obstacle to the dissolution of the marriage.[23] Castigating

---

[18]Mansilla, *Documentación pontificia*, 209-15, no. 196 = PL 214:610. See also ibid., 336-8, no. 305 (20 June 1204) = PL 215:373. Linehan, *History*, 257, remarked that this bull was included in the *Compilatio tertia* and then in the *Liber Extra* (4.20.5).

[19]Leonor died on 12 November 1202 and was buried in San Isidoro de León. The other children were the future Fernando III, who would reunite Castile and León, Alfonso, Constanza and Berenguela. Rodrigo Jiménez de Rada, *De rebus Hispaniae*, 7.24, pp. 246-7; Lucas of Túy, *Chronicon Mundi*, 4:111; González, *Alfonso VIII*, 1:390.

[20]Thirty castles were to be held by Alfonso VIII in the name of Berenguela. González, *Alfonso IX*, 1:104-5, and 2:194-7, no. 135, and *Alfonso VIII*, 1:729-30, and 3:204-8, no. 681.

[21]González, *Alfonso IX*, 1:106, 108, and *Alfonso VIII*, 1:730.

[22]Fernando is recorded for the first time in a royal charter of 5 August 1201; González, *Alfonso IX*, 2:218, no. 155; Julio González, *Reinado y diplomas de Fernando III*, 3 vols (Córdoba, 1980-86), 1:61-3.

[23]Bishop-elect Mauricio of Burgos went to Rome for consecration and probably reported to the pope concerning the status of the marriage. Innocent III commissioned the bishops of Burgos and Osma on 17 June 1203 to inquire into accusations against the bishop of Astorga. Mansilla, *Documentación pontificia*, 307-8, no. 278 = PL 215:96. See also, ibid., 322-3, 328-9, nos. 284 (11 July 1203), 293 (12 January 1204) = PL 215:133, 227. In 1201 Mateo bishop-elect of Burgos went to Rome to be consecrated by Innocent III and probably reported on the situation in Spain. Gonzalez, *Alfonso IX*, 1:106-7, 115, and *Alfonso VIII*, 1:731-2.

the Castilian ruler for giving lip service while refusing in his heart to obey, the pope charged that the king eluded divine censure and the judgment of the church by pleasing words and by blaming another for his own fault. The king of Castile, according to reports received by the pope, had entrapped the king of León, taking advantage of his simplicity. Alfonso VIII had arranged for his own men to hold as Berenguela's dowry many of the best fortresses in the kingdom of León which would remain in her possession should Alfonso IX abandon her. Innocent was especially distressed because Alfonso VIII cunningly arranged for the whole kingdom of León to swear allegiance to the children of this incestuous marriage (probably at the curia of Benavente in 1202)[24] even though the pope, denouncing them as spurious, had declared that they would never have any right of succession. Accusing the king of Castile of having put a bit in the mouth of Alfonso IX, leading him at will and disposing of his kingdom as though it were his own, Pope Innocent now demanded the dissolution of 'all alliances of iniquity' and the return of Berenguela to her father's house. Otherwise the pope promised to take such action against Alfonso VIII and his kingdom 'as seems expedient to us'. There could be no doubt that the threat of excommunication and interdict was implied.[25]

Alfonso VIII apparently concluded that he could not escape ecclesiastical censure much longer. Inasmuch as Berenguela now had four surviving children, including two boys, the king of Castile bowed to papal pressure and at Valladolid in April 1204 acquiesced in the dissolution of the marriage. From May onward Berenguela was no longer recorded in Alfonso IX's charters as his queen.[26]

Archbishop Martín of Toledo and Bishop Fernando of Burgos wrote to inform the pope that Berenguela had indeed separated from her husband and was repentant. Therefore, Innocent III on 22 May 1204 instructed the two prelates and Bishop Martín of Zamora to absolve her from the sentence of excommunication.[27] He sent a similar letter to Archbishop Pedro of Compostela and Bishops Martín of Zamora and Arderico of Palencia on 19 June ordering them to absolve Alfonso IX, his counsellors and supporters from excommunication and to lift the interdict on his kingdom.[28] Through his *nuntius* Magister Lope, Alfonso VIII asked the pope not to require him to give up the castles which Alfonso IX had given as dowry to Berenguela; the king of Castile argued that the castles belonged to

---

[24]The coincidence of Infante Fernando's birth in August 1201, the convocation of the curia six months later and the pope's letter of June 1203 suggests that the recognition ceremony did take place at Benavente in March 1202. Joseph F. O'Callaghan, 'The Beginnings of the Cortes of León-Castile', *American Historical Review* 74 (1969), 1520-1.

[25]Mansilla, *Documentación pontificia*, 305-6, no. 276 = PL 215:82.

[26]González, *Alfonso VIII*, 1:733-4, and *Alfonso IX*, 1:117, citing her motto from a charter: 'Domine, doce me facere voluntatem tuam.'

[27]Mansilla, *Documentación pontificia*, 332, no. 299 = PL 215:345.

[28]Mansilla, *Documentación pontificia*, 335-6, no. 304 = PL 215: 376.

Berenguela, rather than himself. Innocent III saw through this attempt to retain the castles for Castile. In a third letter dated 20 June he instructed the Archbishops Pedro of Compostela and Martín of Toledo and Bishops García of Tarazona and Pedro of Coimbra to require Berenguela to restore the castles once the king of León was absolved. If she did not the pope authorized the bishops to excommunicate her and her parents. [29]

Not surprisingly hostilities between the kings of Castile and León erupted shortly concerning the disposition of the castles in question.[30] That prompted Innocent III to demand that the archbishops of Compostela and Toledo and the bishops of Coimbra and Tarazona proceed as he had already commanded them to arrange the differences between Castile and León (2 March 1206).[31] Even before the pope's letter was received the two kings reached a new agreement at Cabreros on 26 March 1206; Fernando, the oldest son of Alfonso IX and Berenguela, would succeed to the Leonese throne and would receive Berenguela's dower lands.[32] Alfonso IX seems not to have been entirely satisfied by this and sought an alliance with King John of England, whom Alfonso VIII had offended in 1204-1205 by claiming and invading Gascony as the dowry of his wife, Queen Leonor of Castile.[33] In a letter of 7 August 1207 John asked Alfonso IX to send a discreet and faithful representative to discuss the matter further.[34] Perhaps on that account Alfonso VIII agreed to a new settlement with León at Valladolid on 27 June 1209.[35] That concluded the matter and there is no record that Innocent III troubled himself further about it. Linehan pointed out, however, that the pope had not legitimated Fernando III, an action that was taken by Innocent's successor, Honorius III, in 1218.[36]

---

[29]Mansilla, *Documentación pontificia*, 336-9, no. 305 = PL 215:373; González, *Alfonso IX*, 1:116-17, and *Alfonso VIII*, 1:733-5.

[30]*Chronique latine*, 17, pp. 53-4; González, *Alfonso IX*, 1:119, and *Alfonso VIII*, 1:390-1, 735-8. Innocent III ordered Archbishop Martín of Toledo on 28 January 1206 to settle a complaint of the knights of the Hospital who protested that Alfonso VIII, during the conflict with León, had seized their castles of Fraxina and Paradinas and three villages of Torisella, Tarauca and Porta. Mansilla, *Documentación pontificia*, 353-4, no. 326 = PL 215:782.

[31]Mansilla, *Documentación pontificia*, 358, no. 331 = PL 215:810.

[32]González, *Alfonso IX*, 1:121-3, and 2:284-91, no. 205, and *Alfonso VIII*, 1:738-40, and 2:365-74, no. 782.

[33]*Chronique latine*, 17, pp. 51-4; Rodrigo Jiménez de Rada, *De rebus Hispaniae*, 7.34, p. 256.

[34]Thomas Rymer, *Foedera, conventiones, litterae et cuiuscunque acta publica inter reges Angliae et alios quovis imperatores, reges, pontifices, principes*, 3rd edn, 10 vols (The Hague, 1739-45), 1:45; González, *Alfonso IX*, 1:123-4, and *Alfonso VIII*, 1:739-40, 873.

[35]González, *Alfonso IX*, 1:129-31, and 2:341-5, no. 251, and *Alfonso VIII*, 1: 741-44 and 3:479-84, no. 845.

[36]Linehan, *History*, 258-9. See González, *Alfonso IX*, 2:460-2, no. 352 for the pact between Alfonso IX and Fernando III, and Demetrio Mansilla, *La documentación pontificia de Honorio III* (Rome, 1965), 141-2, no. 179 (10 July 1218).

THE PACIFICATION OF CHRISTIAN SPAIN

The resolution of the marriage conflict went a long way toward the establishment of peaceful, if not friendly, relations between Castile and León, but the pope was also concerned about relationships among the other Christian states of Spain. Both the tiny kingdom of Navarre set in the foothills of the Pyrenees and Portugal, a kingdom stretching along the Atlantic coast, were resentful of Castilian designs on their territory.

The kings of Castile and Aragón planned since the second quarter of the twelfth century to divide Navarre between them.[37] The truce with the Almohads and the resolution of differences with León in 1197 enabled Alfonso VIII to turn against Sancho VII of Navarre (1194-1234) with whom he had a long-standing quarrel over frontier lands.[38] Celestine III's legate Cardinal Gregory had excommunicated Sancho VII and imposed an interdict on the kingdom of Navarre because he broke a truce with Castile.[39] Intent on dividing Navarre between them, Alfonso VIII and Pedro II of Aragón (1196-1213) invaded that kingdom, but Sancho VII temporarily averted disaster by agreeing to the marriage of his sister to the Aragonese king. Noting that the couple were related within the third degree and that Sancho VII's oath was invalid due to duress, Innocent III on 11 February 1199 absolved the king of Navarre from any obligation to abide by his oath.[40] Unable to resist the kings of Castile and Aragón, Sancho VII fled to the court of the Almohad caliph in Morocco but received only financial aid to defend his kingdom. Thus Alfonso VIII was able to occupy Vitoria, Guipúzcoa and Alava in 1204-1205 and compel the king of Navarre to come to terms.[41] Innocent III instructed Archbishop Pedro of Compostela and Bishop García of Tarazona on 16 June 1205 to procure peace between Castile and Navarre,[42] but two years elapsed before a five-year truce was concluded; Castile remained in possession

---

[37]O'Callaghan, *Medieval Spain*, 225, 232, 235, 240.

[38]González, *Alfonso VIII*, 1:842-5; O'Callaghan, *Medieval Spain*, 236, 239.

[39]In his instruction to Rainier on 16 April 1198, Innocent III noted this. On 15 July 1198 the pope authorized Bishop García of Pamplona to celebrate divine office during the interdict under certain limitations. Mansilla, *Documentación pontificia*, 169, 187, nos. 138, 162 = PL 214:79, 244.

[40]Mansilla, *Documentación pontificia*, 197-8, no. 181 = PL 214:509; Gonzalez, *Alfonso VIII*, 1:845-8. Pedro II requested Sancho VII's sister in marriage, but the king of Navarre demanded that the invaders first leave his kingdom. Alfonso VIII refused, so Sancho VII agreed to a truce and to the marriage.

[41]*Chrónicon Burgense, ES* 23:310, records the burning of Vitoria in era MCCXL [1202]; Rodrigo Jiménez de Rada, *De rebus Hispaniae*, 7.32, pp. 253-4; *Chronique latine*, 16, pp. 50-1; Gonzalez, *Alfonso VIII*, 1:848-54.

[42]Mansilla, *Documentación pontificia*, 347, no. 315 (no text), citing Ferran Miquel, *Regesta de letras pontificias del Archivo de la Corona de Aragón. Sección Cancillería real* (Madrid, 1948), 44, no. 55.

of the recently conquered provinces.[43] Aragón and Navarre also made peace in 1208 and renewed it in the following year,[44] but there is no evidence that Innocent III was directly involved.

Portugal's relations with Castile and León were also difficult. Once a county within the kingdom of León, Portugal had claimed its independence under Afonso I (1128-1185), but the neighboring kings, Fernando II of León (1157-1188) and Sancho III of Castile (1157-1158), had agreed to partition that realm between them.[45] On 16 April 1198 the pope urged Rainier, using excommunication and interdict if necessary, to bring together the rulers of the three kingdoms with other kings, presumably those of Navarre and Aragón 'so that they may strive to reform an alliance of peace' – 'inter se pacis studeant federa reformare'.[46] Even before the pope wrote his letter, Alfonso VIII and Sancho I of Portugal (1185-1211), probably in the fall of 1197, had concluded a peace treaty, but as Innocent III remarked, certain wicked persons were trying to undermine it; therefore he ordered Rainier on 6 June 1198 to use excommunication and interdict if need be to thwart such efforts.[47] From the pope's point of view Sancho I's decision to pay arrears of tribute, owed ever since his father Afonso I declared himself a papal vassal, was immensely gratifying. The king admitted to Rainier that he owed an annual tribute of four ounces of gold and sent five hundred *maravedís* to Rome by the hand of Alfonso, the Master of the Hospital in Spain. Pope Innocent told Rainier to remind the king to fulfill his obligation regularly.[48] The marriage in 1208 of Alfonso VIII's daughter Urraca to Infante Afonso, the heir to the Portuguese throne, also solidified peaceful relations between Castile and Portugal.[49]

PREPARATIONS FOR THE CRUSADE OF LAS NAVAS DE TOLOSA

By the end of 1209 the Christian rulers were finally at peace with one another, a fortunate circumstance because the truce with the Almohads was about to expire.

---

[43]The truce was concluded at Guadalajara on 29 October 1207; González, *Alfonso VIII*, 1:873-4, and 3:424-9, no. 813.

[44]The treaty was concluded at Monteagudo on 2 February 1208, and renewed at Mallén on 4 June 1209. Ambrosio Huici, *Las grandes batallas de la reconquista durante las invasiones africanas (Almorávides, Almohades y Benimerines* (Madrid, 1956), 219-27.

[45]González, *Alfonso VIII*, 1:667-70, and 2:79-82, no. 44, and *Regesta de Fernando II* (Madrid, 1943), 28-35, 241-3, no. 1.

[46]Mansilla, *Documentación pontificia*, 168-70, 172-4, nos. 138 (16 April 1198), 141 (24 April) = PL 214:79, 82. The pope had already written to the Spanish prelates (the letter is not extant) telling them to abide by whatever the legate determined in these matters.

[47]Mansilla, *Documentación pontificia*, 185, no. 157 (6 June 1198) = PL 214:214; González, *Alfonso VIII*, 1:722.

[48]Mansilla, *Documentación pontificia*, 193, no. 170 (9 December 1198) = PL 214:425.

[49]*Chronique latine*, 18, p. 54; Lucas of Túy, *Chronicon Mundi*, 4:111; González, *Alfonso VIII*, 1:203-4.

Given the existing peace among the Christians, Innocent III on 26 February 1210 urged Archbishop Rodrigo Jiménez de Rada of Toledo and his suffragans to encourage Alfonso VIII to imitate the example of Pedro II of Aragón who was preparing to go to war against the Saracens. If the king could not be persuaded, he was forbidden to prevent any of his subjects from aiding Pedro II. The archbishop and his suffragans were authorized to offer remission of sins to their people who elected to join the king of Aragón.[50] In a letter addressed to the archbishops and bishops of Spain, the pope lauded the intention of the Castilian Infante Fernando who wished 'to dedicate the first fruits of his knighthood to Almighty God by driving the enemies of the Christian name from the bounds of his inheritance which they impiously occupied'. Although the pope did not say so, it seems likely that Infante Fernando made the crusader's vow. The pope urged the prelates to promise remission of sins to those kings who were not bound by truces with the enemy and lent their aid. The same remission was granted to pilgrims who set out to carry on the work (10 December 1210).[51] Reiterating his words of praise on 22 February 1211, the pope authorized Archbishop Rodrigo of Toledo and the bishops of Tarazona, Coimbra and Zamora to impose ecclesiastical censures on any king of Spain who, while Alfonso VIII and Infante Fernando were attacking the Saracens, violated the peace or truce made with Castile.[52] On the same day, citing the disturbed condition of the times, the pope turned down Alfonso VIII's request that he appoint a legate for Spain, no doubt to encourage the campaign against the Moors, though he hinted that he might do so later.[53]

As the truce with the Almohads expired and the Christians commenced raids against Muslim territory, the Caliph an-Nasir (1199-1213), known to the

---

[50]Mansilla, *Documentación pontificia*, 436, no. 416; Javier Gorosterratzu, *Don Rodrigo Jiménez de Rada, Gran Estadista, Escritor y Prelado* (Pamplona, 1925), 411, no. 1 (16 February 1210). The pope approved Rodrigo's election on 27 February 1210; ibid., 411-12, no. 2; González, *Alfonso VIII*, 1:391, 982-3.

[51]Mansilla, *Documentación pontificia*, 472-3, no. 442 = PL 216:353; Gorosterratzu, *Don Rodrigo*, 414-15, no. 8; González, *Alfonso VIII*, 1:391, 985.

[52]Mansilla, *Documentación pontificia*, 474-5, no. 446 = PL 216:379; Gorosterratzu, *Don Rodrigo*, 415, no. 9. Ibn 'Idhârî, *al-Bayân al-Mugrib fi Ijtisâr Ajbâr Muluk al-andalus wa al-Magrib*, trans. Ambrosio Huici Miranda, *Colección de Crónicas árabes,* 3 vols (Tetuán, 1953), 2:266, reported that the bishops (the imams of the infidels) received an envoy from Rome instructing them to maintain the peace.

[53]A papal letter to the same effect was sent on the same day to Infante Fernando. Mansilla, *Documentación pontificia*, 475-7, nos. 447-8 = PL 216:380; Gorosterratzu, *Don Rodrigo*, 415-16, no. 10; González, *Alfonso VIII*, 1:391, 985-6. Bishop-elect Tello of Palencia was the Castilian envoy to Rome.

Christians as Miramamolín, crossed the Strait of Gibraltar in May 1211.[54] Advancing northward from Córdoba, he stopped in July to besiege the castle of Salvatierra, guarding the road to Toledo, which served as the headquarters of the Order of Calatrava since the loss of the fortress of Calatrava itself in 1195. The knights of Calatrava successfully defended the castle through the summer until the king, unable to assist them, authorized them to surrender in September. Although Salvatierra fell into enemy hands, the caliph decided to terminate the campaign and returned to Córdoba.[55] Infante Fernando, meantime, died suddenly in October 1211 before he could fulfill his great desire.[56]

In preparation for the renewal of war in the following spring, Alfonso VIII, after taking counsel with the archbishop, bishops and magnates of the realm, concluded that it was preferable 'to prove the will of heaven in the danger of battle than to witness the ruin of the fatherland'.[57] Appealing to Innocent III for help, the king voiced his determination to oppose the Almohads on the battlefield, 'choosing to die rather than witness the ruin of the Christian people'. For that reason he summoned his army to engage the enemy in a pitched battle in the octave of Pentecost. The pope therefore, on 31 January 1212, called on Archbishop Pierre of Sens and his suffragans in France to offer remission of sins to all those who aided the king of Castile in person or in goods.[58] A few days later (4 February) the pope informed Alfonso VIII that he had sent letters to that

---

[54]Matthew Paris, *Chronica Majora*, ed. H. R. Luard, 7 vols, RS (London, 1872-1883), 2:559-66, related that King John of England sent envoys to the caliph, offering his realm to him and promising to pay tribute and even to convert to Islam. The caliph concluded that John was a fool. Nevertheless, John, whom the chronicler despised, encouraged the caliph's invasion (p. 565): 'non sine, ut dicitur, regis Joannis assensu, fines Hispaniae potenter disposuit occupare'. Matthew says he heard this story from the envoy Robert of London.

[55]Rodrigo Jiménez de Rada, *De rebus Hispaniae*, 7.34-35, pp. 256-7; *Chronique latine*, 18-19, pp. 55-8; Lucas of Túy, *Chronicon Mundi*, 4:111; *Anales Compostelani*, ES 23:324; Ibn 'Idhârî, *al-Bayân al-Mugrib*, 2:261-8; Joseph F. O'Callaghan, 'The Order of Calatrava: Years of Crisis and Survival, 1158-1212', in *The Meeting of Two Worlds: Cultural Exchange between East and West during the Period of the Crusades*, ed. Vladimir P. Goss and Christine Verzár Bornstein (Kalamazoo, 1986), 427-8.

[56]*Anales Toledanos I* and *Annales Compostelani*, ES 23:324, 396 record his death on 14 October; Rodrigo Jiménez de Rada, *De rebus Hispaniae*, 7.35, p. 257; *Chronique latine*, 20, pp. 58-9; González, *Alfonso VIII*, 1:986-96.

[57]Rodrigo Jiménez de Rada, *De rebus Hispaniae*, 7.36, pp. 258-9: 'melius esse in bello voluntatem coeli sub discrimine experiri quam videre mala patriae'.

[58]Mansilla, *Documentación pontificia*, 497-8, no. 468 = PL 216:514; Gorosterratzu, *Don Rodrigo*, 417, no. 15: 'mandamus quatinus subditos vestros sedulis exhortationibus moneatis in remissionem omnium peccatorum ex parte Dei et nostra vere penitentibus iniungentes, ut ei prescripto termino in hoc necessitatis articulo succurrentes, necessarium impendant auxilium in rebus pariter et personis; ut per hec et alia bona que fecerint celestis regni gloriam consequi mereantur; pari quoque remissione gaudere concedimus peregrinos qui propria devocione undecumque processerint ad idem opus fideliter exequendum.'

effect to the prelates of France and Provence.[59]

How the crusade privilege was perceived in Spain is revealed in the report of the *Anales Toledanos I* that the pope granted 'such liberty throughout the whole world that all should be absolved from their sins, and this pardon was [granted] because the king of Morocco said that he would fight against those throughout the world who adored the cross'.[60] The remark attributed to the caliph probably was employed by preachers to arouse the faithful. The *Latin Chronicle,* written perhaps by Bishop Juan of Osma, narrated that when Alfonso VIII sent his envoys to seek aid in France and in other Christian lands, the king of Morocco declared that he would wage war against all who adored the sign of the cross.[61] Archbishop Arnald Amaury of Narbonne used the same language in his account of the crusade.[62] Both were referring to a false letter of the caliph Miramamolín dated 8 October 1211 that apparently circulated widely.[63]

---

[59]Mansilla, *Documentación pontificia,* 500-1, no. 470 = PL 216:513; Gorosterratzu, *Don Rodrigo,* 417, no. 14; González, *Alfonso VIII,* 1:997-8. Bishop Gerardo of Segovia was the royal envoy to Rome.

[60]*Anales Toledanos I, ES* 23:396: 'dio el Apostoligo a tal soltura a por tod el mundo que fuesen todos soltos de sus pecados; e este perdon fue porque el rey de Marruecos dixo que lidiare con quantos adoraban Cruz en todo el mundo.'

[61]*Chronique latine,* 23, p. 67: 'fertur dixisse rex marroquitanus quia ipse potens erat bellare contra omnes qui signum crucis adorabant'. Lucas of Túy, *Chronicon Mundi,* 4:111: 'Rex Miramamolinus, ut haec audivit, valde pertimuit et doluit se verbum superbiae protulisse, scilicet quod vinceret in campo omnes adorantes crucem Christi.' Michele Maccarrone, 'La crociata e la sua predicazione nel programma e nell'azione di Innocenzo III', in his *Studi su Innocenzo III* (Padua, 1972), 94.

[62]Archbishop Arnald said that Miramamolín 'sicut audivimus a plerisque, bellum indixerat omnibus illis qui crucem adorant'. The archbishop continued: 'ab illis eisdem qui crucem colunt bello campestri devictus est et fugatus'. Archbishop Arnald's account of the campaign was addressed to the Cistercian General Chapter, which usually met on 14 September each year. See the text in Marqués de Mondéjar, *Memorias históricas de la vida y acciones del Rey Don Alfonso el Noble Octavo del Nombre* (Madrid, 1783), Appendix, CIII-CVII (for the quotation see CIV); Ferdinando Ughelli, *Italia Sacra,* new ed. Nicolai Coleto, 10 vols (Venice, 1717-23), 1:188. There is probably an echo of this in Alberic of Trois Fontaines, *Chronica,* MGH SS, 23:894, who reported that 'rex Sarracenorum in Hispania qui dicebatur Mammelinus aggressus est fines Hispanensium christianorum et locutus est in magna superbia contra christicolas et optulit eis bellum'.

[63]The text is given in the Austrian *Continuatio Lambacensis,* MGH SS, 9:557-8. The letter is addressed 'omnibus regibus et principibus christianorum et maxime regi Aragonum et comiti de Baruh, iram et indignationem'. The caliph mentions that Muslim arms had cleansed Jerusalem of the filthiness of the Christians – 'purgaverunt ab immundiciis christianorum' – and that he had now taken Salvatierra, a fortress in which the Christians had invested their pride. He then commented that the 'lex Sarracenica melior est quam vestra' and urged the Christians to submit to his rule and to accept Islam – 'quatenus subdatis vos imperio nostro et transeatis ad legem nostram'. If not, he told them to assemble 'omnes qui signum crucis adorant et nobis occurrite ad conflictum et ibi experiemini enses nostros'. Addressing the king of Aragón, the caliph commented that it was at the king's suggestion and counsel that great harm had been done to the Saracens, and that he had done so on the advice of the pope. He then concluded, promising to fight unceasingly and to proceed on to Rome and to subject the lord of Rome to contumely and misery.

Meanwhile the king sent Archbishop Rodrigo Jiménez de Rada of Toledo to seek help from King Philip Augustus of France. In his letter to the French king, Alfonso VIII declared that if he should die in the coming battle against the Moors he would 'truly be counted among the martyrs'.[64] Although Archbishop Rodrigo offered 'remission of sins' to those who would defend the faith and who would 'fortify themselves with the sign of the cross', he had not much success.[65] While the archbishop's plea fell on deaf ears, the royal physician Master Arnald had greater success in gaining recruits in Poitou and Gascony.[66]

Innocent III on 5 April 1212 commanded the archbishops of Toledo and Compostela, using ecclesiastical censures if necessary, to demand that the kings of Spain maintain the peace and truce with one another during the war against the Saracens. The kings ought also to lend mutual assistance 'against the enemies of the cross of the Lord who not only aspire to the destruction of the Spains, but also threaten to vent their rage on Christ's faithful in other lands and, if they can, which God forbid, oppress the Christian name'. Singling out King Alfonso IX of León, the pope prohibited anyone, under pain of excommunication and interdict, from joining the Saracens or lending them aid and counsel against the Christians. The resolution of all disputes would be postponed until a suitable time when the parties could send their procurators and witnesses to the papal court where the pope promised to render the plenitude of justice.[67] Acting on Innocent III's instructions, the two archbishops sent a copy of the papal letter to Alfonso IX of León and ordered him to maintain peace with his Christian neighbors and to lend his assistance against the Saracens.[68] The king of León, however, still angry with Castile, and more concerned to take advantage of the death of Sancho I of

---

[64]González, *Alfonso VIII*, 1:999, and 3:557-8, no. 890: 'nihil dubitantes quod si sanguis noster in conflictu Christi respondet sanguini, vere poterimus inter martyres computeri'. Goñi Gaztambide, *Historia*, 114, n. 13.

[65]Lucas of Tuy, *Chronicon Mundi*, 4:110: 'ad defensionem fidei convenirent, data illis remissione peccatorum et eos crucis signaculo muniendo'. Rodrigo Jiménez de Rada, *De rebus Hispaniae*, 8.1, p. 259.

[66]Speaking of Archbishop Rodrigo's mission, the *Chronique latine*, 21, pp. 60-1, remarks: 'neque uerbum bonum habere potuit ab ore eius [the king of France] . . . sed nec unum ex eis [the French magnates] mouere potuit'. The troubadour Gavaudan appealed to the emperor and the kings of France and England to aid the king of Spain; Carlos Alvar, *Textos trovadorescos sobre España y Portugal* (Madrid, 1978), 91-4; Goñi Gaztambide, *Historia*, 113-15.

[67]Mansilla, *Documentación pontificia*, 501-2, no. 471 = PL 216:553; Gorosterratzu, *Don Rodrigo*, 416, no. 13. A similar fragmentary text dated 5 April 1211 published by Mansilla, *Documentación pontificia*, 480-1, no. 452, and Gorosterratzu, *Don Rodrigo*, 416, no. 11, probably was misdated by a copyist and should be dated 5 April 1212. Goñi Gaztambide, *Historia*, 116.

[68]Archivo de la Catedral de Toledo, A.6.H.1.37, and Madrid, Archivo Histórico Nacional 996B, fol. 39vb-40ra, cited by Francisco J. Hernández, *Los cartularios de Toledo. Catálogo documental* (Madrid, 1985), 329, 651, nos. 328, 649. The letter of the two prelates is undated. González, *Alfonso IX*, 1:143-4.

Portugal in May 1211, opted not to participate in the coming crusade.[69] At the pope's direction, the men, women and clergy of Rome, on Wednesday 16 May, within the octave of Pentecost, while observing the fast, went in procession to the Lateran basilica praying 'that God might be propitious to those engaged in battle' with the Saracens in Spain.[70] The French Cistercian chronicler Alberic of Trois Fontaines related that 'litanies and prayers were offered in France for the Christians who were about to fight in Spain'.[71]

THE CRUSADE OF LAS NAVAS DE TOLOSA

During the octave of Pentecost 'the faithful of Christ gathered at Toledo from all parts of the world because of the remission granted by the Lord Pope, the vicar of the Lord Jesus Christ to those going off to give battle in support of Christendom in Spain'.[72] Included in the 'army of the Lord' – 'exercitus Domini' – were Alfonso VIII, Pedro II of Aragón, Archbishops Arnald Amaury of Narbonne and Guillaume of Bordeaux, several counts and viscounts from southern France, the knights of the Military Orders of Calatrava, Santiago, the Temple and the Hospital, as well as the Castilian nobles and the urban militias. Sancho VII of Navarre joined them shortly.[73] As the Christians advanced southward the French became angry with the lack of booty and withdrew. Nevertheless, the Spanish Christians emerged triumphant in a fierce battle with the Almohads at Las Navas de Tolosa on 16 July 1212.[74] In an exultant mood, Alfonso VIII sent the standard

---

[69]Alfonso IX attacked the Castilian frontier during the campaign of Las Navas but made a truce with Castile and Portugal on 11 November at Coimbra. González, *Alfonso VIII*, 3:576, no. 900, and *Alfonso IX*, 1:144-7.

[70]Mansilla, *Documentación pontificia*, 503-4, no. 473 = PL 216:698. The pope had granted the indulgence to those pilgrims who went in procession asking God to aid the enterprise.

[71]Alberic of Trois Fontaines, *Chronica*, MGH SS, 23:894, also recorded portents in the sky: 'quod ea die cum fierent letanie et preces in Francia pro christianis qui pugnaturi erant in Hispania, visus est sol circa horam nonam in antea salire et reverti et nunc esse rubeus, nunc hiacinthinus; non fuit eclipsis solis, utpote luna plena, sed lune potius eclipsis poterat dici, si de nocte occurrisset'. See the excerpt from Alberic's *Chronica* in Mondéjar, *Alonso el Noble*, Appendix, CXXII.

[72]See Archbishop Arnald of Narbonne in Mondéjar, *Alonso el Noble*, Appendix, CIV: 'Siquidem cum de universis mundi partibus fideles Christi propter remissionem quae a domino Papa Domini Jesu Christi vicario proficiscentibus ad indictum bellum in Christianitatis Hispaniae subsidium est indulta . . .'.

[73]*Chronique latine*, 21, pp. 60-63; Rodrigo Jiménez de Rada, *De rebus Hispaniae*, 8.1-4, pp. 259-64. Archbishop Arnald of Narbonne related that he visited the king of Navarre 'qui tunc inimicatur domino Regi Castellae' and persuaded him to collaborate in the enterprise. See the text in Mondéjar, *Alonso el Noble*, Appendix, CIII-CVII; Ughelli, *Italia Sacra*, 1:188; González, *Alfonso VIII*, 1:1003-57.

[74]Rodrigo Jiménez de Rada, *De rebus Hispaniae*, 8.8-11, pp. 264-75; *Chronique latine*, 24-25, pp. 67-71; Lucas of Túy, *Chronicon Mundi*, 4:110-11; *Anales Toledanos I*, *ES* 23:397; Ibn 'Idhârî, *al-Bayân al-Mugrib*, 2:269-73; Alberic of Trois Fontaines, *Chronica*, MGH SS, 23:894-5; *Continuatio Claustroneoburgensis* II, MGH SS, 23:622; Ricardo de San Germano, *Chronica*, ed. C.A. Galufi,

and the tent of the Almohad caliph to Innocent III as a sign of the Christian victory,[75] together with a detailed account of the crusade:

On their side 100,000 armed men or more fell in the battle, according to the estimate of the Saracens whom we captured. But of the army of the Lord . . . incredible though it may be, unless it be a miracle, hardly twenty-five or thirty Christians of our whole army fell. O what happiness! O what thanksgiving! though one might lament that so few martyrs from such a great army went to Christ in martyrdom.[76]

On receipt of the king's letter Innocent III summoned the clergy and people of Rome to give thanks to God and ordered the letter to be read to everyone. The pope credited the victory to God, who laid low the pride of the infidels who did not recognize Him. It was 'the sword of God not of man . . . that struck down the enemies of the cross of the Lord'.[77]

Rerum Italicarum Scriptores, 7 vols (Bologna, 1958), 7.2:35-46.

[75] Alberic of Trois Fontaines, *Chronica,* MGH SS, 23:895, reported that the caliph's lance and standard were sent to Rome where 'adhuc in ecclesia beati Petri in loco eminentiori posita favorem et misericordiam Christi qua suos licet paucos respectu hostium in predicto bello victores fecit, in perpetuum representat'. Rigord, *Gesta Philippi Augusti,* in *Oeuvres de Rigord et de Guillaume le Breton, historiens de Philippe-Auguste,* ed. H. François Delaborde, 2 vols (Paris, 1882-1885), 1:241, repeated Alberic's words. Ricardo de San Germano, *Chronica,* 7.2:35, reported that the caliph's tent, all of silk, and his standard worked in gold were sent to Rome, and the standard was hung in the basilica of St Peter: 'Mittit etiam de acceptis Sarracenorum spoliis eidem honorabilia exenia, tentorium uidelicet totum sericum et uexillum auro contextum. Quod in principis apostolorum basilica in laudem nominis Christi appensum est.' The caliph's tent remained in the Vatican basilica until the end of the sixteenth century; Maccarrone, 'La crociata', 99, n. 3.

[76] González, *Alfonso VIII,* 3:566-72, no. 897; Mansilla, *Documentacion pontificia,* 511-15, no. 483 = PL 216:699; Maccarrone, 'La crociata', 94-9; Linehan, *History,* 295-6.

[77] Mansilla, *Documentacion pontificia,* 519-21, no. 488 (26 October 1212) = PL 216:703: 'Ista enim victoria proculdubio non humani operis exstitit set divini; et gladius Dei, non hominis, immo verius Dei hominis, inimicos crucis dominice devoravit.' The letter is also in Giulio Cipollone, *Cristianità – Islam: cattività e liberazione in nome di Dio. Il tempo di Innocenzo III dopo 'il 1187'* (Rome, 1992), 534-6, no. 43. Riley-Smith, *The Crusades,* 140, translated Innocent III's letter in part: 'God, the protector of those who hope in him, without whom nothing is strong, nothing firm, multiplying his mercy on you and the Christian people and pouring out his anger on races that do not acknowledge the Lord and against kingdoms that do not invoke his most holy name, according to what had been foretold long ago by the Holy Spirit, has made a laughing stock of the races which rashly murmured against him and a mockery of the peoples thinking empty thoughts, by humbling the arrogance of the strong and causing the pride of the infidels to be laid low . . . It was not your highness's hands but the Lord who has done all these things . . . For that victory took place without doubt not by human but by divine agency . . . So do not walk proudly because those who work wickedness have fallen there, but give glory and honour to the Lord, saying humbly with the prophet the *zeal of the Lord of Hosts* has done this. And while others exult in chariots and horses you ought to rejoice and glory in the name of the Lord your God.' Archbishop Arnald of Narbonne in Mondéjar,

For Pope Innocent the triumph at Las Navas de Tolosa meant that the Almohad peril had been contained and that the danger to Christendom in the west had been relieved. The death of the Almohad caliph by the end of 1213 and the ensuing minority of his successor surely convinced the pope that for some years to come there would be little to fear from Morocco. Moreover, the death of Alfonso VIII in late 1214 and the accession of his underage son, Enrique I (1214-1217), meant that the continuance of a truce with the Almohads would be imperative for several years. Thus Pope Innocent had every reason to believe that he could safely focus the crusading energy of western Europe exclusively on the recovery of the Holy Land.[78]

With that goal in mind on 19 April 1213 the pope summoned all the prelates of Europe to the Fourth Lateran Council.[79] At the same time he also revoked the remission of sins granted to those waging war against the Moors in Spain or the Albigensian heretics in southern France because success had been achieved by crusades in both regions. He did promise, however, to reconsider should that situation require it.[80] When the council met in 1215 a tax of one twentieth on ecclesiastical income for three years was proclaimed in support of the Fifth

---

Alfonso el Noble, Appendix, CVI, commented on the victory: 'Benedictus per omnia Dominus Jesus Christus qui per suam misericordiam in nostris temporibus sub felici Apostolatu domini Papae Innocentii de tribus generibus petulantium hominum & inimicorum Ecclesiae S. suae, videlicet orientalibus schismaticis, occidentalibus haereticis, meridionalibus Saracenis, victoriam contulit catholicis Christianis.' In this way the archbishop linked the Fourth Crusade which assaulted Constantinople and destroyed the Byzantine Empire, the Albigensian Crusade proclaimed against the heretics in southern France, with the Crusade of Las Navas de Tolosa.

[78] Innocent III instructed his legate in Provence, Archbishop Arnald of Narbonne, not to invite the faithful to seek the papal indulgence granted for the crusade against the Albigensians (15 January 1213): 'Accepimus siquidem quod rex sarracenorum partes suas armat ad prelium, nitens fortius in fidei christiane cultores insurgere, quo lapsu graviore succubuit sub populo christiano; immo sub Christo causam suam propitio nobis iuditio iudicante'. The legate was also instructed to consult Pedro II of Aragón about establishing the peace and truce of God throughout Provence. Mansilla, *Documentacion pontificia*, 522-3, no. 491 = PL 216:744. Pedro II proposed that the counts of Toulouse, Comminges, Foix and Béarn might be permitted to make satisfaction for whatever excesses they had committed in the Albigensian affair 'vel in frontaria sarracenorum eundo in subsidium christianorum cum militibus suis vel in partibus transmarinis'. Innocent III ordered Simon de Montfort to restore lands to the vassals of Pedro II seized while the king was engaged in the war against the Saracens. Mansilla, *Documentacion pontificia*, 523-5, nos. 492-3 (16-17 January 1213) = PL 216:741, 839; Goñi Gaztambide, *Historia*, 131.

[79] Mansilla, *Documentacion pontificia*, 543-5, no. 503 = PL 216:823; Goñi Gaztambide, *Historia*, 131-2.

[80] PL 216: 820: 'Et propter eandem causam remissiones et indulgentias hactenus a nobis concessas procedentibus in Hispaniam contra mauros vel contra haereticos in Provinciam revocamus, maxime cum illis concessae fuerint ad tempus quod jam ex toto praeteriit, et istis ob causam quae iam ex majori parte cessavit; utroque negotio per Dei gratiam adeo prosperato ut vehementem instantiam non requirat; et si forte requireret, nos ingruenti necessitati prospicere curaremus.' Goñi Gaztambide, *Historia*, 132; James M. Powell, *Anatomy of a Crusade, 1213-1221* (Philadelphia, 1986), 20-1.

Crusade. The Spanish bishops, who had already contributed heavily to the Crusade of Las Navas de Tolosa,[81] were unhappy at the prospect of this new levy and attempted to avoid it in every way possible.[82] No doubt on that account the archbishops of Compostela and Toledo and all the Spanish bishops attending the council asked Innocent III to extend the indulgence given to the Holy Land to those fighting the Saracens in Spain. He replied that if a war against the Muslims were undertaken there he would gladly do so;[83] but he obviously knew that that was unlikely so long as the king of Castile was a minor and a truce existed with the Almohads. The death of Pope Innocent III on 16 July 1216 left this issue as well as the prosecution of the Fifth Crusade in the hands of his successor, Honorius III.

In evaluating Innocent III's relationship to the kingdoms of Castile and León one has to conclude that he had only mixed success. Alfonso IX and Berenguela separated when it suited them, even though the pope had threatened them with dire ecclesiastical penalties. The pope's efforts to bring about the pacification of Christian Spain and to organize a united Christian offensive against Spanish Islam were successful only when the kings of Castile and León, who seemed to have evaded compliance with papal demands as long as possible, concluded that it was to their advantage to agree with one another. On the other hand, Pope Innocent's concession of crusading privileges and his encouragement of French support transformed the campaign of Las Navas de Tolosa into a real crusade and helped to bring about victory. It is not clear, however, why he opted not to appoint a legate to command that enterprise, especially when the king of Castile had requested one. The pope's concentration on the recovery of the Holy Land after 1212 made sense in view of the circumstances then prevailing in Morocco and Spain, but his insistence that the Spanish clergy contribute financially to the Fifth Crusade probably encouraged the archbishop of Toledo, for one, to think about ways of organizing peninsular crusades that would keep Spanish money at home. Above all, Innocent III's policy had much to do with the development of the idea of the crusade in Spain in the thirteenth and later centuries.

---

[81]The Castilian clergy gave half their revenues for the Crusade of Las Navas. *Chronique latine*, 21, p. 62: 'Vniversus clerus regni castelle ad peticionem regni medietatem omnium redituum suorum in eodem anno concesserant domino regi'.

[82]Goñi Gaztambide, *Historia*, 135; Demetrio Mansilla Reoyo, *Iglesia castellano-leonesa y curia romana en los tiempos del rey San Fernando* (Madrid, 1945), 50-3; Peter Linehan, *The Spanish Church and the Papacy in the Thirteenth Century* (Cambridge, 1971), 5-6.

[83]See the letter of the Portuguese bishops to Honorius III in September-October 1217 in Mansilla, *Honorio III*, 76, no. 95: 'ut remissionem quam Terre Sancte subvenientibus concesserat, concederet et in Yspania expugnantibus sarracenos et responsum fuisset eis a domno papa de consilio cardinalium quod si guerra esset contra sarracenos in Yspaniam libenter ibidem plenam concederet remissionem'. Riley-Smith, *The Crusades*, 142.

Innocent III and the Kingdom of Castile

Antonio García y García

By the expression Castile we mean the two kingdoms of León and Castile, even though their separation was of short duration and the history that we will narrate here relate equally to Castile and León. Both kingdoms were united until the eleventh century and were definitively reunited as one kingdom in 1230. The territory to which we now refer included in Innocent III's time the greater part of the Iberian peninsula, namely, the present autonomous regions of Castile-León, Galicia, Asturias, Cantabria, the Basque Country, Extremadura, New Castile and that part of Murcia and Andalucía reconquered from the Muslims.[1]

---

[1]The author and the editor wish to express their appreciation to Joseph O'Callaghan for translating this paper from the Spanish.

Abbreviations:

AHC = *Annuarium Historiae Conciliorum.*

CCQL = Antonio García y García, *Constitutiones Concilii quarti Lateranensis una cum Commentariis Glossatorum (Monumenta iuris canonici.* Series A: Corpus glossatorum, vol. 2) (Città del Vaticano 1981).

G = Giessen, Universitätsbibliothek, MS 1105.

HS = Hispania Sacra.

ISD 1-2 = Antonio García y García, *Iglesia, Sociedad y Derecho* (Bibliotheca Salmanticensis. Estudios 74 and 89) (Salamanca, 1985-1987).

Mansi = J. S. Mansi, *Sacrorum conciliorum nova et amplissima collectio.* 22 vols (Venice, 1768).

Mansilla = Demetrio Mansilla, *La documentación pontificia hasta Inocencio III (965-1216)* (Monumenta Hispaniae Vaticana, Sección Registros I) (Rome, 1955).

MIC = Monumenta Iuris Canonici.

TR = J. Tejado y Ramiro, *Coleccion de cánones y de todos los concilios de la Iglesia Española traducida al castellano con notas e ilustraciones de J. Tejada y Ramiro,* vol. 3 (Madrid, 1851).

T¹ = Toledo, Biblioteca del Cabildo, MS 15-22 (now conserved in the Biblioteca Nacional of Madrid

Some ten years ago, in a small study dedicated to the theme 'Alexander III and the Iberian kingdoms', I stated that there are two constants in the action of the medieval popes in the Iberian Peninsula that are clearly perceptible during different pontificates.[2] The first is their recognition of the plurality of the peninsular kingdoms, to which the popes accorded equality of rights. The second consists in the eight-centuries-long struggle against Islam. The Holy See continually tried to encourage it and to unite the forces of the Christian kings behind it. This observation is also applicable to the pontificate of Innocent III, to which indeed a third reality may be added, namely, the Fourth Lateran Council celebrated by the pope in 1215.

I will try, therefore, to develop these themes under the six headings into which this small study is divided. All the rest of the documentation of Innocent III directed to Castile during his pontificate relates to local matters that were the same or quite similar to those in the different kingdoms of Christendom at that time: matters concerning jurisdiction, property, benefices, politics etc. The best documentary collection of papal letters directed to Spain is that of Demetrio Mansilla.[3]

I. THE IBERIAN CRUSADE

Among all the letters of Innocent III sent to Castile, there is only one document relative to the Oriental Crusade.[4] On the other hand, there are at least seven documents in which Innocent III concerns himself with the Iberian Crusade. In the first of those, dated 10 December 1210, he urges the bishops of Spain to aid the kings in the struggle against the Saracens.[5] In February 1211, he ordered the archbishop of Toledo and the bishops of Coimbra and Zamora to assist Infante Don Fernando in the reconquest and to assure peace among the kings.[6] On the same date he informed King Alfonso VIII of Castile that he could not send (*propter impacata tempore*) a papal legate as the monarch had requested, but that he was writing to various bishops to support the struggle against the Muslims.[7]

MS Vi.15 no. 5).

T² = Toledo, Biblioteca del Cabildo, MS 42-21 no. 1.

Z = Zurich, Zentralbibliothek, MS Car. C. 148.

[2]That study was published in F. Liotta, ed., *Miscellanea Rolando Bandinelli papa Alessandro III* (Siena 1986), 237-57. The passage referred to is found on p. 244.

[3]Mansilla, nos. 130-568, pp. 160-385. One should note that the the documents of Innocent III are almost four times greater in number than those of all his predecessors together. The majority of those pieces addressed to persons in the territory which is now Spain refer to Castilian affairs.

[4]Mansilla, no. 241, pp. 269-70 = PL 214:934, which concerns the collection of tribute from all the monasteries of Spain and Gascony intended for the liberation of the Holy Places in Palestine.

[5]Ibid., no. 442, pp. 472-3 = PL 216:353.

[6]Ibid., no. 446, pp. 474-5 = PL 216:379.

[7]Ibid., no. 447, pp. 475-6 = PL 216:380.

On the same day, he informed the oldest son of the king of Castile that he had ordered various bishops to take an interest in the prince's planned campaign against the Moors.[8] On 5 April, he commanded the archbishops of Toledo and Santiago de Compostela to encourage the kings of Castile and León to make peace in order to prosecute the reconquest.[9]

Papal diplomacy was directed not only to the bishops and kings of Castile and León but was also projected beyond the Iberian Peninsula. In effect, on 31 January 1212, Innocent III ordered the archbishop of Sens in France and his suffragans to aid the king of Castile, who was preparing for battle against the Muslims, a campaign that resulted in a battle and a great victory for Christian arms over the Muslims at Las Navas de Tolosa in 1212.[10] On 5 April 1212, he commanded the archbishops of Toledo and Compostela to pressure the Iberian kings to maintain the peace and to give mutual support in the struggle against Islam.[11]

Pope Innocent III ordered the celebration of solemn rogations in diverse places in Rome to pray for the success of the Spanish crusade.[12] The regulations set forth by the pope in his letter in this regard are interesting: women should go to the Roman basilica of Santa Maria Maggiore, clerics to that of the Twelve Apostles and men to that of Santa Anastasia, and then to the Campo Lateranense, while the bells of the churches of Rome pealed. The cross of Santa Maria Maggiore was carried at the head of the company of women, while the cross of the priestly confraternity preceded the clerics, and the cross of St Peter before the men. The company of the pope, cardinals and bishops was supposed to enter the basilica called *Sancta Sanctorum* (the present *Camara Santa*) where they would receive the *lignum Sanctae Crucis* to go in procession to the bishop of Albano's palace, on whose front steps the pope would preach a sermon to all the people. Once the sermon was finished, the women would return in procession as they had come to the basilica of Santa Croce de Gerusalemme, where a cardinal priest would await them to celebrate holy mass, during which the oration 'Omnipotens, sempiterne Deus, in cuius manu sunt omnes potestates, etc.' would be said. The women would then return at once to their homes. The pope, with the bishops, cardinals and chaplains would leave the palace and go to the Lateran Basilica, where the clergy would enter through the portico, and the laity through the borgo (*per burgum*). After the celebration of mass, and having recited the oration already mentioned, the clergy followed by the laity would proceed in bare feet to

---

[8]Ibid., no. 448, pp. 476-77 = PL 216:380.
[9]Ibid., no. 452, pp. 480-1.
[10]Ibid., no. 468, pp. 497-8 = PL 216:514.
[11]Ibid., no. 471, pp. 501-3 = PL 216:553.
[12]Ibid., no. 473, pp. 503-4 = PL 216:698.

the basilica of Santa Croce, and the ceremony would conclude. On that day, it was expected that all except the sick would fast on bread and water, pray and offer alms. This penitential celebration took place on 16 May 1212, which that year fell on a Wednesday.

The battle and the Christian victory of Las Navas de Tolosa (in the present province of Jaén) took place on 16 July 1212. The victory opened the gates to Christian arms for the reconquest of western Andalucía. The Muslims defeated at Las Navas belonged to the sect known as Almohads, who under the command of the Caliph Ya'qûb had inflicted a terrible defeat on the Christians at Alarcos (in the present province of Ciudad Real) on 19 July 1195. Returning again to Spain under the command of Ya'qûb's son, called Miramamolín al-Nâsir Muhammad ibn Ya'qûb, they were defeated at Las Navas by an army composed of contingents from Castile and the other Iberian kingdoms, with the solid support of crusaders from beyond the Pyrenees.[13] In a letter of 1212-1213 Innocent III confirmed for the archbishop of Toledo the donations that Alfonso VIII of Castile had granted him for his services to the king in the affair of Las Navas de Tolosa.[14] Another concession that the pope made to the archbishop of Toledo was the administration of dioceses after they were reconquered and before they had their own bishop.[15]

II. RELATIONS WITH PORTUGAL

Soon after his accession to the papacy (8 January 1198), Innocent III wrote on 6 June of that year to his legate Rainier ordering him to see to the observance of the peace established by the kings of Castile and Portugal.[16]

When Portugal gained its independence in the twelfth century, it had not been foreseen nor determined which dioceses, in addition to those of Astorga, Coimbra, Porto, and Viseu, were suffragan to the metropolitan see of Braga. It was precisely in the twelfth century that the see of Santiago de Compostela emerged first as a simple bishopric but then as a metropolitan see by reason of the transferral of that status from Mérida to Compostela. As a consequence, the sees of the province of Mérida both in Castile and in Portugal were now assigned to Compostela. It was as difficult for Braga to exercise its metropolitan jurisdiction in Spain as it was for Santiago to do so in Portugal. The suffragan dioceses that Santiago had in Portugal until 1383 were Lamego, Idanha (Guarda), Évora, and

---

[13] See the succinct account in the *Enciclopedia Universal Ilustrada Europeo-Americana (Espasa)* 37 (Madrid, 1918):1299-1302.

[14] Mansilla, no. 489, pp. 521-2 = PL 216:743.

[15] Ibid., no. 512, pp. 552-3 = PL 216:943.

[16] Ibid., no. 157, p. 185 = PL 214:214, in which it is indicated that a similar letter was sent to the king of Portugal.

Lisbon. In turn Braga had as suffragans in Spain the sees of Mondoñedo, Lugo, Orense, Tuy and Astorga.

Meanwhile there were frequent attempts to modify this anomalous situation, but a satisfactory solution was not reached until the end of the fourteenth century. Innocent III preferred to maintain the status quo, and so, on 2 June 1199, he informed the archbishop of Santiago that Lisbon and Évora belonged to the metropolitan see of Santiago de Compostela.[17] Three days later Pope Innocent sent a similar letter to the archbishop of Braga in which he affirmed that the see of Zamora was suffragan to Santiago and not to Braga.[18] On 6 July 1199 Innocent III confirmed the pact which the two archbishops of Braga and Santiago concluded, which permitted each one to carry the cross on high in the other's province.[19] But on 11 July 1199 Innocent III declared that in the registers of Eugene III a bull was found whereby that pope had incorporated Zamora into the metropolitan jurisdiction of Braga.[20]

The struggle between Braga and Santiago to extend their metropolitan jurisdiction over the dioceses of Lamego and Idhanha, as well as over Coimbra and Viseu, resulted in Innocent III's letter of 12 July 1199 in which he established that the first two were suffragans of Santiago de Compostela and the other two were suffragans of Braga.[21] In a letter of 12 July 1199, he informed the archbishop of Braga that the sees of Lisbon, Évora, Lamego and Idanha pertained to the ecclesiastical province of Compostela.[22] On 21 July 1199, the pope notified the bishops of Lisbon, Évora and Lamego, who were affected by these arrangements, that they should obey the archbishop of Compostela.[23] The diplomacy of both parties in this struggle continued indefatigably during the month of July 1199. Thus, on 20 July, only three days after the previous letter, Innocent III wrote to the archbishop of Braga telling him that five bishoprics belonged to Braga: Tuy, Orense, Mondoñedo, Lugo, and Astorga. In passing he also confirmed that the sees of Coimbra and Viseu belonged to Braga.[24]

---

[17]Ibid., no. 198, pp. 215-20 = PL 214:653. This is an interesting document because the history of the entire affair is presented..

[18]Ibid., no. 199, pp. 220-6 = PL 214:657; the previous history of this affair is also presented.

[19]Ibid., no. 200, pp. 226-7 = PL 216:663.

[20]Ibid., no. 568, p. 585.

[21]Ibid., no. 204, pp. 230-40 = PL 214:680. This is interesting for the amount of detail that it provides in tracing the previous history of these four bishoprics and their relations with their respective metropolitans.

[22]Ibid., no. 205, pp. 240-1 = PL 214:689. Aside from the text in the Vatican register, there is a copy in the Archivo de Simancas and a third copy in MS Vat. Lat. 12125, fol. 203r.

[23]Ibid., no. 207, pp. 242-3 = PL 214:690. Mansilla mentions another copy in the Archivo de Simancas.

[24]Ibid., no. 215, pp. 250-1 = PL 214:703 . Mansilla mentions another copy in the Archivo de Simancas.

After all this dance of metropolitans and suffragan sees, there were still those who wondered to which metropolitan Zamora belonged; so the pope named a commission on 21 July 1199 to resolve it.[25] The definitive resolution of this question was not reached during the time of Innocent III.

III. RELATIONS WITH THE CASTILIAN-LEONESE MONARCHY

Innocent III, like other medieval popes, exercised a moderating role in relation to each of the monarchies, especially when the weaker ones were confronted by the stronger ones. Castile was the last one to throw off the Muslim yoke, inasmuch as it only completed the conquest of Granada in 1492, but that also required her to develop a military power not needed by either Portugal or Aragón, who had already expelled the Moors from their territory. In fact, Castile's territory was equal to that of Aragón and Portugal combined. For all that, Portugal and Aragón were natural allies of one another and they also sought the protection of the Holy See against eventual Castilian expansion. For that reason they became vassal states of the Holy See in the time of Innocent III.[26]

By contrast, the breadth of the territories of Castile resulted in its being the last one to conclude the reconquest of its lands from Muslim power. Hence the intense activity of the popes and above all of Innocent III to support Castilian efforts in order to encourage the reconquest, of which we have spoken above.

The moderating role of Innocent III in the case of Castile was evident, moreover, in numerous other aspects. Thus, for example, the pope wrote to his legate Rainier on 6 June 1198 ordering him to see to the observance of peace established between the kings of Castile and Portugal.[27]

The marriage of King Alfonso IX of León with Doña Berenguela, in violation of the impediment of consanguinity in the third collateral degree, prompted Innocent III to send four letters to the Leonese king on this matter. The pope on 16 April 1198 ordered his legate Rainier to declare the marriage null and reminded him also that he should see to it that the kings of Spain maintained the peace.[28] On 25 May 1198, the pope ordered the archbishop of Compostela and the bishops of the kingdom of León to observe the sentence of interdict on the kingdom because of the king's marriage contrary to the norms of the church.[29] On 5 June 1203, the pope ordered the king of Castile to dissolve the marital union

---

[25] Ibid., no. 216, pp. 251-2 = PL 214:705. Mansilla mentions another copy in the Archivo de Simancas.

[26] Portugal became a vassal state in 1210 and Aragón declared itself a papal fief on 10 November 1204, when King Pedro II of Aragón was crowned in Rome by Innocent III, to whom he swore an oath of fealty, declaring himself a vassal of the Holy See. See Mansilla, no. 307, pp. 340-41 = PL 215:550.

[27] Ibid., no. 157, p. 185 = PL 214:214.

[28] Ibid., no. 138, pp. 168-70 = PL 214:79.

[29] Ibid., no. 196, pp. 209-15 = PL 214:610.

between his daughter Berenguela and King Alfonso IX of León.[30] Finally on 19 June 1204, Innocent III ordered the archbishop of Santiago de Compostela and the bishops of Zamora and Palencia to grant absolution to the Leonese king and to lift the interdict on his kingdom.[31] Again on 20 June 1204, the pope ordered the archbishops of Compostela and Toledo and the bishops of Zamora and Coimbra to compel Doña Berenguela to restore the castles that she had received in dowry from the king of León.[32]

The abuses of the king of Castile, who violated the liberties of the church in the economic sphere (especially in the matter of tributes, which the secular authority did not demand of Jews and Moors) did not escape the notice of Innocent III.[33] This violation of ecclesiastical liberties in Castile and other kingdoms of Christendom at that time was not typical or exclusive to the pontificate of Innocent III, but occurred with frequency throughout the Middle Ages in different Christian kingdoms.[34]

IV. CASTILIAN PARTICIPATION IN THE LATERAN COUNCIL OF 1215

Three documents of the thirteenth century give us some indication of the Spanish prelates who attended the Fourth Lateran Council of 1215. Two of them are from Toledo,[35] while the third is the work of a German monk and is conserved in Zurich.[36]

This theme has been debated for a long time. In 1593 there was published a long Toledan account of the discussion between the archbishop of Toledo,

---

[30]Ibid., no. 276, pp. 305-6 = PL 215:82.

[31]Ibid., no. 304, pp. 335-6 = PL 215:376.

[32]Ibid., no. 305, pp. 336-9 = PL 215:373.

[33]Ibid., no. 312, pp. 344-5 = PL 215:616.

[34]A vibrant document on this point is the *Summa de libertate ecclesiastica* of Egas de Viseu, ed. by myself in my book entitled *Estudios sobre la canonística portuguesa* (Madrid, 1976), 219-81. Curiously all nine known codices of this *Summa* are found in Castile, which means that this text was as current in the Castilian kingdom as in the Portuguese.

[35]García de Loaysa, *Collectio conciliorum Hispaniae* (Madrid, 1595), 87-92, reproduces the codex of Madrid, Biblioteca Nacional, MS Vitr. 15, n. 5, fol. 22r-23v, originally in the Biblioteca Capitular de Toledo, where it had the signature 15-22. This text was then reproduced in various conciliar collections, for example, Mansi 22:1071-75. In my book *ISD* 2:203-8 I give a new transcription of this text from the manuscript cited. The second Toledan text (taken from MS 42-21, n. 1, fol. 1 – a folio later added to the original codex – of the Biblioteca Capitular de Toledo) was edited by Juan Francisco Rivera Recio, 'Personajes asistentes en 1215 al IV Concilio de Letrán', *HS* 4 (1951):335-55.

[36]The Zurich document was published by J. Werner, 'Die Teilnehmerliste des Laterankonzils vom Jahre 1215', *Neues Archiv der Gesellschaft für älteste deutsche Geschichtskunde* 31 (1906):575-93, who showed it to Achille Luchaire, 'Un document retrouvé', *Journal des Savants* (1905):557-68, whence it was taken by Karl Hefele and Henri Leclercq, *Histoire des Conciles,* 5.2 (Paris, 1913), 1722-33.

Rodrigo Jiménez de Rada, and his opponents, the archbishops of Braga, Santiago de Compostela, Tarragona and Narbonne in the Council of 1215 concerning the Iberian primacy.[37] From these three documents there emerges a list that is now definitive of the bishops from the kingdom of Castile who attended the Fourth Lateran Council in 1215: Juan, bishop of Oviedo, Mauricio of Burgos, Rodrigo Álvarez of León, Rodrigo Jiménez de Rada, archbishop of Toledo, García of Cuenca, Giraldo of Segovia, Melendo of Burgo de Osma, Hispano of Segorbe, Pedro Muñiz, archbishop of Santiago de Compostela, Gonzalo of Salamanca, Martín Paes of Guarda (then belonging to the archdiocese of Santiago de Compostela), Martín Lombardo of Ciudad Rodrigo, Juan of Ávila, Juan of Calahorra, Pedro Andrés of Astorga, Pelayo Cebeira of Mondoñedo, and Fernando Méndez of Orense. Out of the total of twenty-one episcopal sees then in Castile, sixteen, or seventy-six per cent, of the Castilian bishops, attended Innocent III's council.

What were the likely expectations of the Castilian bishops that would prompt them to attend the council convoked by Innocent III in 1213 and celebrated in 1215? The hopes of the Castilian, and the Iberian episcopate in general, were more or less identical in general lines to those of any other part of Christendom. The only differential note lay in the fact that the Spaniards were then involved in the hard task of the reconquest of the ancient territory of the Visigothic monarchy from the hands of the Muslims. The kings pressured the bishops and abbots to gather the funds necessary to carry out the reconquest and the prelates of the church pressured the faithful to obtain those funds. In addition, the bishops and abbots often litigated with one another to obtain churches with substantial revenues. The participation of the bishops in military incursions against the Muslims in the south aroused in them the hope of sharing in a substantial part of the booty taken from the Moors. The kings were not of the same mind, however, and often forgot to reward the bishops for their collaboration and effort.[38]

Pope Innocent III hoped to obtain from the council of 1215 'the reform of the universal church and above all the liberation of the Holy Land'.[39] The first of these ideals perhaps did not arouse much enthusiasm among the Spanish bishops. As for the recovery of the Holy Land, they had nothing against that idea, but they were still engaged in the reconquest of extensive territories in the peninsula still in the power of the Muslims. Perhaps they thought of the possibility that, in the

---

[37] See above, note 35.

[38] On this theme see Peter Linehan, *The Spanish Church and the Papacy in the Thirteenth Century* (Cambridge, 1971); there is a Spanish translation by P. Borges Morán (Salamanca, 1975). Also, Linehan, *Spanish Church and Society 1150-1300* (Variorum Reprints CS 184) (London, 1983).

[39] Innocent III, *Desiderio desideravi*, 11 November 1215; *Vineam Domini*, 19 April 1213, Mansi 22:960-8; PL 216:823-5.

context of the Oriental crusade, help might also be secured in an efficacious way for the Iberian reconquest, as had recently happened in the victory of Las Navas de Tolosa. The convocation of an ecumenical council was then (and indeed is now) an event that stirs the people and even the bishops. In addition, a visit to Rome enabled the bishops in the thirteenth century and still enables them today to settle their pending affairs and those of their dioceses in the presence of the Roman pontiff and the curia.

The first Toledan document mentioned offers us an interesting detail, in that it indicates the principal persons who accompanied each bishop. Thus the bishop of Cuenca had in his company his chaplain, the archdeacon 'Optensis' [Huete], and the archpriest of Cuenca. The bishop of Segovia brought the dean of the chapter and two canons who had the title of *magister*, and two others described only as canons. The bishop of Siguenza was accompanied by an archdeacon and a canon. The *magister* and prior of the chapter of Burgo de Osma accompanied their bishop. The archbishop of Toledo had in his retinue at least ten persons, among them, 'Magister Michael Scotus', and even a cook.

One should recall that no Iberian prelate seems to have attended the first two Lateran Councils of 1123 and 1139. Somewhat less than twenty were at the third. The twenty-seven Iberian bishops attending the Fourth Lateran Council of 1215 represented, out of a total of some 404 bishops, a percentage of Hispanic prelates identical to the Council of 1179 celebrated by Pope Alexander III.

V. THE DISCUSSION OF THE IBERIAN PRIMACY IN THE FOURTH LATERAN COUNCIL OF 1215

Aside from the documents that we alluded to in the previous section, there is a third that I found in MS 1105 in the Universitätsbibliothek of Giessen, Germany, and which has great importance for the history of the Fourth Lateran Council, and not only for the Spanish question of the peninsular primacy. The document was edited and studied by Professor Stephan Kuttner and myself.[40] On fol. 59r-60v of the codex one finds this reference to the discussion of the primacy in the Iberian Peninsula: 'Tercia uero die litem que inter Compostellanum et Tolletanum super optinendo primatum hucusque durauit, dominus papa dirimere et rationabiliter inde deffinire conabatur.'

The author of the discussion of the Iberian primacy alluded to in the text that we have just described was an anonymous monk of the German Cistercian abbey of Aulesburg, an abbey transferred in 1221 to Haina (Hesse) and suppressed in

---

[40]Stephan Kuttner and Antonio García y García, 'A New Eyewitness Account of the Fourth Lateran Council', *Traditio* 20 (1964):115-78, reproduced by Professor Stephan Kuttner in his book *Medieval Councils, Decretals and Collections of Canon Law* (London, 1980), to which he added some interesting 'Retractationes'. I also reproduced it in my book *ISD* 2:61-121.

1527.[41] The other contemporary chroniclers of the council do not mention the discussion of the Iberian primacy.

But the testimony of the chronicler that we have just cited is undeniable, and it also validates the first of the Toledan documents cited above, in which the author, certainly someone from the Toledan ambiance, describes in detail the development of the discussion of the primacy. We will not transcribe it now because we have done so elsewhere,[42] so we will limit ourselves to giving a brief résumé of it. According to the anonymous monk of Giessen, the pope tried to bring the litigants to agreement, but failed to do so, so that the question remained a dead letter once more, as the Holy See made no decision concerning it. This episode took place on 13 November 1215. The document edited by Loaysa was questioned by the judgment of historians, but nevertheless it fits the true historical context, even though not each and every detail that it offers is confirmed by other sources. Thus, for example, the faculty to create chapters in all the new cathedrals seems hardly credible. Equally, when it affirms that the discussion of the primacy took place 'in pleno consistorio', one has to understand it in the sense that it occurred in the council and not in what was technically a consistory of the pope and the cardinals.

The different protagonists of this history who participated in the discussion of the primacy employed arguments usual in these cases. The archbishop of Toledo, Don Rodrigo Jiménez de Rada, alleged ancient documents which, according to him, were kept in the see of Toledo. The archbishop of Compostela replied that his church was older because it had been founded by the Apostle St James. Don Rodrigo denied the historicity of the preaching of the Apostle St James in Spain. He added that even if it were true, the Mother of Christ had made an appearance in Toledo, appearing to the Toledan archbishop St Ildefonse; that gave this see a greater dignity than that of Santiago de Compostela, which had only been visited by one of the apostles. The archbishop of Tarragona, also present in Rome, was represented by the bishop of Vich, who limited himself to denying the Toledan primacy in the Peninsula. One can well understand why, as the chronicler of the Giessen codex asserts, Innocent III could not satisfactorily settle this discussion.

In any case, Innocent III's thought was favorable to the Toledan primacy in the Peninsula, as appears from a letter of 16 April (there is no year) in which the pope said that: 'venientem ad nos venerabilem fratrem nostrum Rodericum archiepiscopum Toletanum benigne recipimus, et inspectis predecessorum nostrorum privilegiis primatus dignitatem per uniuersa Hispaniarum regna, iuxta eorundem privilegiorum tenorem, confirmavimus . . . mandamus quatenus

---

[41] On fol. 61r and on fol. 142rv of Giessen MS 1105 there is this notice: 'Liber gloriose (al. sancte) uirginis Marie de Aulesburg'.

[42] *ISD*, 2:205-8.

tanquam primati vestro eidem absque ulla contradictione canonicam obedientiam et debitam reverentiam exhibere curetis.'[43]

Another affirmation of the first Toledo document (T[1]) is that Don Rodrigo Jiménez de Rada, the archbishop of Toledo, obtained the post of papal legate in the Peninsula for a term of ten years, with authority to dispense 300 persons from the irregularity of illegitimate birth so that they could receive orders and dignities and obtain benefices; he also received the power to dispense certain excommunicated, sacrilegious, irregular and concubinary persons. T[1] also contains the information that as soon as Seville was liberated from Saracen power, it would be subjected *iure primatus* to the see of Toledo. That see would also have the right to create new chapters of canons in the churches that would be reconquered from the hands of the Moors.

We do not know any other historical source that confirms these last papal concessions to the archbishop of Toledo. In addition, it is not clear what their connection was with the fact that Toledo should be the primatial see.

On the other hand, all these concessions were relatively frequent in the canonical order and practice of that time. This is confirmed, for example, by the fact that Doña María de Portugal, the wife of Alfonso XI of Castile, requested and obtained on 16 January 1343 that twenty-eight persons whom she named would be invested by the bishop of Palencia as canons in as many canonries in the cathedrals of the realm.[44]

Nevertheless, the sermon that, according to the Toledan document T[1], Archbishop D. Rodrigo Jiménez de Rada preached in the council, does not seem to merit any credibility:

In hoc generali sinodo Rodericus archiepiscopus Toletanus et Yspanie primas de licentia Innocentii tertii pontificis proposuit uerbum dei, incipiens et finiens in latino sermone. Set quia de diuersis mundi partibus tam clerici quam layci ibidem conuenerant, ut omnibus satisfaceret, suas in predicando pausaciones et interpollationes faciendo easdem a[u]ctoritates et rationes propositas in latino exposuit laycis et illitteratis in linguagiis maternis uidelicet Romanorum, Teutonicorum, Francorum, Anglorum, Nauarrorum et Yspanorum.

Huiusmodi autem predicationis expositio placuit in conspectu omnium non solum subtile set pocius admirabile reputantes, cum a tempore apostolorum uix crederetur seu ab aliquo audiretur uel scriptum repertum fuisset aliquam

---

[43]Mansilla, no. 530, p. 564.

[44]Antonio García y García, Francisco Cantelar Rodríguez and Miguel Nieto Cumplido, *Catálogo de los manuscritos e incunables de la Catedral de Córdoba* (Salamanca, 1976), 82. This case happened 142 years after 1215, but the canonical order of the church was substantially the same.

aliam sub tot modis ydiomatum seu linguarum in uno et eodem sermone
uerbum Domini predicando taliter exposuisset.[45]

That Rodrigo Jiménez de Rada preached a sermon alternately using seven
languages (Latin, Italian, German, French, English, Basque and Spanish) seems
somewhat picturesque, although not impossible, given that he undoubtedly knew
three of the languages mentioned (Latin, Basque and Spanish) by reason of his
status as a Navarrese, and it would not be difficult in Rome at that time (nor even
now) to find native speakers of each of the other four languages to make a
translation. The decisive difficulty against that affirmation of T[1] lies in the fact
that contemporary chroniclers who concerned themselves with the council of
1215 refer to other sermons, but not to this supposed sermon of the archbishop of
Toledo, which undoubtedly would have drawn their attention .

VI. APPLICATION OF THE FOURTH LATERAN COUNCIL IN CASTILE
The application of the Fourth Lateran Council was very uneven in the different
kingdoms and churches of the epoch. In general terms, one can affirm that it was
well received in England[46] and France[47] as well as in the kingdom of Aragón,
while in the Empire,[48] Castile and some other areas, application was weak. As for
Castile, it is undeniable that there was no local reform council until the legatine
council of Jean d'Abbeville, celebrated in Valladolid in the year 1228.[49]

Innocent III died a few months after the celebration of the Fourth Lateran
Council of 1215. For that reason he had little time at his disposal to concern
himself with how his council could bring about reform in the Castilian church.
On the other hand, his successors, and especially the immediate one, Honorius III,
attended to this matter, sending a harsh letter to Archbishop Rodrigo Jiménez de

---

[45]*ISD*, 2:204.

[46]See my article entitled 'El Concilio IV Lateranense (1215) y las Islas Británicas', *Synodus: Beiträge zur Konzilien- und allgemeinen Kirchengeschichte Festschrift für Walter Brandmüller* (Paderborn, 1995-96), 276-92, where the sources and bibliography on this subject are cited.

[47]See my article 'El Concilio IV Lateranense y Francia', *AHC* 26 (1994):61-86, where the sources and bibliography on this subject are cited.

[48]See P.B. Pixton, *The Episcopacy and the Implementation of the Decrees of the Fourth Lateran Council 1216-1245. Watchmen of the Tower* (Leiden, 1995); *idem*, 'Cardinal Bishop Conrad of Porto and the Implementation of Innocent III's Conciliar Decrees in Germany', *Xth International Congress of Medieval Canon Law, Syracuse University August 1996* (in press in the series *MIC* of the Biblioteca Apostolica Vaticana).

[49]*TR*, 3:324-9 and my critical edition in my article entitled 'Legislación de los concilios y sínodos del Reino Leonés', *El Reino de León en la Alta Edad Media, 2: Ordenamiento Jurídico del Reino (Fuentes y estudios de historia leonesa* 49) (León, 1992), 7-114.

Rada of Toledo which begins: 'Expectantes hactenus expectauimus'.[50] But this reprimand was somewhat relative if one takes into account that the same document was sent on different dates to numerous distinct and distant addresses, as we shall point out shortly. The same letter, dated a month later (21 November 1219) without indication of the addressees, is found in MS 10 of the Biblioteca del Cabildo de Córdoba (first third of the thirteenth century) in the appendix to the *Compilatio IV Antiqua*. Keep in mind that this codex is composed of two manuscripts that were originally different: one in a Bolognese hand coming from Italy, and the other in a French hand, in which inscriptions are recorded indicating that the manuscript went from Bologna to Burgos, and from the latter city to Córdoba. We do not know to whom this text was previously addressed nor to whom it was of interest nor why it was included in the Córdoban codex, together with another letter that follows and begins: 'Super speculum Domini licet immeriti, des . . . causaueritis promouere'.[51]

Among the addressees of the letter 'Expectantes hactenus expectauimus', aside from Rodrigo Jiménez de Rada, we count at least the following: (1) the same letter, dated only a month later, appears as already noted, in the codex of Córdoba, though we do not know to whom this text was addressed; (2) the same document was sent to the Irish bishops on 19 November 1219;[52] (3) with the same date, to the patriarch of Antioch and the Swedish bishops;[53] (4) the same letter was sent to the archbishop of Bourges in 1227 and in 1241;[54] (5) in the MS Can.19 of the Staatsbibliothek of Bamberg, fol. 255rb-vb, the same document appears, without indication of addressees, as an appendix to the *Compilatio IV Antiqua*, the same as in the codex of Córdoba, already mentioned; (6) the same is true for MS 2183 fol. 105-108 of the Nationalbibliothek of Vienna;[55] (7) the same text was edited by Mansi, without any indication of the source from which he took it;[56] (8) a fragment of this letter was also included in the *Compilatio V Antiqua*;[57] (9) the

---

[50]Toledo, Archivo Capitular, I.5 A.i.i., transcribed by Burriel, Biblioteca Nacional de Madrid, MS 13116, fol. 10r-11v (dated 26 October 1219) and edited by Demetrio Mansilla, *La documentación pontificia de Honorio III* (Rome, 1965), no. 246, pp. 190-2.

[51]There is a partial edition of this letter in 5 Comp. 5.2.1, and 5.12.3 (X 5.5.5, 350.10 and 5.33.28).

[52]Pott. 6163. Maurice Sheehy, *Pontificia Hibernica. Medieval Papal Chancery Documents concerning Ireland (640-1260)*, 1 (Dublin, 1962), does not include this in his edition, even though it had been published by Mansi, as we shall see.

[53]Pott. 6166 for the Swedes.

[54] Pott. 11052 (see Pott. 8025).

[55]See Stephan Kuttner, 'The Barcelona Edition of St. Raymond's Treatise on Canon Law', *Seminar* 8 (1950):65.

[56]Mansi, 22:1098-1100.

[57]5 Comp. 3.24.1 (X 3.41.10). Saint Raymond of Peñafort cited this decretal of Honorius III as 'extra titutlos Expectantes'. See *San Raimundo de Peñafort, Summa iuris*, ed. José Rius Serra (Barcelona, 1945), 49. See also Xavier Ochoa, A. Diez, ed., *Sanctus Raumundus de Pennaforte,*

Scottish bishops on 19 June 1225 also received a letter which is an abbreviation of 'Expectantes hactenus expectauimus', on which we are commenting.[58]

The scanty presence of manuscripts of the Fourth Lateran Council in Castile could reflect the minimal application of the council in Castilian lands. In fact, there is only one codex in Toledo and one other in El Escorial.[59] But this argument has little value, since none is conserved in the kingdom of Aragón, and yet the application of the council there in the thirteenth century was notable, although it declined in the fourteenth and fifteenth centuries. In Castile, on the other hand, it was poorly applied in the thirteenth and early fourteenth centuries, but somewhat better after the legatine Council of Valladolid in 1322.

Finally, one should add that the projection of the Fourth Lateran Council was far from over in the thirteenth century, where we noted that it was better applied in Aragón than in Castile. In the fourteenth century, the legatine Council of Valladolid held by the legate Cardinal Guillermo Peyre de Godin[60] introduced the Lateran reform into Castile, and the council included it in its reforming legislation.

Such then, in broad strokes, are the relations of Innocent III with the Kingdom of Castile.

Summa de iure canonico (Rome 1975), 47, where only the *Compilatio V Antiqua,* the *Liber Extra* and the edition of Mansi are cited. See Peter Linehan, *La Iglesia española,* 10, n. 54.

[58]D. Wilkins, *Concilia Magnae Britanniae et Hiberniae* (London, 1737), 548-51.

[59]Described in *CCQL,* 30:126-7, 133.

[60]*TR,* 3:477-504 (bilingual edition in Latin and Castilian). See my article entitled 'Las constituciones del Concilio legatino de Valladolid (1322)', *Ecclesia militans. Studien zur Konzilien und Reformationsgeschichte Remigius Bäumer zum 70. Geburtstag gewidmet,* 1 (Paderborn, 1988):111-27, which contains a register and the rubrics of the titles and chapters that do not appear in the edition cited.

Mass, the Eucharist and the Cross: Innocent III and the Relocation of the Crusade

Christoph T. Maier

Innocent III ascended the papal throne just over one hundred years after Urban II had founded the crusade movement. After Urban, Innocent was arguably the most influential pope for the development of the medieval crusade. His role in reshaping and revitalizing the crusade movement at the beginning of the thirteenth century is well known and has been described at length. By enlarging its scope, Innocent used the crusade to fight the papacy's political enemies, to combat heresy and to expand the frontiers of Christendom. He tried to establish rigorous papal leadership of the crusade by reorganizing propaganda and logistics, and he undertook efforts to increase the military strength of crusade armies by excluding non-combatant elements. To this end, Innocent made provisions in canon law for the commutation and redemption of crusading vows, and he granted partial indulgences for material contributions to the crusades. In addition, he established regular liturgies in aid of the crusaders in the field and instituted universal taxation to help finance the crusades. With all these he designed an institutional and legal framework which gave the crusade movement its distinctive shape and character for centuries to come.[1]

---

[1] The standard work on Innocent III and the crusades is still Helmut Roscher, *Papst Innocenz III. und die Kreuzzüge*, Forschungen zur Kirchen- und Dogmengeschichte 21 (Göttingen, 1969). But see also Jonathan Riley-Smith, *The Crusades: A Short History* (London, 1987), 119-45. Maureen Purcell, *Papal Crusading Policy, 1244-1291*, Studies in the History of Christian Thought 11 (Leiden, 1975), passim. Donald E. Queller and Thomas F. Madden, *The Fourth Crusade: The Conquest of*

There has, however, been a tendency to view Innocent's achievements primarily in terms of his integration of the crusade into his grand political strategies. Another area in which Innocent's lasting influence on the crusade movement has rightfully been acknowledged is canon law. But, as is well known, Innocent III was not only a politician and legislator. He also showed great concern for pastoral matters and the spiritual constitution of the church.[2] This is also true with regard to the crusade. So far historians have perhaps underrated Innocent's efforts in the field of the theology of the crusade and his advancement of crusade spirituality.[3] Innocent's vision of the crusade extended far beyond the politics of the crusade, its legal justification and practical organization. His was a vision of a Christian society organized for the *negotium crucis*. He expected people generally to get involved in the crusade, not only in the military campaigns as such but also in the spiritual and devotional aspects of the crusade movement. It is these points that I want to consider in the following, primarily by concentrating on the theme of crusade liturgy.

Following the battle of Hattin in 1187 and the shock waves which this defeat of the Christian forces in the Holy Land sent throughout Europe, the popes called for a series of new crusades to the East and, for the first time, instituted intercessory liturgies to be performed throughout Christendom in support of these crusades. As with so many other aspects of the crusade, it was Innocent III who established intercessory liturgies, processions and prayers on the home front as a regular feature of the crusade movement.[4] One of the most striking liturgical events of this kind was staged by Innocent III in Rome on 16 May 1212 in support of the crusade in Spain. After the recent loss of Salvatierra to the Muslims earlier that year, the Spanish crusade must have seemed in particular need of liturgical support.[5] Innocent III knew that King Alfonso VIII of Castile had announced that he would engage the advancing Muslim forces in a decisive battle in the week

---

Constantinople, 2nd edn (Philadelphia, 1997), passim. James M. Powell, *Anatomy of a Crusade, 1213-1221* (Philadelphia, 1986), 1-65. For canon law see James A. Brundage, *Medieval Canon Law and the Crusader* (Madison, 1969), passim. For finance see William E. Lunt, *Financial Relations of the Papacy with England to 1321*, Studies in Anglo-Papal Relations during the Middle Ages 1 (Cambridge, Mass., 1939):420-32. For liturgy see Christoph T. Maier, 'Crisis, Liturgy and the Crusade in the Twelfth and Thirteenth Centuries', *Journal of Ecclesiastical History* 48 (1997), 628-57.

[2] See Brenda Bolton, *Innocent III: Studies on Papal Authority and Pastoral Care*, Collected Studies Series: CS 490 (Aldershot, 1995).

[3] See, however, John Gilchrist, 'The Lord's War as the Proving Ground of Faith: Pope Innocent III and the Propagation of Violence (1198-1216)', in *Crusaders and Muslims in Twelfth-Century Syria*, ed. Maya Shatzmiller, The Medieval Mediterranean 1 (Leiden, 1993):65-83.

[4] Maier, 'Crisis, Liturgy and the Crusades', 631-4.

[5] Charles J. Bishko, 'The Spanish and the Portuguese Reconquest, 1095-1492', in *A History of the Crusades*, 3, ed. Kenneth M. Setton (Madison, 1975):396-456, here pp. 422-4.

following Pentecost.[6] The pope, therefore, planned a magnificent procession in support of this crusade to coincide with the time of the battle. As the date, he chose the first day of the Pentecost Quatember, the Wednesday after Pentecost. This was traditionally a date for special penitential services and the beginning of the Quatember fast which continued on the Friday and Saturday of the same week.[7] Even though in the event the battle of Las Navas de Tolosa did not take place until two months later, on 16 July, Innocent was convinced that the overwhelming victory that the crusaders carried that day had been won primarily because of divine help. As if to acknowledge the successful intercessory efforts of those who took part in the Roman Quatember procession, a triumphant Innocent later publicly read out King Alfonso's report about the victory to the citizens of Rome.[8] There is no doubt that the pope believed that the procession, which begged God for his assistance, had had a direct influence on the outcome of the battle.

The instructions for carrying out the lavish liturgical event of 16 May 1212 have survived in the papal registers.[9] The event was organized with reference to the customs of the Roman Quatember celebrations. The pope ordered the whole of the population of Rome to congregate early in the morning on the Wednesday after Pentecost. Only those people with mortal enemies who could not show themselves in the streets were excused. The women were to gather at Santa Maria Maggiore, the men at Santa Anastasia and the clergy at Santi Apostoli. These three churches were most certainly chosen because, in the normal liturgical year, they were the *stationes* designated for the Tuesday after Pentecost (Santa Anastasia) and Quatember Wednesday (Santa Maria Maggiore and Santi Apostoli).[10] At the churches, the collect for the day was sung and, to the tolling of the church bells, the three processions set out on prescribed routes towards the open space in front of the Lateran. Strict instructions were given for the order within the processions. The women walked behind the festive cross of Santa Maria Maggiore, with nuns in front and the secular women following. No one was to wear gold, jewelry or silk. The men followed the cross of Saint Peter with the *hospitalarii* in the lead. The clergy followed the cross of the Fraternity with monks and regular canons in front of the rectors and the other clerics. Everybody walked barefoot and people were expected to pray, grieve and lament on route.

---

[6]PL 216:513-14.

[7]Ludwig Fischer, *Die kirchliche Quatember. Ihre Entstehung, Entwicklung und Bedeutung in liturgischer, rechtlicher und kulturhistorischer Hinsicht*, Veröffentlichungen aus dem Kirchenhistorischen Seminar München (Reihe 4), 3 (München, 1914).

[8]PL 216:703-4.

[9]PL 216:698-9.

[10]Johann P. Kirsch, *Die Stationskirchen des Missale Romanum*, Ecclesia Orans 19 (Freiburg i.Br., 1926):227-8. Fischer, *Die kirchliche Quatember*, 85-7.

Once arrived in front of the Lateran church, the three groups were to gather separately in different parts of the square while remaining silent.

Meanwhile the pope, the bishops and cardinals and the papal chaplains proceeded to the chapel of the Sancta Sanctorum, where they fetched the relic of the True Cross. This they took in procession to the square by the Lateran where everybody was by now assembled. They stopped at the palace of the cardinal bishop of Albano and sat on the palace steps while the pope preached a sermon to the people. After the sermon the assembly split up. The women continued their procession to Santa Croce where the presbyter cardinal said mass followed by a special prayer of intercession. From there, they were to return to their homes in peace. The men, however, entered the Lateran church in solemn procession, each group along a different route: the pope and his party through the palace, the clergy through the main entrance of the church and the laymen through the *castellum*. There they celebrated mass and only then proceeded to Santa Croce to say the special prayer, presumably once the women had left. After this everybody went home. To finish the day of intercessory worship, people were instructed to hold a strict fast of bread and water. Exceptions were only made for the sick, but meat, fish and undiluted wine were strictly forbidden to everyone. Lastly those who could were encouraged to give alms to the poor.

The entry in the papal registers is the only evidence we have for this liturgical event, but it seems reasonable to assume that it took place more or less as prescribed. The reason why these instructions were recorded in the registers was probably that Innocent regarded them as a model for similar intercessory events in the future. There is, in fact, evidence that both Honorius III and Gregory IX repeated this kind of procession, in 1217 and 1240, also in support of the crusade.[11]

I have described this event in such great detail in order to make two points. Firstly, it serves as a typical illustration of Innocent's vision of a society involved in the crusade. Just as in this case the pope expected the entire population of Rome to join in intercession for the crusade, so he was convinced that only a concerted effort by all the faithful in Christendom could lead to success of the crusade movement as a whole. This belief was derived from Innocent's theological concept of the crusade. In his opinion, God called for the crusade and expected everybody to respond to this call.[12] Like his predecessors, Innocent also firmly believed that it was God's will and power which engineered the outcome

---

[11]*Regesta Honorii papae III*, ed. P. Pressuti (Rome, 1888, 1905), 149-50, no. 885. *Annales Placentini Gibellini*, ed. Georg H. Pertz, MGH SS 18 (Hanover, 1863):457-581, here p. 428. In both cases it is mentioned that the pope carried the heads of Saints Peter and Paul in procession.

[12]See *Conciliorum Oecumenicorum Decreta*, ed. Josepho Alberigo (Basel, 1962), 244.

of the crusade.[13] For Innocent, the success of the crusade, therefore, depended on how many people got involved in the business of the cross and whether those who participated were in God's favour.[14] Contrary to his predecessors, however, Innocent drew far-reaching practical consequences from this theological position. Since it was neither possible nor feasible for everybody to join a crusade army, it was necessary in Innocent's view to create ways in which those who could not go on crusade personally could still make a meaningful contribution to the movement as a whole. To this end, I believe, Innocent introduced the commutation and even more importantly the redemption of crusade vows, and this was also why he instituted partial indulgences for those who contributed money to finance the crusade.[15] For the same reason, he ordered regular communal liturgies to be performed in every parish for intercession in aid of the crusade.[16] With all these, Innocent broadened the base of the crusade movement by multiplying the ways in which people could take an active part in the movement. According to Innocent's theological concept of the crusade, only a society which was properly organized for participation in the crusade and in which everybody contributed to the business of the cross could sway God's favour and ensure the success of the movement.

The second remarkable point about the procession in aid of the Spanish crusade in 1212 concerns the specific crusade spirituality it represented. The liturgical setting of the event and the symbolism with which it was imbued reflected a pastoral message that tells us a great deal about Innocent's view of the spiritual significance of the crusade for the individual. The liturgical setting was the mass, the symbolism was that of the cross. For all three groups worship began with penitential prayers at their respective starting points, the three churches from where the processions set out. The day's event ended for all with the celebration of the eucharist and a special prayer at Santa Croce. The entire event can, therefore, be described as one long, drawn-out mass, interrupted in the middle by two processions – one from the respective churches to the Lateran and another one from there on to Santa Croce – and a sermon delivered by the pope in front of the Lateran.

In addition, the day's event was dominated by the symbolism of the cross of Christ. Firstly, the three processions were headed by three prominent liturgical crosses. Then, on the square in front of the Lateran basilica where everybody

---

[13]For one of the clearest expressions of this position see PL 216:702-4.

[14]On this see also Gilchrist, 'The Lord's War', 69-74, albeit with a different emphasis.

[15]The most elaborate regulations of this kind appear in *Quia maior* (G. Tangl, *Studien zum Register Innocenz' III.* [Weimar, 1929], 88-97 and PL 216:817-22) and in *Ad liberandam* (*Conciliorum Oecumenicorum Decreta*, 243-7).

[16]Maier, 'Crisis, Liturgy and the Crusades', 631-4.

assembled, the relic of the True Cross was displayed and served as the visual focus for the congregation during the pope's sermon. Unfortunately, we do not know what Innocent said in his sermon. But it is likely that, as in most other sermons connected with the crusade of that period,[17] the symbolism of the cross was a central theme, all the more because of the prominent presence of the relic of the True Cross. Lastly, the day's event culminated in a special intercessory prayer at Santa Croce, the church dedicated to the cross of Christ. In fact, the symbolism of the cross had such an outstanding place in this event that it must have been deliberately planned in this way.

Seen in terms of a ritual, the day's event was an enactment of the meaning and mechanism of salvation. In the first part, during the prayers of the collect and the penitential procession to the Lateran, the participants ritually proclaimed their sinfulness and their need to be heard, forgiven and saved by God. At the Lateran they came face to face with Christ on the cross in the moment in which he redeemed mankind, symbolized by the relic of the True Cross. From there they proceeded to join in the act of salvation by celebrating the ritual of the eucharist. The changing mood of the day's event echoed this ritual progression. It started off noisily with the vociferous declamation of the participants' sinfulness and contrition and their need for salvation. This was accompanied by the chiming of the church bells during the first part of the procession. During the exposition of the relic of the True Cross in front of the Lateran, the mood suddenly changed to solemn silence. From there it continued in solemn and peaceful calm for the rest of the day.

The mass as the setting and the prominence of the symbolism of the cross represented a distinct type of crusade spirituality. Innocent III more than any of his predecessors saw crusade spirituality in terms of the personal relationship between the individual crusader and Christ. Of course, the aim of the crusades, also in Innocent's view, was to fight the enemies of the Christian religion. But for him crusading, in essence, represented a spiritual value. Innocent described the crusader as a follower of Christ who served Christ by following him and defending his honour and patrimony.[18] Again, this is a traditional representation

---

[17]For example the sermons by Henry of Strasbourg (*Historia peregrinorum*, ed. Anton Chroust, MGH SS n.s. 5 (Berlin, 1928):116-72, here pp. 122-4), Martin of Pairis (Gunther of Pairis, *Hystoria Constantinopolitana*, ed. Peter Orth, Spolia Berolinensia: Beiträge zur Mediävistik 5 (Hildesheim and Zürich, 1994):111-14. See also Penny J. Cole, *The Preaching of the Crusades to the Holy Land, 1095-1270*, Medieval Academy Books 98 (Cambridge, Mass., 1991), 62-141. Christoph T. Maier, 'Kirche, Kreuz und Ritual: Eine Kreuzzugspredigt in Basel im Jahr 1200', *Deutsches Archiv für Erforschung des Mittelalters* (forthcoming).

[18]See, for example, Reg. 1:13, p. 22 (= PL 214:11), 2:259 (271), p. 498 (= PL 214:833), PL 215:1339-40, PL 216:817.

of the crusader,[19] but Innocent went much further, giving the idea of the crusader following Christ a new dimension and meaning. In his view, the crusader repaid Christ for his suffering on the cross by undergoing the hardship and dangers of the crusade. In a letter to Duke Leopold VI of Austria, written in February 1208, he spelled this out very clearly:

We have learned through experience that you have not heard and left unheeded the words that were spoken in the gospel to those who want to follow the Lord, since you have wondered with a religious mind how to repay the Lord for all the things he himself has given you and you have disposed yourself humbly to imitate Christ, who made himself obedient for you unto death, even to the death of the cross; and for love of him you are going to leave your beloved wife, your sweet children, your delightful fatherland, dear relatives, copious riches and worldly honours, so that in the end by denying yourself, together with your fleshly desires, you may the more freely follow him. You wish, we have heard, to carry your cross and you are girding yourself to hurry with a burning desire to the place where your salvation hung on the cross, so as to place yourself under the banner of the victorious cross to oppose the endeavours of the perfidious men whom we have already seen banish the Crucified One from part of the cross's heritage and who are striving to dispel him altogether. This intention is a very devout one and a heavenly inspiration, because by taking the cross you intend to repay in your turn Christ, who on it bore your infirmities and carried your sorrows.[20]

---

[19]Ernst-Dieter Hehl, 'Was ist eigentlich ein Kreuzzug?', *Historische Zeitschrift* 259 (1994):297-336, here pp. 316-18. Jonathan Riley-Smith, *The First Crusaders, 1095-1131* (Cambridge, 1997), 62-4.

[20]PL 215:1339-40: 'Experimento didicimus quod verbum non fueris obliviosus auditor quae volentibus ire post Dominum in Evangelio proponuntur, cum religiosa mente recogitans quid retribuas Domino pro omnibus quae retribuit ipse tibi, Christum, qui est usque ad mortem, mortem autem crucis, obediens pro te factus, humiliter imitari disponis, et pro ejus amore charam conjugem, dulcem prolem, delectabilem patriam, amabilem parentelam, divitias copias, ac mundanos relicturus honores, ut demum te ipsum cum carnalibus desideriis abnegando, liberius sequaris eumdem, desideras, ut accepimus, tollere crucem tuam, et illuc ubi tua salus in cruce pependit ardenti succingeris desiderio festinare, ut in crucis victoriosae vexillo te contra perfidorum conatus opponas, qui de crucis haereditate in parte jam expulisse videntur et in toto nituntur expellere crucifixum. Vere pium est hoc propositum et tibi coelitus inspiratum. Intendis enim suscipiendo crucem reddere vicem Christo, qui tuos languores in ipsa pertulit, doloresque portavit.' Translation from Louise and Jonathan Riley-Smith, *The Crusades: Idea and Reality, 1095-1274*, Documents of Medieval History 4 (London, 1981), 91.

In this letter Innocent described the act of crusading as an imitation of Christ's suffering on the cross, even if he was quick to point out that the crusader's act could not be compared with that of Christ in terms of its spiritual merit.[21] Nevertheless, Innocent clearly represented the crusade with its hardships and sacrifices as a ritual imitation of the redemptive act of Christ.

Innocent's concept of the crusade had thus strong eucharistic undertones. What connected the eucharist and the crusade was the idea of redemption. For the individual believer, the rituals of the eucharist and the crusade were significant for dealing with the consequence of sins. In the eucharist the church ritually commemorated the redemptive act of Christ in which, according to Christian doctrine, he had made it possible for believers to escape the damnation which followed sin.[22] The eucharist, therefore, represented the underlying mechanism of salvation on which the concept and doctrine of the indulgence were also based. In turn, the spiritual profit which the crusader gained was the fullest possible effect of Christ's act of redemption in the form of the plenary indulgence. In the popular mind this promised the almost certain entry to heaven. Innocent III fully exploited this close conceptual link between the crusading indulgence and the eucharist: if the eucharist was the ritual re-enactment of the redemptive act of Christ, the crusade was the ritual imitation of that same act. Innocent III thus gave the christocentric concept of crusade spirituality an emphasis which sharply focused on the crusader's experience of the redemptive power of Christ.

The parallel between the crusade and the eucharist opened new possibilities for crusade propaganda. As mentioned above, one of Innocent's main aims was to involve the whole of Christian society in the crusade movement. In order to do this, he had to convince everybody of the value of participating in the crusade and he had to provide a meaningful way for them to do so. An important element in this effort was to explain to the faithful how exactly the mechanism of the indulgence worked. By focusing the spirituality of the crusader on the redemptive act of Christ, Innocent suggested that the working of the indulgence followed the same mechanism as that of salvation represented in the eucharist. His arguments, centered on the cross of Christ and the act of redemption, were clad in symbolic language and biblical metaphor which people who went to mass and who knew

---

[21]PL 215:1340: 'Verum licet sit devotio satis magna, multum est tamen vicissitudo dissimilis, quia praeter gratiae differentiam quae videtur consistere in alterutro, si quod Dominus Redemptor pro servo redempto pertulit, demum servus redemptus perferat pro Domino Redemptore, inter crucis Christi patibulum et crucis tuae signaculum valde refert; cum etsi crucis una sit gloria, dispar tamen sit in te ac Domino ejus poena.'

[22]On the social and spiritual meaning of the eucharist see Miri Rubin, *Corpus Christi: The Eucharist in Late Medieval Culture* (Cambridge, 1991), 12-82. *Eadem*, 'What did the Eucharist mean to Thirteenth-Century Villagers?,' in *Thirteenth Century England IV: Proceedings of the Newcastle Upon Tyne Conference 1991*, ed. Peter R. Coss and Simon Lloyd (Woodbridge, 1992), 47-55.

the basics of the story of salvation could understand. If the salvific mechanism of the crusade in essence was the same as that of the eucharist, it made sense that the indulgence could also in principle be enjoyed by those people who did not actually go on crusade.

The rapprochement between eucharistic and crusade spirituality thus allowed Innocent to create a devotional context for all those who were expected to contribute to the crusade movement without actually taking part in a crusade. The regular liturgy for the support of the crusade which Innocent established was aimed at combining the two principal elements of crusade spirituality: firstly, the christocentric element that was rooted in the conviction that the crusader was a soldier of Christ – and in the Innocentian interpretation, an imitator of Christ's suffering on the cross – and that the ritual association with Christ was central to the experience of crusading; secondly, the redemptive element expressed in the crusader's act of penitence and embodied in the indulgence. This combination is why Innocent chose the moment during mass right before the celebration of the eucharist with its christocentric and redemptive focus for the intercessory prayers in aid of the crusade which were to be performed regularly by the whole church community.[23] In the more elaborate, special liturgies like the event in Rome in 1212, that was discussed above, the ritual and symbolic setting was even more clearly geared towards representing this kind of spirituality, focusing on the association with Christ and his power of redemption. In their procession to the Lateran, the participants approached Christ, represented by the relic of the True Cross, as penitents. They stood in his presence before the relic, which symbolized the moment of salvation. After this, they celebrated the eucharist and with it the absolution from their sins through Christ's act of salvation. In the course of this ritually enacted meeting with Christ, the role which the participants assumed changed. In the beginning they appeared as sinners striving to be saved by Christ, in the middle they became supplicants of Christ and at the end, after partaking in Christ's act of salvation, they were penitents reaffirming their reconciliation to Christ. These liturgies were important because they gave people who did not actually join a crusade army an appropriate devotional context to express crusade spirituality and allowed them to take an active public role in the crusade movement, while redeeming their crusade vows for money or supporting the crusade financially in return for partial indulgences.

Innocent III thus relocated the crusade in two ways. Firstly, the crusade was relocated in a spatial sense. Through the involvement in the crusade movement of a large part of society in these liturgies, the crusade no longer only took place in the actual theatres of war. The institution of regular crusade liturgies carried

---

[23] See also Maier, 'Crisis, Liturgy and the Crusades', 638-40.

the crusade into the churches of Christendom at large. There were now meaningful ways of actively supporting the *negotium crucis* on the home front by way of prayers, processions and material assistance. Secondly, Innocent shifted the understanding of crusade spirituality further towards christocentrism and a more radical interpretation of the crusade as *imitatio Christi*. Participation in the crusade movement was no longer exclusively defined as the experience of joining the army of the crusade. As concerns the role of the individual participant, crusading was primarily seen in devotional terms. In Innocent's definition and representation, the crusading experience was in essence one of associating with Christ and imitating his suffering on the cross. More than ever before, crusading could now be seen as one of the many forms of the *imitatio Christi* which became increasingly popular in the thirteenth century.[24] This two-fold relocation of the crusade marked a clear shift in crusade mentality and radically influenced crusade propaganda, which after 1215 was aimed as much at people who supported the crusade on the home front as at actual participants of the crusades. As the thirteenth century progressed, this may well have helped to draw many more supporters of the crusade into active participation in the movement.

---

[24]On the *imitatio Christi* in this period see Giles Constable, *Three Studies in Medieval Religious and Social Thought: The Interpretation of Mary and Martha, The Ideal of the Imitation of Christ, The Orders of Society* (Cambridge, 1995), 198-228.

Innocent III and the Saracens: Between Rejection and Collaboration

Giulio Cipollone

Innocent III, who considered himself and was considered *arbiter mundi* during a time of unusual balance between the *sacerdotium* and *imperium*, had varied attitudes toward the Muslims: rejection, tolerance and finally benevolence.

The purpose of this study is to show Innocent's different attitudes toward Muslims and the effect they had on his conduct, which appears neither homogeneous nor logically derived from the interpretative principles of theology and canon law. This is a matter of 'faith more than religion' and/or of a calibrated political calculus that dispenses from the intransigent demands of religious behavior. This also throws light on the fact that papal politics were demonstrably adaptable and elastic beyond the dogmatic positions taken in the sphere of the purely religious.

These different attitudes are revealed by a threefold typology of papal letters, documents distinguished by the different tones used in approaching the addressees, who were Christian rulers and commoners as well as Muslim rulers and social groups present in Christian lands.

Innocent's attitudes toward Muslims were armed and disarmed. On the one hand, the pope sought Christian rearmament; on the other, he allowed Muslim-Christian coexistence and sought dialogue on the basis of common interests. The purpose of talking together was always the same: to further the interests of Christ and Christianity in spite of the Muslim enemy.

Except for the crusade, little study has been done on the relationship between Innocent and the Muslims. Therefore, it is necessary to examine the phenomenon of captivity and liberation in light of the complex relationship between the pope and the Islamic world. The two attitudes, armed and disarmed, are not always easily definable. Each attitude is put into action at different times. In fact, although it seems to be an incomprehensible politics for us moderns, each attitude seems to support the other. The following section of this paper provides a chronology of Innocent's actions based on his correspondence. The two attitudes of armed and disarmed will help us understand the direction the pope set in his overall policy.

I. INNOCENT III: *POTIORA* AND *PRECIPUA*, THE CONTEXT OF LIBERATION

When he was elected pope at thirty-eight, Innocent III succeeded Celestine III, a man in his nineties. In addition to his theological and legal training in the rich cultural settings of Paris and Bologna, Innocent's temperament made him a 'robust choice' for the governance of the church and the leadership of Christendom. His pontificate (1198-1216) came at the midpoint of two centuries during which the crusades and Muslim counterattacks reached their climax. Crusade and *jihād al-saghīr* – small *jihād* – respectively: *iter Domini*, and *fī sabīl Allāh*, on the way of God.

Innocent showed his political and diplomatic skills in dealing with governmental affairs and political strategies that were especially important to him. He described his preoccupation with the Holy Land's liberation as *sollicitudo potior* and *precipuum studium* ('great concern and special eagerness').[1] We must emphasize that as the pontiff approached the end of his life, the goal of liberating the Holy Land – an effort that had been the driving force of his thought and will – once again became the objective to which he devoted his enormous diplomatic and political skills. In any discussion of Innocent's relations with the Muslims, the liberation of the Holy Land stands out as his pre-eminent concern precisely because it was the most traumatic. Traumatic in this sense: Innocent, the man who held absolute power as the vicar of Christ, was impotent before the Muslims, who were outside the *dominium Christi*.

Because Innocent's pontificate was a season of 'peace during rearmament', one can say that his papacy was a time that favored solving the problem of captivity. In fact, except for the celebrated and victorious campaign of Las Navas de Tolosa (1212), Innocent's pontificate was entirely free of major wars against the Muslim foe. This fact provides a useful perspective on the Fourth Crusade (1202-1204):

---

[1]Reg. 1:355, pp. 515-17, 1:438, pp. 661-2.

although it was planned for a far different end – a *peregrinatio ad liberandum*, a voyage to liberate the Lord's sepulcher, the Holy City, and the land 'where his feet have stood' – the Fourth Crusade produced the slaughter of Christian brothers and sisters. Innocent's pontificate, then, is remembered as a time of truce between Christendom and Islam. Even if this peace was a forced one, it was still an armistice on the official level.

This overall evaluation of Innocent's papacy is based on the experience of Las Navas de Tolosa and the tension of the *bellum Domini* ('the war of the Lord') that the pontiff tenaciously pursued. By temperament and deep theological conviction, Innocent was a man who gave up nothing; rather, he was unyielding in his militant determination to free the Holy Land. His initial efforts in this direction came at the beginning of his pontificate and also appeared at its end. At the Fourth Lateran Council, Innocent published a kind of spiritual testament 'for the whole world'. In this document, he expressed his sorrow and hope for the holy places. The pope wrote of his decisions and actions that were to have universal importance, a significance as wide as Christendom. Innocent III died dreaming. His pontificate was a time of truce, just as it was a time of rearmament.

The treaty concluded with Saladin in September 1192 brought the Latin kingdom of the East a period of tranquillity that lasted for three years and three months. Following Abū Shāma,[2] al-'Ādil concluded a truce with the Franks for a period of five years and eight months beginning on 14 Sha'ban 594 AH or 21 June 1198. An armistice was a time both to count the captives who had not returned home and to mourn the dead who would never return. Truces were also an opportunity to rearm and build up strength for the next holy war. In any case, these temporary suspensions in warfare were times when the fire smoldered under the ashes; a time, however, that included actions of disturbance and piracy that led to sackings and booty. The same Abū Shāma refers to eight important actions of invasion and sacking carried out by Christians and Muslims in 594/1198 and 607/1210.

In addition to these sporadic actions and local events, a concern remained for both the honor of the Christian name recently dishonored by a terrible defeat at Muslim hands and the desire to start doing something. All these facts pressured the young pope to dedicate himself to a reversal of the situation. Inevitably, he began with the most urgent matter: the liberation of the holy places. Hence, the need for rearmament. During his pontificate, Innocent organized the free liberation of captives. Tens of thousands of Christian captives were in Muslim

---

[2]Abū Shāma, *Le livre des deux jardins. Histoire des deux règnes, celui de Nour ed-Dīn et celui de Ṣalāḥ ed-Dīn*, in *Recueil des Historiens des Croisades*. Historiens Orientaux, 5:153-8.

hands. According to 'Imād ad-Dīn,[3] in 1187 the Muslims held 100,000 Christians in bondage.

With regard to the Muslims, one can see a clear difference in the complex plans of the pontiff. Innocent expressed different attitudes on three levels: first, concrete daily choices that came from hostility; second, the reducing and even censuring of relations with Muslims; third, peaceful and even benevolent cohabitation with the Muslim enemy. The core of this basically anti-Muslim policy, therefore, was a plan for rearmament on the international level and humanitarian initiatives. Papal policy expressed the objectives of an inextinguishable theological remembrance of captivity and liberation. Innocent's clear resolve to liberate was evident on these three levels. Indeed, the image of liberation characterized his whole pontificate. This was a double and paradoxical liberation: a liberation through ransoming captives and a liberation of the holy places – by force of arms (*militaribus armis*) – that increased the number of Christian captives.

Following the current theology, tradition and canon law, Innocent wisely controlled relations with the Muslims. He tailored his policies according to each of the following: circumstances, the addressee of his letter and the complex requirements of the moment. Apart from his writings on the crusade, the pontiff's correspondence on the Muslim problem is concentrated in the years 1198-1199 and 1212-1213. One can divide this body of literature on the basis of its addressees. They fall into three main groups: the Christian faithful and clergy, the Christian princes and the Muslim rulers. As stated before, Innocent dealt directly or indirectly with Muslims for various reasons. Nevertheless, his rationale for doing so can be described as follows: first, the pope sought to foster peace among the Christian rulers and have them break their alliances with their Muslim counterparts. Second, he endeavored to heal the wounds of past Muslim persecutions. Third, he hoped to avoid renewed persecution. Fourth, Innocent planned to liberate the holy places and aid impoverished fellow-Christians in foreign lands. Fifth, the pontiff worked to end commercial relations between Muslim and Christians while preventing Muslims from gaining any economic advantage. Sixth, Innocent had to deal with Muslim converts. Finally, he needed to propose an ideal plan by Christians for the liberation of prisoners of war. The barbarous raids of Markward of Anweiler in Sicily forced the pope to adopt a policy of benevolence toward the Muslims. He even wrote to express his solidarity with Christians who suffered in different ways at the hands of Muslims.

---

[3]'Imād ad-Dīn al-Iṣfahānī, *Al-Fath al-qussi fī' l-fath al-qudsī* trans. H. Massé, *Conquête de la Syrie et la Palestine par Saladin* = Documents relatifs à l'histoire des Croisades, 10 (Paris, 1972):38.

II. INNOCENT III AND THE PHENOMENA OF CHRISTIAN DIVISION, CHRISTIANS VERSUS CHRISTIANS AND PRO-MUSLIM CHRISTIANS

Innocent ruled both the clergy and the Christian faithful; these were the groups which the pope addressed most frequently. They were not always docile, but they represented the more secure part of the pontiff's possible audiences. They were more likely to listen to what Christ's vicar had to say. One series of Innocent's letters is occasioned by war among some Christian princes. Unholy alliances between the same Christian rulers and the Muslim 'enemy' provided another reason for the papal correspondence. Nonetheless, the goal of liberating the holy places remained the basic goal in Innocent's correspondence with Christian princes.

The possibility of an unholy alliance[4] between Christian and Muslim provided hard evidence of the internal discord of Christendom. At times, Christian rulers had much better relations with the infidel than with their brothers in the faith, that is, those who had been redeemed by the same blood and were allied with the same God. Innocent had to act as if such *impia foedera* ('unholy alliances') had not occurred. He undertook the difficult task of checking, inducing, admonishing, threatening, punishing and reuniting Christendom's secular rulers. His efforts produced little in the way of positive results. All Christian rulers had the obligation of fostering Christendom's unity, but politics and self-interest often undercut this duty.[5]

From the letters of Innocent III, three 'scandalous' situations appear: the divisions among Christians; Christians against other Christians (*fratres cohuterini*, 'blood brothers'); and finally, Christians who were 'friends' who favored the Muslims. In fact, the pope acted simultaneously with two intentions: to lead the Christians to re-establish peace among themselves and to underline the urgency of their organizing themselves and arming themselves against the Muslims. The different situations in Spain and the holy places are united in a global experience against the Muslim enemy.

Throughout Innocent's correspondence, there is scattered evidence that Christian rulers evaded alliances with their co-religionists and maintained unholy alliances with the Muslim foe. The earlier history of conflict between Christians and Muslims was still alive in Christian memory. Given this fact, Innocent sought to draw Christians to support his plans for dealing with the Muslims.

---

[4]G. Vismara, 'Impium foedus. La illeceità delle alleanze con gli infedeli nella "Res Publica Cristiana" medievale', in *Comunità e diritto internazionale* = Scritti di storia giuridica, 7 (Milan, 1989):77-8; G. Balladore Pallieri and G. Vismara, *Acta pontificia juris gentium usque ad annum MCCCIV* (Milan, 1946), 274-6, nos. 65-74.

[5]G. Cipollone, *Cristianità - Islam cattività e liberazione in nome di Dio. Il tempo di Innocenzo III dopo 'il 1187'* = *Miscellanea Historiae Pontificiae* 60 (Rome, 1992, repr. 1996), 331-6.

On 26 April 1213, Innocent wrote two letters: one 'humbly' to Saladin's brother the sultan of Damascus and Babylon,[6] and another of quite different tone to Albert the patriarch of Jerusalem.[7] Innocent told Albert to take appropriate steps to end the *detestabilis conversatio* ('detestable condition') of the Holy Land's Christians. In spite of the unbending perfidy of the Muslims before the humility of the Christians, Innocent wanted a delegation sent to the sultan to deal with the problem of the Holy Land. The pope also called on John king of Jerusalem, the Hospitallers and the Templars *cum peregrinis pariter et indigenis* ('together with pilgrims and natives equally') to come to the Holy Land's defense. The pope also invited the patriarch, if the circumstances were favorable, to intervene at the aforementioned general council and to be accompanied by well-informed persons.

Lateran III and IV enacted severe judicial sanctions as a decisive means of ending commercial relations between Christians and Muslims. Christians who violated these clear instructions were described as having fallen prey to worldly temptations contrary to the cause of God himself. One finds still more directives concerning the unavoidable contact between Christians and Muslims. Ecclesiastical laws sought both to maintain the advantage of Christians in commercial dealings with Muslims and to force Muslims to wear distinctive apparel as a means of controlling them.

In its constitution 68, the Fourth Lateran Council (1215) ordered that Jews and Muslims wear distinguishing apparel to prevent these unbelievers from having any relations with Christian women and to prevent Christians from having any relations with Jewish and Muslim women. This legislation was also to prevent Jews from insulting the Crucified when Christians celebrated the mysteries of his passion.[8] Innocent intervened in the council because of questions surrounding the following: the religiosity of the Muslims, their faith, their rites, their conversion, the baptism they might receive and the possible marriages they might have.

One of Innocent's personal frustrations was the elusive Markward of Anweiler,[9] who acted violently in his domain and in the kingdom of Frederick II. Markward, who once humbled himself before the pontiff, scorned papal authority until his death in 1202. In January 1199, the pope addressed the clergy, barons, judges, knights and all the people of Capua.[10] He called on them to obey King Frederick of Sicily and to fight against Markward margrave of Ancona and duke of

---

[6]PL 216:831-2, no. 37; *Cristianità - Islam*, 543-4, no. 46.

[7]PL 216:830-1, no. 36.

[8]*Constitutiones Concilii quarti Lateranensis una cum Commentariis glossatorum* = Monumenta iuris canonici, series A: Corpus Glossatorum, 2, ed. A. García y García (Città del Vaticano, 1981):107-8, no. 68.

[9]*Cristianità - Islam*, 339-40.

[10]Reg. 1:555 (558) = PL 214:513.

Romagna and Ravenna. To those who would overcome the violence of Markward and his supporters, the pope granted the same remission of sins as offered to those who joined in the defense of the eastern province against the wickedness of the Saracens. The massacres carried out by Markward in Sicily were the occasion for a sorrowful letter sent to the counts, barons and inhabitants of Sicily.[11] Innocent first compared Markward to Saladin and then went on to say that Markward had allied himself with Muslims of Sicily against the king and that he had let them have their way with captured Christian women. If Muslims remained faithful to King Frederick, the pope was inclined to love and support them and to increase their goods; however, he would not support those who helped Markward. Innocent suggested that if Sicily should come under the control of the Saracens, there would be no hope left for the liberation of Jerusalem. In 1199, the idea of a political crusade took root because of Markward's raids. Innocent even tried to include the Muslims in resistance to Markward. In fact, a few days after addressing Sicily's nobility, Innocent wrote to the island's Muslims inviting them to remain devoted and faithful to him.[12] The pontiff praised the Muslims for their fidelity in the practice of their rites, exhorted them to remain loyal to King Frederick and urged them to imitate the constancy of their ancestors by committing themselves to fight against Markward, an action that would protect and increase their goods.

This letter is important precisely because it is so unusual on several counts. First, in this document, the pontiff addressed 'the enemy' and promised protection to those Saracens who fought against Markward, a Christian son turned enemy. Second, Innocent wrote of honor given to God through the shedding of Muslim blood. Third, the pope discussed Muslim rites and observances. Fourth, he referred to the right of plundering the enemies of religion. Finally, Innocent mentioned that good Muslim customs favored the well-being of Christians. After several years, in 1206, Innocent again addressed the nobles and Muslims of Sicily. He offered them tolerance and benevolence. The pontiff praised them and implored them to remain faithful to the king in spite of many trials. In fact, Innocent wrote with unusual benevolence to the Muslims, who occupied the Lord's inheritance and the Christian land of Spain.

Was this a matter of strategy or a profound sense of tolerance? Who was the real Innocent? Was he a man who could sacrifice his religious commitments for the sake of politics, or was he a man able to live with those of another religious tradition? Throughout his correspondence, Innocent displayed self-interest and political prudence that excluded tolerance for those of other religions. Nevertheless, he also showed great flexibility in dealing with the Muslims. As we will see

---

[11]Reg. 2:212 (221) = PL 214:780.
[12]Reg. 2:217 (226) = PL 214:786.

later, Innocent showed great flexibility in his dealings with the Muslims when he knew that he could not strike at their weaknesses and when he needed their cooperation. This flexibility will be critical in his program for ransoming Christian captives.

The way Innocent availed himself of the services of the Templars, of the Hospitallers of St John of Jerusalem of Calatrava and of the Trinitarian Ransomers-deliverers shows the different approaches the pontiff took in dealing with the Muslims. The service of Christ embraced both enlisting in the *militia* and unarmed labors.

III. INNOCENT III, THE CHRISTIAN PRINCES AND THE MUSLIMS

Conscious of his limits and the greatness of his mission as Christ's vicar, Innocent was aware of his role in solving the problems of Christendom. With an absolute if fragile realism based on the realities of his time, Innocent admonished, exhorted, excommunicated and pardoned Christian rulers. He saw his own power as the authority to bind and loose. In dealing with concrete facts and everyday realities, the pontiff knew that excommunication failed to strike many with fear. In spite of this, Innocent never relented in pushing Christian rulers to liberate the holy places. This was his dream; indeed, it was the dream of Christendom itself.

With regard to the Muslims, the pope directed his correspondence to securing Christian cooperation in the liberation of the Holy Land. Sometimes, he addressed himself to those who suffered directly at the hands of the Muslims. The goal was to liberate Christ the exile and captive. As we have seen, however, Innocent was more interested in the liberation of the holy places – hence, the holy work of rearming – than in the liberation of captives. His was a rather vague and indirect interest in the fate of the captives, a fate that in fact coincided with the liberation of the Holy Land and the Christian lands of Spain.

As early as March 1199, Innocent intended to launch an expedition for liberation. In August 1198, he wrote of this plan in letters addressed to Philip king of France (1180-1223) and Richard the Lion-hearted, king of England (1189-1199). On the same date, he also described his plans in letters sent to the prelates of these two kingdoms.[13] In these documents, the pontiff laid out a plan for the liberation of the Holy Land, a design that required peace among the Christian rulers. Fratricidal war was a grave impediment to this liberation. War among Christians had caused the destruction of two kingdoms, great losses for Christians, massacres in the province of Jerusalem and captivity for the Christian faithful, since men of both kingdoms were captive because of the dissension between the two kings. That Christians delivered other Christians into captivity

---

[13]Reg. 1:355, pp. 530-2; see *Cristianità - Islam*, 493-7, no. 20.

meant that there were fewer believers ready to fight the Muslims. This blocked the way to recovering the Holy Land. With the same goal of freeing the Holy Land, Innocent addressed Alexius III Comnenus, emperor of Constantinople (1195-1203). The pontiff placed on Christ's lips a reproach to Alexius who had failed to do his utmost in the liberation of the Holy Land: 'Jesus Christ himself warns you with these words, "I was a stranger and you did not welcome me; I was sick and you did not visit me, I was in prison and you did not come to me."' Innocent added that foreigners had come into the Lord's inheritance and profaned his temple, 'or rather, Jesus Christ himself, since they captured the wood of the holy cross'. Again the pope wrote of Christ in exile.[14]

According to Innocent, the idea of captivity and liberation applied with singular force to Christ. His land was a reality in which all Christians had to feel involved; indeed, it was a matter of the Last Judgment. Once again, the pontiff proposed the biblical theme (Mt 25:43) to the Emperor Alexius, warning him that at the last judgment, he would have this gospel passage thrown at him, 'I was a stranger and you did not welcome me, I was sick and in prison and you did not come to see me.' Writing about the enemy, Innocent called them Saracens, pagans, and alluded to the Antichrist.[15] In December 1199, Innocent directed an earnest appeal to King Philip of France and King John Lackland of England (1199-1216), who had succeeded Richard the previous May.[16] In his letter, the pope wrote about the Holy Land's misery and the necessity of liberating it. This document provided the pontiff with an opportunity to reaffirm a theme dear to him, namely, that of Christ *similiter* and *quasi* captive. Innocent noted that if vassals were obliged to free an earthly king, then how much more were Christians obliged to free the heavenly king now captive in enemy hands. The pope voiced his admiration for King Peter of Aragon (1196-1213), who wanted to liberate that land 'which, formerly, Christian kings and Catholic princes defended with the shedding of their own blood'.[17] Naturally, Innocent noted that without the help of Spain's other monarchs, Peter could never succeed against the Muslims and free the Christian lands that had fallen to the Muslims. On 14 February 1204, in the same letter, Innocent showed his intention regarding the king: 'Now we persist more strongly in our intention . . . to the same degree that the hostile party seems to grow stronger in that the king of Morocco has triumphed over the king of Majorca . . .' (in 1203).

The scope planned for this study does not allow us to linger with the correspondence of Innocent in which the pope tried to lead the Christian rulers to liberate

---

[14]Reg. 1:353, pp. 526-8; see *Cristianità - Islam*, 498-9, no. 21.
[15]*Cristianità -Islam*, 342.
[16]Reg. 2:241 (251), pp. 459-62.
[17]Reg. 6:234 (235), pp. 395-6.

the holy places and to rearm themselves for this goal. However, one can conclude that Innocent's correspondence with the Christian princes indicated some of the pontiff's different attitudes toward the Muslims. In general, the pope was interested in liberating the holy places and in freeing Christian captives, and the fight against the heretics was an obstacle to this overall goal.

With regard to Innocent's correspondence with the Muslim rulers, we know four letters that the pontiff addressed to Muslim rulers in 1199, 1211, 1213 and a final one written in 1215 or 1216. The first document, written on 8 March 1199,[18] was addressed to Abū 'Abd-allāh Muḥammad an-Nāṣir, amīr al-mu'minīn, *regi marrochetano*, prince of believers. The letter concerned a most representative prince of the Almohad dynasty. Given the extraordinary importance of this document, we shall write of it later in this study.

On 7 June 1211,[19] Innocent approached Malik az-Zahir al-Ghazi, sultan of Aleppo (516-613/1186-1216) and recommended the patriarch of Antioch to him. The pontiff praised the conduct of the sultan who, even if he had not yet received baptism, nevertheless honored the Catholic faith and deferred to the faithful of Christ. It was unusual for Innocent to thank a Muslim ruler for defending a Christian prelate from attacks and 'Christian' annoyances. The remarkable character of this document becomes all the more evident when one sees how Innocent wrote on the same day to Peter Pedemontano, patriarch of Antioch (1209-1217).[20] After consoling and encouraging the patriarch, Innocent invited him to make every effort with divine assistance 'to eliminate from the Holy Land the filth of the pagans '.

As the sultan of Aleppo, the addressee of the letter of 26 April 1213 is a ruler of the Aiyubids dynasty, Malik Al-'Ādil Sayf ad-Dīn Abū Bakr, sultan of Damascus and Egypt (592-615/1196-1218). The point of this message to the sultan was the double captivity endured by the Christians: the first was the captivity of the holy places; the second was the actual enslavement of Christian captives. Forcefully expressing himself, the pope presented the risk involved in the useless shedding of human blood. Moreover, with exact and measured language, Innocent expressed himself in an unusual way: *cum humiliter hoc petamus et suppliciter imploremus* ('since we humbly seek and implore with

---

[18]*Reg.* 2:9, pp. 16-17; K. E. Lupprian, *Die Beziehungen der Päpste zu islamischen und mongolischen Herrschern im 13. Jahrhundert anhand ihres Briefwechsels* = Studi e testi, 291 (Città del Vaticano, 1981), 107, no. 1; *Cristianità - Islam*, 506, no. 26.

[19]PL 216:434, no. 69; K. E. Lupprian, *Die Beziehungen*, 108-9, n. 2; *Cristianità - Islam*, 528-9, no. 39.

[20]PL 216:435-6, no.72. The patriarch is also known as Peter of Lucedio. See John C. Moore, 'Peter of Lucedio (Cistercian Patriarch of Antioch), and Pope Innocent III,' *Römische Historische Mitteilungen*, 29 (1987):221-49, esply 236.

bended knee').[21] Innocent wrote this letter fifteen years after the beginning of his pontificate. During those years, the pontiff had experienced the worldliness and disunity of the Christian faithful for whom the liberation of the Holy Land was not a matter of popular enthusiasm. Between 1213 and the last year of his pontificate, 1216, Innocent again wrote to the same sultan. He asked for the restitution of the province of Jerusalem to Christendom. The pope's religious conviction remained unshaken, but the experience of his pontificate and his diminishing energy had weakened his voice. Nevertheless, the pope died convinced of his dream.

IV. INNOCENT AND ABŪ 'ABD-ALLĀH MUḤAMMAD AN-NĀṢIR, AMĪR AL-MU'MĪNĪN

In the first year of his pontificate, Innocent showed interest in the liberation of captives because of his contact with the Trinitarian Ransomers-deliverers. At the start of his pontificate's second year, Innocent took the initiative of writing to the king of Morocco, the 'prince of believers'. He wrote of a humanitarian undertaking, one in harmony with the evangelical command of merciful charity. The letters of 17 December 1198 and 8 March 1199 both are given unusual *incipits* in the papal chancery, respectively: *Operante divine dispositionis* and *Inter opera misericordie*.[22] One notes an important active and passive in the presentation of the Christian project to the Muslim ruler: *regulam et ordinem invenerunt . . . ut paganos captivos a christianis redimant, est concessum* ('they have founded a rule and order . . . so that it has been granted to them that they may redeem pagan captives from Christians').

The ruler addressed in the famous letter of 8 March 1199[23] was among the more representative figures of the Muslim world. According to his father's will, Muḥammad an-Nāṣir was selected as his successor at the end of January 1199. This papal document is often quoted because in it the pope deals with relations between Islam and Christianity and the relations between the papacy and Islam, and it is considered a truly exceptional document because correspondence between the pope and a Muslim leader is rare.

In this document, Innocent spoke of the Muslim ruler as amīr al-mu'minīn, prince of the believers (in Latin: *miramolino*) and *regi marrochetano*, king of Morocco. An-Nāṣir was more than a king, however; he was a sort of emperor, the leader of all the Almohads, who dominated North Africa from Tunisia to the

---

[21]C. J. Hefele/H. Leclercq, *Histoire des Conciles* (Paris, 1907-38), 5:1733.
[22]Reg. 1:481, pp. 703-8; 2:9, pp. 16-17.
[23]See above, note 18.

Atlantic and Muslim Spain.[24] An-Nāṣir died in 1213. An-Nāṣir's chancery does not provide us with his response to the papal letter. This Almohad ruler proved to be a more modest ruler than his father. When writing of his reign, historians emphasize the conquest of Majorca, the continuous struggle with the indomitable Almoravids and the terrible defeat suffered in Las Navas de Tolosa in 1212 at the hands of the Christians.

These historical events certainly affected Innocent and led him to prefer an-Nāṣir, ruler of the Muslim West, to one of his counterparts in the Muslim East. This is a theme that deserves deeper study. The following remarks provide an explanation for Innocent's preference of a western rather than an eastern Muslim ruler. First of all, an-Nāṣir, who had recently ascended the throne, was the sole ruler of a large part of the Muslim world. We do not know if Innocent was aware of an-Nāṣir's youth, nor do we know if Innocent realized that an-Nāṣir controlled the western part of Islam. One can argue that Innocent tried a western approach in his quest to deal with the problem of the Christian captives. Perhaps he thought this was an easier route that would eventually get him to Alexandria and Damascus. Further, it is possible that the pope believed that a western Muslim ruler would provide him with safe passage for the Christian ransomers. The foregoing possibilities are matters for speculation. From the text, we know that the pope presented the Christian ransomers and deliverers as acting in the name of Christianity; he also included their rule, which was a clear novelty in the project of Christian liberation.

The letter is of exceptional importance because in it the pope expressed an entirely novel and singular official approach to Muslims. Innocent quickly referred to the purpose of his letter, namely, a work of mercy. Such an opening differed from those of Innocent's other letters to Muslim rulers. He wrote: 'Among the works of mercy which Jesus Christ, our Lord, recommends in the gospel to his faithful, the ransoming of captives figures in no small way.' The pontiff, therefore, took the initiative from a disarmed position, namely, from mercy. To this end, nothing was more fitting than to draw from the gospel itself, from the fullness of revelation, from the definitive text. The ransom of captives was presented as an evangelical command, a command that was by no means the least in importance.

---

[24]Regarding the Almohads and Muhammad an-Nāṣir in particular, one can consult the following: E. Levi-Provençal, 'Un recueil de lettres officielles almohades', *Hespéris* 28 (1941), passim; R. Bourouiba, 'La doctrine almohade', *Revue de l'Occident musulman et de la Méditerranée* 13-14 (1973):141-58; *Recueil des Historiens des Croisades. Historiens orientaux,* 4:491-6; N. Barbour, 'The Relations of King Sancho VII of Navarra with the Almohads', *Revue de l'Occident musulman et de la Méditerranée* 4 (1967):9-21; Ibn al-A t̲ī̲r, *Annales du Maghreb et de l'Espagne*, trans. E. Fagnan (Alger, 1898), 613.

The work of liberation that the pope presented to an-Nāṣir was not one that he had conceived; rather it came from a faithful Christian, a Provençal educated in Paris,[25] a teacher of theology, a priest.[26] This project had already been tried on the level of the local church and had received the support of many followers and benefactors. Innocent, however, now made this plan his very own. He proposed it as the plan of liberation in Christianity's name. There were no other plans on such a comprehensive scale. 'In reality, some men, from whose number come the bearers of this letter, were inflamed by God a short while ago and have established a rule and an order. The foundation of this institution is the requirement that they spend one third of their income, which they possess now or will possess in the future, on the ransoming of captives.' The pope then defined the Trinitarian Ransomers-deliverers as simply *viri quidam* ('some men'). There was a certain caution in Innocent's language. The pope assumed that the Muslim ruler would have difficulty in understanding just what sort of 'Christian religious' he was describing. These men were neither esteemed monks nor Greek or Latin prelates. Furthermore, they were not the fierce enemy identified with other men of religion, namely, the Templars and Hospitallers. We have many testimonies that Muslims treated Templars and Hospitallers 'without pity' and without possibility of pardon. *Viri quidam*, then, was not so much a matter of imprecision as an attempt at respect for Muslim sensitivity. In addition, it is worth emphasizing the expression *nuper divinitus inflammati* ('inflamed by God a short while ago'). The pope meant to trace the Christian Deliverers to a divine plan.[27] Their work was not a political plan, nor did it result from worldly calculations. The novelty of this project that aroused interest and resolve to carry it out was based on the practice of the taking one third of all their revenue – both their present and their future revenue. The specific requirement left no way out. If, then, it was a rule[28] of a perpetual, public obligation of charity, then the only thing left to do was to convince a religious enemy who had the interests of another God.

Indeed, this was an atypical letter because in it Innocent contacted a Muslim ruler out of disinterested charity. In his other letters, Innocent expressed benevolence, a desire to exhort and threat – according to requirements of the situation. In this letter, the pontiff tried to present a project undertaken by a Christian group in the name of Christianity itself. In describing a project of liberation to a Muslim, the pope actually engaged in propaganda on behalf of this

---

[25]G. Cipollone, *Studi intorno a Cerfroid prima casa dell'Ordine trinitario (1198-1429)* (Rome, 1978, repr. 1997), 34-43.

[26]*Cristianità -Islam*, 430-1.

[27]G. Cipollone, *Il mosaico di San Tommaso in Formis a Roma (ca. 1210). Contributo di iconografia e iconologia* (Rome, 1984, repr. 1997), 36-42.

[28]Reg. 1:481, pp. 703-8.

undertaking. This project was one that strikes us as modern. It was the best Innocent could propose – because he had nothing else to offer. It was the first project born of Christianity, invented 'on the scale of Christianity'. The pope described the Trinitarians to the Muslim ruler: they were unarmed Trinitarians, Christians unable to fight, harmless souls. Thus, they were remarkably different from the usual 'armed Trinitarians'.

In making this project of liberation his own, the pope equipped it with a special prerogative: the revolutionary concession of the commutation. It was a concession that gave room to the gospel; however, it was a concession that ran the risk of coming into conflict with the politics and interests of the Christian princes. The private and political interests of the Christian rulers were more important than liberative mercy for their fellow Christians. In any event, the work of ransom began and it was a revolutionary action that contravened canonical norms: one could ransom Muslims in order to free Christians held by the Muslims. Innocent espoused this project of an evangelically free group of Christian Ransomers-deliverers and, with great satisfaction, informed a Muslim about it. The pope wanted an-Nāṣir to know that there was a group of ransomers: absolutely unarmed men who would pay for ransom, men who had the ecclesiastical privilege of redeeming captives. This group carried another cross.

Evidence that Christians found Muslim captives a very good investment is found in the following fact. In 1212,[29] Innocent urged the Templars and the overseas Christian princes to exchange their Muslim captives for their baptized brothers and sisters who had been captured by the Muslims and who were in danger of apostatizing because of their suffering. The ransomed Christians would render the same service to their Christian liberators as they had given their Muslim masters. Nevertheless, the military religious orders and the Christian princes showed no enthusiasm for Innocent's proposal. For these Christian rulers, power over the pagan, evil, enemy Muslim captive only enlarged their power and gave glory to God. The pope insisted that ransoming the Christian captives was a useful goal. Indeed, charity was always useful. But politics can prevent a solution to human misery.

Interest in these Christian Ransomers was strong because they were men ready to repatriate an-Nāṣir's fellow Muslims. This project, which was based on the gospel and free of politics, was different: the Ransomers would pay in person. They relied on the free charity of the poor. They came unarmed and with an attitude of mercy. The difficulties they faced in dealing with demanding Christians who held Muslim captives would show the obstacles placed before this completely free project, a return home in complete liberty. The letter of 13

---

[29]*Cristianità - Islam*, 529-34, nos. 40-2.

January 1212 to the patriarch of Jerusalem clarified the difference of this project. This letter was in fact an answer to the request of the patriarch of Alexandria and the Christian captives themselves. The project of the captives and the patriarch of Alexandria sought the preservation of the faith rather than apostasy caused by the awful sufferings of the captives. The captives simply wanted to be exchanged. They were willing to remain in bondage and serve Christian owners. They were content to render the same service and receive the same treatment. How different was the project of the Ransomers. But the Christian rulers resisted this.

In 1213, the invitation to Sayf ad-Dīn was presented with great humility.[30] Innocent trusted the sultan's discretion. Freeing the captives of both sides would amount to acting on the failure of the liberation project that had been presented to the Christian princes and the Christian military religious orders.

Lateran Council IV, which was announced by Innocent at the end of the second year of his pontificate[31] and called for in 1213, provided an overall assessment of what had been done and what remained to be done in order to liberate the Holy Land and Spain. In other words, it provided a general picture of relations with the Muslims. Some decisions were needed on the liberation of captives. All Christendom was asking for such a decision. Christians insisted on the liberation of the holy places, but they had nothing to say about the liberation of the Christian captives. In two constitutions, Lateran IV treated relations with the Muslims. In constitution 68, the council required distinctive signs that would allow immediate recognition of Muslims.[32] This would prevent intermingling with Christians: *dampnate commixtionis excessus* ('the excesses of this condemned mixture'). Constitution 69 removed the practice of allowing Jews to hold public offices. The constitution also extended this prohibition to pagans. The final constitution of Lateran IV dealt with the liberation of the Holy Land. It began as follows: *Ad liberandam terram sanctam de manibus impiorum* ('for the liberation of the Holy Land from the hands of the impious'). In the context of liberation, tension with the Muslims was discussed and then the prohibition of commerce with them was reaffirmed. The activity of privateers was referred to the Muslim enemy.

During the final months of Innocent's pontificate, the last attempts at the Holy Land's liberation were made. Christians were to confront and never retreat before the Muslim foe. From the rubrics of the eighteenth year of Innocent's pontificate, we know of a letter sent to all Christians. By force of arms, they were to aid Christians who were fighting overseas. Finally, just a few months before Innocent's death, the letter of 8 January 1216 was written and sent to all the

---

[30]Ibid., 543-4, no. 46.
[31]Reg. 2:200, p. 388.
[32]*Constitutiones Concilii quarti Lateranensis*, 107-8, no. 68.

crusaders in the province of Bremen. Soon after the general council, and after a pontificate spent in continuous and frustrated efforts to liberate the holy lands, Innocent continued to insist on the liberation of the holy places. This letter had the same insistent tone found in the *littera generalis* of April 1213.[33] In this letter, however, Christians captured by the Muslims were not mentioned. The liberation of the holy places was the essential work.

One was to liberate the land even if that meant not liberating human beings. With his absolute power, Innocent permitted everything in relations with the Muslims: force and humility, threats and indulgence, rigidity and conciliation, esteem and contempt, alliance and rejection. As regards Christians, they were obliged to enter into holy war, the *opus Dei* ('work of God'), against the Muslims. They participated in such war by enlistment or by investment of their money and goods in the struggle against the unbelievers. Excommunication awaited those who dared to have personal relationships with the Muslims. There were prophetic exceptions to these patterns: unarmed Christian 'dreamers' who were far from the armed strategy of the central power. Perhaps this was the extraordinary political and diplomatic ability of a pope like Innocent: he was the vicar of Christ and arbiter of the world. The only thing above him was heaven. But the whole earth followed its own course.

---

[33]PL 216:817-22, no. 28; *Cristianità - Islam*, 536-7, no. 44.

Index

INDEX